RESEARCH METHODS

RESEARCH METHODS

A Process of Inquiry

ANTHONY M. GRAZIANO
MICHAEL L. RAULIN
STATE UNIVERSITY OF NEW YORK AT BUFFALO

HARPER & ROW, PUBLISHERS, New York
Cambridge, Philadelphia, San Francisco, London,
Mexico City, São Paulo, Singapore, Sydney

1817

To Sheila and Sheryl

Editor in Chief: Judith Rothman
Project Editor: Vivian Koenig
Text Design Adaptation: Barbara Bert/North 7 Atelier Ltd.
Cover Design: Michel Craig
Cover Art: *Vie No. 1*, Auguste Herbin. Allbright-Knox Art Gallery, Buffalo, New York.
  Gift of the Seymour H. Knox Foundation, Inc., 1966.
Text Art: ComCom Division of Haddon Craftsmen, Inc.
Production Manager: Willie Lane
Compositor: ComCom Division of Haddon Craftsmen, Inc.
Printer and Binder: R. R. Donnelley & Sons Company
Cover Printer: NEBC

RESEARCH METHODS: A Process of Inquiry

Library of Congress Cataloging-in-Publication Data

Graziano, Anthony M., 1932–
    Research methods : a process of inquiry / Anthony M. Graziano,
Michael L. Raulin.
      p.   cm.
    Bibliography: p.
    Includes index.
    ISBN 0–06–042479–6
    1. Research—Methodology.   I. Raulin, Michael L.   II. Title.
Q180.55.M4G7   1988
507.2—dc19   88–16503
                                                      CIP

88   89   90   91   9   8   7   6   5   4   3   2   1

CONTENTS

12 CONTROL OF VARIANCE THROUGH EXPERIMENTAL DESIGN: FACTORIAL DESIGN 240

13 FIELD RESEARCH: A SECOND LOOK AT RESEARCH IN NATURAL SETTINGS 267

APPENDIX A   Writing a Research Report: APA Publication Style   329

APPENDIX B   Statistical Tables   342

APPENDIX C   Statistical Computation Procedures   357

INSTRUCTOR'S PREFACE

This book has evolved over several years of teaching research methods. The challenges of organizing and presenting this material for its best use by students are well known to all of you. Our goals are to have students learn *concepts* of research, rather than cookbook-like strategies, and to develop a substantial and durable understanding of research as both an integrated *process of thinking* and an exciting enterprise.

In order to become good scientific researchers and/or research consumers, students need to understand the methods of science. While science is not the only way of understanding nature, it is a unique and particularly powerful way of doing so. Science emphasizes the continuous interplay of rationalism and empiricism, a combination that makes stringent and unique demands on the nature of evidence and the procedures used to arrive at conclusions about the universe. These demands of science constitute the core of the material that must be mastered in any study of research methods.

Science is not the only way of thinking about and understanding the universe; humans have developed many competing bases for understanding the world. Some of the competing systems are, for example, accepting an idea as true because (1) it has been accepted as true in the past, (2) it feels intuitively true, or (3) someone with authority says it is true. In order to understand science, students must examine those competing systems and know their limitations. They must come to ask for evidence, that ideas be logically consistent and clearly observable and to see science as a uniquely powerful method of testing ideas. In the first two chapters we focus on these and other basic ideas and build a foundation to prepare students for the subsequent presentation of research methods.

PROGRAMMATIC NATURE OF THE TEXT

In writing this text we have been committed to the idea that difficult concepts are best taught programmatically. A concept, validity for example, is introduced and defined early in the text, but only to the degree needed for that introductory discussion. Concepts are then systematically reexamined throughout the text, new facets are added to them, and they are integrated, which progressively builds a more complete and sophisticated conceptualization.

This programmatic development influenced the form of this text, and it has several implications for teaching. The text provides students with material for systematic, progressive mastery of ideas, beginning with basic levels and building up to more complex and complete concepts. This form results in sequential, rather than independent, chapters, with each chapter building upon earlier material. Thus, we suggest that the text will be used best when the chapters are assigned in their present order.

This approach requires repetition—the same concepts are discussed repeatedly in the text, but at progressively higher levels of sophistication. At times this may seem to be only repetition; however, what may appear to be mere repetition to the sophisticated instructor can be useful rehearsal and summarizing for the student who is just learning. Thus, repetition and internal summaries have been built in as pedagogical aids throughout the text.

TREATMENT OF STATISTICS

Students often believe that researchers begin by designing a study, then gather data, and only after the data are gathered do they select appropriate statistical procedures for the analyses. There are two problems with this conceptualization, and both are addressed in this text. First, we emphasize to the student that the decisions regarding statistical analyses are not made after data collection, but are an integral part of the design process. Accordingly, basic statistical concepts are introduced early in the text (Chapters 4 and 5), and their integration into the design process is maintained throughout. Second, choosing an appropriate statistical procedure often appears to students to be more difficult than it really is. The choice of appropriate statistical analyses is not made from a chaotic array but stems systematically from the design characteristics of the study. We have attempted to teach students how to select analysis procedures in a systematic fashion. In Chapter 14 we have included what we believe to be a unique section in research methods texts: *Decision-tree flowcharts* that lead the students step by step through any basic research design to the choice of an appropriate statistical procedure. The students' use of these flowcharts with exercises given in the text and in the study guide, as well as with any assignments the instructor adds, provides practice in determining the appropriate statistical procedures to use and in critically evaluating research reported by others. In our classes we have found the flowcharts to be valuable teaching aids.

The statistical material in the text has been prepared for students who have not had a statistics course as well as for those who have. The latter students can use the material as review and for experience in integrating statistical procedures with other aspects of research design. The flowcharts should be of value to all students. Appendix C provides more detail on statistical procedures. The instructor, of course, can emphasize this statistical material or not, depending upon the level and type of course being taught.

LEVELS OF RESEARCH

A major aim of this text is to teach students that there are several levels at which research can be conducted. Experimental research, which is covered in Chapters 8–12, is the most rigorous and allows us to answer questions of causality. But other questions are possible: questions about the strength and direction of relationships among variables, questions about differences between already existing rather than experimentally manipulated groups, questions concerning a single individual, and questions about observations leading to the formation rather than the testing of causal hypotheses. All are properly scientific questions about observed relationships among variables and all can be answered systematically. We believe that it is important for students to learn that appropriate scientific research design is largely dependent upon the nature of the question asked (the level of inquiry) and that research at all levels—whether naturalistic, case study, correlational, differential, quasi-experimental, or experimental—is appropriate and useful. As the text builds conceptual foundations to the level of experimental research, it does so by developing each of the other levels of inquiry, thereby providing students with a full spectrum of research knowledge and skills. Chapters 6, 7, and 13 focus on nonexperimental research procedures.

Ethical issues are important in all research. When we decide to use living organisms as subjects, we must be concerned with their welfare and ensure that our procedures do not violate their health, safety, or rights. Because of the importance of ethical issues, we have introduced the topic early and, consistent with the text's general organization, we return to it at later points for further discussion.

In writing this text we have kept our focus on the primary audience: undergraduate students. Several reviewers, however, have suggested that the text may also be useful as supplemental, review, or introductory material in graduate courses.

SUPPLEMENTS

Instructors will find in some instances that our particular interpretations and procedures are unlike their own. In the instructor's manual we have tried to anticipate where there is room for different views and provide material for additional class discussion. In those instances instructors can bring in additional material or organize lectures to incorporate their differing views and interpretations or to emphasize areas of particular importance or interest to them. In addition, the instructor's manual includes a substantial test item file to simplify the task of assessment.

We have also prepared a study guide to supplement the text. Like the text, the study guide structures the learning process for students. Each study guide chapter starts by reviewing basic concepts and terminology, and then proceeds to develop these concepts to increasingly higher levels of understanding. Students should find this study guide a valuable resource and instructors will find that it frees them from the task of preparing routine exercises. Evaluation sheets are provided in the instructor's manual and the study guide, and we welcome any comments and suggestions you may have as you use this text.

ACKNOWLEDGMENTS

The manuscript has gone through many revisions. We used it in prepublication form as a text in two undergraduate research methods courses. These trials were most helpful in identifying sources of ambiguity for students and allowing us to refine our presentation of the material. During the writing process several successive panels of reviewers offered valuable comments and insights. We believe that the process of review and revision has substantially improved the text, allowing us to present complex material in a manner understandable to students. We wish to thank the following reviewers for their comments: Vincent J. Adesso, University of Wisconsin, Milwaukee; Lawrence R. Gordon, University of Vermont; Bert R. Brown, Rutgers—The State University of New Jersey; Charles G. Halcomb, Texas Tech University; Madeline Heilman, New York University; John P. Hostetler, Albion College; Daniel W. Leger, University of Nebraska; Daniel D. Moriarty, Jr., University of San Diego; James L. Pate, Georgia State University; Samuel L. Seaman, Baylor University; Robert M. Stern, The Pennsylvania State University; and Lois E. Tetrick, Wayne State University.

In addition to the reviewers listed above, others have contributed to this text. Several faculty colleagues provided valuable consultation, including Erving Biederman, B. Richard Bugelski, Edwin Hollander, Mark Kristal, Murray Levine, Kenneth Levy, Brenda Major, John Meacham, Dean Pruitt, James Sawusch, and C. James Smith. Two students, Cathleen Carter and Kevin Gorey, made helpful comments on an early draft of the manuscript. Valuable secretarial assistance was provided by Janice Mings, Mary Steves, Lee Gordon, Bridget Winter, and Elaine Weiner. Finally, we express our appreciation to the editorial staff of Harper & Row, including our sponsoring editors, Leslie Carr and Susan Mackey; project editor, Vivian Koenig; and copyeditor, Wendy Polhemus-Annibell.

Anthony M. Graziano

Michael L. Raulin

STUDENT'S PREFACE

For most of us, our image of a scientist is someone who wears a white coat and spends his or her time peering at complicated equipment in shining and mysterious laboratories. But a scientist can operate very scientifically while sitting under a tree in the woods, thinking through a problem, and using apparatus no more technical than a pad and a pencil. This image is important because it emphasizes that the essence of science lies in its logic. Science is above all a way of thinking. The laboratories, the equipment, the computers, in short, all of the hardware, are tools used to promote and support the scientist's central activity: creative, systematic thinking. That intellectual activity is incorporated into a process of inquiry in which the scientist asks and answers questions about nature. That process of inquiry is what we mean by scientific research, and it is the focus of this text.

We ask questions every day. To answer many of those questions we tend to rely on our feelings about things, on our hunches, on already existing ideas, and on respected authorities. Seldom do we seek answers in the systematic manner of science. Although thinking scientifically is unfamiliar to most of us, we can learn to think scientifically. This is the major challenge of this course. Excitement, hunches, and flashes of insight are very much a part of science. So are plodding hard work, rigorous, systematic thinking, and procedures that put our ideas to many demanding tests. All are part of the creative and exciting endeavor of scientific research.

You will find that a research methods course is quite demanding, but the concepts are not really difficult. What may be difficult is learning to think in a different manner than you do now, to think critically and systematically, to phrase questions in such a way that they can be answered clearly, and to apply the many demands of science to the nature of your evidence and to the procedures you use. You will learn to have more confidence in those ideas that survive the rigors of scientific scrutiny and to discard those that do not.

This text has been designed for your *active,* rather than passive, use. You will find questions and problems posed in both the chapters and the exercises at the end of each chapter. There is an index and a glossary. Work through the problems and exercises; consult the glossary when necessary; and if you need more information on some concept, use the index to direct you to more discussion on that topic in the text. The chapter footnotes and the text's references are good sources for further reading.

A study guide has also been prepared, and you are urged to use it *actively* to aid in your mastery of the material. The purpose of the study guide is to organize the information and to structure the studying of each chapter. The study guide starts by summarizing the material and identifying key terms for each chapter, and then goes on to encourage you to actively check your knowledge of the material with test questions in a variety of formats. Answers are provided so that areas of confusion can be identified and corrected before the course examinations.

We welcome your comments and evaluation of this text and urge you to use the evaluation sheets that have been included in the text and study guide.

Anthony M. Graziano

Michael L. Raulin

CHAPTER 1

CURIOSITY, CREATIVITY, AND COMMITMENT

SCIENCE IS A WAY OF THINKING

Scientists seek answers to their own questions. Their work is built on highly refined skills in asking and answering questions: Knowing how to ask questions is as important as knowing how to go about answering them. The essence of *science* is the process of carefully composing questions and then systematically seeking their answers to gain a better understanding of nature. Science involves a *process of inquiry,* a particular way of thinking.

From this process of inquiry many tools and useful products are created, such as laboratory equipment, statistical procedures, computers and computer programs, space flight, new medicines, more powerful detergents and, unfortunately, even more powerful weapons. The tools and applied products of science are too often mistaken for the essence of science. They are not. The essence of science is the scientist's ways of thinking, the logic used in systematically asking and answering questions. A scientist can operate scientifically while sitting under a tree in the woods, thinking through a problem and using apparatus no more technical than paper and pencil. A scientific discipline such as chemistry is not made more scientific than another such as psychology by virtue of its bubbling liquids and laboratory equipment. Likewise, knowing how to use an electron microscope or how to run a computer program does not make a scientist out of a laboratory technician. Our modern television-sustained image of the white-coated laboratory worker surrounded by machines with blinking lights and computers fed by whirling tapes is an effective visual metaphor, but it does not validly portray the essence of science any more than, to use another metaphor, a skyscraper really scrapes the sky. *The essence of modern science is the way of thinking, the discipline in asking and answering questions. It is the intellectual and logical processes of thought and demands for evidence, and not the technologies, which characterize science.*

ASKING QUESTIONS

Asking questions, of course, is not new. Socrates and his followers over 2400 years ago used a highly developed system for asking questions. As in a balanced equation, a question is one side of an idea; on the other side is an unknown quantity, a potential answer. Every question points to the existence of an unknown, to some area of human ignorance or uncertainty. Socrates knew, apparently to his delight, that by posing systematically sharp questions about religion, politics, and morality he could spear even the most dignified citizens, revealing their ignorance and uncertainties, and driving them to extreme discomfort. Unfortunately for Socrates, the good citizens were made so uncomfortable that they executed him as a subversive and corrupter of youth. It was thus established early in history that asking questions may be hazardous to one's health. But risk-taking is part of any scientist's work. Numerous social and political strains have been caused by those who raise questions and expose ignorance, and these people often suffer serious reprisals. Leonardo da Vinci and Galileo posed serious threats to church dogma in the Renaissance; Charles Darwin, Alfred Russel Wallace, and a number of nineteenth-century geologists presented data that seriously questioned the biblical account of creation and the biblically dated age of the earth (see Box 1.1). Lest

Box 1.1 CHARLES DARWIN AND ALFRED RUSSEL WALLACE

Charles Darwin (1809–1882) is one of the most important scientists in history. His work, *On the Origin of Species* (1859), has had profound effects on science, philosophy, religion, and even on political debate.

After completing his famous journeys, Darwin spent the next 21 years (1838–1859) in England, working on his notes and refining his ideas for the eventual publication of *On the Origin of Species.* In June 1858, when his book was still far from completion, Darwin received a package in the mail. The package contained a manuscript in which his own thesis had already been written! Darwin had been preempted by another naturalist, Alfred Russel Wallace (1823–1913).

According to Arthur Keith (1954), Wallace, unlike Darwin who had inherited wealth, was a poor man who had to live off of the earnings from the specimens he collected. Like Darwin many years before, Wallace traveled and studied in the Amazon valley and in the South Pacific. Wallace was impressed by the great diversity of life he had observed during his travels and he followed, completely independently, the same line of reasoning as Darwin in making sense out of the observed data. The result was Wallace's manuscript on the biological operation of

natural selection in the origins of new species. Wallace mailed his discovery to Darwin for comment.

Who was to be the first to present this momentous discovery to the world? Darwin's associates arranged to have the two men's work presented simultaneously at a meeting of the Linnean Society of London on July 1, 1858. Thus Wallace and Darwin are credited equally with the discovery. Long before, the Greeks had developed a concept of evolution. However, it was Wallace and Darwin who gathered the mass of data and created the concept of natural selection that made their evolutionary theory so important.

During the following year, Darwin completed with new urgency *On the Origin of Species,* and soon became the acknowledged originator of the idea of natural selection and the model that derived from it. Wallace, apparently content with this, made no great efforts to share in the subsequent acclaim and the two men remained life-long friends. He outlived Darwin by 31 years, and died in 1913. Wallace contributed many important books and papers to science and is recognized by biologists as an eminent naturalist. However, it is Darwin who is remembered for the great biological discovery.

one believe that reprisals occurred only in the historical past, consider what the Germans did to their Jewish scientists in the 1930s and 1940s or the fate of scientists in Russia even now. The free *skepticism* of scientists cannot be tolerated in authoritarian states. But even in the United States, the free pursuit and exchange of knowledge has been often interfered with by government officials. Scientific knowledge has become so important in our modern world that competing governments impose constraints of secrecy on their own scientists to prevent the leaking of information (see Box 1.2). Science, its questions, its answers, and even its dissemination, make many people very uncomfortable indeed.

Although scientists are not necessarily uncomfortable with uncertainties, they do attempt to resolve them—not by denying the questions and reasserting old beliefs, but by studying the questions and seeking new answers. The scientist is a pervasive skeptic willing to tolerate uncertainty and who finds intellectual excitement in creating ques-

---

Box 1.2   AN EXAMPLE OF STATE CENSORSHIP OF SCIENCE

In August 1982 scientists and engineers from 30 countries met in San Diego at the Annual International Technical Symposium of the Society of Photo-Optical Instrumentation Engineers. They came to exchange ideas both formally and informally, in symposia, papers, workshops, and displays. On opening day a rumor began that 100 scheduled papers had been suddenly cancelled under orders of the Department of Defense. In addition, the Department of Commerce issued a warning to all American participants that if they revealed any "strategic" information they would be in violation of regulations concerning the export of technology.

The rumor was true. United States government agents were there to see that the papers were not presented, and a chilling effect spread through the conference. Those whose papers had been cancelled did not know why, since their work had not been classified for restricted use by the Department of Defense. The other American participants were uncertain about their own participation, fearing legal action and interrupted research support if it were later decided they had revealed "strategic" information.

The government was concerned that some of the information might be of future strategic (usually meaning military) value, and thus should not be made available to the participating Russian scientists. National security is a legitimate concern, and the freedom to exchange ideas must be balanced against it. The problems arise in how to achieve that balance, how to protect security while avoiding overreaching censorship by government. Many at the conference believed that the government's actions in this instance were too sudden and too sweeping.

---

tions and seeking answers about nature. Asking a question is a creative endeavor. A question brings together two or more ideas which, at least for the moment, pose something new. The formation of something new provides the scientist with the personal satisfaction of indulging one's own curiosity and exercising one's own creativity.

Scientists agree that sheer curiosity is one of their major motivators and curiosity is a major component of their work. "What?" "How?" and "What if?" are among the scientists most basic vocabulary. Curiosity may have killed the cat, according to the old saying, but curiosity also sustains the scientist. J. Robert Oppenheimer, speaking about the commonalities of physics and psychology, notes that the sciences are "responsive to a primitive, permanent, pervasive human curiosity" (1956, p. 128). According to Linus Pauling (1981), satisfying one's own curiosity is one of life's greatest sources of happiness. B. F. Skinner also emphasizes the importance of indulging your curiosity in science, even if it pulls you away from more systematic work: "When you run onto something interesting, drop everything else and study it" (1956, p. 223).

The scientist's pursuit of curiosity follows unknown paths, sometimes resulting in dramatic and unanticipated discoveries that can appear to the public as accidental, a matter of "luck." But when scientists drop everything to indulge their curiosity, they do so with what has been called a prepared mind—a disciplined curiosity that makes them sharply alert to the possibility of unanticipated discovery. "A discovery," as Albert Szent-Gyorgi notes, "is said to be an accident meeting a prepared mind" (quoted in Bachrach, 1981, p. 3). Expressing the same point, George Nelson (1970) recounts a comment made by Louis Pasteur when he was the guest of honor at a large reception: "Isn't it extraordinary these days," someone said to Pasteur, "how many scientific achievements are arrived at by accident?" "Yes," replied Pasteur, "it really is remarkable when you think of it, and furthermore, did you ever observe to whom the accidents happen?" (p. 263).

Scientists' curiosity is not idle, but active. That active curiosity leads to discoveries not out of aimless luck but because it is embedded within a prepared mind and long hours of research. It is a highly disciplined curiosity, sharpened and aimed by labor and frustrations, as well as by successes.

SCIENCE AND ART

Although we have attributed certain characteristics to scientists—curiosity, creativity, skepticism, tolerance for ambiguity, and commitment to hard work and a way of thinking that searches for answers to questions—these characteristics are equally well developed in poets, sculptors, painters, composers, philosophers, writers, and others. All engage in a mix of artistic and intellectual endeavors and share the following qualities: they indulge their own curiosity; they explore their worlds with skeptical questioning and sharp observations; and they attempt to answer their own questions and to represent parts of the world through their own particular medium—whether it is color, shape, sound, language, the plasticity of clay, or the solidity of stone. Their representations of ideas become part of the public domain where they may be viewed, criticized, discussed, accepted, rejected, or worse, ignored. In each of these endeavors, we see people compelled by a combination of curiosity and creativity who delight in their discoveries of relationships in nature and in their created representations of nature. Their statements are tentative. Whether a symphony, a painting, or a research investigation, they are presented not as fixed or complete truths but as tentative statements of their own understanding at a given point in time. This is not to argue that science and art are the same. They are not. Yet each employs variations of the same themes: human curiosity, combined with a commitment to ideas, to disciplined processes of inquiry, and to producing the representations of their ideas. Although artists and scientists comprise only a small part of the world's population, they have created a large and enduring array of the ideas and products that have significantly affected the world.

The belief that art and science are so totally different that artists and scientists must be thoroughly alienated from each other is not uncommon. We often hear statements that suggest someone is the artistic type (poet, musician, and so on) and therefore has no capacity for science or math, or that a science or math person cannot appreciate art and literature. However, these assumptions are most often not the case. For example, consider the 40 national winners of the annual Westinghouse Science Talent Competition. Many of these young people of high achievement in science, mathematics, and technology are also talented in other creative activities such as music, writing, and visual arts. As we will see later in this chapter, art, science, and technology were all generated from the same pool of human skills and curiosity early in civilization. Art and science, although different from each other, share many characteristics.

COMMON METHODS OF ACQUIRING KNOWLEDGE_____

The essence of science is its systematic, disciplined way of thinking aimed at gaining *knowledge* about nature. Science places heavy demands on the adequacy of its information and on the processes applied to that information. Science can be described as "common sense" developed to a highly disciplined level. However, science is not the only way of thinking about the world.

G. C. Helmstadter (1970) has labeled the common methods of acquiring knowledge as tenacity, intuition, authority, rationalism, empiricism, and science. These methods are ranked from low to high, in the order of the demands made on the adequacy of the information that each is willing to accept and on the nature of the processing of that information. The methods of science, which include rationalism and empiricism, are the most demanding in these respects, whereas tenacity, intuition, and authority make few demands on information and require minimal processing.

Tenacity

Tenacity describes a willingness to accept an idea as valid knowledge because that idea has been accepted for a long period of time. Tenacity requires no evidence for a belief except that the belief is already accepted. An example of a tenacious idea, held in spite of a lack of evidence, is the belief by some psychotherapists that treating enuretic (bedwetting) children with conditioning therapies will lead to symptom substitution and the possibility that children will develop even more serious symptoms.

Intuition

Intuition supposedly operates directly, without any intellectual effort or, according to some, without any involvement of sensory processes. Examples of such supposedly direct-access knowledge include extrasensory perception (a contradiction in terms), which has been claimed by self-styled psychics, and knowledge received directly from God, claimed by persons who have had powerful religious experiences.

Authority

Authority as a method of acquiring knowledge is the acceptance of an idea as valid knowledge because some respected source—such as religious writings, Aristotle, the Communist Party Central Committee, the President, the Pope, or Sigmund Freud— claims it is valid.

The tenacity, intuition, and authority methods of knowing make few demands on their information and processes. In essence they assert that "we know this is true because (1) it has always been so, (2) because we feel it is so, or (3) because the authority says it is so." What they share is an uncritical acceptance of their information and conclusions and limited skepticism about their methods. All of us, even scientists, use some of these methods in everyday life and are willing to make some decisions based on an uncritical acceptance of information. Such methods have value in smoothing our personal lives. We might, for example, accept religious teachings intuitively or on authority, and experience personal satisfaction in sharing religious ceremonies with others. We can easily act upon our strong urge that tells us we would rather have steak than spaghetti for dinner, accepting it as valid knowledge of what we really want, without any need for further evaluation of the information. But would we also uncritically agree to saunter across a six-lane freeway with our eyes closed because our companion tells us that he knows intuitively through his psychic powers that we will be perfectly safe in spite of the 360 cars per minute hurtling by at high speed from both directions? Clearly, for some kinds of decisions, we must demand that our information and the processes used to gather it be more adequate. In this regard both *rationalism* and *empiricism* give us a much firmer basis for accepting information as knowledge.

Rationalism

Rationalism is a way of thinking in which knowledge is developed through reasoning processes alone. In the rationalistic approach, information is carefully stated and logical rules are followed to arrive at acceptable conclusions. Consider this classic deductive syllogism:

> All crows are black.
> This is a crow.
> Therefore, this crow is black.

The conclusion is logically derived from the major and minor premises. The same logic, however, would lead us to reject the following conclusion:

> All crows are black.
> This is black.
> Therefore, this is a crow.

In the rationalistic approach the conclusion is reached through the *logic* of the procedure, which is a more reliable way to arrive at knowledge than tenacity, intuition, or authority. However, using rationalism alone has its limitations. Consider this syllogism:

> All 4-year-old children develop fears of the dark.
> Lisa is a 4-year-old child.
> Therefore, Lisa has developed fears of the dark.

The logic is clear and the conclusion is correct, unless of course Lisa has not developed fears of the dark. What is the limitation? Suppose it is not true that all 4-year-old children develop fears of the dark, or suppose Lisa is actually 7 and not 4 years old, or suppose Lisa is a yacht and not a child at all. Although essential, rationalism alone has its limitations in science; that is, *the major and minor premises must be true as determined by some other evidence* to arrive at the correct conclusions. Attaining knowledge, then, depends not only on the reasoning process but also on the accuracy of the premises. There is no provision for assessing their accuracy in the pure rationalistic approach.

The rationalistic approach allows us systematically and logically to develop a tentative statement (hypothesis) that can then be tested in some other manner. Each premise is a hypothesis, which, if shown to be true (valid) on the basis of external data, can be used rationally in drawing conclusions. In summary, the logic of rationalism is used in modern science to aid in developing hypotheses that can then be tested against external criteria. Further, for testing against external criteria, science must depend on still another way of knowing, empiricism.

Empiricism

Empiricism is a way of gaining knowledge through observation of real events; that is, *knowing by experiencing through our senses.* It is a method that is as old as civilization. For the empiricist, it is not enough to know through reason (or tenacity or intuition or authority) alone. It is necessary to experience events through the senses, to see, hear, touch, taste, and smell. "I won't believe it unless I see it!" is the empiricist's motto. Thales, Hippocrates, Galen, Copernicus, Galileo, and Darwin all based their important conclusions about nature largely on their observations of events. They rejected the more widely held, nonempirical alternative conceptions provided by mythology, religion, appeal to authority, and rationalism. On a more modern and personal note, when we are ready to leave our home in the morning and we see that the sky is dark and filled with clouds, and we hear approaching rumblings of thunder in the distance, we are good empiricists if we take a hat or umbrella—our senses are telling us something.

Empiricism alone, however, has its limitations. For example, suppose that a psychoanalyst concluded that all enuretic children (children over the age of 4 who do not control urination and who repeatedly wet their bed or clothes) suffer from unresolved Oedipal conflicts. These conflicts, according to this psychoanalyst, cause the enuresis and also cause all enuretic children to be highly anxious and phobic. Therefore, all enuretic children need intensive psychoanalytic treatment to get to the basic causes of their problems. This psychoanalyst did not base her conclusions on an unthinking acceptance of Freud as an authority but on her own empirical observations over more than 20 years in private practice. During that time, more than 100 enuretic children had been brought to her by their parents for treatment and each child was viewed by the analyst as being seriously troubled by the Oedipal conflict and as highly anxious and phobic. There was not a single exception to these observations and interpretations. With such consistent observations of so many cases over so many years of experience, she was extremely confident in her conclusions. As carefully empirical as she tried to be, her conclusions about all enuretic children might be resoundingly incorrect! Here we pose a problem for the reader: Can you see in what ways this psychoanalyst's empiricism might have been misleading? Think it through, and then check your ideas against the discussion in Chapter 2.

Science

From our discussion so far the student should have recognized that *science* brings together elements of both rationalism and empiricism. Science employs rational logic and checks each step with empirical observation. The scientist is constantly shuttling between empirical observation and more abstract rational thought and general principles and back again to further empirical observation of specific facts. It was this repeated returning to empirical observation in an otherwise rationalistic process that marked the sixteenth century's apparently sudden surge into science. Much of the progress in scientific procedure since then has been in strengthening the empirical component by developing more precise methods of observation.

Science is a way of thinking that involves a continuous and systematic interplay of rational thinking and empirical observation. Observed events, whether the movements of planets observed by an astronomer or the behavior of children observed by a psychologist, constitute the major facts of a discipline. But the empirical observation of events and the resulting identification or listing of facts is not sufficient in science. We must go beyond the immediately observable facts, using them in rational processes of abstract thought to construct general principles and understandings and to make new predictions about nature. Science, then, involves the continuous systematic interplay of facts and rational thought. The scientist remains curious, skeptical, and committed, using processes that identify or discover facts and that then integrate those facts into coherent predictions, explanations, and general principles.

EMERGING MODERN SCIENCE

Modern science emerged in the fifteenth and sixteenth centuries. This observation sometimes misleads readers into thinking that science was suddenly created and that there had been no science in the world before Copernicus, Galileo, or Newton. That, of course, is not true. Science has been one of western civilization's alternative methods of acquiring knowledge since the Greeks of 2400 years ago, and its antecedents date back still further, possibly 8000 years. It was not until the late Renaissance in the seventeenth century that science was able to acquire enough independence, social importance, and recognition to begin its rapid acceleration into the powerful social movement it is today.

To understand the development of science, remember that it offers a way of thinking that integrates systematic rationalism with direct empirical observation, the latter serving both as a way of testing prior observations and making new observations to serve as a basis for further rational development. Science is uniquely different from other ways of knowing. A look at the history of science suggests that empiricism was the first to develop, followed by the emergence of rationalism, which, in turn, developed into a sophisticated and competing system. The two were integrated and, finally, the combined process, science, gained social support. Each step represented a major change, and major changes do not occur quickly in history. The long history of science is rooted in ancient intellectual systems, which eventually became the modern social movement.

Early Civilization

Civilization is a process of developing from the primitive, nomadic hunter's existence to a socially organized, cooperative life-style. Civilization operates on a broad array of collective human skills that evolved slowly over millennia and were taught to successive generations. Then, in the relatively short period from about 6000–4000 B.C., the long accumulation of human skills coalesced, enabling a remarkable surge of progress from the late neolithic period of polished stone tools into the age of metals. In growing urban settlements, people integrated and applied the technological, social, and intellectual tools of early civilizations. Humans had spread around the eastern Mediterranean and by about 6000 B.C. had established an astonishing array of skills. The magnificent civilizations of the Babylonians, Egyptians, and others had long flourished and their people had lived in complex, stable societies. The great array of human skills and achievements that were passed on to the Greeks included architecture, agriculture, animal husbandry, preparing and preserving foods, mining, smelting and refining metals, forming carefully combined alloys, and manufacturing a great variety of stone and metal tools. Complicated business and commercial skills were developed that depended on long-distance land and sea navigation. They could weigh, count, do arithmetic, write and maintain permanent records, and keep track of seasons with their accurate calendars. Scholars had developed astronomy, medicine, surgery, and mathematics and, by 4000 B.C., important books on those subjects were available. Early scholarly interests also included imaginative and mystical conceptions of the universe with ideas of gods, demons, and spirits. Early cosmologies were mystical views propounded by the growing class of priests, and they provided a unified conception of the universe.

By 1000 B.C. there was a rich legacy, a complex background of human skills. Benjamin Farrington (1949) has emphasized two characteristics of that array of skills. First, they were practical skills aimed at the everyday demands of making a living. There was little value attached to abstract thinking, in knowledge for the sake of knowledge. By contrast, much value was placed on practical knowledge about agriculture, manufacturing, commerce, and so on. Practical skills and knowledge had been developed from long involvement in the direct, concrete, and objective manipulation of the real, physical environment. They were, in a word, *empirical* skills.

The second characteristic emphasized by Farrington is that from the long involvement in practical skills, there gradually developed more abstract, general ideas about nature. Agriculture and metallurgy are good examples of Farrington's point. In exercising their practical skills the early farmers observed weather phenomena, floods, moon phases, and other changes in the sky for cues to help in their farming. As a result they developed accurate calendars, they learned about using fertilizers and something of the processes of plant growth, and they developed enough practical mathematics to enable them to measure plots and set boundaries. The Egyptians, for example, could accurately measure the annual fall of the Nile River within a few inches.

With metallurgical knowledge artisans could recognize various types of ores and the conditions under which they could best be mined. They knew, for example, about the action of heat in transforming solids into liquids. They were able to measure by weighing and to understand proportionality so as to reproduce reliably the particular mixes needed for various alloys. In these skilled crafts there was considerable abstract, general information about nature, gathered and refined through generations of empirical observations and concrete manipulations. Such abstract knowledge was important only in relation to carrying out practical tasks. The young apprentice did not study abstract astronomy, biology, chemistry, or mathematics—yet we can see embedded in the crafts early elements of those later, more abstract, bodies of knowledge. Thus, in the early Mediterranean civilizations, the components of modern science were found to be in the arts. Science, art, and technology were inseparable in practice.

Another important principle in the development of science is the *"orderliness belief"* (Whitehead, 1925). Science rests on the implicit belief that the universe operates in an orderly, lawful manner. If it did not or if we did not hold this belief, says Whitehead, there could be no science. If the universe were not orderly and predictable, it would not stay the same long enough to be studied. To apply their skills in a reliable manner, the artisans of 1000 B.C. had to expect orderliness in the physical world. How else could they depend on *this* type of rock, when heated, to release *that* kind of metal, which will always have *these* particular properties, and to do so each time regardless of the different pieces of the rock used?

Greek Science

By 600 B.C. the basic components necessary for the emergence of science had been developed. There was as yet no articulate science to organize or to transmit skills or ideas. However, there were other social mechanisms: pragmatic skills and close-to-the-facts abstractions were transmitted by the artisans, tradesmen, and other practically oriented people, while more imaginative, speculative, and less empirically based notions about the universe were transmitted through mythology, drama, and religion. In religion, gods and demons, humans and animals coexisted in a complicated universe that was both material and mystical, but was always orderly. Both the artisans and the priests accepted the orderliness notion. The artisans set their orderliness within pragmatic, concrete experiences; the priests set their orderliness within imaginative, abstract, and mystical cosmologies.

The pre-Socratic Greek period, about 600–400 B.C., was one of developing empirical science. Thales (ca. 640–550 B.C.) is credited as the first Greek philosopher to combine an empirical-rational view of the universe, a view that rejected the prevalent religion and mysticism. Thales lived in Ionia, a Greek colony whose citizens developed a highly commercial level of skills and interests and were pragmatic realists. The skills of the artisans, the farmers, and the tradesmen were of great importance. Empirical knowledge was a basic part of their culture and when some, like Thales, turned to philosophy, they developed a clearly empirical view of nature. Thales' philosophy stressed the observation of natural events in a natural universe and rejected the mysticism of gods, demons, or spirits. He speculated about a natural cosmology in which water was the basic substance from which all else developed and to which all will ultimately return. He learned enough about Babylonian astronomy to predict accurately the solar eclipse that took place on May 25, 585 B.C. He developed an empirical-rational approach that was scientific, albeit in primitive form, because his observations were based on experimentation and on what Whitehead (1925) terms "the painstaking attention to observational details." Thales is the founder of abstract geometry and Ionian philosophy, and is considered to be the "father" of science.

Thales' naturalistic rather than mystical speculations were continued by others. Anaximander's (611–547 B.C.) observations of a shark that had mammalian characteristics led him to develop the concept that higher order creatures, including humans, developed from lower animals, specifically fishes, and gradually emerged from the seas to dry land. It is clear that a concept of the evolution of life on earth was in early development in Greek science. Empedocles (ca. 500 B.C.) created observable demonstrations of the existence of air by using inflated wine skins. Xenophanes (ca. 600 B.C.), having observed rock imprints of fish and seaweed high on mountains and in landlocked stone quarries, developed a systematic theory of geological change over time.

About midway through the development of Greek philosophy, around 450 B.C., Hippocrates emerged with radical ideas for treating illness. At the time, most believed that human illness was caused by demons and spirits invading the body, and treatment involved prayers, incantations, and exorcisms. Hippocratic teachings clearly rejected this mysticism and attributed all mental and physical illnesses to natural events. For Hippocrates, no demon, spirit, or god played any part in disease and no prayers, incantations, or exorcisms could make a sick person well. The Hippocratic physician relied on careful, clinical observations of patients through the course of the disease, and on systematic, rational thought in trying to understand illness. Although the Hippocratic teachings were a major alternative to mysticism and demonology, the Greeks had no science of anatomy, physiology, or chemistry, and therefore had few effective treatments.

In the Ionian development of empirical-rational science from Thales through Hippocrates we see a major emphasis on the careful observation of events in natural, uncontrolled conditions. Thales' scientist and Hippocrates' physician were careful observers and systematic thinkers, but were not systematic manipulators of events. It would be a later Ionian, Strato, who would develop the next important step: making the scientist an active observer who manipulates and controls the conditions of observations. Strato developed Ionian science to the level of actual experimentation.

Strato, one of the last empirical philosophers, was a successor to Aristotle at the Lyceum from 287–269 B.C. He accepted the Ionian cosmology with its emphasis on natural events, its basic belief in the universe as orderly and knowable, and its rejection of mysticism. For Strato, the best method of acquiring knowledge was that of empirical manipulation and observation, that is, *experimentation*. He performed numerous experiments on air and water, demonstrating many of their properties and changes under different conditions. From his experimental work Strato developed some general, explanatory principles about nature.

By Strato's time, however, Ionian science was already in decline, overshadowed by other developments. By 400 B.C. a naturalistic, scientific view stood as an alternative to the generally accepted, mystical beliefs propounded by religion and, later, by philosophers such as Socrates and Plato. Then, as now, these incompatible models—empirical sciences versus mysticism—conflicted, leading to the near-total suppression of one by the other. The early empirical science was virtually lost for the next 1900 years, until the late Renaissance. A condition that might have been partly responsible for the demise of empiricism in Greek science was the growing stratification of society into occupational and status classes. Manual labor and technological skills, with their pragmatic and empirical focus, became separated from the more socially desired and leisurely pursuits of priests, scholars, and ruling classes. Slavery became a major Greek institution for carrying out the manual labor and technical tasks necessary to maintain society. Plato and Aristotle, for example, defended slavery as a necessary and desirable institution, allowing people at higher levels to function in a more ideal manner.

After Socrates, the highest ideals were religion, politics, and rationalistic, mystical philosophy. The pursuit of practical goals was recognized as necessary and left to slaves, laborers, artisans, farmers, and tradesmen, while the pursuit of pure reason and abstract truths was the ideal and reserved for the upper-social levels. As a result theology and abstract philosophy were carefully taught and scrupulously preserved in writing, while the technical, empirical skills and knowledge, not admitted into the realm of scholarship, remained in the oral tradition and were not as fully recorded or preserved. Although social stratification may have helped to separate empiricism from the mainstream of scholarship, more specific attacks on empiricism and naturalism were also occurring. Religion was gaining social power, promulgating its mystical cosmology while attacking the natural philosophy of the Ionians as atheistic and therefore not only factually wrong but also a subversive danger.

The genius of the early Greeks had created empirical, rational science and generated the profound idea of searching for abstract and general principles that would explain observed events. The later highly articulated rational philosophies that culminated with Aristotle (384–322 B.C.) described an orderly universe that operated according to a few basic principles and in which all of the variety of specific, empirically observed events are but manifestations of these basic principles. This contribution of Greek philosophy—so thoroughly transcending immediate, objective reality and conceptualizing a universe of such magnificent orderliness that all of its seeming variation could be understood through discovery of a small number of basic principles—is one of humanity's major intellectual developments. It has profoundly influenced modern thought.

The movement of scholars away from empiricism and pragmatism after about 400 B.C. was led by Socrates, Plato, and to some extent Aristotle despite his strong empiricism. The Greeks developed both rationalism and empiricism, but it was the pursuit of pure reason with which they culminated their philosophy. As Farrington (1949a) comments, "When Plato died (about 347 B.C.) he left behind him a mystical view of the universe set forth in his dialogues in a unique combination of logic and drama. Its weakness was not that it lacked supports in argument, but that it was not open to correction from experience" (p. 13). From 400 B.C. Greek philosophy became increasingly abstract, rational, and mystical, relegating empirical knowledge to less importance and, eventually, joining the attacks on empiricism.

As philosophers became increasingly mystical in their pursuit of the ideal, there was a growing affinity of religious and philosophical mysticism. The universal orderliness such as that observed in astronomy (e.g., it was believed that planets moved in perfect circles) and the beautiful regularity of number relationships discovered by the Pythagoreans were taken as evidence that nature was controlled by divine intelligence. An important shift in the goals of philosophy and science was occurring. Whereas the earlier investigators made observations of nature and rationally analyzed their observations to understand and control nature, the later philosophers began to observe and to think about nature to discover, understand, and illustrate the existence of divine intelligence. In other words, science was beginning to be used in the service of religion, a role that was to be continued and magnified in the Christian era for more than a thousand years and into the Renaissance.

Medieval Science

After centuries of persecution Christianity was accepted as one of the Roman empire's religions at the start of the fourth century, and, by the end of that century was virtually the sole state religion. Christianity grew increasingly powerful as a religious-philosophical movement, a social institution, and a political power, pervading virtually all thought and action in western Europe for the next thousand years.

Although it has been said that Greek empirical science was suppressed by the medieval Christians, that suppression had actually begun with the later Greeks, long before Christianity. The Greeks' increasing reliance on intuition and pure reason rather than empiricism as methods of acquiring knowledge was continued by the medieval scholars, just as they continued so much of the Greco-Roman beliefs and traditions in creating the Christian philosophical-religious stand. The medieval scholars, like the Greeks, believed that divine intelligence controlled an orderly and knowable universe. Probably the most basic tenet in medieval thought was the unshakable belief that the scriptures were the ultimate source of truth. In those instances where specific knowledge was not revealed in the Bible, the rational thought and/or intuition of church authorities substituted as truth. Theology was the reigning study; revelation, rationalism, and authority were its major methods of acquiring knowledge, and all other areas and methods of study were secondary. Empiricism had its place within medieval science, albeit a secondary one. While the Christian scholars continued empirical study in astronomy, optics, and zoology, their empiricism was in the service of religion (Nagel, 1948).

By the thirteenth century, however, some churchmen such as Thomas Aquinas and Roger Bacon, perhaps partly influenced by the rediscovery of early classical scholarship, recognized the value of using the senses for acquiring knowledge about God. Bacon and other medieval scientists repeated a number of optical experiments that had been performed long ago by Islamic scientists. A Dominican, Dietrich of Frieberg (ca. 1300), used water-filled glass balls to experiment with the visible spectrum, discovering that colors are reflected on the inside of spherical water drops. At about the same time Jordanus DeNemore experimented with various types of levers and the equilibrium of weights on inclined planes. In 1269 Peter the Stranger of Maricourt published his empirical experiments with magnets and his work was "a model of the observational and experimental techniques in physics" (Clagett, 1948, p. 119). The increased influence of empiricism is illustrated by a comment attributed to Dietrich of Frieberg, which states that the usual appeal to authority notwithstanding, "one ought never to renounce what had been made manifest by the senses" (cited in Clagett, 1948, p. 119).

During the twelfth and thirteenth centuries great secular changes in politics, art, commerce, exploration, and even the technologies of warfare occurred. People increased their interest and involvement in the present, real world and began to believe in values other than their belief in an afterlife. During this time there occurred a revival of the ancient Greek, Greco-Roman, and Islamic scholarship. As western Europeans increased their explorations and trade around the Mediterranean world, they came into contact with Mohammedan scholars who had been part of the Moorish high civilization in Spain in the tenth century. The Mohammedans had brought with them Arabic versions of classical works. Over the next two centuries these were gradually translated into Latin and by the end of the twelfth century the medieval scholars were becoming familiar with Hippocratic and Galenic writings in medicine, Euclid's mathematics, Ptolemy's astronomy, Archimedes' physics, and a large variety of Hindu mathematical works. Under this influence medical schools were established in southern Italy and later in other parts of Europe. In these new centers the ancient, empirically based study of medicine, mathematics, and physics was revived. Empiricism and rationalism applied to the study of natural phenomena were again viewed as major ways of studying nature and acquiring knowledge. As empirical science grew in strength it did so while still within the bounds of theology where, for a while at least, there was room for science to grow. Soon, however, empirical science challenged these limits and, by the seventeenth century, began to escape from them.

There are two major theological constraints in empirical science that were set in place by the later Greeks and then adopted and strengthened by the Christian theologians for the next thousand years. First, and most importantly, empirical science was not allowed to contradict any theological dogma. If a dispute arose between knowledge gained through the senses and knowledge arrived at by revelation or from church authority, the resolution was simple: truth lay with theology and any contradictory ideas were false. Secondly, when empiricism was used, it was in the service of religion. The value of empirical science for the medievals was to help illustrate divine workings. Both of these constraints were challenged by the reviving empirical sciences.

The second of those major theological constraints was challenged in the thirteenth century by the revival of classical and Islamic empirical science and its institutionalization in schools of medicine. Scholars asserted that the use of empiricism toward development of practical, applied knowledge for the betterment of humanity (in this instance to understand and combat sickness) was a worthwhile goal. The theological grip on empirical science was thus loosened as science began to focus more on service to humanity than on service to God. The church tolerated this application of science to humanity so long as it did not directly challenge church dogma. In time, of course, this conflict did occur in the revolutionary struggles of science in the fourteenth through seventeenth centuries.

The Scientific Revolution

The classical revival of the thirteenth century occurred when western society was beginning major changes, shifting its focus of interest to greater concerns with the present life in this world. Given new strength by the developments of the thirteenth century, science became established in the new medical centers and a change of major significance began to occur. Scholars began to recognize and accept the potential value of science in the service of humanity. This theme would become a major point in the development of science, a point that Francis Bacon would stress in the sixteenth century. By the beginning of the fourteenth century, although science began to focus more on human goals, it remained largely under the control of the religious and political authorities. The growth of science into its independent status occurred during a seething 400 years of major social changes in virtually every area of human experience. The emergence of an independent science was but one of many areas in which old political and religious authority weakened, with people establishing new values and skills, particularly those aimed at achieving a better life.

During the thirteenth to sixteenth centuries scientists made an increasing number of discoveries and developed new hypotheses about nature that conflicted with religious dogma and with some tenacious beliefs about nature. Established institutions fought what they perceived to be the scientists' attack on religious truth, just as they resisted most of the other social and intellectual pressures for change. Eventually, however, revolutionary changes did occur and, by the beginning of the nineteenth century, science had not only been re-established and strengthened but, for the first time since about 400 B.C., had achieved an independent status as an important alternative way of understanding nature.

By the eighteenth and nineteenth centuries scientific centers for research and learning were established in universities, social resources were made available to support science, and the work of scientists became sought after by industries, universities, and governments. (As will be discussed in the next section, the science of psychology emerged in the latter part of the nineteenth century as an outgrowth of fields such as philosophy, biology, and physics.) By the twentieth century, science had become an accepted social institution with the force of a major social movement.

It has been in the latter part of the twentieth century that science has seen its most rapid development. Building on its earlier base, science has advanced enormously in the past 30 years. The current status of the scientific enterprise is dependent on a vast, heavily endowed, social structure including research centers, universities, industrial and private agencies, as well as many university departments created for the education and training of scientists. Large networks of scientific societies have been set up with annual meetings in which scientists communicate their findings and lobby for greater public resources. The scientists also communicate with the general public in many different ways, including newspapers, magazines, radio, television, and books. Scientists and their work have become part of our general information, maintained by the general public, as well as by many special groups such as industry, government, and even some religious leaders.

Scientists have investigated many areas of physical and social phenomena and have created a large variety of special disciplines, each with its own content and procedures. The multiplicity of scientific disciplines is usually viewed as one measure of the complexity of the natural universe. The phenomena differ from one area to another, with observational and methodological procedures differing according to the kinds of questions being asked and the technologies associated with each area. These differences among the scientific disciplines are primarily determined by the particular segments of nature that each area has chosen to investigate. But whatever their specialized differences, all of the sciences share not only a strong curiosity about nature, but a commitment to science—combined empiricism and rationalism—as a way of thinking and of understanding nature.

If modern science represents a way of thinking about nature, then, as outlined above, people began thinking scientifically a very long time ago. But the public's general conception of science appears to stress its recency, its marked differences from the less-enlightened, prescientific views of earlier times, with the result that science is popularly seen as a recent development. If science is so old, what makes it appear so new? Several factors may be involved. First, consider that in the 1700s science was still an obscure pursuit barely known beyond a minority of educated people. But the general level of awareness of science has grown enormously, particularly in the past generation, which in itself may have fostered the perception of science as a recent development.

Secondly, science is only one of several ways of knowing. At any given time we can find most or all of the ways represented, some ascendant and others muted, only to shift to other orderings at other times. Some modes of thinking became associated with powerful political systems or they became so generally socially accepted that they achieved controlling power, making it difficult for alternative views to develop. The social and political power of the medieval church is an example. With the decline of such power, the previously overshadowed scientific ideas became more visible, developed, and refined. Thus, one reason for the apparent recency of science may be the release of political and social constraints that allowed the further development of science.

A third possible factor is the closeness with which science and technology are perceived, and the general perception that because technology is always new, then so must science be new. Consider, for example, the development of the airplane. In 1903, after several years of research, Orville Wright took off from wooden rails and hopped through the air for twelve seconds in the world's first powered, heavier-than-air flight before losing control and crashing.[1] He survived that crash and lived until 1948, missing by only a few years being witness to the first manned flight into space by Yuri Gagarin in 1961. Could he have imagined at the turn of the century, when he and Wilbur were experimenting with their wind machines and models of wing surfaces, that a flight into space and back would occur almost within his lifetime?

Technological advances have helped to produce a world barely suggested at the beginning of this century. Such technological burgeoning overpowers us with its wonders, providing us with a continuing procession of new things and new procedures. Our sharp and constant awareness of new technology and our tendency to link technology and science may help to bolster the impression that science, too, is one of those new, marvelous developments. But, as we have noted, science has a long history and cannot accurately be considered a recent or modern occurrence.

---

[1]Although the Wright brothers made the first powered heavier-than-air flight, they drew on the work of many earlier pioneers, such as Otto Lilienthal of Germany. Lilienthal was the first person to make controlled heavier-than-air flights. Between 1891 and 1896, Lilienthal made more than 2000 successful glides in biplanes and monoplanes, which he designed and constructed. By 1896, he was working on a design for a powered airplane, but was killed in a crash of one of his gliders. Lilienthal's studies and technical writings provided major information for the Wright brothers' later work.

THE SCIENCE OF PSYCHOLOGY

Psychology as an independent scientific discipline is just over a hundred years old, having started with Wilhelm Wundt's psychological laboratory in Germany in 1879. Of course, there had been psychological research and speculations about psychological phenomena long before that, but Wundt's was the first formal laboratory in the new discipline. Psychology had evolved from earlier interests in philosophy, biology, mathematics, physiology, physics, and even astronomy.

Throughout its history, psychology's unique contribution has been to extend our understanding of many dimensions of human and animal functioning. These include learning and motivation, memory, personality, physiological influences on behavior, sensation and perception, intelligence, language and problem solving, emotion, development, psychopathology, and social influences on behavior. Today, psychology is an independent scientific discipline, but in many areas it overlaps with other disciplines. For example, biopsychology combines biology and psychology; cognitive psychology overlaps with computer science and linguistics; the psychological study of the sensory processes of vision and hearing involves knowledge of the physics of light and sound.

Psychology is now a large discipline, with more than 61,000 psychologists in the United States who are members of the major professional organization, the American Psychological Association (APA), and another 3,500 psychologists who are members of the Canadian Psychological Association (CPA). In addition, many psychologists are members of other associations such as the Psychonomic Society, Society for Research in Child Development, and school-related and management professional groups. The discipline of psychology, like science as a whole, is divided into a number of subdisciplines, each with its own focus. The diversity in psychology is reflected by the many divisions within the APA (see Box 1.3). Although all psychologists receive scientific education, many work professionally in applied settings such as hospitals, clinics, schools, industry, and governmental service, rather than in research settings.

Psychology is often considered to be a social science, as are anthropology, economics, history, and sociology. However, as noted above, psychology is also grounded in the natural sciences such as biology. In fact, many would argue that the research methods used in psychology are primarily drawn from the natural sciences. There are many areas of research within psychology, each with its own particular interests, content, and methods. But in all areas of psychology, the scientific model is used to study the behavior of living organisms. In the remainder of this book we will focus on the use of scientific research methods in psychological inquiry.

SUMMARY

Common to all art and science is the essential activity of asking questions. Science may be thought of as a systematic way of asking and answering questions, a disciplined curiosity, a set of procedures by which we make inquiries about the universe.

Box 1.3   DIVISIONS WITHIN THE AMERICAN PSYCHOLOGICAL ASSOCIATION (APA)

The diversity of interests of psychologists is seen in the large number of special interest divisions within the organization. Listed here are the current active divisions of the APA.

 1. General Psychology
 2. Teaching of Psychology
 3. Experimental Psychology
 5.[a] Evaluation and Measurement
 6. Physiological and Comparative Psychology
 7. Developmental Psychology
 8. Personality and Social Psychology
 9. The Society for the Psychological Study of Social Issues
10. Psychology and the Arts
12.[a] Clinical Psychology
13. Consulting Psychology
14. The Society of Industrial and Organizational Psychology
15. Educational Psychology
16. School Psychology
17. Counseling Psychology
18. Psychologists in Public Service
19. Military Psychology
20. Adult Development and Aging
21. Applied Experimental and Engineering Psychologists
22. Rehabilitation Psychology

[a]There are no divisions 4 and 11.

23. Consumer Psychology
24. Theoretical and Philosophical Psychology
25. Experimental Analysis of Behavior
26. History of Psychology
27. Community Psychology
28. Psychopharmacology
29. Psychotherapy
30. Psychological Hypnosis
31. State Psychological Association Affairs
32. Humanistic Psychology
33. Mental Retardation
34. Population and Environmental Psychology
35. Psychology of Women
36. Psychologists Interested in Religious Issues
37. Child, Youth, and Family Services
38. Health Psychology
39. Psychoanalysis
40. Clinical Neuropsychology
41. Psychology and Law
42. Psychologists in Independent Practice
43. Family Psychology
44. Society for the Psychological Study of Lesbian and Gay Issues
45. Society for the Psychological Study of Ethnic Minority Issues
46. Media Psychology
47. Exercise and Sport Psychology

Basic ways in which people have accepted information as being true are tenacity, intuition, authority, rationalism, empiricism, and science. Science combines rationalism and empiricism. Scientists order their thinking rationally and seek facts through empirical observations. It is the inclusion of empiricism that enables scientists to verify their rational conclusions through external validation.

This combination of rationalism and empiricism was first developed in ancient Greece, but was later weakened by a shift to more rational and abstract approaches to knowing the world, particularly as influenced by Plato. Later, medieval Christian scholars maintained science, but as a method it was secondary to theology. Scientific thinking increased through the Renaissance, emerging by the seventeenth century as largely independent from religion. Scientific thinking was becoming increasingly important as humans turned more to concerns about understanding and controlling the physical world and the human position in it.

In the twentieth century science has developed into a major and increasingly powerful and important way of thinking about the universe. Our contemporary lives are largely organized by modern advances in many scientific fields.

Psychology is a relatively recent scientific discipline that studies the behavior of organisms. By combining rational thinking and empirical observations, psychologists create ideas of how organisms function, and those ideas are then used as bases for further study and discovery.

REVIEW EXERCISES

I. Define the following key terms. Be sure you understand them. They are discussed in the chapter and defined in the glossary.

Science	Authority
Scientist	Rationalism
Process of inquiry	Logic
Technology	Empiricism
Skepticism	Orderliness belief
Knowledge	Experimentation
Tenacity	Scientific Revolution
Intuition	Psychology

II. Briefly answer each of the following questions. Check your answers in the chapter.

1. Explain this statement: For some types of decisions, most of the common ways of knowing are not sufficient, and we need the precision of science.
2. What is meant by the statement that "science involves a process of thinking"?
3. Science and technology are overlapping but different. Explain this statement.
4. What is creative about science?
5. What is meant by a prepared mind and how does that concept help to explain the so-called accidental discoveries made by scientists?
6. What are some of the major characteristics of scientists as a group?
7. In what ways are science and art similar?
8. Define and give two or three examples of each of the different ways of knowing or bases on which we accept information as valid knowledge.
9. What are the limitations of rationalism? Of empiricism?
10. What is the orderliness belief? What has it to do with modern science?
11. What is the relationship of the early crafts, such as metallurgy, to the later emergence of abstract science?
12. How did science survive under the domination of the religious thinkers?

III. Think about and work the following problems.

    1. Your friend asserts that scientists "can't make up their minds—they argue with each other over their different views, and they even change their views from one time to another. So how can they claim they know what they are talking about, when they can't even stick to their views or even agree with each other?" How would you answer this?

    2. A common belief is that scientists and artists are fundamentally different types and that they have little in common. A science person supposedly cannot appreciate art and the artistic person cannot understand science and math. If you were in conversation with someone who asserts this, how would you respond?

    3. Suppose you are in a discussion or a debate and the topic is hard sciences versus soft sciences. It is argued that psychology is not a true science at all. How would you defend the proposition that psychology is a true science?

    4. If you were discussing science with your friend, how would you explain that the person sitting under a tree and just thinking could be operating scientifically?

RESEARCH IS A PROCESS OF INQUIRY

Research is a systematic search for information, a process of inquiry. A systematic search for information can be carried out in libraries, laboratories, schoolrooms, hospitals, clinics, and factories, in the pages of the Bible, on street corners, in meadows and woods, in homes or in a herd of elephants. Indeed, research can be carried out anywhere, on virtually any phenomena in nature and by many different people, with varying interests, goals, beliefs, and procedures. Scientists, rabbis, and head chefs can all carry out systematic inquiry in their own domains. Further, the research process itself can be based on several ways of knowing, as discussed in Chapter 1. Although all true research is a systematic process of inquiry, not all research is scientific. A religious scholar might read, study, and research religious writings. The scholar's research is a serious, carefully systematic process of inquiry, but it is not, and it is not meant to be, scientific. What distinguishes scientific research from other research are the same characteristics that distinguish science in general from other ways of knowing—scientific research is that systematic process of inquiry that is based on combined empirical-rational principles. That combination makes heavy demands on the adequacy of the information it uses.

BASIC ASSUMPTIONS OF SCIENCE

An *assumption* in science is an idea or statement that is tentatively accepted as being true without further examination. Scientists make assumptions that are not yet known to be true, often because the knowledge or procedures for testing the ideas are not yet available. By accepting a basic idea *as if* it were true, scientists can then proceed through further investigations. Modern scientists, whatever their particular discipline, share several basic assumptions about nature and the role of science in understanding nature:

1. A true, physical universe does exist.
2. While there is randomness and thus unpredictability in the universe, it is primarily an orderly system.
3. This real and orderly universe is knowable through human intelligence, particularly through scientific research.
4. Our knowledge of the universe is incomplete because new knowledge can alter current knowledge. Therefore, all knowledge is tentative.

OBSERVATION AND INFERENCE: FACTS AND CONSTRUCTS

At a minimum, scientific research involves:

1. Creating and posing a question.
2. Determining how to go about answering the question.
3. Planning for and making appropriate empirical observations.
4. Rationally making sense out of those observations.

Scientists carefully observe events, try to reason about why things occurred, and then try to make predictions based on the ideas developed during the reasoning process. The elements of observation and rational abstraction are brought together to create a coherent understanding of the phenomenon.

In scientific research empirical observations constitute the facts of research. In a somewhat circular fashion, *facts* are those events that can be directly, empirically observed. Each scientific discipline has its own particular kinds of facts. In psychology, observed facts include the physiological structures of the subjects, the physical conditions around them, the behavior of other organisms including the researcher, and, of course, the subject's own behavior. The major category of fact that is observed in psychology is the *behavior of organisms.* The behavior observed can include verbal behavior, nonverbal communication such as gestures, small and large muscle activity, social behavior, and so on. In human research, we can observe the behavior of children at play, shoppers in stores, subjects responding to various perceptual stimuli, clients talking about their inner feelings, parents describing their children's problem behavior, workers at machines, or senators in debate. We can also study animal behaviors in the laboratory and in the natural environment. All of these behaviors can be objectively observed and recorded. *Observation* is the empirical process of using our senses to recognize and to note factual events.

In addition to studying behavioral facts, psychologists also study memory, emotion, intelligence, attitudes, values, creativity, thinking, perception, humor, and so on. These are not behavioral events. They are not directly observable and thus are not facts. We cannot directly observe intelligence or thinking or perception, but we can observe behavior that we believe to be related to those nonobservable events. For example, in some early work with autistic children (Graziano, 1974), we observed that the children frequently exhibited highly disruptive behavior in which they injured themselves and others and caused upheaval in their therapy program. Their behavior was a *fact;* it was repeatedly and clearly observed by many people, was measured by observers, and its sounds and forms were recorded on audio- and video-tape. As we worked with the children to help them reduce their disruptive behavior, we found that both its intensity and duration were reduced significantly, but not its frequency of occurrence. That is, the children were "blowing up" just as frequently as before treatment, but the episodes were each lasting only about half an hour instead of two hours and were less intense. We were able to observe the children, the conditions around them, their disruptive behavior, and the improvement in their behavior as the treatment program progressed. But it became clear that our procedures did not have any effect on the frequency of the disruptions. We thus posed the question, "Having reduced the intensity and duration of these outbursts, can we now reduce their frequency?"

To answer the question we continued to observe the children and soon saw that just prior to each outburst there was an observable, momentary change in the behavior of the child: activity stopped, facial expressions became contorted and mobile, limbs stiffened, and the severe behavior "exploded." It did not take much for us to infer that just prior to their outburst, something was happening inside the children. They were feeling some intense internal arousal, and that arousal might have served as the major cue for the emission of the outburst. Thus, we reasoned, to reduce the frequency of the outbursts we would have to control the internal arousal. But how were we to accomplish this? From our knowledge of the behavior therapy research literature, we selected an approach developed by Joseph Wolpe (1958), systematic desensitization, which employs relaxation training as a first step. Although used with adults, it had not to our knowledge ever been applied to children and particularly not to autistic children. But in light of our inference that the aroused state of the children lead to their outbursts, it seemed a reasonable approach to try. We trained the autistic children in relaxation and, in time, the frequency of their outbursts diminished to none. (We will have more to say later about this study.)

What is important here is our distinction between our *observations* of behavior (the outbursts) and our *inferences* of an internal condition (arousal). The internal condition is not observable. It is inferred, and those inferences are drawn from the observations of behavior—from the facts. Note that the inference is an intellectual process in which conclusions are derived from observed facts or from other ideas.

From empirical observations, events are inferred that cannot be observed; in this instance we inferred a condition of internal arousal. Most of the work that psychologists do, both applied and research work, is focused on inferences. When we study the anxiety of a client or the intelligence of a student or the memory of a subject, we are working with inferences. It is important for the student to recognize that inferences are largely drawn from empirical observations (the facts). Unless the observations are carefully made, little confidence can be placed in any inference drawn from them. In research, precisely defined empirical methods are used to develop a factual, observational base for drawing inferences about events that cannot be directly observed. Inferences can also be drawn from other inferences, but in science an important starting point for making inferences is careful observation. In general, the better the observational base and the more ties our inferences have to that observational base, the more confidence we have in the inference. When making inferences, we are cautioned to stay close to the data. As Detective Sergeant Joe Friday used to say to the witness in the old "Dragnet" television series, "Just give us the facts ma'am." He might have added, "We'll draw our own inferences."

Making an inference is a process that is engaged in by the researcher, with the inference residing in the researcher and not in the subject. The process involves the researcher's rational activity of tentatively accepting the sensory data (the observations) as true and then drawing from them an idea (inference) about nonobservable events. With the autistic children we used the inferential process and concluded that a state of arousal existed (Graziano, 1974). The inferred state of arousal was not a fact; it was an idea that we inferred. In other words, the inference, "arousal," was *not* in the child; it was an idea we created. We have no direct observation of what was really going on in the child. Our hypothesis of an internal arousal, although plausible, is simply an explanatory idea, not reality. It helped to explain the behavior observed, and it helped us to generate a possible course of action that proved to be effective. This is an extremely important point. Those nonobservable inferred events such as gravity, electricity, intelligence, memory, anxiety, perception, id, and ego are all *rational ideas that have been constructed by the researcher.* They are not facts! Not surprisingly, the ideas constructed in this way by the researcher are called *constructs.* Once these ideas are constructed by the researcher, they are used analogically; that is, *as if* they exist in fact and *as if* they really have a relationship with observable events. With the autistic children, we never observed the reduction of their internal state of arousal. We operated *as if* the inferred state actually existed and would be reduced if we trained them in relaxation. Further, we predicted that if the inferred state were indeed reduced, then we would observe a reduction in the frequency of the disruptive behavior (Graziano, 1974). To repeat, psychological constructs are ideas constructed by the researcher through a rational process of inference based on empirical observation as well as on other constructs. The constructs are used in further thinking and research *as if* they do exist and *as if* they have observable effects.

An important caution must be noted here. The analogical nature of constructs must be kept clearly in view. Too often a construct becomes so commonly used that people begin to think of it as a *fact,* a directly observed event, and they lose sight of its very tentative, analogical nature. For example, some people may believe there really is an id, an ego, and a superego inside each of us. These constructs take on a reality they were never meant to have. Confusing a construct for a fact is a logical error known as *reification of a construct.*

CONCEPTUAL MODELS IN SCIENCE

In the example of autistic children referred to earlier (Graziano, 1974), note the relationship between the construct of internal arousal and the observed facts. First, the construct was *inferred* from observed behavior. Then the construct was used as a *basis for predicting* some new behavior that could be observed (we predicted that if the internal arousal were reduced, we would then observe a reduction in disruptive behavior). Thus, the construct is related to observed facts in two ways; it was derived from the observations and it served as a basis for predicting future observations. The construct, in effect, helps us to show and explain tentatively a relationship between two sets of facts. In this instance, the two sets of facts were observations of behavior; one made before training, and the other made after the children had received training in relaxation. This use of constructs to explain relationships among two sets of observed facts is a very important part of the thinking process in science. Recall that a critical characteristic that makes the scientific thought process different from other ways of gaining knowledge is the continual, interactive movement between empirical observation and rational abstractions. Now you can see that this interactive movement is between observations and constructs. The scientist moves from one to the other and back again, at each step refining constructs from observations and predicting observations from constructs. During that process, we build up limited descriptions or explanations of relationships among facts and constructs. With the autistic children, the observations-constructs relationship provided a description or partial explanation of an observed phenomenon, in this case the disruptive behavior. We then used the description as if it adequately represented what was really happening, even though we could not observe all of the parts. By using the interactive observations and constructs in this descriptive and explanatory manner, we had constructed an analogue or *model* to represent reality.

The real universe and any phenomenon within it can be represented by models of reality, models that help us organize our knowledge about the full reality the models represent. The word *model* derives from the Latin *modulus,* meaning a small measure of something. It has come to mean in science a miniature representation of reality. A model is a description or analogy to help understand something that is usually unseen and/or more complex.

A model airplane is a good example of a model. It clearly is not equivalent to a real airplane. It has the general form of the real thing with many of the characteristics of a real airplane such as wings, propellers, wheels, and so on, which correspond quite faithfully to those of a real airplane. However, it is not an exact replica of the real airplane. It is smaller, it does not have all the working parts, and it may be constructed of balsa wood or plastic instead of aluminum. If the model airplane could be improved, making it progressively more like the real one, then eventually it would be a full-size, fully operational airplane, a replica of the original and fully equivalent to it.

But the model only *represents* reality, it does not duplicate it. It is useful because in constructing and examining a model to represent reality we organize knowledge and hypotheses about that reality. We can examine a model, observe relationships among its parts, and observe how it operates. New ideas can be generated from the model about how the reality is constructed and how it operates. For example, a model airplane in a wind tunnel can give us ideas about how the real airplane might behave and can lead us to new ideas or hypotheses about design and operation of the real airplane. Likewise, our model of the relationship of internal arousal and disruptive behavior in autistic children led us to new applications of behavior therapy.

Models can be constructed to represent any aspect of the universe that we wish to study. We can build models of airplanes or the solar system, of an atom or an amoeba, of wave motions, neurons, memory, thinking processes, or genetic structure. Our knowledge of any phenomenon can be organized into models to represent reality. Further, the models need not be physical in their construction such as a balsa wood airplane, but can be abstract or conceptual models, constructed of ideas and expressed in verbal and/or mathematical language. The classical model of human memory is a good example of an abstract model. It assumes multiple levels of memory, each having its own characteristics. The sensory store is assumed to hold information for a very short period of time (about 1 second) to allow further processing, but it is able to hold a very large amount of information. The short-term memory holds information longer (about 15 seconds) but has a much more restricted capacity. The long-term memory provides the long-term, high capacity storage that we usually think of when we think about memory. Few cognitive psychologists believe such structures exist or that their model is the way we process and store information. But a model does not have to be real or true to be useful. It only has to make accurate predictions about relationships between observable events. The classical model of memory is a strong one because it is based on hundreds of independent observations of behavior and the relationship of behavior to other observable events. In other words, the model is closely tied to the observational base on which it was first developed. Further, the model proved useful

"This is Gronski's new model of the synaptic transmission mechanism. Nobody understands it, but it won third prize in the campus art competition."

in that it correctly predicted a number of new observations that were confirmed by careful scientific study. It is not a perfect model of memory and will be replaced by better models as research identifies behavioral relationships that cannot be predicted or explained by the model. In fact, this model of memory has already been seriously challenged. Nevertheless, it is convenient and useful and has contributed enormously to our understanding of how we remember things.

All models share the following characteristics:

1. Models are constructed representations of parts of the real universe, and they have point-to-point correspondence with some of the characteristics of the reality being represented.
2. Models provide a convenient, manageable, and compact representation of the larger, complex, and mostly unknown reality.
3. Models are incomplete, tentative, and analogical.

Models are extremely useful. Manipulating models helps us to organize information, to illustrate relationships among parts, and to create new ideas and predict new observations.

The ancient religious cosmologies were models of the universe. Some of them pictured a flat earth riding on the back of a massive turtle paddling across a large lake, which was in turn held in place by the arching coils of a huge snake whose body defined the arc of the sky across which the gods rode each day in a blazing chariot. We are now reasonably certain that while there was some point-to-point correspondence between those models and reality (both include water, the earth, and the heavens), and while they may have predicted and explained many observable events (such as the daily movement of the sun across the sky), those ancient models were not accurate representations of reality. An example of an early Renaissance scientific model is the Copernican model of the solar system. An elaborate and elegant model, it was constructed in mathematical terms. The resulting model represented the solar system and its parts, spatial and temporal relationships among them, as well as the phenomena of regularity and change in the real solar system. Using his model, Copernicus and others developed hypotheses about the operation of the real solar system. Some of the hypotheses conflicted with religious dogma, creating difficulties not only for Copernicus but for others such as Galileo, 85 years later. Copernicus, in fact, delayed publication of his work for 13 years from 1530 to 1543 because he feared reprisals from the church. In time, the Copernican model proved to be a reasonably accurate model of the solar system, and it was of immense importance in later astronomy and physics. The Copernican model, though incomplete and in some ways inaccurate, nevertheless provided far more accurate point-to-point correspondence with the real solar system than had any model before it. As such, it allowed more accurate predictions of several phenomena that previously could not be predicted with any consistency.

INDUCTIVE AND DEDUCTIVE THINKING

Sherlock Holmes buffs will probably tell us that the great detective never said it, but the statement attributed to Holmes, perhaps first voiced in a movie version, has entertained and perhaps misled us for some time. We all know the scene: at the site of the crime Holmes inspects the room, his keen eyes darting and his nose alert to the lingering tobacco smoke. Suddenly, with an explosive "Aha!" he pounces on a partially burnt matchstick cracked in the middle with a small flake of tobacco stuck to its tip. Holmes examines it closely and then announces, "Our culprit, Watson, is forty-four years old, five feet eight and a half inches tall, one hundred eighty three pounds. He is right handed, a veteran of the India conflicts and still carries a lead ball in his right calf. He is a gentleman, Watson, and had no intention of committing a crime when he entered this room. He left hurriedly by way of that window when he heard us at the door and, if I am not mistaken, he will return here to confess his crime and will knock on that door precisely . . . now!"

A tentative knocking is heard at the door. Watson opens it revealing the gentleman so precisely described by Holmes.

"Egads 'Olmes!" says Watson, wide-eyed. " 'Ow did you ever know that?"

"Deduction, my dear Watson," says Holmes. "A simple process of deduction."

Of course, it was not deduction alone. Holmes had confused two terms and what he should have said was, "Induction-deduction my dear Watson. A simple process of induction-deduction!" Assuming that the great Holmes could in fact have drawn such complete conclusions from such limited evidence, his process was one familiar to all of us. He observed some specific clues and inferred (induced) something he could not directly observe (i.e., the type of person who would have committed such a crime, leaving those clues). Holmes then made the prediction (the deduction) that the man would return. When we reason from the particular to the general, we are reasoning inductively; when we use the more abstract and general ideas to return to specifics (i.e., to make predictions about future observations), then we are reasoning deductively.[1] Induction and deduction are rational processes that are used constantly by the scientist. In terms of our earlier discussion, it is the *combination* of these two kinds of thinking—induction and deduction—that characterizes science. When the researcher begins with empirical observations and then infers constructs, she is engaged in inductive reasoning. When the constructs then serve as the basis of making predictions about new, specific observations, she has engaged in deductive thinking. The scientist must use both processes to build conceptual models effectively as well as to validate the models.

Inductive-deductive reasoning is used not only by scientists but is part of our everyday behavior. When I return from work on a cold winter day and find the front door left partly open and a single muddy sneaker on the hall rug, I *in*ductively conclude that "the kids are home from school." Knowing a good deal about these kids, I can also *de*ductively predict that "right now Lisa is upstairs on the telephone talking with one of her friends," and I can go upstairs to make observations and check the accuracy of my predictions. From the specific observation to the general idea; from the general idea back to the more specific observation; induction and deduction. In everyday affairs, people have been thinking inductively and deductively all of their lives, although probably not with the precision of the scientist. We would like to emphasize this last point. Although the scientist uses the same kind of reasoning process used in everyday life, the scientist must use the process with a precision rarely seen in everyday life. Indeed, the entire scientific research enterprise can be seen as the development of a framework within which the scientist can carry out inductive and deductive reasoning under the most precise conditions. Here we can add to a point made early in Chapter 1: the essence of science is its process of thinking, and that process entails systematic inductive-deductive logic. In this process, science, more than any other way of gaining knowledge, bases its inductive reasoning in careful facts (i.e., empirical observations), and making these observations or getting the facts is one of the critical components of scientific research. Thus, the enterprise of scientific research uses facts to fuel the inductive-deductive process and obtains the facts with the greatest precision possible. Making empirical observations is the focal point around which the inductive-deductive process revolves. The observations provide the data on which theories are inductively produced. Data are also gathered later to test the predictions deduced from the theory during the process of validation.

[1]In psychology, we tend to use the concepts of induction and deduction as discussed above. However, philosophy students will recognize this distinction between induction and deduction as being incomplete, distinguishing only one kind of induction from one kind of deduction. In fact, according to Reese (1980), this distinction is no longer respectable among modern philosophers. A more accepted distinction is the degree of certainty assumed in the two modes of thinking. That is, induction allows partial conclusions and alternatives; deduction allows that the conclusions be either entirely conclusive or entirely inconclusive. Interested students are referred to Reese (1980), Skyrms (1966), and Salmon (1963).

MODELS AND THEORIES IN SCIENCE

It should be clear that science has many goals, such as generating and testing hypotheses, solving practical problems like building bridges and curing disease, developing an understanding of nature, and making new discoveries about the universe. However, the goals of science can be seen as being incorporated into the major goal of developing theories; that is, it has been said that the major aim of science is theory and that there is nothing as useful and practical as a good theory.

What is theory? For purposes of this text, let us consider a *theory* to be a formalized set of concepts that organizes observations and inferences and predicts and explains phenomena. A great deal of research must go into the development of theory. A good theory demands a solid empirical base of evidence and a set of carefully developed constructs, neither of which can be created offhandedly. Thus, scientists do not create theories out of mere guesses and hunches, and their theories are not flimsy and ephemeral flights of fancy. Theories are carefully constructed from empirical observations, constructs, and inductive and deductive logic. In building theories, the scientist brings together and integrates what has been learned about the phenomena under study. To develop an adequate theory that will organize, predict, and explain natural phenomena is a major goal of scientists.

There is a continuing debate in psychology about the value of formal theory. Marx (1963) describes four types of theories used in psychology—inductive theory, deductive theory, functional theory, and models—that vary in the degree to which they emphasize induction or deduction. All theories involve both induction and deduction, but they differ in the degree to which they emphasize one or the other.

An *inductive theory* begins with a solid data base of empirical observations and gradually builds up to more abstract levels of explanations in the theory. The inductive theorist follows the data wherever they may lead. Skinner epitomizes this inductive method of theory construction. A *deductive theory* is more the traditional, formalized theory in which constructs are of major importance. The constructs (the ideas) guide the researcher in making and testing deductions from the constructs. The deductions are empirically tested through research, and thus support or lack of support for the theory is obtained. The formal learning theory of Clark Hull (1943) is an example. Most psychological theories are *functional theories* involving about equal emphasis on induction and deduction. All three types of theories have the characteristic functions of organizing knowledge, predicting new observations, and explaining relationships among events. It should be apparent to you that constructing theories is of major importance if we are to develop coherent knowledge about nature.

The fourth type of theory discussed by Marx (1963) is the *model.* Remember that we described a model as an analogical representation of reality. It is not a duplicate of reality but only a representation. We use models analogically, as if they correctly represent reality. As we discussed earlier, the major function of a model is to organize existing information, much as do theories. A model, however, in contrast to formal theory, usually does not do very well in predicting new observations or in explaining phenomena. Thus, a model is somewhat less developed than a formal theory, and models are sometimes referred to as "minitheories." Models are often used as steps in the development of theory.

A final point should be made here: a theory is never "right" or "wrong." Rather, it is judged by how *useful* it is in organizing information, explaining phenomena, and generating accurate predictions.

A MODEL OF THE RESEARCH PROCESS

Almost any phenomenon can be studied scientifically, and a model can be developed to represent the phenomenon. One purpose that a model can serve is to help organize the activities of the person using the model. We will develop a model in this section to serve as an outline for the text. We will study a category of events or a portion of reality that we will call *psychological research methods.* To help us organize our study, we will propose a model of the universe of the research enterprise.[2] Like any model, this model is not a complete representation of reality. The model tries to simplify the complexity to help emphasize some of the most important aspects of research. It is based on the assumption that there is a large, complex, and highly active area of reality that we call psychological research and it is, by and large, orderly, predictable, and knowable. The conceptual model that we are presenting is consistent with the nature of scientific research, but like all scientific models, it is necessarily an incomplete and tentative representation to aid in organizing our knowledge about research.

We will label our model *Research: A Process of Inquiry.* If we were to observe scientists engaged in the research process, we would see their major activity as a sequence of asking and answering questions about a particular phenomenon under study. The answers are tentative and often raise new questions. Scientists never run out of questions.

Phases of Research

Psychological research usually proceeds in an orderly manner, through successive phases, from the beginning to the end of a particular project. However, this sequencing of phases can vary under special conditions. The most general sequence of research events is described here.

Table 2.1 presents each of the phases of research. The concept of *phases of research* provides one dimension of the conceptual model on which this text is based. Note in Table 2.1 that research begins with ideas and flows through the successive, overlapping phases of this process. Each phase has its own characteristics and different work is accomplished in each, preparing for the next phase.

Idea-Generating Phase   All research must begin with an idea, sometimes quite vague, in which the researcher has interest. The interest of the researcher is critical, particularly in the beginning phases of research. For example, a researcher may have interest in children's aggression but have no further idea for a research project. The interest, however, is enough to point the researcher to an area within which more

---

[2]The model of research presented here is not original with us, but similar to a model presented by Hyman (1964).

Table 2.1 THE PHASES OF A RESEARCH STUDY

Idea-generating phase Identify a topic of interest to study.

Problem-definition phase Refine the vague and general idea(s) generated in the previous step into a precise question to be studied.

Procedures design phase Decide on the specific procedures to be used in the gathering of the data.

Observation phase Using the procedures devised in the previous step, collect your observations from the subjects in your study.

Data-analysis phase Analyze the data collected above using appropriate statistical procedures.

Interpretation phase Compare your results with the results predicted on the basis of your theory. Do your results support the theory?

Communication phase Prepare a written or oral report of your study for publication or presentation to colleagues. Your report should include a description of all of the above steps.

defined ideas can be developed. It is our personal judgment that for the young new researcher in particular, interest in the area to be studied is critical in helping to sustain the long, hard work to follow. This, of course, repeats a point made in Chapter 1 that the scientist's curiosity is a basic component in research, both in helping to generate research ideas and in sustaining the researcher's efforts.

The idea phase can begin with vague thoughts, and initial ideas can emerge in very nonscientific ways. Archimedes is supposed to have had a flash of creative thought while sitting in a bath. Ideas can be generated while in conversations, reading novels, watching television, walking in the woods, buying a hamburger, crossing the street, or even while dreaming. They can be born of vaguely perceived fleeting thoughts. Lest we leave the impression that getting research ideas is all so unsystematic, we should stress that ideas are also generated in a highly systematic fashion from other research results. Most psychological research is stimulated by previous psychological research. Research ideas vary from unsystematic hunches to highly systematic and precise steps in logical thinking. The former is most characteristic of exploratory research, which occurs in the early history of a research area, whereas the latter is characteristic of research at more advanced levels of the research area.

In the early idea-getting activities, we ought not to be too critical of our relatively unformed ideas because premature criticism might serve to interrupt and choke an emerging good idea. The early ideas ought to be nourished and thought about and taken quite seriously, at least for a while. Critical ingredients are curiosity, interest, and enthusiasm for an area under study. Once an area of interest is identified, it is useful to dive right in by reading articles and books, talking with people who work in the area, and thinking about the area.

There seems to be a general lack of information and understanding about the processes involved in the creative idea-generating phases of research. Indeed, here is a good area for research—how are creative ideas generated? Can you think about this and generate some interesting research questions? Perhaps somewhere in one of these research methods classes there is a young student who will eventually make some important contribution to the scientific understanding of generating creative ideas.

What seems clear is that productive scientists have many ideas. For example, when asked in a television interview, "Where does a scientist get a good idea to study?" Linus Pauling replied, "Well, you have *lots* of ideas, and you throw out the bad ones."

Problem-Definition Phase Identifying an area of interest and generating some beginning ideas for study occur at the very start of the research process. Vague ideas alone are not sufficient. In good scientific tradition, we must put more demands on the ideas to clarify and refine them. In this part of the process, the scientist will examine the research literature and learn how other researchers have conceptualized, measured, and tested these and related ideas. We continue working on the ideas, clarifying, defining, specifying, and refining them. Our goal is to produce one or more clearly posed questions based on a well-developed knowledge of previous research and theory as well as on our own thinking.

How carefully we conceptualize and phrase a research question is important, because everything we do in the remainder of the research process will be aimed at answering that research question. Think of it this way: the questions we ask will largely control the way we conduct the rest of the research process. The questions might involve highly specific and precisely drawn hypotheses or they might be phrased in a much more general manner, typical of exploratory research. The way we ask the question will often determine how we should carry out the study.

The activities that make up the problem-definition phase are highly rational, abstract processes that manipulate and systematically develop ideas toward the goal of refining them into researchable questions. Here our rationalism is used to prepare for the next phase in which we design the procedures to make the observations.

Procedures Design Phase As the researcher prepares to make appropriate observations it must be determined which observations are to be made, under what conditions they will be made, which methods will be employed for recording the observations, what the measurements will consist of, which statistical methods we should use for analyzing the data, and so on. In this phase, we also make decisions about who the subjects will be. In essence we are making decisions about how we will use living organisms for purposes of research, which, of course, immediately brings ethical concerns into the process. The ethics of scientific research include guidelines for humane, sensitive treatment of subjects. Before the researcher contacts a single subject he or she must be sure the research plan stands up to ethical evaluation. For human subjects, issues of informed consent, use of deception, invasion of privacy, and physical and psychological harm must be considered. The research plan must be modified whenever the ethical guidelines are not met. Only when the plan can stand up to ethical demands do we proceed with the next phase, making the observations. The ethics of psychological research is a major area that every researcher must know, understand, and apply. (Ethics will be discussed in more detail in later chapters.)

As can be seen, the phase of designing the procedures is active, systematic, and complex. Much of the content of research methods courses focuses specifically on this phase.

Observation Phase   Making the observations (getting the facts) is the most familiar to beginning students who often see this as "actually doing the research." In this phase, the researcher carries out the procedures that were determined in the previous phase, so as to make observations of the subjects' behavior under the conditions specified in the earlier phase. The observation phase is central in all science. Note that the earlier phases serve as preparation for making the empirical observations and the remaining phases focus on using those observations (i.e., processing, understanding, and communicating them). Scientific research can thus be seen as a process of inquiry that revolves around its most central aspect, making empirical observations.

Empirical observations constitute the facts of the research. When the researcher records observed facts, the record constitutes the research data. When a subject answers "Yes" to an item on a questionnaire or shows an increase in physiological activity when a certain stimulus is presented, this information becomes part of the data. In the remainder of the research process, it is the data that are processed, interpreted, and communicated.

Data-Analysis Phase   By the data-analysis phase of research the empirical observations have been made and recorded as data. Remaining are the primarily abstract, rational tasks of processing and making sense out of the data and communicating the results. In almost all psychological research the data will be in the form of a numerical record representing the observations made, and the numerical data must be put into some order and further processed or analyzed. Statistical procedures are used to describe and to evaluate numerical data and to help determine the statistical significance of the observations. The statistical procedures might be as simple as counting responses and drawing graphs to show response changes over time, or they may be as complex as a two-way analysis of variance (described in Chapter 12). Whatever the statistical procedures may be, the important point to be made here is that the researcher must choose statistical procedures that are appropriate to the question being asked and to the observational procedures being used. As we will see in Chapter 14, the choice of statistical procedure is not difficult to make. The choice is determined by the nature of the question and the observational procedures.

Interpretation Phase   Having statistically analyzed the data, we continue to make sense out of them by interpreting the statistical results in terms of (1) how they help answer the research question and (2) how this answer contributes to the knowledge in the field. Here we put the findings into a context that helps to relate them not only to the original questions but also to other concepts and findings in the field. In many ways this stage represents the flip side of the problem-definition phase. When defining the problem we use theories to guide us to important questions. Now we use the answers we have generated to those questions to determine how well they fit into our theoretical predictions. In the problem-definition phase we use deductive reasoning—from the general theory to the particular prediction. In the interpretation phase, we use inductive reasoning—from the specific results of the study back to the generality of the theory. In many cases, the results of a study will suggest ways to expand or modify the theory to increase its usefulness and accuracy.

Communication Phase   As noted in Chapter 1, science is a public enterprise, and one of its most basic components is detailed communication of work among scientists. Scientific communication occurs through oral presentations at scientific meetings and through written accounts in journals and books. Note that it is not only the results that are communicated but also the procedures used in all phases of the research and the rationales behind them. Specific guidelines are needed to organize in a concise manner all of the information needed in a research report. Such guidelines are provided by the *APA Publication Manual* (1983). (A discussion of how to write a research report is presented in Appendix A.)

Publication of scientific research requires that procedures be described in detail not only so that other scientists can understand the research but also to allow them to *replicate* (repeat) it if they wish. Replication is very important, for if some reported research finding cannot be replicated, then considerable doubt is placed on the genuineness of that finding. By presenting full accounts of research rationales, procedures, findings, and interpretations, the researcher is contributing to public scientific activity, and the work can be fully evaluated by others even to the point of replicating the research. (Further discussion of the importance of replication will be presented in Chapter 9.)

Each finished project can serve as the basis for further questions and further empirical research. Here we come full circle, back to the beginning phase of generating ideas. In a developing field of research, the ideas for asking new questions and making new observations are mainly ideas that have been systematically generated by previous research. Scientists are stimulated by the work of their colleagues and derive research questions from them. In turn their own work stimulates others.

Scientists use two major avenues for communicating their work. The most formal is written communication in books and scientific journals. These reports become a permanent record, part of the archives of a scientific discipline. They are preserved and can be retrieved and studied by colleagues soon after publication or many years later. A minor disadvantage of written reports is that it usually takes a year or more after the research has been completed for the publication process to make written reports available in journals and books.

More immediate and more interactive communications are the oral and poster presentations researchers make at scientific meetings and the informal communication among colleagues. Scientists visit each other's laboratories, talk on the telephone or during parties or poker games, exchange letters, and so on. This informal, highly interactive network of communication has been called the "invisible college," and it serves the important function of keeping scientists in communication with each other. Indeed, some believe it is the most critical means of communication among scientists. It is important for the young researcher, seriously interested in a research career, to become involved actively in this "invisible-college" network of communications.

The research process we have briefly described is common to all sciences. The particular observations made in the various disciplines vary from one to the other because each discipline is interested in observing and understanding quite different phenomena. But the basic processes and the systematic way of thinking through the processes are common elements of science regardless of each discipline's particular observations. It is the process and not the content that distinguishes science from other ways of knowing, and it is the content—the particular phenomena and facts of interest—that distinguishes one scientific area from another.

Although it is generally true that research proceeds in the sequence described—from the initial idea phase through the communication phase—the sequencing of the phases is not rigid. New ideas might occur while the researcher is involved in the data-processing phase, and he or she might design and run another study before interpreting and communicating the results of the first study. It is also common for some of the phases (such as the data-processing phase and the interpretation phase) to overlap as the researcher moves back and forth between the phases.

The empirical observation phase is the center of the research process. We first generate and refine ideas, sharpening them into answerable questions. We then carefully make many decisions about what procedures we will use to answer the questions. All of that work is in preparation for the central activity, making empirical observations. The remaining phases are then focused on analyzing the empirical observations, and determining and communicating their importance. It is that central activity, making empirical observations within a systematic rational process, which characterizes science as a method different from other ways of seeking knowledge. Notice that in this process the scientist moves through a systematic, successive cycling of rational thinking, empirical observations, back again to rational thinking, and so on. Science is rationalism and empiricism combined.

Research in psychology as in any other science revolves around that empirical component. Observed facts are the most basic unit in psychological research. It should be clear then, that the more systematically and carefully we make the observations, the more solid will be the data base on which we can continue to build a greater understanding of psychological phenomena.

Levels of Constraint

Recall that in Chapter 1 we noted the various ways people have used to pursue knowledge—tenacity, intuition, authority, rationalism, empiricism, and science. In the order listed, these approaches range from low to high demands on the adequacy of the information each is willing to accept and on the nature of the processing of that information. Of all these approaches, science is the most demanding.

Now let us add to that idea; within science itself, already at the high-demand end of this continuum, there are many approaches to gaining knowledge, which range from lowest to highest demands made on the adequacy of the information and the nature of the processing of that information. Thus, within scientific research some methods are more demanding than others, but they all have their useful place in the scientific research scheme.

Within each phase, the researcher must make a number of decisions about how to develop the research. The decisions may be fairly general in which the ideas, questions, and procedures are left relatively unrefined, as in some of the exploratory research undertaken early in the investigation of some phenomenon. On the other hand, the decisions might involve highly specific and refined ideas, with precise hypotheses, detailed procedures, complex statistical analyses, and so on. In each of these two extremes, the researcher moves through all of the phases, but each is obviously at a different level of refinement. In comparing the two projects, we can see that the exploratory research makes relatively few demands for structure or precision on the procedures in each phase. In contrast, the highly refined research project demands a great deal more structure and precision in its procedures.

For example, suppose we are operating a special training program for exceptional children and have just admitted some moderately retarded children. In order to plan adequately, we might want to know, among other things, whether moderately retarded children behave aggressively. Answering that question would not be difficult; we can ask the parents or we can go into a room with several moderately retarded children and simply watch them for a few hours. Both are observational procedures designed to answer the question. From those observations of parents and/or children, we can arrive at some tentative ideas about moderately retarded children and their aggressive behavior. Continuing the research process, we can report our observations to our colleagues in the program, perhaps in a staff meeting. The point is, that as simple and imprecise as this seems, we have gone through a process of empirical research from original idea to communication of results. It was not highly detailed or structured, but it was research nonetheless. Note that because of the noncomplex nature of the question and the observational procedures, there was little demand that the question or procedures be precise, complex, or highly structured. If, while watching the retarded children, we had decided suddenly to change the observation procedure and try to talk with or otherwise make contact with the children instead of passively watching them, that change in procedure for that particular research would have been acceptable. Here, the activities in each phase are very flexible. As the research questions become more complex and precise, the activities in each phase of research must become correspondingly more demanding, precise, and controlled. Increased control is most readily seen in the observation phase of the process. As noted above, in some research the observations are made in a very flexible, low-control manner, whereas in other research greater control over the conditions of observation is demanded. As we increase control over the conditions and methods of observation, we are imposing *constraints* on our freedom to be flexible. In essence, in the search for precision, we give up flexibility. In almost all research decisions, we are required to make certain trade-offs, and every design decision we make has a price associated with it. Beginning students often believe that the best way to conduct research is always to be precise and controlled. But precision and control may not always be the ideal, because often the loss of flexibility is too great a price to pay for the increase in precision and control.

The idea of constraint provides a second dimension for our model of the research enterprise. The two dimensions are as follows:

1. *The phases of research.* Each complete research project proceeds along this dimension from original ideas to final communication.
2. *The levels of constraint.* This dimension is one of precision, structure, and control. Projects of the highest precision demand the greatest constraint on activities in each phase, the constraint being seen most clearly in the controls imposed in the observation phase. By *levels of constraint* then, we mean *the degree to which the researcher imposes limits or controls on any part of the research process.*

These concepts of phases of research and levels of constraint, when combined, form a two-dimensional descriptive model of research, which is outlined in Figure 2.1. Notice in Figure 2.1 that we have given names to the successive levels of constraint ranging from the lowest constraint (naturalistic methods) to the highest constraint (experimental methods). All of the constraint levels represent scientific research. There is an unfortunate view held by some that only the high constraint methods can properly be considered scientific. In our model all are proper scientific methods, and all can be effective when properly used. The use is determined by the nature of the question being asked and the precision of the existing knowledge about the question. When the question is a low-constraint question, then low-constraint methods are appropriate, and so on. When Jane Goodall (1971) was interested in learning about the social behavior of chimpanzees, the naturalistic observation methods were the most appropriate methods to use, even though they were at a low-constraint level. Her research resulted in new knowledge about those animals. Her questions were general and flexible so the level of research had to be equally general and flexible. High-constraint research would not have been appropriate and could not have given the information sought. The general nature of Goodall's questions was not a flaw in her work. Any scientist breaking new ground must start with just such low-constraint questions.

It is important to understand that all levels of research are properly scientific when used appropriately and the nature of the question determines the level of constraint used in answering the question. Problems arise when researchers inappropriately mix constraint levels, such as when researchers try to interpret low constraint-data in highly precise, predictive, and/or generalized ways. This is essentially the problem in the hypothetical example given in Chapter 1 of the psychoanalyst who observed enuretic children. She employed low-constraint, case-study observations but tried to apply her conclusions to all enuretic children, a step that properly requires high-constraint sampling methods to be certain subjects adequately represent the total population of enuretic children about whom the generalization is to be made.

Figure 2.1   A TWO-DIMENSIONAL MODEL OF SCIENTIFIC RESEARCH

	Phases of Research						
	(1) Idea-generating	(2) Problem-definition	(3) Procedures design	(4) Obser-vation	(5) Data-analysis	(6) Interpre-tation	(7) Commu-nication
Levels of Constraint							
Naturalistic observation							
Case-study method							
Correlational research							
Differential research							
Experimental research							

Consider the researcher who applies highly complex and sophisticated statistical techniques to low-constraint research under the mistaken belief that in good research, high-powered statistical analyses must always be used. This idea is not correct. In fact, there are many important research questions that are most appropriately and most correctly investigated with low-constraint, relatively simple methods, including simple statistical analyses. What is important to impress on the beginning researcher is this: in doing research, we should refine our question so it can be answered using the highest constraint level that is possible given both current knowledge in that field and practical and ethical constraints on the researcher. Once the constraint level of the question has been determined, then the remainder of the research process must be carried out at that same level of constraint. When we mix constraint levels, we run the serious risk of distorting or losing important information.

How can we ever move from low- to high-constraint research? Conclusions drawn from well-executed low-constraint research can serve as the starting points for high-constraint questions and research methods. For example, when the psychoanalyst had observed high anxiety and Oedipal problems in her clinical sample, she could have asked a question like this: "Now that I have observed these consistencies in my clinical sample, do the same consistencies hold in the general population of enuretic children or is this some pecularity of this clinical sample?" This question could lead to research utilizing more careful sampling procedures in selecting subjects who more adequately represent the general population of enuretic children. In this example, the psychoanalyst had made a large leap from her low-constraint data to higher constraint conclusions and failed to develop the intervening steps to justify her conclusion. By asking the question as posed above, she could have moved correctly from low to higher constraint research.[3]

Like the phases of research, the constraint levels in our model are overlapping rather than clearly demarcated. This constraint dimension should be understood as forming a continuum and the labels (naturalistic, case study, and so on) as indicating bands or portions of the continuum. The number of levels we choose to identify in our model of research is not critical in understanding the research activity that the model seeks to represent. The important concept is that constraint ranges from low to high, and the five labels and their descriptions given below are adequate for describing most of the various kinds of psychological research. In later chapters, we will discuss the levels of constraint in more detail. Here we want to define briefly each of the levels.

Naturalistic Observation The *naturalistic* observation level of constraint requires the researcher to observe the behavior of subjects in their natural environment. There is no attempt made to change or limit the environment or the behavior of the subjects. The only constraints that do exist are those that researchers impose on their observational methods. However, the researchers usually are not bound by strong hypotheses that demand a particular set of observational procedures. Therefore, the researchers are free to shift their attention to any behaviors that seem interesting.

---

[3]We do not always move from low-constraint research to high-constraint research. There are times when we want to move in the other direction. As we will discuss later, it is sometimes useful to test findings from high-constraint research in low-constraint, naturalistic settings.

Case-Study Method of Observation   *Case-study* research is somewhat higher constraint because the researcher does intervene with the subject's functioning to some degree. Case-study research might include, for example, asking questions of a subject. Even though slightly more constrained than naturalistic research, the case-study method still allows the researcher flexibility to shift attention to whatever behaviors seem most interesting and relevant at the time. In our usage, case-study research is *not* limited to research on psychopathology or psychotherapy. Rather, it is a set of methods that can be applied to many human issues.

Correlational Research   The *correlational* level of constraint requires much greater constraint on the procedures used to measure behavior. In this method, the setting can range from a naturalistic setting to the highly constrained setting of a scientific laboratory. However, because we are interested in quantifying the relationship between two or more variables in the correlational method, we must use precise (constrained) procedures for measuring each variable.

Differential Research   The *differential* level of constraint involves an explicit comparison between two or more groups of subjects. To make the comparison meaningful, all groups must be treated in exactly the same ways except for the variable that defines the groups. That is, the settings and observational procedures must be constrained across groups. If done properly, the only thing that is not identical across the groups is the variable that defines the groups. In differential research, the variable that defines the groups is a *preexisting variable* not under the researcher's control. Such preexisting variables can include clinical diagnoses, age, IQ, sex, socioeconomic class, and so on.

Experimental Research   *Experimental* research is the highest constraint research. In experimentation, explicit comparisons are made between subjects under different conditions. A major difference between the differential-research approach and the experimental-research approach is the way subjects are assigned to the groups or conditions. The experimental-research method demands that the subjects be assigned to the groups or conditions in an unbiased manner, such as with random assignment. In contrast, in differential research assignment of subjects is based on some preexisting variable that is not within the researcher's control.

   The concept of level of constraint does not represent a single, simple dimension. Some levels differ on the basis of the constraint applied to the setting in which the observation takes place, some differ on the basis of the constraint placed on the measurement procedures, and others differ on the basis of the constraint placed on the subject assignment procedures. But as we move from low-constraint methods to high-constraint methods, more constraint is placed on more aspects of the research study. In pure naturalistic observation, there is little constraint placed on any aspect of the study. In pure experimental methods, every aspect of the study is planned in advance, and explicit procedures must be followed throughout the study. Table 2.2 summarizes these various levels of constraint. A particular research study may not fit neatly into one of these five categories because there is much overlap between categories. We

Table 2.2 LEVELS OF CONSTRAINT OF SCIENTIFIC RESEARCH

Naturalistic observation   This involves the observation of subjects in their natural environment. The researcher should do nothing to limit or change the environment or the behavior of subjects.

Case-study method of observation   This involves moving the subject into a moderately limiting environment, intervening to a slight degree, and observing the subject's responses.

Correlational research   Here the focus is on quantifying the degree of relationship between two variables. The measurement procedures must be carefully defined and precisely followed.

Differential research   Here two or more preexisting groups of subjects are compared. The setting is usually highly constrained, and the measurement procedures must be carefully defined and precisely followed.

Experimental research   Identical to differential research except that the subjects are randomly or in some other way assigned without bias to the various groups or conditions in the study. This is the highest constraint level of research.

present this model only as a way of conceptualizing the many kinds of research studies that can be carried out.

A final point about levels of constraint should be introduced here, and it will be discussed again in later chapters. All research involves the study of relationships among events, and the types of relationships that can be discovered vary from one constraint level to another.

SUMMARY

Based on specific empirical observations, the researcher employs a rational intellectual process of inductive inference to develop more general constructs that represent events that cannot (yet) be observed. Using the more general constructs as bases, the researcher can then make deductive inferences or predictions about future specific observations. The inductive-deductive process (specific-to-general-to-specific process) is highly interactive, and it ties together the empiricism and rationalism that is basic to scientific thinking.

Research is a process of inquiry in which the researcher carefully poses a question and proceeds systematically to gather, analyze, interpret, and communicate the information necessary to answer the question. The central part of this research process is making empirical observations. All activities that take place prior to the observation phase are designed as preparation for the actual gathering of data (making observations). All activities following the observation phase focus on analyzing, interpreting, and communicating those observations.

We have presented a two-dimensional model of the research enterprise to help organize knowledge about research. The two dimensions are (1) the phases through which each research project progresses and (2) the levels of constraint that distinguish the severity of the demands made on the information and the procedures used in each research project.

REVIEW EXERCISES

I. Define the following key terms. Be sure you understand them. They are discussed in the chapter and defined in the glossary.

Assumptions of science
Facts
Behavior of organisms
Observation
Inference
Constructs
Inductive reasoning
Deductive reasoning
Theory
Inductive theories
Deductive theories
Functional theories
Model
Phases of research
   Idea-generating phase

Problem-definition phase
Procedures design phase
Observation phase
Data-analysis phase
Interpretation phase
Communication phase
Replicate
Levels of constraint
   Naturalistic
   Case-study
   Correlational
   Differential
   Experimental
Preexisting variable

II. Answer each of the following. Check your answers in the chapter.

1. Comment on this statement: "Only scientists can do research."
2. What are the basic assumptions of science?
3. What are *facts?* What is the major category of facts in psychology?
4. Distinguish between *observation* and *inference.* Give examples of each.
5. Distinguish between *facts* and *constructs.* Give examples of each.
6. Explain this statement: "Well-accepted ideas such as gravity, anxiety, and superego do not refer to facts at all."
7. Explain the two ways in which constructs are related to facts.
8. What are the major characteristics of scientific models?
9. What kinds of information do scientific models provide?
10. Explain this statement: "Models are used analogically."
11. In what ways are inductive and deductive reasoning commonly used in everyday life?
12. Explain this statement: "Making empirical observations is the focal point around which the inductive-deductive process revolves."
13. Identify and describe the *phases* of a research project.
14. What is meant by *data* in research? How are data obtained?
15. Explain this statement: "In the problem-definition phase we are engaged in deductive reasoning; in the interpretation phase we are engaged in inductive reasoning."
16. Distinguish between inductive theories, deductive theories, and functional theories.

III. Think about and work the following problems.

1. As an exercise, think of common issues or events in your life and try to generate as many general research ideas as you can. You might begin some of your questions with "I wonder what would happen if . . .?" or "I wonder why . . .?" For example:

   I wonder why I wake up every morning just a moment or two before my alarm rings? Do I have some inner time sense?

2. A professor asserts that only high-constraint, highly controlled, experimental research is worth doing. You bravely raise your hand and are recognized. Now, how do you respond to that assertion?

3. Generate some examples of the inappropriate mixing of constraint levels in a research project.

4. Following are some brief descriptions of research. For each one identify the level of constraint.

   a. A therapy researcher has several clients with very similar problems. He compares their statements in therapy to see what might be common among all of the cases.

   b. A researcher compares subjects' reaction times to visual stimuli in a laboratory setting.

   c. Two groups of rats are compared for their accuracy in running a maze. One group was fed just before the comparison, and the other had not been fed for four hours.

   d. A third-grade class and a sixth-grade class are compared on their taste preferences.

   e. A researcher observes prairie dog colonies to learn more about their behavior.

   f. A researcher analyzes data on the relationship between the number of calories consumed and weight.

5. Following is a repetition of a question you were asked at the end of Chapter 1. Now you should be able to give a more complete answer: In a discussion or debate it is argued that social sciences such as psychology are not true sciences at all, as are sciences like chemistry and physics. How would you defend the proposition that psychology is a true science?

CHAPTER 3

THE STARTING POINT
Asking Questions

ASKING QUESTIONS

Asking a question is the usual starting point for research. A *question* is a problem or statement in need of a solution or answer. "How can we reduce the disruptive behaviors of autistic children?" "Do whales vocalize?" "How can we get drunk drivers off the road?" These are questions that have served as starting points for research. But from where do the starting points come? Beginning students are often at a loss to get an idea for a research project and, unfortunately, too often believe it to be far more difficult than it really is. Starting points for research are all around us, and all we have to do is observe and be curious! As we shall see, research ideas in psychology are readily derived from a variety of common sources.

Sources of Questions

Researcher's Personal Interests and Observations   Our own interests and observations are important, particularly for new researchers, because they not only point to directions for research, but also may be important in sustaining our work, particularly when the going gets tough. Most of us can readily identify interests in psychological questions, which can serve as our starting points for research. For example, we might be interested in emotion or, more specifically, in positive emotions like love or joy. We might be interested in memory, creativity, musical ability, or social processes, or we might wonder about some aspect of ourselves or our family members. Any of these interests or observations can serve as the starting point for research.

Other Investigators' Theories and Research   One of the interesting and useful things about research is that it raises more questions than it answers, and the new questions can serve as starting points for more research. Freud's psychoanalytic theory, whatever one may think of its adequacy, nevertheless raised many questions and has generated a vast amount of research. Other examples of ideas and research that have generated a great deal of study are Skinner's (1938, 1972) research on learning, Miller's (1971) work on physiological influences on motivation, Bandura's (1969) research on modeling, Festingers's (1957) theory of cognitive dissonance, and Lovaas's (1973) research with autistic children. To derive ideas from other research, scientists communicate with each other at scientific meetings, in laboratories, through personal communications, and by studying published research literature. The more knowledge we have of a research area, the stronger base we have for generating new research ideas. For beginning students it is difficult to read journals and recognize what new questions are explicitly and implicitly being posed. Better sources of ideas for beginning students are secondary sources, such as textbooks in introductory psychology, or specialty areas, such as cognitive, social, or abnormal psychology. These sources are designed to teach the reader about a particular area and they devote considerable space to explaining ideas. In contrast, research journals have severe space restrictions, and most articles are condensed and difficult to understand unless you already have a good background in the area under study. As you gain sophistication in research and in a particular area of research, journal articles will become more useful and eventually will represent the major source of information. Published research studies can be a major source of new ideas. Another major source is the *Annual Review of Psychology,* which presents updated reviews of psychological research areas.

Fortunately for researchers, libraries have well-organized systems of journal abstracts and cross-referencing systems by topics and authors, which allow us to locate quickly most relevant research. In psychology the *Psychological Abstracts* are the primary source of such data. Other abstracts often used by psychological researchers include *Index Medicus* and the *Social Sciences Citation Index.* In many large university and research center libraries there is a growing trend to make these abstracts part of a computer data base, which makes it even easier to locate appropriate references. It is important for the researcher to become thoroughly familiar with these abstract systems.

Theories and research raise questions for further research in two general ways: heuristically and systematically. Heuristic influence occurs when a theory or research such as Darwin's or Freud's generates a great deal of interest, sometimes even disbelief and outright antagonism, and in that process also suggests further areas of study. The impact of these theories on furthering research has been enormous, but not necessarily in a systematic manner. The systematic influence occurs when theories or research make very explicit, testable propositions as the next step for research. Research in respondent and operant conditioning, for example, has systematically generated considerable research. Both influences, heuristic and systematic, are important in the continued development of science.

Seeking Solutions to Practical Problems   Much of psychology is *applied psychology,* and much of the research is therefore *applied research* in which the goal is to provide solutions to practical problems. Two applied questions were mentioned earlier, one concerning autistic children and the other concerning drunk drivers. Both questions arose out of concerns for practical issues: therapy for children and public safety. Applied research questions in psychology are fairly easy for the beginning student to generate. Here are some examples (try generating some of your own):

How can we better train people to be good drivers?

What can department stores do to reduce shoplifting?

How can we help an underachieving child to improve academically?

What are the best placements of dials and levers on certain machines so as to reduce worker fatigue?

What is an effective approach to calming children before and after surgery so as to improve their recovery?

How can we design nuclear power plant control rooms to minimize the chance of operator error?

How can we best educate the public so as to reduce the incidence of diseases such as lung cancer and AIDS?

Research can be categorized as *applied* or *basic* research. *Basic research* (also known as fundamental or pure research) is carried out to add to our understanding and store of knowledge, but without any particular practical goals. Basic research findings are often eventually incorporated into applied research. For example, basic research findings about the language development of children might be used to develop language training methods for language-deficient, disturbed, or retarded children. Unfortunately, it is often more difficult for basic researchers to obtain support than it is for applied researchers, perhaps because those who allocate funds do not realize the importance of basic research as necessary background for most applied research. It is difficult for even the most creative of individuals to imagine what applications an area of research might have until some basic understanding of that area is achieved. (See Box 3.1.)

REFINING QUESTIONS FOR RESEARCH

The beginning of a research project is a question. Perhaps first only vaguely considered, the question is gradually examined and refined until it becomes specific enough to provide the researcher with a clear direction for answering the question. The initial question, once developed, is much more than just a point from which to begin research; the very nature of the question determines much of how we carry out the rest of the research process. Thus, developing the initial question is of considerable importance. Beginning students may wonder at what level of constraint they should carry out a particular research project or how to determine what specific observational methods to use or how to select the right statistical test from the confusing array of available statistics, and so on. At least part of the answer to those and similar issues lies in the nature of the question we are asking. Once we refine the initial question, then many of those other decisions will follow.

Suppose, for example, that a psychologist studying animal behavior is interested in the parenting behavior of elephants in the wild and wants to know how long the baby elephants are dependent on their parents or other adults. The psychologist also wants to know other things such as whether and to what degree male and female elephants engage in parenting, and whether the baby's care is shared by other adult elephants. If we refine these questions further we might restate them as follows:

1. In their natural habitat, which (if any) adult elephants assist in the birth and early care of the infant elephants and in the primary care of the growing young?
2. At what age do young elephants raised in their natural habitat become independent from the parents and/or caretakers?

Having posed those questions, the first thing to do is search the literature for previous work on these and related questions. We do this to determine whether the questions have already been answered and, if not, what methods have been used by other investigators in answering similar questions. Let us assume in this case that these particular questions had not yet been asked or answered so that we may proceed with the example.

Box 3.1   SENSORY DEPRIVATION: APPLIED RESEARCH BECOMES BASIC RESEARCH

Basic research is often the foundation for applied research. But sometimes it can be the other way around as, for example, the research on sensory deprivation. The original research, which was funded by the Canadian Government and conducted at McGill University (Heron, Doane, & Scott, 1956), was stimulated by reports that communist countries were using brain-washing techniques involving sensory deprivation. Because western scientists knew virtually nothing about the effects of sensory deprivation, it was important to understand this phenomenon.

At McGill, a chamber was constructed to provide sensory isolation for subjects. Subjects wore translucent goggles to eliminate any pattern of stimulation to the visual system. Their hands were covered with cuffs that reduced sensory stimulation. An exhaust fan provided the only auditory stimulation—a constant low-frequency hum. In the original study using college students as subjects, students were paid $20 per day to remain in the chamber as long as they were willing to. Because this research was conducted in the early 1950s, $20 per day was a good payment (comparable to approximately $100 per day now). Even with this incentive, however, over half of the students quit the experiment within 48 hours. Almost all of them found the experience unpleasant, and many began to have vivid hallucinations.

These powerful findings created a great deal of interest and excitement among other researchers. Special laboratories were set up to explore the phenomenon in research centers in Canada and the United States, and knowledge about the phenomenon accumulated. But real understanding came only when scientists started relating the findings to other findings within the scientific literature and theorists began to integrate the findings into a coherent scientific theory. This tied the new body of research to established lines of scientific investigation. It stimulated new ideas and new ways of thinking about phenomena that had been studied for years. Basic research on sensory processes was alive with a new excitement and new sets of ideas.

In this situation, a line of applied research, born out of the cold war tensions of the late 1940s and early 1950s, stimulated basic research in many other areas. The findings on sensory deprivation are valuable contributions to understanding human sensory processes. But perhaps even more important, this research stimulated basic research that has since been used in dozens of applied research projects.

Notice two important points about the initial questions. First, the questions themselves have begun to specify the behavior we are going to observe (parenting behavior of the adults and independent behavior of the young). Secondly, the conditions under which the observations are to be made (the elephants' natural habitat) have also been identified in the question. These constitute two categories or sets of events that are of major interest to the researcher. Each is a complex and variable set of events; that is, both the behavior to be observed and the conditions of observation could vary in many ways.

Each set of varying events of interest to a researcher is a *variable.* A variable is defined as any set of events that may have different values. Height can be a variable because people, other organisms, and inanimate objects exist at different heights. Sex is a variable because there are two sexes. Behavior is a variable because a great number of behaviors can be performed. Any specific behavior (such as aggression) can be a variable because it can occur in different degrees or not occur at all. Some variables can be easily manipulated; for example, the amount of food one eats is a variable that an experimenter can manipulate. Manipulating a variable such as the amount of food eaten might change other variables such as one's weight (at least that's our hope when we go on those diets). In the study of elephants' behavior, two variables of interest are (1) the setting under which we observe the elephants and (2) the behavior of the elephants. We could observe elephants in many different settings. We have chosen to exercise some control by saying that we are interested only in settings that qualify as the "natural habitat of the elephant." We will not observe elephants in a zoo or in a circus. But there will still be variability in the observational settings. The elephants' behavior is even more variable, and, in fact, it is likely to be so variable and complex that we will want to simplify it by establishing broad categories into which it can be classified.

Note that the initial questions have also begun to narrow the choices of just how we are going to design and conduct this research. Obviously, by specifying the natural habitat as one variable, we will have to make observations in low-constraint natural settings. But more is involved. Because we have posed a question about the normal flow of behavior under natural conditions, we do not want to manipulate or control any of the variables. Instead, we will use naturalistic observation of the animals without any manipulation of the animals' behavior on our part.

In formulating initial questions, researchers proceed through an often lengthy process of thinking about their area of interest, posing loosely defined questions at first, studying their own previous work and the work of others reported in the literature, and gradually refining their general or vague ideas into initial research question(s). This process might take them far from their starting point, and their refined questions might be quite different from where they began.

The process of refining originally vague or general ideas does not stop when we arrive at an initial question; rather, the question is further refined into a more specific *statement of the problem* that we wish to investigate, and that statement is still further refined into a specific *research hypothesis*, which we then test in a specific research project. It is the research hypothesis that is tested in any study, and by testing the research hypothesis we thereby gain information about the original questions. Developing the statement of the problem and the research hypothesis are formal processes that will be more fully discussed in Chapter 8 as we approach the experimental level of constraint. The important point here is that the starting point may be vague or general ideas; these are refined into initial questions which, in turn, are further refined into problem statements and research hypotheses.

Once refined, the initial question implicitly helps to identify the major variables of interest and helps to structure the ways in which we will proceed to design and carry out the research. The level of constraint of a research project, and therefore the degree and types of controls, the kinds of observations, the type of data and measurement, and even the kinds of statistical analyses to be used all depend to some extent on the nature of the question that is asked. In general, we try to develop the initial question to the highest level of refinement possible, given the state of knowledge about the particular area of interest. The more we know about an area, the more refined will the question be and the more likely that high-constraint research methods will be used to answer the question. In areas where we do not already possess a great deal of information, the initial question will be correspondingly unrefined and less specific, and the procedures will therefore be carried out at lower constraint levels. In the example of elephants' parenting behavior, the question was general rather than highly detailed because we assumed that little was known about such behavior in elephants. We were unable to define exactly what behavior we were going to focus on because we were not sure what behaviors might be included in the broad category of parenting. We would not want to constrain our observations by trying to be overly specific about what behaviors to observe and how and when to observe them for fear that we might miss something important that we had not expected. In this case we want to maintain maximum flexibility in the research, so we place no constraints on the behavior of the subjects (the elephants), and we place few constraints on the researcher other than the constraint that we not manipulate or interfere with the subjects. If we knew more about elephants before we began the research, our questions would be considerably more specific and our behavior as researchers would be more constrained by our specific focus. The nature of the question determines much about how we carry out our research project.

TYPES OF VARIABLES IN RESEARCH

There are several important ways of classifying variables in psychology: in terms of behavioral variables, stimulus variables, and organismic or subject variables, or independent and dependent variables.

Behavioral Variables

Any overt (i.e., observable) response of an organism is a *behavioral variable.* This includes a rat running a maze, a chimpanzee opening a puzzle box, a child playing with a toy, a subject pressing keys in an experiment, a person playing the piano, people talking to each other, and so on. Behavioral variables can range from relatively simple behavior, such as a single key-press, to quite complex responses, such as social and verbal behavior. Because psychology is defined as the study of behavior, behavioral variables are of particular importance in psychology. *The variables most often observed in psychological research are behavioral variables.*

Stimulus Variables

Behavior always occurs in a context. The context is the total situation surrounding the behaving organism and all of the many different stimulus events that make up the situation. The events that have an actual or potential effect on the organism's response are *stimulus variables.* In psychological research the stimulus variables may be highly specific and readily measurable and controllable, such as a flashing light or a buzzer as a signal for the subject to respond. They also may be more general, such as the total situation surrounding the subject being observed. An example would be the habitat in which we observe elephants' behavior or the condition of a classroom in which we observe a child. Stimulus variables range from simple, such as a light signal, to complex, such as a controlled, contrived, social situation to which we assign subjects. In psychological research it is the stimulus variables over which we exert various degrees of control, and the response variables that we observe. In general, as we move from lower to higher levels of constraint (see Chapter 2), we apply greater degrees of control over stimulus variables.

Some stimulus variables, however, are internal to the subject and cannot be directly manipulated by the experimenter. For example, stimuli for balance, sympathetic nervous system activity, and so on are internal stimuli. Even though these variables are not under the control of the experimenter, they are still a part of the subject's environment and can affect behavior.

Organismic or Subject Variables

Organismic or *subject variables* are the characteristics of the subjects, such as age, sex, height, weight, intelligence, neuroticism, racial attitudes, musical ability, psychiatric diagnosis, socioeconomic class, educational level, and so on. Some of the subjects' characteristics, such as weight, height, and sex, can be directly observed and are referred to as *observed organismic variables.* Other subject characteristics, such as neuroticism, racial attitudes, and intelligence, cannot be directly observed but are inferred from the subject's behavior. These are called *response-inferred organismic variables.* (You should have noticed that response-inferred organismic variables are also constructs, which were discussed in Chapter 2.)

Organismic variables can be used to classify subjects. For example, we might measure neuroticism of a group of subjects, and then divide the subjects into three groups (high, moderate, and low neuroticism) based on their scores. It should be noted that some variables can be classified under more than one of these categories depending on the way they fit into the research situation. For example, educational level would normally be thought of as an organismic variable—it is a characteristic of subjects. But educational level could also be a stimulus variable if the researcher provided an educational experience for subjects as part of a study. It might also be a behavioral variable if we are interested in the behavior of obtaining more education and what factors might influence that behavior. In other words, it is not just the characteristics of the variable itself that allows us to classify it as behavioral, stimulus, or organismic, but also how the variable fits into the research project.

Independent and Dependent Variables

As noted above, one way of classifying variables is in terms of behavioral variables, stimulus variables, and organismic variables. Another way is to classify variables as *independent* and *dependent* variables. In the research with autistic children, disruptive behavior (a behavioral variable) changed from a high frequency of occurrence when there was no relaxation training to a low frequency of occurrence after relaxation training. The researchers manipulated relaxation training (a stimulus variable) and observed the presumed effects of that manipulation on disruptive behavior. Because disruptive behavior was thought to be *dependent upon* the manipulation of relaxation training, it is therefore labeled the *dependent variable.* In experimental research, the dependent variable is not directly manipulated by the experimenter. It is the independent variable that is directly manipulated by the experimenter; the changes that occur in the dependent variable are observed and measured.

The *independent variable* in the above research was the relaxation training. It was hypothesized that the independent variable would have a measurable effect on the dependent variable. There are two kinds of independent variables: (1) manipulated independent variables and (2) nonmanipulated independent variables. *Manipulated independent variables* are those that the experimenter controls by actively manipulating them, such as the relaxation training in the above study. *Nonmanipulated independent variables* are variables that are not directly under the experimenter's control. The largest category of nonmanipulated independent variables in psychology are *organismic* or subject variables; that is, those variables that are preexisting characteristics of the subjects, such as IQ, religious affiliation, age, motor coordination, political affiliation, and so forth. The researcher does not actively manipulate such variables but assigns subjects to groups based on the organismic variables. For example, suppose we wanted to test the hypothesis that moral problem-solving skills are affected by religious affiliation. We would assign subjects to groups based on their identified religious affiliation. We would then have all subjects take the Moral Problem-Solving Test and would compare the scores of the religious affiliation groups on the test to determine whether there were significant differences between them.

Researchers often hypothesize a causal relationship between independent and dependent variables. A causal relationship between two variables exists when changes in one variable result in a predictable change in the other. However, as we will discuss in later chapters, it is difficult to draw a causal conclusion without the control provided by actively manipulating the independent variable. Thus, conclusions about causal relationships in a study with organismic independent variables (subject variables) are extremely tentative conclusions. Later chapters will further discuss manipulated and nonmanipulated variables. For now it is important that the student be able to make two distinctions: (1) the distinction between the independent and the dependent variable, and (2) the distinction between manipulated and nonmanipulated independent variables.

The independent-dependent variable distinction is most important in high-constraint experimental research where a major assumption is that the experimenter's manipulations of the independent variable are *causally related* to the observed changes in the dependent variable. It thus becomes important in experimental research, if one is to have any confidence in the assumption of causality, to distinguish between the two and to apply carefully all of the operations necessary to insure that the independent variable will be as precisely defined and fully controlled as needed, and that the dependent variable will be adequately measured.

In lower constraint research such as correlational research, there is no assumption of a causal relationship. Thus, the independent-dependent variable distinction is not needed. In some research, such as naturalistic observation, there may be no clearly defined independent variable. In such research the behavior being observed is not properly a dependent variable. It is simply a variable of interest—an observational variable. In differential research, the independent variable is not directly manipulated by the experimenter but rather is a variable that already characterizes the subjects. It still serves in research as an independent variable and as a guide for observing and interpreting the changes in the dependent variable. Thus, although the independent-dependent variable distinction is most importantly applied in higher constraint experimental research, it is nevertheless used in lower constraint research, often as a convenience to distinguish between the two variables of interest.

The independent variable in psychological research is usually a stimulus variable (in the case of manipulated independent variables) or an organismic variable (in the case of nonmanipulated independent variables). The dependent variable is usually a response variable. We should also note that an independent variable in one study may be a dependent variable in another. For example, in a learning study, the researcher might manipulate, as the independent variable, the amount of time that visual stimuli are presented to subjects. The dependent variable in this study might be the accuracy of the subjects' recognition of the stimulus figures. In another study, the researcher might manipulate as the independent variable the complexity of visual stimuli presented. The dependent variable in this second study might be the amount of time needed by the subjects to identify the stimuli. Thus, in the first study, the amount of stimulus presentation time is controlled by the researcher and is an independent variable. In the second study, the amount of stimulus presentation time required by the subjects to identify the stimuli is the dependent variable.

VALIDITY AND THE CONTROL OF EXTRANEOUS VARIABLES

Validity is one of the most important concepts in research and a central theme throughout the remainder of this text. Validity is a complex idea and there are many types of validity. When the researcher asks, "Does this study really answer the question it posed?" or "Does this test really measure what we want it to measure?" or "What does this laboratory study tell us about the 'real world'?" he or she is asking questions about validity. In essence, validity refers to how well a study, a procedure, or a measure does what it is supposed to do. One of the fundamental tasks of research is to ensure the validity of the procedures by applying controls. We have referred several times to *control* or *controlled research* but have not yet defined what we mean by those terms.

Let us begin to think of control in research by recognizing that empirical observation is a central point in the scientific research process. Observations in psychological research are usually observations of the behavior of organisms. The behavior under observation may be influenced by many different variables, some of which are known and many of which are unknown to the researcher. Further, some of the variables may be of research interest to the researcher while others may be extraneous and even interfering factors. If the extraneous factors are numerous or powerful in the research, then their interference might make it impossible for the researcher to draw meaningful conclusions about the operations of the variables of interest. In effect, the influence of extraneous variables can reduce the methodological soundness or *validity* of the research findings. That is, *extraneous variables* are threats to the validity of the study.

It is thus important to reduce the influence of extraneous variables on the behavior being observed. However, it is not only the behavior of subjects that can be influenced by extraneous variables but also the behavior of researchers doing the observing. Extraneous influences on researchers might so powerfully bias their observational methods as to invalidate the research or at least make it difficult to draw clear conclusions from the results. Therefore, it is important in research to reduce the effects that extraneous variables might have on the behavior of subjects being observed and on that of researchers doing the observation.

The procedures used to reduce such extraneous influences are what we mean by controls in research. Thus, the concept of *control in research* refers to the *systematic methods employed by the researcher to reduce threats to the validity of the study posed by extraneous influences on the behavior of both the subjects and the observer.* Although detailed, systematic control methods become most important in higher constraint research, they are nevertheless part of the procedures at all levels. For example, in a case-study research project where we might want to observe the solutions of some problems by children working individually, it would be important to prevent the child from being interrupted in the problem-solving tasks by other children who might make distracting noises or perhaps become interested themselves and volunteer their own solutions. These would be extraneous factors, and we would probably arrange to test the children individually in a quiet room safely separated from the rest of the class. In effect, we would have exerted some control over the observational setting as a method to reduce the effects of those and perhaps other extraneous variables.

There are two ways of controlling extraneous variables. One is to use higher constraint research designs whenever possible. The second set of control procedures, *general control procedures,* can be incorporated in research at many different levels of constraint. They can effectively compensate for some of the controls that are not available in lower constraint research. For example, at all levels of research careful measurement of the variables is an important general control procedure. (Controls in research will be discussed further in later chapters.)

RESEARCH ETHICS

The research process involves a series of decisions that must be made by the researcher before observing even a single subject. These decisions include subject selection and assignment, controls, definition and measurement of variables, the statistical analyses to be used, and so on. One important set of decisions involves the ethics of psychological research, or *research ethics.* These issues are so important that we have included this section early in this text, so the ideas will be familiar to students as they progress through most of the text. As noted in Chapter 2, researchers make decisions about how they will use living organisms, human and nonhuman, for research purposes, and this demands that ethical concerns be included in the decision process. The ethical guides for scientific research extend to both human and nonhuman research (the latter is often referred to as "animal research"), and emphasize humane, sensitive treatment of subjects who are often put at varying degrees of threat or risk by research procedures. Before the researcher contacts a single subject, he or she must be sure that the research plan stands up to ethical evaluation. Ethical concerns, therefore, are an integral part of the preobservation decision-making process in research.

Although the following discussion will focus on ethics in research, it is important to note that ethical concerns also apply to other activities of psychologists such as psychological testing and psychotherapy.

Ethical Guides for Human Research

Concern over potential inhumane treatment of human subjects was generated by post World War II revelations of what German researchers did to people including children in the name of science. International groups as well as United States professional organizations (such as the American Psychological Association and the American Medical Association) began to examine their own research practices. Although no other people were found to approximate the German inhumanities, considerable concern developed that even in the United States some research subjects might be treated in less than humane ways. In the 1950s and 1960s there were growing criticisms of some of the methods used in biomedical research in the United States, which placed human subjects at considerable risk without subjects' knowledge of the risks. In some instances, live disease organisms were injected into subjects or new surgical techniques were practiced on patients who were undergoing surgery not related to the new techniques, without subjects' or patients' knowledge or permission. Researchers were careful to provide the best-known medical safeguards for their subjects, but the point remains that the procedures were carried out without subjects' full knowledge and consent.

By the mid-1960s, many writers were expressing concern over these and other practices. Numerous journals published articles in this new area of concern for research ethics, and at least one journal, *Daedalus* (1969), devoted an entire issue to research ethics. To tell a subject only that they were to be given a test of biological resistance, while withholding the information that the substance injected into them contained live cancer cells, in order to determine how readily the body rejects them, is at the very least a serious deception. Writers maintained that research subjects must be protected against deception, dangerous procedures, and invasion of privacy. Subjects, they said, have a right to know what is going to be done to them and to be given enough clear information so that they can freely give their consent or refuse the experimental procedures.

Psychological research with human subjects is rarely physically intrusive, and the risks to subjects are not as great as in some biomedical research. Nevertheless, issues of *deception, invasion of privacy,* and *subjects' rights* to be informed so as to be able to make a free choice still apply to psychological research. Potential invasions of privacy occur when researchers examine highly personal and sensitive areas of psychological adjustment, such as sexual behavior, private thoughts and fears, or relationships between couples. Social scientists often gain access to confidential records of patients in hospitals or of children in schools for research purposes. Deception in psychological research has become standard in some areas of study, although in nearly all instances the deception is mild. When a social psychologist tells a group of children he wants to see how well they can judge the length of lines drawn on the blackboard, but in fact really wants to know how much the least and most popular child influences the other children's judgments, he is practicing a mild form of deception.

At the center of these issues lies a genuine conflict of interests and a moral problem. On the one hand, society demands scientific solutions to a large array of problems. On the other hand, there are times when searching for such solutions may violate individuals' rights to privacy and to proper treatment. If we are going to meet society's demands to develop new knowledge and new medicines and treatments for illness, to solve problems such as juvenile delinquency, depression, psychosis, or aggression, or to develop improved teaching methods, we must be able to carry out scientific research and that requires the cooperation of subjects. It is our position that it is in the long-term interests of society for individuals to contribute to scientific efforts. One way is by participating as subjects in research. This is not to say that we expect all individuals to accept whatever subject's role is presented, but rather, responsible people will seriously consider donating their time, effort, and information as subjects to promote scientific knowledge, even when they do not personally benefit by their participation. The potential benefits to society constitute an important criterion. Of course, the decision is up to each individual.

The moral dilemma arises because research, even with its potential benefits to society, sometimes exposes subjects to potential risks. In attempting to solve this dilemma, most research agencies, universities, and professional organizations have adopted a position that accepts the following basic ideas:

1. Scientific research offers potential benefits to society in general as well as to specific disciplines.
2. It is reasonable to expect that individuals will behave in a socially responsible manner and contribute to the research enterprise by participating as subjects in research.
3. Individual subjects have basic rights when they elect to participate in a research study. They have the right to privacy and to protection from physical and psychological harm. They should also be given clear and sufficient information on which to make their own decision as to whether they will or will not serve as subjects in any given research project.
4. It is the responsibility of the researcher to conduct research in such a manner as to respect and maintain subjects' rights and to protect subjects from possible physical and/or psychological harm.

The American Psychological Association (APA) was one of the first professional organizations to develop ethical guidelines for research. The latest guidelines (1981) are organized into ten ethical principles, reprinted in Box 3.2. Psychological researchers must be thoroughly familiar with these principles.

The APA recognizes both the need for research and the rights of subjects in its attempt to reconcile the two or at least to reduce conflicts. This position recognizes that some research, in order to obtain the information it seeks, employs deception, makes subjects uncomfortable, or pries into personal areas. These and other conditions of some research are considered to place the subjects at risk. To say that the *subject is at risk* means that the potential exists for some subjects to suffer physical or emotional

Ethical Principles in the Conduct of Research with Human Participants

The decision to undertake research rests upon a considered judgment by the individual psychologist about how best to contribute to psychological science and human welfare. Having made the decision to conduct research, the psychologist considers alternative directions in which research energies and resources might be invested. On the basis of this consideration, the psychologist carries out the investigation with respect and concern for the dignity and welfare of the people who participate and with cognizance of federal and state regulations and professional standards governing the conduct of research with human participants.

A. In planning a study, the investigator has the responsibility to make a careful evaluation of its ethical acceptability. To the extent that the weighing of scientific and human values suggests a compromise of any principle, the investigator incurs a correspondingly serious obligation to seek ethical advice and to observe stringent safeguards to protect the rights of human participants.

B. Considering whether a participant in a planned study will be a "subject at risk" or a "subject at minimal risk," according to recognized standards, is of primary ethical concern to the investigator.

C. The investigator always retains the responsibility for ensuring ethical practice in research. The investigator is also responsible for the ethical treatment of research participants by collaborators, assistants,

students, and employees, all of whom, however, incur similar obligations.

D. Except in minimal-risk research, the investigator establishes a clear and fair agreement with research participants, prior to their participation, that clarifies the obligations and responsibilities of each. The investigator has the obligation to honor all promises and commitments included in that agreement. The investigator informs the participants of all aspects of the research that might reasonably be expected to influence willingness to participate and explains all other aspects of the research about which the participants inquire. Failure to make full disclosure prior to obtaining informed consent requires additional safeguards to protect the welfare and dignity of the research participants. Research with children or with participants who have impairments that would limit understanding and/or communication requires special safeguarding procedures.

E. Methodological requirements of a study may make the use of concealment or deception necessary. Before conducting such a study, the investigator has a special responsibility to (1) determine whether the use of such techniques is justified by the study's prospective scientific, educational, or applied value; (2) determine whether alternative procedures are available that do not use concealment or deception; and (3) ensure that the participants are provided with sufficient explanation as soon as possible.

F. The investigator respects the individual's freedom to decline to participate in or to withdraw from the research at any time.

The obligation to protect this freedom requires careful thought and consideration when the investigator is in a position of authority or influence over the participant. Such positions of authority include, but are not limited to, situations in which research participation is required as part of employment or in which the participant is a student, client, or employee of the investigator.

G. The investigator protects the participant from physical and mental discomfort, harm, and danger that may arise from research procedures. If risks of such consequences exist, the investigator informs the participant of that fact. Research procedures likely to cause serious or lasting harm to a participant are not used unless the failure to use these procedures might expose the participant to risk of greater harm or unless the research has great potential benefit and fully informed and voluntary consent is obtained from each participant. The participant should be informed of procedures for contacting the investigator within a reasonable time period following participation should stress, potential harm, or related questions or concerns arise.

H. After the data are collected, the investigator provides the participant with information about the nature of the study and attempts to remove any misconceptions that may have arisen. Where scientific or humane values justify delaying or withholding this information, the investigator incurs a special responsibility to monitor the research and to ensure that there are no damaging consequences for the participant.

I. Where research procedures result in undesirable consequences for the individual participant, the investigator has the responsibility to detect and remove or correct these consequences, including long-term effects.

J. Information obtained about a research participant during the course of an investigation is confidential unless otherwise agreed upon in advance. When the possibility exists that others may obtain access to such information, this possibility, together with the plans for protecting confidentiality, is explained to the participant as part of the procedure for obtaining informed consent.

harm as a result of participating in the study. The ethical principles are an attempt to help researchers conduct research while at the same time minimize those risks to subjects.

Perhaps the most important safeguard built into these guidelines is this: it is the *subject* who decides to participate in research. The subject has the right to refuse to participate or the right to discontinue at any time even after having agreed to participate. The ethical researcher is bound to honor this right and can neither coerce subjects into participating nor prevent subjects from withdrawing if they so decide. Researchers may not proceed to gather data until they have received the unequivocal consent of the subjects. Further, *informed consent* is an important safeguard; that is, the researcher must provide subjects with enough information about the research to enable them to make informed decisions about their participation.

When the subjects are children or are in some way incapacitated as is the case with hospitalized mental patients or retarded people, they may have difficulty in understanding the information or in giving consent. Under those conditions, greater responsibility is placed on both the researcher and some designated person who acts on behalf of the subjects to insure that their rights and well-being are protected. These representatives may include parents, school administrators, or other institutional officials.

As first pointed out by Vinacke in 1954, *deception* is frequently employed in some types of psychological research. Although nearly always innocuous and mild in nature, the use of any deception places the subject at risk. Therefore, when deception is used, even mild deception, safeguards must be employed. The most common safeguards are (1) the researcher's judgment that the deception poses no serious or long-term risks and (2) that the true nature of the research, including an explanation of the deception, be communicated to the subject in a postexperimental debriefing. This is designed to let the subject know exactly what the procedures were and to counter any lingering misconceptions, possible discomfort, or risk that may have been generated by the research.

Another important basic safeguard concerns the responsibility of the researcher to maintain strict confidentiality of any information gathered about subjects. This is particularly important when the research deals with sensitive personal information about the subjects or information that was derived from normally confidential personal records such as hospital or school records. Researchers commonly use number codes rather than subjects' names on any records that contain sensitive information. It is the researcher's responsibility to insure that such information does not become known to others who may be in a position to misuse it.

The major ethical responsibility falls on the researcher. In planning any research with human subjects, the researcher must judge the research in terms of its value, the amount of risk it poses, whether the potential benefits outweigh the risks, and whether adequate safeguards have been built in to minimize the risks. It must be emphasized that should the risks to the subjects outweigh any potential benefits of the research, the ethical researcher will necessarily redesign or discontinue the research project.

A point seldom made, but one we believe to be of considerable ethical importance, concerns the potential value of the research. If the research is badly designed without proper attention to details so that its results are of little or no value, then (1) the potential informational value to society and to the discipline will be minimal, and (2) subjects' time will have been wasted and perhaps the subjects will have been exposed to some risks in a largely valueless endeavor. Thus, in addition to all the other value in good research design, it is also an ethical responsibility of the researcher to develop well-designed projects and execute them with care.

Ethical Checks   Let us assume that we are designing a research project with human subjects. We have identified an area of interest and refined the initial question. We have also identified and defined the major variables and have determined the nature of the subjects, how they will be selected, and how we propose to observe them. We still have many detailed decisions to make before we can begin our observations, but at this point it is necessary to make the *ethical checks* by asking these questions:

Is the proposed research sufficiently well designed to be of informational value?

Does the research pose any risks to subjects such as physical or psychological harm, use of deception, obtaining sensitive, personal information, using minors as subjects or others who cannot readily give consent?

If risks are placed on subjects, does the research adequately control those risks by including procedures such as debriefing, removing or reducing risks of physical harm, guaranteeing through the procedures that all information will be obtained anonymously or, if that is not possible, then guaranteeing that it will remain confidential?

Have I included a provision for obtaining informed consent from every subject or, if subjects cannot give it, from responsible people acting for the benefit of the subject? The informed consent should also make it clear to the subject that he or she is free to withdraw from the experiment at any time.

By subjecting the research plan to ethical checks, we can identify and correct most of the potential ethical problems. When the study has been completely designed, repeating the ethical checks is necessary as a final check before submitting the proposal to the institutional review board.

Institutional Review Boards (IRBs)   To assist researchers and help protect subjects, *institutional review boards* consisting of the researcher's peers and members of the community at large have been set up in virtually all universities, research institutes, hospitals, and school systems, wherever research on human subjects is carried out. The task of a review board is to review every research proposal submitted to it, to determine whether the proposal meets the ethical guidelines determined by the IRB, and if it does not, to suggest appropriate changes. Every institution that receives federal funding— including virtually all research agencies—is required to submit all human subject research proposals to a duly appointed review board. Members of the board are usually appointed by the president or other administrator of the institution. It is the responsibility of the individual researcher to be sure that his or her proposal is submitted to the appropriate IRB and is approved by the IRB before gathering any data.

When it functions well, the IRB is a helpful advisory group of colleagues that expedites the research, advises the researcher, and suggests improvements. In our experience the IRB has worked reasonably and quickly without creating undue delays for the responsible researcher and has, in addition, often been helpful to the researcher. It must be emphasized that the IRB acts as an additional safeguard, assisting researchers in clarifying potential ethical issues. The IRB, however, does not replace or reduce the researcher's ethical responsibility to design acceptable research. *The final ethical responsibility always rests with the researcher.*

Ethical Principles in Research with Animals

In our view, concern for the ethical and humane treatment of animal subjects in research is as important as the concern for human subjects. A great deal of animal research is being conducted in many biomedical disciplines, and large numbers of animal subjects are used each year. The APA estimated in 1985 that over 3000 psychologists use animals in their research.

The major ethical concerns revolve about two basic issues: (1) animals are captive subjects and, of course, are not capable of providing informed consent and (2) the nature of the research carried out on animals is generally more invasive than that carried out on humans. Thus, there are many more serious risks to individual animal subjects than there are in human research. Therefore, much more responsibility is placed on the researcher to ensure that animal subjects are treated humanely.

For years, professional and governmental organizations have followed ethical guidelines in the use of animal subjects. The APA, for example, has had ongoing professional committees to address issues of animal research since 1925. That early concern has evolved into a set of standards and principles in animal research, and these standards are periodically reviewed. The National Science Foundation updated its policy for care and use of vertebrate animals in late 1985, and the APA did the same in 1986 with publication of *Guidelines for Ethical Conduct in the Care and Use of Animals*. Researchers who publish in APA journals and who use animals in their research must attest that the research was conducted in accordance with APA guidelines. The guidelines cover areas such as adequate and humane housing, preoperative and postoperative care, concerns about inflicting as little pain and discomfort as possible, and the need to have as much confidence as possible that the proposed research is necessary and is well designed.

There has been recent increased interest in reducing the number of live animals used in experimentation and research training. These reductions are being accomplished in medical and biological laboratories in several ways. One way is to sharpen the designs of the experiments so that fewer animals are needed. Other ways of reducing the number of animals include substituting computer simulation for live animals and by using cells cultured in laboratories rather than live animals. In training researchers and practitioners such as in schools of veterinary medicine, the number of live animals used in teaching has been reduced by substituting full-sized, realistic models of animals. However, it is much more difficult to develop alternatives to live animals in behavioral studies such as are conducted in psychology. Intact, functioning animals are needed if we are to observe changes in their behavior.

Recently there has been considerable controversy about the use of animals in research. Many people have argued that some animals have been mistreated in the name of research. The latest guidelines on the ethical treatment of animals in research are designed to minimize such problems. It has been argued by some that animal research is unnecessary and does not contribute meaningful information. Nothing could be further from the truth. As Neal Miller (1985) has pointed out, animal research has not only contributed knowledge that has improved services and reduced risks for human beings, but has often lead to more effective and humane care for animals and solutions to problems that animals face in natural environments. For example, behavioral research on taste aversion has led to humane alternatives to shooting or poisoning animals, such as deer, coyotes, geese, crows, and others, that destroy crops or attack livestock. Behavioral and biological research has led to improved habitat preservation for wildlife, to successful reintroduction of Atlantic salmon and other fish to areas where they had been killed off, and to successful treatment for and vaccination against many diseases of pets, livestock, and zoo animals. Animal research has also led to successful medical and psychological treatments of human disorders, such as enuresis and encopresis, scoliosis (a severe curvature of the spine), anorexia, life-threatening vomiting in infants, retraining use of limbs following accidents or surgery, and many other disorders. Miller's article is highly recommended reading.

Concern for humane and ethical treatment of animals in research is legitimate, and few researchers would deny the importance of that concern. On the other hand, research with animals has made enormous contributions to our understanding of nature. As with all research, the costs in terms of risks to the subjects must be balanced by the potential benefits to society.

SUMMARY

The starting point for research is finding an area of interest and generating a researchable question. Research questions can be readily developed from our own personal experiences and interests, from the published theoretical and empirical work of others, and from attempts to solve practical problems. New research can be generated from current research both heuristically (by stimulating interest and even opposition) and systematically (by making precise predictions about the needed next step in the research process).

Psychological research can be categorized as (1) basic research in which we attempt to develop new information without any particular practical goals and (2) applied research in which we attempt to answer questions to help solve practical problems.

The initial questions may be quite vague, and must be refined and sharpened until we have attained the most precise questions possible given the state of knowledge in that particular area. The refined question is of considerable importance because the nature of the question will influence how we will proceed with the remainder of the research. Refining the initial question implicitly helps to identify the major variables of interest and to structure the ways in which we will proceed to design and carry out the research. The level of constraint of the research project, and therefore the degree and type of controls, the observational procedures, the methods of measurement, the type of data and the statistical analyses to be used, all depend to a great extent on the nature of the question that is asked.

It is important to identify not only the variables of interest, but also variables in which we have no interest, but which might affect the outcome of research. These extraneous variables must be identified so that appropriate procedures can be developed for controlling or minimizing their effects on the variables we want to study.

One group of important preobservational decisions to be made concerns ethics. The rights of the individual must always be balanced against society's need for scientific information. Ethical guidelines have been developed by the APA for psychological research with human subjects. The basic focus of the guidelines is to insure that subjects are not coerced into cooperating in research, that such research is meaningful, and that it poses no undue hazards to subjects. It is the responsibility of the individual researcher to see that risks to subjects are minimized and to have each project reviewed by an appropriate IRB for their department or agency. However, the ultimate responsibility for insuring subjects' rights lies with the researcher.

Ethical concerns in the use of animal subjects are equally important. The guidelines for animal research focus on the adequacy of housing and general care of laboratory animals, and on minimizing pain or other discomfort that might result from the research procedures.

REVIEW EXERCISES

I. Define the following key terms. Be sure that you understand them. They are discussed in the chapter and defined in the glossary.

Applied psychology
Applied research
Basic research
Variable
Statement of the problem
Research hypothesis
Validity
Types of variables
   Behavioral variables
   Organismic variables
   Subject variables
   Observed organismic variables
   Response-inferred organismic
      variables
   Stimulus variables
   Independent variables
   Dependent variables

Manipulated independent
   variables
Nonmanipulated independent
   variables
Extraneous variables
Controlled research
Validity
Control in research
General control procedures
Research ethics
Deception
Invasion of privacy
Subjects' rights
Subjects at risk
Informed consent
Ethical checks
Institutional review boards (IRBs)

II. Answer each of the following. Check your answers in the chapter.

1. Explain this statement: "Freud's research was of considerable heuristic value."
2. Name and briefly describe the three main starting points for research.
3. To review an earlier concept, what is meant by *levels of constraint*?
4. Name and define the classes of variables discussed in this chapter.
5. For each of the following variables, determine the class of variables to which it belongs: academic achievement; aggressive behavior; number of correct answers on a test; giving one group of rats sugar and another group saccharine; height of subjects; socioeconomic class of subjects; subjects' general health status; amount of light at a desk in research on office working conditions; psychiatric diagnosis of subjects.
6. Distinguish between an independent and a dependent variable.
7. In the research on autistic children described in the chapter, identify the independent variable and the dependent variable.
8. Distinguish between the two types of independent variables.
9. Explain this statement: "The independent-dependent variable distinction is most important in high-constraint experimental research."
10. Exactly what is meant by "manipulating the independent variable"?
11. What is the major assumption about the relationship between variables in experimental research?
12. Distinguish between basic and applied research. Give examples of each.

13. What are extraneous variables? Give some examples.
14. What is deception in research with human subjects, and what is the major safeguard for deception? Give examples of deception in research.
15. Identify and explain the moral problem that lies at the center of research ethics.
16. If proposed subjects are minors or are mentally incapacitated, what is the standard ethical procedure to safeguard their rights?

III. Think about and work the following problems.

1. At the end of Chapter 2 we asked you to generate some research questions. Now we want you to generate more, but this time try to refine them further by clearly identifying the major variables that are included in the questions. For example:

   Question: How much does alcohol affect driving?
   Variables: Alcohol; driving.

2. Following are some brief descriptions of research. For each one you are to (a) identify the variables, (b) indicate the class of variables to which each belongs, and (c) identify any potential extraneous variables.
   a. You are investigating the relationship between children's ethnic prejudices and their socioeconomic status.
   b. In a study on the effects of alcohol on driving, subjects are randomly assigned to seven conditions of alcohol consumption: 0.0, 0.5, 1.0, 1.5, 2.0, 2.5 and 3.0 ounces, respectively. Subjects in each condition are tested in a driving simulator and the number of driving errors is measured. The hypothesis is that higher consumption of alcohol will cause greater driving errors.
   c. Shoppers are asked to compare two laundry products while being videotaped for a television commercial. During the comparison the products' labels are covered, supposedly so the subjects cannot identify them. The subjects know they are not supposed to see the labels. However, the covering on one product, the sponsor's product, is thinner than the other, and the subjects can actually see what the label says. Will the sponsor's product be chosen more than the other as the superior product?
   d. You are investigating the relationship between size (a height-weight measure) and peer status in sixth-grade children.
3. Following are some research situations. What are the potential ethical problems in each? Where you can, indicate what safeguards you would use.
   a. A researcher is going to test third and fourth graders to compare boys and girls on their interest in math problems.
   b. A study of small-group interactions with adults as subjects is being conducted. The subjects are observed in small groups of five people. The subjects do not know that three of the five subjects in their group are actually assistants of the researcher and that their behavior during the small-group meeting has been planned ahead of time.
   c. A researcher wants to examine the files on hospitalized schizophrenics to obtain basic information about their families.

4. Suppose you are a researcher who has designed a research project using human subjects, written a research proposal, and submitted it to your institutional review board for clearance on ethical issues. The board returns your proposal as "ethically unacceptable" because the design is so flawed that the information from the study would be meaningless. There is no other issue raised. Why is this criticism of your proposed design an ethical issue and not just a design problem?

5. Think of several examples of variables that could be independent variable in one study and dependent variable in a different study.

DATA AND THE NATURE OF MEASUREMENT

In Chapter 2 we developed the idea that observation is the pivotal phase in the research process. In Chapter 4 we will take a closer look at observations, how to go about making them, and how to put them into a form most useful for research.

RESEARCH VARIABLES

As introduced in Chapter 3, every research project, whatever its level of constraint, includes one or more sets of events or variables that the researcher manipulates and/or observes and measures. A *variable* is any characteristic that can take more than one form or value (e.g., anxiety, intelligence, height, reaction time, fear). Because scientific methods of research can be used to study any natural phenomena, any varying event or set of events can become a research variable. For example, the study of autistic children (Graziano, 1974) introduced in Chapter 2 has two major variables: (1) relaxation training and (2) children's disruptive behavior. Intelligence as measured by a standard IQ test can be a variable in research because in any group of subjects the score will differ or vary from one subject to another. The number of correct answers on an arithmetic test can also be a variable because that number will differ from one subject to another and can change from one condition to another. Suppose, for example, we measure the number of correct answers given by one group of students under quiet classroom conditions and the number of correct answers given by another group under noisy classroom conditions. In each example, the variable (relaxation, disruptive behavior, intelligence, or academic performance) is a complex event that varies from one subject to another and/or from one condition to another. If the events of interest are static with no variation, they cannot serve as research variables. Simply put, a variable must vary. The major task in measurement is to represent the research variables numerically.

In research there are usually at least two variables of interest: (1) the independent variable (which may or may not be manipulated by the researcher) and (2) the dependent or response variable (which is observed and measured by the researcher). The distinction between independent and dependent variables is often blurred or not wholly necessary in some low-constraint research and is used largely as a convenience.

MEASUREMENT

In scientific research variables must be measured. To measure a variable is to assign numbers that represent values of the variable. When each subject has been measured on the variable, the measurements constitute the numerical or quantitative data, and the data are the basic units for subsequent data analyses and interpretation. Further, the particular statistical analyses chosen by the researcher will be determined largely by the way the dependent variables are measured. Beginning students are often confused when faced with the question, "What statistical procedures should be used in this study?" As we will see later (in this chapter and in Chapter 14), choosing appropriate statistical procedures is often relatively simple once the observational procedures have been designed and the ways in which we will measure the dependent variable have been determined.

Measurement of a variable is essentially the process of assigning numbers to that variable. In assigning numbers to a variable, the researcher works with two major sets of information. The first set is the abstract number system with all its characteristic rules and procedures. The second set is the variable to be measured with all of *its* particular characteristics. The task for the researcher is to bring the two systems together, to apply one to the other so the numbers will accurately represent the variable. The task becomes complicated because the two systems do not necessarily function according to the same rules. The abstract number system has specific and well-defined characteristics and rules. However, variables in psychology, as in many sciences, are not usually so well defined and well understood, and they do not necessarily function according to the same clear rules as the abstract number system. Thus, the two systems cannot always be easily matched. It is necessary for the researcher to determine how the characteristics of a particular variable might fail to match those of the abstract number system, so as to construct appropriate measures of the variable and to use the appropriate statistical methods of analysis. Serious errors in data analysis and interpretation can occur when the researcher misapplies the number system.

The characteristics or properties of the abstract number system are identity, magnitude, equal intervals, and a true zero. Identity means that each number has a particular meaning. Magnitude means that numbers have an inherent order from smaller to larger (5 is of greater magnitude than 3). Equal intervals means that the difference between units is the same anywhere on the scale (the difference between 2 and 3 is the same as the difference between 99 and 100). The zero on the abstract number scale is a true zero. Because of these properties, we can add, subtract, multiply, and divide the numbers. However, if we apply the abstract number system to a psychological variable such as intelligence, we would find that the abstract number system and intelligence do not match exactly. The number system has a true zero point but the psychological variable, intelligence, does not have a zero point. That is, in the unlikely event that a person were to score zero on an intelligence test, we could not conclude that he or she had zero intelligence. Thus, the score zero does not indicate zero intelligence on the psychological variable. In this situation, the number system and the psychological variable do not match exactly. In the abstract number system, 100 is exactly twice as much as 50, but because the psychological variable has no zero point, we cannot say that an intelligence test score of 100 shows twice as much intelligence as a score of 50.

Suppose we were doing a study of taste preferences. We give our subjects samples of solutions to taste and ask the subjects to rank them according to which one they liked the most, which one second, third, and so on. We assign numbers to the ranks (1, 2, 3, etc.) and report that number 1 was most preferred, 2 was second, and so on. But it would not make sense to report that the difference in preference between 1 and 2 is the same as between 2 and 3. Suppose, for example, you were asked to rank Coke, Pepsi, and vinegar from most to least preferred. Now, unless you have strange tastes, your rankings would probably be either 1–2–3 or 2–1–3 for Coke, Pepsi, and vinegar. Clearly, the difference in preference between Coke and Pepsi is much smaller than between either of those drinks and vinegar even though the difference in rank orderings is the same. Similarly, it makes no sense to say that the drink ranked 1 is three times as preferred as the drink ranked 3. In these examples, the characteristics of the variables as they are measured do not match the characteristics of the real number system, and so we are limited in the type of mathematical operations we can perform on the data.

In some cases, however, the variable and the number system can be matched. An example is the research with autistic children discussed in Chapters 2 and 3 (Graziano, 1974), where the dependent variable is disruptive behavior. Each disruptive outburst was observed and recorded for each child. At the end of each six-hour observation period, the number of outbursts was summed to yield a score for the total number of outbursts for each child in each period. Table 4.1 shows sample data for five days of observation for ten children.

The data in Table 4.1 give us considerable information. Because of the nature of the data, we can apply all of the mathematical operations to them. We can add the number of daily outbursts for each child and arrive at each child's total number of outbursts for that week. If you look across each row in Table 4.1 at the totals for each child, you will see that child no. 02 had a total of only two outbursts, whereas child no. 04 had a total of 22 outbursts. This large difference suggests that the children are quite different from each other with regard to disruptive behavior. We can subtract the totals or divide one by the other and can report that in this particular week of observation, subject no. 04 had 20 more outbursts or eleven times as many outbursts as subject no. 02. We also can divide the total for the week by the number of children and report the children's average number of disruptive responses for the week. The point is that when we have a dependent variable such as the number of responses made by a subject, it provides a good match with the real number system. The variable shows a magnitude in the same direction as the real number system so that 22 responses are more than

Table 4.1 **FREQUENCY OF DAILY DISRUPTIVE OUTBURSTS OF TEN AUTISTIC CHILDREN FOR FIVE CONSECUTIVE DAYS**[a]

| Subjects | Days | | | | | Totals |
	Monday	Tuesday	Wednesday	Thursday	Friday	
01	1	2	1	1	1	6
02	0	0	1	0	1	2
03	4	2	3	3	3	15
04	6	4	5	3	4	22
05	1	3	1	0	2	7
06	2	0	2	1	0	5
07	2	3	1	2	2	10
08	2	0	1	1	0	4
09	1	1	0	2	1	5
10	4	3	5	3	3	18
Totals	23	18	20	16	17	94

[a]These are not the actual data from the study referred to earlier (Graziano, 1974), but are facsimile data that have been created for this illustration. The actual data are similar but more complex than is needed for our illustration.

20 responses. This particular dependent measure also has equal intervals so that the difference in response between 4 and 6 is the same as the difference between 10 and 12. Finally, the dependent variable in this study has a true zero point, which means that a child with a score of zero had no outbursts during the observation period. Because of this match of the characteristics of the dependent variable with those of the real number system, we are able to perform all of the mathematical operations on the data—we can add, subtract, multiply, and divide. This in turn allows us to use some of the more powerful statistical tests, which cannot properly be used with dependent variables that are not as well matched with the real number system.

SCALES OF MEASUREMENT

Some of the variables used in psychological research (such as the number or duration of responses, the number of items answered correctly on a test, the amount of weight a subject can lift) have characteristics that closely match those of the real number system. Other variables (such as scores on intelligence or personality tests, academic standing in class, attitudes) are not so well matched with the number system. To help identify the closeness of match, Stevens (1946) classified variables into four levels or scales of measurement. The scales, arranged from least to most "matching" with the real number system, are the nominal, ordinal, interval, and ratio scales of measurement.

Nominal Scales

Nominal scales are at the lowest level of measurement, the scales with the least matching to the number system. As their name suggests, nominal scales are *naming* scales, and their only mathematical property is the property of identity. Dependent variables such as place of birth (Chicago, Boston, Nyack), brand name choice (Chevrolet, Ford, Plymouth), political affiliation (Democrat, Republican, Socialist, Independent), diagnostic category (paranoid, schizoid, bipolar disorder), sex of the subject, or any other way of categorizing subjects are all nominal scales of measurement. The differences between the categories of nominal scales (e.g., Ford, Chevrolet, Plymouth; Republican, Democrat; male, female) are qualitative and not quantitative. We can assign numbers to represent different categories. For example, we could label Chicago as 1, Boston as 2, and Nyack as 3, but the numbers are only arbitrary labels for the categories. *Except for identity,* these numbers have none of the mathematical properties of the real number system, and therefore we cannot meaningfully add, subtract, multiply, or divide them. Is Chicago with its assigned number of 1 to be understood as only one-third of Nyack with its assigned number of 3? Nominal scales have no zero point, cannot be ordered low to high, and make no assumption about equal units of measurement. In other words, they are not numbers at all, at least not in the sense that we usually think of numbers. Nominal scales of measurement classify or categorize each subject, and we work with the number or frequency of subjects who fall into each of the categories. The data of nominal scales are called *nominal data* (also sometimes called categorical data). In statistical analyses of nominal data, we cannot use statistical procedures that assume the data are ordered or have a true zero point or have equal units of measurement. Some common uses of nominal scales are the numbers on an athlete's jersey, a social security number, or a telephone area code.

Ordinal Scales

Ordinal scales, as their name suggests, order the data or measure a variable in order of magnitude. Thus, ordinal scales have the mathematical property of magnitude as well as identity. In ordinal scales, numbers are assigned to categories or groupings that are arranged in order so that some numbers represent more of the variable than others. For example, using socioeconomic class as a variable, we could categorize subjects as belonging to the low, middle, or high socioeconomic class. There is a clear underlying concept here of order of magnitude, from low to high. Other examples of ordinal scales are measurements by rankings, such as a student's academic standing in class, a subject's taste preferences, or children ranked by height in a nursery school; or measurements by ranked categories, such as low, medium, or high anxiety, low, medium, or high artistic ability, or grades of A, B, C, D, or F.

Ordinal scales tell us about the *relative order of magnitude* (nominal scales do not), but they do not give us any information about the differences between categories or ranks. If we rank students on class standing, for example, we can determine from the data which student was first, second, and so on, but we cannot determine *how much* higher the first ranked student is compared to the second. That is, the numbers tell us about ranks or relative positions but not about the distances or intervals between ranks. The differences in academic achievement between students ranked 1 and 2 might be very small (or large) compared with the difference between students ranked 12 and 13. As illustrated earlier in the example of ranking preferred taste of Coke, Pepsi, and vinegar, the intervals in ordinal scaling are not necessarily equal. In fact, it is usually assumed that they are unequal. Therefore, it is inappropriate to try to analyze ordinal data with statistical procedures that require equal intervals of measurement.

Interval Scales

When the measurement conveys information about the ordering of magnitude of the measures and about the distance between the values, we have interval scaling. *Interval scales* have the properties of ordinal scales and the property of equal intervals between consecutive values on the scale. Thus, interval scales come close to matching the real number system but still do not have a true zero point. The most commonly used example of an interval scale is the measurement of temperature on either the Fahrenheit or Celsius scale. The units of the thermometer are at equal intervals representing equal volumes of mercury. We know that 90°F is hotter than 45°F. We also know that the difference in temperature between 60° and 70°F is the same as the difference in temperature between 30° and 40°F. However, the zero point on the scale is arbitrary and not a true zero point. Zero degrees on the scale does not indicate a total absence of heat. Interval scales thus give us order and equal intervals but no true zero point. Most variables in psychology are measured in interval or near-interval scales (e.g., IQ test scores, neuroticism scores, attitudes). With an IQ test, for example, we can report that the measured IQ difference between two people with IQs of 60 and 120 is 60 IQ points. However, because there is no true zero point on the IQ scale, we cannot say that the first person is half as smart as the other.

Ratio Scales

Ratio scales have all of the properties of the preceding scales (identity, magnitude, and equal intervals) as well as a true zero point. Thus, ratio scales provide the best match to the real number system, and we can carry out all of the possible mathematical operations (addition, subtraction, multiplication, and division) on such scales. When the variable is some physical dimension, such as weight, distance, length, volume, number of responses, or time duration, we can use a ratio scale of measurement. We refer to such scales as ratio scales because dividing a point on the scale by another point on the scale (taking a ratio of values) gives a legitimate and meaningful value. For example, a person who runs 10 miles is running twice as far as a person who runs 5 miles and five times as far as someone who runs 2 miles. It is the true zero point that gives the ratio scale this property. Although some variables in psychology can be measured on ratio scales, most variables can be measured only on ordinal or interval scales of measurement. The characteristics of the various scales of measurement are summarized in Table 4.2.

TYPES OF DATA

It is critical that the researcher be able to identify the level of measurement of the dependent variable in order to select the appropriate statistical analysis. This identifi-

Table 4.2   SOME ASPECTS OF SCALES OF MEASUREMENT[a]

| | Levels of measurement | | | |
	Nominal	Ordinal	Interval	Ratio

Examples	Diagnostic categories
	Brand names
	Political or religious
	   affiliations
		Socioeconomic class
		Ranks
			IQ test scores
			Personality and
			   attitude scales
				Weight
				Length
				Reaction time
				Number of responses

Mathematical properties	Identity	Identity Magnitude	Identity Magnitude Equal intervals	Identity Magnitude Equal intervals True zero point
Mathematical operations	None	Rank order	Add Subtract	Add Subtract Multiply Divide
Type of data	Nominal	Ordered	Score	Score
Typical statistics used	Chi-square	Sign test Mann-Whitney U-test	t-test ANOVA	t-test ANOVA

[a]Many more examples of the various scales and additional appropriate statistical procedures could be given.

cation is usually not difficult. The summary of the scales of measurement and some of their characteristics in Table 4.2 can serve as a useful guide for such identification. Notice that the four scales yield three types of data:

1. Nominal data (associated with nominal scales).
2. Ordered data (associated with ordinal scales).
3. Score data (associated with both interval and ratio scales).

For most psychological research, it is not too important to distinguish between interval and ratio scales as they are treated much the same statistically. Hence, these will be combined into one category that we will call score data. As the researcher prepares to select an appropriate statistical test, one of the questions to ask is, "Which type of data is produced by measurement of the dependent variable—nominal data, ordered data, or score data?"

Nominal Data

Nominal data are generated by nominal scales of measurement. Identity is the only mathematical property that nominal data reflect. Data made up of the number of subjects assigned to each of several qualitatively different categories are nominal data. Table 4.2 gives several examples of such categorical or nominal data. Various forms of chi-square are the most commonly used statistical tests for nominal data.

Ordered Data

Ordered data not only reflect identity but also order or magnitude. Whenever we can arrange subjects' responses in order of magnitude and we cannot assume equal intervals in the scale of measurement, we have ordered data. Table 4.2 gives several examples of such scales of measurement. The most commonly used statistical tests with ordered data are nonparametric tests, such as the Mann-Whitney *U*-test, the sign test, or the Wilcoxon matched-pairs signed-rank test. Nonparametric tests compare two or more groups on an ordinal dependent measure. If the relationship between two ordinal measures is to be quantified, then a rank-order correlation is most appropriate.

Score Data

Based on ratio or interval scales, *score data* will reflect properties of identity, magnitude, equal intervals, and, if based on ratio scales, a true zero point. Examples of score data are given in Table 4.2. A variety of statistical techniques are typically used for score data, including *t*-tests, analysis of variance (ANOVA), and product-moment correlations. The statistical procedure used with score data will depend both on what question is asked and on the design of the study. These and other tests typically used with score data make fairly demanding assumptions about the nature of the data. One of the important assumptions is that the measurement scale is based at least on equal intervals between scores. Sometimes researchers will use what at first appear to be score data, but on closer inspection, the assumption of equal intervals is questioned. Under these conditions, to be conservative in the statistical analysis, researchers often treat data as ordered rather than score data.

MEASURING AND CONTROLLING VARIABLES

Now that we have defined different types of variables, scales of measurement, and types of data, we should consider how to measure and manipulate variables. Let us start with a fairly simple problem so that we can easily follow the steps required to solve it. Assume that we are interested in the effects of food intake on weight for human subjects. In this example, food intake is the independent variable, the variable to be manipulated in the study. We want to know what effect manipulations of food intake will have on subjects' weight, so weight is the dependent variable. We are hypothesizing that weight fluctuations will be dependent on the manipulations of food intake.

Measurement Error

Consider the problem of measuring weight. Suppose we have the subject stand on a standard doctor's scale. If the subject were to lean against the wall, the weight reading would be distorted. If the subject were weighed at one time while wearing a heavy coat and boots and the next time while in bare feet and no coat, the two weights would not be comparable. Factors such as these are sources of *measurement error.* Measurement error can distort the scores so that the observations are no longer an accurate reflection of reality. Measurement error can also attenuate (reduce) the observed strength of a relationship between variables, giving the impression that two variables are unrelated when in fact they are related to one another.

Another source of measurement error is the problem of *response-set biases.* One of the most powerful response-set biases is *social desirability.* Social desirability is the tendency of many subjects to respond in what they believe to be the most socially acceptable manner. For example, suppose we were studying the relationship between level of food intake and weight in a weight-loss program. Have you ever cheated when you were on a diet? If you did, would you always be willing to admit it to people? There is a good chance that you would not admit it because you would find it embarrassing. In this case, some subjects might not be willing to report their true level of food intake because they do not want to admit to socially undesirable behavior such as cheating on a diet. This social desirability response set would obviously affect the validity of the measurement and constitutes measurement error in the study.

In research it is important to minimize measurement error. This is best accomplished by developing a well thought out operational definition of the measurement procedure and by diligently using the operational definition in the research.

Operational Definitions

Measuring a person's weight is not difficult. Most of us measure our own weight periodically by standing on a scale and reading the weight from a dial or a balance scale, which is easy because the scales are already developed and readily available. However, consider exactly how we weigh ourselves. What we are doing in this process is operationally defining the measurement of weight. An *operational definition* is a definition of a variable in terms of the procedures used to measure or manipulate the variable. That is, an operational definition specifies the activities of the researcher in measuring and/or manipulating a variable (Kerlinger, 1986). In research, even for such simple measures as weight, every step of the measurement procedure should be carefully planned in order to avoid confusion.

Measuring a variable such as food intake requires a scale different from the weight scale. We know from past research that food intake is measured in terms of calories and that foods differ in their level of calories. If we know the calorie level of each type of food, we can compute the total calorie intake for each subject without much difficulty. This process of measuring food intake is based on a good deal of research and theory. We can be reasonably sure that this approach to measuring food intake is effective because it has worked well for researchers in the past—a fact we can confirm by reading some of the earlier research.

In many psychological studies the researcher wants to create a particular response in subjects, such as increasing their levels of motivation, anxiety, or alertness. These are factors that are within the subject and are therefore difficult to measure or manipulate. But such variables can be studied by operationally defining the set of procedures for manipulating the variables. In a study discussed earlier, the relaxation level of autistic children was manipulated to see whether it would have any effect on the level of disruptive behavior (Graziano, 1974). The manipulation was defined in terms of a set of explicit procedures that was followed by the researcher. The following example of some of the specific procedures used in the study of autistic children shows how much detail and specificity is needed to define such a manipulation effectively.

A specific area of the room was selected and for three days prior to the initiation of relaxation training the children were told about "relax time" and shown the "quiet spot" where the training would occur. Characteristically, they asked no questions nor exhibited any reaction to the announcements. The first training session was announced simply: "O.K. kids, now it's relax time." The lights were turned out, and the children were led to the "quiet spot" and instructed to lie down on a clearly defined blanket on the floor. The therapist gently, quietly, and in a soft, almost "lullaby" cadence, told them, ". . . Close your eyes, now, just like when you're in bed, nice and comfortable. That's it, eyes closed. Breathe slow and easy, slow and easy, that's it, good job, nice and easy, nice and slow, nice and relaxed, good job, calm, slow, easy, relaxed. That's right. That's it. Real good, real relaxed!" The therapist continued her quiet instructions to breathe easily and be calm, settled and relaxed. After two minutes of quiet cooperation, Cathy got up and walked away. The therapist then ended the training session, and the children resumed their usual program.

The training sessions occurred once daily, always following snack time, and just prior to resuming the academic session. The children continued to experience relaxation not only lying down, but gradually also sitting and standing. The therapist continued her soothing, quiet instructions and paired the gentle manipulation of arms, legs and necks, with the verbal instructions to relax. Any sign of approximating relaxed behavior was given immediate verbal reinforcement and, eventually, the children learned to relax on verbal instruction alone. (Graziano, 1974, p. 170)

The first training session was about one minute in duration, increasing daily until a criterion of five consecutive minutes of relaxation had been reached for twelve consecutive training sessions. Relaxation involved the child's being quiet, still, without talking or squirming, and with no perceptible rigidity or tension in the muscles of the arms, legs, shoulders, and stomach.

The operational definition above gives a description of the procedures used with the subjects and the criteria to be achieved. Although a somewhat wordy operational definition, it does serve the purpose of giving researchers a fairly clear set of operations or instructions to define the independent variable. Once the independent variable is operationally defined, we refer to it simply as "relaxation training" with the understanding that it refers to the entire set of procedures. A good operational definition of a procedure defines the procedure so precisely that another researcher could perform the same procedure by simply following the description. Good operational definitions make replication of research possible.

In the study of disruptive behavior in autistic children (Graziano, 1974), an operational definition for the dependent variable of disruptive behavior was also needed. In a staff-training manual (Graziano, 1963) disruptive behavior had been defined in terms of its frequency, duration, and intensity, as follows:

> Disruptive behavior is any observed, sudden change in a child's behavior from calm, quiet, cooperative, and appropriate behavior to explosive, loud, screaming and tantrums, including sudden attacks on people, smashing and throwing objects, throwing oneself into walls, or on the floor, self-abuse such as head-banging, biting, scratching, picking sores and so on, all carried out in rapid, near "frenzied" manner. Each disruptive behavior incident will be considered to have ended when the child has returned to the previous level of calm, appropriate behavior for at least three consecutive minutes.
>
> *Frequency.* Each occurrence of disruptive behavior is recorded as a single event. The frequency score per child is then the total number of events.
>
> *Duration.* Each disruptive event is timed by stopwatch from the observed beginning to its end, as defined above.
>
> *Intensity.* Each disruptive event is rated by the observers on a three-point scale of intensity: low, moderate, high. The rating is made immediately after the event is over and is made for the perceived peak of intensity for the incident. (Graziano, 1963, p. 3)

It is important to note that developing an operational definition involves a combination of drawing on the wisdom reflected in past research and making some arbitrary decisions. The arbitrary decisions should be based on some common sense ideas of how best to measure a variable from both a theoretical and a practical sense. For example, the decision to set the relaxation criterion at five consecutive minutes for 12 consecutive sessions is at least partly judgmental. Instructions to use a "soft, gentle, calm, voice" leave some margin for interpretation by any other researcher who may want to replicate the study. Perhaps with more research on the use of relaxation with autistic children we will be able to define the variables operationally in a more precise manner. The point is that operational definitions used in research vary in constraint. Under some conditions, such as in nonlaboratory settings, it is more difficult to create precise operational definitions for the variables. Under other conditions, such as in measuring physiological responses to a series of carefully constructed visual stimuli in a laboratory, we can operationally define both variables far more precisely. In any study the researcher should operationally define the independent and dependent variables as clearly and precisely as possible. The completeness and detail of operational definitions will depend to a great extent on the nature of the issues being investigated, the subjects used, and the settings in which the observations are made.

Reliability, Effective Range, and Validity

Whatever we wish to measure, it is important that we measure it in such a way that the measure would agree with anyone else's measure of the same variable measured in the same way. The reproducibility factor of the measure is referred to as the *reliability* of the measure. In measuring weight, for example, a scale is said to be reliable if it always gives the same reading when measuring the same object assuming the object remains constant in weight. Because weight fluctuates, we might want to use some standard that is unlikely to fluctuate (e.g., a 100-pound lead weight) to test the reliability of the scale. If the scales are of the type that can be adjusted, we can also use a standard weight to standardize the measuring instrument so that it reads the correct weight for any standard that we put on the scale.

The same procedure can be used to establish the reliability of many other kinds of psychological measures. If the measure involves some sort of rating of behavior by a human observer, it is necessary to have at least two observers independently rate the same sample of behavior to see how well they agree with one another. To rate independently of one another, both raters must be blind to the ratings of the other. This type of reliability is referred to as *interrater reliability* and should be evaluated whenever a rating or judgment is required of the researcher. A measure is not wholly reliable or unreliable but, rather, varies in its degree of reliability. If two raters always agree with one another, then the interrater reliability is perfect. If their ratings are unrelated to one another, then the interrater reliability is zero. However, the actual level of reliability is likely to be somewhere in between. A correlation coefficient can be used to quantify the degree of reliability, although other, more sophisticated indices are also available (see Nunnally, 1967).

If we measure variables that should be stable over time, then a reliable measure of the variables should give the same reading at different points in time. If we measure a group of subjects on that variable at time 1 and then remeasure the same subjects at some later point in time, we want the measures to be consistent. This type of reliability is known as *test-retest reliability.* Like interrater reliability, test-retest reliability is not an all-or-nothing phenomenon and is usually quantified with a correlation coefficient.

Another type of reliability is referred to as *internal consistency reliability,* which is relevant when we make several observations to obtain a score for each subject. This might be the case if we had subjects complete a test with several items or if we observed their behavior under several different conditions. Internal consistency reliability is high if each of the items or each of the behavioral observations correlates with the other observations; that is, if all of the items are measuring the same thing. A measure that is internally consistent measures one construct with several independent observations or items. Discussing all of the ramifications of internal consistency reliability is beyond the scope of this book, but one principle important in research should be mentioned. Generally speaking, *the more observations we make to obtain a score for a person, the greater will be the reliability of that score.* Take for example the typical tests that are used in courses to determine the grade for each student. The test could be considered an operational definition of the level of knowledge of the students in that particular course. A test with many questions covering all of the different topics in the course should give a consistent indication of how much students know. Asking only one or two questions, on the other hand, will not provide the same level of consistency, because it is possible that students will misinterpret any given question and answer it incorrectly even though they know the material. This same principle holds for behavioral observations as well. It is better to have several observations of behavior on which to base the measurement of a construct than to rely on only a few.

The concept of reliability of measures is critical in research because if the measures we use in a study are not reliable then the study cannot produce useful information. The factors that contribute to reliability include (1) the precision and clarity of the operational definition of the construct, (2) the care with which we carry out the measures and the precision with which we follow the procedures outlined in the operational definition, and (3) the number of independent observations on which the score is based. (Discussion of all the potential issues in measuring and improving the reliability of measures is beyond the scope of this book. See Anastasi [1982] for further discussion.)

Another factor to consider in measuring variables is the *effective range* of the scale. If we are interested in weight changes in people, a normal bathroom scale will usually have sufficient range because it typically can weigh objects between 0 and 300 pounds. But weighing very large or very small objects (like elephants or mice) would require different scales, scales capable of accurately measuring weight in whatever range necessary. Although the concept of weight is the same for both mice and elephants, it is unlikely that a scale constructed to measure one can also measure the other. The heavy duty construction required of a scale to measure an elephant would make the scale quite insensitive to the relatively light weight of a mouse. The same is true of most psychological measures. A test of mathematical skills sensitive enough to detect different skill levels in college math majors would be too difficult to detect differences in math skills among third-grade students. A measure of social skills designed for use with children would probably not be appropriate for use with adults. A measure of memory ability that is challenging enough to detect differences in college students would be too difficult to detect memory ability differences in retarded adults. Procedures designed to effect some change with one group of subjects, such as inducing anxiety or relaxation, may not be appropriate for other subjects. The procedures lack the range to work with any and all subjects. When designing or selecting measures for research, therefore, we must keep in mind who the subjects will be so that we can select measures that will be sensitive to the differences in the variables that the subjects are likely to show.

The third factor that must be considered is the *validity* of the measure. When we say that the scale to measure weight is valid, we mean that the readings are accurate reflections of the true weight of the subjects. That is not the same as reliability, which refers to how consistently the weight is measured. A scale for measuring weight, for example, might not be properly adjusted, thereby giving a reading 10 pounds lighter than the object really is. The scale is reliable if it consistently gives the same weight, but it is not valid because that weight is not the true weight. It is important to note that *a measure cannot be a valid measure unless it is a reliable measure, but a measure can be reliable without being a valid measure of the variable of interest.* It is also important to realize that validity, like reliability, is not an all-or-nothing concept. There are degrees of validity from none to perfect validity. Once again, a correlation coefficient is used most often to quantify the degree of validity. There are also different types of validity, which will be discussed in detail in Chapter 8.

Scale Attenuation Effects

A problem that is related to the effective range of a measure is *scale attenuation effects.* In this context attenuation refers to restricting the range of a scale. Using a measuring scale with a restricted range—not ranging high enough or not ranging low enough, or both—can result in data showing subjects bunched up near the top or bottom of the scale. For example, suppose that we are conducting a study on changing high school students' attitudes toward tobacco use. For obvious health reasons we hope to bring about more negative attitudes. We administer our pretest of negative attitudes toward tobacco use, and we find that virtually all subjects score very near the top of the scale. The subjects show at pretest, at least as measured by that scale, already high negative attitudes toward tobacco use. Suppose we then proceeded to apply the attitude change intervention and then take postintervention measures of attitudes. The posttest results *could not* show much change toward greater negative attitudes *even if the intervention was actually highly effective.* The subjects, already at the top of the scale before the intervention, simply have no room to show change toward still higher scores. This direction of scale attenuation is called a *ceiling effect.* It should be clear that such a restricted scale will have serious effects on the research findings.

A scale can also be attenuated by having a restricted lower range, thus creating a possible *floor effect.* In this situation subjects would tend to score near the bottom of the scale only because the scale does not allow a sufficiently low range. A floor effect would occur if an instructor gave an examination that was too difficult for the class and almost all students scored low. That is, if the scale had a greater lower range, the students' scores might be more spread out rather than bunched at the bottom of the scale.

Ceiling and floor effects (scale attenuation effects) restrict the range of possible scores for subjects' responses; that is, they reduce the potential variability of the data. As we will discuss at some length in Chapter 10, because restricting variability results in serious errors, sufficient variability is essential in research.

THE NEED FOR OBJECTIVE MEASUREMENT

All sciences stress the need for objectivity, or *objective measures,* but often scientists do not make it clear why objectivity is so important. Vague references to how objectivity is somehow more accurate than subjectivity are common, but *why* is it more accurate? One reason is that subjective measures are person-specific; that is, they represent the judgments of only one person. To the extent that another person in the same situation might make a different judgment, then the findings are not reproducible.

A hallmark of all science is that the laws of nature should hold no matter who tests them. There may be many reasons why two people might disagree on their subjective impression of a phenomenon. If we take an example from physics, the judgment of temperature, John might judge a room to be hotter than Jerry because John is accustomed to cooler temperatures and so by comparison the room seems hot. Another reason for John and Jerry's disagreement about the temperature of a room might be a differential sensitivity to features other than heat, such as humidity. Yet another reason might be a physiological deficiency in one or both in their ability to sense temperature. Even with something simple like temperature, subjective impressions pose many problems. If an objective measure of temperature (the thermometer) had not been developed, most of the physical laws relating temperature to other phenomena would have remained undiscovered. The thermometer measures temperature independently of other variables such as humidity. It can measure temperature reliably and across a much greater range than we could accomplish without such an instrument. Finally, the thermometer provides at least an interval scale of measurement of temperature. Although this concept may be difficult to grasp on the basis of our brief discussion, it is important to note that an interval scale greatly simplifies the mathematical description of the relationship of temperature to hundreds of other physical phenomena.

If so many problems can emerge with subjective measures when considering a relatively simple issue such as temperature, imagine the problems that might arise when trying to measure some complicated construct in psychology, such as anxiety. Many phenomena that psychologists need to measure are events that all people have feelings about. These feelings can systematically distort perceptions of the phenomena. For example, a person who is easily upset by an angry outburst might be more sensitive to the presence of anger in an individual who is being frustrated as part of a study on frustration and aggression. Good research, therefore, demands objective measures that can be performed by anyone properly trained to use them and that give the same results regardless of who does the measuring.

Statistical Analyses

The use of mathematics and statistical procedures are a central part of all modern sciences. They are powerful tools for accurately describing phenomena. They also provide objective ways of evaluating patterns of events by computing the probability of observing such patterns by chance alone. Insisting on the use of statistical analyses on which to draw conclusions is simply an extension of the argument that objectivity is critical in science. (In Chapter 5 we will discuss some basic statistical procedures.)

SUMMARY

In research we study relationships between variables. A variable is one or more sets of events that the researcher manipulates and/or observes and measures. In assessing how much effect the independent variable has on the dependent variable or the amount of relationship among variables, or in observing the magnitude, frequency, or duration of some behavioral variable (as in naturalistic observation), it is necessary to quantify the observations we make.

The quantification process (measurement) involves the application of the real number system, with all of its characteristics, to the variable, with all of its characteristics. The number system has many properties—identity, magnitude, equal intervals, and absolute zero. But in any science the characteristics of the variables seldom perfectly match the properties of the real number system. Consequently, in applying the real number system to variables (i.e., in measurement), we find that some variables match the number system well whereas others do not. Four levels of matching in measurement have been described: nominal, ordinal, interval, and ratio measurements. These levels of measurement constitute different types or levels of data.

> Nominal measures—nominal data
>
> Ordinal measures—ordered data
>
> Interval and ratio measures—score data

After the observations have been quantified and the level of the data is determined, the selection of an appropriate statistical test is a fairly straightforward decision. (Selecting statistical tests will be discussed further in Chapter 14.)

The operational definition for a psychological variable describes precisely what operations will be performed to measure the variable. The specifications should be as precise as possible to reduce the likelihood of inaccurate measurement, to increase the reliability and validity of the measure, and to make replication of the research possible. The reliability of a measure is an index of how consistent the measure is. The validity of the measure is its effectiveness in tapping the characteristic measured. A measure cannot be valid unless it is first reliable; but a measure can be reliable without being valid.

Objectivity is an essential part of research in any science, including psychology. Well-conceived operational definitions of variables can improve objectivity in the measurement process. The use of statistical procedures provides objectivity in the analysis and interpretation of data. Objectivity will normally improve reliability and make it more likely that researchers can discover valid relationships between variables.

REVIEW EXERCISES

I. Define the following key terms. Be sure you understand them. They are discussed in the chapter and defined in the glossary.

Variable	Types of data
Causally related	Nominal
Data	Ordered
Scales of measurement	Score
Nominal	Measurement error
Ordinal	Response-set biases
Interval	Social desirability
Ratio	Operational definition

Reliability	Validity
Interrater reliability	Scale attenuation effects
Test-retest reliability	Ceiling effect
Internal consistency reliability	Floor effect
Effective range	Objective measures

II. Answer each of the following. Check your answer in the chapter.

1. What is the major task in measurement?

2. Explain this statement: "In measuring variables, the researcher works with two major sets of information."

3. What are the important characteristics of the abstract number system?

4. Why is it important in measurement to match the characteristics of the dependent variable with those of the number system?

5. What type of data is generated by each level of measurement?

6. Define *reliability* and the different types of reliability.

III. Think about and work each of the following problems.

1. Following is a list of possible dependent variables. For each one identify its level of measurement and the type of data it generates. Be sure that you understand why each is at the level you indicate.

IQ scores

Number of disruptive outbursts

Time needed (number of seconds) for a response to occur

Place or position of each runner at the end of a race

Speed of each runner during the race

Annual income of subjects

Car preference of each subject

2. Following are brief descriptions of research projects. For each one identify the (a) independent variable and type of independent variable it is; (b) dependent variable(s); (c) level of measurement and type of data for each dependent variable.

a. In a study on the effects of television violence on aggressive behavior, schoolchildren are assigned to two conditions. In condition A the subjects watch a typical half hour of television in which eight violent acts are portrayed (aggressive TV condition); in condition B the subjects watch a half hour of television in which no violent acts are portrayed (nonaggressive TV condition). Following each TV condition, the subjects in each condition are observed in a playroom. Observers record all aggressive acts. The hypotheses are that the group exposed to aggressive TV (i) will have a greater number of aggressive acts and (ii) the acts will be rated as more highly aggressive in nature than the subjects who were in the nonaggressive TV condition. The rating will be done using a five-point rating scale in which the units are not equal intervals.

b. College students are observed as they try to solve a series of puzzles. The subjects are compared on how many minutes it takes each subject to solve all of the problems. One-third of the subjects are told they will be paid more if they solve the problems quickly; one-third are told they will be paid a fixed amount; and one-third are not told anything about being paid.

3. How would you explain to someone who does not know measurement that an IQ of 140 does not indicate twice as much intelligence as an IQ of 70?

4. Write an operational definition for each of the following variables:

Racial attitudes	Ego
Intelligence	Criminality
Neurosis	Hyperactivity
Age	Aggression
Reading ability	Creativity
Fear	Deafness

STATISTICAL ANALYSIS OF DATA

Once a decision on how to measure the research variables is made, as discussed in Chapter 4, the next step in designing research is to determine how to analyze the data statistically. Statistical procedures are powerful research tools for organizing and understanding large sets of data. They provide ways to represent and describe groups, summarize results, and evaluate data. Without the use of statistics little could be learned from most studies.

Further, it is important to understand statistical procedures in the context of research design. The two domains are interrelated; when designing research, plans for statistical analyses must be incorporated *as part of the research design.* Although this chapter review cannot replace a good course in statistics, it is designed to introduce some basic statistical concepts (or refresh the student's memory of them) and to place statistical analyses in the context of research design.

There are two major uses of statistical procedures: (1) *descriptive statistics* simplify and organize data, and (2) *inferential statistics,* which go beyond simple description of data, help make inferences about what the data mean. Both descriptive and inferential statistics are important tools for the research scientist.

INDIVIDUAL DIFFERENCES AND STATISTICAL PROCEDURES

Statistical procedures depend on variability or differences in responses among subjects. No two subjects or groups will respond in exactly the same manner, and measurements of their responses will show variability.

Suppose, for example, we are studying the effects of memory training. We predict that subjects who are trained will perform better on a memory task than those who are not trained. In a study designed to test the hypothesis, subjects are assigned to either of two conditions: (1) memory training or (2) no training. All subjects are given a memory test, the dependent variable. Let us suppose the test yields scores from 0–100. Hypothetical data are shown in Table 5.1. When we examine the two groups of data we see that there is a difference in mean (average) scores *between* the groups. (The mean for each group is shown in Table 5.1.) There are also differences among the scores *within* each group. That is, the scores in Group A range from 66–98 and those in Group B range from 56–94. The variation within each group illustrates that there are *individual differences* in memory skills. Some people, with or without training, are better able to remember things. Others cannot seem to remember very much, and most people fall somewhere in between. All subject variables that we study in psychology—anxiety, intelligence, reaction time, social skills, hormonal levels, and so on—show individual differences. Therefore, in the study of the hypothesized effects of memory training on memory, we cannot be sure whether the memory training is the reason for the apparent differences between the groups, or whether the subjects in the training group have better memories and would have performed better regardless of the training. Most of the variables that are manipulated in psychology make only a small difference in how

Table 5.1 HYPOTHETICAL DATA AND DESCRIPTIVE
STATISTICS FOR TEST RESULTS OF
TRAINED AND NONTRAINED SUBJECTS

	Group A (trained)	Group B (nontrained)
	98	94
	93	88
	90	82
	89	77
	87	75
	87	74
	84	72
	81	72
	78	67
	71	61
	66	56
Median	87	74
Mode	87	72
Mean	84	74.36

people perform compared with the differences that already exist between people. There-fore, it is important in psychological experimentation to demonstrate that any differ-ences on dependent measures that we find between groups are due to the research manipulations and not merely to already existing individual differences.

We can use our example study of the effects of memory training to define further what we mean by descriptive and inferential statistics. Whenever we study a group of subjects there will be many measures or scores. Also, because of individual differences the scores will vary from subject to subject. With so many measurements and so much variability, a way is needed to organize and simplify the numbers, to help make some sense out of them, and to describe and represent the groups. *Descriptive statistics* are used to summarize and simplify a large number of measurements and to describe numerically and represent groups of measurements. *Inferential statistics,* on the other hand, are used to help interpret what the data mean rather than only describing the data. For example, in the study on memory training, the means of the two groups are different, with the trained group showing a higher mean score than the nontrained group (as predicted by our hypothesis). But we must also ask whether that difference is due only to chance variations or is it beyond a chance occurrence? That is, is the difference we found between the groups so large that the difference probably did not occur by chance? Inferential statistics are used to help answer questions such as this.

DESCRIPTIVE STATISTICS

There are three important groups of descriptive statistics: (1) frequency counts and frequency distributions, (2) graphical representations of data, and (3) summary statis-tics. The hypothetical data in Table 5.2 represent responses from 24 subjects attending

Table 5.2   RAW DATA FROM 24 SUBJECTS WHO ATTENDED A PARTICULAR
             MOVIE

Subject	Age (in years)	Income	Number of movies seen in last year	Sex	Political affiliation[a]
A	28	$17,000	5	M	R
B	46	34,000	3	M	D
C	33	28,000	6	F	D
D	40	29,000	7	M	R
E	21	14,000	10	M	R
F	26	19,000	0	F	O
G	39	26,000	1	M	O
H	23	17,000	9	F	D
I	20	11,000	33	M	O
J	26	15,000	3	M	R
K	29	23,000	0	F	R
L	24	18,000	7	M	D
M	34	28,000	2	M	O
N	35	29,000	3	M	O
O	52	30,000	1	M	O
P	31	23,000	4	F	D
Q	30	27,000	8	M	R
R	45	31,000	4	F	D
S	18	12,000	14	M	O
T	29	28,000	5	M	R
U	26	22,000	6	F	D
V	23	21,000	24	M	O
W	47	32,000	4	M	D
X	53	35,000	3	M	D

[a]R = Republican; D = Democrat; O = other.

a particular movie. The information gathered from each subject included (1) the subject's age, (2) the subject's income, (3) the number of movies (at theaters) that the subject had seen in the last 12 months, (4) the sex of the subject, and (5) the political affiliation of the subject (coded as Democrat, Republican, or other).

What type of data do we have for each of these variables? The subject's age, income, and the number of movies seen are measured on a ratio scale (score data). Each of these variables has the property of magnitude (34 is older than 25, $20,000 is more than $15,000, and so on). All three variables have the property of equal intervals (e.g., the difference in age between people who are 25 and 20 is the same as the difference between people who are 38 and 33). The variables are measured on ratio scales because they have not only the property of equal intervals but they each have a true zero point. A person who is zero years old is just being born; a person whose income is zero doesn't earn anything; a person who has seen zero movies in the last 12 months has seen no movies in that time. The other two variables, sex of the subject and political affiliation, are measured on nominal scales. These data are nominal or categorical, and there is no logical way of ordering the categories. (For further information on how to identify scales of measurement, see Chapter 4.)

Frequency Counts and Distributions

Nominal and Ordinal Data   For most kinds of nominal or ordinal data, statistical simplification involves computing frequencies (i.e., the number of subjects who fall in each category). Table 5.3 shows the distribution of frequencies of sex for the data from Table 5.2. Note that when we sum across all categories, the total should always be equal to the number of subjects initially measured. It is often helpful to convert frequencies to percentages. This is done by dividing the frequency in each cell by the total number of subjects and multiplying each of these proportions by 100 as has been done in Table 5.3.

Sometimes it is useful to categorize subjects on the basis of more than one variable at the same time. This is called *cross-tabulation.* For example, subjects can be categorized on the basis of both the sex and political affiliation of the subject. *Cross-tabulation* can help us to see relationships between nominal measures. In our example, we have two levels of the variable sex (male and female) and three levels of the variable political affiliation (Democrat, Republican, and other) giving a total of six (2 × 3) possible joint categories. The data are arranged in a 2 × 3 matrix where the numbers in the matrix are the frequency of people in each of the categories. Table 5.4 gives the cross-tabulation for these two variables. Note that if we add all of the frequencies in the six cells, they sum to the total number of subjects. Also note that the row and column totals represent the *univariate* (one-variable) frequency distribution for the political affiliation and sex variables, respectively. For example, the column totals in Table 5.4 of 17 males and 7 females represent the frequency distribution for the single variable of sex and, not surprisingly, are the same numbers that appear in Table 5.3.

Score Data   Different kinds of statistical procedures are used with score data. The simplest way to organize a set of score data is to create a *frequency distribution.* If we

Table 5.3   FREQUENCY OF MALES AND FEMALES IN SAMPLE OF 24 SUBJECTS ATTENDING A PARTICULAR MOVIE

	Males	Females	Total
Frequency	17	7	24
Percentage	71%	29%	100%

Table 5.4   CROSS-TABULATION BY SEX AND EXPRESSED POLITICAL AFFILIATION FOR 24 SUBJECTS WHO ATTENDED A PARTICULAR MOVIE

	Males	Females	Total
Democrat	4	5	9
Republican	6	1	7
Other	7	1	8
Totals	17	7	24

look at the variable "number of movies seen in the last 12 months," we will probably find it difficult to organize all 24 scores. Note that some of the subjects have not seen any movies in the last year whereas one subject (I) attended 33, but where do the rest of the subjects tend to fall? A frequency distribution will organize the data to answer a question such as this at a glance. Frequency distributions list each possible score and the frequency of that score in a given group of subjects. There may be no subjects for some of the scores, in which case the frequency list for the score would be zero. Table 5.5 shows the frequency distribution for the number of movies seen in the last year.

If there is a large number of possible scores, such as 25 or more, between the lowest and the highest scores, then the frequency table will be very long and almost as difficult to read as the original raw data. In this situation we use a *grouped frequency distribution,* which shortens the table to a more manageable size by grouping the scores into intervals, usually about 15 intervals. A grouped frequency distribution is required if you are working with a continuous variable. In a *continuous variable* there are, theoretically, an infinite number of possible scores between the lowest and the highest score. In the frequency distribution example in Table 5.5 there are 34 possible scores, and if we group the scores in groups of 2, we will have 17 intervals. Note that the intervals all must be the same size. Table 5.6 gives the grouped frequency distribution for the same data listed in Table 5.5.

Graphical Representation of Data

It has often been said that a picture is worth a thousand words, and this is especially true when dealing with statistical information. Graphs often clarify a data set or help interpret a summary statistic or statistical test. Most people find graphic representa-

Table 5.5 FREQUENCY DISTRIBUTION FOR THE VARIABLE OF THE NUMBER OF MOVIES SEEN IN THE LAST 12 MONTHS

No. of movies seen	Frequency	No. of movies seen	Frequency
33	1	16	0
32	0	15	0
31	0	14	1
30	0	13	0
29	0	12	0
28	0	11	0
27	0	10	1
26	0	9	1
25	0	8	1
24	1	7	2
23	0	6	2
22	0	5	2
21	0	4	3
20	0	3	4
19	0	2	1
18	0	1	2
17	0	0	2

**Table 5.6   GROUPED FREQUENCY DISTRIBUTION
FOR THE VARIABLE OF THE NUMBER OF
MOVIES SEEN IN THE LAST 12 MONTHS**

Interval	Frequency	Interval	Frequency
32–33	1	14–15	1
30–31	0	12–13	0
28–29	0	10–11	1
26–27	0	8–9	2
24–25	1	6–7	4
22–23	0	4–5	5
20–21	0	2–3	5
18–19	0	0–1	4
16–17	0		

tions much simpler to understand than other statistical procedures. The use of *graphs* and *tables* as supplements to other statistical procedures is encouraged.

Frequency or grouped frequency distributions can be represented by a graph called a *frequency polygon.* Figure 5.1 shows a frequency polygon representing the movie data summarized in Table 5.5. The frequency polygon represents data on a two-dimensional graph where the horizontal axis *(x-axis or abscissa)* represents the range of scores for the variable and the vertical axis *(y-axis or ordinate)* represents the frequency of the scores. The location of the point above each score on the *x*-axis represents the frequency of that score in the group. To aid in the interpretation of the frequency polygon, it is important to carefully label both axes.

One of the advantages of a frequency polygon is that two frequency distributions can be compared by putting them both on the same graph. To compare the distributions, each is graphed independently with different colors or different types of lines (e.g., solid versus dotted) to distinguish one distribution from the other. Figure 5.2 gives an example of two frequency distributions, each represented by its own frequency polygon.

With small group sizes, the frequency polygon usually appears to be rather jagged. There often is an overall shape to the distribution, but the lines connecting the points will go up and down from one interval to another. The distributions graphed

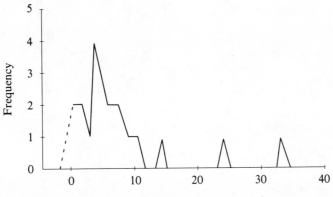

No. Movies Seen (variable)

Figure 5.1   A FREQUENCY POLYGON

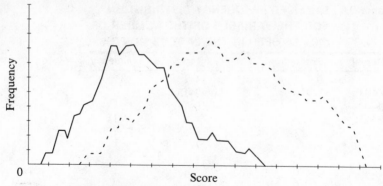

Figure 5.2   USING TWO FREQUENCY POLYGONS TO COMPARE TWO DISTRIBUTIONS

in Figures 5.1 and 5.2 have this jagged appearance. As the group size increases, the frequency polygon tends to look more like a smooth curve. Data in textbooks are often described by drawing smooth curves even though such curves are seen only when the group sizes are extremely large.

Figure 5.3 represents several different smooth-curve drawings of frequency poly-

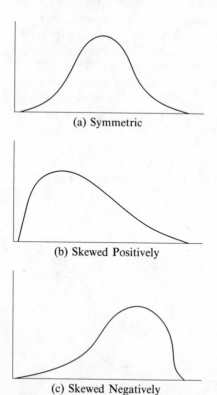

(a) Symmetric

(b) Skewed Positively

(c) Skewed Negatively

Figure 5.3   FREQUENCY POLYGONS OF SYMMETRIC AND SKEWED DISTRIBUTIONS

gons that illustrate various distribution shapes. Figure 5.3(a) shows a common shape for a symmetric distribution, a bell-shaped curve. In a symmetric bell-shaped curve most of the subjects are near the middle of the distribution. We refer to distributions with this shape as *normal curves* or *normal distributions.* The normal curve is actually a mathematical curve defined by an equation, but many variables in psychology form distributions that are similar in shape to a true normal curve. Figures 5.3(b) and 5.3(c) represent *skewed distributions.* In a skewed distribution, the scores tend to pile up on one end of the distribution or the other. The direction of the skewness is indicated by the tail of the curve. In Figure 5.3(b) the curve is *positively skewed,* with most of the scores piled up near the bottom (the tail points toward the high or positive end of the scale, thus the distribution is positively skewed). Even though the group size is quite small, you can see that the number-of-movies-attended data that are graphed in Figure 5.1 also represent a positively skewed distribution. Figure 5.3(c), on the other hand, is *negatively skewed.* Note the tail is toward the negative end of the scale. We might see such distributions on an easy classroom test where almost everyone does well with only a few people doing poorly.

These are the distribution shapes most likely seen when variables of interest to psychologists are measured. In addition to the shape, we describe distributions in terms of their location on the *x*-axis (the *central tendency* of the distribution) and their horizontal spread (the *variability* of the distribution).

Summary Statistics

Summary statistics serve two purposes. The first is to describe the data with just one or two numbers, which makes it easier to compare several different groups quickly. The second is to provide a basis for later analyses in which inferential statistics will be used. Normally, we would compute a measure of central tendency and a measure of variability.

Measures of Central Tendency: Mode, Median, and Mean Measures of central tendency describe the typical or average score. They are called measures of central tendency because they provide an indication of the center of the distribution where most of the scores tend to cluster. There are three measures of central tendency used in describing psychological data: the mode, the median, and the mean. The *mode* is the most frequently occurring score in the distribution. In the example shown in Table 5.1, the mode for group A is 87 and for group B is 72. If the data are more complicated and a frequency distribution like the one in Table 5.5 has been prepared, the mode can be computed by finding the largest number in the frequency column and noting the score with that frequency. In Table 5.5 the mode is 3. A distribution may have more than one mode. If there are two, then the distribution is *bimodal;* if there are three, it is *trimodal.* The mode has the advantage of being easily computed but the disadvantage of being unstable, which means that it can be affected by a change in only one or two scores. The mode can be appropriately used with all scales of measurement.

A second measure of central tendency is the *median.* The median is the middle score in a distribution where the scores have been arranged in order from lowest to highest. The median is also the 50th percentile, which means that half of the scores fall below the median and half are above the median. The median is easily computed if there are few scores and they have been ordered from lowest to highest. With an odd number of scores, the median is the $(N + 1)/2$ score where N is the number of scores. In Table 5.1 there are 11 scores. Therefore, the sixth score [$(11 + 1)/2$] will be the median. Note that the sixth score in a group of 11 scores will be exactly in the middle with 5 scores above it and 5 scores below it. In Table 5.1 in Group A the median is 87; in Group B it is 74. If there is an even number of scores, there is not one middle score but two middle scores. The median is the average of the two middle scores. With a large number of scores and many people with each possible score, a more complicated formula is used (the formula is given in Appendix C). The median can be appropriately used with ordered and score data but not with nominal data.

The most commonly used measure of central tendency is the *mean,* the arithmetic average of all of the scores. The mean is computed by summing the scores and dividing by the number of scores as follows:

$$\text{Mean} = \bar{X} = \frac{\Sigma X}{N} \tag{5.1}$$

The term $\bar{X}$ (read "X bar") is the notation for the mean. The term ΣX (read "sigma X") is the summation notation and simply means to add all of the scores. Table 5.7 shows a sample computation of a mean. The mean is appropriately used only with score data.

Table 5.7 SAMPLE COMPUTATION OF A MEAN

Compute the mean for the following ten scores: 12, 7, 8, 5, 10, 8, 9, 13, 9, 6

1. Start by listing the scores in no particular order in a column labelled X at the top.
2. Sum the column.
3. Use the computational formula below to compute the mean.

X
12
7
8
5
10
8
9
13
9
6
$\Sigma X = 87$

Computing the mean

$$\bar{X} = \frac{\Sigma X}{N} = \frac{87}{10} = 8.7$$

The mean and the median are used extensively to describe the average score. The median gives a better indication of what the typical score is if there are some very deviant scores in the distribution. This property is shown in the example given in Table 5.8. The mean, on the other hand, is more useful in other statistical procedures such as inferential statistics.

Measures of Variability: Range, Variance, and Standard Deviation   In addition to measures of central tendency, it is also important to determine how variable the scores are. The concept of variability of scores is best illustrated by the two curves shown in Figure 5.4. Both curves represent symmetric frequency distributions with identical means. But curve A is narrower—the scores are bunched closer together. Curve B is more spread out than curve A, with fewer people close to the middle of the distribution; that is, the scores in curve B are more variable, have greater dispersion, or have a greater spread or range than curve A. All of these are different ways of saying the same thing: variability of scores is greater in curve B than in curve A. As another example, consider the ages of people who attend county fairs and those who attend rock concerts. If we measured their ages we would probably find that county fair-goers range from infants in arms through the oldest farmers in the region (perhaps from less than a year to over 90 years old). However, if we measured the ages of rock concert-goers we would probably find that most are in their teens and early twenties, with few preteens and people over 30. Clearly, there is far more variability in the age of attendees at a county fair than at a typical rock concert.

The concept of variability is one of the most important concepts in research and

Table 5.8   AN EXAMPLE OF THE EFFECTS OF A SINGLE DEVIANT SCORE ON THE MEAN AND MEDIAN

Assume we have two companies (Company A and Company B), each with five employees. Listed below are the annual salaries of each employee in each company.

Company A	Company B
$16,000	$16,000
18,000	18,000
20,000	20,000
22,000	22,000
24,000	124,000
$\Sigma X = \$100,000$	$\Sigma X = \$200,000$

The salaries of the employees in both companies have been ordered for ease of comparison between companies. Note that four of the salaries paid out to employees are exactly the same in both companies. Only the top salary is different in the two companies. In Company A the top salary is $24,000, whereas in Company B the top salary is $124,000.

$$\text{The mean for Company A} = \frac{\$100,000}{5} = \$20,000.$$

$$\text{The mean for Company B} = \frac{\$200,000}{5} = \$40,000.$$

The median (or middle score) is the same for both companies ($20,000).

Which measure gives the most typical salary in each company?

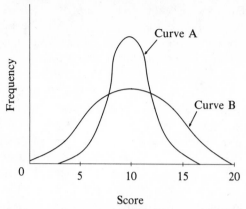

Figure 5.4 TWO DISTRIBUTIONS WITH THE SAME CENTRAL TENDENCY BUT DIFFERENT LEVELS OF VARIABILITY

will be discussed in increasing detail as we proceed through later chapters. It is important for students to gain an early understanding of the concept of variability. Variability is a fact of life. Individuals differ from one another and they differ in their responses to different stimuli. But this natural variability among subjects can often mask the effects of variables we are studying. Thus, many of the sophisticated research designs and statistical procedures used in research were developed to control or minimize the effects of natural variability of scores.

But as critically important as the concept of variability is, it is an easy concept to understand. Subjects differ from one another, and those differences are reflected in differences in scores on whatever variable we are measuring. On some variables there are large differences between subjects; on other variables there are only small differences between subjects. For any given variable, there may be numerous reasons why scores among subjects vary as they do, but we need not worry about the reasons for the variability at this point. The important point to remember for now is that the scores do vary and that the degree of variability can be quantified.

There are many ways in which the variability of the scores can be measured; for example, by using the *range,* the *variance,* and the *standard deviation.* The simplest measure of variability is the *range,* which is the distance from the lowest to the highest score. Although the range is easy to compute, it is too unstable to describe consistently the variability in data because it depends on only two scores—the highest and the lowest. A single deviant score can dramatically affect the range of scores. For example, in Figure 5.4 the scores for curve A range from 4–16 (a range of 12) and the scores for curve B range from 1–19 (a range of 18). However, if one more score were added to curve A (a score of 22), the range for curves A and B would be equal. Still, even with the addition of this one deviant score, the scores are more tightly clustered or less variable in curve A than in curve B.

A better measure of variability is the *variance.* The variance utilizes all of the scores (instead of just the lowest and highest scores) in quantifying the degree of variability in the data, and it has the statistical properties that make it useful in inferential statistics. The variance measures the average squared distance (deviation)

Box 5.1 DEGREES OF FREEDOM

Degrees of freedom is a basic statistical concept needed in many computations. It refers to the number of scores that are free to vary. For example, suppose you are asked to pick *any three numbers.* There are no restrictions and the numbers are completely free to vary. They could be any three values. In standard terminology, there would be three degrees of freedom; that is, three numbers are free to vary. Now suppose you are to choose any three numbers, but they *must* total 15; that is, there is one restriction on the numbers. Because of the restriction you will loose some of the freedom to vary the three numbers you choose. For example, if you freely chose the numbers 5 and 1 as the first two numbers, you *must* choose 9 as the third number to arrive at the total of 15. If instead you freely chose the numbers 8 and 11 as the first two numbers, the third *must* be −4 in order to total 15. In both examples, two numbers are free to vary, but one is not free to vary. In standard terminology there are two degrees of freedom; that is, two numbers are free to vary. In comparison to the first example where there was no restriction on what the total had to be and all the scores could be freely selected, we now can freely select only two scores. We have lost a degree of freedom.

Now suppose that you are to choose three scores where (1) the total *must* be 15 *and* (2) the first score *must* be 7. Notice there are two restrictions placed on these scores: the total and the value of the first score. Because of the two restrictions, two degrees of freedom have been lost, leaving only one degree of freedom. The only score that can vary freely is the second score.

In statistics the restrictions imposed on data are not arbitrary such as in our examples. Instead, they are determined by the demands of the statistical procedures used. Many statistical procedures require that estimates be made of certain values such as the mean. These estimates constitute restrictions. The more such restrictions there are, the more degrees of freedom are lost. In the computation of the variance, one such restriction is imposed and consequently the degrees of freedom are reduced by one. Hence, the denominator is $N - 1$.

of each score from the mean. The deviations from the mean are squared to make them all positive. Without squaring each deviation before adding them together, we would always find that the average deviation from the mean was zero no matter how variable the scores were, which would make the index quite useless. The notation s^2 refers to variance. The definitional formula for variance is:

$$s^2 = \frac{\text{SS (Sum of Squares)}}{\text{df (degrees of freedom)}} = \frac{\Sigma (X - \bar{X})^2}{N - 1} \tag{5.2}$$

That is, variance equals the sum of the squared differences of each score from the mean (the sum of squares) divided by the number of scores minus one (the degrees of freedom). The degrees of freedom is an important concept in statistics referring to the number of scores that are free to vary (see Box 5.1). To use Formula 5.2, we first compute the mean of the scores. We then subtract the mean from each score and square that difference. We then sum the squared differences to calculate the numerator of Formula 5.2, which is called the *sum of squares.* The sum of squares is short for "the sum of squared deviations from the mean" and is often abbreviated in formulas as SS. We then divide the sum of squares by $N - 1$ to obtain the variance. In Table 5.9 the variance is computed for the data presented in Table 5.7 using Formula 5.2.

The definitional formula for the variance (5.2) is unnecessarily tedious to use for computation. A much simpler computational formula is given below:

$$s^2 = \frac{SS}{N - 1} \tag{5.3}$$

where

$$SS = \Sigma X^2 - \frac{(\Sigma X)^2}{N} \tag{5.4}$$

In Table 5.10 the above computational formula is used to compute the variance for the same data in Table 5.9. In Table 5.9 the definitional formula for the variance was used. Because the data set in Tables 5.9 and 5.10 are the same, we would expect

Table 5.9   AN EXAMPLE OF THE VARIANCE USING THE DEFINITIONAL FORMULA

Compute the variance for the data from Table 5.7.

Steps in computing the variance using the definitional formula

1. Start by listing the scores in no particular order in a column labelled X at the top.
2. Label two other columns $(X - \bar{X})$ and $(X - \bar{X})^2$.
3. Compute the mean as was done in Table 5.7.
4. Compute the values for the second and third columns using the mean. Then add up the numbers in each column. If the computations are done correctly, the second column will always add to zero. Column 3 gives you the numerator for your variance computation.
5. Use Formula 5.2 to compute the variance.

X	$(X - \bar{X})$	$(X - \bar{X})^2$
12	3.3	10.89
7	−1.7	2.89
8	−0.7	0.49
5	−3.7	13.69
10	1.3	1.69
8	−0.7	0.49
9	0.3	0.09
13	4.3	18.49
9	0.3	0.09
6	−2.7	7.29
$\Sigma X = 87$	$\Sigma (X - \bar{X}) = 0.0$	$\Sigma (X - \bar{X})^2 = 56.10$

Computing the mean and variance

$$\bar{X} = \frac{\Sigma X}{N} = \frac{87}{10} = 8.7$$

$$s^2 = \frac{\Sigma (X - \bar{X})^2}{N - 1} = \frac{56.1}{10 - 1} = \frac{56.1}{9} = 6.23$$

Table 5.10   COMPUTATION OF THE VARIANCE AND STANDARD DEVIATION USING THE COMPUTATIONAL FORMULA

Compute the variance and standard deviation for the following ten scores: 12, 7, 8, 5, 10, 8, 9, 13, 9, 6

1. Start by listing the scores in no particular order in a column labelled X at the top.

2. Label an adjacent column X^2.

3. Square each value in the column labeled X and put it in the adjacent column.

4. Sum both columns of numbers.

X	X^2
12	144
7	49
8	64
5	25
10	100
8	64
9	81
13	169
9	81
6	36
$\Sigma X = 87$	$\Sigma X^2 = 813$

Computing the variance and standard deviation[a]

$$\text{SS} = (\Sigma X^2) - \frac{(\Sigma X)^2}{N} = 813 - \frac{(87)^2}{10} = 813 - 756.9 = 56.1$$

$$s^2 = \frac{\text{SS}}{N-1} = \frac{56.1}{10-1} = \frac{56.1}{9} = 6.23$$

$$s = \sqrt{s^2} = \sqrt{6.23} = 2.50$$

[a]Answers have been rounded to two decimal places.

the variance to be the same even though different formulas are used. In both cases, the variance is equal to 6.23.

The variance is an excellent measure of variability and is used in many inferential statistics. But the variance is expressed in squared units whereas the mean is expressed in the original units of the variable. A measure called the *standard deviation* can be computed to transform the measure of variability into the same units as the original scores. The standard deviation is equal to the square root of the variance. Like the mean, the variance and standard deviation are appropriately used only with score data.

$$\text{Standard deviation} = s = \sqrt{s^2} = \sqrt{\text{variance}} \qquad (5.5)$$

Measures of Relationship (Correlations)   We know now that measures of central tendency and variability are basic descriptive statistics that tell us something about the distribution of a variable. At times, however, we need to know more about a variable, such as what relationship the variable has to other variables. This relationship or association between one variable and any other variable is best indexed with a *correla-*

tion coefficient. A correlation is another descriptive statistic in that it describes some aspect of the data. However, it is different from the other descriptive statistics in that it always involves at least two variables. There are different correlation coefficients for different types of data. With score data the Pearson product-moment correlation should be used; with ordered data the Spearman rank-order correlation should be used.

The *Pearson product-moment correlation* is by far the most widely used correlation index. (The computational procedures of the Pearson product-moment correlation are detailed in Appendix C.) The product-moment correlation can range from −1.00 to +1.00. A correlation of +1.00 means that the two variables are perfectly related in a positive direction; in other words, as one of the variables increases the other variable will increase by a predictable amount. A correlation of −1.00 represents a perfect negative relationship—as one variable increases the other decreases by a predictable amount. A correlation of zero means that there is no relationship between the variables. The strength of the relationship is indicated by the absolute value of the correlation coefficient. For example, a correlation of 0.55 indicates a stronger relationship between two variables than a correlation of 0.25, and a correlation of −0.85 indicates an even stronger relationship. The sign of the correlation indicates the direction of the relationship rather than the strength of the relationship.

The Pearson product-moment correlation is an index of the degree of *linear relationship* between two variables. What that means is best illustrated if we look at scatter plots. A *scatter plot* is the graphic technique used to represent the relationship between two variables. To construct one, standard *x*- and *y*-axes are labeled with the names of the two variables of interest. Each axis must then be divided into a sufficient number of equal intervals to handle the range for the variable represented by that axis. A scatter plot for the relationship between age and income using data from Table 5.2 is graphed in Figure 5.5. As indicated in the figure, subject A is 28 years old and earns $17,000 a year. The point representing subject A is directly above $17,000 on the *x*-axis

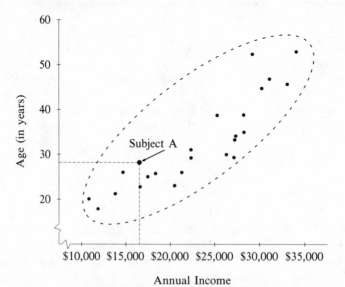

Figure 5.5 **SCATTER PLOT OF THE RELATIONSHIP BETWEEN AGE AND INCOME**

and directly across from 28 on the y-axis. To complete the scatter plot, each person's set of scores is plotted in the same way.

The pattern of scores in the scatter plot can tell us a great deal. For example, in Figure 5.5 the dots are not scattered randomly but in a pattern. The people with the highest incomes are all older; young people tend to have lower incomes. One could draw a straight line through the middle of the dots from the lower left to upper right of the graph with most of the dots falling close to that line—this is a good example of a linear relationship. The points of a scatter plot seem to cluster around a straight line. It is a positive relationship because incomes are higher for older subjects. It is not a perfect relationship—in a perfect relationship all of the dots form a straight line.

The scatter plots in Figure 5.6 illustrate other types of relationships. Figure 5.6(a) illustrates a *negative correlation.* Figure 5.6(b) illustrates a *perfect positive correlation.* Figure 5.6(c) represents the random scattering found when no relationship exists. Finally, Figure 5.6(d) depicts a *nonlinear relationship.* We might have seen a nonlinear relationship between age and income if we had included many older, retired persons. When the relationship between two variables is not linear, it is *not* appropriate to use a product-moment correlation to quantify the strength of the relationship.

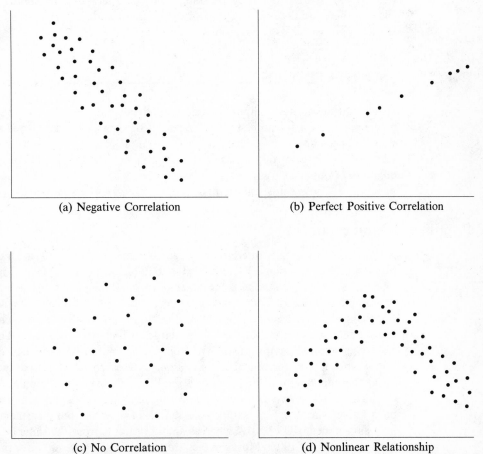

(a) Negative Correlation   (b) Perfect Positive Correlation

(c) No Correlation   (d) Nonlinear Relationship

Figure 5.6 SCATTER PLOTS OF VARIOUS RELATIONSHIPS

If either or both variables are ordinal (and neither variable is nominal), the appropriate coefficient is the *Spearman rank-order correlation* (the computational procedures are included in Appendix C). The Spearman rank-order correlation is interpreted like the product-moment correlation: A correlation of -1.00 is a perfect negative relationship; a correlation of $+1.00$ is a perfect positive relationship; and a correlation of 0 means that no linear relationship exists. Scatter plots can be drawn using the ranking of each subject on each variable.

Summary of Descriptive Statistics

Descriptive statistics help us to summarize and describe large quantities of scores in only a few numbers. They are a vital first step in interpreting research data. Even when more complicated research designs are used, describing data will always be the first step in any data-analysis procedure. Frequency distributions and graphical representations of data are often helpful. Summary statistics simplify data further. There are summary statistics to indicate the typical score (measures of central tendency), including the mean, the median, and the mode. There are summary statistics to indicate the variability of the scores, including the range, the variance, and the standard deviation. Finally, there are descriptive statistics to indicate the degree of relationship between two or more variables (correlations).

INFERENTIAL STATISTICS

Using statistics to help simplify and describe data is only the first step in the analysis of the results of a research study. The rest of the analysis is concerned not so much with the specific subjects we have tested (the sample), but with what those subjects can tell us about a larger group of people (the population). That is, we use statistical analysis of the data obtained from the sample to draw *inferences* about a larger group, the population. These statistical methods are called *inferential statistics*.

Populations and Samples

Although we are usually interested in large populations of subjects, it is rarely possible to test whole populations. Therefore, we obtain data on samples from populations. In human research, a *population* is the larger group of all the people of interest from which the sample is selected. The *sample* is a subset of people drawn from that population. For example, a researcher might be interested in the population of high school students in a county, but the population is too large to include in a study. Therefore, the researcher selects a sample of students from the population. A sample is used as if that sample adequately represents the population. In research we want to draw conclusions about the population on the basis of a small sample from that population.

However, no two samples drawn from the same population will be exactly alike on any given variable. For example, one sample of subjects from the general population may have a mean IQ of 101.2 whereas another sample from the same population will have a mean IQ of 100.3. Most samples are reasonably representative of the population from which they are drawn, but sometimes samples are unrepresentative of the population even though the sampling procedure may have been carried out flawlessly. The variation among different samples drawn from the same population is referred to as *sampling error*. In a sense, the term *sampling error* is misleading in that it does not represent a mistake of any kind but rather refers to the small chance variability among samples. Because samples are not perfectly representative of the population from which they are drawn, we cannot be sure that the conclusions drawn from the samples will generalize to the entire population. In fact, we can *never be sure* that inferences drawn from a sample are valid for the population; the best we can do is calculate probabilities about the inferences. The idea of probability is important and is the major issue addressed by inferential statistics.

Suppose, for example, we were interested in reaction time in schizophrenics and in normal subjects. The variable, reaction time, is measured by recording how quickly subjects press a button in response to an auditory signal. The samples used would be drawn from the population of schizophrenics and from the population of normals. Suppose we found that mean reaction time from the samples was 0.268 seconds for schizophrenics and 0.254 seconds for normals. Clearly, the sample means are different but not very different. However, we are actually interested in the *population* of schizophrenics and the *population* of normals. That is, we want to draw conclusions about characteristics of the populations from the results of the samples. Would the observed difference in mean reaction time in the samples of schizophrenics and normals lead us to believe that a similar difference exists between the populations of schizophrenics and normals or could the observed difference simply be a result of sampling error? This kind of question (comparing population means) is the type most often raised in such research. Suppose for the moment that the reaction time means for the populations were *not* different. In this case, samples drawn from the populations should have approximately equal mean reaction times. Returning to our example, are mean reaction times of 0.268 and 0.254 approximately equal? Are they close enough to infer that the populations means (unknown to us) are also approximately equal? Here we are testing the null hypothesis, which in this case is that the population means are not different from one another.

The Null Hypothesis

The *null hypothesis* is a general hypothesis that can be applied to many types of comparisons. In the situation discussed above, it is the population means that are being compared. Null is from the Latin *nullus,* meaning "not any." Thus, the null hypothesis in this situation is that there is "not any" statistical difference between the population means. Inferential statistics are used to test the null hypothesis. If the observed sample means were very different, then we would reject the null hypothesis and conclude that the population means are not equal. But how different is "very different"? Inferential statistics give a probabilistic answer to this question.

Before proceeding further, let us distinguish between a population parameter and a sample statistic. If we compute a characteristic of the population (such as the mean) by testing everyone in the population, we refer to the value as a *population parameter*. If we compute the same characteristic on a sample drawn from the population, we refer to the value as a *sample statistic.* Our task is usually to estimate population parameters and to draw conclusions about population parameters on the basis of sample statistics.

Statistical Decisions and Alpha Levels

Inferential statistics are used to compute the probability of obtaining the observed data if the null hypothesis is true. If the probability is small, then it is unlikely that the null hypothesis is indeed true. We would therefore conclude that the null hypothesis is false. A somewhat arbitrary cutoff point called the *alpha level* (written α) is used for making this decision. Traditionally, we set alpha to a small value such as 0.05 or 0.01. To clarify these difficult but important concepts, let us refer back to our example. We are interested in the reaction time of schizophrenics and normals. The null hypothesis is that the mean reaction times are the same in the schizophrenic and normal populations. The inferential statistical procedure evaluates the size of the observed mean difference between the samples. If the sample means are so different that it is unlikely the samples could have come from populations with equal means, then we reject the hypothesis that the population means are equal (the null hypothesis).

Type I and Type II Errors

The alpha level that we select guides us in rejecting or not rejecting the null hypothesis—the hypothesis that there is no difference between the means. When the probability exceeds the alpha level, we retain the null hypothesis; when the probability is at or less than the alpha level, we reject the null hypothesis.

Of course, there is always the chance that the researcher might be wrong in his or her decision. For example, the researcher might reject the null hypothesis and conclude the population means are not equal when, in fact, the population means are equal. In this case, the researcher has made a *Type I error.* The probability of this error occurring is equal to the alpha level we set. If an alpha of 0.05 is used, Type I errors will occur 5 percent of the time. If the alpha is 0.01, Type I errors will occur 1 percent of the time. The alpha level is the proportion of Type I errors one could expect to make if the study were repeated many times.

If alpha is the level of Type I error and the researcher decides what alpha to use, why not set alpha to zero to avoid all Type I errors? The reason is that there is another possible error known as a Type II error. A *Type II error* occurs when we *fail to reject* the null hypothesis when it is false. Ideally, we do not want to make either kind of error, but because we can never be sure what the real state of nature is, there is always the chance for error in our decision. It is important to realize that if we decrease the Type I error rate (without doing anything else), we will automatically increase the Type II error rate. Therefore, the two types of error have to be balanced against one another. Table 5.11 summarizes the definitions of Type I and Type II errors.

Testing for Mean Differences

As we know, inferential statistics are used most frequently to evaluate mean differences between groups. Such statistical techniques are extremely useful in research because we often can specify the research hypothesis in terms of group differences. There are a number of commonly used tests for evaluating mean differences in two or more groups, including the simple *t*-test, correlated *t*-test, and analysis of variance (ANOVA).

Table 5.11 TYPE I AND TYPE II ERRORS

		Researcher's decision	
		Reject the null hypothesis	Retain the null hypothesis[a]
True state of nature	Null hypothesis is true	Type I error	Correct decision
	Null hypothesis is false	Correct decision	Type II error

[a]Technically, we never actually accept the null hypothesis. Instead, we retain or fail to reject the null hypothesis. The interested student should consult an introductory statistics textbook for the reasoning behind this subtle distinction.

Simple *t*-Test The simple *t*-test (sometimes referred to as the *t*-test for independent groups) is typically used with score data from two independent samples of subjects. The samples are independent if different subjects appear in each sample and if the subjects in the two samples are not matched in any way. The null hypothesis is that there is no difference in the two population means; that is, the observed difference between the sample means is due only to sampling error. The test statistic is called *t*. Computational formulas for *t* can be found in Appendix C. The general procedure in this and most other inferential statistics is to compute the test statistic and then to compare that value with a critical value of the statistic. The critical value, which is looked up in a table, provides a basis for statistical decisions. The tabled critical values are based on factors such as the alpha level chosen and sizes of the samples. Appendix B includes most of the commonly used statistical tables, including a table of critical values of *t*. Procedures for using these tables are described in Appendix C and, where appropriate, in the text itself.

Correlated *t*-Test In some research designs we do not have independent groups. One such design is called a *within-subjects design*, where the same subjects appear in each group. In this design the groups represent different conditions under which the subjects are tested. Another design is the *matched-subjects design*, where all subjects are matched in pairs and then randomly assigned so that one member of the pair goes into one group and the other member goes into another group. (We will discuss these designs in further detail in Chapter 11.) In either case, a correlated *t*-test would be the appropriate test to use to analyze the results of the study. (The computational procedures for the correlated *t*-test are included in Appendix C.)

Analysis of Variance (ANOVA) When we have more than two groups and want to test for mean differences among the groups, an *analysis of variance (ANOVA)* is the appropriate test. The term *analysis of variance* is confusing because the test actually compares the means of the various groups. But it compares the means by computing and comparing different population variance estimates. (Explaining how this is accomplished is beyond the scope of this book; we will focus only on the conceptual basis of ANOVA in this section. Standard terminology and interpretation will be discussed in Chapters 10 through 12, and computational procedures are included in Appendix C.)

One reason analysis of variance is such a useful tool for analyzing the results of research is that it is flexible. We can analyze the results of studies that use one independent variable and of studies that use two or more independent variables. If we have more than one independent variable, the independent variables are referred to as *factors* and the research design is said to be *factorial.* We refer to the analysis of a study with only one independent variable as a *one-way ANOVA,* with two independent variables as a *two-way ANOVA,* and so forth. Each factor can have many levels or groups. Also, ANOVAs can be used to analyze data from studies where different subjects appear in each condition (a between-subjects design) or where the same subjects appear in all of the conditions (a within-subjects design). An ANOVA used to analyze data from a within-subjects design is referred to as a *repeated measures ANOVA.* (We will discuss analysis of variance further in Chapters 10 through 12, when we describe the research designs that would use ANOVA to test research hypotheses.)

SUMMARY

Statistics are tools that help us interpret the results of experiments and observational studies. The interpretations made on the basis of statistical calculations are limited by (1) the quality of the data gathered, (2) the appropriateness of the statistic for the data gathered and the question we want to ask, and (3) the accuracy with which we compute and interpret the statistic. Some statistical procedures are designed solely to describe the data from a study (descriptive statistics). Other statistics (inferential statistics) are designed to help interpret the data. Whatever our purpose in using statistics, the appropriate statistic(s) will depend on the nature of the data and of the question we are asking.

In this chapter we have discussed the most commonly used statistics. Procedures for computing frequently used statistics are included in Appendix C. In addition, Chapter 14 presents a flowchart for selecting the appropriate statistical technique based on the research design.

REVIEW EXERCISES

I. Define the following key terms. Be sure you understand them. They are discussed in the chapter and defined in the glossary.

Statistics	*x*-axis or abscissa
Descriptive statistics	*y*-axis or ordinate
Inferential statistics	Symmetric curve
Individual differences	Normal distribution
Cross-tabulation	Skewed distribution
Univariate	Skewed positively
Frequency distribution	Skewed negatively
Grouped frequency distribution	Summary statistics
Continuous variable	Central tendency
Graphs	Variability
Tables	Mode
Frequency polygon	Median

Mean

Range

Variance

Standard deviation

Sum of squares

Relationship

Correlation

Correlation coefficient

Pearson product-moment correlation

Scatter plot

Linear relationship

Nonlinear relationship

Perfect correlation

Positive correlation

Negative correlation

Spearman rank-order correlation

Inferential statistics

Population

Sample

Sampling error

Null hypothesis

Population parameters

Sample statistics

Alpha level

Type I error

Type II error

Simple t-test

t-test for independent groups

Correlated t-test

Within-subjects design

Matched-subjects design

Analysis of variance (ANOVA)

Factors

Factorial design

One-way ANOVA

Two-way ANOVA

Repeated measures ANOVA

Statistical symbols: Σ (sigma); $\bar{X}$; N; s; s^2; SS; α (alpha); t

II. Answer each of the following. Check your answers in the chapter.

1. With what kind of data do we use frequency distributions?
2. Draw a graph showing a negatively skewed distribution and one showing a positively skewed distribution.
3. What are the different kinds of summary statistics?
4. Name and define the measures of central tendency and of variability.
5. Is it possible for a distribution of scores to have more than one mode? More than one mean?
6. Suppose you are the teaching assistant in this course. How would you present and explain variability and its measures to students?
7. Why is the variance a better measure of variability than the range?
8. Why is the mean a better measure of central tendency than the mode.
9. How does a correlation differ from other descriptive statistics?
10. Which correlation coefficient would you calculate for each of the following: (a) age and height; (b) class rank and IQ; (c) grade (number correct) on two different exams?
11. How do inferential statistics differ from descriptive statistics?

III. Think about and work the following problems.

1. For each of the following data sets, (a) draw a descriptive graph, (b) compute the measures of central tendency, and (c) compute the measures of variability.
   a. 20 scores: 8; 6; 4; 3; 9; 5; 7; 8; 6; 7; 9; 5; 9; 8; 9; 7; 4; 8; 7; 9
   b. 15 IQ scores: 104; 121; 94; 107; 81; 96; 100; 96; 102; 115; 87; 101; 91; 114; 111

2. In the following research projects identify: (a) the independent variable and the type of independent variable (manipulated or nonmanipulated); (b) the dependent variable(s); (c) the level of measurement and the type of data for each dependent variable. (Refer to Chapter 4 if you have difficulty with this exercise.)

a. Thirty rats are randomly assigned to one of three groups (10 rats per group). Each group of rats is under different amounts of food deprivation (4 hours; 8 hours; 12 hours). The rats are then tested to see how many trials are required to learn a standard maze.

b. Twenty 2-year-olds and twenty 3-year-olds are compared on their enjoyment of toys. Each child is allowed to play for a period of 30 minutes in a playroom. An observer rates each child on a five-point scale on the child's enjoyment.

c. Birth records of 250 schizophrenic patients and 250 randomly selected individuals are compared on the frequency of birth complications in each group. The birth record for each subject is categorized as normal (no complications) or abnormal (complications reported).

NATURALISTIC AND CASE-STUDY RESEARCH

In this chapter we will discuss the naturalistic and case-study research methods in more detail, including the conditions under which they are appropriately used, the kinds of important information they provide, the limitations of the methods, and some procedures for minimizing the limitations. Finally, we will introduce some of the procedures used to analyze data generated by naturalistic and case-study research.

The naturalistic and case-study methods are at the lowest levels of constraint in scientific research. Here researchers observe the behavior of subjects in a flexible way, which allows them to take advantage of unexpected occurrences and new ideas developed during the observations. The focus of low-constraint research is on the natural flow of behavior. Therefore, the investigator intervenes as little as possible, imposing few, if any, controls or constraints on subjects' behavior. Naturalistic research is carried out in the subject's natural environment. Case-study research is slightly higher in constraint because the researcher does intervene to some degree. Naturalistic research methods have been used by ethologists and comparative psychologists studying the behavior of animals in their natural habitats, and by sociologists and social psychologists interested in the natural behavior of human groups under various conditions that cannot be duplicated in the laboratory. Case-study research methods have been used to study subjective processes such as thinking and problem solving in children and personal adjustment in both adults and children. Most often case-study research is carried out with one subject at a time, usually in an interactive or face-to-face situation.

It is tempting to think that, because the researcher imposes few controls and can make observations in a flexible manner, naturalistic and case-study research are relatively easy to carry out. As in all research, however, a great deal of care and effort is required, even at low-constraint levels. Indeed, the very lack of high-constraint controls and procedures actually adds to the researcher's burden in many ways in that the researcher cannot depend on the usual, reliable supports found in laboratory settings.

To illustrate the particular difficulties faced in low-constraint research, suppose you want to study the mating, nesting, and rearing behaviors of a certain rarely seen bird. Before going into the field you must search the literature and communicate with other ornithologists to learn what is known about the species and the best methods by which to study the species. Assume also that you have identified the bird's natural habitat, outfitted your expedition, and traveled there. You probably have with you audiotape and videotape recording equipment, camping supplies, food, and so on. If your research grant permits it, you have an assistant to help carry the load. If not, you do it yourself. There are long hours of searching for this rare bird and when you find it, you spend long days, perhaps weeks and months, waiting for opportunities to observe the behavior you wish to study. Because you are not in control of the bird's behavior, you have to "take it as it comes," which results in a long, tedious, and laborious enterprise, often carried out under difficult and uncomfortable conditions. After the observations have been successfully made, you must analyze your data—often a mammoth task in naturalistic research—then interpret the data, and finally communicate the results.

Researchers face the same problems, although perhaps not quite so dramatically, when they observe human behavior in natural settings. Because you are a passive observer, you must locate the subjects, make yourself as unobtrusive as possible, and then wait for your subjects to display the behavior you want to observe.

Note that in naturalistic and case-study research the constraints or controls are primarily on the observer, with as little control as possible exerted on the behavior of the subject. As we move to higher constraint levels, the controls are increasingly placed on the subjects, so as to specify and delimit the behavior to be observed.

EXAMPLES OF NATURALISTIC RESEARCH

A classic example of naturalistic research is that of Charles Darwin who voyaged five years on the HMS *Beagle* while compiling descriptive data in the form of notes, drawings, and specimens from a large area of the world. Darwin carefully observed animals and plants in their natural settings, as well as weather and geological formations. Over time he began to see patterns in his data and to form ideas about how the great variety of life might have developed. The more familiar he became with the data, the more clues and patterns there seemed to be. Over a number of years Darwin integrated his observations and ideas and eventually formulated his theory of evolution. However, Darwin was not the first person to propose the idea of biological evolution. Over 2000 years earlier Greek philosophers had developed some concepts of animal and human evolution. Also, Alfred Russel Wallace proposed the concept of natural selection in the origin of species just prior to Darwin's publication of *On the Origin of Species*. But it was Darwin who was most influential in bringing the wealth of data and the interpretations of those data to the attention of other scientists and the public.

A more recent example of naturalistic study of animals is Jane Goodall's (1971, 1986) study of chimpanzees in their natural habitat in Tanzania. Beginning in the early 1960s, Goodall persisted two years in the forests under difficult conditions before she was even able to begin making substantial observations and then many more years to carry on her work. Her research, primarily low constraint and naturalistic, has given ethologists new information and presents a remarkable picture of the now endangered chimpanzee as a highly social creature.

A similar example of naturalistic research is the work of Diane Fossey who for years studied the now rare mountain gorilla in its natural habitat in Africa. In her book, *Gorilla in the Mist* (1983), Fossey describes her discovery that the gorilla is a complex, highly social, responsive, and even gentle animal—far different from the earlier, distorted assumption of the gorilla's ferociousness and danger to humans.

Naturalistic methods can also be applied to human behavior. Anthropologists and sociologists have used these methods extensively. When anthropologists such as Margaret Mead live among the people of a different culture, they are obviously not inconspicuous, but they are in a position to make direct observations of everyday behavior over a long period of time. They observe and record behavior and then organize and interpret the data to produce a detailed account of the ways in which the people function. From the descriptive data, inferences are made about the culture's values, religious and other beliefs, power status, organization, and so forth. The detailed descriptions are valuable in understanding behaviors and processes, such as parenting, growing into adulthood, divisions of labor, conflicts, and a host of other issues.

"DR. HODGES, HERE, IS FROM ENGLAND, AND HE'S BEEN OBSERVING US FOR 14 YEARS. MR. FERRELL, AN AMERICAN, HAS BEEN HERE ONLY THREE WEEKS. MONIQUE CORVEAU, FROM PARIS, HAS PRACTICALLY BEEN LIVING WITH US FOR ABOUT NINE YEARS..."

Reprinted by permission of S. Harris.

A recent example of naturalistic methods used in sociological research is Adeline Levine's (1982) study of the Love Canal disaster in Niagara Falls, New York. Just after World War II, the city of Niagara Falls built a grammar school in the middle of a covered-up toxic dumpsite. The area surrounding the dump was developed for residential use. For a long time nothing seemed amiss. But unknown to the residents, the thousands of metal drums of toxins were slowly and quietly corroding underground, releasing their toxins into the surrounding soil. Over the next two decades the toxins seeped into the underground springs, into the creeks and rivers and, pushed during the 1970s by the pressure of a slowly rising water table, made their way into the cellars of the homes above and percolated up to the surface of the soil. There were reports of unaccountable small explosions in the area and of "brown ooze" that clung to the legs of schoolchildren. The "ooze" and the smells became so bad that the school playground had to be placed off limits after heavy rains. Sump pumps in cellars began to corrode, and more ominously, pets began to die and several children were burned by the chemicals. The people gradually began to perceive that there seemed to be an unusually high occurrence among their neighbors of cancer, miscarriages, and children sick with intestinal and serious respiratory diseases. By 1978, more than 25 years after the toxic dump had been covered up, the residents (several thousand in number) suspected that their entire area, including the air, water, and even their homes, had been permeated with dangerous toxins. They were in peril and many hundreds of families had to abandon their homes. The disaster had enormous impact on the people's physical and psychological health as well as their financial conditions.

Levine (1982) and her students, using naturalistic methods, studied the Love Canal disaster. They used historical records and documents prepared by investigating committees, met with the residents, attended public meetings, communicated with state and federal officials and with groups of scientists appointed to study the problems, read newspaper reports, and monitored local television and radio broadcasts. Using this mass of observation Levine documented the disaster and its psychological, social, and financial impact on the people of the Love Canal neighborhood. Levine's study illuminates the social and psychological factors in this disaster and their personal impact on people. She examined the political and social interactions of the chemical company that had created the dump site, the government agencies involved, the people residing in the area, and the many scientists who had been involved in the disaster. Levine's investigation is a major sociological study with important implications for federal and state policy-making. Such a study could not have been carried out in any way other than through the use of naturalistic research methods.

Naturalistic methods are used in psychology; for example, in studies of human behavior in public places. Researchers have studied smoking and eating behavior in restaurants, drinking behavior in bars, drivers' behavior while at intersections, and so on. The social behavior of children on schoolgrounds or in class has been studied as well as that of shoppers in stores. There are many examples in the research literature; the interested student is encouraged to find and examine these reports.

A particularly interesting naturalistic study was carried out by David Rosenhan (1973) who investigated the use of psychiatric diagnoses and the experiences of mental patients in hospitals. Rosenhan asked eight "pseudopatients"—perfectly normal people—to admit themselves to various mental hospitals on their feigned complaints of hearing voices that said "thud," "hollow," and "empty." The pseudopatients were asked to display no other signs of mental disorder during their initial examination at the hospital, during their stay, or at their discharge. In fact, once they were admitted to the hospital, each patient was to behave in their normal manner and give no indication of their supposed hallucinations. During their hospital stays, the patients (actually Rosenhan's researchers) made observations of the hospital conditions, of their treatment, and of the staff and patients. Much like an anthropologist in a strange culture, each researcher made naturalistic observations and kept detailed notes on what they observed. The 8 researchers had been admitted to 12 different hospitals and, apparently, none of the hospitals' staff ever discerned that they were not real patients. In fact, the only people who did realize it were some of the other patients. In the Rosenhan study, the researchers, like anthropologists, were more than neutral observers; they were participant observers. Again, as in the Levine study, the use of naturalistic methods was not only appropriate for the investigation but was probably the best way to investigate the issue.

EXAMPLES OF CASE-STUDY RESEARCH

Like naturalistic research, case-study research falls on the low-constraint band of our continuum, and there is overlap of the two areas. Case studies focus on the subject's behavior with little influence or constraint forced on the subject by either the researcher or the setting. In case-study and naturalistic research, the investigator does not manipulate independent variables. Both research approaches utilize flexible observational methods in an effort to record the subject's natural behavior. Case-study research *is* naturalistic research but with somewhat more constraint imposed on the procedures. What are those constraints? First, case studies are not typically carried out in natural environments but in special settings in which the researcher does intervene somewhat. Secondly, case-study research is typically focused on individuals. Finally, case-study research usually looks at limited classes of behavior rather than being interested in the total context and natural flow of behavior. Thus, we can see that case studies, by imposing a few constraints, narrow the focus somewhat but retain their essential interest in subjects' natural behavior.

Probably the most widely known example of case-study research is that carried out by Sigmund Freud. Beginning in the late nineteenth century, Freud accumulated a mass of observation from which he eventually formulated psychoanalytic theory and clinical treatment procedures. His method was to interview patients intensively, not in the natural environment but in the mild constraints of his office. Although Freud worked almost completely outside of the mainstream of academic psychology, his impact on the field has been enormous. Specifically, Freud was one of several investigators who countered the dominant focus of early psychology on laboratory experimentation of adult human consciousness. Freud and his many followers believed their clinical observations were more useful than laboratory observations in studying the highly subjective events that seemed to be critical in the understanding of the psychological dysfunction of their clients.

Freud's work had an enormous impact on the early psychology of consciousness. Freud popularized an alternative to the psychology of consciousness in which he focused on the psychology of unconscious processes. Also, more than any other person, Freud established case-study methods in psychology as a major way of studying human subjective phenomena. Both influences were not only substantial at their time but have endured, continuing to be powerfully evident even today.

Freud's case-study methods consisted of interviews with his patients in which they free-associated, allowing their thinking free reign. The patients told of their early lives, their dreams, their fears, their current and past fantasies, and so on. From this mass of verbal behavior—obtained over many years and from many patients—Freud began to see patterns in his work, much as Darwin had in his observations. Freud observed the verbal behavior and drew inferences about clients' subjective functioning.

These inferences eventually were integrated into his psychoanalytic theory and techniques.

Another early proponent of the case-study method was a psychologist, E. L. Witmer, who had studied with Wundt in Germany. In 1896, Witmer began teaching at the University of Pennsylvania where he founded the first psychological clinic. (See Brotemarkle, 1966; Boring, 1950.) His clinic treated children with learning and behavioral problems. Witmer used careful medical and psychological examinations of each child in an effort to determine whether the child's problems were due to some brain pathology or to inadequate teaching and learning. He developed a treatment-educational approach to children, which became known as psychoeducation and applied psychological procedures, many based on those used in the laboratory in a highly individualized, intense, single-case study method that he called the new "clinical psychology."

Jean Piaget's work provides us with another example of the use of case-study methods in research. Both Freud and Witmer used case-study methods to provide services to individuals with psychological problems and to serve as a basis for inferences about human psychological functioning in general. Piaget's case-study methods, on the other hand, were completely aimed at research and he was not particularly interested in abnormal conditions. He was interested in gaining knowledge about children's normal cognitive development.

Studying one child at a time in informal settings, Piaget asked questions and presented tasks to the children and observed how they answered. He did not follow any carefully detailed set of procedures. Rather, he left the procedures quite flexible, taking advantage of ideas or observations that occurred during the interviews to alter the methods or follow up on something new the child might have said or done. Piaget did impose some mild constraints. The interviews were usually carried out in simplified settings where there would be little interference. The tasks themselves, although presented in a nonstandardized manner, did serve as stimuli that were controlled by Piaget and to which the child responded. The child's responses, both verbal and motor, were then observed by Piaget. The degree of constraint was somewhat more than that found in naturalistic observation studies and was consistent with case-study methods.

Based on his observations of children, Piaget developed inferences about intellectual functioning at different ages and about cognitive development in children. Many of Piaget's concepts have been examined in higher constraint research by other psychologists, with a good degree of support being found for many of the ideas. Piaget's flexible case-study methodology resulted in important knowledge about children's intellectual development and, as many writers have pointed out, might not have been arrived at if Piaget had insisted on high-constraint, experimental research.

By now it should be apparent that low-constraint naturalistic and case-study research can be valuable when used appropriately. Low-constraint research, when done well, should not be thought of as merely sloppy research; it has its uses and must be carried out as carefully as any level of research. To demonstrate this we need to discuss further the conditions under which low-constraint research should and should not be used, the kinds of information it can generate, and its strengths and weaknesses, along with some of the issues and procedures involved in carrying out low-constraint research.

THE VALUE OF LOW-CONSTRAINT METHODS

Conditions for Using Low-Constraint Research

From the examples given earlier, we can begin to see the conditions under which low-constraint research can be useful. Obviously, when the question concerns the natural flow of behavior in natural settings, then low-constraint observational research is appropriate. For example, if we are interested in studying the peak hours of aircraft take-offs and landings at an airport, or the flow of traffic in certain kinds of intersections, or the pattern of seating in theaters, or the flow of events in a disaster or crisis, or the relative amounts of positive and negative feedback given to students by teachers in a typical day—then the best methods will involve direct observations of those events as they occur in their natural settings.

Another condition under which low-constraint research is appropriate is at the beginning stages of research in a new area. For example, it seems fairly certain that adults can organize their behavior with reference to time, but how well do young children do so? The researcher might be well advised to begin studying this question at a low-constraint level by observing young children in some normal setting, such as a nursery school or playground. By doing so, the researcher might be able to develop some ideas or hypotheses for higher constraint research. Thus, low-constraint research is useful in new areas to generate ideas for further, presumably higher constraint, research. Naturalistic observation is also an excellent way for researchers to familiarize themselves with subjects or settings that are new to them, although not a new research area. For example, you might be interested in replicating or extending some part of Piaget's work on conservation of shape in young children. It may be that you know the previous research and the concepts and procedures but have had little experience working with young children as subjects. It would be useful for you to spend a few hours familiarizing yourself with young children by observing a nursery-school class.

Low-constraint procedures also can be used to demonstrate a new research or treatment technique. Here the only question is whether the technique is feasible. The researcher is not attempting to test a prediction or develop new hypotheses but only to see whether some method can be carried out.

An often overlooked use for case-study and naturalistic research is their potential contributions to *generalizability* of research findings. This is a problem faced constantly by psychologists who conduct most or all of their research in highly constrained laboratory settings. The advantages of laboratory research are enormous, and it is therefore not surprising that so much laboratory research is conducted. But a problem with such research is that we are never really sure that the behavior we see in the laboratory is representative of the behavior we would see in the natural environment. Naturalistic research methods, and to some degree case-study research, can be used to test the generalizability of the theories developed or refined on the basis of laboratory studies. Any laws of behavior that are generalizable to other settings must be able to make accurate predictions in those settings. The most useful laws of behavior are those that predict behavior in natural environments. Thus, naturalistic observation is not only useful in the early stages of research on a particular topic but can also be helpful in establishing the generalizability of findings during the more mature stages of behavioral research.

The most common justification for case-study research is the situation where the question being asked concerns the specific individual or case who is the object of the study, such as when psychological tests are administered to a client to learn more about that particular person. Under such conditions there is no concern for developing inferences and concepts that can be generalized to a population, as is the case in high-constraint research. (See Box 6.1.)

A final point should be made: naturalistic and case-study observation procedures constitute low-constraint research, but the observational methods might nevertheless employ highly sophisticated instrumentation. In the naturalistic observation of the rare bird in its habitat, for example, the investigator might have used the most advanced, lightweight, portable equipment, including telephoto lenses and highly sensitive microphones. In case-study research we might employ computerized psychophysiological testing equipment. The research is still naturalistic or a case study; the technological equipment does not define the level of constraint.

Information Gained from Low-Constraint Research

Naturalistic and case-study research can give us only certain kinds of information. First, observation of relatively unconstrained subjects can give us new, descriptive information. For example, Goodall (1978) reported her observations that one group of chimpanzees in the wild attacked and killed another group. This was the first observation of anything that resembles warfare among chimpanzees, and as such, it is new information. These observations cannot explain the event or tell us what caused it or whether it is a commonly occurring behavior among chimpanzees. But, Goodall's observations did establish a new fact never before observed.

Evidence from low-constraint, naturalistic, and case-study research can be used to negate a general proposition. Suppose that prior to Goodall's observation some naturalist had stated the general proposition that "chimpanzees are known to act aggressively toward each other in individual conflicts, but they do not engage in any concerted or group aggression resembling warfare seen in certain insects and in man." Quite obviously, Goodall's observations show that this general proposition is incorrect; she observed at least some chimpanzees engaging in warlike behavior. Another example involves the statement, "man's superiority over other creatures is due to the fact that man is the only tool-making and tool-using animal." Again the naturalistic observations of Goodall effectively refute this general proposition. She observed chimpanzees select and pull twigs from a bush or tree and strip off the leaves so as to fashion a slender, tapering, flexible rod. The chimps then carefully inserted the twig into a termite nest, waited a moment, then withdrew the twig and licked off the termites clinging to it. This was not accidental behavior; it was purposeful, smooth, and was repeated. The chimpanzees not only selected but modified a natural object, preparing it for use as a food-gathering tool.

A final example involves some of our early research with autistic children (Graziano & Kean, 1968). Psychologists who had pioneered in the use of relaxation in

Box 6.1 THE THERAPIST AS SCIENTIST

The case-study method of research is a powerful tool that can be used in settings not normally thought of as research. For example, the therapist is faced in clinical practice with the constant problem of gathering information. But more than simple information gathering is required; the therapist is constantly trying to generate hypotheses about the reasons for the behavior of the client and ways in which problem behaviors can be modified, reduced, or replaced. This process is a part of therapy whether the therapist is a classic psychoanalyst, a behavior therapist, or any other kind of therapist. Although there is a certain amount of art to therapy and interpersonal contact is a critical part of any therapy, the effective use of research methods, especially methods of inference, can greatly improve the effectiveness of a therapist. The phases of research presented in Chapter 2 are equally applicable to the therapy session. The therapist is faced with a variety of information about the client. From that information and the theoretical biases of the therapist, the therapist generates ideas about what problems the client possesses, how the problems developed, and how they might be corrected. The usual situation is vague, allowing several possible ideas to be developed. These raw ideas are then translated into specific hypotheses by the clinician and plans for testing the hypotheses are developed. The observation phase of research may be no more than asking the client a specific question or it may involve closely observing how the client responds to particular actions by the therapist or others. The analysis phase relies less on statistics and more on logic and the analysis and interpretation phases are difficult to separate. Most therapists record their observations in some sort of progress notes so that the information will be readily available to them or to other clinicians who might work with the client at some later point in time. The important point to note here is that a clinician, in gathering the information necessary for treatment planning, is operating much like a research scientist. It is probably no accident that the most widely accepted model for the training of a clinical psychologist is the *scientist-practitioner model*. Understanding the way scientists gather information and draw conclusions can sharpen the clinician's skills in information gathering and treatment planning.

behavior therapy had noted that neither children nor psychotic people, including autistic children, could be taught relaxation. Ignoring the general proposition, we succeeded in training four autistic children in relaxation skills, procedures that have been repeated many times with other children. This research was low constraint with no experimental controls and only four subjects. However, as with the observations in the naturalistic research noted above, this case study successfully negated the general proposition that children cannot be taught relaxation skills.

We see then that low-constraint research can negate a general proposition, but can it establish one? The answer is no, it cannot. We cannot conclude from Goodall's observations that chimps, in general, engage in warfare; or from the Graziano and Kean study that autistic children, in general, can be taught relaxation skills. We do not know whether those single observations are truly representative or whether they were one-shot phenomena. This limitation in representativeness is related to issues of sampling, which we will discuss in more detail later in this chapter and again in Chapter 9.

Another important kind of information provided by naturalistic and case-study research involves observations about the relationships among variables. All research seeks to identify and understand relationships among variables. The type of relationship among variables that is studied varies from one level of constraint to another. In experimental research we apply systematic controls and we manipulate variables so that we can identify causal relationships among variables. In low-constraint research, however, such causal inferences cannot be made. Nevertheless, we can obtain other useful information about relationships among variables in low-constraint research. For example, in case-study research with autistic children (Graziano & Kean, 1968), we had noted a sudden, momentary but observable change in the children's behavior immediately prior to one of their severe disruptive outbursts. Repeated observations led to the idea that when that behavior occurs, it will most likely be followed by the disruptive outbursts; when X occurs, then Y will probably occur. Note that this does not state that X causes Y but only that there is a high probability of one occurring when the other is present. It is a statement of probability, and it helps to identify and describe a relationship between two variables. An example from naturalistic research is Niko Tinbergen's (1951, 1963) observation that the parent herring gull readily provides food for its chick when the young bird pecks on or near a particular spot on the adult's bill. The chick's pecking is a stimulus for the parent's feeding behavior; further, a red spot on the parent's bill seems to be a stimulus for the chick's pecking behavior. When the young bird pecks on the parent's bill there is a high probability that the parent will provide food. As another example, suppose you are observing the aggressive behavior of kindergarten boys in a naturalistic manner and you note that the aggressive behavior seems to increase sharply as soon as the dismissal bell rings: when the bell rings the aggressive behavior becomes more probable.

In the above examples the relationship among the variables is one of probability; given X, then Y is highly probable. This kind of relationship is referred to as a *contingency;* feeding seems contingent on pecking; pecking seems contingent on the presence of a red spot; disruptive behavior seems contingent on muscular tension; aggressive behavior seems contingent on the dismissal bell. Naturalistic and case-study research can reveal many such contingent relationships among observed variables, and these contingencies can then become the bases for higher constraint research. This is exactly what Tinbergen did once he noticed the contingent relationship between the chick's pecking and the adult's feeding behavior. Having made the observation in relatively uncontrolled situations, actual experimentation was later carried out in which conditions were systematically varied to gain more information. Contingent relationships that are observed in low-constraint research can be extremely valuable bases for hypotheses and higher constraint research, which is one of the major values of low-constraint research. An advantage of both naturalistic and case-study research is that they can be carried out in a flexible manner. Unlike the formal, high-constraint experiment, the researcher in low-constraint studies is free to vary procedures during the study, changing the focus on the basis of the obtained data or the changing interests of the researcher.

To summarize, then, low-constraint naturalistic and case-study research is *not* necessarily poor research. It is useful and sometimes the only way to proceed, and it can yield important information when used carefully and appropriately. In general, low-constraint research is appropriate for low-constraint questions; questions about unconstrained behavior in natural settings. Some of the conditions under which we can best use low-constraint research are:

1. When we are beginning to investigate a new area in which little information is available.
2. When the researcher wishes to gain familiarity with typical characteristics of settings or subjects before planning high-constraint research for similar settings or subjects.
3. When the questions asked specifically focus on the natural flow of behavior and/or on the behavior in the natural environment.
4. When the study is of a single individual, group, or set of events, and the questions are specifically about those particular people, settings, or events.
5. For demonstrations or illustrations, such as demonstrating a new procedure.
6. As a way of discovering contingencies that can then be used as a basis for higher constraint questions and research.
7. When, on completing high-constraint research, we might want to know if the relationships we have discovered and demonstrated under laboratory conditions hold true for behavior in the natural environment.

Further, naturalistic and case-study research can provide:

1. Description of events, including events never before observed.
2. Identification of contingent relationships among variables.
3. Bases for hypotheses to be used in higher constraint research.
4. Observations to negate general propositions.

However, low-constraint research cannot establish general propositions or causal inferences.

PROBLEM STATEMENTS AND HYPOTHESES IN NATURALISTIC AND CASE-STUDY RESEARCH

In Chapter 3 we noted the importance of developing a statement of the problem for each research project. Although problem statements and their ultimate development into one or more research hypotheses are most formalized and best developed at the experimental level of constraint, they represent important steps in the research design process at *all* levels of constraint. Problem statements help us to organize our thinking, to specify how we are going to carry out our research, and to focus on the kinds of inferences we can confidently make based on data obtained in the research. The inferences we are able to make with confidence are different at different constraint levels: at the experimental level problem statements and research hypotheses are focused on questions of causality; in differential studies they are focused on determining differences between groups; at the correlational level they are focused on the direction and strength of relationships between two or more variables; at the naturalistic and case-study levels problem statements and research hypotheses are focused on identifying contingencies (i.e., on what variables seem to go together). Research hypotheses can be tested at any level of constraint, but research hypotheses concerning causality can be tested with confidence only at the experimental level where the most complete controls are applied.

It is often tempting to try to draw causal inferences from low-constraint research when we observe some clear contingency in which variable *Y* seems to occur whenever we also observe variable *X.* But as we have emphasized here and will discuss again later in this chapter, *we cannot confidently draw causal inferences from low-constraint research.*

USING NATURALISTIC AND CASE-STUDY METHODS

As mentioned earlier, the central phase of any research project is the observational or data-gathering phase. This is especially true in the naturalistic and case-study methods. In some of the higher constraint research, before we do any observation, we make detailed and highly specific plans of how to observe and record the data and how to analyze the data once it has been collected. In lower constraint research methods planning is much less formal and plans are much more fluid. The researcher is free to change hypotheses and modify procedures in the middle of the observations. It is not unusual, for example, for the observer conducting naturalistic and case-study research to design a whole new ministudy based on some of the initial observations made by the researcher.

Making Observations

There are two ways the researcher can choose to make observations in naturalistic research: as an unobtrusive observer or as a participant observer. As an *unobtrusive observer,* the researcher tries to avoid responding in any way to the subject who is under observation. In other situations the investigator may choose to become a *participant observer* and modify his or her own behavior and become a part of the environment being observed. Here the scientist who is observing the situation is also very much a part of the situation and, in some ways, contributes to it. The contribution might be the normal contribution that almost anyone would make in that situation or it might be carefully planned and executed changes in the researcher's behavior as a way of tentatively testing specific hypotheses that the researcher has generated. The work of Dr. Levine mentioned earlier utilized participant observation in some aspects of her study of the Homeowners' Association during the Love Canal crisis.

One advantage of participant observation is that by actually manipulating your own behavior as an observer, you are able to test some hypotheses by creating some situations that are unlikely to occur naturally. The case-study method often uses participant observation. For example, Piaget did not passively observe children. Instead, he asked questions, created test situations, interacted with the children, and observed their responses. Another advantage of the participant observer method is that it often makes the observer less obtrusive and in so doing can reduce the likelihood that the observer will influence the subject to behave in particular ways. The term *measurement reactivity* refers to the phenomenon of subjects behaving differently than they might normally because they know they are being observed. Some measures *(reactive measures)* are particularly prone to such distortions, while other measures *(nonreactive measures)* are not affected by the subjects' knowledge that they are being observed. Measurement reactivity is not unique to social science research. In physics, for example, simply measuring the movement of an electron changes the motion of that electron so that a physicist is never actually capable of observing continuously the motion of so small a particle. In psychology and other social sciences, the reactivity is often a function of what the subject believes is the appropriate behavior in that particular situation. All of us have a tendency to behave in ways we think are appropriate when we know we are being observed. How much more likely is it that you will use a fork and a knife to eat your chicken if you are dining in a restaurant than if you are eating that chicken at home in front of the television with no one else present?

The problem of reactivity in social science research has spawned a variety of interesting concepts, the best known of which is the unobtrusive measure. *Unobtrusive measures* are measures of a person's behavior that are not obvious to the person being observed and, consequently, are less likely to influence the person to behave in particular ways. Webb, Campbell, Schwartz, and Sechrest (1966) describe a number of clever ways of measuring a phenomenon without appearing to measure it. Some of the measures they describe are designed to provide information about phenomena that have already occurred. These *archival records* are often readily available in libraries, schools, or town halls. They may include school records, marriage and divorce records, driving records, or even general census data. Many of the records are protected from unlawful use even by well-intentioned researchers.

It might appear that simply using archival records, records that already exist, is a sloppy way to measure a phenomenon. But that need not be the case. Some of the most sophisticated research studies on the genetic influences in psychopathology were essentially archival studies (Kety, Rosenthal, Wender, & Schulsinger, 1968; Wender, Kety, Rosenthal, Schulsinger, Ortmann, & Lunde, 1986). These investigators used records from a variety of sources to track the rates of psychopathology in both the adoptive and biological families of severely disturbed adults who were adopted as infants.

National governments gather archival data routinely to identify nationwide problems quickly. Statistics computed from such archival data, such as the "Index of Leading Economic Indicators," can be accurate predictors of future events. Data gathered from hospitals about the diseases under treatment have allowed government officials to identify new diseases like Toxic Shock Syndrome or AIDS and isolate the probable causes of the diseases. The key to the effectiveness of any use of archival data is the quality of the data itself and the degree of relevance of the data to the question being asked.

Archival records are only one type of unobtrusive measure available to psychological researchers. Webb et al. (1966) describe several clever ways of measuring constructs of interest to the psychologist. For example, suppose you want to measure the level of interest of particular museum exhibits. You first need some sort of operational definition of *interesting*. (Remember from Chapter 4 that an operational definition is a statement of the procedures or operations that the investigator will perform to measure a specified variable.) One operational definition of *interesting* is the average of many people's interest ratings. You might ask each of the first 200 people who walked by the exhibit to rate how interesting it is on a 10-point scale. Such a measure would hardly be unobtrusive because each subject would be well aware that something about them— their level of interest in an exhibit—is being measured. The measure would therefore have the potential for being reactive because subjects may behave differently because they know they are being measured.

An alternate operational definition of the level of interest is the number of people who choose to view a particular exhibit. We could measure this in many different ways. One way might be to ask each person who viewed an exhibit to sign a log. Such a measure would be obtrusive and the person would know that something about them (their presence) was being recorded. A less obtrusive measure would involve having someone who is standing off to the side count the number of people who approach the exhibit. One advantage of having an observer do the counting is that the observer can code other information, such as how long people observed the exhibit, the subject's sex, approximate age, and so on. We could automate the counting procedure by using an electric eye and an electronic counter. But there are also simpler yet equally effective measures that might give us the information we desire. One procedure suggested by Webb et al. (1966) is to note the degree of wear on the tiles of the floor surrounding the exhibit. The tiles around very popular exhibits have to be replaced every few weeks, whereas the tiles around other exhibits will last for several years. Another clever method suggested by Webb et al. is the nose-print approach. In this approach, the exhibit is put in a glass display and arranged so that people can get the best view by putting their faces right up to the glass. The glass is cleaned at the start of each day. At day's end the glass is dusted with the same powder police use to dust for fingerprints. The number of nose prints is then counted. Of course, not everyone will leave a nose print, and some people will press their nose to the glass in several places, so this method will not give us an accurate count of how many people viewed the display. But remember, this is not what we wanted to measure anyway. We want to measure how "interesting" the exhibit is, and the number of people who viewed the exhibit is an operational definition of that interest. The number of nose prints is an equally reasonable operational definition of interest level and may in some ways be superior to our head-count method.

The above suggestions are not intended to be specific suggestions for research measures. Instead, the examples are designed to get you to think more creatively when you develop your own measures. There is nothing wrong with asking people to rate museum exhibits on how interesting they are, but it is often valuable to get some independent data to substantiate the ratings.

Ethical Issues

Research ethics is an important issue when using unobtrusive measures. A basic ethical principle is the concept of informed consent. Each potential subject in a research study should be made aware of the procedures of the study in order to make an informed decision. The principle is not absolute, however. If it were, unobtrusive measures could never be used. But for a research scientist to justify unobtrusive measures in a study, the researcher must show that nondeceptive measures would not work. The investigator must also show that no significant risk of harm (including embarrassment) would result from use of the measure. Note that these are judgments and are not easy ones to make. As mentioned earlier, this is one of the reasons for having a formal review process of all studies using human subjects.

Sampling of Subjects

It should be clear now that deciding on the best way to observe subjects is an important matter. An equally demanding task is to decide what subjects will be observed. We use the term *sampling* to refer to the selection of subjects. Sampling is important to any kind of research study but is particularly important in higher constraint research. (We will discuss sampling in much more detail in Chapter 9.) The issue of sampling that we need to understand now is the concept of *representativeness* and its relationship to generalizability.

In naturalistic and case-study research sampling is often not much of an issue, for in many cases we do not actually select the sample of subjects for study. If we are psychotherapy researchers, the clients who come to us for treatment constitute the sample. If we are investigating behavior of human beings during a natural disaster, the people unfortunate enough to be present when the disaster occurs represent the sample. In both cases, however, we must address the question of how representative the samples are of the broader population. In the psychotherapy example we might expect that people who come to a therapist for help may well be different from people in general. They probably have more psychological problems and are more concerned with those problems than is the typical person. They may be wealthier than the typical person since they can afford the cost of psychotherapy or have insurance that will cover the cost. To the extent that there are differences between the sample and the general population, the sample is said to be unrepresentative of the population. Whenever a sample is not representative of the general population, we must be very careful in generalizing the findings. *We generalize the findings when we assume that what we observed in the sample of subjects would also be observed in any other group of subjects from the population.* We want to be able to generalize the findings, but we can do that only if the sample is truly representative of the population in which we are interested. In our psychotherapy example, suppose we found that all of the male clients expressed hatred for their mothers. Could we then conclude that all men hate their mothers? We certainly could not because the sample is not representative of all men. It may be that men who hate their mothers are more likely to develop psychological problems or that people with psychological problems tend to hate their mothers. Could we generalize the findings to a more narrow population? Could we conclude that all men who have psychological problems hate their mothers? We cannot even draw that conclusion safely because there may be many people with psychological problems who do not seek therapy and who may be different from those people who do.

In most case-study and naturalistic research we do not usually have the opportunity to select our own samples. Therefore, we must make some judgment of how well the sample represents the population to which we want to generalize the results. The more representative of the population a sample is, the more confident we can be in making generalizations. However, with low-constraint research we should always be cautious in making generalizations. We should think of such generalizations as tentative hypotheses that can be tested with higher constraint research methods. As we will see later in the text, when we are allowed to control the sampling procedures, we can almost guarantee the representativeness of the sample.

Sampling of Situations

The sampling of situations also can affect generalizability. Suppose, for example, we want to study work habits. As part of the study, we install a television camera to monitor employees' behavior. From the previous section's discussion we know that the presence of the camera may be reactive; that is, the subjects may behave differently because they know they are being watched. But we can view this same problem from another perspective, that of sampling. Our sample of behaviors comes from a situation that is different from the situations to which we want to generalize (i.e., the typical factory). Because closed circuit TV is not used to monitor employees in most factory settings, this situation is not representative of the population of settings to which we wish to generalize our results, and so we cannot generalize our findings with confidence.

The sample of situations can be distorted in numerous ways. Some variables are beyond our control and others can be controlled only at great cost or inconvenience. Suppose we want to study animals in the wild. Many animals behave differently during different seasons of the year, being active during some seasons and inactive during other seasons. Most animals show the same kind of fluctuations in activity level on a daily basis. If we observe the animals only during the morning hours of spring and summer because these were convenient and comfortable times to make such observations, we might get a distorted picture of the behavior of the animals under study. An even worse violation of this principle would be to study only animals in zoos because they are close and easy to find. The situation in even the best of zoos is dramatically different from the natural environment to which we want to generalize our findings. Therefore, a good rule of thumb in early study of any population is to sample as widely as possible the many situations the subjects are likely to face in their daily existence. The broader the sample of situations studied and the broader the sample of subjects, the more confidence we can have in the generalizability of the findings.

Sampling of Behaviors

A related issue is the importance of adequately sampling behaviors within any given situation. In any particular situation, organisms may behave in many different ways. Therefore, a single observation of behavior in a particular situation could lead to an incorrect conclusion about how the organism behaves in that setting. However, by sampling behaviors repeatedly in each situation, it is possible to identify whatever behavioral variability actually occurs.

EVALUATING AND INTERPRETING DATA

Once observations are made and data are gathered, we need to evaluate and interpret the results of the study. This step usually involves statistical analyses. In many low-constraint studies direct statistical analysis is not possible until some coding of the data is accomplished. In low-constraint studies we often observe and record everything that happens. The data set might be a verbal description of everything we observed or it might be a video- or audiotape of the action. For example, if we were studying the process of labor contract negotiation, the data set might be the transcripts of all negotiation sessions. In analyzing the data we might code the interactions in terms of categories such as hostile comments, request for information, suggested solution, and so forth. Dean Pruitt and his colleagues (Kimmel, Pruitt, Magenau, Konar-Goldband, & Carnevale, 1980; Pruitt & Lewis, 1975; Schulz & Pruitt, 1978) have used similar categories in a series of studies of the negotiation process. Once the data have been coded, we can count up the numbers of each type of interaction. For lower constraint studies the statistical procedures used may be no more complicated than means and standard deviations or simple frequency counts. There may be some natural comparisons to be made, such as between different groups of subjects or among the same subjects under more than one condition. In the above example, we might want to compare the verbal statements of the labor and management negotiators, or the negotiation sessions that were fruitful with sessions that were not. If such comparisons are needed, we would use the appropriate inferential statistic. (Procedures for selecting the appropriate statistical test are reviewed in Chapter 14.)

Regardless of the statistical procedures used it is important to realize that *we must be cautious* when interpreting the data from a low-constraint research study. By its very nature low-constraint research employs few controls. The purpose of control is to eliminate alternative explanations for results, making it easier to draw a single strong conclusion. Because those controls are absent from this level of constraint, we will seldom be able to draw strong conclusions from a low-constraint study. Further, these limitations cannot be corrected by applying sophisticated statistical analyses. *No statistical analysis will create the controls that were not part of the original study.*

LIMITATIONS OF NATURALISTIC AND CASE-STUDY METHODS

We have noted the positive values of low-constraint research. But it also has limitations. Consider some of the limitations of one example already given, Freud's psychoanalytic theory and the observational methods on which it is based. Freud's case-study methods exemplified so well many of the strengths and weaknesses associated with this level of research. As noted earlier, psychoanalytic theory has had a powerful influence on many disciplines. Psychoanalytic ideas generated by Freud and his early followers have had creative, heuristic impact on many areas of research. Today, half a century after Freud's death and a full century since his early work, researchers are still investigating his concepts and methods. There are, however, some weaknesses in the research on which psychoanalytic theory is based, many of which have yet to be corrected.

Poor Representativeness

One of the major weaknesses in the use of low-constraint methods is its poor representativeness. Recall that an appropriate use of low-constraint research is in answering questions about the particular group or person being studied. The conclusions in low-constraint studies almost always must be limited to those individuals who are directly studied and cannot be generalized to a wider population. But Freud drew inferences from his limited sample, which were presented and accepted as universally applicable to all people of all ages in all cultures and across all time. The phrase *sweeping generalization* certainly applies here. Freud studied only an extremely limited sample of adult, neurotic, well-to-do, turn-of-the-century Europeans and he rarely, if ever, directly studied children. The unwarranted overgeneralizations led, for example, to the remarkable situation where psychoanalytic theory was enthusiastically accepted by many professionals as the major and most definitive theory of child development, even though Freud never directly treated a child during the development of the theory. If psychoanalytic theory is to be generalized to all children, then a sample of children who adequately represent the population must be studied. Indeed, more recent psychoanalytic investigators have tried to do this and the late Anna Freud's work, for example, focused primarily on children. But even in Anna Freud's work, her low-constraint case studies of children do not allow us to generalize the findings beyond the individuals studied unless they have been carefully selected as representative samples. We do not know, for example, how Freud's patients might have been different from people in general. They may have been more troubled than most people because they sought psychological help, or they may have been simply more willing to seek psychological help. We know they were more wealthy because they could afford treatment. (There were no insurance reimbursements at the time.) Any clinical sample, including Freud's, is going to be a biased rather than a representative sample because the subjects have selected themselves for therapy and not every person in the population is equally likely to seek therapy. Therefore, generalization of findings from clinical samples to any group other than those who seek therapy is unwarranted without additional research with representative samples. (See Box 6.2.)

Poor Replicability

Another limitation of low-constraint research is related to the very characteristic that gives it its greatest strength—flexibility. Because observations of naturally occurring behavior are made in settings where the observer has imposed few if any constraints on the behavior of the subject, it is often difficult to replicate (repeat) such research. Different investigators studying the same phenomenon through low-constraint methods will probably make different observations and different inferences. In order for *replication* to be possible, the researchers must clearly state all details of their procedures. Freud, for example, never made his methods of observation and inference explicit, so it is impossible to replicate them. In addition, Freud published a total of only six psychoanalytic case studies (two of which were not his own cases). This is another weakness because the small number of cases cannot adequately represent the true variability among human beings. Many more cases would be necessary.

Causal Inference and Low-Constraint Research: The *Ex Post Facto* Fallacy

As mentioned earlier, drawing causal inferences from case studies is virtually impossible. Freud listened to his clients talk about their subjective experiences. He noted that

Box 6.2 FOR WHAT IS A SCIENTIST REMEMBERED?

A scientist is not always remembered only for research. Sometimes the ideas of a scientist can capture the imaginations of many people in many areas, even though the level of research support for these ideas is quite minimal. The work of Sigmund Freud and E. L. Witmer provides an interesting contrast for those students interested in studying the sociology of science.

Freud and Witmer were contemporaries. Both men, working in the early 1900s, emphasized and developed case-study methods applied to services for people with psychological problems. Both pushed their colleagues to seek new directions and applications in their professions. They also contrasted sharply. Whereas Freud worked with adults and never directly studied or worked with children, Witmer focused his clinical work almost exclusively on children. Freud based his inferences on his clients' verbal self-reports; Witmer included self-reports but also used more objective medical and psychological testing approaches. Freud never went beyond the clients' self-reports for any corroborating evidence; Witmer sought information from parents, teachers, and others to provide some degree of external validation for his inferences. Freud worked with individual adults, virtually all of whom were well-to-do; Witmer worked with individual children across all social classes and had an additional and apparently quite intense concern for social conditions as well as issues of individual psychology.

Thus, both men emphasized the development of case-study methods, but Witmer did so at what appears now to have been a more scientifically sophisticated level than Freud. Given the apparent superiority of Witmer's work, the final comparison leaves us with a puzzle: Freud's influence on anthropology, drama, literature, psychiatry, psychology, social work, sociology, and on popular culture generally has been enormous and sustained; Witmer is ordinarily accorded a footnote here and there. We will not attempt to solve this puzzle here—perhaps some interested student might do some research (low-constraint, historical research, of course) and shed some light on the puzzle.

certain past experiences seemed to be associated with current functioning in certain ways, and he drew *causal inferences* about these relationships (i.e., specific past experiences helped to bring about or cause current problems). *Ex post facto* ("after the fact") reasoning is a major part of Freud's research approach; he observed events after the fact, such as current neurotic symptoms, and then searched the client's reported history for clues about what earlier events might be causally related. This type of speculative and tentative identification of contingencies is useful in suggesting hypothetical relationships. However, as a research approach it does not provide the controls needed to rule out the possibility that other factors may have influenced the observed symptoms, and so we cannot properly state that we have demonstrated a causal relationship.

Case studies are by their nature *ex post facto* approaches lacking control over independent variables and unable to rule out the possible effects of other variables. It is because of this that we cannot have confidence in any causal inference we might be tempted to draw. Such inferences must be treated as no more than speculative hypotheses for further research. For that purpose—generating higher constraint research—case-study methods can be useful.

The *ex post facto* fallacy is a common and serious error because it can mislead investigators into severe misinterpretation of data. Some common examples of *ex post facto* fallacies follow. You should note the logical fallacy is obvious in some of the statements, whereas other, exactly parallel statements seem quite reasonable. There may even be some assertions in the list that you have heard many times before and may have accepted without giving them much thought.

1. "Hard drug users all smoked marijuana before turning to hard drugs; therefore, marijuana use leads to hard drug addiction."
2. "Alcoholics started with beer and wine; therefore, beer and wine lead to alcoholism."
3. "Child-abusing parents were abused themselves as children; therefore, being abused as a child leads to becoming an abusive parent."
4. "Most of the inmates in urban jails are black; therefore, being black leads to crime."
5. "Nearly all institutionalized juvenile delinquents are from urban backgrounds; therefore, growing up in cities leads to juvenile delinquency."
6. "Aggressive children watch a great deal of television; therefore, watching a great deal of television leads to aggressive behavior in children."

If each of the above statements is taken as a speculative hypothesis rather than a confident statement of causality, then they can be useful for further research. In this case we view them as tentative statements to be tested rather than already established conclusions. When we interpret and use low-constraint results as if they were equivalent to high-constraint research results, we not only draw conclusions that are likely to be false but we might also damage the credibility of other research, even well-designed high-constraint research.

Limitations of the Observer

Another issue in low-constraint research concerns the limitations of the observer. When Freud listened to his clients, were they giving spontaneous verbalizations or were they saying what they thought Freud wanted to hear? Did he influence their verbalizing, perhaps by emitting an interested "mm hmm" whenever the client touched on some sexual fantasy? The issue is one of *experimenter reactivity* or *experimenter bias* (Rosenthal, 1976). To obtain natural behavior the observer must be noninvolved. In case studies it is difficult for observers to control their own reactivity, to control the many possible subtle influences they might have on the subject. In higher constraint research controls can be used to minimize the observer's possible reactivity, which might influence the results.

It is important for researchers to understand the limitations of low-constraint methods. Knowing the limitations will allow us to use the methods appropriately, as in studying particular individuals or in generating hypotheses for further research. When used appropriately, naturalistic and case-study methods can be extremely useful. The dangers are more in our temptations to infer causality erroneously, to generalize beyond the subjects studied, to consider the finding certain rather than tentative, and to fail to recognize how the observer may be reactive, therefore influencing the behavior of the subjects. These and other limitations are adequately dealt with in higher constraint research by the careful addition of various controls. With controls in place we are able to use high-constraint experimental research as a basis for making causal inferences and for generalizing the results from the research subjects (sample) to the larger group (population).

SUMMARY

In naturalistic and case-study research little constraint is placed on the behavior of subjects. Although the behavior of the observer may be tightly constrained by the observational techniques employed, it need not be by these methods. In fact, one of the biggest advantages of lower constraint research methods is the flexibility they allow the researcher.

The most common error in interpreting low-constraint research is to overinterpret the results; either to generalize the results to a broader population than actually sampled in the study or to draw a causal inference from the observed relationships in the study. Even though we cannot easily generalize to other populations or draw causal inferences, naturalistic and case-study methods can provide useful information. These methods can help us describe events not previously observed. They can inform us about relationships and contingencies. We can then speculate about the causal bases of these relationships and test those speculations with higher constraint research methods. And, finally, they can negate a general proposition if an appropriate counterexample can be observed. Some kinds of research can be done only with naturalistic research methods, such as when we study the unconstrained behavior of subjects in their natural surroundings.

The key issue in low-constraint research is the observation of behavior. Whether that observation is made with only our senses or highly sophisticated equipment, the same general principles apply. We should make observations in ways that will allow us to generalize to the population of interest. The way the measures are taken will influence the validity of the data. Neither the actions of the researcher nor the process of measurement should affect the behavior of subjects if we want to measure validly their natural behavior. As with any research project, ethical issues in low-constraint research are important and must be considered carefully during every phase of the study.

REVIEW EXERCISES

I. Define the following key terms. Be sure you understand them. They are discussed in the chapter and defined in the glossary.

Generalizability	Unobtrusive observer
Scientist-practitioner model	Participant observer
Contingency	Measurement reactivity

Reactive measures
Nonreactive measures
Unobtrusive measure
Archival records
Sampling
Representativeness

Replication
Causal inference
Ex post facto fallacy
Experimenter reactivity
Experimenter bias

II. Answer each of the following. Check your answers in the chapter.

1. What are the two essential characteristics of low-constraint research?
2. Differentiate between case-study and naturalistic research methods.
3. Explain and discuss this idea: "In naturalistic research, the constraint or controls are placed on the researcher."
4. Under what conditions do we use low-constraint research methods?
5. Sometimes naturalistic research allows greater generalization than does laboratory research. How?
6. Explain how naturalistic research can negate a general proposition but cannot establish a general proposition.
7. What kind of relationship among variables is sought in naturalistic research?
8. Explain the concept of measurement reactivity.
9. What are the major criticisms of Freud's research methods?
10. What is experimenter reactivity?

III. Think about and work the following problems:

1. Explain this statement: "Freud's case-study research had poor validity."
2. You are in a discussion about research and someone asserts, "The only worthwhile research is high-constraint experimentation!" You jump into the discussion and explain how low-constraint research can be valuable. Develop your argument. Make it as strong as you can.
3. What is the *ex post facto* fallacy? Develop ten examples of research conclusions in which the *ex post facto* fallacy occurs.
4. For each of the following research areas assume that you will perform some of the ground-breaking research. Because there is no prior research in the area to draw on, you will need to utilize the flexible naturalistic and case-study approaches to identify critical variables, formulate initial hypotheses, and so on. Develop an initial research plan to accomplish these goals.
   a. Some people are concerned about the possible effects of televised wrestling on viewers and on society in general. How would you begin to study such an issue?
   b. Studies have shown that seatbelts dramatically reduce your risk of injury or death in the event of an accident. In spite of this, many people continue to avoid the use of seatbelts. The issue of concern to you is how one might increase seatbelt use among the average driver.
   c. Many naturalists and others are concerned about the welfare of animals in the natural environment because of increasing incursions of human activity.

Most people seem to be little concerned with the fate of wildlife or with the effects of hunting, habitat destruction, environmental pollution, and so on. You are to develop ways to sensitize people to greater concern for wildlife and greater efforts to reduce human incursions. What research would you develop toward these goals?

d. Shoplifting costs retail businesses and consumers many millions of dollars annually. You have been hired by a national retail consortium to study shoplifting and make recommendations toward control of this problem. How would you begin such a study?

CHAPTER 7

CORRELATIONAL AND DIFFERENTIAL METHODS OF RESEARCH

In the naturalistic research method we observe the behavior of organisms in natural settings. The case-study method limits the setting but does little to constrain the reactions of subjects. Our focus in this chapter on the correlational and differential methods of research will be on the measurement of relationships between variables (correlational) and differences between groups defined by preexisting variables (differential). As we will see, correlational and differential methods, although different, have important similarities.

CORRELATIONAL RESEARCH METHODS

In *correlational research* the strength of a relationship between two or more variables is quantified. The variables must be quantifiable and usually represent at least an ordinal scale of measurement.

In many ways the correlational research approach is an extension of naturalistic research. As in naturalistic research, variables are not usually manipulated in correlational research, and there is usually a single group of subjects that is a sample of a larger population. However, there are important differences between correlational and naturalistic research. The correlational research design always measures at least two variables, and plans for measuring variables are designed prior to any actual measurement.

Most texts on statistics and experimental design caution that a correlation cannot imply causality, and that caution is important. If the purpose of science is to understand natural events, what value is an observed correlation if it cannot be used to determine causality? The observed correlations between two variables serve two useful functions in science. The first is that any consistent relationship can be used to predict future events. Prediction is possible even if we have no idea why the observed relationship exists. It is not unusual in science to become accurate at predicting events long before we understand why the events occur. For example, as early as 140 A.D., Ptolemy had developed a complicated system to predict the movements of the planets. Although his predictions were remarkably accurate, he had little understanding of how the planets actually moved. In fact, his tentative model of planetary movement—that all celestial bodies revolve about the earth—was clearly wrong. But his assumptions do not diminish the accuracy of the predictions that could be made using his system.

A second valuable function of correlational research is to provide data that are either consistent or inconsistent with some currently held scientific theory. A study, correlational or otherwise, cannot prove a theory correct, although it can negate a theory. For example, the question of what intelligence is and how it should be measured has been debated for over half a century. British psychologist Charles Spearman (1904) proposed that there is a dominating general intellectual trait that governs performance in all areas of cognitive functioning. He referred to this trait as a "*g*" (general) factor. Spearman's theory can be validated or invalidated by research data. The process of validating a theory requires the scientist to derive predictions from the theory, predictions that can then be tested by gathering the appropriate data. One prediction that could be derived from Spearman's *g* factor theory is that there should be a strong correlation between different cognitive abilities, because each ability is affected primarily by the dominant *g* factor. Suppose we decide to test a randomly selected sample of subjects on both math and vocabulary skills and find the two to be highly correlated; that is, people who score high on the math skills measure also tend to score high on the vocabulary measure. Do the data confirm Spearman's theory? No, they do not. The data show only that one relationship out of thousands of possible predicted relationships exists. To prove the theory one would have to test every possible prediction from the theory; a task that is usually impossible to accomplish because many theories make an almost infinite number of predictions. The data are consistent with the theory and as such provide a small increment in the confidence that we place in the theory. Suppose we also test reading ability, abstract reasoning, short- and long-term memory, and the ability to solve riddles and find that all possible correlations between the measures are large and positive. Have we then proved the theory correct? The answer is still "no" because there remain other predicted relationships that we have not tested. However, we do have considerably more confidence in the theory because all predictions of the theory we tested are confirmed. But suppose we find that memory and math ability are virtually uncorrelated. What do these data mean? If the procedures were done correctly, we have to conclude that Spearman's *g* factor theory is incorrect. In other words, *a correlation cannot prove a theory but can negate a theory.* Notice that this function of correlational research is similar to a function of naturalistic and case-study research discussed in Chapter 6—in naturalistic and case-study research we cannot establish a general proposition but we can negate a general proposition. Again, correlational research is in many ways an extension of naturalistic and case-study research.

As noted in Chapters 2 and 6, research involves the study of relationships among variables. In correlational research we seek the strength of relationships among variables so that one variable can be predicted from the other variable. Thus, the relationship sought in correlational research can be described as a predictive relationship.

DIFFERENTIAL RESEARCH METHODS_____

In *differential research methods* we observe two or more groups that are differentiated on the basis of some preexisting variable. Groups can be determined by some qualitative dimension (such as the subject's sex, religion, political party, or psychiatric diagnosis) or by some quantitative dimension (such as the subject's age or number of years of education). Whether the variable that differentiates the groups is qualitative or quantitative, the group differences *existed before any research study was conducted.* The researcher measures the variable and assigns subjects to groups based on their scores. This classification variable is called the *independent variable* and the behavior measured in the different groups is called the *dependent variable.* More specifically, as discussed in Chapter 3, independent variables in differential research are *nonmanipulated independent variables* rather than *manipulated independent variables.* In differential research the independent and dependent variables are measured by the researcher and neither is directly manipulated. In experimental research the independent variable is not only measured but is actually manipulated by the researcher. Because differential research involves only measuring variables and not manipulating them, we are actually studying relationships between variables. Thus, differential research is conceptually similar to correlational research. The conceptual similarity of differential research to correlational research means that the same general principles will be used in interpreting the results from each of these research approaches. We must be as cautious in drawing causal interpretations from differential research studies as we are in correlational research studies. The structural similarity of differential research to experimental research (that is, there are different groups defined by an independent variable with a dependent measure taken on all subjects in each group) means that we will use essentially the same statistical procedures to evaluate the data from these two approaches. Thus, differential research is similar in many ways to both correlational and experimental research.

Recall our discussion in Chapter 6 of naturalistic research used to study outbursts in autistic children (Graziano, 1974). Had we wanted to know more about the outbursts of autistic children and how they compared with the behavior of normal children, we would have had to use the higher constraint research strategy of differential research. Instead of observing only autistic children, we would have also observed a group of normal children, which would give us a basis for comparison. A simple two-group research design is diagramed in Figure 7.1. The addition of a comparison group gives us more power to address several valuable questions that might further our understanding of autism—questions like "Are the outbursts of autistic children qualitatively different from the outbursts of normal children or simply more frequent and intense?" "Does the pattern of behavior immediately prior to and after the outbursts differ in the two groups, possibly suggesting that different mechanisms are responsible for the outbursts in the two groups?"

Artifacts and Confounding Variables

Adding one or more additional groups forces the researcher to standardize (i.e., constrain) the observational methods. In the naturalistic methods we could easily change our observational method or focus of observation to study any phenomenon that captured our interest. In differential research we compare observations in one group of subjects with observations in other group(s). We can legitimately compare observations from two or more groups only if the observations were made in the same way in each group. If we use different methods to observe and measure a phenomenon in two groups, any differences we observe between the groups could be real differences *or* they could be a function of the different observational procedures. We would have no way of knowing which of these possibilities is correct. In such a case, we speak of the two variables as being *confounded*. The two variables in this case are the group the subjects

Figure 7.1 A SIMPLE TWO-GROUP RESEARCH DESIGN

Define the group	Gather the data	Analyze the data
Autistic children	Observe the autistic children	Compare the groups
Normal children	Observe the normal children	

were in and the different methods of observing and measuring in the two groups. When we say they are confounded, we mean that they both vary at the same time—as the group variable changes, the method of observation variable also changes. Because the two variables change together, we can never know which of them is responsible for any observed changes in the dependent variable. The only way to avoid confounding variables is to make sure that they vary independently of one another, and the simplest way of ensuring this is to hold one of the variables constant. *The variable that should be held constant is the variable we have no interest in, and the variable we want to focus our attention on is the variable we allow to vary.* In the example of outbursts in autistic children we are not as interested in the effects of different observational procedures on the data recorded as we are in how autistic children's outbursts differ from normal children's. Therefore, we will hold the observational method variable constant and allow the group variable to vary. That is, we will observe a group of autistic and a group of normal children using the same observational procedures in each group. We must define in advance exactly what variables we will measure and how we will observe and measure the variables. Once the study starts, we are constrained by those design decisions, and we must use the same observational and measurement procedures throughout the research study.

We gain power to answer research questions by using the higher constraint differential research method instead of lower constraint naturalistic and case-study observation methods. The additional power comes from the ability to compare groups of subjects who differ on some important variable such as diagnosis. But a price is paid for this additional power—a loss of flexibility. When we have only one group we can modify procedures easily. But when we have more than one group we must use the same observational and measurement procedures in each group if we want to make valid comparisons between them. Failure to constrain the procedures can lead to *artifactual* findings. An *artifact* is any apparent effect of an independent variable that is actually the effect of some other variable that was not properly controlled (in this case, held constant). That is, an artifact is a result of confounding. Therefore, if we had used different measurement procedures for the autistic and control groups, the observed differences between the groups might actually have been an artifact of changes in the measurement procedure rather than real differences in subjects' behavior.

In higher constraint research where precise and consistent observational procedures are required, more detailed planning is also necessary prior to any data collection. How can a researcher make such detailed plans before a study even begins? If the study is the first being conducted on a particular topic, the researcher cannot make such detailed plans. Detailed planning is possible only if the phenomenon under study is already reasonably well understood. High-constraint research is thus seldom used in the early stages of studying a problem. Instead, the flexible low-constraint methods allow the researcher to explore the phenomenon and to gain a sense of what to expect. Such an understanding is necessary for any investigator to be able later to state hypotheses in explicit terms and to design procedures for measuring variables that will test hypotheses. Research on a particular topic usually begins with low-constraint methods and proceeds to higher constraint research only after a basic understanding of the phenomenon is achieved. Scientists often study topics that other people have already studied extensively and thus often do not need to start with low-constraint research. However, most researchers choose to do at least some low-constraint research to gain familiarity with the phenomenon that would be difficult to gain solely from the published accounts of other investigators.

WHAT MAKES DIFFERENTIAL RESEARCH HIGHER CONSTRAINT THAN CORRELATIONAL RESEARCH?

Conceptually, both correlational research and differential research measure relationships between variables. But for several reasons we have listed differential research as higher constraint in our model. One reason is that differential research is structurally similar to experimental research when comparisons of two or more groups are made on a dependent measure. However, there are other, more relevant issues that define the level of constraint for differential research.

In many cases the researcher conducting differential research is actually interested in addressing causal questions. Ideally, in addressing a causal question experimental research should be used. But often ethical or practical constraints prevent the use of an experimental procedure. For example, it is not possible to randomly assign subjects to groups of schizophrenics and controls. The advantage of random assignment of subjects to groups or conditions is that it will tend to equate the groups on potential confounding variables so that the only consistent difference between the groups is the level of the independent variable. Consequently, it is relatively safe to conclude that any observed differences in the dependent variable are the result of the manipulation of the independent variable. With differential research subjects are assigned to groups on the basis of some preexisting variable, and often the groups will differ on several variables other than the independent variable. For example, chronic schizophrenics tend to be from lower social classes, have fewer relationships in adolescence and early adulthood, and spend more time in hospitals than a randomly selected group of people from the general population. These particular differences are predictable and are well established by past research. If we find differences between a group of chronic schizophrenics and a general control group on some dependent measure (such as style of processing visual information), we have no way of knowing whether the differences are due to schizophrenia, to social class differences, to social experiences during adolescence, or to effects of hospitalization. In other words, all of the group differences, other than diagnosis, are potential confounding variables. In this example, knowing which variable(s) is(are) responsible for the differences on the dependent variable is impossible.

As we will see later in this chapter, researchers using differential methods are rarely content with this state of affairs. Instead of selecting a general control group, the researcher might select one or more specific control groups using selection criteria that will assure that a given control group is comparable to the experimental group on some potentially confounding variable. For example, if the researcher suspects that social class might well affect the scores on the dependent variable, he or she might select a control group that is, on average, of the same social class as the experimental group. Thus, social class could not confound the findings. The active control over sampling by the researcher is a form of constraint, which minimizes confounding and therefore strengthens the conclusions drawn from the study. There is no comparable control used in correlational research. Hence, differential research has more control procedures available and is higher constraint than correlational research. The more controls that can be applied, the stronger the conclusions one can draw from the study.

WHEN TO USE CORRELATIONAL AND DIFFERENTIAL RESEARCH

Differential research designs are used most often in situations where the manipulation of an independent variable is impractical, impossible, or inappropriate. If a psychologist wants to know about the relative effectiveness of two theories of education in creating an environment that fosters learning, he or she might set up two separate schools and for each school institute a different curriculum, randomly assign a pool of students, and then evaluate the amount of learning by students. But the expense of setting up such a research program would make the study impractical. An alternative would be to use two existing schools that already have the kinds of curricula that the researcher is interested in evaluating. Because these groups are naturally occurring instead of experimentally manipulated groups, this would be a differential research design. In other instances a differential design could be used because the experimental manipulation we are interested in is physically impossible to accomplish. That might be the case if we were interested in the social development of individuals with superior intelligence. There is no way that we could raise or lower the intelligence of newborns so that we could randomly assign them to normal and superior intelligence groups and observe their subsequent social development. But we could select children of high and average intelligence, assign them to two groups, and follow their social development. Finally, there are many cases in which experimental manipulation of a particular variable is possible but to do so would be unethical. We might hypothesize that a prolonged separation from one's parents during the first two years of life might lead to permanently retarded social development. It would be unethical to select infants randomly and separate them from their parents to test the hypothesis experimentally. But some children are separated from their parents for reasons that are beyond the researcher's control. Such a naturally occurring group might be a suitable population to study in order to explore the hypothesis.

Another field that uses correlational and differential research designs almost exclusively because of ethical considerations is the area of clinical neuropsychology. A neuropsychologist uses psychological measures of human behavior to infer the structural and functional condition of the human brain. The neuropsychologist administers tests to patients to determine what the patients can and cannot do. The patterns of such abilities and disabilities can often suggest where in the brain a particular problem such as a tumor might be located. The wealth of background data that neuropsychologists draw on when they evaluate a particular person is gathered from previous patients with neurological problems. If a particular pattern of abilities and disabilities is consistently found for patients later diagnosed as suffering from a particular type of problem in a particular location of the brain, then it is reasonable to predict that a new patient with that pattern might well be suffering from the same neurological dysfunction. The data gathering in this case is correlational, because the researcher is trying to identify relationships between behavior and brain functioning. Granted, some of the relationships observed are not easily quantifiable in terms of a simple correlation coefficient, but they are relationships nevertheless. Note that by mapping these relationships carefully and accurately we are able to obtain an accurate prediction of one of the variables (brain functioning) on the basis of knowing the other variable (the person's behavior). Accurate prediction is a principle goal of correlational research.

CONDUCTING CORRELATIONAL AND DIFFERENTIAL RESEARCH

Conducting correlational and differential research is among the most difficult tasks faced by the research scientist. Two factors contribute to this difficulty. On the one hand, they are relatively high constraint research approaches, which require the investigator to prepare detailed procedures prior to any data collection and then follow through on the procedures throughout the study. On the other hand, the investigator often is unable to use some of the most powerful research procedures such as those available in experimental research.

Conducting Correlational Research

In correlational research we seek to quantify the direction and strength of a relationship between two or more variables. (Our discussion here will focus on the relationships between two variables only.)

Measurement   Developing effective operational definitions of the variables is as important here as in any other kind of research. Measurement—the assignment of numbers to variables (see Chapter 4)—depends on the adequacy of operational definitions.

Once the investigator selects the measures to be used, the next step is to determine procedures for collecting the data. *As in any other research,* we want to avoid the possibility that the researcher might unintentionally influence the subjects. Ways to avoid influencing subjects include never allowing the same researcher to collect both measures on the subject, or never allowing the researcher to know subjects' scores on the first measure until after the second measure is taken. Two effects need to be controlled: (1) the tendency of investigators to see what they expect to see and (2) the tendency of investigators to influence the behavior of subjects. The latter problem is referred to as *experimenter reactivity* (see Chapter 6). The tendency of investigators to see what they expect to see is minimized by using objective measures whenever possible so that little subjective interpretation is necessary. The problem of experimenter reactivity may require the use of two independent researchers. The researcher's influence on the subject is particularly likely when the subject is being asked to give a voluntary response with the researcher present. (Experimenter effects on subjects will be discussed in more detail in Chapters 8 and 9.)

Another potential problem in correlational research is the subject's own influence on the measures. Subjects like to be consistent, especially when they believe they are being observed and evaluated. This is a variation on the *measurement reactivity* problem discussed in Chapter 6. Such contrived consistency can create strong relationships between variables when such relationships do not exist in real life. There are a number of ways of reducing this effect. One way is to disguise the self-report measures by including *filler items,* so that the subject is not sure of what the investigator is interested in studying. Filler items are not meant to measure anything but to draw the subject's attention away from the real purpose of the test. A second method of controlling the subject's influence on data is to rely on one or more unobtrusive measures. In this way subjects are unaware that they are being observed and are thus less likely to control their own behavior. A third method is to separate the measures from one another, which can be done by taking measurements at different times or by having different researchers take the measurements. Probably the best way to deal with the problem of measurement reactivity is to use measures that are beyond the control of the subject. If we want to measure anxiety, for example, we might rely more on psychophysiological measures than on self-reports or behavior as the index.

Sampling   In most research obtaining a sample that is representative of the population to which we want to generalize the results is a major concern. Another sampling issue important in correlational research is whether the relationship between the two variables is the same in all segments of the population under study. If we have any reason to believe that such differences exist, we might draw samples from separate subpopulations. For example, if we suspect that males and females might demonstrate a different relationship between two variables, either in direction or strength, we should select samples of males and females separately and compute separate correlations for each group. In this example the sex of the subject would be a *moderator variable;* that is, any variable that seems to modify the relationship between other variables. Sex of subject is a commonly used moderator variable. If different subgroups in a population show different relationships between two variables, the relationships can be obscured if the variable that defines the subgroups is not included in the study as a moderator variable. For example, if two variables such as dependency and hostility are positively correlated in males but negatively correlated in females, the correlation in a mixed group of males and females will probably be close to zero, suggesting no relationship. The opposite relationships in the two groups cancel each other. In this example sex is a moderator variable in that the sex of the subject modifies the relationship between the variables of dependency and hostility. Recognizing potential moderator variables requires a thorough knowledge of the area under study. When in doubt it is always better to compute correlations for different subgroups. If the same relationship is found in all of the groups, we can be more confident that the relationship will hold for the entire population sampled.

Analysis of Data   In correlational research, data analysis involves computing an index of the degree of relationship between variables under study. The correlation coefficient computed will depend on the level of measurement used for both variables. If both variables are measured on at least an interval scale of measurement (i.e., both measures produce score data), then a Pearson product-moment correlation coefficient should be computed. If one variable is measured on an ordinal scale and the other variable is at least ordinal, then the appropriate coefficient is a Spearman rank-order correlation. Both correlation coefficients accomplish the same thing; that is, they indicate the degree of linear relationship between the two variables. Both range from -1.00 to $+1.00$. A -1.00 means a perfect negative relationship exists (as one variable increases, the other decreases in a perfectly predictable fashion). A $+1.00$ means a perfect positive relationship exists. A correlation of 0.00 means there is no linear relationship between the two variables. (See Figures 5.5 and 5.6 for examples of correlation scatter diagrams. The computational procedures for these correlation coefficients are shown in Appendix C.)

The most frequently used correlational procedures are the Pearson and Spearman correlations, both of which quantify the relationship between two variables. However, there are research situations that demand more complicated correlational analyses, such as correlating one variable with an entire set of variables (multiple correlation) or one set of variables with another set of variables (canonical correlation). It is also possible to correlate one variable with another after statistically removing the effects of a third variable (partial correlation). Detailed discussion of these more sophisticated analytic procedures is beyond the scope of this book [see Nunnally (1967) or Timm (1975)]. However, it is important to realize that such procedures do exist to meet a variety of research needs.

Interpreting the Correlation   The first step in interpreting the correlation is to note its direction and size. Is the correlation a positive relationship between the variables or a negative relationship? Is the relationship small (close to zero) or relatively large (close to $+1.00$ or -1.00)?

The next step is to test for the statistical significance of the correlation; that is, test to see whether the observed correlation is large enough for us to believe there is a nonzero correlation between the variables in the population from which the current sample was drawn. To state it another way, we are testing the null hypothesis that there is a zero correlation between the variables in the population. We use tables to answer this question, which contain critical values for the Pearson correlation and the Spearman correlation (see Appendix B, Tables B.4 and B.5). If the absolute value of the observed correlation from the sample exceeds the appropriate critical value, we conclude that the correlation is *statistically significant.* This finding is taken as evidence that a nonzero correlation exists in the population from which the sample is drawn. Suppose that we select ten subjects and compute a Pearson correlation between two variables. The correlation is $+0.69$, and we want to test the null hypothesis that there is no relationship between the variables in the population. The critical value is a function of the sample size and the designated alpha (Type I error) level. The critical values for the product-moment correlation are in Appendix B, Table B.4, which is organized by degrees of freedom. (The degrees of freedom are easily calculated in this case by subtracting two from the sample size.) We traditionally set alpha to 0.05. In our example we sampled ten people and computed a product-moment correlation of 0.69. With an alpha of 0.05 and the degrees of freedom equal to 8 $(10 - 2)$, we look in the second column of correlations in Table B.4 on the row for 8 degrees of freedom and read the critical value of 0.6319. If the absolute value of the obtained correlation exceeds this critical value, we conclude that there is a relationship between these variables in the sampled population. Because 0.69 does exceed the critical value (0.6319), we conclude that there is a relationship in our population.

When using correlation coefficients it is useful to calculate the *coefficient of determination* by squaring the obtained correlation. If the obtained correlation was 0.50, then $r^2 = 0.25$. We can convert 0.25 to a percent by multiplying by 100 (100 $\times$ 0.25 = 25%). A correlation of 0.50 indicates that 25 percent of the variability in the first variable can be accounted for or predicted by knowing the scores on the second variable. We shorten this statement by referring to r^2 as the "proportion of variance accounted for." This procedure allows us to estimate how useful the relationship might be in prediction. However, it is appropriate to take r^2 seriously only if we have a good-sized sample (a minimum of 30 subjects).

Conducting Differential Research

Measurement   In differential research we distinguish between the independent variable and the dependent variable. The dependent variable is usually a continuous measure but it might also be a discrete (categorical) measure. For example, it may be a measure of performance on a particular task, an index of anxiety level, or a physical characteristic such as a person's weight. All of the previously discussed issues of operationalizing the dependent variable are relevant here. It is important to select an operational definition for the dependent measure that can be clearly stated and communicated to other researchers.

In differential research the nonmanipulated independent variable is typically a discrete variable. For example, it might be a diagnostic category with two values such as manic patients and depressed patients. In differential research the independent variable is measured rather than manipulated. For example, suppose we need a procedure to measure the diagnosis of the patients. We need to operationalize the procedures for making that diagnosis. We might use a structured interview to gather information about symptoms from each patient and some clearly defined, easily replicable criteria for making the final diagnosis. Note that the issues that apply to creating operational definitions for the independent variable are exactly the same issues that apply in defining operational procedures for measuring the dependent variable. It is always possible to take a continuous variable, such as anxiety level, and break it into discrete intervals, such as high anxiety, moderate anxiety, or low anxiety, and thus convert a correlational research design into a differential research design.

Selecting Appropriate Control Groups   In differential research we have to decide which groups to include in the study. In some cases the decision is simple. If, for example, we are interested in sex differences, sex would be the independent variable, and there are only two possibilities. Because the minimum number of groups required in differential research is two, we would use both a male and a female group. However, such is not the case with other independent variables. If we are interested in studying psychopathology, there are dozens of psychiatric disorders. Choosing which of those particular disorders to compare must be done within a theoretical framework. The theory in any research study should guide the researcher in selecting the appropriate comparisons and control groups. We use the term *control group* to refer to any group selected in differential research as a basis of comparison with the primary or *experimental group.*[1] In some cases the experimental/control group distinction is irrelevant. With the example above of exploring sex differences, it makes little sense to say that one sex represents the experimental group whereas the other sex represents the control group. In other situations the control group is arbitrarily defined as the group that has none of the characteristic that defines the independent variable. For example, if the independent variable is college education and we had three levels (no college, some college, college graduate), it would be customary to refer to the no-college group as the control group.

Recall that control groups are designed to reduce the effects of potential confounding factors. A variable can have a confounding effect in a differential study only if (1) it affects the scores on the dependent variable(s) and (2) there is a difference between the experimental and control groups on the potential confounding variable. For example, suppose a differential design is being used to study sex differences in the ability to perceive details in visual scenes. It is known that visual acuity will affect performance on the task. Therefore, visual acuity is a potential confounding factor. However, if males and females do not differ on visual acuity, then the potential confounding factor cannot differentially affect performance in the two groups. If males and females did differ on visual acuity, then visual acuity would be a confounding factor.

In many differential research designs the control group has to be selected with care if it is to be an effective control. *The ideal control group is identical to the experimental group on all variables except the independent variable that defines the groups.* For example, if we were studying the effects of exposure to toxic chemicals in the work environment on cognitive performance, the experimental group would consist of people who work in industries in which they are exposed to such toxins. An ideal control group would include workers of about the same age, social class, and education level, and who do similar kinds of work, but who work in an industry that does not expose them to these toxins. A group of office workers from the same company as the plant workers in the experimental group might be a convenient control group, but it would *not* make a good control group. The office workers would probably differ from the plant workers on a number of important variables, such as education level, age, and the ratio of males to females. Any of these differences could affect how the subjects might do on the cognitive performance dependent measure and thus constitute potential confounding variables.

Let us consider another example of selecting a control group, this one from the research literature on psychopathology. Suppose we are interested in studying schizophrenia. The experimental group consists of schizophrenic patients. What is a good control group to compare with the schizophrenic group? Our choice will depend on the dependent measure and the confounding variables that might affect it. As noted earlier, a variable can have a confounding effect in a differential study only if (1) it affects the scores on the dependent variable(s) and (2) there is a difference between the experimental and control groups on the potential confounding variable. To select an appropriate control group, we must first identify factors that will affect the dependent measures.

---

[1]Although the term *experimental group* is commonly used, it can be misleading in discussions of differential research. In spite of the common use of the term, differential research is *not* experimental.

These represent potential confounding factors, but they will not actually confound the results unless the experimental and control groups differ on these factors. Therefore, we want to select a control group that is comparable to the experimental group on these potentially confounding factors. Let us assume that we are interested in measuring thought processes in schizophrenic patients. We need to identify variables known to affect performance on the dependent measures. We can find answers to this question through careful library research. Past research using the same or similar dependent measures will often report correlations with potentially confounding variables. Once the potentially confounding variables are identified, we can identify a control group that will not differ from the experimental group on these variables. Potential confounding variables might include amount of education, age, and total amount of psychiatric hospitalization. To reduce the threat of these potentially confounding variables, we select a control group that is as similar to the schizophrenics on these variables as possible. If we can accomplish this, the variables will not confound the results.

As mentioned earlier, it is rare to find an ideal control group. Instead, what we usually try to obtain is a control group that controls some of the most important and most powerful confounding variables. A confounding variable is powerful if it is likely to have a large effect on the dependent measure. In our hypothetical study of the thought processes of schizophrenics, a powerful confounding variable might be education. We can identify education as a confounding variable because the research literature shows that education is highly correlated with measures of cognitive performance.

It is often difficult to find a single, ideal control group matched with the experimental group on all potentially confounding variables. In fact, at times when we select a group to control for a particular confounding variable, we confound other variables with the independent measure. This is why we commonly use more than one control group in differential research studies. Each of the comparison groups will typically control for one or more of the major confounding variables, but no group will control for all potential confounding variables. If each of the comparisons of the experimental group with the control groups gives essentially the same result and leads to the same conclusion, then the researcher can be reasonably confident that the independent variable and not one of the confounding variables is responsible for the observed effect. Most of the research in medicine and the social sciences, because of ethical and practical considerations, relies on such multiple comparisons. It is not always feasible to include all possible comparison groups in one study. Therefore, research often involves multiple studies by different researchers in different laboratories, each using slightly different procedures and different control groups. If the phenomenon under study is stronger than the potential confounding variables, each researcher will come to the same conclusion.

The multiple-comparison approach was used in a recent study of schizophrenic ambivalence (Raulin, 1984). Ambivalence had long been considered to be a primary symptom of schizophrenia (Bleuler, 1911/1950). Surprisingly, in the 70 years since this initial clinical observation, no one had actually tested the hypothesis with a high-constraint design. Raulin (1984) developed a self-report test of ambivalence that showed strong test-retest and internal consistency reliability. The test was then given to a sample of schizophrenics and three control samples: hospitalized depressed patients, outpatient psychotherapy clients, and a nonpsychiatric control sample. Because this was the first measure of ambivalence, there was little existing information available about potential confounding variables. Therefore, three control groups were used and all groups were matched on demographic variables (age, education, social class) that were known to affect responding on other self-report measures. The nonpsychiatric control group controlled for demographic variables because it was matched with the schizophrenic group on these variables; the psychotherapy clients also controlled for psychological distress; and the hospitalized depressed patients controlled for severe psychopathology and hospitalization. The results indicate the importance of the multiple-control group approach. The schizophrenics scored significantly higher than the nonpsychiatric controls on the ambivalence measure (consistent with the hypothesis). The schizophrenics, however, were not significantly different from the psychotherapy clients and scored significantly lower than the hospitalized depressed subjects on the ambivalence test. Had the last two control groups been left out of the study, it might have been mistakenly concluded that ambivalence is characteristic of schizophrenia.

We suspect that some students will find this discussion discouraging in that it seems no matter how hard we try, an ideal comparison cannot be found. This is, in fact, true, and one of the reasons why it is so important to do multiple research studies. In Chapter 10 we will discuss experimental research designs in which groups are not defined on the basis of some preexisting variable, but instead, subjects are randomly assigned to the groups. In this situation we will find that most of the problems described in the preceding discussion disappear and that, by and large, we are able on the basis of a true experiment to interpret findings with a great deal of confidence. Our advice to students interested in studying areas where experimentation is unethical or impossible, is to realize that drawing strong conclusions is very difficult at best and finding answers to any given question is likely to be a long, tedious, and intellectually demanding task.

Sampling Regardless of the type of research, the same issues of sampling always apply. To be able to generalize to a larger population we must sample randomly from the population. Random sampling is a procedure for selecting subjects from a population where each subject has an equal chance of being selected. To study schizophrenics we should ideally utilize a procedure that samples randomly from all possible schizophrenics. In practice that ideal is impossible to attain. It would be much too expensive, for example, to obtain a sample of 30 schizophrenics from many different states and hospitals because the cost of travel alone would be prohibitive. Usually a random sample is selected from all of the subjects that are available to the researcher. Unless there is reason to believe that subjects from one part of the country are different from subjects in another part of the country, the sample need not be from the whole country to be able to generalize to the whole country.

A serious threat to generalizability is the subtle kind of bias that can occur when a researcher has access to only certain groups. For example, if the researcher studying schizophrenics obtained all of the patients from one hospital, the sample might well be unrepresentative of schizophrenia because most psychiatric hospitals specialize in the kinds of patients they treat. Some hospitals handle the more chronic cases that require long-term hospitalization. Any sample from such a hospital would underrepresent those who recover fairly quickly. Private hospitals because of their expense serve patients from higher socioeconomic levels than state-funded hospitals. In fact, choosing patients from only hospitals may even result in a biased sample. Many patients who might be cared for at home, are in hospitals because they have no family or home to go to. A hospital sample of schizophrenics might overrepresent patients from unstable homes.

Researchers studying other problems must also be sensitive to these subtle sampling biases. If we are sampling children from schools, we recognize that a particular school may not have a representative sample of children. Depending on the location of the school, the children may come from higher or lower socioeconomic backgrounds than children in general. They may overrepresent or underrepresent certain ethnic or socioeconomic groups. They may be of higher or lower intelligence than the average child. Any of these variables might affect the results of a study.

Even when we appear to be sampling randomly, it is important to be sensitive to subtle biases. If, for example, we are surveying people randomly in a shopping center, we must still question the representativeness of the sample. A shopping center on the west side of town may have quite different customers than a similar shopping center on the east side of town. A shopping center in the city is likely to have different customers than one in the suburbs. To obtain a representative sample it might be best to sample people from several locations. The time of day or day of the week also could affect the sample composition. If we sampled on a weekday afternoon we would probably overrepresent homemakers; people who work evenings, weekends, or flexible hours; the unemployed; kids playing hooky; or people on vacation. Even if we take all of these exceptions into account, we might still have a biased sample. People who do not like shopping will probably be underrepresented. Finally, the researcher may be making subtle discriminations that could produce a biased sample. Because none of us likes to be turned away, we might choose to approach people who seem more likely to cooperate and avoid those who seem in a hurry. The point is that it is easy to obtain an unrepresentative sample that might threaten the generalizability of a study. An issue and a problem with any research, it is particularly relevant in differential research studies. Because the groups in differential research already differ on some preexisting variable, the likelihood is high that they will differ on other variables that might affect the outcome of the research. The investigator must be careful in sampling subjects in differential research and needs to take measures to assure the representativeness of the sample. When a representative sample cannot be obtained, the researcher must use extra caution in interpreting the findings.

In differential research, especially differential research of diagnostic groups, sampling is usually not the primary factor in determining the generalizability of the study. Instead, the factor that most affects the generalizability of the study is the number of subjects who drop out. Using our hypothetical study of schizophrenics, depending on the task, we might find that many schizophrenics would not or could not perform the task and hence would not be included in the study. To the extent that these patients are different from those who do perform the task, we cannot generalize to the larger population of schizophrenics. If the patients who could not perform the task are more seriously disturbed than those who could, then we have not studied all schizophrenics. Instead, we have studied the less severely disturbed schizophrenics and we can reasonably generalize the findings only to a population of these less seriously disturbed subjects. (Sampling will be discussed in more detail in Chapter 9.)

Analysis of Data In some respects the data produced from differential research studies resemble the data from experimental studies. We will typically have scores from each subject in each group. We will want to compare the scores of the experimental group(s) with the scores of the control group(s). The type of statistical analysis used will depend on the number of groups and the scale of measurement of the dependent variable(s). If the dependent measure represents score data and we have two groups, a *t*-test for independent groups is typically used to compare the two groups. If we have more than two groups and score data, an analysis of variance (ANOVA) is typically used. (Both statistical procedures are described in Appendix C.) If the data are ordinal or nominal, nonparametric statistics are typically used. With ordinal data, a Mann-Whitney *U*-Test is used; with nominal data, a chi-square is used (see Appendix C). (In Chapter 14 we will discuss the selection of the appropriate statistical analyses.)

Interpretation of Data Regardless of what statistical test we perform, we interpret it in the same way. We always compare the probability value produced by the statistic with the predetermined alpha level to determine whether the null hypothesis should be rejected. The null hypothesis in this case is that the population means are equal, and rejecting that hypothesis suggests that at least one population mean is different from at least one other population mean.

Drawing the proper conclusion from the null hypothesis is the easy part of interpreting data in differential research design. The difficult part is taking into account all of the possible confounding factors discussed previously. If we believe the groups are not representative of the populations to which we hope to generalize, we must be especially cautious in making that generalization. If we think the control groups are inadequate to control for all the possible confounding variables, we should acknowledge this in the report of the study.

The possible confounding variables in most differential research make it difficult to draw solid conclusions on the basis of a single research study. Especially in differential research, results should be interpreted in the context of findings from other studies. Therefore, it is critically important for each investigator to describe the research procedures in detail. Whenever possible, confounding variables should be measured and reported. For example, if we were studying psychiatric patients we would want to report the diagnoses of the patients and the procedures used to obtain them. We also should report variables such as subjects' average age, education, social class, amount of hospitalization, and any other patient variables relevant to the interpretation of the study. In this way, we communicate the kinds of information future investigators will need to interpret their studies in the context of our study.

LIMITATIONS OF CORRELATIONAL AND DIFFERENTIAL RESEARCH

Problems in Determining Causation

One of the most severe limitations of differential and correlational research methods is the kind of conclusion that is drawn from the data. Remember, differential research is conceptually similar to correlational research. This means that causal conclusions cannot be safely draw from differential or correlational research. A correlation (i.e., an observed relationship) does not necessarily imply causality. Students may wonder why we keep repeating this point. In the abstract, the point is indeed simple. If A and B are correlated, then three possibilities exist: (1) A causes B; (2) B causes A; or (3) some third factor C causes both A and B. In the abstract, all of these are equally plausible. But in real life situations, one or more of the possibilities may appear implausible and so the student may feel justified in drawing a strong causal conclusion.

Suppose, for example, we find that reading and arithmetic abilities are highly correlated. How do we interpret such a finding? If we are testing Spearman's theory, we want to interpret the data to mean that some third factor (in this case the g factor) is responsible for both reading ability and arithmetic ability. However, there are other possible interpretations. Can arithmetic ability cause reading ability? It might, but it would be difficult to imagine a mechanism by which such a causal chain could proceed (i.e., how arithmetic skills could lead to better reading skills), in which case we might be tempted to dismiss such an interpretation as unlikely. Consider the reverse causal chain. Can reading ability cause arithmetic ability? How did you learn about arithmetic? Your teacher in grammar school taught you basic arithmetic, *and* you read about it and practiced it from your arithmetic textbook. If you had poor reading skills, you might well have been less able to learn other skills including arithmetic. So there is a potential causal chain that seems plausible and could explain how better reading skills can lead to better arithmetic skills.

Another explanation for a strong correlation between arithmetic and reading abilities should be considered. What does it mean when there is a strong relationship between reading ability and arithmetic ability? We are not trying to interpret this relationship but rather to define what it means in operational terms; that is, how we quantified this relationship. We asked a sample of people to take tests of reading ability and arithmetic ability. But what do the scores on the tests really mean? Suppose the arithmetic test includes the following question:

> John goes to the market and buys 5 tomatoes. If tomatoes sell for $3 per dozen, how much change should John receive if he gives the clerk a $5 bill?

Clearly, this question measures the ability to multiply, divide, and subtract. If tomatoes are $3 per dozen, they are $.25 each and therefore 5 tomatoes would cost $1.25. The change John should receive (assuming no sales tax) should be $3.75. It seems simple enough. But what other abilities would this question measure? Consider the following example:

> Jean va au marché et il achète 5 tomates. Si les tomates coute $3 la douzaine, combien de monnaie doit Jean reçevoir s'il donne la vendeuse $5?

Unless you read French, you probably found this question considerably harder to answer, yet it is the same arithmetic question. The example illustrates how important reading ability is in most tests regardless of the material being tested. Therefore, a correlation between reading ability and arithmetic ability may actually be an artifact of the phenomenon that reading ability is required to perform well on either test.

There is one more point often overlooked when interpreting a correlation. When we say that both A and B may be caused by some third variable C, we are not specifying what the third variable might be. In fact, variable C might be anything, so that we do not have three interpretations to choose from but rather hundreds. Suppose we believe that we can eliminate the possibility that arithmetic skills caused reading skills and the possibility that reading skills caused arithmetic skills. Could we then conclude that the third factor (Spearman's g factor) is responsible for both? No, we cannot. Spearman's general intelligence factor is only one of many possible third-factor variables that could account for the observed correlation. General test-taking ability might be a relevant factor. Anxiety level during the testing might be a relevant factor. (Have you ever taken an exam during which you panicked?) The amount of distraction during the testing session might be important or the level of motivation of the subjects or the general quality of their education or any one of a dozen other variables. Most likely, each of these variables contributes to the observed correlation. Yet, it is tempting to conclude that the one causal relationship being hypothesized is the one that led to the observed relationship.

Confounding Variables

Another limitation of differential and correlational research methods is that it is often difficult or impossible to avoid confounding variables. Two variables are said to be confounded when they tend to vary together. Because they vary together, any observed relationships with other variables might be caused by either of the variables or none of them. In differential research in particular, confounding is more the rule than the exception. Some potential confounding variables may be controlled with a carefully selected control group, but rarely will we be able to eliminate confounding. Such problems will always make interpretation difficult, although some researchers choose to think of them as simply making the task more challenging.

SUMMARY

Our discussion groups together correlational and differential methods of research because they share the common characteristic that the measures studied are not systematically manipulated by the researcher. The researcher's only role in correlational or differential research is to measure the variables of interest. By surrendering the opportunity to manipulate variables, the researcher surrenders a great deal of power in interpreting the data obtained. It is difficult to draw causal conclusions from data derived from correlational or differential research.

Correlational and differential research designs are appropriate when the researcher is interested in relationships between variables. Sometimes researchers are interested in a causal relationship but are unable to conduct a true experiment because practical or ethical concerns restrict them to measuring rather than manipulating a variable of interest. In such cases, a differential design is appropriate. The student should not view differential or correlational research methods as inferior to experimental research. It is true that experimental research is often easier to interpret and that causal conclusions are more safely drawn from experimental research, but many questions of interest in psychology and medicine cannot use experimental methods to answer questions posed by researchers. The effective use of correlational and differential research methods, coupled with a thorough knowledge of past research and a sophisticated use of logic, can often answer some of these difficult yet critically important questions.

REVIEW EXERCISES

I. Define the following key terms. Be sure you understand them. They are discussed in the chapter and defined in the glossary.

Correlational research methods   Experimenter reactivity
Differential research methods   Measurement reactivity
Independent variable   Filler items
Dependent variable   Moderator variable
Nonmanipulated independent variable   Statistically significant correlation
Manipulated independent variable   Coefficient of determination
Confounding variable   Control group
Artifact   Experimental group

II. Answer each of the following. Check your answers in the chapter.

1. Explain this statement: "In many ways correlational research is an extension of naturalistic research."
2. In what ways are naturalistic research and correlational research different?
3. Why is it not advisable to try to infer causality from correlational research?
4. If causality cannot be inferred from a correlation, what information can be obtained from a correlation?
5. We keep noting that research at all levels of constraint seeks relationships between variables. What does this mean?
6. What are artifacts in research?
7. Under what conditions would we use differential research?
8. Why can we not infer causality in differential research?
9. What are moderator variables? Give examples.
10. What kind of variable are the independent variables in differential research?
11. What information is gained by squaring the correlation coefficient?
12. What kind of relationship among variables is sought in correlational research? In differential research?

III. Think about and work the following problems.

1. Interpret each of the following correlations (for statistical significance, proportion of variance accounted for, and conceptual interpretation).
   a. A product-moment correlation of 0.41 between age and height in grade-school girls (based on a sample of 60 children).

    b. A rank-order correlation of 0.32 between ranks on a depression scale and rank order of activity level on the ward in a group of hospitalized psychiatric patients (sample size is 18).

    c. A product-moment correlation of 0.20 between two different measures of assertiveness in a sample of 100 college students.

2. For each of the following experimental groups in a differential research study, list two to three possible control groups. For each control group, what possible confounding variables are likely to be controlled and which ones are likely to be left uncontrolled?

    a. Juvenile delinquent boys (aged 10–14) in a study of parenting style and its possible relationship to delinquency.

    b. Data-entry clerks in a study of eye strain from working daily at CRT displays.

    c. Residents of a neighborhood that is known to be contaminated by toxic chemicals in a study of health effects of exposure to such chemicals.

    d. Mildly depressed individuals in a study of the number of negative events experienced in the last two months.

3. We chose to include two apparently different types of research design in this chapter because we believe they are conceptually similar. What conceptual similarities exist between differential and correlational research?

CHAPTER 8

HYPOTHESIS TESTING, VALIDITY, AND THREATS TO VALIDITY

Numerous research concepts have been introduced in Chapters 1–7, some of them familiar to the student and others new. The variety of concepts we have had to include thus far may have been confusing at times. Although some new research concepts are introduced in Chapter 8, our main goal here is to integrate some of the most important concepts to present a more complete and organized picture of the process of research. Such integration is necessary to understand the experimental level of constraint, our focus in Chapters 8–13.

The naturalistic, case-study, correlational, differential, and experimental levels of research are arranged along a continuum of constraint and differ in the degree of demands placed on procedures used in the study. Each constraint level has its own useful applications and the skilled researcher knows when to apply each appropriately. Low-constraint naturalistic and case-study research methods are best used when a research area is new and relatively undeveloped, when the researcher wishes to make observations from which hypotheses can be generated rather than tested, or when the interest is in observing a natural flow of behavior under natural or near-natural conditions. Correlational research methods are applied when we ask questions about relationships among variables and when we measure, but do not manipulate, the variables. Questions about causality cannot be answered with correlational methods. Differential research methods are used when we wish to test the differences between groups where the independent variable is a preexisting factor that can be measured but not directly manipulated. Subjects are not randomly assigned to groups or conditions. Because we measure but do not manipulate the independent variable and we assign subjects to groups based on their scores on the independent variable, differential research is conceptually similar to correlational research. In both, we measure the variables but do not manipulate them. The data from differential research are not sufficient to draw causal inferences.

Experimental research is at the highest constraint level where high demands are placed on both the adequacy of the information and the methods used. At this level of research, subjects are assigned to groups or conditions without bias; for example, using random assignment. Dependent variables are observed and measured and the independent variable is actively and systematically manipulated by the researcher to help answer questions about causality (i.e., "Does change in one variable cause change in another?"). Active manipulation helps to eliminate alternative hypotheses and therefore gives us more confidence in our causal inferences. In summary, the major characteristics that differentiate experimentation from other levels of constraint are (1) there is a high degree of control that the experimenter exerts over the procedures in general and over the independent variable in particular, and (2) the major goal is to draw conclusions about causality from the results.

HYPOTHESIS TESTING

Hypothesis testing is a crucial part of the experimental research process and developing the *research hypothesis* is a major task for the researcher. The research hypothesis in a study has its beginnings in the initial ideas which, as explained in earlier chapters, are often vague or general ideas about natural phenomena. The researcher carefully refines the ideas into a *statement of the problem* drawing on initial observations of the phenomenon as well as a thorough review of previous research. The statement of the problem is converted into a research hypothesis when the *theoretical concepts* in the problem statement are operationalized into specific procedures for measurement or manipulation. The procedure for measuring or manipulating a concept is referred to as an *operational definition* of the concept. By combining the statement of the problem and operational definitions within experimental research, the researcher makes a prediction about the effects of the specific, operationally defined independent variable on the specific, operationally defined dependent variable. The final prediction is the research hypothesis. It is the research hypothesis that is tested through the processes of making, measuring, analyzing, and interpreting empirical observations under controlled conditions. The researcher devotes a good deal of effort to building the research hypothesis. (The flow of the development of the research hypothesis is diagramed in Figure 8.1.)

Our focus here is on developing the research hypothesis at the experimental level. However, it should be understood that problem statements, operational definitions, and research hypotheses are important elements at *all levels* of research. As stressed earlier, we can test hypotheses at all levels of research but the inferences we can confidently draw from the research vary from one level to another.

Statement of the Problem

In designing and carrying out experiments the researcher moves through all phases of the research process beginning with ideas that are refined and developed into one or more specific questions. The researcher then designs the procedures to be used to answer the questions and proceeds with the observations. The design phase is crucial in experimentation. The researcher must carefully plan each step, asking and answering a variety of conceptual and procedural questions to design the controlled observation procedures. The process begins with an idea that is refined into a statement of the problem, which is usually phrased as a question. The initial idea may be somewhat

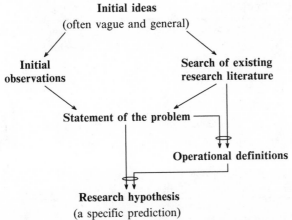

Figure 8.1   **A MODEL OF THE DEVELOPMENT OF A RESEARCH HYPOTHESIS**

vague but does identify the variables to be studied. As an initial idea a researcher might ask, "Does immediate feedback of examination results have any effects on mathematics achievement?" or "What are the effects of relaxation on anxiety?" or "Does the quality of breakfast have any effect on children's academic achievement?" The researcher's initial ideas are then transformed into a statement of the problem by building a prediction into the question. In experimentation the problem statement focuses on a causal prediction. Therefore, the form of the statement of the problem would be "Does variable A cause a specific change in variable B?" A researcher might ask, for example, "Does relaxation reduce anxiety?" or "Does a good breakfast improve academic achievement in grammar schoolchildren?" or "Does immediate feedback of examination results improve arithmetic skills?" Table 8.1 lists other problem statements for which research at the experimental level of constraint is appropriate.

Notice that problem statements are in the form of questions that concern causality—the effects of one variable on another. Further, the direction of the expected effects is clearly suggested—immediate feedback is expected to improve arithmetic skill, relaxation is expected to affect anxiety, and so on. The statement of the problem at the experimental level gives us a good deal of information and a beginning indication of how to proceed with the research. We find (1) a statement about an expected causal effect, (2) identification of at least two variables, and (3) an indication of the direction of the causal effects. Thus, by formulating a clear statement of the problem we have already indicated a good deal about the nature of the research to be done and have helped to point the researcher toward effective design.

Developing a clear statement of the problem requires skill and creative thinking. For example, consider the March 1964 murder of a young woman named Kitty Genovese. Shocking about this particular murder was that the woman was attacked repeatedly in a public parking lot over a 30-minute period while at least 38 of her neighbors heard her screams and/or watched the attack. No one came to her aid. No one even called the police until after she was dead. The questions that occur to us are questions like "How could this happen?" or "Why didn't anyone help her?" These questions are important, but they are too vague to be tested scientifically. If like Darley and Latane

Table 8.1 EXAMPLES OF PROBLEM STATEMENTS AT THE EXPERIMENTAL LEVEL OF CONSTRAINT

1. Does the presence of male hormones increase the aggressive behavior of rats?
2. Does the presence of a mediator increase the likelihood of reaching a compromise in a negotiation setting?
3. Are words that are easily visualized more readily learned than words that cannot be easily visualized?
4. Does the presence of a stranger in the room increase the crying of an infant?
5. Does the administration of stimulants help hyperactive children control their behavior?
6. Does the presentation of contingent reinforcement increase the accuracy of maze-running in mice?
7. Will frustrated people increase their level of aggressive behavior?
8. Will sensory deprivation lead to gross disturbance in thinking and emotional responsivity?

(1968) we were interested in trying to find some answers to these questions, we would have to refine the questions into something more manageable. We would need to study reports of the attack and what the witnesses said about the attack and their behavior in not coming to the victim's aid. We would look for other similar occurrences in police files. We would look in the research literature to see if anyone had studied concepts that might explain what happened to Kitty Genovese. But in the end, we would need to focus our attention on only one or two factors to create a workable statement of the problem. A major factor in this case is that none of the 38 people who witnessed the attack or heard the screams came to the victim's aid. Common sense might lead us to believe that if more people are present, it is more likely that someone will help. But this incident suggests something contrary to common sense; that is, as the number of people present increases, it is less likely that someone will obtain help. This idea has one variable (the number of people) that affects another variable (the likelihood of someone offering aid) in a predictable way. If we develop the idea into a problem statement it would read: "Will bystanders be less likely to help a victim when there are many people present than when there are only a few people present?" The statement of the problem can lead to specific research studies. When Darley and Latane (1968) studied the problem, they found that people are less likely to help if there are other people present. People apparently assume that someone else will take the responsibility. Darley and Latane could have defined other problems from their original vague questions but chose to start with this particular issue.

The statement of the problem, then, is an important early phase in designing research. As noted by Kerlinger (1969), the major criteria of a good problem statement are:

1. The problem should state clearly the expected relationships between variables (in experimentation this is a causal relationship).
2. The problem should be stated clearly in the form of a question.
3. The statement of the problem must at least imply the possibility of an empirical test of the problem.

In the research on the treatment of autistic children discussed in earlier chapters (Graziano, 1974), the major question posed by the researcher was "Can relaxation reduce disruption in autistic children?" The independent variable is relaxation and the dependent variable is disruption. The expected effects are a decrease in disruption brought about by relaxation training. With the statement of the problem clearly defined and, therefore, the major variables identified, the next step in the development of the research hypothesis is to define operationally the variables suggested by the problem statement.

Operational Definitions

Before the dependent variable can be measured it must be defined. Similarly, before the researcher can manipulate the independent variable, relaxation in autistic children, relaxation must be defined. At all levels of research, variables are defined both conceptually and operationally. The *concept* of relaxation refers to an internal state, a condition of people in which they function evenly and without stress or anxiety. We have a fairly good idea of what we mean by relaxation and we would probably agree that the concept refers to an internal, subjective condition. We cannot directly observe that internal condition but can infer it; that is, it is not an observed fact but an inferred *construct.* The conceptual definition of relaxation gives us an idea of what we want to manipulate. But how do we manipulate something that is internal to the subject and thus not directly accessible to the researcher? In this case we need to define operationally how to manipulate the subjects' condition of relaxation. Unless we define precisely how we will manipulate relaxation, other researchers will not be able to repeat our studies. We must therefore develop a construct to the level of an operational definition to manipulate a variable *and* to communicate to other researchers how we manipulated the variable. In this case, we must define relaxation in terms of the procedures (the operations) that will be used to manipulate, control, and measure it. The independent variable, relaxation, is operationally defined in terms of the procedures used in the relaxation training. The definition is clearly spelled out and may be several pages in length. It describes how the researcher should set up the room as well as what should be said and done to "relax" the subjects. Once the definition is created, the term "relaxation training" should be understood to mean all of the detailed procedures. Because the definition provides detailed instructions, other researchers can replicate the procedure. The dependent variable, disruption, can be operationally defined as the (1) frequency, (2) duration, and (3) intensity of each observed disruptive occurrence. "Disruptive occurrence" can be defined behaviorally as any behavior that interferes with an existing activity of staff or other patients. Numerous examples of specific disruptive behaviors should be included in the behavioral description to clarify the concept and to simplify the task of recognizing which behaviors are classified as disruptive. (The actual operational definitions of the two major variables used in this study, relaxation and disruptive behavior, are given in Chapter 4). The operational definitions make it possible for the researcher to proceed a step closer to formulating the research hypothesis.

Research Hypothesis

To gain the information we seek about the effects of relaxation on disruptive behavior of autistic children, we must test our hypothesis. To do that we must develop the problem statement into a specific, testable prediction. The prediction becomes the research hypothesis. Notice that the problem statement has already suggested one basic way to test it: to measure disruptive behavior before and after relaxation training and to see whether there is a difference as predicted—a *pretest-posttest design.* (See Figure 8.2.) As we will see in later chapters, however, a simple pretest-posttest design has weaknesses and there are better methods available to test the hypothesis. However, it helps illustrate the use of operational definitions.

Having operationally defined both the dependent variable (disruptive behavior) and the independent variable (relaxation training), we can now combine the operational definitions and the statement of the problem into a specific prediction—the research

Figure 8.2 A SIMPLE SINGLE-GROUP PRETEST-POSTTEST RESEARCH DESIGN

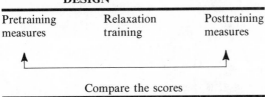

hypothesis. The research hypothesis in this case is: "Following relaxation training, the frequency, duration, and intensity of disruptive behavior will be significantly less than at the pretraining baseline."

Two of the major criteria for good problem statements also apply to research hypotheses. A research hypothesis (1) makes a statement about the relationship among variables and (2) implies clearly that the relationship can be empirically tested. Notice that the research hypothesis is a declarative statement. It is in this form not because we know it is accurate, but because it is a tentative statement that we plan to test. Any research hypothesis at the experimental level of constraint is a tentative statement about the effects of one variable on another and is subject to verification by empirical testing. The research hypothesis, like the statement of the problem, tells us a good deal about the study: it identifies the independent and dependent variables, states a relationship between them, and clearly allows for the possibility of empirically testing the hypothesis. The research hypothesis clearly states how the researcher will go about testing it. The relationship posed in the research hypothesis varies according to the level of constraint. At the correlational level it is a hypothesis about relationships among variables; at the differential level the hypothesis concerns the difference between groups; at the experimental level it is a causal hypothesis.

Testing the Research Hypothesis

The research hypothesis is a complex statement. It is not a single hypothesis at all but actually encompasses three hypotheses, each of which must be carefully checked: the null or statistical hypothesis, the confounding variable hypothesis, and the causal hypothesis.

Suppose we carry out the research with autistic children as follows: (1) we measure the frequency, intensity, and duration of the autistic children's disruptive behavior during a four-week pretraining baseline period; (2) we then train the children in relaxation to the criteria specified (the training requires two months); and (3) after completion of training, we again measure the frequency, intensity, and duration of their disruptive behavior for a four-week posttraining period. This is an example of a simple pretest-posttest design. Now suppose that as we predicted all of the dependent measures of disruption at posttraining are smaller than those taken at the pretraining baseline. With such apparently clear results, can we conclude that the independent variable, relaxation training, did reduce the children's disruptive behavior? Not yet, because to answer the research question we must rule out two other hypotheses. Note again there are *three* hypotheses imbedded in the research hypothesis: (1) the null or statistical hypothesis, (2) the confounding variable hypothesis, and (3) the causal hypothesis (which is the original statement of the problem: will relaxation training reduce disruptive behavior?).

Null Hypothesis Before we can conclude that relaxation does reduce disruptive behavior, we must determine that the posttraining measures of disruption are significantly smaller than the pretraining measures of disruption—that the differences observed are not merely due to chance variation. Thus, the first of the three hypotheses we must test is the *statistical hypothesis*. The *t*- or *F*-test for correlated groups is appropriate because the dependent measure yields score data, and the measures are correlated because they are taken on the same subjects in the pre- and posttraining conditions.

The *null hypothesis* is what its name suggests; null means "none." The null hypothesis states that there is no difference between the two conditions beyond chance differences. If we find a statistically significant difference, we reject the null hypothesis; if we find the differences are within chance limits, we conclude there is not sufficient evidence to reject the null hypothesis. Suppose a *t*- or *F*-test discloses that the posttraining measures are significantly smaller than the pretraining measures—that the differences are not due only to chance. We have rejected the null hypothesis. However, we are not yet ready to accept the hypothesis that relaxation training is responsible for the observed reduction in disruptive behavior.

Confounding Variable Hypothesis Although we have found statistically significant differences in the predicted direction, we still cannot be sure that the observed differences are actually due to the independent variable—relaxation—for they may be due to some extraneous variables that have confounded the research. Testing and rejecting the null hypothesis, while necessary, is not sufficient to draw a causal inference. We must also rule out the possibility that factors other than the independent variable may have had an effect on the dependent variable (i.e., that confounding variables are responsible for any observed effect). The task here is to rule out confounding variables as explanations of the results, which is done primarily during the design phase when we anticipate possible confounding variables and design controls to eliminate their effects on the dependent variable.

The *confounding variable hypothesis* suggests that the observed statistically significant differences may be due to extraneous factors that have systematic effects on the dependent measures rather than being due to changes in the independent variable. In this research we accept the finding that there is a significant difference as predicted, but being systematic scientists we are not yet convinced that the difference we found is due to the independent variable. Rather, we consider it may be due to the effects of confounding factors. For example, we have noted that relaxation training required two months to reach criterion, a long time in the life of a growing child and during which the children could have matured somewhat. The observed improvement might have been due to maturational factors and not to the independent variable, relaxation training. Thus, in this study, the independent variable may have been confounded with maturation. If we are not careful in our enthusiasm at having found a statistically significant difference, we might too readily conclude that relaxation training is the effective variable that brought about the improvement in disruptive behavior. But the confounding variable hypothesis recognizes that the explanation of relaxation training being responsible for the improvement in disruptive behavior may be only one of several possible alternative explanations and to have confidence in our conclusions we must carefully rule out all alternative explanations.

Note that the confounding variable hypothesis is not directly tested as is the statistical hypothesis. Rather, each confounding variable hypothesis is ruled out by first anticipating potential confounding variables, reducing their likelihood by carefully designing the research, and later by carefully inspecting the research design and procedures. This careful designing and inspection shows where the design is weak and where it is strong. The researcher must then judge whether the design is strong enough to rule out the most likely potential confounding variables. As we will see in later chapters, some designs are so powerful that they almost automatically rule out many confounding variables.

The concern for ruling out alternative explanations in science is an important point for students to understand. Research is conducted not only to find evidence to support research hypotheses but also to rule out alternative explanations, which are also known as rival hypotheses. Every confounding variable is a threat to the validity of an experiment. We will discover that certain experimental designs can rule out most of the confounding variables likely to occur in a research project.

Causal Hypothesis   The *causal hypothesis* states that the independent variable has the predicted effect on the dependent variable. Suppose we tested and rejected the null hypothesis and carefully ruled out *confounding variables.* (We will discuss how to control or rule out confounding variables in Chapter 9.) We are ready to return to the original research question, "Does relaxation training cause a reduction in disruptive behavior of autistic children?" Because we found that there is significantly less disruption after training than before training and we carefully ruled out alternative hypotheses, we are then left with one hypothesis, that the independent variable affected the dependent variable as predicted. Note, however, that our assertion is not absolute but is a statement of probability. Our first hypothesis was the statistical hypothesis, which we tested in terms of probability. Even though the data may have been sufficiently persuasive to convince us to reject the null hypothesis of no difference, there is always the possibility that we have made a Type I error. It should be clear that there are so many complicated steps from initial conceptualization to running the study to interpreting the results that we must always be cautious in our interpretations. We can have confidence but not certainty in the results of a well-run study. Every finding in science is considered to be a tentative finding, subject to change due to new observations.

Another important point about developing research hypotheses is that most problem statements can be developed into several different research hypotheses, each of which can then be tested. Thus, we can generate many different studies from the same problem statement. Recall that the problem statement in the research with autistic children is "Can relaxation reduce disruption of autistic children?" The essential question being posed here is whether there is a causal relationship between the child's relaxation and the degree of disruption. In the study described earlier (Graziano, 1974), relaxation is defined operationally in terms of procedures used to train the child to "slow down," and disruption is operationally defined as the frequency, duration, and intensity of each overt behavior that is recognized as "disruptive." These definitions led to the specific research hypothesis that "following relaxation training, the frequency, duration, and intensity of disruptive behavior will be significantly less than at the pretraining baseline."

Now suppose that we want to study another aspect of the relaxation-disruption hypothesis and operationally define relaxation in terms of the pharmacological effects of a particular drug. We give each child a drug that is known to relax individuals. We also modify or redefine the dependent measure of disruptive behavior. The research hypothesis is similar to the original hypothesis but, because we have defined variables in terms of different operations, we are actually testing a different research hypothesis. When we conduct the study using the pretest-posttest design we use our redefined measures of baseline and posttest levels of disruption, and we give the children specific drugs to induce relaxation instead of using a behavioral training approach to teach relaxation. Yet we are still evaluating the same statement of the problem but with a different interpretation expressed as a different research hypothesis.

We can make other changes as well in the way we translate the statement of the problem into a research hypothesis. We could use a different research design. Instead of using the pretest-posttest design we randomly assign each of the autistic children to one of two groups. One of the groups is relaxed with the drug whereas the other group is not given the drug. We then measure the disruptive behavior of all subjects and compare the mean level of disruption in the two groups. This design is called a *two-group posttest-only design* and is illustrated in Figure 8.3. The research hypothesis in this study is stated differently from that of the previous example because the independent variable and the research design have been changed. The new research hypothesis is "Autistic children who are given drugs that relax them will show less disruptive behavior than autistic children who do not receive such drugs." Thus, the same problem statement regarding the hypothesized causal relationship between relaxation and disruption of autistic children can be combined with different operational definitions of the independent and dependent variables and different research designs. This results in the generation of several different research hypotheses and consequently several different studies. In essence, the researcher is able to investigate the same basic problem in different ways, discovering and testing different facets of the same issue. This allows us to *replicate* (repeat) systematically the study of the hypothesized relationship in

Figure 8.3 A SIMPLE TWO-GROUP POSTTEST-ONLY, RESEARCH DESIGN

Autistic children given relaxation drugs	Level of disruptive behavior ←	
		Compare the scores
Autistic children *not* given relaxation drugs	Level of disruptive behavior ←	

several different ways, thus increasing confidence in the conclusions about that hypothesized relationship. Replication is an extremely important part of research (see Chapter 9). Other research hypotheses also can be generated from the basic problem posed in the relaxation-disruption hypothesis.

Summary

To summarize, we carefully refine initially vague or general ideas to formulate a statement of the problem. The statement of the problem in experimentation identifies the variables, implies causality, and indicates the expected direction of the causal effect. Having identified the variables by posing the problem statement, we must then operationally define the variables. Having done that, we can then construct a research hypothesis by combining the operational definitions with the statement of the problem. The research hypothesis states a specific prediction about the specific variables, which then can be tested by the researcher.

Remember, when we test the research hypothesis, we are testing not one but several hypotheses: the null or statistical hypothesis, the confounding variable hypothesis (which itself is often a set of several hypotheses), and the causal hypothesis. We must consider and reject the null and the confounding variable hypotheses before we are able to accept the causal hypothesis.

Psychology majors are well aware of the importance of statistical methods for testing the null hypothesis. It is equally important for the researcher to rule out the confounding variable hypotheses—to be able to recognize potential confounding variables in any proposed research and to rule them out to draw conclusions about a causal relationship between the independent and dependent variables. Statistical tests will tell us only whether there is a significant difference between groups or conditions and not whether the difference is due to the independent variable manipulation. We can draw that conclusion only after we have identified and ruled out competing interpretations. Finally, one problem statement can be developed into several different research hypotheses that lead to several studies, which allows us to examine different facets of the basic problem and to increase our confidence through such replications.

VALIDITY AND THREATS TO VALIDITY

A major concern in research is the validity of the procedures and conclusions. The term *validity* has several meanings. Perhaps the most basic meaning refers to methodological soundness or appropriateness. That is, a valid measure does indeed measure what it is supposed to measure; a valid research design does, in fact, test what it is supposed to test. In general validity concerns whether the concepts being investigated are actually the ones being measured or tested.

At any level of constraint we must be concerned with issues of validity. At the experimental level we are concerned with answering specific questions about causality, such as "Does the independent variable have effects on the dependent variable?" We want to carry out the experiment so it will give us high confidence in the validity of the conclusions about that causal relationship. Because experimentation may involve many factors, all having effects on the outcome, there are likely to be many potential threats to the validity of any experiment. Therefore, two major tasks of the researcher are to (1) anticipate all potential threats to validity and (2) create procedures to eliminate or reduce them. Absolute accuracy or validity cannot be achieved and validity must always be understood in relative terms.

Types of Validity

There are many types of validity. We have chosen to follow and to modify the organization presented by Campbell and Stanley (1966) and Cook and Campbell (1979). The latter discussed four types of validity: statistical validity, construct validity, external validity, and internal validity.

Statistical Validity   When we use statistical procedures to test the null hypothesis we are making a statement about the *statistical validity* of the results; that is, are the results due to some systematic factor (ideally, the independent variable) or are they due merely to chance variations? Ruling out the null hypothesis is a necessary first step in testing the effects of the independent variable.

There are several possible threats to a study's statistical validity and the researcher must carefully prevent them. One such threat is the possibility that the measures used to assess the dependent variable are unreliable. Unreliable measures threaten statistical validity. Another threat to statistical validity is the researcher's violations of the assumptions that underlie the statistical tests. Each statistical procedure makes several assumptions about the nature of the data. Using a statistical procedure in a situation where one or more of these assumptions are not true can threaten the study's statistical validity.

Construct Validity   Every hypothesis tested in research is constructed in a theoretical context of ideas. *Construct validity* refers to how well the study's results support the theory or constructs behind the research and asks whether the theory supported by the findings provides the best available theoretical explanation of the results. To help reduce threats to construct validity the researcher uses clearly stated definitions and carefully builds the hypotheses on solid, well-validated constructs. In brief, the theoretical bases must be clear and well supported with rival theories carefully ruled out.

As an example of dubious construct validity consider the popular books by Erich von Daniken, *Chariots of the Gods* (1970) and *Gods from Outer Space* (1972). Millions of copies of the books have been sold around the world and they have been translated into a number of foreign languages. They have been among the world's best-selling books, supposedly surpassed only by the Bible in total sales. They present Daniken's theoretical proposition that an advanced race of humanoid, extraterrestrial beings who visited Earth thousands of years ago had a great impact on starting humans toward advanced civilization. The author presents an impressive array of evidence to support his hypothesis, including numerous photographs of ancient objects that he claims suggest technical skills far beyond the abilities of primitive humans. Many readers, impressed by his abundant evidence, are convinced of the validity of his theory. But Daniken's particular theoretical explanation of the observed artifacts is only one of at least two alternative explanations. The most plausible rival explanation is that humans, without extraterrestrial help, created the objects themselves. For example, consider a figure that Daniken suggests shows a humanoid in a space helmet hundreds of years before space helmets were even thought of by humans. According to a rival hypothesis, the figure could be a religious symbol, a human figure with a halo of light around the head. In other words, the evidence presented by Daniken does seem to support his theory, but it supports an alternative theory just as well. The construct validity of his theory is in doubt.

An example from a continuing debate in psychology—the nature-nurture issue—further clarifies the concept of construct validity. The nature-nurture question has been raised in many different areas of psychological research from questions about the cause of schizophrenia to exploring the issue of why males usually score higher than females on math skill measures. On the latter issue, a lively debate has raged over how much of the difference is innate and how much is the result of environmental effects (Benbow & Stanley, 1980; Parsons, 1980). Environmental variables alone could shape the differences if males receive more training than females in math or if males are more likely than females to be told that learning math is important if they want to be successful. The issue is whether the data on this question support the idea of an innate, genetically determined characteristic (nature) as being responsible for the observed sex differences or whether the environment (nurture) could have shaped the relationships observed. In many cases, the interpretation of data that one is tempted to make is dependent on the preconceptions of the investigator and not on the nature of the data. For example, the finding that men tend to take more math courses than women would seem to be consistent with the nurture hypothesis that males are better at math because they get more training in math. However, one could interpret that same finding to mean that men take more math courses because they tend to be good at math. Therefore, the data are consistent with both a nature and a nurture hypothesis, and the construct validity of any one interpretation would be in doubt.

External Validity   In its strictest sense, the results of an experiment are limited to those subjects and conditions used in the particular experiment. But when, for example, we test college students' memory ability, are we really interested in how well these particular 20 freshmen in Dr. Perkins' introductory psychology class did on the morning of October 21? No, instead we are interested in memory functions in general. We want to be able to generalize the results beyond the specific conditions and subjects, and to be able to apply the findings to other, similar subjects and conditions. *External validity* refers to the degree to which we are able to generalize the results of a study to other subjects, conditions, times, and places.

The hypothetical example of the psychoanalyst who studied enuretic children (see Chapter 1) illustrates a problem of external validity. The psychoanalyst observed that every enuretic child she treated showed high levels of anxiety and significant Oedipal conflicts. Let us assume that her assessments of the clients are accurate. Can she validly conclude, based on her particular sample of children, that all enuretic children have the same characteristics? Of course, she cannot. Why? Because her particular clients do not necessarily represent the entire population of enuretic children. They were not selected to represent them. Her clients might have been a specific subgroup with characteristics not generally found in other enuretic children. For example, her sample might have been, in addition to being enuretic, emotionally disturbed to such a degree as to warrant professional help. They might represent only those enuretic children whose parents were anxious enough about the problem behavior to seek treatment or who were wealthy enough to afford a private psychoanalyst.

To make statements about the overall population based on the findings of a particular sample, the sample must be selected from the population in such a manner that it adequately represents the population. Problems of generalization from a sample to a population are often best controlled by random selection of subjects from the population (controls are explained further in Chapter 9). In similar fashion, the researcher must be careful about generalizing across times, places, and conditions. To generalize across different times, places, or conditions, one *must* sample across those times, places, or conditions.

Internal Validity and Confounding Variables   *Internal validity* is of great concern to the researcher because it involves the very heart of the experimental goals—the demonstration of causality. In an experiment internal validity concerns the question, "Was the independent variable and not some extraneous variable responsible for the observed changes in the dependent variable?" An experiment is said to be internally valid when it can be concluded with confidence that the independent variable and not some other variable brought about the observed changes in the dependent variable. Any factor that weakens this confidence is a threat to the internal validity of the study.

Suppose, for example, we are interested in the ability of schizophrenic patients to judge time duration. We predict that their time estimation will be significantly disrupted by intrusive auditory stimulation. We test patients for their time estimations of short intervals under two conditions: (1) a high-stimulation condition in which loud, rhythmic music is played during testing, and (2) a low-stimulation condition in which the testing room is kept quiet. Because of scheduling problems in the hospital, patients are available to us only on Monday and Thursday mornings, when the locked-ward and the open-ward patients, respectively, can be tested. We test the Monday patients under the high-stimulation condition and the Thursday patients under the low-stimulation condition. The research hypothesis is that schizophrenic patients under the high-stimulation condition will make significantly more errors than those under the low-stimulation condition. We find, exactly as predicted, that significantly more errors are made under the high-stimulation condition and conclude that external auditory stimulation is a significant factor that affects time estimation in schizophrenics. The major confounding variable in our study should be obvious: the subjects in the two conditions differ not only in terms of the independent variable—high- and low-auditory stimulation—but also because one group consists of closed-ward patients and the other group consists of open-ward patients. There is good reason to suspect that the closed-ward patients are more disturbed than the other group, and it is therefore not surprising that they do much more poorly on the time-estimation task. But we attribute the difference between the two groups to the high- and low-stimulation conditions that we manipulated. We do not recognize that another factor we did not control—severity of illness—might also have influenced the outcome. That the results may be due to severity of illness rather than amount of auditory stimulation provides an alternative explanation.

Until the alternative explanation is clearly ruled out, we cannot confidently conclude that amount of stimulation has much to do with subjects' ability to estimate time duration. In our study, the independent variable—amount of auditory stimulation—is confounded with an uncontrolled variable—severity of illness. When we use the term *confounded* we mean that the independent variable varies with another variable. Because the two vary together we cannot easily tell whether one or the other or both are responsible for the observed changes in the dependent variable. This confounding leaves us with an alternative explanation of the results rather than with a confident conclusion about the effects of auditory stimulation. The confounding variable in this study should have been eliminated in the initial design of the study, long before testing any subjects.

As another example consider the hypothesis worked out earlier concerning the effects of relaxation training on the disruptive behavior of autistic children and the research procedures used to test it. Can we conclude with confidence that the independent variable, relaxation training, is responsible for the observed reduction in disruptive behavior? In short, can we be confident about the *internal validity* of this study? Consider the basic design of the first study, which tried to test the research hypothesis that "Following relaxation training, the frequency, duration, and intensity of disruptive behavior will be significantly less than at the pretraining baseline." To test the hypothesis we measured the disruptive behavior of the autistic children, then provided relaxation training, and then measured disruption again. It required two months for all of the children in the study to reach the criterion of successful relaxation. We found that at posttraining the disruptive behavior was measurably less and the decrease was statistically significant. It is tempting to conclude that the relaxation training was responsible for the decrease in disruptive behavior, but what alternative explanations might there be for the results? What confounds might have been operating to have produced the results? As suggested earlier, the children might simply have improved their functioning naturally over the two-month period, for children can change markedly over two months through natural maturational processes. Perhaps the observed improvement was due simply to maturation of the subjects. If this is the case, the relaxation treatment had little to do with the observed improvement. Maturation is a confounding variable; in this study it supplies us with an alternative explanation of the results, and we cannot be confident that the results are due to the influence of the independent variable.

Another alternative explanation for the observed improvement is that some systematic factor in the research itself, other than relaxation, might have been responsible. After all, the children were in a full-day, five-days-weekly therapy program. Many procedures were used in addition to relaxation training. Might it not be possible that some other factor that was consistently applied to the children during the two months of relaxation training might have been responsible for the improvement? This is an example of the confounding variable of history; that is, during the course of the research many variables besides the independent variable may have been operating.

A phenomenon called regression to the mean might also have been operating here. Any behavior will naturally vary in its frequency, intensity, and duration, going through ups and downs of severity. Perhaps this research had been started at the peak of severity, perhaps begun even *because* the severity was so great. As time passed, the normal variation of the behavior returned to levels of severity closer to the mean, far lower than it was at the high, pretreatment baseline peak of severity. It was then that the posttraining measures were taken. If regression to the mean was indeed operating here, then the relaxation manipulations might have had little to do with the observed improvement in behavior.

There is yet another possible confounding variable that could explain findings of a decrease in disruptive behavior. In the course of the research, the staff making the observations of the children's disruptive behavior may have changed in the ways in which they observed and measured the behavior. They might have gradually become more accustomed to the children's severe behavior and, in time, tended to record it as less severe (i.e., their criteria for observations and not the behavior of the children might have changed during the course of the study).

There are many potential confounding variables such as these in research. In fact, there may be several confounding variables in a study. Where there are multiple confounding variables in a study their effects might all be in the same direction, thus compounding the errors, or in opposite directions countering one another, thus decreasing potential errors. In any event, if we wish to draw valid, confident conclusions about the effects of one variable on another we must carefully anticipate and control potential confounding variables to eliminate rival hypotheses, leaving the research hypothesis as the most likely explanation for the results.

SOME MAJOR CONFOUNDING VARIABLES

Cook and Campbell (1979) have summarized the major types of *confounding variables* that can affect experimental results and thus lead to erroneous interpretations. Some of the major confounding variables that can occur in research follow.

Maturation

In research such as pretest-posttest studies with children, subjects grow older between the pretreatment and posttreatment measures. As they grow older, they may also become more sophisticated, experienced, bigger, stronger, and so on. Natural *maturational* changes can occur in subjects other than children. Adults placed in a new environment tend to make predictable changes (adjustments) over time. Diseases tend to have a predictable course. Thus, observed changes over time may be due to maturational factors rather than to any effects of the independent variable. Researchers must be particularly alert to maturational factors when conducting research with children during which change and growth are virtual certainties.

History

During the course of the study many events that are not of interest can occur and possibly affect the outcome. In general, threats to internal validity due to *history* are greatest with longer times between pretest and posttest measurements. Historical factors are most important to consider when we are measuring dependent variables respon-

"OF COURSE I'VE BECOME MORE MATURE SINCE YOU STARTED TREATING ME. YOU'VE BEEN AT IT SINCE I WAS 14 YEARS OLD."

Reprinted by permission of S. Harris.

sive to environmental changes. For example, weight is more affected by the amount of food intake than is height. Weight shows more natural variation within a subject over time than height. Therefore, historical factors are more likely to be a confounding variable for weight than for height. Most weight-control procedures would be lucky to hold their own if we evaluated them during the holidays when people are constantly exposed to tempting high-calorie foods.

Testing

The effects of repeated *testing* of subjects may be a threat to internal validity because subjects may gain proficiency through repeated practice on the measuring instruments. Testing effects are most pronounced on measures where the subject is asked to perform on some skill-related task. Measures such as memory tests, IQ tests, or tests of manual dexterity fall into this category. Most people will do better on the second administration of the test because of a practice effect.

Instrumentation

Apparent pre-post changes may be due to changes in the measuring *instrument* over time rather than to the experimental manipulation of the independent variable. This is particularly true when the measuring instrument is a human observer. Observers might, in time, become more proficient in administering tests or in making observations. Their criteria for judgments might change as they become familiar with the dependent variable being observed. In the research with autistic children, such changes in instrumentation might have accounted for some of the apparent improvement.

Regression to the Mean

Regression to the mean is one of the most misunderstood concepts in research. Stated simply, the concept of *regression to the mean* suggests that whenever you select subjects *because* their scores on a measure are extreme (either very high or very low), they will tend to be less extreme on a second testing (i.e., their scores will have regressed toward the mean). For most students it is not obvious why this is the case. Suppose, for example, students take a series of tests in a course. Assume that we consider the top 10 percent of the class based on the first exam score. How should the top students perform on the second exam? We would expect them to do well, but would they do *as* well as on the first exam? Would they all be in the top 10 percent the second time around? Probably not. The reason is that some of the students did well on the first exam in part because they were fortunate to have known more about a significant number of questions. We might say they were "lucky." On the second test, however, many of the students who scored high on the first test because of good fortune might have found more questions on material they had not studied, and so they scored lower. If we took the top 10 percent of students on the first test and computed their mean score on both the first and second tests, we would probably find that they scored (on average) lower on the second test—they regressed toward the mean. Similarly, if we took the bottom 10 percent of students on the first test and compute their mean score on both the first and second tests, we would find that they scored (on average) higher on the second test—again, they regressed toward the mean. How much regression occurs will depend on how much of the average test performance is due to variable factors, such as "being lucky," and how much is due to consistent factors, such as skill and good study habits. The more that variable factors contribute to the score, the more regression we can expect to see.

Selection

Confounding due to *selection* can occur when care is not taken to insure that two or more groups being compared are equivalent before the manipulations begin. Under ideal conditions, subjects will be randomly selected and then randomly assigned to different groups. When random selection and assignment are not possible as in much of the naturalistic, case-study, and differential research, then the possibility of confounding due to selection exists.

Attrition

In the normal course of a study, subjects are lost for different reasons; some people go on vacation in the middle of the study, others forget their appointments, others decide they are not interested, some become ill, and so on. If there are no biasing factors, such dropouts will probably be evenly distributed across groups, and they will not differentially affect one group more than others. But confounding due to *attrition* can occur when subjects are lost differentially, such as when there is more drop out from one group than from another, or when subjects with certain characteristics are lost. When we plan research we must be careful not to create situations or use procedures that will bias some subjects against completing the study, thus differentially affecting the outcome of the study. For example, suppose a researcher realized too late that nearly all of the seniors among the high school subjects failed to return for the second half of the experiment because it coincided with school parties, excitement, and general preparation for graduation. Their attrition left primarily underclass subjects in the second half of the study, thus biasing the sample and the results.

Sometimes procedures may tend to cause subjects with certain characteristics to drop out, leaving a biased sample. For example, in an unpublished study conducted many years ago by one of the authors, sixth-grade boys responded diffidently and many dropped out because they said they found the procedures "too girlish." Perhaps in today's more egalitarian mood this particular example might be less likely. In any event, care must be taken to avoid confounding studies by allowing attrition of subjects to have a differential affect on the outcome.

Diffusion of Treatment

When subjects in different experimental conditions are in close proximity, such as children in the same classroom, and are able to communicate with each other, earlier subjects may "give away" the procedures to those scheduled later. Also, experimental subjects who receive some particular treatment may communicate with control subjects who supposedly do not receive that treatment or who may not have known they were in a control group. Such information exchanges may erode the planned experimental differences between groups. The groups become more similar because of the information exchange between subjects.

Diffusion of treatment can affect studies in many ways. For example, a situation encountered by many psychologists is the common practice of using subjects from an undergraduate subject pool. In a setting like this, diffusion of treatment is possible. Students often hear about studies from other students and perhaps even select the study on the basis of what they hear. When they participate, the knowledge of what their friends experienced might affect how they respond regardless of the condition in which they are placed. To compensate for this problem, many researchers try to make their study look the same to subjects in all conditions in an attempt to minimize diffusion of treatments.

Sequencing Effects

Much of the research in psychology is designed so that each subject is exposed to more than one of the experimental conditions. These are called *within-subjects designs*. Although they offer some important advantages over other designs, they also introduce another confounding factor, *sequencing effects*. For example, if a study includes three conditions and each subject is exposed to all three, their experiences with earlier conditions of the study may affect their responses to later conditions. If the order of presentation of conditions for all subjects are always condition A followed by condition B followed by condition C, then systematic confounding effects can occur. To control for sequencing effects we would normally use more than one order of conditions.

Summary

The major objective of an experiment is to demonstrate with confidence that the manipulated independent variable is the major cause of the observed changes in the dependent variable. When this causality is not clear because some variable other than the independent variable may have caused the effects, we have a confounding, a threat to the internal validity of the study. Threats to internal validity reduce our confidence in the causal relationship between the independent variable and the dependent variable. Therefore, it is extremely important for the researcher to plan studies carefully to anticipate and to control potential confounding.

THREATS TO VALIDITY FROM SUBJECT AND EXPERIMENTER EFFECTS

There is a large category of threats to the validity of a study due to subject and experimenter factors. The expectations and biases of both the researcher and the subjects can systematically affect the results in subtle ways, thus reducing the study's validity.

Subject Effects

As discussed by Orne (1962), every psychological experiment is a social situation in which both subjects and researchers participate in a common undertaking, the experiment. Each behaves according to their understanding of how a subject or a psychological researcher should behave. When subjects enter an experiment, they are not entirely naive. They have some ideas, understandings, and perhaps misunderstandings about what to expect in the experimental situation. Subjects enter with a variety of reasons for being subjects. Some do so because it is a course requirement. Others participate because of curiosity or because they will be paid for their participation. Some volunteer because they hope to learn something, perhaps about science or themselves. The point is that subjects enter and carry out their role with a variety of motivations, understandings, expectations, and biases, all of which can affect their behavior in the experimental setting. Further, as we noted several times earlier, an experiment is an artificial, contrived situation, far removed from subjects' natural environments. When being closely observed and measured, people are likely to be more "on guard" and to behave differently than in more familiar situations, which can result in *subject effects*.

Most subjects do their best to be "good" subjects. They want to appear at their best for the researcher. This may lead some subjects to try and discern the research hypothesis so they will know how they are "supposed to behave." Subjects are often particularly sensitive to any real or imagined cues from the researcher, and the researcher, with his or her own expectations and biases, might inadvertently give such cues. Cues given to the subjects that give information on how to behave to satisfy the researcher and demands of the research are called *demand characteristics* of the study. Demand characteristics occur unintentionally, and they include not only characteristics of the setting and procedures but also information and even rumors about the researcher and the nature of the research.

A related phenomenon, the *placebo effect,* can occur when subjects expect some fairly specific effect of an experimental manipulation. For example, some subjects in biofeedback studies of tension reduction or drug studies of pain control enter the study with the clear expectation that the procedures will help, and they actually report feeling better or even show physiological changes, all due to the *suggestion* that the procedure will work. In a number of studies, subjects have reported improvement when given a placebo treatment such as a sugar pill that looks and tastes like the true drug being tested but lacks the active drug ingredient.

Clearly there are many ways that subjects, bringing their own expectations and biases, can react in the experimental situation. Many of their reactions are not part of the experimental plan. Thus, the researcher should include controls for these and other possible subject effects to prevent confounding that can reduce the study's validity.

Experimenter Effects

Experimenter effects also can have significant impact on the outcome of a study. The researcher attempts to carry out the research plan as objectively and as accurately as possible. But researchers, too, are human and carry their own potentially biasing expectations and motivations into the study. The major expectation of the researcher that can operate to bias the results is, of course, that the results will turn out as predicted and the hypothesis will have been supported. But how can such expectations bias the results in an objective experimental situation? *Experimenter expectancies* might cause researchers to bias results in several ways: by directly influencing the subject's behavior toward support of the hypothesis; by selecting data that best support the hypothesis; by using statistical techniques that best show the particular effects predicted, but not other effects; and by interpreting results in a biased manner (i.e., by drawing conclusions that accept improbable explanations consistent with the research hypothesis while ignoring other, more probable and parsimonious explanations that do not support the hypothesis). Common to all of these ways of introducing bias is the idea that the researcher will tend to make decisions and choices that favor the hypothesis being tested. This is not to say that the researcher deliberately and knowingly falsifies data but, rather, behaves in ways that tend to support his or her own expectations and does so without being clearly aware of it. For example, suppose that a researcher has two groups of subjects. The subjects have been randomly assigned to the groups to avoid confounding due to assignment. Subjects in each group are to be tested on a series of arithmetic problems and are timed by the researcher. The prediction is that, because of the difference in instructions to the two groups, the experimental group will take significantly longer than the control group to complete the problems. In this situation there are several ways that experimenter bias can operate. If the researcher knows to which group each subject is assigned and knows the research hypothesis, then it is quite possible that the researcher might tend to time the experimental subjects in a way that would extend their times. The researcher also could influence the results by reading the same set of instructions in a slightly different tone to the two groups, emphasizing speed for the control subjects. In either case, the researcher would probably not be aware of this systematic bias and would deny it. However, the bias, accumulated over all of the subjects in the group, could very well affect the outcome toward support of the hypothesis.

Much of our understanding of experimenter expectancy effects is due to the research of Rosenthal and his colleagues. Rosenthal and Fode (1963a, 1963b) suggest several ways in which the experimenter might unintentionally affect a subject's responses while interacting with the subject and thus bias the results to favor the hypothesis. For example, the researcher might unintentionally present cues by variations in tone of voice or by changes in posture or facial expressions, might unintentionally verbally reinforce some responses and not others, or might unintentionally misjudge and misrecord subjects' responses. Although such experimenter expectancy effects may occur, it has been difficult to demonstrate clearly that they do occur, leaving many researchers to conclude that although this may be a problem in a minority of studies, it does not characterize most research (Barber & Silver, 1968). But what is important here is that in any research where experimenter expectancy effects may occur, the effects may provide an alternative explanation for the obtained results. When, for example, a journal editor reads a research manuscript that has been submitted for possible publication and determines that such expectancy effects may have occurred, just raising this possibility is sufficient to cast doubt on the validity of the experiment and lead to the rejection of the manuscript for publication. The editor need not provide data to support the alternative hypothesis that the obtained results were due to experimenter expectancy effects. If the rival hypothesis could be true, then we cannot accept the researcher's conclusions about the effects of the independent variable. The researcher would have to repeat the experiment, adding controls to eliminate the rival hypothesis. Thus, although Barber and Silver (1968) may be correct in doubting that such effects are as frequent as Rosenthal suggested, the simple existence of the rival hypothesis in a study is sufficient to cast doubt on a researcher's findings, and it is therefore important for the researcher to control for potential experimenter expectancy effects.

We have pointed out that not every confounding variable occurs in every experiment, and therefore, not all of the available controls are necessary in each experiment. However, subject and experimenter effects may occur in virtually any experimental situation and the experimenter should, as a matter of course, take steps to avoid these biases in every experiment. It is important to note that *many of the most important threats to validity will be well controlled if the researcher designs into each experiment the random selection of subjects, the random assignment of subjects to conditions, and a proper control group* (see Chapter 9).

STATISTICAL VERSUS PRACTICAL SIGNIFICANCE

A statistically significant finding is impressive and usually pleases the researcher, especially if it is in the predicted direction. But the mere fact of finding statistical significance can be quite misleading, and we have to be careful not to conclude that because a finding is statistically significant, it is therefore important or of practical or useful significance.

As Lick (1973) points out, a statistically significant finding is not necessarily of personal or practical significance. Suppose, for example, that we compare two groups of seriously obese adults. The experimental group attends a weight-reduction program while the control group is put on a waiting list. After six months the treated group has lost a mean of 3.4 pounds while the control group has gained a mean of 1.2 pounds, and the difference between the groups is statistically significant. Despite the statistical significance, the question must be asked, "Is the loss of just over three pounds after six months of dieting, exercise, and group meetings of any personal importance or significance to those obese people who wanted to lose weight?" Most of those dieters would probably say "No!" Thus, when evaluating the effectiveness of the weight-reduction program in practical terms, we have to be careful not to let the statistically significant findings blind us to the fact that the program was simply not practically or personally successful for those people.

VALIDITY, CONTROL, AND CONSTRAINT

Validity, control, and constraint are closely related concepts. In essence, control procedures are applied to increase the various kinds of validity in research, and constraint is largely a matter of the degree of control, precision, and structure applied in research. Thus, a large component of the difference between low- and high-constraint methods is the greater, more precise, and structured application of controls at high-constraint levels.

SUMMARY

Our focus has been on the development and testing of hypotheses, from initially vague and/or general ideas to specific research hypotheses. The careful construction of the research hypothesis is a critical step in all research, and it is most formalized and most fully developed at the experimental level of constraint. Testing the research hypothesis in any experiment actually involves three hypotheses: the null or statistical hypothesis, the confounding variable hypothesis, and the causal hypothesis.

Also important are issues of validity and threats to validity in research. There are at least four important types of validity with which the researcher must be concerned: statistical validity, construct validity, external validity, and internal validity. Each type of validity can be threatened in a number of ways, and the researcher must anticipate the potential threats and design appropriate controls into the research. The specific controls will vary according to the type of validity being threatened and the nature of the particular threats.

In addition, there is a large area of general threats to validity due to subject and experimenter expectations and biases, and these should be routinely controlled in any study. In general, the two concepts of threats to validity and controls are two sides of the same conceptual coin. Of particular concern are threats to internal validity because these affect the confidence with which we can conclude there is a causal relationship between the independent and dependent variables. In Chapter 9 we will consider controls, paying particular attention to controls for threats to internal validity.

REVIEW EXERCISES

I. Define the following key terms. Be sure you understand them. They are discussed in the chapter and defined in the glossary.

Research hypothesis
Statement of the problem
Theoretical concept
Operational definition
Concept
Construct
Pretest-posttest design
Null hypothesis
Statistical hypothesis
Confounding variable hypothesis
Causal hypothesis
Two-group posttest-only design
Confounding variable
Extraneous variable
Rival hypothesis
Replicate
Types of validity
    Statistical
    Construct

External
Internal
Confounding variables
Maturation
History
Testing
Instrumentation
Regression to the mean
Selection
Attrition
Diffusion of treatment
Sequencing effects
Within-subjects design
Subject effects
Demand characteristics
Placebo effect
Experimenter effects
Experimenter expectancies

II. Answer each of the following. Check your answers in the chapter.

1. What is meant by "testing the research hypothesis actually involves three hypotheses"?
2. How do we deal with the confounding variable hypothesis?
3. Explain why it is so important in experimental research to rule out the confounding variable hypothesis.
4. What are the major types of validity in research?
5. For each of the following independent variables indicate the number of levels of the independent variable and identify each.
   a. We study the effects of high- and low-audio stimulation on subjects' responses.
   b. We use six levels of room temperature in a working-conditions study.
   c. A researcher compares rats' running times. One group of rats is fed one hour prior to running, another group is fed two hours prior to running, and a third group is fed three hours prior to running.
   d. Four different arithmetic workbooks are tested in an elementary school.

6. Why is internal validity of such importance in experimentation?

7. What kind of relationships among variables are studied at each of the five levels of constraint?

8. What are the nine major confounding factors? For each one develop at least three examples of research in which each confounding factor could occur.

9. What is meant by subject and experimenter effects? How do they threaten the validity of a study? Give several examples.

III. Think about and work the following problems.

1. a. Think of five or six experimental research ideas. Create them or obtain them from published reports of studies, such as in textbooks.

   b. Develop each research idea into a clear statement of a problem.

   c. Identify and operationally define the variables suggested by the problem statement.

   d. Combine the problem statement with the operational definitions into a specific prediction and state the research hypothesis.

2. Take the problem statements you developed in the preceding exercise and develop different operational definitions. Then develop several research hypotheses that are different from those developed in the preceding exercise. Why is it important to be able to do this in research?

3. Explain, as if to another student in the course, how replication can be achieved in the process of varying the operational definitions when developing research hypotheses from problem statements. Give examples.

4. Develop a research project in which there are some clear experimenter and subject effects.

CHAPTER 9

CONTROLS TO REDUCE THREATS TO VALIDITY IN EXPERIMENTAL RESEARCH

Control procedures are needed to counteract threats to validity so that we may confidently draw conclusions. Threats to validity and control procedures to reduce threats constitute two sides of the same conceptual coin. In this chapter we will consider the major methods for controlling threats to the validity of experiments.

Control is defined here somewhat more broadly than is usually done in research methods texts as *any procedure used by the researcher to counteract potential threats to the validity of the research.* When we can rule out alternative explanations of the obtained results to improve construct and internal validity, we thereby increase control. Control is increased as well when we reduce barriers to generalization, thus improving external validity, and when we establish statistical validity.

Many control procedures are available to meet the variety of threats to validity. But not every threat to validity is likely to occur in every experiment; thus, not every control measure is needed in every experiment. Although some control procedures are of general value and therefore applicable to nearly all studies, many of the available controls must be carefully chosen to meet the particular threats to validity present in each study. It is also important to recognize that controls are necessary at all levels of research—not only at the experimental level. However, we use experimental research to explain controls in this chapter because controls are most fully developed at the experimental level, where we attempt to answer research questions concerning causality.

THREATS TO VALIDITY

Several kinds of hypotheses are involved in experimental research and the experimenter seeks to insure a high degree of confidence in the validity of conclusions drawn about hypotheses. Researchers are concerned with statistical, construct, internal, and external validity. *Statistical validity* concerns the adequacy of conclusions about the null hypothesis. Examples of threats to statistical validity are the use of unreliable dependent measures and violations of the assumptions of statistical tests.

Confounding, a term we used earlier to refer to threats to internal validity, can also be applied to construct validity. *Confounding* exists when some factor allows a feasible alternative explanation of the experimental results or allows an alternative explanatory or basic construct to be used. With regard to *internal validity,* confounding exists when some uncontrolled factor other than the independent variable may be responsible for the results. Thus, *in a threat to internal validity, it is the independent variable that is confounded.* With regard to *construct validity,* confounding exists when a construct or theory other than those that underlie the experiment allows an alternative explanation to be plausible. Thus, *in a threat to construct validity, it is the theoretical construct that is confounded* because an alternative theoretical explanation is possible for the observed data. (For examples of confounding see "Construct Validity" in Chapter 8.) *External validity* is threatened whenever we cannot confidently generalize results from the study's particular subjects, times, and settings to other conditions. Threats to external validity are controlled by careful subject selection to ensure that subjects accurately represent the population to which we want to generalize the results and by carefully planning the settings to represent other settings, particularly those found under natural conditions.

The methods of control commonly used in experimentation to reduce various threats to validity are of four types:

1. General control procedures (control achieved through preparation of settings, response measurement, and replication).
2. Control over subject and experimenter effects.
3. Control achieved through the selection and assignment of subjects.
4. Control achieved through specific experimental design.

The four categories of controls are arranged from the more general control procedures applicable to most research to the most specific control procedures. In this chapter we will focus on the first three categories of control. The fourth category—control achieved through specific experimental design—is the "essence" of experimentation, and it will be introduced here and discussed at length in Chapters 10–13. Recall that in our research model, experimentation represents the highest level of constraint. We will see that in experimentation we use all available control procedures including controls achieved through specific *experimental design*.

GENERAL CONTROL PROCEDURES

Preparation of Setting

The most general control procedures are those that clearly define the *research setting*—the setting in which the research is to take place. The major advantage of the laboratory setting over lower constraint settings is that many extraneous variables can be eliminated, such as interfering visual and auditory stimuli, the influence of other people and of competing tasks, and so forth. In the laboratory setting we can eliminate competing variables, simplify the situation, and increase control over the independent variable, which permits a greater degree of confidence about the effects of the independent variable. Thus, control by preparation of the research setting helps to reduce threats to internal validity.

In most studies the preparation of settings is designed to increase internal validity. This often results in the lab setting becoming so constrained and artificial that it is unlike the natural situation. Thus, preparation of the lab setting can result in poor external validity. However, external validity need not be compromised if the researcher makes an effort to create a natural environment in the laboratory. For example, in a series of children's fear-reduction experiments (Graziano & Mooney, 1982), the laboratory was a room with a rug, couch, end tables, and easy chairs—a living-room setting with two-way mirrors and ceiling microphones. The laboratory setting was used to train children in fear-control procedures that they would use nightly at home. The living-room setting was used to provide a familiar and reassuring environment for the fearful children and to be similar to their own living rooms so as to enhance generalization (external validity). Thus, preparation of settings in laboratories can enhance external validity as well as internal validity.

Response Measurement

We can increase control by careful selection and preparation of the instruments used to measure the dependent variable. By using measuring instruments of known reliability and validity, we improve both statistical and construct validity. The care with which the researcher selects measuring instruments can have powerful effects on validity. Unfortunately, in our concern for operationalizing and manipulating the independent variable, we sometimes pay less attention to the dependent measures and therefore compromise the validity of the study.

Replication

Replication is not considered by many textbook authors to be a control procedure. However, we believe replication is an important enough issue to be considered a general control procedure. By defining in operational terms and specifying the laboratory setting, conditions, procedures, and measuring instruments we make it easier for ourselves and other researchers to re-create the same conditions and to replicate the research. Therefore, *replication* is a control procedure.

Successful replication provides important information—if a phenomenon observed in one study can be reliably demonstrated a second or third time, confidence in the original observations increases; if the study cannot be replicated, confidence is shaken. Research in extrasensory perception (ESP) (a contradiction in terms) is an example. Some researchers have reported statistically significant ESP results. However, other researchers have not been able to replicate the claimed ESP phenomena, thus leaving the earlier reports open to serious question. (See Edge, Morris, Rush & Palmer, 1986.) If a finding cannot be replicated, then it may be only a chance event and not an indication of a genuine phenomenon. In more statistical terms, the researcher may have made a Type I error. If ESP phenomena cannot be reliably replicated, then we must ask whether the ESP phenomenon exists at all.

We can distinguish between exact replication and systematic replication. *Exact replication* (repeating the experiment as nearly as possible in the way it was carried out originally) is rarely done in psychology. Journals seldom publish exact replication studies and there are no career benefits to be gained by a young researcher in spending time repeating other people's research. Although exact replication is rare, researchers often replicate earlier findings by testing some systematic theoretical or procedural modification of the original work, which is known as *systematic replication*. If, for example, Dr. Marlatt finds an interesting phenomenon in the alcohol research laboratory, a colleague might reason that a certain systematic modification will bring about a certain specific result. The second researcher uses Marlatt's initial work, making a systematic modification, which, if Marlatt's work was correct, should result in the predicted outcome.

There are still other ways to replicate. Recall that most problem statements can be developed into several different research hypotheses, each of which can then be tested (see Chapter 8). Thus, many different studies can be generated from the same problem statement. By combining the problem statement with various operational definitions of the independent and dependent variables or by using different research designs to evaluate the same problem statement, several different research hypotheses and consequently several different studies are generated. In essence, the researcher is able to investigate the same basic problem in different ways, discovering and testing different facets of the same issue. These kinds of replications are sometimes referred to as *conceptual replications*.

Although replication increases confidence in the validity of findings, it does not guarantee validity. For example, suppose that confounding factors in a study brought about certain results. Then, if the procedures are replicated exactly without recognizing and controlling the confounding factors, the replication might well produce the same invalid results as in the initial study. Of course, this is true of all control procedures. No single control procedure can by itself guarantee validity.

CONTROL OVER SUBJECT AND EXPERIMENTER EFFECTS

Experimenter and subject effects, including the influence of *demand characteristics* and *placebo effects,* are serious threats to the validity of an experiment. The behavior of both the subjects and the researcher may be influenced by factors other than the independent variable. Factors such as motivation, knowledge, expectations, and information or misinformation about the study can be powerful influences on behavior. Extra-experimental factors may significantly bias subjects' and researchers' behavior, affecting not only the experimental procedure but also the analysis and interpretation of data.

The possibility that uncontrolled experimenter and/or subject effects may have occurred in a study is sufficient to cast doubt on conclusions about causal relationships between the independent and dependent variables because the possibility constitutes an alternative hypothesis. Subject and experimenter effects are of general importance and must be controlled in virtually all experimentation. Among the useful controls are:

1. Single-blind and double-blind procedures.
2. Automation.
3. Use of objective measures.
4. Multiple observers.
5. Use of deception.

Single- and Double-Blind Procedures

Experimenter effects arise from the experimenter's knowledge of (1) the hypothesis being tested, (2) the nature of the experimental and control conditions, and (3) the assignment of individual subjects to conditions of the experiment. Such knowledge may subtly affect the ways in which the researcher interacts with each subject. In general, to control for experimenter effects, we *reduce the researcher's direct contact with and knowledge about the subjects.* The researcher may employ an assistant who is trained to carry out the procedure with subjects but who does not know the condition to which each subject is assigned. If possible, the assistant should be unaware of the hypothesis being tested. Thus, the assistant is *blind* to these factors and presumably cannot be biased by knowledge of the hypothesis or of the assignment of subjects to conditions. This is called the *single-blind control procedure.*

A more powerful control is the *double-blind control procedure* in which the researcher is blind to the assignment of each subject *and* subjects are blind to their assignments. That is, the experiment is designed so that experimental and control procedures are indistinguishable to subjects. Therefore, subjects do not know whether they are in an experimental or a control group. The double-blind technique is often used in drug studies where the experimental group receives the drug in the form of a pill, for example, and the control group receives a pill that is identical in appearance, weight, smell, and taste but lacks the actual drug (i.e., it is a placebo). Neither the subjects who take the pill nor the experimental assistants who administer it and gather the data know which subjects are receiving the drug and which are receiving the placebo. The use of a placebo control group in research that is purely psychological in nature is more difficult and probably not as effective as in drug studies. For example, suppose a clinical researcher wants to study the effectiveness of systematic desensitization on reduction of adult fears. Subjects are assigned in an unbiased manner to an experimental and a control group; the experimental group is given the systematic desensitization and the control group is presented with a placebo treatment. The placebo treatment must be believable so that subjects do not know they are controls. The design problem is to create experimentally adequate, ethically acceptable, and believable placebo manipulations, a task that is often extremely difficult.

In addition to design problems in the use of placebos, ethical issues should be considered. Can we ethically deny treatment to some subjects? For ethical reasons, subjects should be told they may receive a placebo treatment. For both design and ethical reasons, the use of true placebos in medical and psychological research is not recommended when an effective treatment is available. Instead of comparing a new treatment with a placebo, researchers should compare the new treatment with the currently available treatment.

When actual data collection occurs it is important for the research assistant to be blind to the group or condition the subject is in and to the hypotheses of the study. It is equally important to maintain a blind condition during the scoring of data, especially when the scoring requires many judgments. Knowledge of the hypotheses and of the conditions under which the subject is tested may affect judgments made during the scoring of data.

In some cases, however, it is not possible for researchers to be blind during particular aspects of the study. For example, in a study of sex effects on aggression the researcher testing subjects could not be blind to the knowledge of which subjects are male and which are female. In such a situation the researcher should attempt to be blind in as many ways as possible even if it is impossible at every stage. If, for example, the measure of aggression in the study is verbal behavior, someone otherwise not connected with the study should transcribe the tapes of subjects' verbal responses so that auditory cues of subject's sex are not used when the data are scored. Scoring should then be done by someone other than the person who tested the subjects in the study. Although in this case it may be impossible to test subjects blindly, the data can be scored as a separate procedure by researchers blind to the group membership of subjects. In this study assistants testing subjects should also be blind to the hypothesis even if they cannot be blind to group membership. A general rule of thumb is to *test subjects and score data as blindly as possible to avoid experimenter biases.* Even though there are some difficulties with single-blind techniques and double-blind placebo techniques, these methods can control for a number of potentially biasing subject and experimenter effects and are good controls to employ in many studies.

Automation

Another means of reducing experimenter-subject contact and thus reducing potential biases is to standardize and *automate* instructions to subjects and procedures for obtaining and recording subjects' responses. Instructions to subjects can be tape-recorded and the timing of instructions and recording of subjects' responses can be

"IT WAS MORE OF A 'TRIPLE-BLIND' TEST. THE PATIENTS DIDN'T KNOW WHICH ONES WERE GETTING THE REAL DRUG, THE DOCTORS DIDN'T KNOW, AND, I'M AFRAID, NOBODY KNEW."

Reprinted by permission of S. Harris.

automated with electronic equipment. In this way the experimenter is removed from much of the immediate involvement in giving instructions and recording responses. Effects due to experimenter bias can be dramatically reduced by standardization and automation.

Using Objective Measures

Using *objective measures* of dependent variables is of critical importance. A measure is objective when it is based on empirically observable and clearly specified events about which two or more people could easily agree. In contrast, subjective measures involve the general impressions of the observers, which are often based on poorly specified and/or unobserved events. An example of a subjective measure is an observer's feeling that a person is anxious in a public-speaking situation. It is subjective because the observer does not specify what events were observed. Thus, it would be difficult for another observer to make the same observations and come to the same conclusions about the anxiety level of the speaker.

In contrast, good objective measures precisely define the behaviors to be observed and require minimal judgments on the part of the observer. Consequently, objective measures are less prone to experimenter biases. Such measures usually produce impressive levels of interrater agreement and make replication by other researchers easier. For example, public-speaking anxiety can be operationally defined in terms of empirically observable behavior, such as sweating, stammering, rapid speech, face flushing, and hands shaking. Each of these are empirically observable, clearly specified behaviors that can be observed by one or more researchers. With objective measures, we know what a score means; with subjective measures, we are never sure.

Multiple Observers

In any research, especially when there may be questions about objectivity in making observations, a common control is to employ several observers to record subjects' behavior. Data obtained by *multiple observers* are compared for agreement using interrater reliability coefficients or an index of percent agreement.

Suppose, for example, that two raters are simultaneously observing a videotape of children at play. At random intervals an audio signal occurs and the observers then rate the behavior occurring at that moment as either happy or sad behavior. The observers are separated in booths but are watching the same video monitor. Thus, the observers are independently rating exactly the same behaviors. Ten signals are given and each observer rates ten instances of behavior as happy or sad. The two observers' ratings can then be directly compared, as shown in Table 9.1.

Using Deception

Perhaps the most common control for subject effects is to obscure the true hypothesis of the experiment. The researcher can deliberately misinform subjects about the nature of the experiment or withhold information that might reveal the hypothesis. This

Table 9.1 **COMPUTING PERCENT AGREEMENT FOR TWO OBSERVERS**

Instance of behavior	Rater 1 Happy	Rater 1 Sad	Rater 2 Happy	Rater 2 Sad	Agree	Disagree
1	1		1		1	
2	1		1		1	
3		1	1			1
4		1		1	1	
5		1		1	1	
6		1		1	1	
7	1		1		1	
8	1			1		1
9		1		1	1	
10	1		1		1	
				Totals	8	2

$$\text{Percent agreement} = \frac{\text{no. agreed}}{\text{no. agreed} + \text{no. disagreed}} \times 100 = \frac{8}{8 + 2} \times 100 = 80\%$$

control, called *deception,* is almost always minor, but in some experiments deception can become quite elaborate.

In a procedure known as the balanced placebo design used by G. Alan Marlatt to study the effects of alcohol on behavior, subjects were asked to drink a beverage that contained either tonic only or alcohol and tonic (Marlatt, Demming, & Reid, 1973; Rohsenow & Marlatt, 1981). The deception is that what subjects actually drank and what they were told they were drinking is not necessarily the same thing. Suppose the study included 100 subjects; 50 subjects were given vodka and tonic and 50 were given tonic only. Of the 50 subjects who drank tonic only, half (25) were told that they were in a control condition and that they would be drinking tonic water, and the other half (25) were told they were in the alcohol condition and that they would be asked to drink a vodka-tonic drink. Similarly, half (25) of the 50 subjects who drank vodka and tonic were led to believe that they were drinking only tonic, and the remaining subjects (25) were told they were drinking vodka and tonic. Because vodka is tasteless it is almost impossible to distinguish it from taste alone. To reinforce the deception that subjects were drinking a vodka-tonic mixture instead of only tonic, the drinks were mixed in front of subjects with water (disguised as vodka) carefully measured from a vodka bottle into the drinks and tonic poured from a separate labeled bottle. This design is interesting in many respects. First, because several ethical issues are raised by the deception, appropriate safeguards must be included in the study. Second, it is equally desirable to have the experimenter blind to subject condition. To accomplish this an elaborate coding system is used on the bottles. The experimenter knows which bottle(s) to pour the drinks from but does not know what each bottle contains. According to the ethical standards for research, the use of deception violates subjects' rights and places the subjects "at risk." Therefore, deception should be used only when truly necessary for the conduct of the study, and at completion of the experiment subjects should be debriefed (i.e., told about the deception and the true nature of the experiment and given ample opportunity to ask questions about the procedure).

CONTROL THROUGH SUBJECT SELECTION AND ASSIGNMENT

Subject Selection

Careful *subject selection* in research insures external validity and allows us to generalize the results to a larger population. In nearly all psychological research the investigator's interest is not limited to specific subjects but rather is focused on the larger, more general group—the population. In the hypothetical example given earlier of the psychoanalyst who treated enuretic children (see Chapter 1), there is a major problem with external validity. From a limited sample of clients the psychoanalyst drew conclusions about *all* enuretic children. The client sample had not been selected so as to represent adequately all enuretic children but instead consisted only of those particular children who were brought to that particular therapist for treatment. Thus, the conclusions drawn from the study cannot be generalized to all enuretic children. Therefore, to understand subject selection we must distinguish between (1) populations and samples, (2) target populations and accessible populations, and among (3) representative samples, random samples, stratified random samples, and *ad hoc* samples.

A *population* is the larger group of all events of interest (people, rats, occurrences, and so on) from which a sample is selected. The *sample* is a smaller number of events (people, occurrences, rats, and so on) drawn from that population and used in a specific study as if the sample adequately represents the target population.

The *target population* is the larger population in which we are ultimately interested. It is usually a naturally occurring population, such as all grammar school children, all diagnosed schizophrenics, all registered voters, and so on. Target populations often are not easily available to us. For example, suppose we are interested in the development of temporal concepts in 6-year-olds. We cannot readily sample from all of the 6-year-olds in the country. We do, however, have access to five local public schools that have a total of 400 six-year-old pupils. The 400 children become the *accessible population* from which we will draw (select) the sample. Thus, in this research we must recognize that any generalizations from the results will most confidently be made from the sample to the accessible population, but we must be cautious about generalizing to the larger, target population. Because nearly all psychological research is carried out by sampling accessible populations (e.g., introductory psychology students in a particular university, mental patients in a particular institution, children in a particular school system), *we must always be extremely cautious about generalizations made from the samples to the general population.* If we sample from an accessible population, then we may generalize the results only to that accessible population and not to a larger, target population. In this regard, replication is an important procedure. Each replication may be carried out on somewhat different accessible populations. If the results are replicated with the different populations, our confidence in the generalizability of the findings is increased.

We do not study populations directly. Instead, we usually select a sample from an accessible population. To generalize the findings to the accessible or target population we must be careful to select a *representative sample* which adequately reflects population characteristics. The basic idea of representativeness is simple enough: if the sample is representative, then the characteristics found in the population (e.g., the distribution of sex, age, intelligence, socioeconomic class, ethnicity, attitudes, political affiliations, religious beliefs) will be found in the sample in the same proportions as in the target population. Although the concept is simple, actually obtaining a representative sample is a good deal more difficult. Further, small samples often do not adequately represent populations. In general, the larger the sample, the more likely the sample will adequately represent the population because larger samples tend to reduce the effects of sampling errors. Another issue is that most psychological research is conducted with samples drawn from accessible populations that are not necessarily representative of the larger, target population.

In social science research, sampling of subjects is a critical issue. Many methods have been developed to solve the problems of obtaining representative samples. Although some of the methods are beyond the scope of this text, we will consider three solutions to the problem of selecting a representative sample: (1) random sampling, (2) stratified random sampling, and (3) *ad hoc* samples.

Random Sampling   Random selection of a sample from a target population or from an accessible population means drawing the sample so that (1) every member of the population has an equal chance of being selected for the sample and (2) the selections do not affect each other (i.e., they are independent). With *random sampling* there are no systematic biases that result in some members of the population having a greater chance than others of being selected. If the selection of subjects is truly random, then we assume that the distribution of characteristics of the population, such as age, ethnicity, and intelligence, will be distributed in the sample in the same proportion as in the population.

In the example of the enuretic children, the sample was probably biased; it may have been limited to enuretic children who were also emotionally disturbed or from high socioeconomic homes. Those who were not emotionally disturbed or were from lower socioeconomic homes were not likely to be present in the psychoanalyst's sample. To draw conclusions about all enuretic children a representative sample drawn from the target population (i.e., *all* enuretic children) would be necessary.

The best procedure for drawing an unbiased sample to represent a population adequately is to draw a random sample. This is rather like picking numbers out of a hat. In actual practice, numbers are usually drawn not from a hat but from a *table of random numbers* (see Table B.7 in Appendix B). The random number table was devised to meet the two criteria of random selection: (1) that each number has the same chance of being selected as any other number and (2) that each number is independent of the others. Suppose we want to draw a sample of 60 subjects from the accessible population of 400 six-year-old children in our local school system. We list all 400 children, assign each one a three-digit number such as 001, 002, 003, and so on up to 400. We enter the table of random numbers at any place; we can close our eyes and point at it with a finger and use that as our starting place. We then read three-digit numbers, forward or backward, proceeding up or down the columns in sequence. We record all the numbers that correspond to any of the 400 subject numbers until we have a total of 60 nonduplicated numbers. Thus, 60 subjects will have been randomly selected from the accessible population. The table of random numbers is useful not only for selecting a random sample but also for making any decisions based on the principle of randomness, such as assigning subjects to experimental conditions.

Stratified Random Sampling   In *stratified random sampling* separate samples from each of several subpopulations are drawn. The subpopulations are defined in advance on the basis of one or more critical subject variables, such as age and socioeconomic status, that we expect will influence scores on the dependent measures. Therefore, small variations in the distribution of the variables in a sample can have a large effect on the results. For example, we might suspect that age is strongly correlated with the dependent measure of political preference. Therefore, the sample should approximate closely the distribution of age in the population studied. Rather than rely on chance by sampling randomly, we divide the population into subpopulations on the basis of age. We then create a total sample by selecting the appropriate proportion of subjects from each of the subpopulations. If 16 percent of the population is between the ages of 20 and 25, then we need to select randomly from that subpopulation the number of subjects it would take to represent 16 percent of the total sample. If we want to draw a total sample of 100 subjects, we will need 16 subjects selected from the 20–25 age range. Stratified random samples are used extensively in sophisticated political polling operations. With this technique, samples as small as 1000 people can so closely represent the population that the outcome of elections involving several million actual voters can be accurately predicted.

Although random sampling is a major control for threats to external validity, little psychological research employs random sampling from a target population. Target populations are often not easily utilized. For any large population, target or accessible, listing and numbering every individual to prepare for random selection is a sizable task. Random and stratified random sampling from a target population is important in some research, such as in large-scale surveys of voters where the results will be used to predict a winner, but most psychological research does not employ random selection. The fact is that obtaining a random sample from a target population is difficult and rarely done. In most psychological research, subjects are obtained from an *accessible population* as described earlier, such as introductory psychology students, children from local schools, and so on. Further, subjects are almost always volunteers. Those who do not volunteer are not included and the sample is thus not representative of the target population. The ethical demand that subjects be volunteers makes it difficult for researchers to obtain a random sample of any population. For example, Graziano, Gallipeau, and Graziano (1982) surveyed young adults (18–23 years old) about their experience in having been spanked as children. The subjects were volunteers from large introductory psychology classes at a state university. Kraemer, Hastrup, Sobota, and Bornstein (1985) studied the crying behavior of children and their parents. To obtain subjects they advertised in newspapers offering $20 for each volunteer family. In each of these projects *volunteer* subjects with the required characteristics were obtained from accessible populations.

***Ad hoc* Samples**   How can we generalize results from samples that are not randomly selected from a target population? The answer is twofold: first, as noted earlier, we generalize cautiously and conservatively; second, we generalize only to other people (or to laboratory animals or events or places) who have characteristics similar to those of the sample. That is, *we are careful not to generalize beyond the limits of the sample.* In the two examples given above, researchers may generalize their results only to people who are like those in their studies. In other words, the population to which we generalize is defined by the characteristics of the sample. This type of sample is called an *ad hoc sample,* and is often used in psychological research. In the spanking survey cited earlier (Graziano et al., 1982), it was found that 92 percent of the 600 subjects reported they had been spanked as children. The researchers could not of course suggest that 92 percent of the country's total population of young adults had been spanked as children. However, they could suggest that the findings do apply to people similar to the sample; that is, to other state university undergraduates from working and middle-class families in the northeastern section of the United States. The same research carried out at Columbia, Harvard, Princeton, Vassar, or Yale, with their student populations drawn largely from middle- to upper-socioeconomic classes *might* have produced different results. In the Kraemer et al. (1985) study on crying behavior in children, the generalizations are likewise limited to the characteristics of subjects and by the selection procedure in which subjects were volunteer families who knew they would receive a $20 fee. It may be that affluent families might not have volunteered.

The point is that in most psychological research we do not have random sampling from a known target population; instead, we use *ad hoc* sampling. To generalize beyond the samples and yet maintain external validity, we must know the characteristics of the subjects and keep our generalizations within the limits of the characteristics. It becomes important in using *ad hoc* sampling to obtain descriptive data, such as subjects' age, physical and psychological characteristics, and family socioeconomic data. The more completely we can describe subjects in the sample, the more secure we can be in establishing the generalization limits and the more confidence we can have in making generalizations.

Thus, the researcher is advised to draw a random sample from a known target population whenever it is feasible to do so. In most instances that will not be feasible, and an *ad hoc* sample will be used. Here the researcher should obtain sufficient descriptive information about the subjects to establish the limits for generalization. In this way, threats to external validity can be reduced.

Subject Assignment

Once subjects are selected from a target or accessible population or an *ad hoc* sample has been created, we must then assign subjects to the conditions required by the experimental procedures. Unbiased *subject assignment* is critical in true experiments.

In all true experiments the independent variable is systematically manipulated and the corresponding changes in the dependent variable are observed. For example, suppose we want to test the effectiveness of teaching arithmetic to third graders using a new video-teaching program. In the experimental condition third graders will have arithmetic lessons presented daily through videotapes. In the control condition other third graders will have arithmetic lessons presented in the usual, nontelevised manner. In this experiment there are two levels of the independent variable, video presentation and teacher presentation. Suppose that 60 children have been selected as subjects and we want to assign 30 children to each condition in an unbiased manner. We want to be sure, for example, that we do not assign all female subjects to one condition and all male subjects to the other, or that we do not assign the best math students to the same condition.

Take another example: in a study of office working conditions six groups of typists are compared on their typing speed (number of words per minute) and accuracy (number of errors) under six different conditions of room temperature: 55°F, 60°F, 65°F, 70°F, 75°F, and 80°F. A sample of 48 typists is selected and we must assign them without bias to six groups of eight subjects each. For example, we would not want most of the best typists in one group. The problem of subject assignment is similar to the one above, even though in this experiment the independent variable has six levels.

The ideal experiment would include (1) random selection of subjects from a known population and (2) random assignment of subjects to conditions. The ideal, however, is seldom achieved. As noted earlier, random selection is rare in psychological research. Therefore, we must be cautious in generalizing to other subjects, times, and conditions. *Of far greater importance in a true experiment is random assignment of subjects to conditions.* Random assignment is a powerful control procedure that helps to reduce many known and unknown threats to internal validity—the central issue in experiments. Unbiased assignment of subjects to conditions can be accomplished by free random assignment or by matched random assignment.

Free Random Assignment   *Free random assignment* of subjects to conditions is carried out using a table of random numbers. For example, in the experiment on working conditions, the 48 subjects can be randomly assigned to six conditions, eight subjects per condition. We number the subjects from 01–48, consult the table of random numbers, and assign the first subject number we encounter to the first condition, the next subject number to the second condition, and so on. The seventh subject would of course be assigned to the first condition, eighth to the second, and so forth. We continue in this way until all 48 subjects are assigned to the six conditions. The same random assignment procedure would be used in the experiment on teaching arithmetic to third graders to assign subjects to two conditions with 30 subjects in each condition.

Randomization is a control method used in subject selection and subject assignment to conditions. *Randomization is the most basic and single most important control procedure.* It has several major advantages: (1) it can be used to control threats to internal and external validity; (2) it can control for many variables simultaneously; and (3) it is the only control procedure that can control for unknown factors. When we randomize, subject variables are distributed without biases, even if we have not specifically identified the variables. Other control methods are effective with known extraneous variables that threaten the study, but randomization is effective in reducing the bias of unknown variables. A good general rule for the researcher is: *Whenever possible, randomize.*

Matched Random Assignment   *Matched random assignment* of subjects to conditions is often used in small-sample research. A good deal of psychological research is carried out with small numbers of subjects and we are often faced with the task of assigning 20–30 subjects to two or three conditions. Free random assignment works best with large numbers, but with a small number of subjects to be assigned, randomized groups can be unequal on some important variable. For example, suppose that in the relaxation training study with autistic children (Graziano, 1974) there were only 12 subjects to be assigned to an experimental and a control group. Free random assignment of so small a number might result in unequal groups on important variables. We might find, for example, that the most severely disruptive children or those with best motor control or the oldest were all in one group. Thus, the experimental and control groups would not be equivalent at the start of the study and any results obtained may be due to differences between the groups rather than to the effects of the independent variable, relaxation training. That is, the independent variable may have been confounded by one or more extraneous variables.

To solve the problems of working with small numbers of subjects we can use a matching procedure combined with randomization—*matched random assignment*. To do this we must first decide what variables are the most important potential confounding factors. Suppose we decide that the age of the child is a potential confounding variable in the autistic children study and that the older children are more likely to learn the relaxation procedures more quickly and thoroughly than the younger children. We would then list the children by age, as shown in Table 9.2, and match them on age by taking the children in pairs, successively, down the list. Kathy, the oldest, is matched with the next oldest, Robbie; Matt is matched with Rick, and so on, as shown in Table 9.3. We can now assign the subjects to two groups by using a table of random numbers or by tossing a coin. Using the random number table, the first subject of each pair is assigned to group 1 if the number is odd or to group 2 if the number is even. If a coin toss is used, heads or tails determine group assignment. Whichever method is used, the second subject in each pair is assigned to the other group. This procedure results in the assignment of subjects, as shown in Table 9.4.

As is seen in Table 9.4, the mean ages of the two groups (103.8 months and 104.5 months) are quite close. We have thus assured that groups 1 and 2 are comparable on the age variable and that age will not be a confounding variable. Notice, too, that groups

Table 9.2 SEX AND AGE OF
          AUSTISTIC CHILDREN IN
          THE SAMPLE

Name	Sex	Age (in months)
Kathy	(F)	122
Robbie	(M)	120
Matt	(M)	119
Rick	(M)	115
Terri	(F)	108
Holly	(F)	104
Kevin	(M)	100
Miriam	(F)	98
Debby	(F)	96
Randy	(M)	95
Jimmy	(M)	87
Tommy	(M)	86

Table 9.3   AUSTISTIC CHILDREN MATCHED IN PAIRS BY AGE

Kathy	—	Robbie
Matt	—	Rick
Terri	—	Holly
Kevin	—	Miriam
Debby	—	Randy
Jimmy	—	Tommy

Table 9.4   MATCHED AUTISTIC CHILDREN RANDOMLY ASSIGNED TO TWO GROUPS

	Group 1			Group 2		
	Robbie	(M)	120	Kathy	(F)	122
	Matt	(M)	119	Rick	(M)	115
	Holly	(F)	104	Terri	(F)	108
	Miriam	(F)	98	Kevin	(M)	100
	Debby	(F)	96	Randy	(M)	95
	Tommy	(M)	86	Jimmy	(M)	87
Total females	3			2		
Total males	3			4		
Mean age	103.8 months			104.5 months		

1 and 2 do not have equal numbers of males and females. However, the differences are small and sex is not considered to be a potential confounding variable in the study. (Our expectation, of course, may be incorrect, but given the state of knowledge at the time of the study, it is a reasonable expectation.)

Matching helps to make small-group research more sensitive to the effects of the independent variable by equally distributing known variables that are potentially confounding. We can match for more than one variable. However, it is not feasible to match on several variables simultaneously because the task becomes so cumbersome and difficult that it is more efficient to assign subjects to groups randomly. Matching requires that we identify the variables to be matched and obtain a measure on the variables for each subject. Further, subjects can be matched on any measurable physical or psychological variables (e.g., age, weight, intelligence, neuroticism, attitudes, and so on).

Other Matching Procedures   A number of other matching procedures are available. An alternative to subject-by-subject matching is to match characteristics of groups. This procedure is more commonly used in differential research but can be useful in some experimental situations. In such a situation we would first identify the variables on which the groups are to be matched and obtain measures on the variables for each of the potential subjects. Using a randomization procedure we would assign subjects to one of the two groups and calculate that group's mean and standard deviation on each variable to be matched. We would then select the second group of subjects so that it has a comparable mean and standard deviation on the variables. The two groups would be equivalent on the matching variables but individuals would not be matched as closely. The equal distribution of matching variables is thereby achieved and potential confounding avoided.

A variation of matching is to equate groups by holding the variable constant. For example, if we want to match on age we could use subjects in all groups of approximately the same age. There is little or no variability on this factor between the experimental and control groups, thus increasing our confidence in the effects of the independent variable. However, a disadvantage to matching by holding the variable constant is that it reduces the generalizability (i.e., it reduces external validity). For example, if we used only adult subjects we would be unable to generalize with confidence to adolescents.

Matching by building the variable into the study is another of the many methods of control through matching. (This method creates what is known as a factorial design, which will be discussed in more detail in Chapter 12.) Suppose we want to test the effects of complexity of temporal stimuli on the time-duration estimates of 6-year-old children. The independent variable is the complexity of the temporal stimuli presented; the dependent variable is the time-duration estimates made by the subjects. However, we are concerned about differences in age of only a few months that may confound the results; that is, the older 6-year-olds might do better on the temporal tasks than the younger 6-year-olds. To control for this we make the age variable a part of the study by grouping the 6-year-olds into four groups of three months each, as follows:

1. 6 years 1 month–6 years 3 months.
2. 6 years 4 months–6 years 6 months.
3. 6 years 7 months–6 years 9 months.
4. 6 years 10 months–6 years 12 months (i.e., 7 years).

The subjects in each group are of similar age and we thus are able to determine the influence of the age variable.

CONTROL ACHIEVED THROUGH SPECIFIC EXPERIMENTAL DESIGN

An understanding of the three major groups of methods for achieving control in experimentation—(1) general control procedures, (2) control of subject and experimenter effects, (3) control achieved through subject selection and assignment—is necessary to an understanding of (4) control achieved through specific experimental design. Although the four groups of control methods are classified separately, they are related and overlapping. Indeed, some might argue that all methods are properly subsumed under experimental design. The division here into four groups of control methods is thus somewhat arbitrary, but it is believed useful. (Because experimental design is a major topic, it is introduced here and discussed in detail in Chapters 10–13.)

In any experiment the protection of internal validity is of critical importance because it bears on the very essence of experimentation—the predicted causal relationship between the independent and dependent variables. The control methods we have chosen to list under experimental design primarily focus on protection of internal validity. In general, by *experimental design* we mean the careful arrangement of all parts of the experiment so as to (1) test directly the effects of the independent variable on the dependent variable and (2) protect against threats to internal validity. In experimental design, control to reduce confounding and thus to protect internal validity is a key factor.

The True Experiment

A number of basic experimental designs are available to test hypotheses and protect internal validity (see Chapter 10). However, to introduce experimental design, let us consider a research design that is *not* a true experiment.

In an earlier discussion of confounding (see Chapter 8), a study of the effects of relaxation training on the disruptive behavior of autistic children was described (Graziano, 1974). Recall that a small group of autistic children was observed for disruptive behavior, trained in relaxation over a two-month period, and again observed for disruptive behavior. (The simple pretest-posttest design that was used in the study is illustrated in Figure 9.1.) Suppose that the researcher found a statistically significant difference between the pretest and posttest measures; that is, the null hypothesis was rejected. That finding, however, is not sufficient for the researcher to conclude anything about *causality,* about the hypothesis that relaxation training would cause or bring about the improved behavior. Again, the conclusion cannot be drawn because of possible confounding. To avoid confounding variables (in this case, maturation and history), the experimenter would have to anticipate them and build into the research design suitable controls. In this instance a good control would be a no-treatment control group (i.e., an equivalent group of autistic children who do not receive relaxation training). Suppose there are 20 autistic children in the program. Using one of the methods for unbiased assignment of subjects to conditions, the researcher could assign ten of the children to the experimental condition and ten to the control condition. All of the children would remain in the general program and receive the same general treatment. However, only the experimental group would receive the relaxation training. This is a pretest-posttest, control-group design, as shown in Figure 9.2.

Figure 9.1   A SIMPLE PRETEST-POSTTEST DESIGN

Pretest for disruptive behavior	Relaxation training	Posttest for disruptive behavior

Figure 9.2   A PRETEST-POSTTEST CONTROL-GROUP DESIGN

A. Experimental group	Pretest for disruptive behavior	Relaxation training	Posttest for disruptive behavior
B. Control group	Pretest for disruptive behavior	No relaxation training	Posttest for disruptive behavior

The critical comparison, of course, is to determine if the experimental group demonstrates significantly less disruptive behavior than the control group at the posttest. Suppose this is exactly what the researcher finds. The researcher thus can have considerably more confidence in concluding that relaxation is responsible for the difference because the confounding variables of maturation and history have been controlled. Maturation is controlled because, if the experimental and control groups are equivalent at the start of the experiment, the researcher can expect that if maturation did occur it occurred equally for the two groups. Confounding due to history is controlled in this design because both groups have received all other treatments in the general program. Thus, if some program factor other than relaxation is responsible for the posttest differences in disruptive behavior, it would affect both groups equally.

For the control-group design to be effective it is *essential that the experimental and control groups be comparable at the start of the experiment.* If the experimental group has more of the most capable, older, or better-adjusted children, then confounding due to selection would occur. To control for possible confounding the researcher must carefully assign subjects to the two groups in an unbiased manner. Thus, in this example unbiased subject assignment has controlled for confounding due to selection, and the inclusion of a no-treatment control group has controlled for confounding due to maturation and history. The two control procedures—unbiased assignment and a control group—provide a large measure of control in the experiment.

If in carrying out experiments with between-subjects designs we routinely include three of the basic control procedures—(1) unbiased subject selection or careful definition of subject characteristics to define an *ad hoc* sample, (2) unbiased assignment of subjects to conditions, (3) inclusion of appropriate control groups or conditions—we can control for major potential confounding variables in most studies.

Note, too, in this experiment the independent variable—relaxation training—is presented at two levels, "all" or "none." The experimental group received the training ("all") whereas the control did not ("none"). A characteristic of a true experiment is that the independent variable must be presented at least at two levels. That is, the independent variable must vary; it must be actively manipulated in some way so that it varies from one condition to another. In many experiments there are more than two levels; for example, recall our hypothetical study earlier of typists' productivity at different room temperatures, which included six levels of the independent variable (room temperature). This design does not have one control group but six levels of the independent variable, each of which operates as a control for all other levels.

Scientific research generally is characterized by attention to details, such as developing carefully reasoned and clearly stated concepts, well-developed operational definitions, use of inductive-deductive logic, careful measurement of the observed variables, and careful use of appropriate statistical methods to analyze data. The *true experiment* shares these characteristics but also has the following five characteristics:

1. A clearly stated research hypothesis concerning predicted causal effects of one variable on another.
2. At least two levels of the independent variable.

3. Unbiased assignment of subjects to conditions.
4. Specific and systematic procedures for empirically testing the hypothesized causal relationships.
5. Specific controls to reduce threats to internal validity.

In experiments the task is to answer the question about causality and to control for threats to validity. To do so the experimenter must carefully arrange all parts and procedures of the experiment—formation of a problem statement, operational definitions, and research hypotheses; subject selection and assignment; constructing different levels of the independent variable; creating measures for the dependent variable; creation of specific controls—in such a way as to answer the research question: "Does the hypothesized causal relationship between the independent and dependent variables exist?" The detailed task of arranging the components and procedures is what is meant generally by experimental design. In essence, experimental design gives us a detailed plan for the conduct of the experiment. In developing the experimental design, we specify the procedures. Once the design has been determined and set in place, we must proceed through it step by step as planned. Remember that at the high-constraint level of experimentation we no longer have the flexibility to alter any parts of the design once we begin making observations.

The essence of experimentation is to ask and answer questions about causality. In designing an experiment we must do so in such way that we can clearly test the research hypothesis by ruling out various alternative hypotheses (i.e., the null hypothesis and the confounding variable hypotheses). Our detailed procedural blueprint constitutes experimental design, the focus of the following chapters.

SUMMARY

Four major groups of control procedures used in research are defined: (1) general control procedures, (2) control of subject and experimenter effects, (3) control through subject selection and assignment, (4) control achieved through specific experimental design.

General control procedures include careful preparation of the research setting, specification of measurement instruments, and replication. Subject and experimenter effects are controlled by keeping the researcher and subjects blind to both the hypotheses and the condition under which each subject is tested and by using automated procedures, objective measures, multiple observers, and deception when necessary. Appropriate subject selection (such as random sampling) helps control for threats to external validity whereas random assignment of subjects to conditions helps to control for threats to internal validity.

The essential issue in experimentation is to develop, state, and test a hypothesized causal relationship between at least two variables and to do so in such way as to rule out alternative hypotheses that can explain the results. Procedures to control for threats to validity are at the center of research design. The development of controls to their highest degree is a major factor that distinguishes experimentation from other levels of constraint in research. Control is a basic concept, and students must learn control procedures if they are to become scientific researchers—whether for a semester's course or for a professional career.

REVIEW EXERCISES

I. Define the following key terms. Be sure you understand them. They are discussed in the chapter and defined in the glossary.

Control	Deception
Statistical validity	Subject selection
Confounding variable	Population
Internal validity	Sample
Construct validity	Representative sample
External validity	Target population
Experimental design	Accessible population
Research setting	Random sampling
Replication	Table of random numbers
Exact replication	Stratified random sampling
Systematic replication	*Ad hoc* sample
Conceptual replication	Subject assignment
Demand characteristics	Free random assignment
Placebo effects	Matched random assignment
Single-blind procedure	Experimental design
Double-blind procedure	True experiment
Automation	Experimental group
Objective measure	Control group
Multiple observers	

II. Answer the following. Check your answers in the chapter.

1. Identify and define the types of validity in experimentation. For each type, identify and describe its major threats. (See Chapter 8.)
2. Explain this statement: "Confounding variables can threaten both internal validity and construct validity."
3. What is meant by general control procedures? Give examples of general control procedures and the threats they control.
4. Explain this statement: "Threats to validity and control procedures to reduce threats constitute two sides of the same coin."
5. How is replication a control procedure?
6. Describe single-blind and double-blind procedures.
7. Why is it important to use objective measures in research?
8. How can deception in an experiment be ethically justified?
9. What makes random sampling a powerful control technique?

10. Why is random assignment of subjects to conditions an important control procedure?
11. How is matching subjects a control?
12. Why is internal validity of such importance in experimentation?
13. What is a true experiment?
14. Why is it important in experimentation for experimental and control groups to be equivalent at the start of a study?
15. Why is it important that the independent variable is presented at least at two different levels?
16. What kind of relationship among variables is studied at each of the five levels of constraint?

III. Think about and work the following problems.

1. A researcher selects 30 children from among the 473 enrolled in an elementary school. On completion of the study the researcher wants to discuss the results in terms of all elementary schoolchildren. Identify the various populations and samples involved in this study. What cautions must the researcher be aware of in generalizing the results?
2. If you were the teaching assistant for this course, how would you explain the concept of representativeness of a sample to students?
3. For each of the following independent variables indicate the number of levels and identify each level.
   a. We study the effects of bright and dark illumination on subjects' perception of stimuli.
   b. We vary the amount of noise using four levels in a study of classroom behavior.
   c. A researcher compares children's ability to solve riddles under different conditions. One group of children is given no extra clues, another group is given one extra clue, and a third group is given five extra clues.
   d. Five different kinds of pain-relief medications are tested in a pharmaceutical laboratory.
4. Assume you have 60 subjects. Use the table of random numbers (Table B.7 in Appendix B) to assign subjects randomly to three conditions with 20 subjects in each condition. Show which subjects are assigned to which conditions.

CHAPTER **10**

CONTROL OF VARIANCE THROUGH EXPERIMENTAL DESIGN

Single-Variable, Independent-Groups Design

EXPERIMENTAL DESIGN

All scientific research is concerned with providing answers to questions. It does so by its careful development of concepts and by its use of operational definitions, inductive-deductive logic, careful measurement of variables, and appropriate statistical and reporting procedures. These general research design characteristics are important at all levels of constraint. Careful planning and design are critical to the success of any research project. It is at the experimental level of constraint, however, that the design process is most important and most completely developed. *Experimental design* is thus a special case of the general concept of research design—a detailed customizing process for each specific study. True experiments share general research design characteristics and, in addition, have five specific experimental characteristics. That is, the true experiment:

1. States one or more hypotheses about predicted causal effects of the independent variable(s) on the dependent variable(s).
2. Includes at least two levels of the independent variable.
3. Assigns subjects to conditions in an unbiased manner, such as through random assignment.
4. Includes specific procedures for testing hypotheses.
5. Includes controls for major threats to internal validity.

Experiments attempt to answer questions about causality as systematically and as validly as possible. Planning the design is a critical element in experimental research. The researcher develops a problem statement, identifies and defines important theoretical constructs, identifies and operationally defines independent and dependent variables, formulates research hypotheses, identifies a population, selects and assigns subjects to conditions, specifies the details of observational procedures, anticipates threats to validity, creates controls, and specifies the procedures for data analysis—all of which is carried out before observing a single subject. The activity of planning and integrating all of these details and the resulting detailed research plan for conducting the experiment is what we mean by experimental design. The term *experimental design* thus refers to both the *activity involved* in the detailed planning of the experiment and the *product,* the detailed plan itself. A well-developed experimental design provides a "blueprint" for the experimenter to follow. Developing a clear experimental design *before beginning any observations* is essential in experimental research. We cannot emphasize enough the importance of this detailed planning. Careful planning can build in all the controls necessary to have confidence in conclusions drawn from results. Therefore, *plan the experiment in careful detail and carry it out exactly as planned.* Further, although planning at the experimental level is emphasized here, it should be noted that planning is a crucial ingredient in research at all levels of constraint.

VARIANCE

Variation is necessary to carry out experiments—without variation there would be no differences to test. When we conduct an experiment we predict variation, and we hope to find that the variation between the experimental conditions is due to the manipulated independent variable(s). There must be variation of the independent variable if we are to study causal relationships among variables scientifically. However, as much as we seek variation in experimental designs, we must be cautious about unwanted or extraneous variation. Experimental design is a blueprint for control of unwanted or extraneous variation. Unwanted variation can occur in any study and can threaten the validity of the study by allowing alternative explanations of results. This reduces confidence in drawing causal inferences, in generalizing beyond the sample, and in interpreting results. Experimental design answers research questions by controlling many sources of unwanted, extraneous, and chance variation.

The most basic measure of variation is the *variance,* the *sum of squares* divided by the *degrees of freedom* $(N - 1)$:

$$\text{Variance} = \frac{\text{Sum of squares}}{\text{Degrees of freedom}} = \frac{\Sigma\,(X - \bar{X})^2}{N - 1}$$

Using the concept of variance, the major goals of experimental design can be summarized succinctly by paraphrasing a statement made by Fred Kerlinger: Experimental design has two basic purposes: (1) to provide answers to questions by testing causal hypotheses and (2) to control variance so as to increase internal validity (1964, p. 275). Several concepts used throughout this text—levels of constraint, experimental controls, reducing threats to validity, control of variance—are closely related, all referring to similar issues of control but in different ways. Variance is a major underlying concept among these control issues.

Forms of Variance

Although a fairly easy idea, the concept of variance may seem difficult and at times confusing because it appears so often and in different forms. The different forms of variance are (1) systematic between-groups variance and (2) nonsystematic within-groups variance (called error variance). These are important concepts in the logic of experimentation and in the analysis of data.

Systematic Between-Groups Variance   In an experiment we test the effects of an independent variable on the dependent variable(s). To do so, we set up at least two levels of the independent variable and measure subjects' responses on the dependent variable(s). If, for example, the study included three levels of the independent variable, we would predict that the dependent measures will differ significantly between the three groups; that is, that there will be significant variability among the group means. By "significant variability" we mean that the variability among the means will be larger than the variability expected on the basis of sampling error alone. Recall from Chapter 5 that sampling error refers to the natural variation among samples drawn from the same population. In an experiment we seek a *significantly high variance between the groups.* If we do not find a sufficiently great between-groups variance—that is, if the groups are essentially the same on the dependent measures—then we have not observed an effect of the independent variable. Thus, a significantly high between-groups variance is necessary to support the research hypothesis that the independent variable influenced the dependent variable as predicted.

However, as discussed earlier, if we find a significant difference between the groups (if the between-groups variance is high), we must be careful in drawing a causal inference. The significant difference may be due to either the systematic effects of the independent variable as predicted by the research hypothesis *(experimental variance)* or to the systematic effects of uncontrolled confounding variables *(extraneous variance)* or a combination of the two. That is, *the between-groups variance is a function of both experimental effects and confounding variables* as well as the natural variability due to sampling error.

The systematic between-groups variance in the experiment might be statistically significant, thus tempting the researcher to conclude that there is a causal relationship between the independent variable and dependent variable. But, suppose the between-groups variance is high only because of systematic influence of confounding variables and not because of the independent variable? That is, suppose the observed differences were due to the extraneous variance and not to the experimental variance? Statistical tests will tell us only whether there is a reliable difference between the groups but not whether the observed difference is due to experimental or extraneous variance. If there is any possibility that the differences between the groups are due to extraneous factors, then we cannot draw a causal inference. It is for this reason that we must anticipate possible confounding and plan controls to reduce the systematic between-groups variance due to extraneous variables.

Therefore, systematic, between-groups variance has two sources: (1) systematic between-groups variance due to the influence of the manipulated independent variables (experimental variance) and (2) systematic between-groups variance due to the influence of extraneous, uncontrolled variables (extraneous variance). High experimental variance is important for the experiment. High extraneous variance is a serious problem making it impossible to draw clear conclusions about causality. In testing hypothesized effects of an independent variable on a dependent variable, *we should seek to maximize the experimental variance and control the extraneous variance.* Even when we find a statistically significant difference between groups, if we have not used controls to minimize extraneous variance, we cannot conclude that the obtained difference was due to the independent variable. Note that extraneous variance cannot be measured directly; we try to minimize it by including careful control procedures.

Nonsystematic Within-Groups Variance The term *error variance* is often used to denote the nonsystematic *within-groups variability.* Although systematic variance reflects influences on each group as a whole, error variance is due to random factors that affect only some subjects within a group. For example, some subjects may score as they do because they might not feel well or were anxious or excited that day. Error variance may also be increased by more stable factors, such as *individual differences* in motor coordination, personality, interest, and motivation. Error variance is also increased by experimenter errors or equipment variations that cause measurement errors for some subjects but not for others in the same group. In other words, error variance is the *variation among individual subjects within a group that is due to chance factors.* Because no two subjects are exactly alike and no procedures are perfect, there will always be some error variance, some noise in the system.

The errors are largely random and therefore will have random effects. There should be just as much chance that random errors will occur in one direction as in another and will have as much chance of affecting any one subject in the group as any other. Thus, if random errors cause some subjects to score lower than they ordinarily would, we expect that random error will also cause other subjects to score higher than they ordinarily would. That is, the effects of within-groups random errors tend to cancel each other. While some subjects score too high, others score too low, but the *mean of the group as a whole is not affected; only the variance is affected.* In contrast, systematic between-groups factors influence subjects in a group in one direction. The effects are not random; they do not cancel each other out within the group. As a result, the mean of the group as a whole is moved up or down by systematic between-group factors depending on the direction of their influence.

In summary, the distinction is made between

1. *Systematic between-groups variance,* which includes
   a. Experimental variance (due to independent variables) and
   b. Extraneous variance (due to confounding variables), and
2. *Nonsystematic within-groups error variance* (due to chance factors).

It is important to repeat that the between-groups variance is a function not only of the systematic between-groups variance (experimental and extraneous variance) but also of the nonsystematic effects that are due to sampling error.

The relationship of the systematic between-groups variance and within-groups error variance is important. The way we analyze data is to compare the variation due to an experimental manipulation (between-groups variation) with the variation due to chance or error (within-groups variation) by computing appropriate measures of each and their ratio. As we will see later, the ratio defines the F test.

$$F = \frac{\text{Measure based on between-groups variation}}{\text{Measure based on within-groups error variation}}$$

Without statistical detail let us consider the principles involved in evaluating the relationship of the between-groups variation and the within-groups variation. Because of the way the numerator in analysis of variance is computed, the measure based on the between-groups variation is due to both the systematic effects (experimental variance plus extraneous variance) and the effects of sampling error (error variance). The measure based on within-groups error variation (the denominator) is due only to error variance. These terms are computed in such a way that the error variance is the same value in both the numerator and the denominator of the formula. Therefore, we could rewrite the above equation as

$$F = \frac{\text{Systematic effects} + \text{Error variance}}{\text{Error variance}}$$

Suppose there are no systematic effects. In this case both the numerator and the denominator would represent error variance only and the ratio would be 1.00. Whenever the F-ratio is near 1.00, it means there are no systematic effects present. In other words the between-groups variation is no larger than would be expected by chance alone. On the other hand, suppose the measure based on the between-groups variation is substantially greater than the measure based on the within-groups error variation.

This would suggest that the experimental manipulation may have had the predicted effects and caused differences between the groups that are greater than those due to chance alone. In this case we would conclude the groups do differ. This is the basic idea behind the F-test.

Controlling Variance in Research

To show a causal effect of the independent variable on the dependent variable, the experimental variance must be high and not masked by too much extraneous or error variance. The greater the extraneous and/or error variance, the more difficult it becomes to show the effects of systematic, experimental variance. This idea leads to a general but important rule: *In experimentation each study is designed so as to maximize experimental variance, control extraneous variance, and minimize error variance.*

Maximizing Experimental Variance   Experimental variance is that variance due to the effects of the independent variable(s) on the dependent variable(s). In an experiment there must be at least two levels of the independent variable, such as an experimental and a control group or several experimental groups. In fact, it is advisable to include more than two levels of the independent variable because more information can then be gained about the relationship between the independent and dependent variable(s). To demonstrate a causal effect we must be sure the independent variable really varies; that is, that the experimental conditions truly differ from one another. It is therefore necessary *to design and carry out experiments so that the experimental conditions are clearly different from each other.*

It is often useful when conducting a research study to evaluate the effectiveness of the manipulations of the independent variable by including a *manipulation check.* That is, it is important to evaluate whether the manipulation actually had its intended effect on the subject. Suppose that, in an experiment to evaluate the effect of level of anxiety on performance of a coordination task, we plan to manipulate anxiety by changing the feedback given subjects during a training period. We reason that subjects who think they are doing poorly will be more anxious than subjects who think they are doing well. Therefore, we set up two conditions. In one we tell subjects after the training period that they did quite well and should have no problems during the actual testing period (the low-anxiety group). A second group is told that they did badly during the training and that they must try harder if they want to avoid making themselves look foolish (the high-anxiety group). In this case a manipulation check, such as a simple self-report measure of anxiety, would verify that the groups differ on their level of anxiety and, therefore, the anxiety manipulation was effective. A statistical evaluation would be conducted on the manipulation check. If we find that the groups do not differ statistically on anxiety, then we cannot be sure that the manipulation of anxiety was effective. Consequently, we would not be able to evaluate the effect of anxiety on the dependent measure.

Controlling Extraneous Variance   As discussed earlier, extraneous variables are those between-group variables other than the independent variables that have effects on whole groups and may thus confound the results. (Most of the common sources of extraneous variance are discussed in Chapter 8.) To demonstrate the effects of an experimental manipulation it is necessary to control the extraneous variables and keep them from differentially affecting the groups. In this regard, two important ideas are basic in experimentation: we must be sure that (1) the experimental and control groups are as similar as possible at the start of the experiment and (2) that they are treated in exactly the same way except for the independent variable manipulation. Much of the discussion in Chapter 9 is devoted to controlling extraneous variables; the methods are summarized here:

1. The best way to avoid introducing extraneous variance during the study is to make sure that the independent variable manipulation is the *only* difference in the researcher's treatment of the experimental and control subjects.

The remaining methods for controlling extraneous variance are aimed at insuring that the groups are equal at the beginning of the study.

2. The best general method of controlling for extraneous variance is by randomization, which decreases the probability that the groups will differ on extraneous variables. Thus, *whenever possible, randomly assign subjects to conditions.*
3. If a factor such as age, ethnic identification, social class, intelligence, or sex is a potential confounding variable, we may control it by *eliminating the variable as a factor by selecting subjects who are as homogeneous as possible on that variable.* That is, for example, we can select only males or only females or subjects who are of a limited age range or within a few IQ points of each other. The cost of using this as a control is that we limit generalizability. By using only males or females, for example, we must limit our conclusions to only one sex.
4. A potential confounding variable also can be controlled by *building it into the experiment as an additional independent variable.* Thus, if sex, for example, is a potentially confounding variable, we could compare male and female subjects by adding sex as a nonmanipulated independent variable. There then would be two independent variables in the study, a design known as a *factorial design* (see Chapter 12). Note that sex in this case is not actively manipulated because it is a preexisting factor.
5. Extraneous variance can be controlled by *matching subjects* or by using a *within-subjects design* (see Chapter 11).

Minimizing Error Variance   Error variance is within-groups variance that is due to chance factors and individual differences and that affects individuals within a group rather than the group as a whole. One source of error variance is measurement error; that is, variations in the way a subject responds from trial to trial due to factors such as unreliability of the measurement instruments. To minimize this source of error variance we must *maintain carefully controlled conditions of measurement and be sure that the measuring instruments are reliable.*

Another major source of error variance is *individual differences.* Using within-subjects or matched-subjects designs will minimize this source of error variance. As discussed earlier, there are problems in using within-subjects designs—problems of sequencing and order effects that must be controlled. But the within-subjects design does effectively reduce error variance by eliminating the individual differences among subjects from one condition to another.

It should be clear that this brief discussion of maximizing experimental variance, controlling extraneous variance, and minimizing error variance is a summary of the earlier discussions of control. That is, when we discuss control in experimentation we refer to *the control of variance.* The general control procedures discussed in Chapter 9 deal with the control of error variance. Other control procedures help to control both error variance and extraneous variance. The most powerful control for extraneous variance is a properly selected experimental design in which subjects are randomly assigned to conditions. There are a number of useful experimental designs available as well as statistical tests for evaluating data generated by experimental designs.

NONEXPERIMENTAL RESEARCH DESIGNS

There are several true experimental designs and each has many variations. Earlier we listed five characteristics of true experimental designs and noted that research designs that do not meet the criteria are not true experimental designs. Thus, hypotheses about causal relationships cannot be properly tested with such designs. Unfortunately, some of the designs are still inappropriately used in social science research. To understand the limitations of these designs we need to discuss four of the most commonly used nonexperimental designs:

1. *Ex post facto* studies.
2. Single-group, posttest-only design.
3. Single-group, pretest-posttest design.
4. Pretest-posttest, natural control-group design.

We also need to look at examples of designs, beginning with *nonexperimental designs* and progressing to the most highly controlled, high-constraint, experimental designs. As we progress along this continuum, notice that each successive design controls for more sources of extraneous variance.

Ex Post Facto Design

Ex post facto ("after the fact") studies are commonly used procedures but they are not true experiments. In the *ex post facto* design the researcher observes current behavior and attempts to relate it causally to some earlier factors. (The design is diagrammed in Figure 10.1). A therapist might observe some difficulty in a client and conclude that the problem was caused by earlier life events that the therapist never directly observed

Figure 10.1 *EX POST FACTO* **DESIGN**

Group A	(Naturally occurring events) (No direct manipulation)	Measurement

or manipulated. For example, many people have concluded that abused children become abusive parents based on the observation that a large proportion of abusive parents report that they were themselves abused as children. The conclusion is arrived at in an *ex post facto* manner and, as reasonable as the conclusion seems, we can have little scientific confidence in its validity because there were no controls for confounding factors. If we cannot control for confounding such as by manipulating the independent variable, then we cannot eliminate rival hypotheses. Thus, we cannot infer a causal relationship between the independent and dependent variables.

For example, suppose a researcher suspects that food products or additives such as chocolate and artificial colors, flavors, and preservatives stimulate hyperactive behavior in some children. Obtaining a sample of 30 hyperactive children, the researcher finds that 28 of them (93.3 percent) eat chocolate or foods containing these additives every day. The number seems high to the researcher and the findings are consistent with the researcher's suspicion that there may be a relationship between food additives and hyperactivity. The researcher can even formulate the hypothesis for future testing that food additives stimulate hyperactivity. But, because the researcher followed an *ex post facto* procedure, a valid conclusion that a causal relationship exists between food additives and hyperactive behavior cannot be made.

Although *ex post facto* procedures, like all low-constraint research, have some value in helping us to *generate* hypotheses that can be tested in better-designed studies, they are not capable of *testing* causal hypotheses. The main weaknesses of the *ex post facto* procedure are that no independent variable can be manipulated and, thus, controls to guard against confounding cannot be applied. Consequently, the researcher cannot know which variable(s) may have affected the outcome and is *unable to eliminate rival hypotheses*. That is, any of several confounding variables may have been responsible. Any inferred causal relationship between an observed variable (such as a parent's current child abuse) and an assumed but never manipulated factor (having been abused as a child) is pure speculation. The *ex post facto* design should be used with great caution. However, as we discussed in the sections on naturalistic and case study research, we can speculate about possible contingencies and can use the procedure to help formulate causal hypotheses for future testing. But the *ex post facto* study is not a true experimental design and cannot be used to test causal hypotheses.

Single-Group, Posttest-Only Design

The *single-group, posttest-only* design is at a somewhat higher level of constraint than *ex post facto* procedures because an actual manipulation of a variable is included, but it still is not a true experiment. In this design a variable is manipulated with a single group and the group is then measured.

Suppose, for example, a clinician wants to determine whether eliminating suspected allergenic foods will be of help to hyperactive children. He asks parents of 20 children diagnosed as hyperactive to eliminate the foods from their children's diets for four weeks. At the end of the period the children are tested for hyperactivity and only 4 out of the 16 children are found to be hyperactive. (The single-group, posttest-only design is diagramed in Figure 10.2.) Here, there has been an actual manipulation in the form of the dietary change as well as measurement of posttreatment hyperactivity

Figure 10.2 SINGLE-GROUP,
POSTTEST-ONLY DESIGN

Group A	Treatment[a]	Posttest

[a]The term *treatment* as used in Figures 10.2–10.8
refers to any kind of manipulation of the independent variable.

levels. But there are problems in the design that prevent the researcher from drawing
causal inferences about the treatment having helped to reduce hyperactivity. There are
several confounding factors. Perhaps the children did not change at all. They were just
as active before the treatment but, because there was no pretreatment measurement,
this cannot be known. Perhaps the children did improve but the improvement was due
to some other uncontrolled factor, such as another program in which the children were
involved. Perhaps the children matured over the four weeks of treatment and their low
hyperactivity was actually due to their natural maturation and not to the dietary
program at all. Perhaps they did become less active during the program but it was only
a natural return to their normal activity level. In this case, it may have been a temporary
peak in their activity level that prompted parents to bring their children in for treatment. In other words, the single-group, posttest-only design does not control for the
confounding variables of history, maturation, or regression to the mean. The researcher
cannot even be sure if there was any change in activity level. Even though the single-
group, posttest-only design is a weak design, it is unfortunately commonly used in
clinical settings and in education. Teachers, for example, sometimes apply new teaching
programs to single groups and claim causal effects.

Single-Group, Pretest-Posttest Design

Single-group, pretest-posttest designs are also frequently used but they are weak designs
for inferring causality. They are an improvement over the posttest-only design because
they include a pretreatment evaluation (a pretest). The researcher studying hyperactivity, for example, might select a sample of hyperactive children and (1) observe them
for rates of hyperactive behavior, (2) impose the four-week dietary restrictions, and (3)
observe them again for hyperactivity at the end of the four weeks. This is the single-
group, pretest-posttest design illustrated in Figure 10.3.

Suppose the posttest measurement of hyperactivity is significantly less than the
pretest measurement. The children are indeed better at the posttest; they clearly improved from pretest to posttest. Recall from our earlier discussion that the finding is
not sufficient for us to conclude anything about the hypothesis that restriction of the
foods will decrease hyperactivity. We cannot draw these causal conclusions because the
single-group, pretest-posttest design fails to control for the same confounding variables
as does the single-group, posttest-only design—primarily maturation, history, and
regression to the mean. That is, the measured improvement might have occurred only

Figure 10.3 SINGLE-GROUP, PRETEST-POSTTEST
DESIGN

Group A	Pretest	Treatment	Posttest

because the children matured during the treatment period (maturation), because of some other factor in the program that was operating but was uncontrolled (history), or because the pretest measures of hyperactivity were at an abnormally high peak and they naturally returned in time to about their mean level (regression). To avoid these confounding variables the researcher would have to anticipate them and build in suitable controls.

Pretest-Posttest, Natural Control-Group Design

A good control to add to the above designs is a no-treatment control group. In the *pretest-posttest, natural control-group design,* subjects cannot be randomly assigned to groups as they would be in a true experimental design. Rather, naturally occurring groups are used, only one of which receives the treatment. For example, rather than randomly assign students to two groups, we might use two intact classrooms. The students from one classroom are assigned to the first group and the students from the other classroom are assigned to the second group. In the hyperactivity and food additives example, a control group of hyperactive children would not receive the dietary restriction treatment. Addition of this control group significantly strengthens the design. (The pretest-posttest, natural control-group design is illustrated in Figure 10.4.)

With the natural control-group design, which still has a major weakness, we begin to draw closer to true experimental design. However, its major weakness is that it gives no indication of randomization or any other way to insure that the two groups are statistically equivalent at the start of the study. For example, suppose that in forming the experimental and control groups the researcher asked parents if they were willing to try the four-week dietary restrictions. The children of those parents who were willing to expend the effort were put in the experimental group and those who were not were put in the control group. The serious confounding in this procedure is that the experimental and the control groups are different from each other *at the start of the study* in terms of parents' willingness to try the dietary restrictions. In other words, the dietary restriction treatment is confounded with parents' willingness to cooperate. We might assume that parents who are willing to do everything necessary to change their child's diet in hope of decreasing their child's hyperactivity may be more motivated to help their child change. Any posttreatment differences between the groups on measures of hyperactivity might be due to either factor—dietary restriction or parental willingness to cooperate. The children in the two groups may even have been different on the dependent measure (level of hyperactivity) before the experiment began. It may be that parents with the most hyperactive children are the most desperate and, therefore, the most likely to try *any* kind of treatment. Of course, the pretest in the design would allow us to check this possibility.

Figure 10.4 PRETEST-POSTTEST, NATURAL CONTROL-GROUP DESIGN

Group A (Experimental)	Pretest	Treatment	Posttest
Group B (Control)	Pretest	No Treatment	Posttest

Remember that in a true experiment, when we compare groups of subjects at different levels of the independent variable, it is essential that the groups be equivalent on the dependent measures at the start of the study. Random assignment of subjects to conditions is one way of increasing our confidence that the groups are equivalent at the start of the study.

EXPERIMENTAL RESEARCH DESIGNS

In experiments the control of variance is maximized. More fully than at other levels of constraint, using true experiments protects internal, external, statistical, and construct validity. Two critical factors that distinguish experimental designs from most nonexperimental designs and through which many threats to validity are controlled are *control groups or conditions* and *randomization.*

The addition of one or more control groups to nonexperimental designs can improve them considerably. Including proper control groups helps to control history, maturation, and regression to the mean. The experimental designs discussed here all include at least one control group. To make the control groups effective subjects must be randomly assigned to conditions. Also, the random selection of subjects from a population is a valuable control that helps protect external validity. Randomization is a powerful tool. A good general rule to follow in designing research is to randomize whenever possible.

Because there are so many different experimental designs we need to divide our discussion into several sections. We first need to discuss designs appropriate for testing a single variable using independent groups of subjects (the focus of the remainder of this chapter). Later chapters focus on designs for testing a single independent variable using correlated groups of subjects (Chapter 11); designs used for testing more than one independent variable in a single experiment (Chapter 12); and designs that test causal hypotheses in natural environments (Chapter 13).

Designs for Testing One Independent Variable

Although many variations of experimental designs are possible, there are four basic designs used to test a single independent variable using independent groups of subjects; that is, *single-variable, between-subjects designs.* These include:

1. Randomized posttest-only, control-group design.
2. Randomized pretest-posttest, control-group design.
3. Multilevel, completely randomized, between-subjects design.
4. Solomon four-group design.

Randomized, Posttest-Only, Control-Group Design   Suppose we want to manipulate an experimental treatment to test the effects of relaxation training on disruptive behavior or the effects of a special tutorial program on reading skills or the effects of visual stimulus complexity on time estimation or the effects of food additives on hyperactivity—in each case we wish to manipulate a variable and measure the effects, but in such a way that unwanted variance is controlled and validity is protected. (Note that the terms *treatment* and *manipulation* are used interchangeably throughout this discussion.)

A basic experimental design that answers questions and protects validity is the *randomized, posttest-only, control-group design,* which includes randomization and a control group. In this design we first randomly select subjects from a general or accessible population or carefully define an *ad hoc* sample. Our selected or *ad hoc* subjects are then randomly assigned to the experimental (treatment) and control (no-treatment) conditions. The resulting design, using "R" to indicate randomization, is illustrated in Figure 10.5. The arrows denote the critical comparison to be made to test the hypothesis that the independent variable did significantly affect the dependent measures.

The critical comparison is between the two levels of the independent variable (experimental and control groups) on the dependent variable at posttest. Note that it is critical for this comparison that the two groups are equivalent at the beginning of the study. If they are not, then we cannot know if differences at the posttest are due to the independent variable or to preexisting differences between the groups. Random assignment of subjects to groups increases the probability that the groups are equivalent at the beginning of the study.

Several threats to validity are controlled by the randomized, posttest-only, control-group design. External validity (generalizability of the findings) is protected by random selection or *ad hoc* sample definition. Threats to internal validity from regression to the mean and from attrition are reduced by random assignment of subjects. Threats to internal validity from instrumentation, history, and maturation are reduced by the inclusion of the no-treatment control group. Random assignment helps to insure statistical equivalence of the groups at the beginning of the study.

Randomized, Pretest-Posttest, Control-Group Design   Recall the pretest-posttest, control-group design discussed earlier in the chapter, which is a relatively weak design but not far from being a true experimental design. It is not a true experimental design because it does not use randomization. The *randomized, pretest-posttest, control-group design* is illustrated in Figure 10.6. In this design subjects are randomly assigned

Figure 10.5   RANDOMIZED, POSTTEST-ONLY, CONTROL-GROUP DESIGN

R[a]	Group A (Experimental)	Treatment	Posttest
R	Group B (Control)	No Treatment	Posttest

Compare

[a]"R" means subjects are randomly assigned to groups.

Figure 10.6   RANDOMIZED, PRETEST-POSTTEST, CONTROL-GROUP DESIGN

R	Group A (Experimental)	Pretest	Treatment	Posttest
R	Group B (Control)	Pretest	No Treatment	Posttest

to experimental and control conditions. All subjects are then pretested on the dependent variable. The experimental group is administered the treatment and both groups are then posttested on the dependent variable. The critical comparison is between the experimental and control groups on the posttreatment measure of the dependent variable.

The randomized pretest-posttest, control-group design is an improvement over the randomized posttest-only, control-group design because the former adds a pretreatment measurement of the dependent variable (i.e., a pretest). By adding the pretest we provide further assurance that the two groups are equivalent on the dependent variable at the start of the experiment. Random assignment of subjects and groups also helps to insure the two groups' equivalence. Note that though adding a pretest has some advantages, it also carries some disadvantages, which are discussed later in the chapter.

Multilevel, Completely Randomized, Between-Subjects Design   More complex randomized designs are possible where several levels of a single independent variable are manipulated. The *multilevel, completely randomized, between-subjects design* is a simple extension of previously discussed designs. Instead of subjects being randomly assigned to two conditions, they are randomly assigned to three or more conditions (see Figure 10.7). Pretests may or may not be included in this design depending on the questions the investigator wants to answer. Because this design is only an extension of earlier designs, it controls for the same confounding variables as the simple two-group designs.

Recall the description in Chapter 9 of a study in which room temperature was varied to test its effects on the speed and accuracy of typing—the study uses a multilevel, completely randomized, between-subjects design. Forty-eight typists were randomly assigned to six groups of eight typists each. Each group of typists was tested at a different room temperature (the independent variable) and their typing speed and accuracy were measured (the dependent variable).

Solomon Four-Group Design   The addition of a pretest improves control in experimental design but it also creates a new problem—the possibility that experiencing the pretest will affect subjects in some way. We might expect such pretesting effects to be the same in the experimental and control groups, but interaction effects might occur between the pretest and the experimental manipulation and constitute a potential confounding factor. By *interaction effect* in this situation we mean that the effect of the pretest will not be constant for the groups but will vary depending on the level of the independent variable. For example, suppose a researcher is interested in testing whether

Figure 10.7   MULTILEVEL, COMPLETELY RANDOMIZED,
BETWEEN-SUBJECTS DESIGN

R	Group 1	Pretest[a]	Treatment 1	Posttest
R	Group 2	Pretest	Treatment 2	Posttest
	.	.	.	.
	.	.	.	.
	.	.	.	.
R	Group N	Pretest	Treatment N	Posttest

[a]This design may or may not include a pretest.

adolescents' attitudes toward cigarette smoking can be changed by presenting them with a videotape about the health hazards of tobacco use. One hundred subjects are randomly selected from a high school. They are given a pretest measuring their attitudes toward use of tobacco and are randomly assigned to two conditions, experimental and control. The pretests show that the subjects in the two conditions are statistically equivalent on attitudes toward tobacco use at the start of the study. The experimental group is then shown the videotape and the control group is not. Both groups are then retested on their attitudes toward tobacco use and the experimental and control groups' posttest measures are compared. As well designed as this study may appear, it is still possible that the pretest of attitudes may sensitize the subjects to what the research is about. When the videotape is presented to the experimental group, this sensitization may interact with that new information and have some effect on subjects' responses. The experimenter might erroneously conclude that the observed difference is due only to the videotape, when it may actually be due to the interaction of the pretest and the videotape. If no pretest had been given, the videotape may have been less effective.

In an attempt to reduce such errors Solomon (1949) developed what he termed an *extension of control group design* to control possible interaction effects of the pretest and the manipulation. The *Solomon four-group design* combines the randomized, pretest-posttest, control-group design and the posttest-only, control-group design. (The Solomon four-group design is illustrated in Figure 10.8.) As is seen in Figure 10.8, groups A and B constitute the pretest-posttest, control-group design component, whereas groups C and D constitute the posttest-only design component. Groups A and B are the experimental and control groups, respectively, and they provide the basic comparison needed to test the hypothesis. Groups C and D represent a replication of this basic comparison but without the pretest. The critical comparison, of course, is between the posttest measures of groups A and B. The random assignment of subjects to conditions insures that the groups are statistically equivalent at the start of the study and the pretest gives us the means to test their equivalence. Random assignment also controls for potential confounding due to statistical regression. The potential confounding due to history and maturation are controlled by the inclusion of the control group (group B). Group C, which includes the treatment and posttest but no pretest, controls for the possible interaction effects of the pretest. By comparing the posttest measures of group C and group A, we have the basis for determining whether the pretest in group A did have an interactive effect. The final control, group D, includes only the posttest and provides further control for the effects of maturation. The posttest measures for group D should be similar to those of group B and different from groups A and C.

Solomon's four-group design is powerful, providing good controls and exceeding the requirements for an experiment. However, because it requires the resources of two experiments, it is not recommended for routine use. Rather, it is best used for experiments in a well-developed research program where the basic hypotheses have already

Figure 10.8 SOLOMON'S FOUR-GROUP DESIGN (*Source: Solomon, R. L., 1949, pp. 137–150.*)

R	Group A	Pretest	Treatment	Posttest
R	Group B	Pretest		Posttest
R	Group C		Treatment	Posttest
R	Group D			Posttest

been tested and supported using simpler designs and a test of greater rigor is desired. It is also used in situations where an interaction between the treatment and the pretest is expected.

Summary

Each of the four experimental designs discussed uses randomization to assign subjects to conditions. Actually, what is required is the *unbiased assignment of subjects to conditions,* which is achieved through free random assignment or matched random assignment (see Chapter 9). Thus, we can utilize matching procedures and still maintain a true experimental design. (Designs employing matching procedures are discussed in Chapter 11.)

The most basic experimental design is the randomized, posttest-only, control-group design and it is used in many experimental situations. The other designs are more complex variations of this basic design and are used when more confidence or finer testing is needed. Notice three characteristics of the studies that would be carried out using this experimental design and its variations:

1. The studies to which they are applied are experiments in which only one independent variable is manipulated.
2. The designs are completely randomized because subjects are randomly assigned to conditions.
3. The critical comparison is a comparison between subjects in one group and different subjects in another group; the groups of subjects in the experiment are independent of each other. These are completely randomized, between-subjects designs.

Statistical Analyses of Completely Randomized Designs

Different statistical methods are typically used depending on the level of measurement of the dependent variable (see Chapters 4 and 5). For example, if we test differences between groups and the data are nominal data, chi-square is typically used; if we have ordered data, a commonly used statistic for comparing two groups is the Mann-Whitney U-test; and if we have score data, we would use either a t-test or an analysis of variance (F-test). Score data are most often found at the experimental level of constraint.

t-**Test**   The *t-test* evaluates the size of the difference between the means of the two groups. The difference between the means is divided by an *error term,* which is a function of the variance of scores within each group and the size of the samples. The t-test is easily applied, commonly used, and useful when we wish to test the difference between two groups. Its disadvantage is that it can compare only two groups at a time.

Analysis of Variance (ANOVA)   Many studies are multilevel designs in which more than two groups are used. For those studies an *analysis of variance (ANOVA)* is preferred because it is flexible enough to handle any number of groups. In fact, ANOVA is now so frequently used when there are only two groups that it is beginning to replace the *t*-test. For example, in the typists study described earlier, there are six levels of the independent variable, room temperature. Because there are six groups of subjects, we would not use a *t*-test. Instead, we could use a simple one-way analysis of variance to test whether any of the six groups is statistically different from any of the other groups.

To introduce analysis of variance it is necessary to review some of our earlier discussion of variance. Basically, the ANOVA procedure depends on calculations of the variance of the scores in the distribution. Variance is calculated by finding the difference between each score and the mean, squaring each of the differences and summing those squares to find the sum of squares. The sum of squares is divided by the degrees of freedom to yield the variance. Thus, variance is essentially the average of the squared deviations from the mean.

Variance is a relatively simple concept, but it can seem confusing because, in analysis of variance, variance is calculated more than once based on different combinations of the same data. Analysis of variance uses both the within-groups variance and the between-groups variance. Within groups variance is a measure of nonsystematic variation within a group. It is error or chance variation among individual subjects within a group and is due to factors such as individual differences and measurement errors. It represents the average variability within each of the groups. The between-groups variance is a measure of both the systematic factors that affect the groups differently and the variation due to sampling error. The systematic factors include (1) experimental variance, which is variation due to the effects of the independent variables, and (2) extraneous variance, which is due to extraneous factors. Even if there are no systematic effects, the group means are likely to be slightly different from one another by chance alone due to sampling error. The between-groups variance tells us how variable the group means are. If all groups in the experiment have approximately the same mean, the between-groups variance will be small. However, if the group means are quite different from one another, the between-groups variance will be large.

Further, the researcher should attempt to arrange the experiment so as to maximize experimental variance, control extraneous variance, and minimize error variance. The reasoning behind this principle becomes apparent through knowing how the analysis of variance is computed. The variance is based on the sum of squares, which is the sum of squared deviations from the mean. In an analysis of variance there is a sum of squares on which the between-groups variance is based, a sum of squares on which the within-groups variance is based, and a total sum of squares. In the ANOVA procedure the sum of squares is calculated for each of these; that is, we *partition* the total sum of squares into the between-groups sum of squares and the within-groups sum of squares:

$$\text{Total sum} \atop \text{of squares} = {\text{Between-groups} \atop \text{sum of squares}} + {\text{Within-groups} \atop \text{sum of squares}}$$

These principles can be illustrated by using the example described earlier, the study of the effects of room temperature on typing speed. Forty-eight typists are randomly assigned to six conditions defined by the temperature of the room in which their typing speed is tested. Table 10.1 shows the raw data and the mean scores for the typing speed data for each group of typists. The first step in doing an analysis of variance of these data is to compute each of the sums of squares: the sum of squares

Table 10.1 TYPING SPEED DATA FROM 48 TYPISTS RANDOMLY ASSIGNED TO 1 OF 6 ROOM TEMPERATURES

	55°	60°	65°	70°	75°	80°
	49	71	64	63	60	48
	59	54	73	72	71	53
	61	62	60	56	49	64
	52	58	55	59	54	53
	50	64	72	64	63	59
	58	68	81	70	55	61
	63	57	79	63	59	54
	54	61	76	65	62	60
Means	55.75	61.88	70.00	64.00	59.13	56.50

between-groups, the sum of squares within-groups, and the total sum of squares. (The computational procedures for these values are given in Appendix C.) The results of the computations are recorded in an *ANOVA summary table* (see Table 10.2). The next step is to compute between-groups and within-groups variances, which are called *mean squares*. To compute the mean squares we divide each of the sums of squares by the appropriate *degrees of freedom* (df). The between-groups sum of squares is divided by the number of groups minus one (in this case, $6 - 1 = 5$). The within-groups sum of squares is divided by the total number of subjects minus the number of groups (in this case, $48 - 6 = 42$). The between-groups and within-groups mean squares are then compared by dividing the between-groups mean square by the within-groups mean square. The result is the F ratio, which we will interpret shortly. (All computations are summarized in Table 10.2.) Note that the ANOVA summary table shows the sources of variation in column 1, the degrees of freedom associated with each source of variation in column 2, the sum of squares in column 3, the mean squares in column 4, the value of F (mean square between-groups divided by mean square within-groups) in column 5, and the probability value in column 6.

The statistical significance of the ANOVA is based on the F-*test* (named after its originator, Sir Ronald Fisher). Fisher's F-test involves the ratio of the between-groups mean square to the within-groups mean square:

$$F = \frac{\text{Mean square between-groups}}{\text{Mean square within-groups}}$$

Consider some of the possibilities we might find in this ratio. If there were no *systematic* between-groups differences, there would still be some *chance* differences between the groups. The group differences are due to the normal chance variation found

Table 10.2 ANOVA SUMMARY TABLE FOR STUDY OF TYPING SPEED AND ROOM TEMPERATURE

Source	df	Sum of squares	Mean square	F	p
Between	5	1134.66	226.93	5.51	< .01
Within	42	1731.26	41.22		
Total	47	2865.92			

among subjects and to sampling error in the formation of the groups. In fact, if there were no systematic between-groups differences, both the mean square between-groups (based on between-groups variability) and the mean square within-groups (based on within-groups variability) would be estimates of the same quantity—the within-groups variance. In that case, the F ratio should have a value of approximately 1.00. However, if there are systematic between-groups differences, the ratio would have a value greater than 1.00. Consider also the conditions that would make the F ratio larger or smaller. Any factors that increase the size of the numerator relative to the denominator will make the ratio larger; any factors that increase the size of the denominator relative to the numerator will make the ratio smaller. Thus, the ratio will be made larger by either increasing the between-groups mean square or by decreasing the within-groups mean square. We increase the between-groups mean square by maximizing the differences between the groups. We minimize the within-groups mean square by controlling as many potential sources of random error as possible. In other words, it is desirable to maximize experimental variance and minimize error variance.

Recall that within-groups variation is due to chance factors and between-groups variation is due to both chance factors and systematic effects. Thus, if the mean square between-groups is the same as the mean square within-groups, the differences between experimental conditions are due solely to chance factors and the experimental manipulations have no additional effects. The between-groups mean square must be significantly larger than the within-groups mean square if we are to conclude that the experimental manipulations had effects beyond the chance differences.

The larger the F ratio, the greater the difference *between* groups relative to the chance differences *within* groups. An F value of 1.00 or less indicates there is no significant difference between groups relative to differences within groups. It is this concept that the F-test utilizes. A large F indicates that the experimental manipulations may have succeeded in causing a greater difference between experimental conditions than one would expect by chance alone (i.e., a significant difference between the conditions). In practice if there are no systematic differences between groups, the F ratio will sometimes by chance alone be slightly larger than 1.00. Therefore, we do not reject the hypothesis that there are no systematic differences unless the F ratio is larger than we would expect by chance alone. The researcher evaluates the size of the F ratio by comparing it with critical values (see Table B.3 in Appendix B). The appropriate critical value will depend on the degrees of freedom for both the numerator (df for between-groups) and the denominator (df for within-groups) of the F ratio. The appropriate critical value will also depend on the alpha or Type I error level that is set. For example, in the hypothetical study of the effects of room temperature on typing speed there are six groups and eight subjects in each group. Therefore, the degrees of freedom (df) between-groups is equal to 5 and the degrees of freedom within-groups is equal to 42. The critical value of F from Table B.3 (see Appendix B) for an alpha of 0.05 is 2.44. If there really are no differences between the populations, we will obtain F values this large or larger by chance 5 percent of the time (our alpha level). If the computed value of F exceeds this number, we conclude that we have significant differences among the groups. Because the computed value of F is 5.51, larger than we would expect by chance, we conclude that at least one of the groups is significantly different from at least one other group.

Specific Means Comparisons in ANOVA   Note that the F-test in the analysis of variance tells us if a significant difference among the groups exists but does not tell us which group or groups are significantly different from the others. This is not a problem when an ANOVA has only two groups to compare because the significant F ratio tells us that the two groups do differ. By simply inspecting their means we can see whether the difference is in the predicted direction. But when we have three or more groups to compare, an additional step is needed: we must *probe* to determine where the significant difference(s) occurred. Probing is done by statistically testing the differences between the individual means. Specific comparisons are best carried out as a planned part of the research (i.e., a planned comparison or an *a priori* comparison) in which the experimenter makes predictions before data are collected about which groups will differ and in what directions based on theoretical concepts that underlie the experiment. At times we cannot make an *a priori* prediction, and we carry out an ANOVA to answer the question of whether there are any differences. Under these conditions, if a significant F is found, we compare the pattern of means using a *post hoc* comparison (also called *a posteriori* or incidental comparison). The scientific rigor and informational value is generally greater for the planned comparisons than for the *post hoc* comparisons. There are several statistical procedures that can be used for the specific comparisons depending on whether they are planned or *post hoc*. Thus, if there are two groups, the F-test indicates whether the groups are significantly different from one another, and inspecting the means reveals the direction of the difference. If there are three or more groups to compare, the F-test reveals whether there are statistically significant differences among the groups, and the next step—probing—tells exactly where the differences are. (The student interested in probing procedures can consult Shavelson, 1981.)

Interpreting results is a process of trying to make sense out of complicated findings and a useful first step in the interpretation process is to look at the pattern of means. In the typing speed example we can inspect the means as they are are listed in Table 10.1 and can organize the means into a graph as shown in Figure 10.9. Graphs

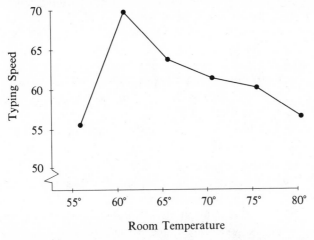

Figure 10.9   PATTERN OF MEAN SCORES FOR THE STUDY OF EFFECTS OF ROOM TEMPERATURE ON TYPING SPEED

are usually easier than tables to read and are particularly helpful when there is more than one independent variable (i.e., factorial designs).

Other Experimental Designs

The simple and multilevel between-subjects, completely randomized designs have served researchers well. They are powerful, commonly used, and are appropriate where a single independent variable is to be manipulated and random assignment of subjects is used. However, there are three general conditions where these designs should not be used.

First, there are many research settings in which complete randomization is not possible. Here a lower constraint design is necessary. Secondly, we know that variables do not necessarily operate singly but often operate simultaneously to affect the responses of subjects. Further, several variables may interact with each other. Thus, there are many research questions in which it may be useful to manipulate more than one independent variable in a single study and to manipulate them in such a way that enables us to assess whether the two independent variables interact with each other when producing their effects on the dependent variable. Here a factorial design is appropriate. Finally, there are research conditions in which it is desirable to have the same subjects tested under each condition. In this case a within-subjects design is used. (Factorial and within-subjects designs are discussed in Chapters 11–12.) It is important to emphasize that the experimental research designs we discuss in this text can be categorized according to two dimensions. First, studies can be independent groups designs, such as between-subjects designs, or correlated-groups designs, such as within-subjects designs. Secondly, studies can be either single-variable designs or multivariable (factorial) designs.

Independent- Versus Correlated-Groups Designs Essentially, *independent-groups* (between-subjects) *designs* have different subjects in each group and the critical comparisons are made between the different groups of subjects. *Correlated-groups designs* have the same or closely matched subjects in each group, and the same subjects' or matched subjects' performance is compared under different conditions. By far the most common correlated-groups design is the within-subjects design. The experimental designs discussed so far are randomized, independent-groups, or between-subjects designs. The correlated-groups designs, however, do not randomly assign subjects to groups because either all subjects are in each group or condition, or subjects in one condition are closely matched with subjects in the other condition(s). (Within-subjects designs and matched-subjects designs are discussed further in Chapter 11.)

Single-Variable Versus Multivariable or Factorial Designs The experimental designs discussed so far in this chapter have been single-variable designs (i.e., in which only one independent variable is manipulated in a study). There are many research projects in which more than one independent variable is manipulated. We call these studies *factorial designs*. These designs have the additional advantage of allowing us to evaluate the *interactive effects* of two or more independent variables. (Factorial designs are discussed further in Chapter 12.)

SUMMARY

Experimental design entails a highly detailed process of developing controls over unwanted variance to reduce threats to validity. Variance includes systematic between-groups variance and nonsystematic within-groups error variance. Between-groups variance is a function of both experimental variance and extraneous variance. A major principle in experimentation is to design the study in order to maximize experimental variance, control extraneous variance, and minimize error variance.

There are many specific experimental designs that can be used to test causal hypotheses and in this chapter they are organized into two groups: (1) specific designs that are appropriate for testing hypotheses when we have a single independent variable to manipulate and (2) specific experimental designs, called factorial designs, which are used when we have more than one independent variable to manipulate in a single study and when we are interested in the interactions among independent variables. In this chapter we also make the distinction between within-subjects and between-subjects designs. This chapter focuses exclusively on between-subjects, single independent variable designs. Chapter 11 presents correlated-groups designs, Chapter 12 factorial designs, and Chapter 13 specialized designs used in field settings (single-subject experimental designs and quasi-experimental designs).

REVIEW EXERCISES

I. Define the following key terms. Be sure you understand them. They are discussed in the chapter and defined in the glossary.

Experimental design
Variance
Sum of squares
Degrees of freedom
Between-groups variance
Experimental variance
Extraneous variance
Within-groups variance
Error variance
Manipulation check
Within-subjects design
Individual differences
Between-subjects design
Control groups
Randomization

Confounding variables
Interaction effects
Nonexperimental designs
   Ex post facto design
   Single-group, posttest-only
      design
   Single-group, pretest-posttest
      design
   Pretest-posttest natural
      control-group design
Experimental designs
   Randomized, posttest-only,
      control-group design
   Randomized, pretest-posttest,
      control-group design

Multilevel, completely randomized, between-subjects design	Mean squares
	F-test
	Independent-groups design
Solomon four-group design	Correlated-groups design
t-test	Single-variable design
Analysis of variance (ANOVA)	Multivariable design
ANOVA summary table	Factorial design

II. Briefly answer the following. Check your answers in the chapter.

1. Review the concepts of deduction and induction.
2. What is extraneous variance? Why is it important to consider in research?
3. Why is it important to maximize between-groups variance?
4. If between-groups variance is high in an experiment, is that enough evidence to conclude that the independent variable had the predicted effect on the dependent variable? Explain.
5. What are the two major sources of between-groups variance in an experiment?
6. What is the relationship between error variance and individual differences among subjects?
7. Why is it important to maximize experimental variance?
8. What is the relationship among these concepts: confounding variables, threats to validity, extraneous variance?
9. Why is randomization the single best way to control extraneous variance?
10. In terms of the F-test, why is it important to minimize the error variance?
11. Define *ex post facto* studies and explain why it is a weak design. What conclusions can you draw from this type of study?
12. Why is it important to be sure that the groups to be compared in an experiment are equivalent at the start of the study?
13. Almost all threats to validity are controlled if we include only two control procedures. What are they and what threats are controlled by their inclusion?
14. Why do we urge researchers to randomize wherever possible?
15. Why is it so important that the independent variable in experiments be presented at two or more levels?
16. Suppose we find a significant difference between groups in an experiment. Are we then justified in inferring that the experimental manipulation caused the difference? Explain.

III. Think about and work the following problems.

1. How do (a) random assignment of subjects to conditions and (b) the addition of a control group reduce threats to internal validity?
2. You are the teaching assistant for this course and you have to explain variability to your students. How would you explain the concept, its major measure, and its importance?
3. Explain this statement: Error variance affects scores in both directions; systematic variance affects scores in only one direction. Why is this so important?

4. For each of the following designs (a) give an example, (b) identify the major threats to validity, and (c) state the limits on the conclusions that can be drawn.

   Single-group, posttest-only design
   Ex post facto design
   Single-group, pretest-posttest design
   Pretest-posttest, natural control-group design

5. As the course teaching assistant you have the task of explaining the F ratio. Define all of its components and explain the logic of the F-test.

6. For each of the following types of experimental design (a) give an example and (b) indicate what threats to validity are controlled.

   Randomized, posttest-only, control-group design
   Randomized, pretest-posttest, control-group design
   Multilevel, completely randomized, between-subjects design
   Solomon four-group design

CHAPTER 11

CONTROL OF VARIANCE THROUGH EXPERIMENTAL DESIGN

Single-Variable, Correlated-Groups Design

An experiment represents high-constraint research aimed at drawing causal inferences. Its characteristics are:

1. A clearly stated hypothesis concerning predicted *causal effects* of one variable on another.
2. At least two levels of a manipulated independent variable.
3. Unbiased assignment of subjects to conditions to insure equivalence of groups at the start of the experiment.
4. Specific and systematic procedures for testing the causal hypothesis.
5. Specific controls to reduce threats to internal validity.

As noted in Chapter 10, single-variable, independent-groups experiments are completely randomized, between-subjects designs in which the requirement of unbiased subject assignment is met by random assignment of subjects to conditions. Random assignment of subjects increases our confidence that the groups are equivalent at the start of the study. The designs allow us to answer questions about causality with considerable confidence.

The characteristics of randomized, between-subjects experimental designs are:

1. Each subject is exposed to only one level of the independent variable.
2. The groups are independent of each other.
3. Only one score per subject on the dependent variable is used in analyzing the results.
4. The critical comparison is the difference between independent groups on the dependent measures.

Randomized, between-subjects experimental designs have been a mainstay in psychological research. They are powerful designs used under many conditions to answer causal questions. Random assignment of subjects to conditions, a principal feature of the designs, is a powerful control and gives us confidence that the groups to be compared are equivalent at the start of the study.

CORRELATED-GROUPS DESIGN

There are conditions in which a causal question must be answered but the researcher decides not to use random assignment of subjects to conditions. Given our emphasis on the importance of randomization, the question is raised, "Is an experimental design possible when random assignment is not used?" There are designs that do not include random assignment but nevertheless *provide equivalent groups at the start of the study* and allow other controls to be applied when necessary. *Correlated-groups designs* allow us to test causal hypotheses with confidence and without randomization. Some researchers do not consider correlated-groups designs to be true experiments because they do not use random assignment. However, others believe they are true experiments because they meet the requirements of equivalence of groups and because most other controls are possible, thereby providing the bases for eliminating rival hypotheses and allowing systematic testing of causal hypotheses with confidence. Further, correlated-groups designs are generally more sensitive than between-subjects designs to the effects of the independent variable (for reasons discussed later in the chapter), and are often preferred by researchers to between-subjects designs. Therefore, correlated-groups designs are considered in this text as a category of experimental design.

Let us consider why these designs are called correlated-groups (or correlated-subjects) designs. Recall that random assignment helps to assure equivalence of groups at the start of the experiment. But there are other ways to assure equivalence. For example, suppose we have only five children and want to study their attention span for complex versus simple visual stimuli. We could measure the attention span of all five children under each of the two conditions. The independent variable—complexity of visual stimuli—is presented at two levels, *simple* and *complex*. The dependent variable—attention span—is measured under both conditions for all children. In this design the subjects who are in level 1 of the experiment are the *same subjects* who are in level 2. Clearly, when the subjects in one group are the same individuals in the other group(s) then the groups are equivalent at the start of the study. Indeed, they are identical. Thus, by using the same subjects in all conditions we guarantee equivalence of groups at the start of the study. The groups are not independent of one another as they are in between-subjects designs but are correlated with each other. Note also that each subject is measured more than once (i.e., repeatedly measured). Hence, the term *repeated measures design* is sometimes used. The strength of correlated-groups designs and the reason they are often preferred by experimenters is their power in assuring equivalence of groups. However, there is potential for confounding that must be controlled. Thus, although random assignment of subjects to conditions is not used with correlated designs, we can still preserve the characteristics of experimental designs so as to have good control and reasonable confidence in testing causal hypotheses. The key idea in correlated-groups designs is that in seeking to insure equivalence of groups, some correlation among subjects in different groups is introduced.

There are two basic ways of introducing the correlation among subjects in correlated-groups designs:

1. Within-subjects designs, in which a single group of subjects is exposed to all conditions.
2. Matched-subjects designs, in which subjects are matched on some important variable(s) and matched sets of subjects are randomly assigned so that one subject of each set is assigned to each condition.

Within-Subjects Design

In *within-subjects designs* all subjects are exposed to all experimental conditions, thereby making the conditions correlated. *In essence, each subject serves as his or her own control.*

Using Within-Subjects Design   Suppose that in a time-perception experiment we want to test whether subjects' estimates of the duration of a standard time interval varies with the amount of information given during the interval. That is, we predict that the interval "filled" with information will be perceived as longer than the "partially filled" or "empty" intervals. Each of six subjects is presented with one filled time interval, one partially filled interval, and one empty interval, all identical in duration. Because each subject appears in each condition, each subject is measured more than once on the dependent variable. (The design of this study is illustrated in Figure 11.1.)

The characteristics of within-subjects designs can be summarized:

1. Each subject is exposed to all levels of the independent variable.
2. The scores in each condition thereby are correlated with each other (i.e., performance in one condition is correlated with performance in each other condition).
3. Each subject is measured more than once on the dependent variable (i.e., each subject is measured under each experimental condition).
4. The critical comparison is the difference between correlated groups on the dependent variable.

In within-subjects designs a sample of subjects is drawn from a population or an *ad hoc* sample is created, and that single sample is exposed to all conditions of the experiment. Notice that the time-estimation experiment described earlier is similar to a single-group, pretest-posttest design (see Chapter 10). In both designs the same subjects are tested under each condition. In the single-group, pretest-posttest design each subject responds to the pretest and the posttest in that order. In contrast, in within-subjects designs each subject responds in two or more conditions and the order of presentation of conditions is not necessarily fixed as it must be in a pretest-posttest study. In the time-estimation study each subject is measured under three conditions. Because it is similar to the single-group, pretest-posttest design, it also has many of the same weaknesses of that design. For example, because we have the same subjects in all conditions, the experience subjects have in one condition might affect how they respond in subsequent conditions. Thus, if we found differences between the conditions in an experiment, they might be due not to the independent variable manipulation but to the confounding effects of one condition on later conditions. This potential confounding, called *sequencing effects,* can occur in within-subjects designs and must be controlled by systematically or randomly varying the order of presentation of conditions. A major control for sequencing effects is *counterbalancing,* in which the order of presentation of conditions to subjects is systematically varied so that (1) each subject is exposed to all conditions of the experiment, (2) each condition is presented an equal number of

Figure 11.1   WITHIN-SUBJECTS DESIGN IN WHICH EACH SUBJECT IS TESTED IN EACH OF THREE CONDITIONS

	Conditions[a]		
	Filled	**Partially filled**	**Empty**
Group A	Measure	Measure	Measure

[a]The order of presentation of conditions will vary from subject to subject, as shown in Table 11.1.

times, (3) each condition is presented an equal number of times in each position, and (4) each condition precedes and follows each other condition an equal number of times. (Sequencing effects and their controls will be discussed further later in the chapter.)

Table 11.1 shows the various orders of conditions for the hypothetical within-subjects experimental study of time estimation. Notice that all four conditions given in the previous paragraph are met with this set of orders. Hypothetical data for the experiment are also in Table 11.1. The data are the number of seconds duration estimated by each subject in each condition. The first column lists the six subjects, the second column shows the order of presentation of the stimulus conditions to each subject, and the last three columns show the time estimations for each of the three experimental conditions.

Analyzing Within-Subjects Design   To analyze the results of within-subjects designs we first organize and summarize the data, as shown in Table 11.1. As shown by the mean values of each condition in the table, the estimates are largest on average for the filled interval, next for the partially filled interval, and lowest for the empty interval. These results suggest that our hypothesis might be supported. But are the differences between conditions large enough for us to state with confidence that similar differences exist in the populations? In other words, "Are the differences statistically significant?"

The most commonly used statistical analysis for the single-variable, within-subjects experiment is an ANOVA similar to the one discussed in Chapter 10. However, the difference is that in the present study the conditions are not independent of each other but are correlated. The ANOVA procedure must be modified slightly to take this correlation into account. In this case the appropriate ANOVA to use is called a *repeated measures ANOVA* in which each subject is measured on the dependent variable under each condition.

The advantage of a within-subjects design is that it effectively equates subjects in different conditions prior to experimental manipulation by using the same subjects in each condition. Therefore, the single largest contributing factor to error variance—individual differences—has been removed. In the language of analysis of variance we have removed the effects of individual differences from the error component. What effect do you think this would have on the F ratio? Because the individual difference

Table 11.1   HYPOTHETICAL DATA FOR THE TIME-ESTIMATION STUDY

Subjects	Order of Presentation	A (filled)	B (part filled)	C (empty)
1	ABC	22	17	15
2	ACB	17	14	14
3	BAC	13	13	12
4	BCA	19	14	11
5	CAB	24	16	14
6	CBA	12	11	10
Mean scores		17.83	14.16	12.66

portion of the error term has been removed, the denominator in the F ratio will be smaller and, therefore, the F will be larger. This means that the procedure will be more sensitive to small differences between groups.

In a repeated measures ANOVA the total sum of squares is computed in the same way as in a simple one-way ANOVA. What is called a between-groups sum of squares in a simple one-way ANOVA is in this case called a between-conditions or simply a between sum of squares. That is, in the repeated measures design there is only one group. The within-groups sum of squares is split into two terms, *subjects* and *error,* in the repeated measures ANOVA. The *Subjects term* is the individual differences component of the within-groups variability. The *Error term* is what is left of the within-groups variability after the individual differences component is removed. In the repeated measures ANOVA we test the null hypothesis that there are no differences between conditions by dividing the mean square between by the error mean square. As in the independent groups ANOVA, the ratio of mean squares is an F ratio and is compared with the appropriate critical value of F, which can be found in Table B.3 of Appendix B. (The computational procedures for a repeated measures ANOVA are given in Appendix C.) Table 11.2 gives the summary table for the repeated measures ANOVA for the data from Table 11.1.

The analysis of variance tests the null hypothesis that there are no differences between any of the conditions. Therefore, a significant F ratio indicates that at least one of the condition means is significantly different from at least one other condition mean. To determine which means are significantly different from which other means we must use one of the statistical tests to probe for specific mean differences. Computational procedures for the tests can be found in most advanced statistics textbooks (Myers, 1972; Shavelson, 1981).

Strengths and Weaknesses of Within-Subjects Design When properly used within-subjects designs have important advantages. First, because the same subjects are in each condition there are no differences between groups due to subject variables, which guarantees that subjects in various conditions are equivalent at the start of the study. If the conditions are not equivalent at the start of the study, we cannot know whether differences found are due to experimental manipulation or to preexisting differences between the conditions.

Another important advantage of within-subjects designs is that they are often a good deal more sensitive than between-subjects designs to the effects of the independent variable. Experimenters have argued that this is so important an advantage that, given the choice, within-subjects designs are preferred to between-subjects designs. Why this sensitivity is greater for within-subjects designs is clear. Remember that the aim of an

Table 11.2 SUMMARY TABLE FOR REPEATED MEASURES ANOVA EXAMPLE

Source	df	Sum of squares	Mean squares	F	p
Between	2	84.78	42.39	10.98	< 0.01
Subjects	5	118.44	23.69		
Error term	10	38.56	3.86		
Total	17	241.78			

experiment is to show the effects of an independent variable upon a dependent variable. Recall that to show that effect we try to maximize the experimental variance (variance due to the effects of the independent variable), to control extraneous variance (variance due to confounding), and to minimize error variance (variance due to individual differences and chance factors) (see Chapter 10). By using a within-subjects design we not only control but *actually eliminate the variance that is due to subject differences, thereby reducing error variance.* In terms of the F-test, the value of F is increased by either increasing the between-conditions variance (the experimental variance) or by decreasing the within-conditions variance (the error variance). The use of within-subjects designs decreases error variance by removing its major contributor, individual differences. As the measure of within-conditions variance decreases, the value of F increases. The greater sensitivity of within-subjects designs to the effects of the independent variable leads many researchers to prefer within-subjects designs to between-subjects designs when given the choice.

Further, fewer subjects are needed in within-subjects designs. For example, an independent-groups design with 10 subjects in each of 3 conditions will require a total of 30 subjects. Using a within-subjects design requires only 10 subjects because each subject is tested under all conditions. In addition, because of its greater sensitivity, the within-subjects design might require even fewer subjects per condition. For example, 7 subjects in a within-subjects design might give us the same sensitivity as 10 subjects per condition in a between-subjects design. Reducing the sample size reduces sensitivity, but we can do it safely here because the greater sensitivity of the within-subjects design will balance the loss of sensitivity from using fewer subjects.

There is yet another advantage of within-subjects designs, one that further increases efficiency. Because the same subjects are tested under several conditions, instructions can be given only once instead of at the beginning of each condition, or the instructions may require only slight modifications for each condition. If instructions are long and/or complicated, or if a practice period is part of the instructions, time savings can be considerable.

Although within-subjects designs have many advantages, they also have some important disadvantages. The disadvantages all stem from the fact that in this design each subject is exposed to each condition. Therefore, subjects' experience in one condition may affect their responses to any or all of the conditions that follow. That is, the major disadvantage of within-subjects designs are sequencing effects, effects of one treatment on another. If sequencing effects occur and are not properly controlled, any significant differences between conditions may be due to sequencing effects and not to the effects of the independent variable. In other words, there would be serious confounding in the study and we could not confidently draw a causal inference about the effects of the independent variable. Sequencing effects can obviously occur in experiments where a treatment has a permanent or long-lasting effect on subjects. Examples can be found in animal experimentation where chemical or surgical changes are brought about or in human experiments in which attitudes are changed or psychotherapy is given. A long-lasting or permanent effect of a condition can certainly affect the subject's response to any other condition that followed it. A within-subjects design should not be used in such a situation. Even if the effects of conditions are temporary, there is always the risk of potential sequencing effects for at least some period of time following the treatment. There are a number of potentially confounding sequencing effects. The two most important are (1) practice effects and (2) carry-over effects.

Practice effects, as the term implies, are caused by subjects' practice and growing experience with procedures as they move through successive conditions. Practice effects are not due to influences of any particular condition but, rather, to subjects' growing familiarity with the task. If, for example, the experiment includes five conditions and they are presented in the same order to each subject, then presumably because of practice effects many subjects might perform better in the last two or three conditions than in the earlier conditions. This enhancement of performance on the later conditions constitutes a *positive practice effect.* On the other hand, if the procedure is lengthy or demanding, subjects might become fatigued as they continued in the experiment. Their performance in later conditions might therefore be reduced by fatigue. This is called a *negative practice effect.* Thus, practice effects may either enhance or reduce performance. In either case, they constitute a potential confounding variable and must be controlled. Note also that practice effects depend on subjects' experience as they move sequentially through the conditions. This means that practice effects occur regardless of the particular sequence of conditions. That is, if the conditions are always presented in the same order, the last few conditions in the sequence could be influenced by practice effects.

In contrast, *carry-over effects* are sequencing effects due to the influence of a particular condition or combination of conditions on responses to the following condition. Carry-over effects may be greatest from one particular condition than from any others, and thus the particular sequence of conditions is a factor. For example, there may be some aspect of condition A that produces an effect on any condition that follows it. Thus, wherever condition A appears in a sequence, the next condition will be influenced. Suppose that in the time-estimation study described earlier the conditions are always presented A, B, C, where A is the filled condition, B is the partially filled condition, and C is the empty condition. Each subject first responds to the two filled conditions before being presented with the empty condition. The sequence effect may be that when subjects reach the empty condition they are still responding to the details of the two filled conditions (i.e., conditions A and B might influence subjects to respond to condition C in a similar fashion). Thus, we might find no differences in response between the filled and empty conditions. On the other hand, experiencing the two filled conditions first and the empty condition last might set up a marked contrast, causing subjects to respond differently to the empty condition, not because of the empty condition itself but because of the contrast with the prior filled conditions. Note that carry-over effects of one condition may be the same on all subsequent conditions or they might affect only some of the subsequent conditions; that is, carry-over effects may be differential. In either case, carry-over effects constitute an extraneous variable and must be controlled.

There are two general types of controls for sequencing effects: (1) holding the extraneous variable constant and (2) varying the order of presentation of conditions. In the time-estimation example presented earlier, to control for positive practice effects we might *hold the practice variable constant* by training all of the subjects to the same criterion of performance before the first condition begins. Thus, all subjects would be familiar with the procedures before they respond to any of the experimental conditions.

A control for fatigue (negative practice effects) could be the inclusion of a rest period between the conditions, allowing fatigue that was building up to dissipate before going on to the next condition. Such procedures can minimize practice effects. However, control is best achieved by varying the order of presentation of conditions.

Carry-over effects can be controlled only by varying the order of presentation of conditions. For example, we should not use the same ABC sequence for all subjects in the time-estimation study. Varying the presentation can be accomplished by random order of presentations or by counterbalanced order of presentations. In *random order of presentation* we randomly order the conditions to be presented to each subject. In this way practice effects are not systematically maximized in one condition and carry-over effects should occur as much to any one condition as to any other. Counterbalancing the presentation is more involved. In counterbalancing we arrange the order of presentations of conditions to subjects so that (1) each subject is exposed to all conditions of the experiment, (2) each condition occurs the same number of times as every other condition, (3) each condition is presented an equal number of times in each position, and (4) each condition precedes and follows each condition an equal number of times. Counterbalancing controls for confounding due to both practice effects and carry-over effects.

In a study with three experimental conditions (A, B, C) there are six possible orders of presentation of conditions, as shown in Table 11.1. Subjects are assigned to orders of presentation with an equal number assigned to each order. If we have 30 subjects, for instance, we can assign five subjects to each of the six orders. Each condition appears in each position an equal number of times and each precedes and follows every other condition an equal number of times. Clearly, counterbalancing is best used in studies with a small number of conditions. Counterbalancing procedures for many conditions can become extremely complicated. With two conditions—A and B—there are only two orders of presentation (AB and BA). With three conditions—A, B, and C—there are six orders of presentation. But with four experimental conditions—A, B, C, and D—there are 24 orders of presentation ($4 \times 3 \times 2 \times 1$). To meet the counterbalancing criteria noted above we would need at least 24 subjects in the experiment. But suppose we have only 10 subjects and four experimental conditions, and we still want to use a within-subjects design and control for sequencing effects? In experiments with three or more conditions we can (1) randomize the order of presentation for each subject, (2) randomly select 10 of the 24 possible arrangements and then randomly assign subjects to those conditions, or (3) use a more formalized design known as a *Latin square design.* Latin squares are counterbalanced arrangements presumably named after an ancient Roman puzzle that required arranging letters in rows and columns so that each letter occurs only once in each row and once in each column.

A word of caution is needed. If strong carry-over effects are expected, the within-subjects design is *not recommended* even if the above controls are included. Although the controls will prevent carry-over effects from systematically affecting the mean scores for the conditions, they will prevent the effects on the variability of scores. Carry-over effects tend to add error variance to scores, which can offset any increased sensitivity normally expected from a within-subjects design. If strong carry-over effects are expected, it is best to use either a between-subjects design or a matched-subjects design.

Readers should note that the within-subjects designs referred to in Chapter 10 are nonexperimental designs (i.e., the single-group, pretest-posttest design). The reason this design is considered nonexperimental, whereas the within-subjects designs discussed in this chapter are considered experimental, is that controls to reduce sequencing effects are not possible in the single-group, pretest-posttest design. We cannot counterbalance the order of presentation because the pretest must always precede the treatment and the posttest must always follow the treatment. To obtain sufficient control over confounding the pretest-posttest design requires a separate control group. Remember, the experimental level of constraint is defined in terms of the adequacy of control over potential confounding.

Summary The within-subjects design is a type of correlated-groups design in which each subject is tested under each condition of the experiment. The major strengths of the within-subjects design are that it equates groups prior to the experimental manipulation and is sensitive to small effects of the independent variable. Its major disadvantage is that potentially confounding sequencing effects are highly likely. Sequencing effects must be controlled by varying the order of presentation of conditions to the subjects.

Matched-Subjects Design

Matched-subjects designs have many of the strengths of within-subjects designs as well as some advantages of their own. Instead of using each subject as his or her own control by testing each subject under all conditions, the matched-subjects design uses different subjects in each condition but closely matches subjects before they are assigned to conditions. This process of matching before assignment to conditions is referred to as *matched random assignment* (see Chapter 9).

The characteristics of matched-subjects designs are that:

1. Each subject is exposed to only one level of the independent variable.
2. Each subject has a matched subject in each of the other conditions so that the groups are correlated.
3. Only one measurement per subject on the dependent variable is used in analyzing the results, but the analysis also takes into account which subjects were matched with which other subjects.
4. The critical comparison is the difference between the correlated groups where the correlation is created by the matching procedure.

Using Matched-Subjects Design Matched-subjects designs are used when the researcher wants to take advantage of the greater sensitivity of within-subjects designs but cannot or does not prefer to use a simple within-subjects design. Matched-subjects designs are most often used when exposure to one condition causes permanent or at least long-term changes in the subject, making it impossible for the subject to appear in the other conditions.

For example, when surgical procedures are used in physiological studies the procedures permanently alter the animal, making it impossible to use the animal in another condition that requires nonaltered subjects. Also, in most learning research where subjects learn a content area or behavior under one condition, they are no longer suitable subjects for testing under other conditions. For example, suppose the Air Force wanted to compare two methods of teaching map reading to its navigation students. If one group of subjects were successfully taught using method A, then those subjects could not be used for testing the effectiveness of method B. A separate group of subjects would have to be trained using method B, and then the two groups would be compared. These are examples of extreme forms of carry-over effects. It is best to avoid within-subjects designs if any large carry-over effects are anticipated and to choose instead a matched-subjects design. Another example is the situation where the demands on subjects' time in each condition are so excessive that it is unreasonable to ask subjects to be tested under all conditions. Researchers may also choose to use a matched-subjects design if they are concerned that subjects who are tested under all conditions might figure out the hypothesis of the study and influence the results through expectancy effects and/or demand characteristics (see Chapter 8).

Therefore, in certain situations within-subjects designs can present problems for the researcher. To avoid them we can choose an independent-groups design and randomly assign subjects to each of the various experimental conditions. However, an independent-groups design relies on chance to equate the groups and, therefore, is not as sensitive to small effects of the independent variable as is a correlated-groups design. Statistical tests must take into account the possibility that independent groups of subjects are not equal on the dependent measure before the study begins. Matched-subjects designs provide a solution to this problem; they make it more likely that the groups are equivalent at the beginning of the study by explicitly matching on the relevant variables.

How would we go about matching subjects for a matched-subjects design? We discussed matching subjects on relevant variables, but what does that mean? Which variables are relevant? In the within-subjects design these questions are irrelevant because each subject serves as his or her own control. Subjects in the various conditions are matched on all variables, whether relevant or not, because they are the same subjects. To obtain the same degree of control over all extraneous variables in a matched-subjects design we would probably have to use only identical twins and even then we would probably still not have perfectly matched groups. Using only identical twins would also significantly reduce the pool of available subjects. However, many factors that differentiate one person from another may be irrelevant for a particular study. For example, eye color may be a relevant variable if we are studying ways of increasing attractiveness but is probably irrelevant if we are studying visual acuity. *A variable is relevant if it can have an effect on the dependent variable in a study.* Subjects' eye color may influence the ratings of their attractiveness but should not influence their level of visual acuity. The more powerful the effect of a variable on the dependent variable, the more important it is to match subjects on that variable to assure comparable groups of subjects. To use a matched-subjects design effectively we must identify the relevant variables and match the groups subject-for-subject on them.

The procedure for matching subjects on a given variable is described in Chapter 9. In the example used there we matched subjects on age. First we ordered subjects by age. Then we divided subjects into pairs by selecting the two oldest, then the next two oldest, and so on. Finally, we randomly assigned one member of each pair to one of the two available groups and automatically assigned his or her partner to the opposite group. The result is two groups of subjects matched on the variable of age. It is legitimate during the pairing process to exclude subjects for whom a close age-mate is not available. One subject may be older than the rest of the children with no other subjects of a comparable age. This subject could not be paired with any other subject and so would not be assigned to any condition. We could have extended this process to three or more conditions by matching in sets of three or more subjects. We would then randomly assign one member from the matched set to the first condition, randomly assign one of the remaining members to the second condition, and so on until there is only one member left in the matched set and only one condition left to which to assign that person. Of course, as we increase the number of experimental conditions to which we want to assign matched subjects, we also increase the likelihood that subjects will have to be excluded because we are unable to find enough close matches for them.

Extending the matching procedure to matching on more than one variable is even more complicated than extending it to matching more than two groups. For instance, matching on age and sex of the subject is relatively simple because one of the matching variables (sex of subject) has only two levels. We could pair subjects just as we did before on age, except that we would pair the male children only with other male children and the female children only with other female children. That way, subjects in each pair will be similar to each other on both matching variables (i.e., they will be the same sex and approximately the same age). We might lose a few more subjects than before from the potential sample because appropriate matches could not be found, but the loss should not be too great.

However, if we match on two variables where both variables are continuous, matching can become tedious and subject loss can be large because an appropriate match for any given subject may be hard to find. For example, if we match on age and IQ we would first want to order all of the subjects on one of the variables (e.g., age). We would then divide the subjects into small subgroups defined by having all of the subjects in each group within a narrow age range. Then within each of these subgroups we would order on the second variable—in this case, IQ. Within each group we would pair as many subjects as possible using as the criteria that each member of the pair must have similar IQs. We would probably find several people in each age group with no close match on IQ and these people would have to be excluded from the potential sample. If the study requires three conditions, we would have to match in triplets, which would make it even more likely that subjects would be excluded because appropriate matches could not be found. A general rule of thumb is that matching on more than one continuous variable is difficult to accomplish and will usually result in significant subject loss. If matching is used as a research strategy, it is best to match on only one or two of the most important and significant variables. Again, *the important variables to match are variables that are strongly related to performance on the dependent measure(s)*. If age makes little difference in how well subjects perform on the dependent measure, it makes little sense to match subjects on age. Because age does not affect the dependent measure, it cannot confound the results. If we have several variables that could have strong effects on the dependent measure, matching on all of them simultaneously is usually not a workable solution. Instead, we should match on those variables that show the greatest natural variability (variance) in the population from which we are sampling. Characteristics that are more variable in the population (such as age, income, IQ) are more likely to show large mean differences by chance in randomly selected groups if an explicit matching procedure is not employed. Therefore, they should be given the highest priority when deciding on which variables to match in a matched-subjects design. For example, with college students as subjects, age is probably not an important variable on which to match because there is little variability in age among college students and a difference of one or two years makes little difference in students' behavior. However, when doing research with young children, age can be an extremely important variable. An age difference in children of even a few months can have major effects on their behavior. Therefore, matching on age may be an important control in many research studies with children.

Although it can be difficult to identify the critical variables on which to match, in many cases the needed information is already available in published studies of other investigators. These studies often report observed correlations of many potential confounding variables with their dependent measure. If we are using similar dependent measures, these correlations will help us decide on which variables to match in our study. Therefore, it is necessary to be thoroughly familiar with past research and with the population we are studying if we want to make good design decisions. This is true regardless of the design we are contemplating but is particularly true in matched-subjects designs. However, even with the information from past research, we might not always be able to identify important confounding variables for matching. Therefore, it is necessary even in a matched-subjects design to assign each subject *randomly* in a matched set to one of the conditions. Random assignment within sets can control for unidentified confounding variables.

Analyzing Matched-Subjects Design Designing a matched-subjects study can be complicated but analyzing data from the design is generally no more complicated than analyzing data from a simple within-subjects design. The key is to maintain the ordering of data, from the matching of subjects at the beginning of the study through the analysis of data at the end of the study. In the within-subjects design the scores from each condition for a given subject are put on the same line, as shown in Table 11.1. In the matched subjects design the scores on a given line represent the scores of different subjects tested under different conditions, but all the subjects in a given line are specifically matched with the other subjects on that line prior to the beginning of the study.

Once we have organized the data, we analyze the data as if all the scores on a given line came from the same subject instead of from matched-subjects. The same statistical procedures used in within-subjects designs are used for matched-subjects designs. The repeated measures ANOVA is used to determine whether the observed mean differences between groups is large enough to assert that real differences exist in the populations (i.e., are the differences statistically significant?). If subjects are carefully matched on relevant variable(s), then their scores on the dependent measures in each condition should be correlated with one another. This design would have the same high statistical sensitivity to small differences between conditions as the within-subjects design but without some of the problems of the within-subjects design (such as carry-over or practice effects).

Strengths and Weaknesses of Matched-Subjects Design The matched-subjects design has similar strengths to but different weaknesses than the within-subjects design. Both designs have greater sensitivity to small differences between conditions than between-subjects designs, which rely on chance to equate groups because correlated designs use selection and assignment procedures that almost guarantee that groups are equivalent. If we can be sure the groups are equivalent before the study begins, the groups do not have to show large differences after the manipulation for us to be convinced that treatment conditions and not just chance differences account for the observed data. The term *power* or *statistical power* refers to the sensitivity of the statistical procedure to the differences being sought. It is important to realize that sensitivity is not only a function of the statistical procedure alone but also depends on the precision of the research design.

Because matched- and within-subjects designs have greater sensitivity, we can use a smaller number of subjects and still be confident in our ability to detect population differences if differences exist. For example, for 3 conditions with 10 subjects in each condition, a between-subjects design will require 30 subjects. However, because of the greater sensitivity of the matched-subjects design, we may need only 8 matched subjects in each condition to test the null hypothesis with the same confidence that we would have using 10 subjects in each condition in the between-subjects design. This is a direct consequence of the increased statistical power or sensitivity of the designs. We can safely decrease sensitivity by reducing the sample size because the design provides a balancing increase in sensitivity.

An advantage of the matched-subjects design over the within-subjects design is that there are no problems of practice and carry-over effects. Therefore, control procedures like counterbalancing are not needed. But there are disadvantages to the matched-subjects design. The most obvious disadvantage is that it can be a lot of extra work. We must decide what variable(s) to match on and must obtain measures from all potential subjects on the variables. The matching process itself can be tedious, especially if we want to match on more than one variable simultaneously. And, finally, the requirement of matching subjects in sets can eliminate many potential subjects because suitable matches cannot be found for them. We may need to pretest a large sample of subjects on the matching variables to obtain a modest sample of matched subjects. It may be more efficient to use large sample sizes in a between-subjects design.

Summary Matched-subjects designs have many of the advantages of within-subjects designs while avoiding the problems of sequencing effects. In the simplest situation (two conditions) subjects are matched in pairs on one or more relevant variables. Then one member of the pair is randomly assigned to one condition and the other is automatically assigned to the other condition, a process known as matched random assignment. In a situation with three conditions subjects are matched in triplets and each member of the triplet is randomly assigned to one of three conditions. The matched-subjects design is used when increased sensitivity is needed and when a within-subjects design is inappropriate.

SINGLE-SUBJECT DESIGN

Single-subject designs are extensions of within-subjects designs. Single-subject designs *are* within-subject designs in that the same subject appears in all conditions and, as its name suggests, there is only one subject in the study. These designs are usually variations on time-series designs where repeated measurements are taken over time and various manipulations are performed at different points in time. Single-subject designs have become highly developed and represent alternatives to some of the more traditional designs. They are especially useful in the evaluation of treatment effects and are used often in research on behavior modification. Because of unique issues associated with time-series and single-subject research, they are discussed further in Chapter 13.

SUMMARY

Correlated-groups designs include both within-subjects design and matched-subjects design. In within-subjects designs there is a correlation between the conditions because the same subjects appear in all conditions. In matched-subject designs the correlation between conditions is created by the researcher who carefully matches subjects on one or more relevant variables. Regardless of the method used, the result is the same—confidence in the comparability of groups before the start of the study. The correlation increases sensitivity when testing for differences between conditions.

Correlated-groups designs raise new issues not found in other designs. For example, in within-subjects designs each subject is exposed to all conditions. This raises the possibility that the exposure to one or more of the conditions may affect the performance of the subject in later conditions (sequencing effects). Matching subjects and assigning one member of each matched set of subjects to each condition eliminates these problems but raises new issues. The most important issue in matched-subjects designs is the selection of the variable(s) on which subjects will be matched. Even when that question is answered, the actual matching of subjects can be a difficult and tedious task. Still, both within- and matched-subjects designs are used frequently in research and provide a powerful way to answer causal questions.

REVIEW EXERCISES

I. Define the following key terms. Be sure you understand them. They are discussed in the chapter and defined in the glossary.

Correlated-groups design	Carry-over effects
Repeated measures design	Random order of presentation
Within-subjects design	Latin square design
Sequencing effects	Matched-subjects design
Counterbalancing	Matched random assignment
Repeated measures ANOVA	Statistical power
Practice effects	Single-subject design

II. Answer the following. Check your answers in the chapter.

1. What is meant by independent-groups designs?
2. Controversy exists over whether correlated-groups designs are true experiments. What are the arguments on this issue?
3. Under what conditions are correlated-groups designs used?
4. As the teaching assistant in this course you have to explain the particular strength of correlated-groups designs. Explain it carefully so your students thoroughly understand it.
5. What is the essential feature of correlated-groups designs that distinguishes them from independent-groups designs?
6. What are the two major types of correlated-groups design? What are the characteristics of each?
7. What does it mean when we say that "within-subjects designs are experiments that are run on a single group of subjects"? How can this statement be reconciled with the requirement that in true experiments the independent variable must be presented at more than one level? Explain.
8. Here is a review of material from earlier chapters.
   a. What are the different kinds of samples used in research?
   b. Distinguish between internal and external validity.
9. Can ANOVA be used to test a null hypothesis in a within-subjects design? If not, why not? If so, are there any special steps that must be taken?
10. What are the major advantages of within-subjects designs over between-subjects designs? Explain how these advantages occur.
11. Explain this statement: "Once we complete an ANOVA and find a significant difference between groups, we still have more analyses to carry out."
12. What are the major disadvantages of within-subjects designs and how are they controlled?

III. Think about and work the following problems.

1. As a review of earlier material, you have 50 subjects to assign to two groups of 25 subjects each. Each subject is numbered (1–50). Using the table of random numbers, randomly assign the subjects to the two conditions.
2. Now assume you have 50 more subjects to assign to two groups, but the 50 subjects are matched in pairs on IQ. Designate the first pair as subjects A_1 and A_2, the second pair as B_1 and B_2, and so on. Use the table of random numbers to assign the pairs to the two groups.
3. In counterbalancing how many possible orders of presentation are there in an experiment with three conditions? With five conditions? With six conditions? Is counterbalancing the order of presentation feasible with a large number of conditions in an experiment?
4. What is meant by the phrase "match only on relevant variables"?
5. What is a major advantage of matched-subjects designs over within-subjects designs?

CHAPTER 12

CONTROL OF VARIANCE THROUGH EXPERIMENTAL DESIGN

Factorial Design

Although the types of experiments discussed in Chapters 10–11 have only one independent variable, we often design research to include two or more independent variables in the same experiment. These are called factorial designs. *Factorial designs* are research designs that include two or more independent variables to study their independent and interactive effects on a dependent variable.

FACTORIAL DESIGN

Suppose we are working with children afraid of the dark and we wish to develop an effective treatment program. Through interviewing the children and their parents we determine that their fear reactions vary considerably from one night to another. On some nights they do not seem afraid and go to sleep with no difficulty. But on most nights they are fearful and have difficulty sleeping. Thus, it appears that, although the children's fears are related to darkness, other variables may also be operating. In further interviews we find that many of the children report vivid and frightening images of monsters, ghosts, vampires, burglars, and so on when they are put to bed and left alone in the dark. Can it be that darkness is a necessary but not sufficient condition for the fear reaction? Might the children's fears be triggered by a combination of being in the dark and having fearful images? That is, darkness alone or fearful images alone may not be sufficient to trigger the severe fear reactions, but the two in combination might constitute the effective stimulus.

The question about the two variables having effects when they are in combination is a question about their *interaction*. As psychological research has become more sophisticated, we have realized that behavior is rarely determined by a single variable but is usually determined by several factors operating together in interaction. An *interactive effect* between two variables is an effect that is greater than summing the effects of the two variables. Rather, the individual effects of the independent variables in interaction somehow enhance each other. A true interaction is not simply additive— it is an enhancement. Recognizing the importance of interactive effects, most modern psychological research involves factorial designs rather than single-variable designs (Edgington, 1974).

In our hypothetical dark-fear research a factorial design can be used to test two independent variables (illumination and frightening images) and their interaction. The independent variables in a factorial design are called *factors*. In this experiment the dependent variable—the children's fear—can be measured by pulse rate, which has been shown in previous research to reflect fear arousal. Measured electronically, pulse rate can be taken under two conditions of illumination (lighted condition and dark condition) and two conditions of visual images (fear and neutral images). That is, factor A (illumination) is presented at two levels (lighted and dark) and factor B (images) is presented at two levels (fear and neutral images). The two independent variables (factors), each presented at two levels, will produce a matrix of four treatment combinations called a *matrix of cells*. The result is a 2 × 2 (read "two-by-two") factorial design, as shown in Figure 12.1.

Figure 12.1 2 × 2 FACTORIAL DESIGN

	Factor A (illumination)	
	Level A_1 (lighted condition)	Level A_2 (dark condition)
Factor B (images)		
Level B_1 (feared)	A_1B_1	A_2B_1
Level B_2 (neutral)	A_1B_2	A_2B_2

The *design notation* for a factorial design (2 × 2, 2 × 3, 3 × 3 × 2, and so on) shows how many independent variables and how many levels of each variable are included. Each number in the notation represents one independent variable and denotes the number of levels for that variable. Thus, the notation 3 × 3 tells us that the design has two independent variables with three levels of each variable; a 2 × 3 × 2 notation tells us that the design has three independent variables with two levels of factor A, three levels of factor B, and two levels of factor C. Note that we can design our dark-fears experiment in which (1) factor A is varied in three ways and therefore has three levels, such as dark, dim, and lighted conditions; and (2) factor B has two levels, fear and neutral images. This would result in a 3 × 2 factorial that produces a matrix of six cells.

In the same way different combinations of factors and levels can produce more complex designs such as 3 × 3, 4 × 3, 2 × 3 × 2, 4 × 3 × 2 × 2, and so on. As we make the designs more complex, more cells are produced and more subjects are required. Further, as factorial designs become more complex through the addition of independent variables, their results become increasingly difficult to interpret. Thus, although any number of factors and levels can be combined in factorial designs, there are practical limits to the complexity of the designs. They can become too unwieldy and too difficult to carry out and interpret, thus not serving the major purpose of providing clear answers to research questions. (Figure 12.2 diagrams several factorial designs.)

Main Effects and Interactions

There are several important aspects of factorial design. First, remember that factorial designs are used to test hypotheses where more than one independent variable is included in the study and where interactions and main effects are tested. The 2 × 2 factorial design results in a four-cell matrix. Factorial designs, like single-variable designs, can be set up as independent- or correlated-groups designs. Consider first the independent-groups, between-subjects factorial designs in which a different group of subjects is assigned to each of the conditions defined by the four cells. Each of these independent groups includes the scores of individual subjects on the dependent variable and a mean of the scores is calculated for each group.

Figure 12.2 VARIOUS FACTORIAL DESIGNS

	Factor A	
	A_1	A_2
Factor B		
B_1	A_1B_1	A_2B_1
B_2	A_1B_2	A_2B_2

(a) 2×2 Design with two factors and two levels of each factor

	Factor A		
	A_1	A_2	A_3
Factor B			
B_1	A_1B_1	A_2B_1	A_3B_1
B_2	A_1B_2	A_2B_2	A_3B_2

(b) 3×2 Design with two factors: Three levels of A, two levels of B

	Factor A		
	A_1	A_2	A_3
Factor B			
B_1	A_1B_1	A_2B_1	A_3B_1
B_2	A_1B_2	A_2B_2	A_3B_2
B_3	A_1B_3	A_2B_3	A_3B_3

(c) 3×3 Design with two factors and three levels of each factor

	Factor C			
	C_1		C_2	
	Factor A		Factor A	
	A_1	A_2	A_1	A_2
Factor B				
B_1	$A_1B_1C_1$	$A_2B_1C_1$	$A_1B_1C_2$	$A_2B_1C_2$
B_2	$A_1B_2C_1$	$A_2B_2C_1$	$A_1B_2C_2$	$A_2B_2C_2$
B_3	$A_1B_3C_1$	$A_2B_3C_1$	$A_1B_3C_2$	$A_2B_3C_2$

(d) $2 \times 3 \times 2$ Design with three factors and two levels of A, three levels of B, and two levels of C

Figure 12.3 shows the 2×2 matrix for our hypothetical children's dark-fears study and includes a mean score for the group of subjects in each cell and the row and column means for each variable. Notice that the matrix is, in a sense, two separate studies that are combined. Figure 12.4a shows that the column means of level 1 and level 2 for factor A can be compared, just as if one were the experimental and the other the control group in a completely randomized, single-variable design. For the dark-fears study this comparison can answer the question, "Is there a significant difference in fear reactions between the darkness and the lighted conditions?" That is, are pulse

Figure 12.3 A 2×2 FACTORIAL DESIGN: CELL MEANS
OF FEAR-INDUCED RESPONSES OF
CHILDREN UNDER LIGHT/DARK (A) AND
FEAR/NEUTRAL (B) CONDITIONS

Factor B (images)	Factor A (illumination)		Row mean
	A_1 (light)	A_2 (dark)	
B_1 (fear)	A_1B_1 (98.3)	A_2B_1 (114.1)	106.2
B_2 (neutral)	A_1B_2 (98.1)	A_2B_2 (99.9)	99.0
Column mean	98.2	107.0	

rates different for children tested under darkness conditions than for children tested under lighted conditions? This much of the matrix looks like a between-subjects, completely randomized, experimental-control group comparison in which a single variable—in this case illumination—is manipulated.

In the same way, if we compare only the two levels of factor B (images), as shown in Figure 12.4b, we see again a comparison of two independent groups. The question answered here is whether there is a significant difference in fear reactions between subjects in the fear-image condition and those in the neutral-image condition. As noted above, this much of the matrix is like a between-subjects, control-group comparison.

In a factorial design comparison of all levels of one factor with each other and the separate comparison of all levels of the other factor with each other constitute a test of the *main effects* of the independent variables on the dependent variable. In the dark-fears study we can test whether pulse rates differ under lighted and dark conditions and whether they differ under feared and neutral images. We can test the questions, "Are there significant main effects of the illumination factor?" and "Are there significant main effects of the images factor?" Thus, factorial designs allow the testing of such main effects. Further, the factorial design allows us a saving, an efficiency in carrying out two studies in one. The questions about main effects could be answered by conducting two separate single-variable studies. However, because we are also asking a question about an interaction, the two variables must be combined in a single study. When we combine the two separate designs by crossing them (as shown in Figure 12.4c), the original 2×2 matrix is formed with four cells within which are the data for testing interactions. This allows us to ask not only about main effects but to ask also, "Are the effects of one variable different depending on the level of the other variable?" This question of interaction is the major one posed in our hypothetical dark-fears study. In most factorial studies the primary focus is on the interaction effects of independent variables on the dependent variable.

Conducting the factorial experiment is similar to but more complex than conducting single-variable designs. We carefully move through all phases of the research design process: we state the problem, operationally define the variables, develop and state the research hypotheses, randomly assign subjects to conditions, determine the dependent measures, and carefully carry out procedures to make measurements of subjects' re-

Factor A
(illumination)

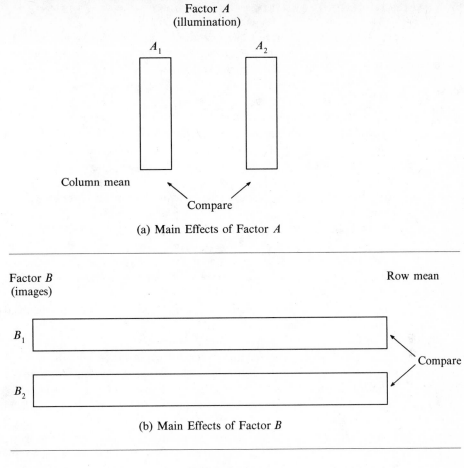

A_1 A_2

Column mean

Compare

(a) Main Effects of Factor A

Factor B
(images)

Row mean

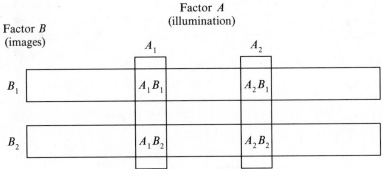

B_1

B_2

Compare

(b) Main Effects of Factor B

Factor B
(images)

Factor A
(illumination)

A_1 A_2

B_1 $A_1 B_1$ $A_2 B_1$

B_2 $A_1 B_2$ $A_2 B_2$

(c) Interactions in a Factorial Design

Figure 12.4   A FACTORIAL DESIGN AS A COMBINATION OF TWO SEPARATE STUDIES

245

sponses. The goal is to test one or more causal hypotheses, just as is done in simpler research designs. That is, we proceed to test the null hypothesis and to eliminate rival hypotheses in order to draw causal inferences.

However, factorial designs are more complicated than single-variable designs. The 2×2 factorial, because it is essentially two designs combined into a single study, *contains more than one null hypothesis.* Further, because there are two independent variables to be manipulated, the potential threats to internal validity are more complex than in single-variable designs. A single-variable experimental design has only one null hypothesis for each dependent measure (i.e., there are no differences on the dependent measure between the levels of the independent variable). But in a 2×2 factorial there are three null hypotheses for each dependent measure: (1) there is no difference between the levels of factor A (no main effects for factor A); (2) there is no difference between the levels of factor B (no main effects for factor B); and (3) there is no significant interaction of factors A and B. With more complex factorial designs in which there are more than two factors, there will be more null hypotheses to test. In factorial designs the null hypotheses are usually tested with an analysis of variance (as we will see by examples later in the chapter).

Suppose that on completion of an analysis of variance for a factorial design there are no significant main effects or interactions. We must conclude that the data fail to support the research hypotheses and thus fail to support the original idea that there is a causal relationship between the independent variables and the dependent variable. Although we cannot proceed further in interpreting the results in terms of the research hypotheses, it can be helpful to examine the procedures to detect possible errors that might help to account for the lack of support of the hypothesis and help to improve the design of the next study. If, on the other hand, one or more of the null hypotheses is rejected—if there are main effects and/or interactions—we must proceed to check for possible confounding so as to rule out alternative explanations of the findings. If satisfied that confounding variables are adequately anticipated and controlled, we can conclude that the data support the hypothesis that there is at least one causal relationship.

Clearly, the hypothesis-testing procedure with its elimination of alternative hypotheses is similar to the procedure used in single-variable designs. The reasoning is exactly the same. The major difference is that because there are more independent variables in the factorial design, there are several null hypotheses to test rather than only one and therefore more chance for confounding to occur. Further, the interpretation of interactions is more complex than the interpretation of differences in a simple, single-variable study (as is made clear later in the chapter).

Possible Outcomes of Factorial Design

There are many possible outcomes of a factorial design. There may be main effects for one or more factors but no interaction; there may be interactions but no main effects; there may be both interactions and main effects; or there may be neither main effects nor interactions. In this section 2×2 and 2×3 factorial designs are shown. The mean score for each cell is shown and the combined means *(row means* and *column means)* for each level of each factor are also indicated. The means are simplified to show basic, general outcomes. For purposes of this discussion, we assume that the observed differences are sufficiently large that they are statistically significant. We also assume that there are an equal number of subjects in each cell, which simplifies the computation of row and column means. For each matrix the same information is shown in graphic form. Figure 12.5 shows a number of possible outcomes and their characteristic graphs.

In Figure 12.5a a 3×2 factorial design is shown using both a 3×2 matrix and a graph illustrating the same results. In this example there are no significant main effects and no significant interaction. Around the margins of the 3×2 table are the means for each level of each variable, (i.e., for level A_1, A_2, A_3, and level B_1 and B_2). Within each of the six cells is the mean score for the specific group in that condition $(A_1B_1, A_1B_2, A_2B_1, A_2B_2, A_3B_1, A_3B_2)$. In this hypothetical experiment the means are all equal and there are obviously no significant differences anywhere in the matrix. Thus, there are no significant main effects for factors A or B and no significant interactions. On the graph the levels of variable A (A_1, A_2, A_3) are shown on the abscissa (the horizontal or x-axis) and the values of the dependent variable with a range sufficient to encompass the cell means are shown on the ordinate (the vertical or y-axis). Means for cells A_1B_1, A_2B_1, and A_3B_1 are all located on the graph at the value 50 and are identified on the graph with small circles. The points are connected to show graphically the overall effect of A on the dependent measure at the B_1 level of B, and that line is labeled B_1. Clearly there is no effect of A on the dependent measure at level B_1 because all values are the same (50). The effects of A at level B_2 are plotted in the same way. In this case they fall on the same points along the same line, all at the value 50. They are marked with stars to locate the B_2 level of B. Again, there is no effect of A at the B_2 level. By inspecting either the table or the graph we can see that there are no main effects and no interaction.

Figure 12.5b illustrates a 2×2 factorial in which there is a significant main effect for factor A, no significant main effect for factor B, and no interaction. As shown on the graph, the B_1 and B_2 lines are the same line and, thus, B has had no effect. But the mean of A_2 is considerably greater than the mean of A_1, illustrating an effect for A. The 2×2 matrix shows the same results with the mean for levels B_1 and B_2 equal (at 45), whereas means for levels A_1 and A_2 are quite different (30 and 60). The interaction is most easily seen in the graph of the cell means with lines that are clearly not parallel. In this example both lines show the same upward swing from left to right, so there is no interaction effect. Thus, there is a main effect for A, no main effect for B, and no interaction.

In Figure 12.5c is a 2×2 factorial design in which there is a main effect for factor B, no main effect for factor A, and no interaction. As shown in both the 2×2 grid and the graph, the means for levels A_1 and A_2 are the same, whereas the means for levels B_1 and B_2 are quite different. In the graph the two separated lines, B_1 and B_2, show that there is a difference between the levels. Because the lines are parallel, there is no interaction between A and B.

Figure 12.5d shows a 2×2 factorial in which there is a main effect for both factor A and factor B but no interaction. The graph shows this clearly where the mean for level A_2 is greater than the mean for level A_1, thus accounting for the slope of the lines. The means for the two levels of B are clearly different, as the points fall along two separated lines. As in Figure 12.5c, the parallel lines indicate that there is no interaction.

	A_1	A_2	A_3	Mean
B_1	50	50	50	50
B_2	50	50	50	50
Mean	50	50	50	

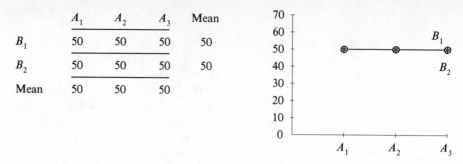

(a) 3 × 2 Factorial (*A*, *B*, and the interaction are not significant)

	A_1	A_2	Mean
B_1	30	60	45
B_2	30	60	45
Mean	30	60	

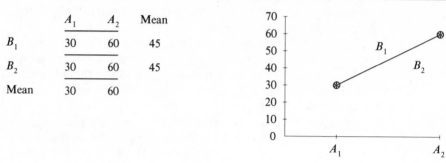

(b) 2 × 2 Factorial (*A* is significant; *B* and the interaction are not significant)

	A_1	A_2	Mean
B_1	70	70	70
B_2	40	40	40
Mean	55	55	

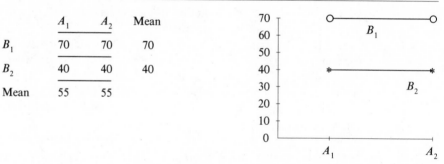

(c) 2 × 2 Factorial (*B* is significant; *A* and the interaction are not significant)

	A_1	A_2	Mean
B_1	10	30	20
B_2	30	50	40
Mean	20	40	

(d) 2 × 2 Factorial (*A* and *B* are significant; the interaction is not significant)

Figure 12.5 SEVERAL POSSIBLE OUTCOMES OF FACTORIAL DESIGNS

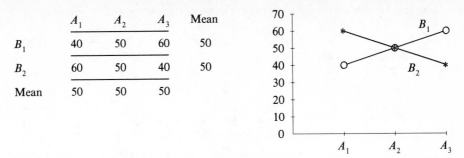

	A_1	A_2	A_3	Mean
B_1	40	50	60	50
B_2	60	50	40	50
Mean	50	50	50	

(e) 3×2 Factorial (the interaction is significant; A and B are not significant)

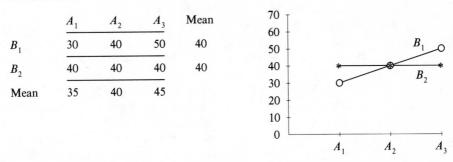

	A_1	A_2	A_3	Mean
B_1	30	40	50	40
B_2	40	40	40	40
Mean	35	40	45	

(f) 3×2 Factorial (A and the interaction are significant; B is not significant)

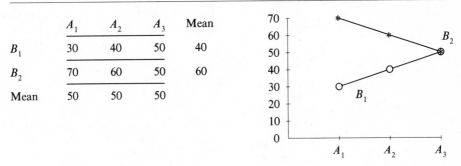

	A_1	A_2	A_3	Mean
B_1	30	40	50	40
B_2	70	60	50	60
Mean	50	50	50	

(g) 3×2 Factorial (B and the interaction are significant; A is not significant)

	A_1	A_2	Mean
B_1	40	40	40
B_2	40	60	50
Mean	40	50	

(h) 2×2 Factorial (A, B, and the interaction are significant)

Figure 12.5 *(cont.)*

A 3×2 factorial showing a significant $A \times B$ interaction but no significant main effects is illustrated in Figure 12.5e. Note that the column means for the three levels of factor A are the same, thus indicating there is no main effect for the A variable. The same is true for the B variable, where the means at levels B_1 and B_2 are the same. Thus, there is no significant main effect for A or B. But when plotted on the graph the two lines cross, giving an immediate clue that there may be a significant $A \times B$ interaction. Indeed, one of the values of drawing a graph is that interactions become readily apparent. Note in graph 12.5e that the slope of line B_1 is from 40 to 50 to 60. Line B_2 changes *in the opposite direction,* decreasing from 60 to 50 to 40. Thus, A when paired with B_1 has a different effect on the dependent measure than when paired with B_2. The effects of A on the dependent variable are clearly influenced by the level of B. This is a classic interaction, where the effect of one variable is systematically influenced by the effect of a second variable.

Note also that the column means and row means in Figures 12.5a and 12.5e are identical. However, in Figure 12.5a the pattern of means within the cells indicates no interaction, whereas the pattern of means in Figure 12.5e does indicate an interaction. This illustrates that the column and row means give us an indication only of main effects, and one has to inspect the individual cells to see any pattern of interaction.

Figure 12.5f shows a main effect for A and an $A \times B$ interaction. When both a main effect and an interaction occur, it is important to interpret the interaction first (the reasons for this are discussed in the next section). The remaining examples can be read in similar fashion.

It is important for students to know how to construct and read these tables and graphs. There are a number of exercises at the end of this chapter that the student should work until satisfied that these concepts and procedures are understood.

An Example: Children's Dark-Fears Study

To illustrate a factorial design let us return to our hypothetical children's dark-fears study, which used a 2×2 factorial design. Suppose that the subjects for this experiment include 40 dark-fearful children—20 boys and 20 girls—drawn from an available population. Subjects are randomly assigned to the four conditions of the 2×2 matrix (10 children per condition). Random assignment helps to insure the equivalence of the four conditions at the outset of the study.

There are two independent variables. Variable A (illumination) is presented at two levels, a lighted and a darkened condition. Variable B (images) is presented at two levels, fear images and neutral images. The dependent variable is the children's fear as measured by their pulse rate. The research hypotheses being tested are that there will be a main effect for factor A, a main effect for factor B, and a significant $A \times B$ interaction. That is, we predict that there will be more measurable fear under conditions of darkness than under lighted conditions, more under the fear-images condition than under the neutral-images condition, and the greatest effects on fear response will occur when the two factors interact (i.e., under the combined darkness and fear-images condition).

Subjects are tested individually while seated comfortably facing a projection screen. A small sensor is placed on a finger to monitor pulse rate. Subjects are told they will be shown ten slides and will be asked questions about them later. Each slide is shown for 15 seconds with a five-second pause between slides. As shown in the 2 × 2 design (see Figure 12.3), cell A_1B_1 represents the lighted-plus-fear images condition. The lights are kept on in the room and the fear-image slides are presented (e.g., ghostly images, commonly feared animals such as snakes, a burglar entering a house, and so on). All ten subjects in condition A_1B_1 are presented the fear images and their pulse rates are recorded at each presentation. Cell A_2B_1 represents the dark-plus-fear images condition. The lights in the room are turned off and all ten subjects in that condition are individually presented the fear images. Each subject's pulse rate is recorded at each presentation. Cell A_1B_2 represents the neutral-images-lighted condition, and cell A_2B_2 represents the neutral-images-dark condition. The general procedures in these two conditions are the same as described above except that the slide images presented are neutral (i.e., nonfearful). Thus, we have scores (pulse rates) for 40 subjects—10 subjects in each of 4 different conditions in the 2 × 2 design.

Figure 12.6 shows hypothetical scores for the ten subjects in each of the four conditions of our study. Note the mean score, shown in parentheses for each condition, and the column and row means for each of the levels (A_1, A_2, B_1, B_2). Thus, the row mean, 106.2, is the mean for *fear images;* the row mean, 99.0, is the mean for *neutral images;* 98.2 and 107.0 are the column means for *light* and *dark* conditions. Further, the scores in cell A_1B_1 are presumably affected by the particular combination of light

Figure 12.6 HYPOTHETICAL PULSE RATES OF 40 DARK-FEAR CHILDREN

Factor *B* (images)	Factor *A* (illumination)		Row mean
	A_1 (light)	A_2 (dark)	
B_1 (fear)	100	118	
	100	117	
	100	117	
	99	116	
	99 (98.3)	115 (114.1)	106.2
	98	114	
	97	113	
	97	113	
	97	110	
	96	108	
B_2 (neutral)	107	109	
	106	107	
	101	104	
	100	104	
	98 (98.1)	100 (99.9)	99.0
	97	98	
	94	96	
	93	94	
	93	94	
	92	93	
Column mean	98.2	107.0	

and feared images. Cell A_2B_1 reflects the combined effects of darkness and fear images. Cell A_1B_2 reflects the combined effects of light and neutral images. Finally, cell A_2B_2 reflects the combined influence of darkness and neutral images.

The experiment is a completely randomized, between-subjects, 2×2 factorial. We are interested in knowing whether there is an $A \times B$ interaction and whether there are main effects for A and B. To test for main effects we have to compare the means of the two levels of each factor. As shown in Figure 12.7a, the means of the two levels of A (98.2 and 107.0) are compared to determine whether there is a main effect for illumination. This is essentially comparing two independent groups in a completely randomized, between-subjects, single-variable study. To determine whether there is a main effect for B we compare the means of the two independent groups, fear and neutral images (106.2 and 99.0), as shown in Figure 12.7b. To determine whether there is an interaction we compare means of the four cells to see whether the effects of one independent variable on the dependent variable are different depending on the level of the other independent variable. The essential issue in interaction is whether the two factors, when they occur together, influence the dependent variable differently than when they occur separately. The interaction is most easily seen in a graph of the data, such as the graphs in Figure 12.5.

As noted earlier, the appropriate statistical test for factorial designs is an analysis

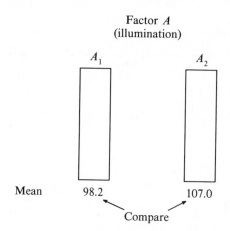

(a) Comparisons needed to test the main effects for factor A

(b) Comparisons needed to test the main effects for factor B

Figure 12.7 TESTING FOR MAIN EFFECTS

of variance (ANOVA). However, before carrying out the ANOVA it is helpful to graph the cell means because it can be seen quickly whether an interaction might exist and whether the mean differences suggest the presence of main effects.

Let us examine the hypothetical results of our children's dark-fears study by looking at the cell means and the row and column means and by drawing a graph. By inspecting the table and graph in Figure 12.8 we can see that the subjects in the dark condition have a higher mean pulse rate (107.0) than the subjects in the lighted condition (98.2). To see this, compare the column means in the table for light and dark conditions. This difference suggests that there may be a main effect for factor A, illumination (i.e., the subjects in the dark condition show higher pulse rates than the subjects in the lighted condition). For factor B the fear images condition has a higher mean pulse rate (106.2) than the neutral-images condition (99.0). The results suggest that there may be a significant main effect for factor B. Now, inspect the same means as shown in the graph. Note that the two lines are not parallel, alerting us to the possibility of an $A \times B$ interaction. The B_1 line slopes upward, moving from a mean

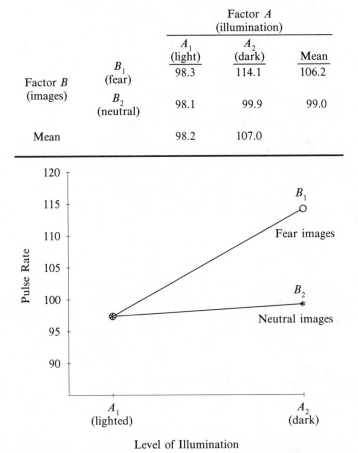

| | | Factor A (illumination) | | |
		A_1 (light)	A_2 (dark)	Mean
Factor B (images)	B_1 (fear)	98.3	114.1	106.2
	B_2 (neutral)	98.1	99.9	99.0
Mean		98.2	107.0	

Figure 12.8   2 × 2 MATRIX AND GRAPH FOR CHILDREN'S DARK-FEARS STUDY

of 98.3 to a mean of 114.1. The slope of that line appears to be due to the elevation of the A_2B_1 cell, where the dark condition and the fear images are combined. The mean of this cell is elevated when compared with the other three cells. Fear images produce high pulse rates but only in the presence of the dark condition. The B_2 line is nearly flat; that is, the amount of light has little effect when neutral images are used. This seems clearly to be an interaction. Thus, we may have an $A \times B$ interaction, a main effect for A, and a main effect for B.

Inspecting the matrix and graph gives us only an approximate suggestion of the results. The next step is to determine whether the differences we observed are large enough that they are unlikely to be only chance differences and instead reflect consistent differences in the response of the children in the different conditions. An analysis of variance is used to test for *statistically significant differences*. Before we can do this, however, another important point should be illustrated. Suppose that the statistical analysis does indicate an $A \times B$ interaction and a main effect for A. The important point here is that when we interpret the results of an analysis of variance in which we have found both an interaction and a main effect, *we always begin the interpretation with the interaction*. The reason for this becomes clear if we reinspect the matrix and graph. Our hypothetical statistical analysis indicates a main effect for A (light versus dark condition). But by inspecting the matrix we can see that light or dark conditions have little effect (means = 98.1 versus 99.9) when the visual images presented are neutral. The effect seems to occur when the dark condition and fear stimuli are combined; that is, the apparent main effect *actually seems to be due to the interaction* and can be best understood in terms of the interaction. We would have to interpret the findings as indicating that light and dark conditions by themselves do not seem to have an effect on fear, but it is the combination of darkness and fear images that appears to have the effect of increasing the children's fear. If we were to accept the finding of a main effect for A in our hypothetical study without interpreting it in terms of the interaction, we could be led to an erroneous conclusion that the darkness itself causes increased fear. Again, *where we find both an interaction and a main effect, all effects must be interpreted in light of the interaction*.

Analysis of Variance in Factorial Design

The appropriate statistical analysis for factorial designs is some form of analysis of variance (ANOVA) (see Chapters 10–11). The calculations for ANOVA are usually carried out by use of computer-analysis programs, such as the *Statistical Package for the Social Sciences* (SPSS), *Biomedical Programs* (BMDP), *Statistical Analysis System* (SAS), and *Minitab*. Computer programs such as these can carry out calculations far more rapidly than we can by hand. However, the researcher must understand experimental design, statistical principles and procedures, and how to use the computer to be able to set up and interpret the computer analysis. Knowledge of computer use is now a virtual necessity for researchers, but that knowledge is not a substitute for understanding the principles of design and the concepts and procedures of statistical analysis. Remember our admonition in Chapter 1—a laboratory technician is not necessarily a scientist; it is not the technician's manipulation of laboratory equipment, including use of computers, that defines the science but, rather, the *process of systematic thinking* that guides the use of laboratory techniques.

Statistical computations for complex ANOVAs are beyond the scope of this text. In this section our goal is an understanding of how to read an ANOVA summary table for a factorial design and how to interpret the results.

ANOVA Summary Table for Children's Dark-Fears Study The results of an ANOVA are typically presented in an *ANOVA summary table.* The summary table in Figure 12.9 shows the results of an ANOVA carried out on our children's dark-fears data. Assume that we have carried out an ANOVA using a computer package and have received the print-out of results, including the ANOVA summary table shown in Figure 12.9.

The first column of the summary table lists the source of variation—between-groups variance for factors A (illumination) and B (images); the $A \times B$ interaction; the within-groups variance (error variance); and the total variance. In the second column the degrees of freedom (df) associated with each source has been entered. Note that associated with the total variance there are 39 degrees of freedom (i.e., one less than the total number of subjects). The total degrees of freedom (39) are then apportioned to factors A and B [two levels of A, thus $df_a = (2 - 1) = 1$; two levels of B, thus $df_b = (2 - 1) = 1$; the degrees of freedom for the interaction ($A \times B$) is the product of the degrees of freedom for the main effects, thus $df_{a \times b} = df_a \times df_b = (2 - 1) \times (2 - 1) = 1$]. The remaining degrees of freedom (36) are associated with the within-groups or error variance and are calculated by taking the total number of subjects in the study and subtracting the number of cells. The third column of the summary table lists the sum of squares (SS) that has been calculated for each source. Notice that the total sum of squares is, in fact, the total—the sum of all component sums of squares will equal the total sum of squares. In the fourth column each sum of squares has been divided by its associated degrees of freedom to yield the mean square (MS), which is the variance as it is calculated by the ANOVA procedure. In the fifth column the mean square for each between-groups comparison has been divided by the within-groups mean square (the error term). This between-groups variance divided by the within-groups variance is the F ratio. Thus, F values for A, B, and the $A \times B$ interaction are calculated and recorded in the summary table. It is the F values that are compared with values in the F table to see whether they are significant. The probability of each F value (p) is shown in column 6 of the summary table.

In our ANOVA there is a significant $A \times B$ interaction. That is, fear, as measured

Figure 12.9 ANOVA SUMMARY TABLE FOR CHILDREN'S DARK-FEARS STUDY

Source of variance	df	SS	MS	F	p
Between-groups variance					
Factor A (illumination)	1	774.4	774.4	41.19	<0.001
Factor B (images)	1	518.4	518.4	27.57	<0.001
$A \times B$ (interaction)	1	490.0	490.0	26.06	<0.001
Within-groups (error variance)	36	676.8	18.8		
Total	39	2459.6			

by pulse rate, is highest when the darkness and fear images are presented together. The summary table also shows significant main effects for both A and B, but they can be understood only in terms of the interaction. That is, as shown in the graph in Figure 12.8 under the neutral-images condition, the light or dark condition does not make a difference; likewise, under lighted conditions the fear images do not cause more fear than do the neutral images. The main effects are due to the interaction, to the condition A_2B_1, in which the fear images and darkness occur together. Remember, in factorial designs, whenever a main effect *and* an interaction involving the significant factors occur, then we interpret the interaction first and the main effects are interpreted in light of the interaction.

The main conclusion that can be drawn from our hypothetical study is that neither fear images alone nor darkness alone appears to be sufficient to stimulate children's night fears, but the two together, darkness and fear images, is a sufficient condition for children's night fears (see Box 12.1).

VARIATIONS OF BASIC FACTORIAL DESIGN

Among several important contemporary trends in psychological research, three are most important. They are the increased use of (1) factorial designs, (2) within-subjects designs, and (3) mixed designs.

The increased use of factorials has come about not only because of their efficiency in testing several causal hypotheses in a single design but also because by testing the effects on behavior of multiple variables in interaction, factorials come closer than do single-variable designs to the multiply determined nature of behavior in natural environments.

The increased use of within-subjects designs reflects the growing recognition of their advantages over completely randomized designs. As discussed earlier, their major advantage is that they are generally more sensitive to the effects of the independent variable because they eliminate a major cause of error variance (individual differences between subjects). Within-subjects designs also require fewer subjects, which can be of enormous value when subjects are difficult to obtain or considerable preparation per subject is required.

Mixed designs blend different types of factors into a single factorial study. This mixing can affect the statistical analyses and the restrictions placed on the interpretation of results. But mixing has its advantages as well. Many studies require the use of mixed designs to investigate the effects and interactions of most interest to the researcher.

Within-Subjects (Repeated Measures) Factorial

In this chapter we have discussed randomized, between-subjects factorial designs in which subjects are randomly assigned to conditions. The basic factorial design, illustrated in the children's dark-fears study, is a completely randomized, between-subjects design in which each subject responds to only one condition. With this design we meet the experimental requirements for unbiased subject assignment and can draw conclusions about causality with considerable confidence.

Box 12.1 ETHICAL CONSIDERATIONS IN THE CHILDREN'S DARK-FEARS STUDY

In our hypothetical study of children who fear darkness, the children are exposed to the very conditions that may be frightening to them, darkness and fearful images. This immediately raises the researcher's ethical concerns of placing the subjects at risk for potential harm. What are the major concerns?

First, the subjects are children. As such, they are presumed to be unable to understand all of the implications of the procedure and, therefore, cannot give their fully informed consent to participate. The standard ethical guidelines assume that children, merely by virtue of being under the age of consent, are automatically subjects at risk in any research. Therefore, steps must be taken by the researcher to reduce risks. One obvious safeguard is to obtain the informed consent of the children's parents. They presumably will be able to understand the situation and make an appropriate decision. Thus, the risks that result from using children as subjects are reduced when the researcher obtains the fully informed consent of the subjects' parents.

Another issue is whether the children want to participate or whether they are being in some ways coerced by both the researcher and the parents. Thus, the ethical researcher will try to obtain the children's assent to participate by explaining the procedure to them and asking whether they want to take part. If a child says no or shows a great deal of reluctance, the researcher must interpret that as a lack of assent. Further, in obtaining consent and assent the researcher should give a full account of the procedures, provide ample opportunity for questions, and answer all questions. Parents and children should also have the opportunity to ask more questions and to seek explanations after the conclusion of the experiment.

With parental-informed consent and the child's assent included in the research procedure, the researcher must then consider other possible risks to the subject, such as undue anxiety and other psychological upset due to the procedures. For example, the children should be assured from the start that they may stop the procedure whenever they want to. Also, the researcher or assistant should be sufficiently experienced with children to observe whether a child is becoming unduly upset so they can (1) make a reasoned decision to discontinue the procedure for that child and (2) soothe and reassure any child who does become upset. The researcher must be as certain as possible that the procedures themselves are not unduly distressing and that only those procedures essential for the study are being used.

Finally, there is an ethical issue that bears directly on the adequacy of the experimental design itself: *it is the responsibility of the researcher to assure that the study is competently designed and carried out so that there can be a high degree of confidence in results and conclusions.* Why is this an ethical issue and not only a design issue? Because it is the researcher's responsibility to insure that subjects' time, effort, expectations, and risk-taking, however minimal, are given in an effort that will likely yield knowledge. The researcher must insure that subjects do not make contributions to a research project that is poorly designed and from which little knowledge can be gained. Subjects' contributions must not be trivialized and wasted by an incompetent design.

Can you see other potential risks for the subjects in our experiment? If so, how would you reduce them?

In factorials, as with single-variable designs, we may choose to employ a within-subjects design in the factorial experiment. This is called a *within-subjects* (or *repeated measures*) *factorial.* If we employ it in the dark-fears factorial study, then each subject is in this case measured under each of the four conditions. The ANOVA carried out to test for statistical significance is a *repeated measures ANOVA,* which takes into account the correlated groups.

Recall from Chapter 11 that using a within-subjects design involves disadvantages that stem from the fact that each subject is exposed to each condition. This means that sequencing effects (practice and carry-over effects) are potential sources of confounding and must be controlled. In some research potential sequencing effects may be so strong that a within-subjects design is not appropriate. However, when not precluded by such strong potential sequencing effects, a within-subjects design has decided advantages over a between-subjects design. As with the single-variable design, use of a within-subjects design in a factorial experiment can (1) provide greater sensitivity to the effects of the independent variable by reducing the individual differences component of the error term, (2) assure equivalence of groups at the start of the experiment because the subjects in each condition are identical, (3) require fewer subjects and, related to the third point, (4) can be more efficient. In the dark-fears study, for example, if we want 10 subjects in each of the four conditions, then only 10 subjects in total are needed for a within-subjects design but 40 subjects are needed for a between-subjects design. This could be a major advantage when subjects are difficult to obtain or when considerable preparation is required for each subject.

Many researchers prefer a within-subjects design over a between-subjects design because fewer subjects are required. This is true for both single-variable and factorial experiments. The repeated measures or within-subjects factorial design is a frequently used and valuable design.

Mixed Designs

When there is more than one factor it is possible that the factors will be of different types. For example, one factor may be a within-subjects factor whereas the other may be a between-subjects factor. This is a mixed design.

The term *mixed design* is used in two different ways, which can lead to considerable confusion. In one meaning mixed design refers to a factorial that includes a between-subjects variable and a within-subjects variable. In the other meaning mixed design refers to a factorial that includes a manipulated variable and a nonmanipulated variable. It is important to distinguish between the two types of mixed design.

Between-Subjects and Within-Subjects Variables In this meaning of the term *mixed design,* where both *between-subjects* and *within-subjects factors* exist in the same study, the critical issue is a statistical one. For example, suppose a study has "level of distraction" as the within-subjects factor and the "amount of potential reward for success" as the between-subjects factor. Each subject would be assigned to one of the potential reward conditions (the between-subjects variable) and tested under all levels of distraction (the within-subjects variable). Of course, for the within-subjects factor the order of presentation of conditions would be counterbalanced to control sequencing effects (see Figure 12.10a).

Figure 12.10 SEVERAL EXAMPLES OF MIXED DESIGNS IN FACTORIAL RESEARCH

	Level of distraction (within-subjects factor)		
	Low	Medium	High
Amount of Reward (between-subjects factor) Small			
Large			

(a) One-between, one-within factorial design in which subjects are randomly assigned to either the small-reward or the large-reward condition and then are tested under all three levels of distraction.

	Level of crowding (between-subjects factor)		
	No crowding	Slightly crowded	Crowded
Sex of Subject Male			
Female			

(b) One-manipulated variable, one-nonmanipulated variable mixed design in which male and female subjects are randomly assigned to one of the three levels of crowding. Both factors are between-subject factors. Subjects are randomly assigned to the level of crowding (manipulated variable) and assigned to male or female based on their sex (nonmanipulated variable).

	Type of words (within-subjects factor)	
	Neutral	Emotional
Diagnosis (between-subjects factor) Schizophrenic		
Normal		

(c) Design mixed in both a statistical sense (one-between, one-within) and an experimental sense (one-manipulated, one-nonmanipulated). Diagnosis is a between-subjects factor whereas type of words is a within-subjects factor, which affects the ANOVA formulas used. Also, diagnosis is an nonmanipulated factor whereas type of words is a manipulated factor, which affects confidence in causal inference(s).

The significance of the mixed design here is that the particular formulas used in the analysis of variance will differ depending on which factors are within-subjects factors and which are between-subjects factors. Recall that in analyzing within-subjects designs the statistical procedures must take into account the correlated nature of the data. Computation of ANOVAs for mixed designs is beyond the scope of this text. In most cases data from such designs are analyzed using statistical computer programs such as BMDP. Further, it is necessary to distinguish between-subjects and within-subjects factors to use the correct statistical procedure.

Manipulated and Nonmanipulated Variables

In this meaning of the term *mixed design,* where both *manipulated* and *nonmanipulated factors* are included, the essential issue is one of interpretation of results rather than statistical procedures. In a mixed design where one factor is a nonmanipulated variable and one factor is a manipulated variable, subjects are randomly assigned to conditions of the manipulated variable but are assigned to levels of the nonmanipulated independent variable based on their preexisting characteristics.

For example, if we are studying the effects of crowding on aggression, we might randomly assign subjects to one of three conditions: alone, slightly crowded, and crowded. We could observe the level of aggression of subjects in each of these conditions. The variable of crowding is a manipulated variable because the condition under which subjects are tested is actively manipulated by the researcher. Suppose we are also interested in sex differences in response to crowding. Here we are asking about an interaction between sex of subject and level of crowding on the dependent measure of aggression. The sex of subjects is the second factor; an organismic factor or subject variable that the researcher cannot manipulate. Instead, the researcher assigns subjects to the male or female group depending on the sex of the subject. The design shown in Figure 12.10b is an example of the second type of mixed design—in which we are not concerned about whether factors are between-subjects or within-subjects but, rather, whether factors are manipulated or nonmanipulated.

The formulas for statistical analysis are not affected by whether the variables are manipulated or nonmanipulated as they are when we are dealing with between- and within-subjects factors. The importance of whether a factor is manipulated or nonmanipulated comes into play when we *interpret* the statistical analysis. Manipulated factors are experiments that allow us to eliminate rival hypotheses involving confounding variables. We can therefore safely draw causal inferences based on analysis of the main effects of the variables. Research designs using nonmanipulated factors are *not* experiments. Instead, they represent differential research (see Chapter 7). Remember that in differential research, because subjects are not randomly assigned to groups, groups may differ on variables other than the independent variable. These potential differences may cause confounding and, unless we can rule out all potential confounding, we cannot draw causal inferences with confidence. Therefore, interpreting the main effects of nonmanipulated factors must be done cautiously and with careful attention to likely confounding variables. In our example we must be cautious about drawing the inference that the sex differences *caused* any observed differences in aggression. Random assignment of subjects in manipulated factors automatically controls for such confounding and makes interpretation much easier. If differences are found in the level of aggression shown at each level of crowding, we can confidently conclude that crowding causes changes in level of aggression. The same caution used in the interpretation of main effects for nonmanipulated factors should be used in the interpretation of any interaction involving an organismic factor. In our example the interaction between sex and level of crowding on aggression should be interpreted as cautiously as the main effect of sex.

Finally, it is possible to have a mixed design that is mixed in both of the ways just described. Figure 12.10c presents such a situation. In this example we want to compare schizophrenics' and normals' accuracy of recognition of neutral words compared with emotionally charged words. We have arranged a factorial design in which both neutral and charged words are presented to schizophrenic and normal subjects for short intervals using a tachistoscope. Note that this is a factorial with one non-manipulated variable (diagnosis) and one manipulated variable (type of words). Although subjects can be randomly assigned to the levels of factor *A* (type of words), we obviously cannot randomly assign subjects to factor *B* (diagnosis). Psychological adjustment (schizophrenic or normal) is an organismic variable (i.e., a characteristic of the subject that preexists the experiment and cannot be manipulated by the researcher). In addition to being a mixed design in the above sense, it is also a mixed design in that one factor (diagnosis) is a between-subjects variable whereas the other factor (type of words) is a within-subjects variable. In this situation we need to classify each factor on the dimension of between-subjects versus within-subjects factors in order to select the appropriate ANOVA formulas for statistical analysis. We then need to classify each factor on the dimension of manipulated versus nonmanipulated factors to interpret the results of the statistical analysis. Again, we must be especially cautious in drawing conclusions based on observed main effects and/or interactions with nonmanipulated factors, because such factors represent differential research and do not have the controls of experimental research that make causal inferences reasonably safe.

Summary There are two meanings of the term *mixed design*. The first meaning affects the formulas we use in the analysis of variance. We label each factor as either a between-subjects factor or a within-subjects factor to identify the appropriate statistical analysis procedure. Once we have completed the analysis, we again label each factor but this time on whether the factor is a manipulated or a nonmanipulated factor. These labels affect the confidence of the conclusions about the causal relationship between the independent variable(s) and the dependent variable.

ANOVA: A POSTSCRIPT

Analysis of variance (ANOVA) is one of the most flexible statistical tools available for the evaluation of data. The basic concept of ANOVA can be easily extended to a variety of situations. The simplest situation is in comparing the means of independent samples of subjects. ANOVA compares the variability of the means against a standard based on the variability of scores within each group. If the means are more variable than expected, based on the variability of scores within groups, it can be concluded that the independent variable had an effect that produced the group differences. The concept of comparing the variability between-groups to the variability within-groups is constant in every ANOVA, no matter how complicated it becomes.

In an ANOVA with three or more groups, if the *F* is significant, specific means comparisons must be made to find which group or groups differ significantly from the others. The specific means comparisons are carried out as *a priori* or as *post hoc* comparisons (see Chapter 10). In a repeated measures ANOVA the same subjects are tested under every condition, which the analysis of variance must take into account in computing the within-subjects variance. The repeated measures ANOVA, a conceptual extension of the simple one-way ANOVA, adjusts for the effects of using the same subjects in each condition.

Finally, with factorial designs the analysis of variance is extended still further. Here the effects of each independent variable and the interactive effects of combinations of independent variables are examined. For example, if we have two factors (A and B), we have three possible effects: the A main effect, the B main effect, and the interaction between A and B. If we have three factors, we may have three main effects (A, B, and C), three two-way interactions (AB, AC, and BC), and one three-way interaction (ABC) for a total of seven different effects. With four factors we have the following possible effects: A, B, C, D, AB, AC, AD, BC, BD, CD, ABC, ABD, ACD, BCD, and ABCD. And, of course, as discussed earlier in the chapter, the ANOVA can take into account which of the factors are within-subjects factors and which are between-subjects factors.

Although it can become complicated as factors are added to a study, extending the logic and the computational formulas of the analysis of variance to factorial designs is not difficult. The formulas themselves can become quite complex but for the most part we rely on computers to perform the actual computation. Because there are many different effects, there are many different F ratios, but each F ratio represents a comparison of between-groups variability to within-groups variability. Further, we interpret the F ratio in these complex designs in exactly the same way as in simpler designs: if the observed F is large (greater than some critical value that can be deter-

"He wouldn't listen to me when he was designing the study — so now he has to interpret a five-way interaction."

mined by consulting a table of F values), we reject the null hypothesis that there are no group differences and conclude that the independent variable(s) had an effect on the dependent variable. The combination of consistency in how the ANOVA is used and the flexibility of the procedure to analyze data from so many different designs make analysis of variance the most widely used statistical technique in psychology.

Given the diversity of ANOVA procedures, it is perhaps not surprising that analysis of variance procedures have been extended into still other designs. These more advanced procedures are generally beyond the scope of this book and are described here briefly.

A widely used but often misused technique, as pointed out by Lord (1967), is *analysis of covariance (ANCOVA)*. Analysis of covariance is used in the same way as analysis of variance with one addition. Before the analysis is conducted, the effects of a theoretically unimportant but nonetheless powerful variable are removed from the dependent measure scores. For example, if we want to study the effects of reinforcement strategies on learning in young children, we could set up a study with two or three levels of the independent variable. We could then randomly assign the sample of children to each condition and measure how well they perform on the measure of learning (the dependent variable). Of course, the age of the children will affect how quickly they learn different material. However, we are not interested in the variable of age in our study. We could hold age constant by using only subjects who are in a narrow age range if we had enough subjects available in a single age range. We could use a matching procedure to make sure the groups are equivalent on age at the beginning of the study. On the other hand, we could randomly assign the subjects to groups and use analysis of covariance to remove statistically the effects of age from the dependent measure. Analysis of covariance would give us a more sensitive test of the hypothesis because unwanted variability due to an extraneous factor is statistically removed as part of the analysis. We must caution, however, that ANCOVA is a complicated procedure with many potential pitfalls. It cannot be used in all situations. Using ANCOVA properly requires a thorough understanding of its procedure.

Another extension of analysis of variance, which is becoming much more popular as sophisticated computer-analysis packages become more available, is *multivariate analysis of variance (MANOVA)*. The difference between a simple ANOVA and a MANOVA is in the dependent variable. In an ANOVA we have only one dependent variable entered into the analysis. In a MANOVA we have more than one dependent variable being analyzed at one time. Conceptually, it is similar to the extension from one-way (one independent variable) ANOVAs to factorial (more than one independent variable) ANOVAs, except that now we are looking at multiple *dependent* measures in the same study. The full power of MANOVA procedures is still being discovered. Just like in analysis of covariance, using MANOVA procedures correctly and interpreting the results accurately require an extensive understanding of the technique.

Clearly, analysis of variance techniques are flexible and powerful procedures for analyzing data from almost any design. With the aid of the computer and some well-written computer programs, the computations can be done quickly and easily. However, the researcher still has to understand exactly what research design is being used in a given study to instruct the program correctly on what analysis to run. Even more important, the researcher needs to understand when ANOVA procedures are appropriate to use. This is a reason why Ph.D. programs in psychology require extensive course work in statistics as a part of the degree requirements. Finally, performing the appropriate statistical analysis is only the first step in the evaluation of data. The next step is interpreting the meaning of the results. Interpreting meaning requires evaluating the entire study on issues such as potential confounding and the adequacy of control procedures. The principles for such an evaluation are the primary focus of this text. Statistical procedures, even clever and useful ones such as ANOVA, do not impart meaning to data. Only the researcher well trained in science can take this last important step.

SUMMARY

Factorial designs include more than one independent variable. They are highly efficient and flexible designs in which we can combine information from the equivalent of two or more single-variable studies. Their greatest advantage is the information they yield about interactive effects of the independent variables.

Factorial designs can be of several types in which the factors are (1) between-subjects variables or within-subjects variables, (2) manipulated variables or non-manipulated variables, or (3) mixed factorials. Nonmanipulated variable factorials and mixed factorial designs have special cautions associated with them. A factorial with a within-subjects component must be analyzed with statistical procedures that take into account the correlated nature of the data; a factorial with an nonmanipulated component must be interpreted cautiously because causality cannot be properly inferred from nonmanipulated independent variables.

ANOVAs are used to analyze factorial designs. It is helpful to graph cell means and, by inspection of the graph, to note whether significant interactions and/or main effects seem likely. When the analysis indicates that both main effects and an interaction are significant, it is necessary to interpret the main effects in terms of interaction.

Several experimental designs are presented: (1) single-variable designs, both independent- and correlated-groups designs; and (2) multivariable or factorial designs, including within-subjects, between-subjects, manipulated and nonmanipulated variable factorials, and mixed designs. All of these designs provide a considerable array of powerful methods for answering questions concerning causality.

REVIEW EXERCISES

I. Define the following key terms. Be sure you understand them. They are discussed in the chapter and defined in the glossary.

Factorial design   Main effects
Interaction   Row means
Matrix of cells   Column means
Design notation   Statistically significant differences

Computer-analysis programs	Repeated measures factorial

Computer-analysis programs
   Statistical Package for the
      Social Sciences (SPSS)
      Biomedical Programs (BMDP)
      Statistical Analysis System
        (SAS)
      Minitab
ANOVA summary table
Repeated measures ANOVA
Within-subjects factorial

Repeated measures factorial
Mixed design
      Between-subjects factors
      Within-subjects factors
      Manipulated factors
      Nonmanipulated factors
Analysis of covariance (ANCOVA)
Multivariate analysis of variance
   (MANOVA)

II. Answer the following. Check your answers in the chapter.

1. What distinguishes factorial designs from designs discussed in Chapters 10–11?
2. Under what conditions would a factorial design rather than a single-variable design be used?
3. For each of the following (a) indicate how many factors are included and (b) for each factor tell how many levels there are.

   2×2 4×3
   2×3 $4 \times 3 \times 2 \times 3$
   $2 \times 3 \times 2$

4. For each of the above draw the appropriate matrix and label the factors and levels.
5. Theoretically, we can handle any number of factors in a factorial design. But there are some important limitations to the number of factors we should include. Identify and explain the limitations.
6. It is noted that testing the research hypothesis in a factorial design is more complicated than in a single-variable design. What is (are) the complication(s)?
7. On completing an ANOVA and finding that there is a statistically significant difference, what other statistical procedures are needed? Why?
8. In a factorial design where both the interaction and significant main effects are significant, why is it important to interpret the interaction first?
9. What are main effects in factorials?
10. What is a mean square in an ANOVA table?
11. What are mixed designs? Explain the three types of mixed designs.
12. What are repeated measures designs? What potential confounding variables are there in repeated measures designs and what control must be used?
13. Explain the cautions in using mixed designs. That is, in one type of mixed design we must be cautious about statistical procedures; in the other, we must be cautious about the interpretation of results.
14. Carefully distinguish within-subjects designs and between-subjects designs. What are the major characteristics of each? Give an example of each.

III. Think about and work the following problems.

1. You are the teaching assistant for this course and are to explain the concept of interaction in factorial design. Organize your presentation by first making the distinction between main effects and interaction effects. Be sure to clarify for your students the distinction between additive and interactive effects.

2. You are the teaching assistant for the course and are to explain to the class that a 2×2 factorial study is, in a sense, two separate studies combined. How would you develop your explanation?

3. Given the following cell means and ANOVA summary table, how would you interpret the results?

Source	df	SS	MS	F	p	Matrix of means	B_1	B_2
A	3	121.5	40.5	1.39	n.s.	A_1	12.1	13.4
B	1	93.7	93.7	3.21	<0.05	A_2	9.5	15.7
AB	3	288.6	96.2	3.29	<0.05	A_3	7.5	17.5
Within	72	2102.4	29.2			A_4	5.9	18.9
Total	79	2606.2						

4. Each of the following matrices shows group means of results of a factorial study. For each one draw and label the appropriate graph. Indicate for each whether interactions and main effects are significant or not significant. (Assume that all differences are statistically significant.)

	A_1	A_2
B_1	10	15
B_2	10	15
B_3	10	15

	A_1	A_2	A_3
B_1	10	15	10
B_2	15	20	15
B_3	25	30	25

	A_1	A_2
B_1	14	22
B_2	26	18

CHAPTER 13

FIELD RESEARCH

A Second Look at Research in Natural Settings

CONDUCTING FIELD RESEARCH

Research in natural settings is introduced in Chapter 6, where our focus is on low-constraint, naturalistic research. In this chapter we need to look again at research in natural settings—or, as it is usually referred to, *field research*—but our focus here is on *experiments* in natural settings designed to draw causal inferences.

Recall from Chapter 12 the three important trends in psychological research: increases in the use of (1) factorial designs, (2) within-subjects designs, and (3) mixed designs. A fourth trend is the growing importance of conducting experimental research in natural settings. For example, there are increasing demands to evaluate the effectiveness of large-scale and small-scale educational, clinical, and public health programs; to test the effects of large-scale natural events, such as disasters and human-caused events (e.g., massive unemployment); and to determine employee reactions to changed work conditions and consumer reactions to new products, procedures, or news about products they are using.

Naturalistic and case-study research allow us to identify contingencies and to form causal hypotheses that can be tested at higher constraint levels. However, naturalistic research methods cannot answer questions about causality. Why? Primarily because they do not allow manipulation of the independent variable and therefore do not rule out alternative hypotheses. Conducting experimental research in natural settings is difficult because it is almost always limited by the demands and characteristics of the natural setting that often cannot be controlled by the experimenter. We often cannot obtain the number of subjects required to create experimental and control groups; random assignment of subjects to groups is often impossible in the field; precise measures of dependent variables is often impossible; manipulation of independent variables is usually difficult and, indeed, in some studies such as a study of the psychological effects of a natural disaster, is sometimes impossible. Finally, it is often difficult to maintain projects in the field because research might be canceled or otherwise interrupted by other people, such as teachers and principals who have decision-making responsibility for the field settings.

Reasons for Doing Field Research

There are three major reasons for conducting experiments in field settings:

1. To test the external validity of causal conclusions arrived at in the laboratory.
2. To determine the effects of events that occur in the field.
3. To improve the generalization across settings.

Experimental research conducted in the laboratory allows us to test hypotheses and infer causality under controlled conditions designed to maximize internal validity. However, with high control and internal validity comes a reduction of external validity. That is, the more precise, constrained, and artificial we become in the laboratory, the less natural are the procedures and findings, with the result that we sometimes have difficulty generalizing laboratory experimentation to the natural environment. As noted by Cook and Campbell (1979):

The advantages of experimental control for inferring causation have to be weighed against the disadvantages that arise because we do not always want to learn about causation in controlled settings. Instead, for many purposes, we would like to be able to generalize to causal relationships in complex field settings, and we cannot easily assume that findings from the laboratory will hold in the field. (p. 7)

For example, suppose we have an experimental grammar school on the university campus. It is staffed by educational psychologists, teachers specifically trained for the school, and graduate student research assistants. We conduct a highly controlled experiment that indicates clearly that a new teaching method A is superior to methods B, C, and D, which are representative of the standard procedures used in schools throughout the state. No matter how much confidence we have in the internal validity of the results, can we assume that when the new teaching method is adopted by many different teachers, in different schools, all operating under a variety of conditions, that the method will still be just as effective? No, we cannot. Why? Because the variety of field situations is not exactly like the laboratory situation, and we cannot easily assume external validity of the laboratory findings. It is necessary to test newly developed instructional procedures in actual field situations in order to have more confidence in the generalizability to other field settings. This is particularly important in applied research where the goal is not only to understand phenomena as it is in basic research but, also, to use the new understanding in some practical way, such as in teaching more efficiently.

The second reason for doing field research is to meet growing demands to test the effectiveness of a large variety of social programs, ranging from special educational programs, public health campaigns, and crack-downs on drunk drivers to programs that give economic incentives such as generous tax write-offs to corporations. Each of these programs has an implicit assumption—the large-scale educational program will lead to massive reduction of illiteracy; the public health program will reduce drug addiction; the drunk-driving crackdown will reduce highway fatalities; the economic incentives to corporations will increase economic growth. Unfortunately, such assumptions are seldom tested. Social programs, as well-meaning as they may be, are usually created through political inspiration and for political ends. Seldom are supporters committed to testing the programs' effectiveness. Politically it may be better not to subject such programs to testing than to find that a costly and fine-sounding project really does not work.

In 1969 the president of the American Psychological Association, Donald Campbell, argued that perhaps it is time for developed countries to carry out social reforms as much like controlled social experiments as possible. The studies would be designed to maximize validity. We would make decisions about retaining, modifying, or ending programs in an objective rather than political manner based on the data. Over the past two decades there has been an increase in demands for careful evaluation of such programs, but we are not yet at the point where such evaluation is routinely carried out.

The third reason for conducting experiments in the field is to take advantage of the potential for greater generalizability of results to other conditions. To understand this we must distinguish three types of generalization:

1. Generalization of results from the subjects in the study to the larger population.
2. Generalization of the results of the study over time.
3. Generalization of results from conditions of the study to other conditions (i.e., generalization to other settings).

The third type of generalization may be enhanced when we carry out experiments in naturalistic settings.

Consider the example given earlier in which we tested the effectiveness of a new elementary school teaching program in a university laboratory school. The high-constraint laboratory setting, although giving us confidence in the *internal* validity of the study, is not necessarily strong in external validity. To test the new teaching program so as to enhance its external validity we should also carry out the research in real schools. If we find that in the natural setting the new program is superior to other teaching methods, we can have greater confidence in inferring that the results are generalizable to other, similar classroom settings.

Difficulties in Field Research

We need to conduct experiments in field settings so as to be able to draw causal inferences, but doing so can be flooded with difficulties. There are many field situations in which we cannot apply the laboratory controls completely and cannot, for example, assign subjects to groups at all, but still wish to draw causal inferences with confidence. This is frequently the situation in natural settings such as schools, hospitals, and neighborhoods, or situations in which natural or contrived events occur and affect a large number of people.

Suppose, for example, some natural disaster has occurred, such as the near-meltdown of a nuclear power plant, a severe smog period, or a major flood. We want to know how much the event has affected residents' psychological stability and/or their physical health. If we consider the natural event as the independent variable and residents' behavior and/or health as the dependent variable, we can see that we have no control over the independent variable—we cannot manipulate it. How then do we measure the reactions and draw causal inferences? To take another example, suppose that in studying children we cannot randomly assign subjects to different groups for treatment because subjects are all part of a single class following a common program. That is, they are always together and whatever is applied to one child is applied to all others. Assigning the children to different groups for purposes of the experimental manipulation will seriously interfere with the ongoing program and the program director will not allow it. We want to conduct research with as much control as possible in order to draw causal inferences, and yet we know that random assignment or, for that matter, any differential assignment of subjects to conditions is not possible. Under these restrictions how might we go about testing the new treatment? The essential question here is: How do we answer questions about causality in natural settings when we cannot utilize many of the usual manipulation and control procedures available in the laboratory?

In this chapter we discuss several possible solutions to this question by way of four main topics: quasi-experimental design, single-subject design, program evaluation, and survey research. The first two terms denote a number of specific research designs that have been developed to answer causal questions in natural settings. The last two, program evaluation and survey research, are not so much methods as they are research areas of growing importance. In program evaluation we try to assess the effectiveness of clinical, educational, rehabilitation, and other programs. In survey research we obtain information about the preferences, attitudes, beliefs, and so on of a specified segment of the population. However, each of the four topics has its focus on research issues in natural settings.

QUASI-EXPERIMENTAL DESIGN

The highest degree of control is obtained with experiments that allow us to draw causal inferences with the greatest confidence. Thus, an experiment would be the preferred procedure for answering causal questions. However, there are conditions when we cannot meet all demands of a true experiment but still want to answer a causal question. In these situations we can use quasi-experimental designs. "Quasi" means "similar to". Thus, a *quasi-experimental design* is one that is like an experimental design but is not quite equal to it. Quasi-experiments have the essential form of experiments including a causal hypothesis and some type of manipulation to compare two or more conditions. They do control for some confounding but do not have as much control as a true experiment. Thus, we can draw causal inferences from quasi-experiments but not with the same confidence as when we use a true experimental design. Quasi-experimental designs are used in situations such as field research where full experimental controls cannot be used but where a causal question must be addressed. Donald Campbell (1969) argues that when experiments cannot be carried out, quasi-experimental designs should be used. In many field situations using quasi-experiments to draw causal inferences with somewhat less than high confidence *will still give us more useful information than not experimenting at all.* (Keep in mind that quasi-experimental designs are different from low-constraint methods—naturalistic, case-study, correlational, and differential research—in that quasi-experimental methods *attempt to answer questions of causality.*)

Quasi-experimental designs have much the same form as experiments but are weak on some of the characteristics. Specifically, whereas quasi-experiments do include a comparison of at least two levels of an independent variable, the actual manipulation is not always clearly defined or under the experimenter's control. For example, if we compare some measures of health before and after a natural disaster such as a destructive tornado, we obviously cannot manipulate the tornado but can compare the health records from the local hospital before and after the tornado struck. Likewise, in many field situations we cannot assign subjects to groups in an unbiased manner; indeed, we often cannot assign subjects at all but must accept the natural groups as they exist. Thus, in quasi-experimental designs:

1. We state causal hypotheses.
2. We include at least two levels of the independent variable *but cannot always directly manipulate the independent variable.*

3. We usually cannot assign subjects to groups but must accept already existing groups.
4. We include specific procedures for testing hypotheses.
5. We include some controls for threats to validity.

Compare these characteristics with the characteristics of an experiment (see Chapter 10).

There are a number of basic quasi-experimental designs, but this chapter focuses on two: the nonequivalent control-group design and the interrupted time-series design. [Students who wish information about other quasi-experimental designs can consult Cook and Campbell (1979).]

Nonequivalent Control-Group Design

The best way to test causal hypotheses with confidence is to compare groups that are created by the researcher through random assignment. This makes it likely that the groups are equivalent at the beginning of the study. Recall that initial equivalence of groups is crucial in experimental design. However, there are conditions under which the groups are not assigned randomly or in some other nonbiased manner and, therefore, may not be equivalent on several variables at the beginning of the study. There are several designs in this category, all of which attempt to solve the problem of comparing two groups that we suspect are not equivalent at the beginning of the study.

In field research we frequently have no choice but to use already existing groups, which means that subjects cannot be randomly assigned. Even though the groups appear to be similar, we cannot assume that they are equivalent at the start of the study. The groups may be different on the dependent variable at the beginning of the study. However, whether they are the same or different on the dependent variable, the groups may differ on other important variables that constitute potential confounding. Box 13.1 lists several examples of research using *nonequivalent control-group designs*.

Campbell and Stanley (1966) popularized the nonequivalent control-group design by suggesting that already existing groups can be similar to one another on most relevant variable even though there is no formal systematic assignment of subjects to groups. As they point out, the more similar natural groups are to one another, the closer the design approximates a true experiment and the more confidence we can have in conclusions. Later, Cook and Campbell (1979) extended these principles to even more extreme situations where there may be clear evidence that naturally occurring groups are not equivalent on potential confounding variables. What Cook and Campbell show is that, even in this extreme situation, it is sometimes possible to draw strong conclusions if the researcher carefully evaluates all potential threats to validity. The ideal, of course, is a true experiment in which subjects are assigned to groups in a nonbiased manner. If this is not possible, the best alternative is to use nonequivalent control groups where the groups give every indication of being similar on most of the relevant variables. But, as Cook and Campbell (1979) point out, even when that requirement cannot be met, careful analysis of the design and the results can sometimes allow the researcher to draw useful conclusions from what appears to be a weak research design.

There are two major problems with nonequivalent groups: groups may be differ-

| Box 13.1 | FIELD SITUATIONS WITH NONEQUIVALENT GROUPS |

1. We want to evaluate the effectiveness of an antismoking campaign using two different schools. We suspect that one school has a higher rate of smoking than the other.

2. A company wants to test their employees' attitudes toward work as they may be affected by new work rules. One department is selected as an experimental group, another as the control group. However, there is evidence that the first department has more positive work attitudes than the second.

3. A psychology professor wants to compare examination results in a research methods course based on two different textbooks. The professor teaches one section of the course at 8:00 A.M. on Monday and the other at 4:00 P.M. on Wednesday. It is suspected that students who chose the early section may be quite different from those who chose the later section.

4. A new treatment approach for hyperactivity is to be tested in a special school using three different classes. The classes, however, are at different levels of hyperactivity.

ent on the dependent measure(s) at the start of the study and there may be other differences between groups that have not been controlled by random assignment. To address the first issue the basic strategy in nonequivalent control-group designs is to measure the experimental and control group on the dependent measure both before and after the manipulation. Then, following the manipulation, the *difference* between the premanipulation and postmanipulation scores for each group is calculated. The *difference score* for each group is then taken as a measure of how much each group changed as a result of the manipulation. The pretest allows us to measure how similar the groups are on the dependent variable(s) at the beginning of the study. This similarity is important—the more similar the groups are, the greater control we have. Notice that as the similarity between groups at the beginning of the study increases, the design approaches the experimental designs discussed earlier.

To address the second issue—that groups may differ on variables other than the dependent variable—it is important to rule out each potential confounding variable. To do this, we must first systematically identify potential confounding variables, measure them, and carefully rule them out (see Chapter 7). A typical nonequivalent control-group design is shown in Figure 13.1.

Causality is inferred when the results show that the control group remains essentially the same from pretreatment to posttreatment measures but the experimental group changes markedly in the predicted direction. Cook and Campbell (1979) note that the nonequivalent control-group design controls for many potential sources of

Figure 13.1 A NONEQUIVALENT CONTROL-GROUP DESIGN

Group A (experimental)	Pretest	Treatment	Posttest	Pretest-Posttest
Group B (control)	Pretest	No Treatment	Posttest	Pretest-Posttest

Compare

confounding but still must be interpreted carefully because some confounding variables may be uncontrolled. The confounding that can affect the outcome will vary from study to study. (A complete discussion of the principles for identifying confounding variables and interpreting their likely effects on a nonequivalent control-group study is beyond the scope of this book. The interested reader is referred to Cook and Campbell (1979) for a more complete discussion.)

As noted, there are two major problems in nonequivalent control-group designs, both related to the fact that the groups exist prior to the study and subjects cannot be assigned to groups in a nonbiased manner. That is, the experimental and control groups may differ on the dependent measures at the start of the study, and/or there may be other differences between groups that were not controlled because nonbiased assignment of subjects is not possible. Thus, there may be confounding due to selection. Figure 13.2 shows six possible outcomes of a nonequivalent control-group design. Figures 13.2a and 13.2b show results where the experimental and control groups are

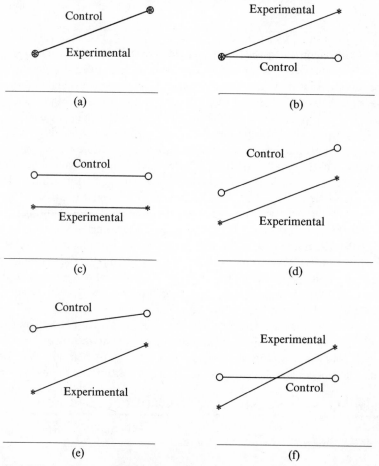

Figure 13.2 **SOME POSSIBLE OUTCOMES FOR NONEQUIVALENT CONTROL-GROUP DESIGNS**

equivalent on the dependent measure at the beginning of the study. Of course, the groups may be different on other important variables, in which case the major issue is to carefully rule out confounding due to selection. In Figures 13.2c–13.2f the groups actually differ on the dependent measure at pretest. In these instances we must rule out confounding due to selection to draw a causal inference, and we must also rule out confounding from sources such as regression to the mean that result from the initial difference on the dependent variable. For purposes of illustration, it is assumed that all changes shown are in the predicted direction.

In Figure 13.2a both the experimental and control groups show an increase on the dependent measure from pretest to posttest. The groups are equivalent at the beginning and show equivalent change over time. Thus, there appears to be no effect of the independent variable. In Figure 13.2b the groups are equivalent on the dependent measures at the beginning of the study. The experimental group shows a large change whereas the control group does not change from pretest to posttest. There does appear to be an effect of the independent variable. However, before drawing this conclusion we must still rule out possible confounding due to selection. In Figure 13.2c neither group changes from pretest to posttest. The obvious interpretation is that the manipulation had no effects. Figure 13.2d shows change in both groups from pretest to posttest at the same rate. With these results we have to conclude that there is a pre-to-posttest difference as predicted but, because both groups changed in the same manner, we cannot attribute the change to the independent variable. It appears more likely that some maturation process or historical event common to both groups may be responsible for the change in scores. Figure 13.2e shows a slight change in the control group but a marked change in the experimental group. With these results we have some confidence in attributing the measured change to the effects of the independent variable. However, there is still the potentially confounding factor of regression to the mean, which limits our confidence in this interpretation. Recall from Chapter 8 that regression is a potential source of confounding whenever we begin an experiment with extreme scores. In Figure 13.2e the marked pretest difference between groups may well represent extreme scores for the experimental group. In the course of the experiment the scores for the group may have returned to the mean level represented by the control group. Thus, the marked change in the experimental group may not be due to the independent variable but, rather, to regression to the mean. Consequently, we cannot be highly confident in attributing the results to the causal effects of the independent variable. In Figure 13.2f the control group does not change but the experimental group changes markedly in the predicted direction, even going far beyond the level of the control group. This is called a *crossover effect*. The results give us considerable confidence in a causal inference. Maturation is an unlikely alternative hypothesis because the control group presumably matured, but actually it did not change. If maturation were responsible, it is unlikely that the effect would be so markedly greater for one group than for the other. Regression to the mean is also an unlikely alternative hypothesis because the experimental group increased not only to the mean of the control group but changed far beyond it. With these results a quasi-experimental design gives us fairly good confidence in a causal inference.

The above examples represent reasonably interpretable data from nonequivalent control-group studies. Other situations, as described by Cook and Campbell (1979), can be far more difficult to interpret—in some cases, impossible to interpret. Using nonequivalent control-group designs and correctly interpreting data from them require considerable expertise and are not recommended to beginning students. A true experiment is the best approach. When a true experiment is not possible, a quasi-experiment where groups are apparently equivalent is the best compromise. Only if neither of these alternatives is feasible should the researcher consider using a quasi-experimental design with a nonequivalent control group.

Interrupted Time-Series Design

In *interrupted time-series designs* a single group of subjects is measured several times both before and after some event or manipulation. Time-series designs are variations of within-subjects designs in which the same subjects are measured in different conditions. In its general form the time-series design is similar to a simple pre-post design, but instead of a single pretreatment measure and a single posttreatment measure of the dependent variable it uses multiple measures taken at several points in time both before and after the manipulation. That is, a series of measures are taken over time, "interrupted" by the manipulation, after which the series of measures are again taken. It is the multiple measures over time that make it a useful design.

The simple pre-post design is weak, leaving so many potential confounding factors uncontrolled that, even if a statistically significant difference is found, we cannot draw causal inferences from the findings (see Chapter 10). Recall the pre-post study of the use of relaxation to reduce disruptive behavior of autistic children. Suppose this study is carried out by taking a pretreatment measure of disruption at one point in time, then applying the relaxation treatment, and then taking a posttreatment measure of disruption at another point in time. Even if we find a significant reduction in disruptive behavior, confounding due to history, maturation, and regression to the mean prevents us from drawing a causal inference.

A major potential confounding factor in the simple pre-post study is *regression to the mean*. The disruptive behavior may naturally fluctuate over time, displaying considerable variability. The intervention might be applied only at a high point in that natural variation, just before the disruptive behavior decreased again. Thus, the observed reduction in disruption may not be due to the treatment at all but only to the natural variability of behavior, and it may thus show the same reduction at that time even if we do not apply any treatment. Because of its multiple measures that give several points of comparison over a long time period, the interrupted time-series design is a useful approach to control for regression to the mean in the single-group situation.

To apply the interrupted time-series design in the study of autistic children we (1) measure disruption at several points in time during a baseline observation period prior to treatment, (2) apply the treatment, and (3) measure the same subjects on the disruptive behavior at several points in time following the intervention. The following example is from the actual results of the study of disruption in autistic children (Graziano, 1974). Disruptive behavior of four autistic children was measured and recorded for a full year as a normal part of the monitoring carried out in the program. The treatment (relaxation training) was applied and the behavioral measures were again taken for more than a year following the treatment. (Figure 13.3 shows the results.)

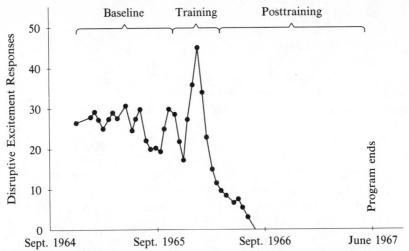

Figure 13.3   INTERRUPTED TIME-SERIES DESIGN SHOWING EFFECTS OF RELAXATION TREATMENT FOR FOUR AUTISTIC CHILDREN (*Source:* **Graziano, 1974, p. 172.**)

Inspection of the graph shows considerable variation during the one-year, pretreatment baseline but none of the variation is comparable to that which occurred after treatment. Following the treatment, the graph shows a marked decrease in disruptive behavior,[1] reaching zero and remaining there for a full year until the program ended. Because so long a pretreatment baseline was used, it is possible to see the magnitude of normal variations over a full year's time and compare it with the marked decrease following treatment. The results suggest that the decrease following treatment is not due to normal fluctuation or regression to the mean. It also seems unlikely to be due to maturation of all subjects all during the same period of time. Although a good demonstration of the effects of relaxation training, there is still a major confounding factor remaining. Can you identify it? (We will return to this point soon.)

By using an interrupted time-series design with a single group of subjects researchers can take advantage of data already gathered over a long period of time. It is a useful design in clinical or naturalistic settings where the effects of some event, naturally occurring or manipulated, may be assessed by taking multiple measurements both before and after the event.

The interrupted time-series design can also be used in large-scale studies and is particularly useful when the presumed causal event occurs to all members of a population. For example, suppose a state government wants to reduce traffic accidents and their resulting injuries and deaths. To accomplish this they reduce the state speed limit from 65 mph to 55 mph. It is important to determine whether the intervention (reduced speed) does result in fewer accidents. Because the new speed limit applies to every driver in the state, there cannot be an experimental group of state drivers for whom the new

---

[1] Notice the peak of disruptive behavior immediately after training began. This peak is a common clinical phenomenon called a *frustration effect,* which occurs when new procedures are initiated with autistic children. Frustration effects are generally temporary. Note too that the disruption dropped dramatically following this short burst.

limit applies and a control group for which it does not. How then might the effects of the intervention be evaluated? One way is to use the interrupted time-series design. Figure 13.4 is a hypothetical time graph showing the number of accidents in the state that involved injury or death over a 16-month period, plotted for several months prior to implementing the new speed limit and for several more months during which the new speed limit is in effect. The time graph shows variation in the number of serious accidents during the preintervention phase, with an overall slight increase throughout the year. Following the new speed limit, there is a sharp reduction that eventually stabilizes at a new, lower level of accidents for the remainder of that year and into the next. Are these results sufficient for us to draw a reasonably confident conclusion that the reduced speed limit is effective in reducing the number of serious accidents? Let us consider the major potential confounding factors.

Selection is not at issue because this is essentially a within-subjects design and the two groups being compared, the state's drivers before and after the decreased speed limit, were thus equivalent at the start of the study. *Testing* effects are not critical because the measures taken are unobtrusive; that is, all measures are taken from traffic records and not directly from subjects. *Maturation* is not an issue because it is most unlikely that all of the state's drivers, of all ages, all became better drivers at the same time through some common maturational process. *Regression to the mean* is not an issue. Note that the postintervention decrease in accidents is much sharper, lasts longer, and reaches a lower mean level than the preintervention normal fluctuations. Thus, the decrease does not seem to be due to regression to the mean. Primarily because of its

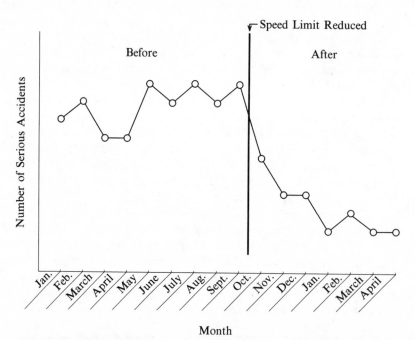

Figure 13.4 HYPOTHETICAL TIME GRAPH FOR INTERRUPTED TIME-SERIES DESIGN SHOWING NUMBER OF SERIOUS AUTO ACCIDENTS BEFORE AND AFTER REDUCTION OF STATE SPEED LIMIT

multiple measures at pre- and posttreatment, the interrupted time-series design does control for most potential confounding. It is a far stronger design than the simple pre-post design where only one measure is taken at each phase.

With time-series designs, however, there are two potentially confounding factors: *history* and *instrumentation.* History can confound results in any procedure that requires a fairly long period of time because any number of other events might occur to account for changes in the dependent variable. In our hypothetical speed-limit example there may be other factors that contributed to or are wholly responsible for the decrease. For example, the state might have also sharply increased the number of patrol cars, the number of speeding tickets, and the severity of penalties for speeding and for drunk driving. Any of these actions may have contributed to the decrease in accidents. Thus, when using the interrupted time-series design, the experimenter must be particularly careful to identify potential confounding due to history and carefully rule it out. In this example we must be sure the state did not initiate these other actions at the same time they decreased the speed limit. (Recall a few paragraphs earlier when you were asked to identify the remaining major confounding factor in the time-series design for the experiment in relaxation training. If you identified it as *history,* you were correct.) Instrumentation is also a potential threat to validity in time-series designs. When people initiate new approaches or programs there also may be an accompanying change in the way records are made and kept. The researcher must be careful to determine that the reduction in accidents is not due to changes in measuring or record keeping.

In a time-series study the change in the time graph must be quite sharp to be interpreted as anything other than only a normal fluctuation. Any postintervention change that is slight or gradual is difficult to interpret as being due to the causal effects of the intervention.

Note two important points about the interrupted time-series design. First, it is a flexible design that can be used in many situations. With it we can evaluate events that are large- or small-scale, that have already occurred, and that are actually manipulated (such as the decreased speed limit) or uncontrolled (such as a natural disaster). Think about this, and see whether you can determine how we might use this design to evaluate, for example, a large-scale natural disaster that has already occurred. Secondly, the time-series design is such that we can use data that already have been gathered and that are unobtrusive, such as data on auto accidents. This adds a great deal to the flexibility of the design.

The interrupted time-series design is a powerful design and is useful in many naturalistic situations. However, it can be improved by adding one or more comparison groups. In our hypothetical study of the effects of a change in speed limit on the number of accidents, we can use comparable data from a neighboring state that did not reduce the speed limit. This would provide a comparison that helps to control for many potentially confounding factors such as history and maturation. For example, Guerin and MacKinnon (1985) studied the effects of the new California Child Passenger Restraint Requirement. This law requires that children under 4 years of age be in federally approved child car seats while riding in cars. Using an interrupted time-series design, the authors examined the effects of the new law on child auto injuries. The number of injuries for children 3 years and younger was taken from state records for a period covering 48 months prior to the start of the new law and for 12 months following its initiation. Any marked effect of the law should be evident in the pre-post comparisons on the interrupted time-series graph. As an added comparison, the researchers recorded auto injury data for children between 4 and 7 years of age (children who were not covered by the law). They predicted that if the law had any effect, there would be a significant decrease for the younger group but not for the older group of children. As shown in Figure 13.5, after the law went into effect there was a sharp drop in injuries to the younger group but not to the older group, and the differences persist over the next 12 months. Statistical analyses were also carried out that showed a significant reduction in injuries for the younger group but not for the older group. In addition, the younger group was compared with a group of young children from Texas, where no such car-seat law exists. The children in Texas did not show any decrease in injuries during the 12 months of comparison.

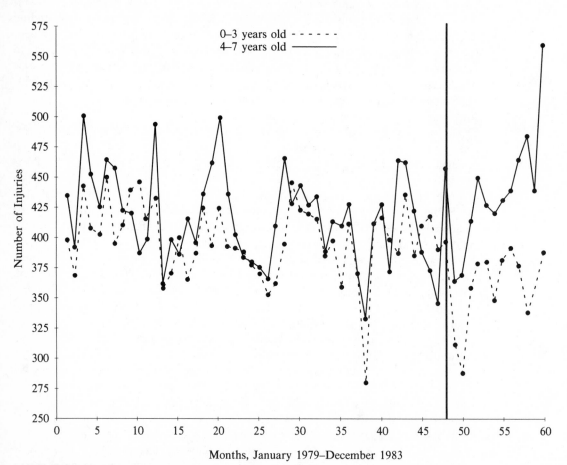

Months, January 1979–December 1983

Figure 13.5   TIME-SERIES DESIGN SHOWING EFFECTS OF CAR-SEAT LAW ON INJURIES IN YOUNG CHILDREN (*Source:* Guerin, D., & MacKinnon, D. P., 1985, p. 143.)

In the Guerin and MacKinnon (1985) study a decrease in injuries is shown for the young group by the interrupted time-series graph, which displays injuries prior to and following the new law. Also, by adding comparison groups of over-4-year-olds in California (for whom the new law did not apply) and the children in Texas (where there was no car-seat law), the effect is further demonstrated. The comparison groups increase the researchers' confidence in concluding that the new law is effective in reducing auto injuries for children.

Interrupted time-series designs provide a good way of testing causal hypotheses under many field conditions in which we cannot apply all of the usual laboratory controls. Cook and Campbell (1979) discuss several variations of the time-series design and interested students are urged to consult their work. Box 13.2 gives examples of published studies in which interrupted time-series designs were used. The references are given so the student can read the original reports.

Graphical presentations of data in the interrupted time-series design can provide considerable information, telling us whether there is a marked change or not. But in a time-series design, simply inspecting the graph does not address the null hypothesis—that the pretest and posttest data are not significantly different. Testing the statistical significance of pre-post differences in time-series designs requires sophisticated procedures such as the Bayesian moving average model (Glass, Wilson, & Gottman, 1975), which tests whether the pretreatment and posttreatment patterns are statistically different. [Such analyses are beyond the scope of this book but interested students should see Glass et al. (1975).]

SINGLE-SUBJECT DESIGN

Single-subject designs are experimental designs that are carried out using only a single subject. They were developed early in the history of experimental psychology and were used in both human and animal learning studies. Since the early 1960s they have become popular in clinical psychology, particularly in research on the effectiveness of clinical treatments. It is important that we not confuse the single-subject experimental designs with the *ex post facto,* single-case study. Recall from our discussion in Chapter 6 that single-case studies using *ex post facto* analyses are frequently used in clinical research to provide in-depth descriptions of single individuals and to generate but not test hypotheses. The *ex post facto,* single-case study is weak, not because it has only one subject (the case), but because the researcher has access to only observed variables and has no control over the independent variables, which are not observed or manipulated but only inferred. Therefore, the independent variable cannot be manipulated to observe its effects on the dependent variable and *alternative hypotheses cannot be ruled out.* In the single-case, *ex post facto* study there are no true dependent and independent variables; there are only observed and inferred variables. However, with single-subject *experimental* designs we are able to manipulate independent variables, to observe their effects on dependent variables, to draw causal inferences, and to do so with a single subject. The power of these designs is in the control of independent variables to eliminate potential confounding factors, enhance internal validity, and thus test causal hypotheses.

Box 13.2   EXAMPLES OF RESEARCH USING INTERRUPTED TIME-SERIES DESIGN

1. Campbell (1969) describes a study of the effects on traffic fatalities of a highway speeding crackdown. The program was initiated by the state of Connecticut after a year of particularly high traffic fatalities. Traffic deaths prior to and following the crackdown are compared.

2. Lawler and Hackman (1969) used time-series designs to test the effects of having employees participate in the planning of an employee bonus incentive plan for reducing absenteeism. Rates of absenteeism were recorded at several points prior to and following the new incentive plan.

3. Using time-series designs, Caporaso (1974) studied the effects of the formation of the European Economic Community (EEC) on the subsequent development of international economic cooperation and interdependencies among the member nations. The EEC was formed in 1958. Caporaso compared a number of measures of dependencies before the EEC was formed (1950–1957) and following the start of the EEC (1958–1970).

4. The on-task school behavior of three overactive preschoolers was improved by Bornstein and Quevillon (1976), who used a time-series design to study the effects of teaching self-instruction skills.

5. Mazur-Hart and Berman (1977) studied the effects of a new no-fault divorce law in the state of Nebraska. They compared the recorded number of divorces for the 3.5 years prior to the new law and the 2.5 years following it. The time-series analyses show that the number of divorces increased prior to the new law and continued to increase at the same rate following it. The new law had no apparent effect on the divorce rate.

6. McSweeny (1978) used a time-series design to study the effects of introducing a small fee for telephone directory assistance (information) on the public's use of the information service. Carried out in Cincinnati with a million telephone users as subjects, McSweeny found that following the introduction of the twenty-cent fee, the number of calls for information dropped by nearly 70,000 each day.

7. Phillips (1983) used time-series designs to investigate the effects of televised violence on homicide rates. Using broadcasts of heavyweight boxing matches as the independent variable and homicide rates as the dependent variable, Phillips found a 12.4 percent increase in homicide rates following telecasts of the boxing matches.

Because of the importance of single-subject designs, they are treated here as a separate category. In essence they are a further development of the basic time-series designs. They are within-subjects designs where the subject serves as his or her own control. There are several variations of single-subject designs, including reversal or ABA designs, multiple baseline designs, and single-subject, randomized, time-series designs.

In this section we will consider why one might want to use a single-subject rather than a multiple-subject design as well as the history of the development of single-subject techniques. Obviously, such designs are appropriate when we have only one subject.

This occurs frequently in clinical treatment situations where we want to know whether a client's problem behavior is improved when a particular treatment is applied. The same situation often occurs in education where we might want to know whether a specific child's academic achievement improves with specific teaching methods. Thus, when we want an intensive study of an individual rather than of a representative group, single-subject designs are useful. In this situation we are not particularly interested in generalizing to a population but wish to limit the conclusions to the individual. Clearly, a single-subject experiment is weak in external validity but can give us valid and reliable information about a single individual.

Sidman (1960) argues that single-subject designs are not only appropriate under certain conditions but are actually preferable to between-subjects, group-comparison designs. The basis for his argument is that, in group-comparison procedures, groups are compared by summarizing each group's performance. In the process of summarizing we may lose important information about the ways in which individuals perform. For example, suppose we have pretested 20 phobic subjects on the intensity of their fears and then randomly assigned them to a treatment and a control condition. We find at posttesting that the treated group has a lower mean fear score than the control group, and it is statistically significant. Assuming that all confounding has been controlled, we can conclude that the treatment is effective, that the independent variable did, indeed, have an effect on the dependent measure of fear.

However, if we examine the scores of individual subjects, we might find that, although the treated group as a whole had lower fear measures than did the control group as a whole, there is considerable variability within each of the two groups—some of the treated subjects may have fear scores that are higher than those of the untreated subjects. Further, if we examined the subject's pretreatment and posttreatment scores, we might find that while most of the control subjects did not improve some of them improved quite a bit, and while most of the treated subjects did improve some of them did not, and some even may have become worse. In other words, individuals respond differently to the same treatment. Although the treatment may be effective when we consider an overall group comparison, it may not be effective for some subjects and it may be effective for some others. This information, according to Sidman (1960), would be more readily apparent if we had used single-subject procedures rather than between-subjects, group comparisons. Thus, he argues, the typical group-comparisons procedures might obscure some important effects.

Such considerations became particularly important in clinical psychology in the 1950s and 1960s when researchers were becoming increasingly critical of traditional psychotherapy, for much of the research failed to support the effectiveness of traditional psychological treatment. Bergin (1966), Bergin and Strupp (1970), and others, using the argument proposed by Sidman (1960), recognized that group-comparison studies of psychotherapy failed to support the hypothesis of the effectiveness of treatment. However, on closer inspection of the data it was clear that some clients improved, some remained the same, and some became worse. When taken together as a group, they tended to cancel each other out, and the overall finding was that psychotherapy was not effective for the group as a whole. Obscured by group-comparison designs was that some clients did improve following psychotherapy. Might it not be important, Bergin suggested, to try to study those individuals who improved to determine whether their improvements were due to some systematic effects of the treatment rather than to chance variation and, if so, to discover whether there are any particular characteristics of clients that make them more responsive to therapy? That is, can we discover whether there are factors that make psychotherapy effective for some people but not for others? Sidman (1960) and Bergin (1966) argued for the development of methods for the controlled study of single individuals.

The intensive experimental study of individuals actually had a prominent place in psychology up to about the late 1930s. Experimental psychology up to that time focused heavily on the detailed study of single subjects in laboratory situations. In our discussion in Chapter 6 of E. L. Witmer's work, we note that in the early 1930s he called for the creation of clinical psychology, which would use as its major methods the intensive experimental study of individual subjects. In the late 1930s, however, psychologists began adopting the new design and statistical procedures that allow for group comparisons. Probably the most influential factor in this shift from single-subject to group comparisons is the publication in 1935 of Sir Ronald Fisher's *The Design of Experiments,* in which he creates the groundwork for the development of multisubject, group-comparison experiments and the statistical procedures for evaluating data from them. In a short time experimental research in psychology was following Fisher's lead and taking advantage of new multisubject design and analysis procedures. However, there is an influential exception to this turn to multisubject procedures: B. F. Skinner (e.g., 1953) continued to develop methods for the intensive, systematic, and controlled study of individual subjects. The experimental analysis of behavior, as these methods became known, was expanded and refined by a number of researchers influenced by Skinner. The single-subject designs discussed here are extensions of the procedures developed by Skinner and his associates.

The controlled study of a single individual has become particularly important in clinical psychology. Modern clinical psychology is now heavily reliant on behavior modification treatment methods and behavior modification research utilizes single-subject research designs refined from Skinner's work. There are many single-subject procedures now available to the researcher. Three of the most frequently used single-subject designs are: (1) reversal or ABA designs, (2) multiple baseline designs, and (3) single-subject, randomized time-series designs. [Students who want to know more about other types of single-subject experimentation can consult Sidman (1960), Hersen and Barlow (1976), and Kratochwill (1978).]

Single-subject experimental designs are variations of within-subject designs because the same subject is exposed to all manipulations. They are also variations of time-series designs. Recall that in time-series designs we have no independent control groups and we take dependent measurements of the same subjects at different points in time. This allows us to compare measures taken before and after some naturally occurring event or an experimental manipulation. Single-subject designs are similar. Measures are taken from a single subject at different points in time, both before and after a manipulation. The basic comparison is between the same subject's own pretreatment and posttreatment responses. Note that at its simplest level, this resembles the pretest-posttest comparison, which is a relatively weak nonexperimental design. Causal inferences cannot be drawn from the pretest-posttest design because so many potential confounding variables are left uncontrolled. The simple use of two conditions alone, pre- and post-, is not sufficient basis for drawing causal inferences. The addition of a control group allows for the control of many potential confounding variables but a control group is not possible when we have only one subject. Single-subject designs improve on the pre-post designs not by adding a control group but by adding more conditions to the experiment. If the dependent variable changes in the predicted direction at each subsequent manipulation, then we have a more confident basis for drawing causal inferences that the manipulation is responsible for the observed change in the dependent variable.

Reversal Design (ABA Design)

In *reversal designs,* also referred to as *ABA designs,* the effects of an independent variable on a dependent variable are demonstrated by measuring the dependent variable at three or four points in time. There is a no-treatment baseline period during which the dependent behavior is only observed, a treatment period in which the manipulation is carried out, and a return or reversal to the no-treatment condition.

The effects of the independent variable (the treatment) on the dependent variable (the behavior to be changed) is demonstrated if the behavior changes in the predicted direction whenever the conditions are reversed. There are numerous published reports of the ABA reversal procedure. A hypothetical study will help to describe the general format used. The study concerns self-stimulatory behavior that is often engaged in by retarded, autistic, or brain-injured children. Such behavior can be self-injurious, such as head-banging, self-biting, and gouging, or otherwise highly disruptive behavior, such as screaming, head shaking, and so on. When the behavior is violent and continual, it interferes with treatment or training programs for the child and is highly disruptive for other children in the same group. It often appears that such behavior may be maintained, at least in part, by the responses of teachers or other staff members. For some children, being ignored seems to help maintain the self-stimulatory behavior; for other children, the staff's attention to the episodes may help maintain it.

Suppose that a retarded child, Betty, displays a complex self-stimulatory behavior that consists of loud, piercing shrieks, grotesque facial grimacing, and rapid, energetic, arm-flapping. The three behaviors occur together, are maintained for as long as 25 minutes, and occur many times each day. The behavior is disruptive, not only preventing Betty from learning all she might in the special classroom but also interfering with the progress of the other children. After observing the child, a psychologist forms the tentative hypothesis that the teacher's attention is the major reinforcement that maintains the behavior. That is, when Betty is not paid attention to, she begins her self-stimulatory activity, which soon brings the teacher to the child to try to soothe and comfort her. The teacher does not realize that it may be her efforts to help Betty control the behavior that are actually helping to maintain it.

To test the hypothesis the psychologist sets up an ABA reversal design, in which condition A, the baseline, involves the teacher's usual approach of attending to Betty whenever she displays the behavior. Condition B is the treatment—a differential reinforcement procedure in which the teacher provides attention and support for Betty whenever she refrains from the self-stimulatory behavior but withdraws all of her attention from Betty whenever she begins or maintains the disruptive behavior. The child is carefully observed and the occurrence of the self-stimulating behavior is recorded during each condition. The observations are carried out for one hour at the same time each day. The graph in Figure 13.6 shows the behavioral changes as the AB conditions are sequentially reversed. In this hypothetical example, the independent variable is teacher attention and the dependent variable is the child's self-stimulatory behavior. The graph suggests there may be a causal relationship between teacher attention and Betty's self-stimulatory behavior. Notice something about the psychologist's approach to the problem. The psychologist has not limited the approach to only three conditions, ABA, but has added another reversal at the end for an ABAB procedure. The ABA sequence is sufficient to suggest causality. Why do you think the psychologist added that extra reversal, back to the B condition? (Think about this. We will return to it shortly.)

In reversal designs we test a causal relationship between an independent variable and a dependent variable. In this case the independent variable is the teacher's attention. It is presented at two levels, (A) baseline in which teacher's attention is given when the self-stimulation occurs and (B) the intervention in which teacher's attention is withdrawn when self-stimulation occurs. The experimental manipulation is the sequential reversal of levels A and B. The dependent variable is Betty's self-stimulatory behavior and is operationally defined in terms of the number of minutes per day in which it occurs. The question being asked is one of causality: Does teacher's attention affect self-stimulation for this particular child? When we find that behavior changes in the predicted direction, increasing or decreasing each time the reversal occurs, then we have a compelling demonstration that the independent variable, and not some confounding variable, has affected the dependent variable.

In this hypothetical example an intervention was tested for reducing undesirable behavior. But the same reversal design has often been used to test the effectiveness of interventions to increase the strength of positive behaviors. For example, Correa, Poulson, and Salzberg (1984) used a reversal design in their study of blind retarded children. Because of multiple handicaps, the children have great difficulty in accurately

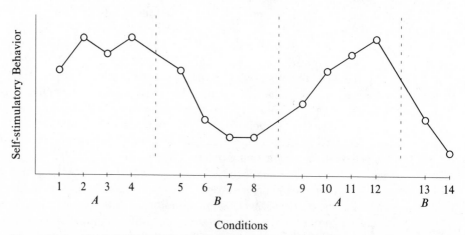

Figure 13.6   ABAB REVERSAL DESIGN SHOWING EFFECTS OF CONTINGENT REINFORCEMENT ON SELF-STIMULATORY BEHAVIOR OF A SINGLE CHILD

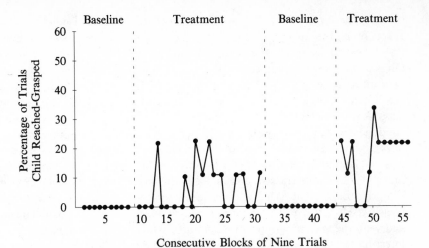

Figure 13.7 STUDY OF PERCENTAGE OF TRIALS IN WHICH SUBJECT (CORY) REACHED AND GRASPED OBJECTS IN BASELINE AND TREATMENT CONDITIONS (*Source:* **Correa, V. I., Poulson, C. L., & Salzberg, C. L., 1984, p. 65.**)

reaching for and grasping objects and hence their general development can be markedly impaired. The researchers set up a treatment procedure to train the children to reach for and to grasp objects accurately. This was the first step in a more general developmental training program. The researchers used a reversal procedure for one child (Cory). They observed Cory's reaching and grasping under both a baseline condition and a treatment condition and repeated the reversal from baseline to treatment one more time. As shown in Figure 13.7 above, Cory's reaching and grasping increased from baseline to treatment at each reversal. Again, why is the last condition (treatment) included? In this case and the example presented earlier, the behavior under the B condition was preferable to the behavior under the A condition. Once we have demonstrated the causal relationship between an independent variable and the dependent variable with an ABA design, it is appropriate to use that relationship to return the subject to the best possible position; that is, to reinstate condition B. In fact, if you think about this, you should see that in many situations we would have an ethical obligation to do so.

Multiple Baseline Design

Although the ABA reversal design is a powerful demonstration of the effect of one variable on another, there are situations in which reversal procedures are not feasible or not ethical. For example, suppose the self-stimulatory behavior of a child is injurious, such as severe head-banging? Or suppose we succeed in improving the academic performance of a child in school? In both cases we would be unwilling to reverse conditions once we achieved improved functioning. For the first child, a return to baseline could risk injury; for the second, it could risk disruption of the improved academic performance. Thus, the ABA reversal design used in the last example might not be acceptable. Instead, we could use a multiple baseline design.

In the *multiple baseline design* there is no reversal of conditions. Rather, the effects of the treatment are demonstrated on different behaviors successively. To illustrate, we will use an example similar to the previous example of an ABA design. Suppose that a fifth-grade boy is doing poorly in both math and reading, although he appears to have the ability to achieve at a high level. He is also a class disruptor, continually interrupting and generally failing to attend to the academic work of the class. A psychologist spends several hours observing the class and notes some apparent contingencies regarding the boy's behavior—the teacher, attempting to control the boy, pays a good deal of attention to him whenever he is disruptive. The teacher scolds, corrects, and lectures him, draws the attention of the class to his antics in an effort to make him feel embarrassed, and makes him stand in front or in a corner of the class. The psychologist notes that the boy seems to accept the attention with a good deal of pleasure. However, on those rare occasions when he does his academic work quietly and well, the teacher ignores him completely for fear that if anything is said it might interrupt him and stimulate his disruptive behavior. "When he is working, I leave well enough alone," the teacher says. "I don't want to risk stirring him up."

Based on these observed contingencies, the psychologist forms the tentative hypothesis that the contingent teacher attention to the boy's disruptive behavior may be a major factor in maintaining the disruptive behavior, whereas the teacher's failure to reward the boy's good academic work may account for its low occurrence. The psychologist sets up a multiple-baseline design to test the hypothesis about the importance of teacher attention on both disruptive and academic behavior. Note that the independent variable here is teacher attention and the dependent variables are the child's (1) disruptive behavior, (2) math performance, and (3) reading performance. The independent variable is presented at two levels—presence of contingent teacher attention and absence of contingent teacher attention.

Figure 13.8 shows the sequence of phases of the hypothetical study. During baseline all three dependent variables are measured while the teacher continues the usual procedure of trying to punish the disruption while ignoring the effective academic behavior. As seen in Figure 13.8, disruptive behavior is high and math and reading performance are low. In the second phase the teacher's attention to disruptive behavior is withdrawn and is, instead, focused on reading performance. In the third phase both reading and math performance receive the teacher's attention whereas disruption continues to be ignored. The measured changes in the dependent variables associated with the independent variable manipulations provide evidence for the hypothesis that contingent teacher attention is an important controlling factor in the child's behavior.

Single-Subject, Randomized, Time-Series Design

As noted earlier, there are conditions in which a reversal design is not appropriate (e.g., when the behavior is injurious or when we have succeeded in improving some behavior and do not want to risk returning it to its original baseline). The multiple baseline procedure meets these objections but sometimes it is not feasible, such as when there is only one behavior at issue. The *single-subject, randomized, time-series design* is used to overcome these limitations. This design is essentially an interrupted time-series

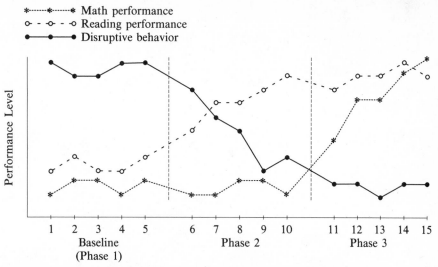

············* Math performance
o - -o- -o Reading performance
●——●——● Disruptive behavior

**Figure 13.8   HYPOTHETICAL RESULTS OF A MULTIPLE-BASELINE DESIGN
SHOWING IMPROVEMENT IN DISRUPTIVE BEHAVIOR, MATH
PERFORMANCE, AND READING PERFORMANCE FOR A SINGLE CHILD
CONTINGENT ON TEACHER ATTENTION**

design for a single subject with one additional element—the randomized assignment of
the manipulation in the time-series.

The single-subject, randomized, time-series design could be applied to the single-
subject experiments described above, but let us take another example. Suppose that
Joey, another child in the special class, does not complete his daily work. During the
15-minute lesson periods in which he is supposed to be responding to a workbook lesson
and marking answers on the page, Joey looks around the room or just closes his eyes
and does no work. Frequent reminders by the teacher might rouse him briefly but not
enough for him to complete the lessons. The teacher is convinced that Joey has the skills
to do the academic work but how can the teacher help him to show it?

An effective motivational intervention with children is a token reinforcement
system in which paper or plastic tokens are given to the child whenever he engages in
the desired behavior. The tokens serve as immediate secondary reinforcement for the
desired behavior and are saved by the child and cashed in for items and privileges that
the child prizes. If we are to employ a single-subject, randomized, time-series design,
we might decide to measure the child's arithmetic achievement for six weeks (30 school
days), which would yield a time graph of 30 measurements. We devote a number of
days, perhaps the first five and the last five (1–5 and 26–30) to measure his arithmetic
achievement. This insures adequate pretreatment and posttreatment measures. We then
use a table of random numbers to select randomly one of the middle 20 days as our
point for introducing the manipulation. The manipulation is the use of token reinforcement for arithmetic achievement. Suppose that we selected the number 9 from the table
of random numbers, thus the beginning of the ninth day becomes our point for introducing the token reinforcement. The beginning of the manipulation is preceded by eight

"Hey, Dad! Who sez you guys could play with _my_ tokens!"

days of arithmetic achievement measured under the usual nontoken condition, and then this would be followed by 22 days of measurements of the dependent variable under the token reinforcement condition. If the time graph shows a marked improvement in arithmetic achievement coincident with the ninth measurement (as shown in Figure 13.9), we have a convincing illustration of the effects of the token reinforcement. Note that it is highly unlikely that such marked improvement would occur by chance at exactly the point at which we have *randomly* introduced the treatment. It is also highly unlikely that this particular time-series pattern would have occurred because of maturation or history.

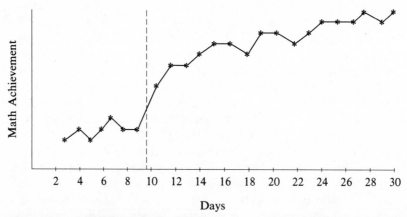

Figure 13.9   HYPOTHETICAL RESULTS OF A SINGLE-SUBJECT, RANDOMIZED, TIME-SERIES DESIGN SHOWING IMPROVED MATH ACHIEVEMENT BY A SINGLE CHILD

PROGRAM EVALUATION_____

Program evaluation research is one of the fastest growing areas of psychological research. The task in this type of research is to evaluate how successfully a program meets its goals. For example, we may need to evaluate the food-stamp program, a state highway speed-control program, or the effectiveness of rehabilitation programs for criminal offenders. In these days of budget deficits a key word is *accountability*. The goal of a good program evaluation is to provide evidence on whether the money being spent on the program is accomplishing the goals intended. The situation presents a number of unique research challenges.

Program evaluation is not a set of research designs distinct from the designs discussed earlier in the text. Instead, in program evaluation designs such as those discussed are modified to meet the particular constraints of the situation. Of course, we always want to use the best possible research design—the design that will permit us to draw causal inferences about the effectiveness of the program with the greatest degree of confidence. However, program realities frequently restrict our choice of design.

Practical Problems in Program Evaluation Research

Perhaps what separates program evaluation research from many other types of research are the unique practical considerations involved. In lower constraint research, such as naturalistic research or case studies, we observe subjects and record observations of them. Subjects are observed in natural or only slightly constrained settings even though we realize it is difficult to impose effective controls in such settings. We normally would restrict ourselves to observing the public behavior of subjects. An unobtrusive study of the sexual behavior of married couples generally would be considered unethical, not to mention illegal. In higher constraint research we bring subjects into laboratory settings that allow us to exercise more control of the situations. Again, we are usually ethically restricted to studying public behavior, although in theory we could get the permission of the subjects to study normally private behavior. Masters and Johnson (1966), for example, obtained subjects who agreed to allow the researchers to observe and measure details of their physiological response during sexual activity, a normally private behavior. In program evaluation research we evaluate the effectiveness of a program that operates in a complex and often uncontrolled natural setting. Further, we are often interested in how effective the program is in meeting the needs of clients, often a private and personal matter for each client. Finally, in most cases the participants in the program generally are not people who have volunteered for a research study. Rather, they have become involved in the program because they have certain needs that the program is designed to address. Therefore, the program evaluator is faced with difficult practical and ethical considerations that many other researchers can avoid.

Ethical constraints are common in any kind of program evaluation. Often the program is designed to meet an urgent need that cannot be ignored. The ideal research design from the perspective of internal validity would randomly assign subjects to one of two conditions—the program group and the no-program group. But is it ethical to deny at random some individuals food stamps to see whether they really suffer malnutrition more than individuals who are given food stamps, or to deny some children access to a special education program designed to overcome learning disabilities so we can evaluate the program? Sometimes, more than ethical concerns restrict the researcher. In our earlier example one could argue that the learning disabilities program is experimental and may not work at all. In fact, it may do more harm than good, in spite of the effort that went into designing it. Therefore, denying some subjects access to the program to allow a cleaner evaluation of its effectiveness is reasonable from an ethical perspective. However, it may not be acceptable from a political perspective. Depending on the perceived value of the program by the parents of children who might benefit from it and the availability of other programs, the school board may believe that it is politically impossible to deny some students access to such a program. Any of these issues can prevent use of a randomly assigned control-group design in the evaluation.

Another ethical issue affecting program evaluation research is that of informed consent. Voluntary consent to participate in research is the cornerstone of most ethical guidelines. But many people who are being served by particular programs may feel obligated to participate even if they do not wish to. They may fear that some of the benefits they receive from the program will be cut off if they do not cooperate. The program evaluator must be careful to minimize this kind of subtle coercion.

There are also some practical issues that make program evaluations more challenging. Unlike most controlled studies, which are conducted in the laboratory where the researcher can control most aspects of the study, the program is in a natural setting and usually not under the control of the evaluator. The staff is interested in doing the best job they can in applying the program and the evaluation of the program is often secondary. A good program evaluator needs excellent political skills to convince staff to cooperate in the evaluation and to maintain their cooperation throughout the evaluation. Often when staff are involved in an evaluation they resent the time that is taken away from their important work of providing services. If the evaluator is not sensitive to these realities, the relationship between the evaluator and staff in a program can become hostile, with the staff feeling that the evaluator is only trying to find their every flaw and the evaluator feeling that the staff is trying to sabotage the evaluation process. The program evaluator must be aware of potentially biasing factors in the data being gathered. A staff is generally interested in showing the program in its best possible light, not only because it is their program but because a program that appears to be ineffective might not get continued funding. Clients may have a vested interest in the program if they believe it has been helpful and they may, therefore, inflate their ratings of its effectiveness. On the other hand, some clients may believe that better programs could be implemented; therefore, they deflate their ratings of effectiveness. Such potential biases make it especially important that the evaluator rely on many different data sources, at least some of which are objective measures.

Issues of Control

Control in program evaluation research is as important as in any other type of research. A major difficulty is that, because of the more naturalistic nature of the program evaluation setting, it is difficult to apply all of the controls that would be ideal. Despite these difficulties, however, many controls can be applied, three of which are discussed here. Keep in mind that the purpose of control is to enhance the validity of the evaluation.

Selecting Appropriate Dependent Measures   Most programs are developed with several goals in mind. Therefore, the program evaluator needs to use several dependent measures to evaluate the effectiveness of the program in meeting each of the intended goals. Some of the measures focus on actual change in the individuals served by the program and some focus on changes outside the program (such as enhanced economic activity in the community). It is useful to include measures of satisfaction with the program, both from the people served by the program and from the community in general. Although these measures do not indicate the actual effectiveness of the program, they are factors that can influence future effectiveness. An effective program that is politically unpopular will need some work to address this issue or continued funding will be jeopardized.

Minimizing Bias in Dependent Measures   In any research it is essential to minimize measurement bias. This is particularly important in program evaluation research where the possibility of bias is high because data are often collected by the same people who run the program. Program evaluators try to minimize such bias by using objective rather than subjective measures and by using people who are not involved directly in the administration of the program to gather data. Many broad-based programs are intended to have community-wide effects that can be monitored using routinely available data such as census data. No technique for minimizing bias will be completely effective in all situations. One of the better approaches is to use several different dependent measures. If each is a good measure and they all point to the same general conclusion, there can be more confidence in the results.

Control Through Research Design in Program Evaluation   As with any research project the major controls are incorporated into the research design. In program evaluation the strongest research design is an experimental design with random assignment of subjects. When this cannot be done the strongest alternative design available should be used.

Typical Program Evaluation Designs

Dozens of different designs have been used in program evaluation research but two or three major designs account for most of this research.

Randomized Control-Group Design   The ideal design to use in program evaluation is a control-group design with random assignment of subjects to conditions. This design provides maximum control. The control group may be either a no-treatment control, a waiting-list control, or some alternative treatment strategy. Ethical considerations often dictate the nature of the control group. For example, under some conditions it might not be ethical to assign some subjects to a no-treatment control group. In such situations we may use the best treatment currently available as a control against which we compare the experimental procedure.

Single-Group, Time-Series Design   If a control group is not possible, the best alternative strategy for evaluation is a time-series design. Repeated measures on the dependent variables before, during, and after the program can control for many typical threats to internal validity. Depending on the funding source, pretest measures may be difficult to obtain because there would be pressure to begin services as soon as funds are released. Still, this design is flexible and useful in many situations. In fact, even when a control group is possible, using a time-series strategy with repeated preprogram and postprogram measures would increase confidence in the evaluation of the program's effectiveness.

Pretest-Posttest Design   As discussed in Chapter 10, the pretest-posttest design is weak. Unfortunately, it is used much too often in program evaluation research. With only two measures and no control group, almost none of the threats to internal validity is controlled. The simple pretest-posttest design is thus not recommended.

Summary of Program Evaluation

In program evaluation the researcher faces the major problem of attempting high-constraint research in low-constraint naturalistic settings. Compromises are often forced on the evaluator by limitations of the setting. However, program evaluation is a valuable tool in the management of limited resources because ineffective programs spend dollars that could have been spent on effective programs. Program evaluation is both a science and an art. Not only are good research design and statistical analysis skills needed, but also excellent political and communication skills are required. More than any other kind of research project, program evaluation depends on the ability of the researcher to gain the full cooperation of people who are not necessarily committed to the cause of maximizing internal and external validity.

SURVEY RESEARCH _____

Survey research is not a single research design (Schuman & Kalton, 1985). Rather, it is an area of research that utilizes several basic procedures to obtain information from people in their *natural environments.*

The basic instrument used in this research is the *survey,* a set of one or more questions presented to subjects. A survey asks people about their attitudes, beliefs, plans, health, work, income, life satisfactions and concerns, consumer preferences, political views, and so on. Virtually any human issue can be surveyed.

Types of Surveys

Status Survey   A survey can be relatively simple, such as a *status survey* in which the information sought is a description of the current status of some population characteristic. For example, conducting a survey to determine what proportion of voters are Republican, Democrat, or Independent or what proportion of teachers are satisfied with their professions are status surveys. Status surveys were in use as long ago as the nineteenth century in England when some people began investigating working conditions for young children and adults in the mines and factories during the Industrial Revolution.

Survey Research   In contrast to simple status surveys, *survey research* is relatively new, having been developed by social scientists in the twentieth century. It is also a good deal more complex than status surveys, as it seeks not only the current status of population characteristics but also tries to discover relationships among variables. In this sense it is a variation of a correlational research design. For example, survey research could be conducted to determine whether teachers' job satisfaction is related to teacher training, income, age, type of school, grade level taught, and so on. An example is a large-scale survey carried out by Campbell, Converse, and Rodgers (1976) in which they measured the perceptions, evaluations, and satisfactions of Americans to assess the quality of American life. They examined the relationships among demographic variables, such as age, education, income, social class, and the sense of satisfaction that Americans have with critical domains of their lives, such as marriage, jobs, and housing. The researchers were not primarily interested in the *status* of characteristics they measured but in the relationships among the variables.

Steps in Survey Research

Developing the Instrument   The steps involved in survey research are fairly clear, although each step can be quite complex. First, the survey researcher must know the general area of information that is to be obtained and must identify the population from whom to obtain it. For example, in the Campbell et al. (1976) survey the general area studied is Americans' perceived quality of life and the target population is Americans over 18 years of age.

The researcher must determine exactly what questions are to be asked and what other items (such as scales) are to be used. That is, the survey instrument needs to be constructed. It is advisable to pretest the survey to identify and correct ambiguities or confusing items. Developing the survey instrument is often a difficult task. The survey instrument has to be constructed so that it adequately covers the area in which information is sought and the items must be written so that the information can be reliably and validly obtained. The construction of the survey instrument also depends on the procedure to be used in administering it. That is, a face-to-face interview procedure often uses a much more detailed survey instrument than is typical for a telephone survey. The latter usually includes only a few simple items and requires no more than a one- or two-minute telephone conversation. In contrast, personal interview surveys can include many questions, many opportunities for the interviewer to probe for more information, and may require several hours to complete. Construction of an adequate survey instrument can be the most time-consuming step in the survey research process.

Sampling Considerations   Having constructed and tested the survey instrument and identified the population to be studied, the researcher must also specify the sampling procedures. The essential approach of survey research is to draw a *sample* of people from a known population and then to administer the survey directly to each subject. The survey can be administered by mail, telephone, or personal interview. The most information and generally best results are obtained when the survey is administered in a personal, face-to-face interview. In the Campbell et al. (1976) study each of 2164 people was personally interviewed. The personal interview is effective but is also time-consuming and expensive.

Survey information is obtained from a sample but the goal is to learn about the *population* from which the sample is drawn. The survey researcher wants to draw inferences from the procedures and data of the sample in order to be able to describe characteristics of the whole population. Using the terminology developed earlier in the text, whenever we use a sample as a basis for generalizing to a population, we are engaging in a process of inductive inference (from the specific sample to the general population). It should be clear that inductive reasoning is the general process involved in use of inferential statistics. It should also be obvious that, if we are to have confidence in inductive inferences from sample to population, then the sample must be carefully drawn to *represent adequately the population to which we want to infer.* The heart of survey research is the careful selection of representative samples. Without it the results of survey research can tell us only about the sample and are not meaningful or useful in learning about a larger population.

Sampling Procedures Sampling procedures fall into two major categories: (1) nonprobability sampling and (2) probability sampling.

Nonprobability sampling methods include, for example, carrying out a survey by interviewing the first 50 people whom you meet on the street or as many people as you can interview who are coming out of a polling place at election time. Newspaper, TV, and radio surveys are often carried out in this way because a quick public response to an issue needs to be obtained while it is still a current news item. The advantage of nonprobability sampling is the ease with which it can be carried out. Its weakness is that the first 50 people, or whatever other nonprobability sample is obtained, might not be a representative sample of the total population and the survey results might therefore be biased.

Probability sampling procedures give us greater confidence that the sample adequately represents the population to which we want to infer. In probability sampling each population element (i.e., each person) has some known, specifiable probability of being included in the sample. The two major probability sampling methods are simple random sampling and stratified random sampling.

In *simple random sampling* every member of the identified population has an equal chance of being selected. There is no systematic bias in simple random sampling that can lead to persons with certain characteristics having a higher probability of being selected than persons without those characteristics. Simple random sampling, however, requires that we have a list of all members of the population. Clearly this would be difficult to obtain if the population is large, such as all people living in the United States or all children and youth enrolled in primary and secondary schools. With such large populations we cannot use simple random sampling. If the population is more limited, such as all children in a specific school or all psychologists in private practice in a certain city, the initial list (called a *sampling frame*) is much more feasible, and we could randomly select from such sampling frames without much difficulty. Thus, simple random sampling is used for survey research in which population size allows a workable sampling frame from which individuals can be randomly selected. For example, suppose we want to survey 50 of the 317 families in a city who have a mentally retarded child in a special class. The sampling frame would consist of the names of all 317 children. Each would be assigned a number from 1–317 and we would use a table of random numbers to select randomly the sample of 50 families.

Stratified random sampling procedures are used when it is important to ensure that subgroups within a population are adequately represented in the sample. In essence the researcher divides the population into subgroups or strata and a random sample is taken from each stratum. Suppose we want to conduct an in-person, detailed survey on 100 of the 1737 students in McKinley High School. We would not want to bias the results by over- or underrepresenting any groups (e.g., freshmen, sophomores, juniors, seniors, minority students, males, females, and so on). A stratified random sample, drawing randomly from each of the strata, would be used. The number drawn from each stratum would be based on the proportion of students in that stratum in the population. In this way we can have confidence that the sample accurately represents the population, at least on the dimensions on which we stratified the sample.

Sample Size and Confidence Intervals   Having developed the survey instrument and determined the sampling procedure, the researcher must also determine the size of the sample that will be needed. In general larger samples represent populations better than do smaller samples. But exactly how large a sample should be must be determined for each project. Considerations of costs and time are important in determining how large a sample can be handled in a project. But more importantly, the size of the sample needed to represent a population adequately depends on the degree of homogeneity or heterogeneity in the population. In general, if the population is homogeneous, then smaller sample sizes are possible. On the other hand, the more heterogeneous the population, the more diversity there is that must be represented in the sample. Therefore, the sample must be larger to represent that diversity accurately. Thus, in determining how large a sample must be to be representative of the population we must make an estimate of the variability of the characteristics of the population; that is, we estimate the size of the standard deviation of the population for the characteristic we want to measure. With this we can then determine the confidence limits for estimating population characteristics based on the measured sample characteristics. [Methods for calculating required sample size are beyond the scope of this text; interested students are referred to Rossi, Wright, and Anderson (1983).]

Research Design of Surveys

Having developed and tested the survey instrument, determined the population to be surveyed, and drawn the sample, the researcher must also determine the research plan or design to be used in gathering the survey data. Two basic designs are used in survey research: (1) the cross-sectional design and (2) the longitudinal or panel design.

Cross-Sectional Design   *Cross-sectional design* involves administering the survey in "one shot" (once) to a sample, yielding data on the measured characteristics as they exist at the time of the survey. The information can be completely descriptive, such as a status survey, or can involve testing relationships among population characteristics.

A variation of the cross-sectional design allows comparisons to be made of population characteristics at different points in time, such as surveying Americans' perceived quality of life in 1965, 1975, and 1985 to determine whether there have been changes over time. The successive surveys would use independent samples of respondents.

Longitudinal Design The *longitudinal* or *panel design* is a within-subjects survey research design in which the same group or panel of subjects is surveyed successively at different times. Longitudinal surveys make it possible to assess changes over time within individuals. It is often difficult, however, to obtain subjects who are willing to be surveyed several times and often large numbers of subjects drop out of the study before it is completed.

Summary of Survey Research

Survey research is probably the type of social research most familiar to the public. A good deal of important information on a variety of human issues has been gathered through surveys. Because of the central importance of representative sampling, survey researchers have contributed much to the procedures for drawing representative samples from populations.

LONGITUDINAL AND CROSS-SECTIONAL RESEARCH

Research can be categorized as either longitudinal or cross-sectional. Most of the research designs discussed in earlier chapters are cross-sectional. The research designs discussed in this chapter represent longitudinal research. In *cross-sectional research* subjects are measured at only one point in time. In *longitudinal research* subjects are measured at more than one point in time. Longitudinal research is common in developmental psychology where we are interested in changes over time. Much research does not involve changes over time and thus cross-sectional designs are frequently used. Designs such as posttest-only, randomized, control-group designs and differential research designs are examples of cross-sectional research.

SUMMARY

Low-constraint research enables us to observe the natural flow of behavior in natural settings, to try out new procedures, initiate research in new areas of inquiry, negate general propositions, and, most importantly, to observe contingencies and develop hypotheses that can be tested at higher constraint levels. With low-constraint methods, however, we cannot rule out alternative hypotheses and, therefore, cannot test causal hypotheses. In this chapter we return to a discussion of research in naturalistic settings, first presented in Chapter 6. Here, however, we discuss *experimental* research procedures in naturalistic settings with which we are able to test causal hypotheses. Four major topics are discussed: quasi-experimental designs, single-subject designs, program evaluation, and survey research.

Specific quasi-experimental and single-subject designs, as well as their strengths and weaknesses are discussed. Program evaluation involves the use of many of the designs to evaluate the practical effectiveness of programs carried out in naturalistic settings, such as education and therapy programs, public health programs, traffic control, and so on. Although program evaluation is difficult because of many constraints imposed by the natural setting on the researcher, it has become a major area of applied research in the social sciences. Survey research is a large and growing area of research in the natural environment. Researchers directly ask questions of subjects concerning virtually any issue. The heart of survey research is the sampling methods used to insure a representative sample.

REVIEW EXERCISES

I. Define the following key terms. Be sure you understand them. They are discussed in the chapter and defined in the glossary.

Field research
Quasi-experimental design
Nonequivalent control-group design
Difference scores
Crossover effect
Interrupted time-series design
Regression to the mean
Single-subject design
Reversal (ABA) designs
Multiple baseline design
Single-subject, randomized,
   time-series design

Program evaluation
Survey
Status survey
Survey research
Nonprobability sampling
Probability sampling
Simple random sampling
Stratified random sampling
Cross-sectional design
Longitudinal (panel) design
Cross-sectional research
Longitudinal research

II. Answer each of the following. Check your answers in the chapter.

1. Naturalistic research is the focus in Chapter 6 and research in naturalistic (field) settings is the focus in this chapter. How do the research discussed in Chapter 6 and that discussed here differ?

2. What are the reasons why naturalistic research, as discussed in Chapter 6, cannot answer questions of causality?

3. Why would we want to conduct experiments in field settings?

4. Distinguish between applied and basic research. Give at least two examples of each.

5. What are quasi-experimental designs? Under what conditions would we want to use these designs? Give an example.

6. What are the major characteristics of experiments?

7. Name and define the two kinds of quasi-experimental designs discussed in this chapter. Give at least two examples of each.

8. As a review, define *ex post facto* research and discuss its limitations.

9. Under what conditions do we use single-subject designs?

10. What is the major weakness of single-subject designs?

11. What types of single-subject designs are there? Name and define each.

12. Distinguish between longitudinal and cross-sectional research.

13. What is meant by program evaluation?

14. What is the importance of program evaluation?

15. What are the major difficulties in doing program evaluation?

III. Think about and work the following problems.

1. The following graphs represent results in several nonequivalent control-group designs. How do you interpret each? (Assume that the differences are statistically significant.)

* = Control group
O = Experimental group

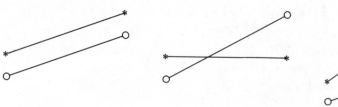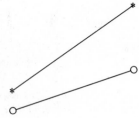

2. How would you interpret the following results of time-series designs?

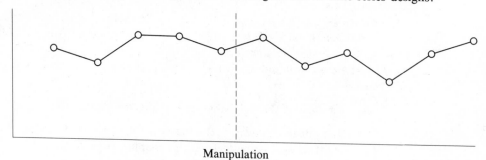

Manipulation
(a)

Manipulation
(b)

3. Explain how we determine causality from single-subject designs.
4. You are the teaching assistant in this course and you have to explain to the class that there are important trade-offs in doing highly controlled experimental research in the laboratory, rather than doing research in field settings. What are the trade-offs? Explain this carefully to the class.

CHAPTER 14

SELECTING APPROPRIATE STATISTICAL PROCEDURES

Research is a systematic process of inquiry. It proceeds across the phases of research from initial ideas through problem definition, design, observation, data processing, interpretation, and communication. At each phase the researcher makes important decisions to design and carry out the research. As explained in Chapter 2, research proceeds not only across the phases of each project but is also carried out at various levels of constraint, ranging from naturalistic research through experimentation. As the level of constraint increases, more is demanded of the researcher and of the procedures used.

The first three phases of research—ideas, definition, and design—involve rational thinking in which we develop and plan the details of the research in preparation for the empirical observation phase. One of the important decisions to be made in the design phase is to determine exactly what statistical procedures to use in analyzing the results. Note two important points. First, the decision about how to analyze data should be made *before* data collection. This demand is relaxed somewhat at the more flexible naturalistic level but becomes increasingly important at higher levels of constraint. Secondly, at higher constraint levels much greater demands are placed on the validity of the procedures, including statistical validity. At the experimental level where causal inferences are to be drawn, we must be particularly careful about the validity of the statistical procedures we will use. In research in general, and particularly at the higher constraint levels, we must carefully plan the details of statistical analyses *before* we make any observations.

Choosing the most valid statistical procedures is often a difficult task for the beginning student. Because there are so many different research designs, a large array of questions that can be asked in each design, and a variety of statistical procedures, students sometimes have difficulty proceeding beyond the data-analysis phase. As illustrated in the accompanying cartoon, sometimes the vast amount of information with which one is faced makes it difficult to know where to focus. But like everything else in research, careful systematic steps can simplify the decisions and bring the process under control. It is this set of decisions—how to select appropriate statistical analyses—that is the focus in this chapter.

AN INITIAL EXAMPLE

As in most aspects of research a systematic approach is needed to select the appropriate statistical procedure. The groundwork for systematic procedures is presented in Chapters 5 and 10–12. Students familiar with the earlier discussions have worked through several research designs and determined what statistical procedures are appropriate.

Appropriate statistical procedures are determined by the characteristics of the research, such as the number of the independent variables, type of relationship studied (e.g., correlational, causal, and so on), and level of measurement for each dependent variable. Thus, in determining what statistics to use we must know in detail the important characteristics of the study. To do this we first carefully describe the study. Let us take an example of a relatively simple study and determine how to analyze it

"You don't often see a real silk lining, these days. . . ."

Drawing by Spencer; © Punch/Rothco. Reprinted by
courtesy of *Punch.*

statistically. Remember, the first step is to describe the research carefully so as to
identify its important characteristics.

Incidental Learning in Rats

An experimenter has hypothesized that laboratory rats can learn incidentally without
specific rewards. Twenty rats are used in the experiment. As a control, all rats are
first exposed to several different mazes for two hours. After the exposure, none of
the animals shows any signs of stress when placed in new mazes. The 20 maze-
adapted animals are randomly assigned to two conditions, 10 animals per condition.
The experimental group is allowed to explore the test maze for one hour, without any
rewards. The control group does not explore the test maze. All animals are then given
learning trials in the test maze and each successful trial is reinforced with food reward.
The experimental and control groups are compared on the number of learning trials
needed to reach a learning criterion of five successive correct trials. The research
hypothesis is that the experimental group, having explored the test maze prior to their
reinforced learning trials, needs significantly fewer learning trials to reach criterion
than does the control group.

Our task is to determine the appropriate statistical procedure to use in the research on learning in rats. The preceding description provides all the information we need. Remember that the characteristics of the research determine what statistical procedures to use. Thus, we need to refer to the description and ask questions that will identify the characteristics of the research.

1. *What is the level of constraint for the research?* Experimental.
2. *What are the independent variables?* There is one independent variable: Exploration of the maze prior to learning trials.
3. *What are the levels of the independent variable?* There are two levels: Prior exploration and no prior exploration.
4. *What type of design is the research* (i.e., independent-groups, correlated-groups, mixed, and so on)? Independent-groups design.
5. *What are the dependent variables?* There is one dependent variable: Maze-learning (i.e., the number of trials needed to reach criterion).
6. *What are the dependent measures* (i.e., how is the dependent variable to be measured)? There is one dependent measure: Number of maze-running trials needed to reach criterion.
7. *What is the level of measurement of the dependent measure?* Ratio.
8. *What type of data is generated for the dependent measure?* Score data (the absolute number of trials).
9. *What is (are) the research hypothesis (hypotheses)?* There is one research hypothesis: The experimental group requires fewer learning trials than the control group to reach criterion.
10. *What kind of test is needed* (i.e., a test of relationship or a test of differences)? A test of differences (i.e., a test of the null hypothesis of no differences between groups).

As we can see, our example study is an independent-groups design in which an hypothesized difference between two groups is tested. There is only one dependent variable, maze-learning, and measuring it yields score data. The appropriate statistical procedure is one that can test differences between independent groups and is typically used for score data. Recall from earlier discussions that the *t*-test for independent groups or the one-way ANOVA are most commonly used.

Before carrying out inferential statistics, it is helpful to calculate descriptive statistics in order to summarize data and give us a first look at the results.

In our simple example the decision about what statistical procedure to use is easily made. In more complex research, where there may be several research hypotheses and several dependent measures, we may need a number of statistical procedures, perhaps a different one for each hypothesis. In such complex research the decisions are not so readily apparent but the procedure to arrive at them is essentially the same: First we describe the research; then we ask a number of questions to identify the important characteristics of the research; finally, we use the characteristics identified and proceed to make decisions to arrive at the appropriate statistical procedures. This sequence of steps has been incorporated into the following discussion of a decision-tree model.

A DECISION-TREE MODEL

The remainder of this chapter focuses on a decision-making model that helps the researcher to organize the process of systematically determining appropriate statistical procedures for complex and simple research designs. The model is called a *decision-tree model*. In this model we follow a line of thinking, reach a decision point, make the decision, and then systematically branch off in appropriate directions based on the decision. These lines of thinking and the branching-off process are organized in five *decision-tree flowcharts,* which are shown below in Figures 14.1–14.5.

To use the model the researcher begins by describing the research, asking questions to identify the major characteristics of the research, and proceeds through the flowcharts until the appropriate statistical procedures are determined. As we move through the flowcharts each decision moves us closer to a particular statistical procedure. The questions to be answered in the decision-tree model are discussed in detail in earlier chapters. There are no new concepts in this chapter; rather, the decision process is made more formal and systematic.

Decision-Tree Flowcharts

In this section we present five decision-tree flowcharts (see Figures 14.1–14.5).[1] Each is an organized sequence of ideas through which the decision-making process flows. Because the procedures discussed may not be clear after a first reading, it is recommended that students reread them and complete the exercises at the end of the chapter until the procedures are understood. In the next section we present an example of research and proceed through the flowcharts to determine the appropriate statistical procedures.

In most research studies more than one research hypothesis is tested and more than one dependent measure is taken to answer questions. Therefore, in most research studies more than one statistical procedure is carried out. Descriptive statistics are first computed for all variables in the study. If there are separate groups, the descriptive statistics are computed for each group. In lower constraint research descriptive statistics may be all that is needed. In higher constraint research, however, we generally have refined the questions and designed the study to answer specific questions about differences between groups. Therefore, at the higher constraint levels we want to use the power of inferential statistics to determine answers to questions. In most cases we cycle through the flowcharts several times to determine appropriate statistical procedures before all questions are answered.

Figures 14.1 through 14.5 present the flowcharts for determining the appropriate statistical procedure. Figure 14.1 shows the overall structure of the decision-tree model; it is the initial flowchart. Figures 14.2 through 14.5 present specific sections of the overall flowchart given in Figure 14.1. Although the flowcharts may look imposing they are easy to follow. To illustrate the process we need to use the flowcharts to determine the set of statistical analyses for a hypothetical study of social problem-solving skills in young children.

[1]The flowcharts are also provided as tear-out sheets in the Study Guide.

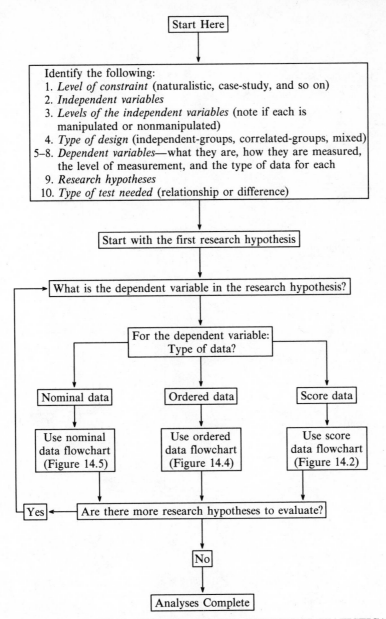

Figure 14.1   INITIAL FLOWCHART FOR SELECTING STATISTICAL ANALYSES

Identifying Research Variables

To use the decision-tree flowcharts we need to identify and organize key aspects of the research design. First, we must describe the research. Then we must identify its major characteristics, such as the level of constraint, the research hypothesis, the independent variables and their levels and types (manipulated or nonmanipulated), and the depen-

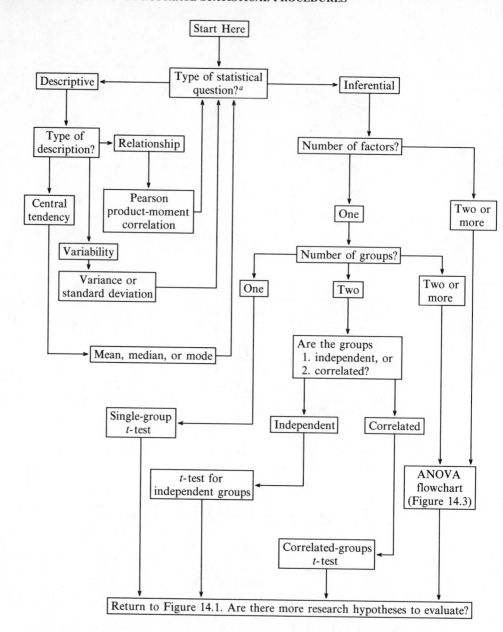

^aIt is best to start with descriptive statistics.

Figure 14.2 SCORE DATA FLOWCHART FOR SELECTING STATISTICAL ANALYSES

dent variables and the level of measurement for each. A simple list of relevant factors helps to organize the analysis of data from the study.

Our hypothetical research study is of social problem-solving skills in sixth-grade children using several different measures. We are interested in comparing boys and girls

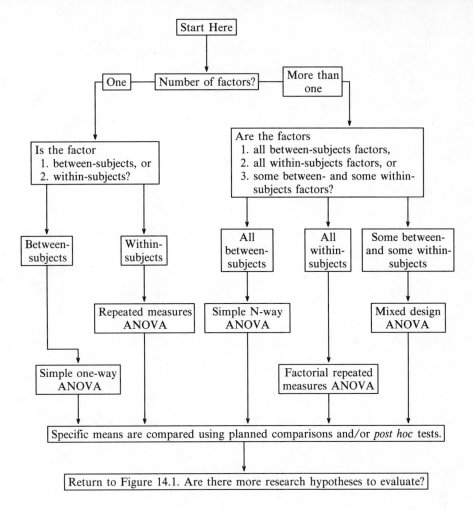

Note: Most formulas for the various ANOVAs and related statistical tests can be found in Appendix C. For additional computational procedures, consult an advanced statistics text (e.g., Myers, 1972; Winer, 1971).

Figure 14.3   ANOVA FLOWCHART FOR SELECTING STATISTICAL ANALYSES

in their problem-solving skills. The research is considerably more complex than the animal learning study presented earlier. For example, instead of only one research hypothesis, this study tests several research hypotheses. Thus, we need to determine several statistical analyses rather than only one. No matter how complex the study may be, the procedures for determining an appropriate statistical analysis are the same as in the simpler example:

1. Describe the study.
2. Identify the study's major characteristics.
3. Make systematic decisions, but now using the flowcharts.

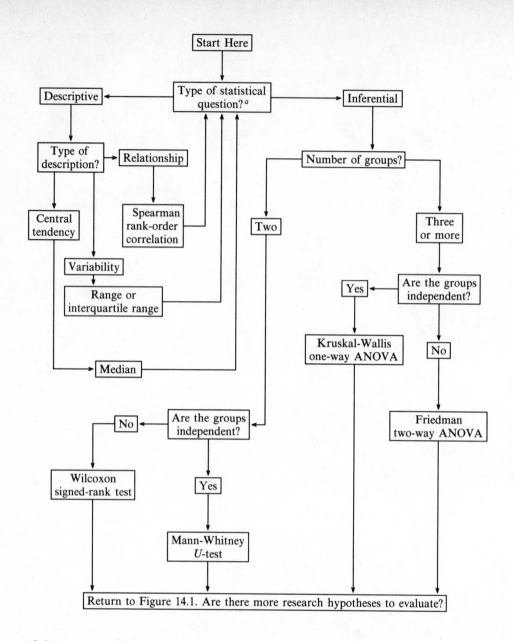

Start Here

Type of statistical question?[a]

Descriptive

Inferential

Type of description?

Relationship

Number of groups?

Central tendency

Spearman rank-order correlation

Two

Three or more

Variability

Are the groups independent?

Range or interquartile range

Yes

No

Median

Kruskal-Wallis one-way ANOVA

Are the groups independent?

Friedman two-way ANOVA

No

Wilcoxon signed-rank test

Yes

Mann-Whitney U-test

Return to Figure 14.1. Are there more research hypotheses to evaluate?

[a] It is best to start with descriptive statistics.

Note: Computational formulas for the statistical procedures described here can be found in Siegel (1956).

Figure 14.4   ORDERED DATA FLOWCHART FOR SELECTING STATISTICAL ANALYSES

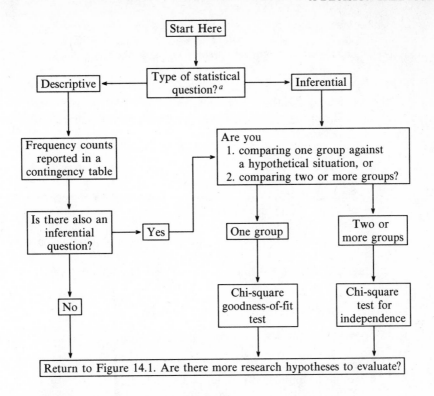

^a It is best to start with descriptive statistics.

Figure 14.5 NOMINAL DATA FLOWCHART FOR SELECTING STATISTICAL ANALYSES

Sex Differences in Children's Social Problem-Solving Skills

The study compares sixth-grade boys and girls on their problem-solving skills in social situations. Twenty boys and 20 girls are randomly selected from the sixth grade of a local grammar school.

Three different measures are taken in the study. In the first measure subjects are tested individually. Ten social situations are described to each subject. In each of these situations one or more social problems or conflicts will be included (e.g., another student pushes ahead in line). Three ways to solve the conflict are described for each situation and the subject is asked to choose one of the three solutions (i.e., a multiple-choice test). For each problem one solution is clearly most socially appropriate and, therefore, is considered to be the correct answer. Each subject's score is the number of correct choices for the ten social situations. The task is presented to the children on audiotape with a coordinated filmstrip to standardize the presentation and to maximize the children's attention.

The second dependent measure is teacher's ranking of the children on social competence. The ranking is based on observations of the children's behavior in three different settings—in the structured classroom, in an unstructured social activity within the classroom, and during recess.

For the third dependent measure an independent rater classifies each of the children as either "generally competent socially" or "generally incompetent socially" based on standardized information provided by the teachers.

The research focuses on sex differences in problem-solving skills. The statement of the problem is: "Is there a sex difference in problem-solving skills for sixth-grade children?" The problem statement combined with operational definitions leads to three research hypotheses:

1. Sixth-grade boys and girls differ in the identification of the correct social response in a multiple-choice task.
2. Sixth-grade boys and girls differ in their ranking on social competence based on observations in three behavior settings.
3. Sixth-grade boys and girls differ in the proportion classified as either "generally socially competent" or "generally socially incompetent."

Having described the study, the next step is to identify its major characteristics.

Identifying Major Characteristics of the Study

1. *Level of constraint?* Differential (i.e., differences between two preexisting groups).
2. *Independent variables?* There is one independent variable: The sex of subjects. It is a nonmanipulated independent variable.
3. *Levels of the independent variable?* There are two levels of the independent variable: Boys and girls.
4. *Type of design?* Independent-groups, differential design.
5–8. *Dependent variable(s)?* There are three dependent variables (5). Their measures are listed below (6), along with the level of measurement for each (7), and the type of data generated by each measure (8).

Dependent Measure	Level of measurement	Type of data
a. Score on the social-skills multiple-choice test.	Ratio	Score
b. Ranking of subjects on social competence.	Ordinal	Ordered
c. Independent classification of social competence.	Nominal	Nominal

9. *Research hypotheses?* There are three research hypotheses:
   a. Sixth-grade boys and girls differ in the identification of the correct social response in a multiple-choice task.
   b. Sixth-grade boys and girls differ in their ranking on social competence based on observations in three behavior settings.
   c. Sixth-grade boys and girls differ in the proportion classified as either "generally socially competent" or "generally socially incompetent."
10. *What kind of test is needed?* For each hypothesis a test of differences between independent groups is needed.

As we can see, the study is a differential, independent-groups design with two levels of the nonmanipulated independent variable. The dependent measures generate three different levels of data. Therefore, different statistical procedures are used to analyze data from each dependent measure. In the study hypothesized differences between groups are tested.

Selecting Appropriate Descriptive and Inferential Statistics

After the major characteristics of the study are identified, the next step is to determine the appropriate procedures for descriptive statistics and inferential statistics for each of the three hypotheses. It is most often useful to begin with descriptive statistics.

Statistical Procedures for the First Hypothesis   For the first hypothesis in our hypothetical study, the multiple-choice test is the dependent measure. We start by calculating *descriptive statistics* and do so for each of the two groups (boys and girls) separately. The flowcharts help us select the appropriate statistics. By turning our attention to the initial flowchart (Figure 14.1) we see that we have already accomplished the first task, identifying the major characteristics of the study. Therefore, we move down the flowchart and begin with the first research hypothesis. The first hypothesis is: "Sixth grade boys and girls differ in the identification of the correct social response in a multiple-choice task." The dependent variable for the hypothesis is the social-skills multiple-choice test. We follow Figure 14.1 to the point where the flowchart inquires, "For the dependent variable: Type of data?" As we have already determined, the type of data for this dependent variable is score data. Therefore, following the flowchart we find that for score data we are directed to use the score data flowchart (Figure 14.2).

We are interested in descriptive statistics at this point, so we move to the left branch of Figure 14.2. Here we are asked, "Type of description?" Normally for score data we want both a measure of central tendency and a measure of variability. The flowchart tells us that the mean, median, and mode are appropriate measures of central tendency and the variance and standard deviation are appropriate measures of variability for score data. We ordinarily compute only the mean as the measure of central tendency. Thus, the mean, variance, and standard deviation are computed as the descriptive statistics for each of the two groups.

Now that we have determined the appropriate descriptive statistics for the first hypothesis, we turn to *inferential statistics* for the first hypothesis. The score data flowchart (Figure 14.2) directs us back to the box asking, "Type of statistical question?" We are interested in an inferential question, so we branch to the right in Figure 14.2, where it asks for the number of factors. Because we have one factor (the independent variable—sex), we follow that branch to where it asks for the number of groups. Because we have two groups (boys and girls), we can go in either of two directions. The rightmost branch takes us to a simple one-way analysis of variance (see Figure 14.3). The middle branch leads us eventually to a *t*-test (for independent groups). In this instance, both are correct procedures for the analyses and lead to the same conclusions about differences between the groups. Having selected an inferential statistical procedure for the first research hypothesis, we return to Figure 14.1. Thus, we determine that for hypothesis 1 we calculate means, variances, and standard deviations as descriptive statistics and use an independent-groups t-test or a simple one-way ANOVA for the inferential statistic.

Statistical Procedures for Other Hypotheses   As we move down the initial flowchart (Figure 14.1), we are asked whether there are more research hypotheses to evaluate. Because there are, we look to the middle portion of the flowchart where it asks, "What is the dependent variable in the research hypothesis?" We identify the variable and move down to where it asks what type of data it represents. For the second research hypothesis, the dependent measure is the teacher's rankings of the children's social competence (ordered data). The flowchart tells us to consult Figure 14.4, the ordered data flowchart. We are interested in descriptive statistics, so we branch to the left and are informed that the median is an appropriate measure of central tendency and the range or the interquartile range is the appropriate measure of variability for ordered data. Having determined the appropriate descriptive statistics for the second research hypothesis, we now turn to the inferential statistics. We follow the flowchart back to the box asking, "Type of statistical question?" We branch right to find an appropriate inferential statistical procedure. If we follow the flowchart correctly (for two independent groups), it will suggest a Mann-Whitney U-test.

The third research hypothesis uses a dependent variable that is measured on a nominal scale, and we are therefore directed by the initial flowchart to use Figure 14.5 (the nominal data flowchart). If we follow the flowchart correctly, we determine that frequency counts in a contingency table is an appropriate descriptive statistic. Likewise, an appropriate inferential procedure is a chi-square test for independence.

If our study were a larger study with more research hypotheses, we would continue this process of using the flowcharts to find the correct descriptive and inferential statistics and compute the statistics for all remaining dependent measures in the study. The example illustrates the need to be well organized during the work because of the many different decisions to be made. Carefully labeling the results will minimize errors during later analyses and report-writing. The study is not particularly complicated for a research study. Most research studies employ more than one measure and test more than one research hypothesis. Although computers can simplify the task of computation, the researcher still needs to decide what statistics to compute, and to label and organize the computer output carefully to avoid later confusion or error.

It is important for students to use the flowcharts with other research examples. With practice, students will become familiar with the rules in the flowcharts and eventually will not need to refer to them. Indeed, that is a goal. But, initially, when learning to make decisions, the flowcharts provide a convenient way to organize necessary information when selecting a statistical procedure.

Secondary Analyses

After completing descriptive and inferential analyses, we often carry out secondary analyses. *Secondary analyses* typically fall into three categories: (1) *post hoc* analyses, or planned comparisons to look at specific mean differences after conducting an overall ANOVA; (2) analyses designed to help explain the pattern of results; or (3) unplanned exploratory analyses (sometimes referred to as data snooping).

***Post hoc* Analyses**   When doing an ANOVA with more than two groups, specific mean comparisons are the logical next step in the interpretation of significant F ratios. The significant F in a one-way ANOVA, for example, tells us only that at least one of the means is significantly different from at least one other mean. It does not tell us which means are different from which other means. Most often, the interpretation requires this more specific information, which can be provided by a variety of *post hoc* tests or planned comparisons.

Secondary Analyses to Help Explain Results   Another set of secondary analyses involve looking at variables that may help to explain the observed set of results. Suppose that differences are found but that they are difficult to interpret because we cannot be sure some confounding variable was adequately controlled. This kind of problem is less common in experimental research because the high level of control minimizes potential confounding. In lower constraint research, particularly in differential research, these issues can be real problems and secondary analyses are often essential to interpret data adequately.

A set of secondary analyses that should be included in the report of any research project regardless of its level of constraint are descriptive statistics on the demographic characteristics of the sample of subjects (e.g., age, social class, level of education, and so on). These statistics allow us to compare different studies in terms of the populations being studied. They also give us information needed to determine the limits of generalizability of the findings.

These are only some of the uses of secondary statistical analyses to help interpret findings of a primary analysis. Some of the analyses in this category are quite sophisticated and beyond the scope of this text. It is important to realize, however, that in many lower constraint research studies the secondary analyses may far outnumber the primary analyses and be as important in terms of interpreting results of the study.

Data Snooping   The third set of secondary analyses are what we have called *data snooping*. Here researchers can play their hunches and see whether, for example, there are any relationships, differences, or interactions that were not predicted. Data snooping is useful in large-scale, lower constraint studies where clues to many potential relationships between variables may be buried in the mass of data. Good data snooping is as much an art as a science. However, it is important to note that one must be cautious in interpreting relationships discovered in such a *post hoc* treasure hunt. Even though we must be cautious, data snooping is a rich source of hypotheses for later research and it should not be overlooked. At least one high level text is devoted entirely to this art (Tukey, 1977).

Caveats and Disclaimers

The flowchart system outlined in this chapter is designed as a teaching device—a way to organize and formalize what is often a difficult task for students. The inferential statistics portion of this system focuses on the kinds of questions asked most often in psychological hypotheses—specifically, are there mean differences between groups on the dependent measure? There are other kinds of questions—such as, "Are there differences in the variability between the groups?"—that are not covered by the set of

Box 14.1 THE ROBUST NATURE OF PARAMETRIC STATISTICS

At several points in the text it is noted that statistical tests make certain assumptions about data. For example, an implicit assumption of parametric statistics (e.g., *t*-test, ANOVA) is that data are on at least an interval level of measurement (score data). But most parametric tests make several other assumptions about data, which are not highlighted in the text because they are not critical. Sometimes an assumption on which an inferential statistical procedure is based can be violated without threatening the validity of the conclusion drawn from the statistical test. In such a case, we say that the statistical procedure is *robust* to violations of the assumption. For example, many statistical tests assume that scores in the population are distributed normally (i.e., they form a symmetric bell-shaped distribution). If the population of scores is actually skewed, we have violated an assumption of the statistical test. If that statistical procedure is *not robust* to this assumption, the violation leads to distortions in the procedure and makes any conclusions drawn from the statistical analysis suspect. Fortunately, most parametric statistics are robust to violations of assumptions about population distributions. We can use them confidently regardless of the shape of the distributions.

As it turns out, most parametric statistics are quite robust to violations of almost all assumptions on which they are based. It is especially true if the sample size in each of the groups is approximately equal (Glass, Peckham, & Sanders, 1972). The conclusion is based on a series of computer simulation studies known as *Monte Carlo studies* (named after the famous gambling resort). In a Monte Carlo study the computer is used to simulate sampling of subjects from populations with known characteristics. In this way the researcher can see what effect violations of certain assumptions have on the accuracy of decisions. The approach has been used to investigate the effects of violations of single assumptions or violations of more than one assumption at the same time (Levy, 1980). The procedures continue to show remarkable robustness of most statistics to assumption violations *when sample sizes are equal*. Consequently, these assumptions are not emphasized in the text and are not built into the decision rules of the flowcharts.

Note the emphasis above on equal sample sizes. Unless sample sizes of groups are approximately equal, violations of assumptions may affect the validity of statistical procedures. Hence, from a design perspective, particularly for the novice researcher, it is beneficial to try to have approximately equal sample sizes.

flowcharts. For such questions other reference sources need to be consulted (Runyon & Haber, 1980; Shavelson, 1981). However, for a large majority of the typical questions investigated in psychological research the flowcharts will identify an appropriate statistical procedure to use.

The statistical procedures suggested by the flowcharts are not the only appropriate procedures for answering a specific question. In almost all cases there are alternative data-analysis approaches available. The statistical procedures given in Figures 14.1–14.5 are the ones most commonly used in these situations, but other procedures may also be appropriate. Therefore, the flowcharts are more helpful in finding a statistical procedure to use in a study than in evaluating whether a particular statistical approach used by some other researcher is appropriate. (See Box 14.1.)

SUMMARY

Selecting an appropriate statistical procedure is often one of the most confusing steps in the research process for beginning students. A flowchart system is presented that organizes for students a process of selecting appropriate statistical procedures. The flowchart system requires that students begin by describing the major characteristics of the research study—a process with which students should be familiar. Information from the summary is used to answer a series of questions, which lead students step-by-step toward the selection of appropriate statistical procedures. The flowcharts help to organize this task. A major goal is for students to learn the decision-making procedures so that eventually the flowcharts will not be needed.

REVIEW EXERCISES

I. Define the following key terms. Be sure you understand them. They are discussed in the chapter and defined in the glossary.

Decision-tree model
Decision-tree flowcharts
Descriptive statistics
Inferential statistics

Secondary analyses
Post hoc analyses
Data snooping
Robust

II. Answer each of the following. Check your answers in the chapter.

1. What does it mean when we say that a statistical test is robust to a particular assumption?
2. What measures are available to quantify relationships among variables? When should each of the measures be used?
3. What are the major measures of central tendency and variability?
4. What is the difference between a planned comparison and a *post hoc* test? (If necessary, refer to Chapter 10.)
5. In what situation can the researcher use either a *t*-test or an ANOVA to compare group means?

III. Think about and work the following problems.

For each of the following situations study the research plan and identify:
    a. Level of constraint
    b. Independent variable(s)
    c. Levels of independent variables
    d. Type of design
    e. Dependent variable(s)
    f. Dependent measure(s)
    g. Level of measurement for each dependent measure
    h. Type of data generated from each dependent measure

       i. Research hypotheses

       j. Kind of statistical test that is appropriate for the research hypothesis

Use the flowcharts to identify the following for each hypothesis:

       k. Appropriate descriptive statistics

       l. Appropriate inferential statistic(s)

1. Thirty hypertensive subjects are randomly assigned to three groups of ten each. Group 1 is taught muscle relaxation training. Group 2 is taught cognitive relaxation training. Group 3 is a no-treatment control. After the manipulation, blood-pressure readings are taken on all subjects. Blood pressure is represented by two numbers. The systolic blood pressure represents the maximum blood pressure at the point that the heart is actually beating. The diastolic blood pressure represents the minimum blood pressure between beats. Both are measured in terms of the number of millimeters of mercury that can be pushed up in a column by the pressure. The researcher wants to know (a) whether relaxation training reduces hypertension and (b) whether one type of relaxation training is more effective than the other.

2. A researcher has the hypothesis that (a) people with phobias are particularly sensitive to minor levels of stimulation and (b) females with phobias are particularly sensitive. Three hundred college freshmen are given a fear survey questionnaire. Fifty of the 300 students have high phobia scores. From the nonphobic subjects, 30 females and 20 males are randomly selected. Thus, a group of 50 (30 female, 20 male) phobics and a group of 50 (30 female, 20 male) nonphobic subjects are constructed. All subjects are tested on their sensitivity to minimal stimuli, a task that yields a simple score of the number of correct responses.

3. In a study of the effects of teacher feedback on accuracy of performance, ten children (five males and five females) are tested under three different conditions: immediate feedback, delayed feedback, and no feedback. All ten children are included in each condition. The order of presentation of feedback conditions is counterbalanced. The children are tested on their reading accuracy (the number of reading errors is counted).

4. The study focuses on the effects of smiling on children's evaluation of adults and on accuracy of learning and recall. Thirty children (15 males and 15 females) are randomly assigned to three conditions. Each condition presented a videotape showing a teacher reading a story. The same teacher and the same story are used in each condition. In the first condition the teacher smiles 60 percent of the time. In the second condition the teacher smiles 30 percent of the time and in the third condition the teacher does did not smile. After viewing the tape, the children are given (a) a learning test scored on the number of correct answers to questions about the story, and (b) a rating on a 1–5 scale of how much they like the teacher (assume an ordinal scale). Two weeks later the children are tested for retention of material from the story (scored on the number of correct answers to questions about the story).

5. A psychiatric survey is conducted in a large metropolitan area. A random sample of 2000 residents is chosen. Each resident is interviewed and diagnosed

into one of six categories as follows: (a) well—no psychiatric symptoms; (b) mild—mild psychiatric symptoms but person is functioning adequately; (c) moderate—some symptoms but little apparent interference with life adjustment; (d) impaired—moderate symptoms with some interference in life adjustment; (e) severe—serious symptoms, functioning but with great difficulty; (f) incapacitated—seriously impaired, unable to function. The number of people from each social class is calculated for each category.

6. Thirty parent/child pairs are involved in a research study focusing on fear. Three hypotheses are tested in the study: (a) the number of fears reported by the parent is correlated with the number of fears reported by the child; (b) the degree of fear reported by the parent is correlated with the degree of fear reported by the child; (c) the number of fears and the degree of fear reported by both the parent and the child are reduced by the introduction of a fear-reduction program. Both parent and child are given a fear survey schedule, which measures the number of fears reported. In addition, both parent and child are rated on an index of fear severity with a range of 1–7 (assume the rating scale is an ordinal scale). After the initial measures, parents are randomly assigned to one of two groups: one group receives a fear-reduction program whereas the other group receives no treatment. At the end of this part of the study the fear survey schedule and the rating scale of fear intensity are readministered to all parents.

CHAPTER 15

RESEARCH METHODOLOGY
An Evolving Discipline

NEW DIRECTIONS IN RESEARCH METHODOLOGY
New Questions and New Methods
SCIENCE: AN INTERACTION BETWEEN EMPIRICISM
   AND RATIONALISM
REVIEW EXERCISE

In this text, the concept of research is presented as an active thinking process of asking and answering questions in which constant interplay takes place between inductive and deductive thinking. Few rules for students are presented because it is believed that rules tend to oversimplify the tasks of designing, conducting, evaluating, and interpreting research findings. Research is a process of inquiry. The methods selected to answer any particular question depend on many factors, including practical and ethical constraints and the desire to get the most precise answer possible given the question being explored. Many traditional methods of research used in psychology and in other biological and social sciences are presented. Basic concepts, such as validity, threats to validity, and control, are presented from a conceptual perspective and designs are explained in terms of these concepts.

The research approaches discussed in this text are by no means all inclusive. Many other research approaches have been and continue to be used in answering questions about behavior. As noted earlier, there is no single "best way" of answering a question in science. The approaches that are most effective for answering a question will largely depend on the kind of question asked. However, regardless of the kinds of questions asked or the procedures used to answer them, there are defined phases in every research project. The research begins with a general idea that is carefully refined into a specific question or problem. Procedures are selected, modified, and adapted to answer particular questions raised. Observations are made and data are analyzed using statistical procedures. Finally, data are interpreted and results and conclusions are communicated to other professionals. Regardless of the level of sophistication of the research method or the type of question asked, the phases of research remain the same.

Another idea emphasized throughout the text is the concept of levels of constraint. It is argued that good research can be conducted at many different levels of constraint. In this respect we differ from some of our colleagues who argue that the best and most effective way of answering a question is always with experimental research. It is agreed that experimental research does provide a more unambiguous answer to a causal question than do other levels of research. However, many questions of interest to psychologists cannot be answered with experimental research. Under some conditions, manipulating variables may be outside the practical control of the experimenter or may represent severe ethical violations. These restrictions, however, make the question no less worthwhile. Therefore, a significant portion of the text is devoted to the concepts and procedures of what is labeled lower constraint research. It should be emphasized again that low-constraint research methods are not considered sloppy research. Instead, they are considered appropriate and useful procedures for answering certain kinds of questions. Low-constraint research procedures are especially important in the early stages of a research program, in which the flexibility of low-constraint methods makes it more likely that we will be able to gather the breadth of data needed to understand the broad conceptual issues being addressed by the project. Remember, too, that at all levels of constraint we study relationships among variables. The types of relationships studied differ from one level of constraint to another (i.e., contingent relationships, predictive relationships, differences between groups, and causal relationships). But at all levels of constraint we seek to understand relationships among variables.

NEW DIRECTIONS IN RESEARCH METHODOLOGY

Science is continually evolving as new questions are raised and new people become involved in the process of finding answers to these questions. As science evolves, so does its methodology. New research methods are developed in every science and old methods are revised and updated to meet the needs and curiosity of scientists. New perspectives on a question create new problems and the various disciplines search for techniques to find the answers.

New Questions and New Methods

The Evolution of Research Questions and Methods   Changes in methods used to study a problem evolve slowly over many years as questions change. Different methods are used to study any given problem and to answer proposed questions. As answers to questions are found, new issues and new questions arise, which may require new methodologies. Therefore, the methods used in a research area change as original questions are answered and new questions are formulated.

An example is the historical sequence of the study of genetic influences on schizophrenia. One of the initial questions asked whether genetic factors contribute to schizophrenia. Subsequent clinical observations *suggested* that schizophrenia runs in families but the observations were informal and less than systematic. In time, more precisely controlled research was carried out and verified the initial clinical observations. Verification was accomplished through differential research in which the rates of schizophrenia were carefully measured in samples of families of schizophrenic patients and control families (families of nonschizophrenics). But, as you may have recognized, a major confounding variable (environmental influences) was uncontrolled in the studies. That is, the higher frequency of schizophrenia in the families of schizophrenics might have been caused by either genetic influences or environmental conditions. Research methods were needed to separate the influences of genetics and environment. One of the ways developed was to study patients who had been adopted as infants and later became schizophrenic. The patients had a set of relatives who shared their genetic heritage (their biological relatives) and a set of relatives who shared their environment (their adoptive relatives). The rates of schizophrenia in each of these sets of relatives indicated the contributions of genetics and environment to the development of schizophrenia. The studies showed that schizophrenia is more likely in the biological relatives than in the adoptive relatives of schizophrenic patients who had been adopted at birth. Data from such studies answered the initial question and made it clear that genetics plays an important role in the development of schizophrenia.

With that question answered, new questions were raised. For example, if genetics plays a role, what role is it and what is the role of other factors in the eventual development of the disorder? The new question was addressed by looking back into the developmental histories of schizophrenics for clues. But this is an *ex post facto* approach to research and it does not allow us to test any causal hypotheses. A better method was needed. Because it was known that genetics strongly influenced schizophrenia, Mednick and Schulsinger (1968) suggested studying individuals who are genetically related to schizophrenics—the offspring of schizophrenic mothers. The approach was called "high-risk research" because the subjects identified for study had a much higher risk of developing schizophrenia than did an unselected sample.

The example illustrates how questions help shape research designs. Studies designed to answer one question often raise other questions in the process. The new questions sometimes require new research approaches, which are often created by scientists as a byproduct of a "need to know" the answer. We cannot predict what the next major research approach in the study of the genetics of schizophrenia will be. It will be selected and/or created as the need develops, and the need to do so will be shaped by answers to current questions. But the principles behind any new research approach in this area will be the same principles underlying the designs discussed in the current text.

The Impact of Other Disciplines Developments in related disciplines can have a significant positive impact on the discipline of psychology. One of the best examples is the study of neurological influences on human behavior.

Developments in the field of biochemistry, which permitted much finer analyses of organic chemicals, made possible the discovery that there are many more neurotransmitters involved in the functioning of the central nervous system than previously believed. This explosion in the number of known chemical transmission agents required scientists to rethink the role of neurotransmitters. The concept of specific transmitter influences in precise locations within the brain and other parts of the central nervous system became a much more intellectually appealing theory. But how do we study specific influences of specific neurotransmitters in specific locations in the brain? Much of the previous research on neurotransmitters operated under the assumption that there are general levels of the chemicals in the system, and the procedures used for measuring the chemicals were usually nonspecific with respect to the location of the action of each transmitter. There was a need to develop techniques to sample from specific locations within the brain. Because brain-functioning processes are part of the living organism and not only a matter of the structure of the organism, one had to accomplish the sampling without damaging the organism. A sampling of brain tissue at autopsy would provide little information useful to the new questions. Even more importantly, it would be enormously helpful if some experimental procedure could be developed for specifically manipulating neurotransmitters at specific locations. A procedure known as *microiontophoresis* (Curtis & Crawford, 1969) was developed that allowed the researcher to inject specific amounts of certain neurotransmitters into the synapses of individual neurons while the animal was awake and functioning. For the first time this new technology offered the possibility of using experimental methods to investigate the relationship between neurotransmitters applied to specific locations of the brain and their effect on the behavior of living organisms. As is always the case in science, these new techniques are providing the answers to some important questions and in the process are raising yet more questions that demand still newer techniques. Here the developments in one science, biochemistry, have affected research in another science, psychology.

Multidisciplinary Research As a science grows there is increasing specialization so that researchers seem to work in ever more narrow areas. Such specialization is important as it focuses the researcher's efforts on specific problems and allows the development of sophisticated approaches to problems. With such specific details established, researchers can then turn to integrating the information into a broader understanding. In this endeavor we find researchers from different disciplines coming together to pool their knowledge in interdisciplinary research projects.

An example of this interdisciplinary approach is the newly emerging area of *behavioral medicine.* The field has brought together physicians, researchers in neurology, physiology, and several different areas of psychology. Another example is the interdisciplinary research integrating sociology, law, and psychology (Levine, 1974, 1980; Levine & Howe, 1985). Still another example is the rapidly growing field of *artificial intelligence.* In this interdisciplinary field, mathematicians, psychologists, and computer scientists developed models of thinking that can be programmed on computers to solve complex problems. We expect interdisciplinary research to continue to increase and to provide greater integrations in the understanding of human functioning.

Moving Research out of the Laboratory Many psychologists are rediscovering old methods as a result of their concern for external validity in current research approaches. For example, naturalistic and case-study research is becoming more common in many areas that previously relied almost exclusively on higher constraint research. Mark Freeman (1984) argues that understanding the development of a person requires that we take a historical perspective, noting the developmental influences that color his or her current perspective on life. The more individualized approach to developmental psychology is different from what has been the tradition over the last few decades. It reinforces the point made throughout the text—lower constraint research is a legitimate way of looking at certain research questions and, from some perspectives, may even be the best way to study a phenomenon.

Also, as discussed in Chapter 13, well-controlled experiments can be carried out in natural settings. The effects of natural events on human behavior, large-scale interventions such as Head Start programs, and policy decisions such as seat-belt laws are best studied in real-world settings. In response to demands for such real world information researchers have increased their research efforts in natural settings. Conducting research in natural settings is difficult and challenging but the reward of good generalization of results to other real-world settings makes the effort worthwhile.

The Impact of Computers In a relatively short period of time computers have had a major impact on research. Perhaps not since the Industrial Revolution has so much changed so quickly. In a fascinating book Christopher Evans (1979), an experimental psychologist and computer scientist, points out some of the reasons for the monumental growth of computer technology. One reason is the enormous increase in the efficiency of modern computers. Since their introduction, computers have become much more powerful, more reliable, and less expensive and require far less energy to operate. Today's typical desk-top computer can perform all the functions of a 1950's computer that had to be housed in five floors of a large building—and today's computer will do the work far more rapidly and more reliably. Dr. Evans (1979) dramatizes the pace of improvement with an analogy:

Suppose for a moment that the automobile industry had developed at the same rate as computers [over the last 30 years]. . . . Today you would be able to buy a Rolls-Royce for $2.75, it would do three million miles to the gallon, and it would deliver enough power to drive the Queen Elizabeth II. And if you were interested in miniaturization, you could place half a dozen of them on the head of a pin. (p. 76)

In the few years since these words were written, the pace of computer development has quickened. Dr. Evans' comparison now would allow you to buy a Rolls-Royce for a few pennies.

Computers have become as common in psychological laboratories as typewriters in offices. The introduction of computers to the laboratory has meant a dramatic increase in efficiency. Some tasks that once took an enormous amount of time can now be done in only minutes. The most obvious benefactor of this improved efficiency is the data-analysis phase. Students who have worked through something as complex as a two-way ANOVA on a pocket calculator can appreciate the time savings of computer analyses. The computer can run ten thousand or more analyses in less time than it takes most people to compute a simple mean from a data sample. The increased efficiency has allowed the development of complex and labor intensive analysis procedures, such as multivariate ANOVAs and factor analyses, which use complex computational techniques to obtain precise estimates of population parameters. This has created an explosion in the number and sophistication of analysis procedures. We may be reaching the limit of this growth in data analysis, however, not because computers cannot do the computations but because humans may not be able to comprehend the results. For example, the computer can easily analyze a factorial study with a dozen or more factors. The mathematical formulas for computation are easily generalized to more complex designs and computers can perform the computations quickly. But few people can actually visualize and understand the meaning of, for example, a five-way interaction— five different factors combining in a unique way to affect the dependent variable.

Such development in computerized data analysis may also have created some problems. Perhaps data analysis has become too easy and some of the care that used to be exercised on the design and execution of studies may have been lost. A colleague worked her way through graduate school in the early 1950s by conducting factor analyses. The analyses were carried out using the most modern calculating instruments of the time, mechanical calculators. A typical analysis required nine months of working 20 hours per week to complete. Today, the same analysis is completed by a computer in less than a second and costs only a few pennies. The entire analysis can be set up by a knowledgeable student in a few minutes. When an analysis takes nine months to complete and costs thousands of dollars, one makes sure that the data being analyzed are as precise and accurate as possible and that the analysis is appropriate for the data available and the question(s) being asked. It is not clear whether the same care goes into these aspects of the research now that the analyses are so easy and inexpensive to accomplish.

Despite such potential problems, there are other ways in which the computer can improve the efficiency and quality of psychological research. Laboratories are now beginning to use computers to interact with and to gather data from subjects. This may reduce the number of experimenter errors that can result in lost or distorted data. The computer can carry out complex procedures flawlessly for one subject after another.

This also has the potential of minimizing experimenter bias. Computers can take and record measures in a completely objective manner, they can present stimuli to different groups of subjects in exactly the same way, and they can perform all of these tasks in a perfectly replicated manner in study after study.

Some common laboratory paradigms in use today would not be possible without the aid of computers. The computer is not limited to simply presenting stimuli in a single predetermined sequence. Rather, it is capable of recording the responses of subjects, evaluating the responses, and choosing the next stimulus to present based on subjects' responses. This permits us to test much more complex hypotheses than are possible with a static presentation of a given set of stimuli. Of course, mechanical equipment that is responsive to the subject in a study has been available for years. The Skinner box is the best known example. What the computer adds is an expansion of the range and level of complexity of response. It also dramatically simplifies the task of modifying procedures to test new hypotheses. With the old mechanical equipment, modifying procedures often meant physically changing the equipment or designing and building new equipment. With computer-controlled studies, often little more than software changes are required.

The computer also may offer us some totally new ways of understanding phenomena. An example of such a new approach is the computer modeling of cognitive processes (Marr, 1982). Computer modeling is an idea that is borrowed and adapted from the artificial intelligence field. In artificial intelligence computers are programmed to behave intelligently, to solve problems, and to react to stimuli. When building artificial intelligence systems we are not particularly interested in duplicating human functioning. However, when building computer models of cognitive functions we do attempt to duplicate human functions. Instead of developing complex abstract models of cognitive processes and designing factorial studies too complicated for anyone to understand, we create a computer model of functioning that we can manipulate to observe the effects of manipulation. The goal in computer modeling is to find a model that can reproduce exactly what we see in human behavior in comparable situations. The idea is directly analogous to using scale models of airplanes and testing them in wind tunnels. We have theories and formulas that predict how certain factors will affect the aerodynamics of an airplane. However, so many factors come into play in real-life situations that we can make only educated guesses about what would happen to a real airplane. But with a model and the wind tunnel to simulate flight conditions, we can actually test our guesses and fine-tune a system that has become so complex that it strains the limits of human understanding. We may soon be able to accomplish similar goals with computer models of cognitive functioning.

The impact of computers on psychological research is only beginning to be felt. The directions for the future will be shaped by the inventiveness of the scientists of today. Computers are becoming so inexpensive that in the near future every active laboratory in the country will have computing power available. There are many who believe that computers will offer whole new ways of looking at questions and will permit new research paradigms that will answer questions yet to be imagined. It is an exciting period for science. But we must not forget that it is the scientist's imagination that is fueling this explosion and not the silicon of the computer chips. The computer is a powerful resource but it is human thought and creativity that harness this resource.

Basic science is unlikely to be changed by the computer. The computer will add efficiency but the scientist will still ask the questions, decide the best ways to search for the answers, set up the studies, and evaluate the results.

SCIENCE: AN INTERACTION BETWEEN EMPIRICISM AND RATIONALISM

It is important to restate a point made in Chapter 1: New technologies used in the research laboratory do not define science or a particular discipline of science. Rather, any discipline is defined by its subject matter and by the processes that are used to answer the questions of interest to that discipline.

In Chapter 1 science is defined as a combination of empiricism and rationalism. By requiring that scientific theories conform to both logical restrictions and to the realities of the world about us, we demand more of scientific theories than is demanded of any other system of knowing. Few scientific theories stand up to this kind of double scrutiny. Theories are constantly being rejected because they are either logically inconsistent (a rational criterion) and/or they do not accurately predict data (an empirical criterion). Science progresses by rejecting inadequate theories and proposing and testing new theories that will stand up better to the rigorous demands of rationalism and empiricism. Initially students may find this process to be negativistic—researchers always try to criticize and reject theories rather than try to prove them. However, it is not negativism but rather *skepticism* that characterizes science. Theories are used but we never really accept them. We are constantly questioning theories. A good scientist expects that all theories will eventually be shown to be false or not completely true and be replaced by better theories. In science we accept little on faith, except for the method of science itself.

Science has become a major enterprise in today's world. Millions of people work in and around scientific laboratories. Scientific disciplines have become increasingly more specialized as their knowledge base grows. As the discipline develops, the research techniques used by the discipline will evolve to handle the specific questions of that discipline. Therefore, different scientific disciplines appear to be using different research methods. In this text we cover many of the most commonly used research techniques in the discipline of psychology. The techniques covered differ somewhat from those used in other sciences. But the differences are more surface differences than conceptual differences. A research biologist would have no trouble conceptually understanding the research methodology of chemistry or psychology and vice versa. In this text we try to present concepts and build specific research techniques on them. If students understand the concepts that underlie the techniques, it will be relatively easy to understand new research techniques—whether they are from the discipline of psychology or some other science.

New research techniques are an almost inevitable result of a developing science. New scientific disciplines are inevitable as the knowledge base of science builds and increased specialization is required. What was once philosophy is now a dozen different basic sciences. What was once physics is now physics, astronomy, and chemistry. Specialization is necessary given the incredible complexity of many disciplines, but it tends to isolate disciplines from the ideas and discoveries of other sciences. Organizations such as the American Association for the Advancement of Science (AAAS) strive to unite the many subdisciplines of science and maintain a healthy level of communication among disciplines. This effort is supported because it is believed that the method of science (empiricism coupled with rationalism) is a strong bond between apparently diverse areas. It is hoped that students gain from this text a good understanding of research approaches in psychology, as well as a good understanding of science and scientific thought and how the specific research approaches in psychology are applications of basic scientific processes to a particular subject matter—the behavior of organisms.

It is appropriate to end the text by repeating an idea that is stressed throughout: The essence of science is its *way of thinking.* The important tools of scientists are their skills in systematically combining rational thinking and empirical findings to ask and answer questions about nature. The scientist's enthusiasm, skepticism, and creativity are essential components in the process of scientific thinking, as are the technologies of each discipline. But mostly, it is the *thinking process that constitutes the essence of science.* To emphasize this point, recall the imagery used in Chapter 1: A scientist can operate scientifically while sitting under a tree in the woods, thinking through a problem, and using apparatus no more technical than a pad and pencil.

REVIEW EXERCISE

Think of the scientist sitting under the tree "being scientific." Your task as teaching assistant for the course is to explain to students how it is that a person can be scientific in these surroundings, apparently so inactive and so far away from the laboratory. How can you explain it in enough detail to answer students' questions?

WRITING A RESEARCH REPORT

APA Publication Style

Publication is a critical part of the research process. Literally, *publication* means "to make public." Making science a public discipline serves two purposes. First, it facilitates building on old knowledge by making the knowledge accessible to everyone. Secondly, it subjects each finding to the scrutiny of many qualified scientists who can independently review the logic, procedures, results, and conclusions from a given study.

There is much to communicate in a research report, yet space restrictions demand that a report be concise. Thus, it is necessary to have guidelines to aid communication while minimizing the journal space used. The publication manual prepared by the American Psychological Association (1983) is used as a guide by most psychology journals as well as journals in several other disciplines. Psychology majors, particularly those planning to attend graduate school, should purchase a copy of the manual.[1]

STRUCTURE OF A RESEARCH ARTICLE

Organization is one key to a good research article. The American Psychological Association recommends that the body of a research article be organized into four parts: introduction, method, results, and discussion. In addition, the report should have a title page and a short (100–150-word) abstract. The abstract briefly describes the study and its findings, permitting readers to ascertain what the article is about so as to decide whether it is of interest and should be read more thoroughly. The abstract is also published in one or more journals that specialize in abstracts (e.g., *Psychological Abstracts*). These journals are cross-referenced to make it easier for a researcher to identify relevant research. The *reference* section provides details on where the reports of previous research can be found. There are specific standards on how to record that information so that it can be presented in a concise and complete manner. Occasionally, additional attachments are included at the end of an article in the form of appendices. These can contain extended information, materials, or scales that are not readily available elsewhere. The major sections of a journal article are shown in Table A.1.

WRITING THE RESEARCH REPORT

It is necessary to know how to prepare each section of a research report. Clarity and precision in the presentation of research results are important. Where appropriate, specific information on APA publication style is given.

Using Levels of Headings to Organize

An *outline* is one of the best ways to organize any kind of report. The familiar indentation pattern of the outline makes it easy to see the overall structure of the intended report. A well-written article follows the organization of an outline. In the

---

[1]The *Publication Manual of the American Psychological Association* can be purchased directly from the American Psychological Association, 1200 17th Street NW, Washington, DC 20036. The current cost to members and student affiliates is $12.50 ($16.50 for nonmembers). The book can also be purchased in many university bookstores.

**Table A.1 MAJOR SECTIONS AND
SUBSECTIONS OF A MANUSCRIPT**

1. Title Page
2. Abstract
3. Introduction
4. Method
   a. Subjects
   b. Apparatus
   c. Procedure
5. Results
6. Discussion
7. References
8. Appendices
9. Footnotes
10. Tables
11. Figure captions
12. Figures

article, however, different *levels of headings* are used instead of indentation to indicate the outline organization. Table A.2 presents examples of five different levels of headings that can be used in a research report.

Sections of a Research Report

Title Page   The title page includes the title of the article, the list of authors, and the institutional affiliations of the authors. The title should be concise while still describing the focus of the study. Phrases such as "A report on" or "A study of" add little information to the title and should be avoided.

Abstract   The abstract summarizes the research paper. In 100–150 words it must include all elements of the research report. Enough information should be given so that anyone who reads the research study after reading the abstract will not be surprised by what they find in the article. Even though the abstract appears first, it is usually written by the researcher last because it essentially summarizes the work. Further, although the abstract is one of the shortest sections of the study, many researchers find it is the most difficult to write because so much must be said in limited space.

Table A.2 FIVE LEVELS OF HEADINGS

THIS IS A CENTERED UPPERCASE HEADING (LEVEL 1)

This is a Centered Upper- and Lowercase Heading
(Level 2)

This is a Centered, Underlined, Uppercase
and Lowercase Heading (Level 3)

This is an Uppercase and Lowercase Side Heading (Level 4)

This is a paragraph heading (level 5). The paragraph heading is in lowercase, is underlined, and should end with a period as shown.

Note: If only one level of heading is needed in a report, use level 2; if two levels are needed, use levels 2 and 4; if three levels are needed, use levels 2, 4, and 5; and if four levels are needed, use levels 2, 3, 4, and 5.

Introduction The introduction states the research problem and discusses prior research. It begins with a broad or general statement of the research problem and proceeds to narrow the focus to the specific research being reported. A good introduction need not be long but it must be well organized. One should focus only on those prior research studies directly relevant to the current research study and should not attempt to review all of the research in a broad area. The introduction usually ends with a specific statement of the hypotheses to be investigated. A good rule of thumb is: If the hypotheses seem to follow naturally from everything that precedes them, then the introduction is well organized and well structured. If, on the other hand, a reader finds some or all of the hypotheses to be surprising in light of what is stated previously, then the introduction is not well focused and fails to provide the rationale for the current research study.

In the introduction other research is referred to by naming the researcher(s) and the date when the research was published. With this information the reader can turn to the reference list and find where the work was published. There are two standard forms for referring to other published work, as shown in the following examples:

> In previous research, most subjects found the situation to be quite realistic (Johnson & Hall, 1979).

> Johnson and Hall (1979) found that most subjects considered the procedure to be quite realistic.

For citing several studies, we can use the following format:

> Several investigators have found this situation to be realistic for their subjects (Johnson & Hall, 1979, 1980a, 1980b; Kelley, 1976; Michaels, Johnson, & Smith, 1981; Smith & Rodick, 1977).

The forms tell the reader what had been found, which researchers made the observation, and when. You may have noticed that the APA conventions are used throughout the text to refer to research discussed.

It is important to note that each reference that appears in a research article must appear in the reference section. In addition, all references that appear in the reference list must have been referred to somewhere within the paper itself.

Method The purpose of the method section is to describe exactly how the research was carried out. We must describe the subjects and how they were selected, the apparatus, equipment and/or materials, and the procedures used. These are typically discussed in separate subsections.

The *subjects* subsection describes how subjects were selected and what subjects were like including demographic characteristics (such as age, education, and sex), from where subjects were obtained (from a college student subject pool, a psychiatric hospital, or a local shopping mall), and what inducements were used to obtain their cooperation (money, experimental credit for students, and so on). In addition, the researcher should describe how subjects were assigned to groups. If it is a differential research study where the assignment is based on classifying the subjects, the procedures used to classify the subjects should be described. If subjects drop out of the experiment or decline to participate, the number of such subjects and the groups they were in should be reported. There should be enough information to allow a researcher to compare the sample with samples from similar research projects.

The next subsection will depend on the study. It might be called the *apparatus* or *equipment* subsection, *materials, instruments,* or *measures* subsection, or some combination of these terms. In this subsection all physical aspects of the research study are described. If the study involves equipment, the type of equipment used and the dial settings of the equipment should be reported. If psychological tests are used, we should describe them and give a reference to where they can be obtained. If the test forms are unique or custom made for the study, they should be either included as an appendix or made available to any reader on request. The goal of the apparatus or equipment subsection is to provide readers with sufficient information to allow them to replicate the study.

The *procedure* subsection describes how we carried out the study. If additional manipulation of data is carried out after the subject has left the experiment, it should be described in the procedure section. For example, if particular scoring procedures were used, they should be described. If specific instructions were given to the subject, the instructions should be included. In other words, the procedure subsection should tell the reader everything that the subject and the researcher did during the course of the study.

Results The purpose of the results section is to tell the reader what was found in the study. A statistical description of the results is usually needed as well as appropriate statistical tests. Reporting statistical findings in a concise yet understandable way requires that the writer follow certain conventions. The usual convention is to present the descriptive statistics first followed by the results of the inferential statistical tests. When reporting inferential statistics one should report what statistic was used, the number of degrees of freedom, the computed value of the statistic, and the probability of obtaining the computed value of the statistic by chance. Each of these is organized in a precise order (see Table A.3). All non-Greek, single-letter terms used in reporting statistical results (e.g., F, t, p) should be underlined in the manuscript. With this format

Table A.3 ORGANIZING COMMON STATISTICS IN THE TEXT OF A RESEARCH REPORT

Reporting t-tests
Boys were found to be significantly more aggressive than girls in the playground situation, $t(28) = 2.33, p < 0.05$.

Reporting ANOVAs
There was a significant difference in performance between the three distraction conditions, $F(2, 27) = 3.69, p < 0.05$.

Reporting chi-squares
Psychology majors were significantly more likely to classify themselves as "humanistic" than were engineering majors, $\chi^2(1, N = 60) = 4.47, p < 0.05$.

readers can easily interpret the importance of certain results even if they are not familiar with the statistical procedure used, because the probability value at the end of the report will mean the same thing. Anytime p is less than 0.05 (a traditional value of alpha), we would conclude the findings are unusual enough that it is unlikely they could have occurred as a result of chance. Although it is important to express the statistical significance of comparisons made in the study, it is equally important to give the reader the information needed to interpret the results, such as the actual mean scores or frequencies.

Often the most effective way of presenting statistical information is to organize it in a table or figure. Tables and figures should be carefully labeled for the reader. Tables should give the reader enough information so they can be interpreted without information from the text. Each table should be numbered using Arabic numerals starting with number 1. The first line of the table should read "Table" and the number. The next line of the table should be a brief title. An example of a typical table title might be "Mean Reaction Times for Distracted and Nondistracted Subjects." The title should be underlined. If the title is more than one line long, it should be double-spaced. The actual values in the table will be arranged in columns and rows with the columns and rows clearly labeled. The columns should be labeled at the top of each column and the rows at the far left-hand side of the table. If additional information is necessary to interpret the table, it should be included at the bottom in the form of a footnote. An example of a typical table format is in Table A.4.

Figures can also be an effective way of presenting information. It is important, however, to label a figure completely. Both the x- and the y-axis should be labeled, and each figure should have a title. Figures should be numbered sequentially starting with number 1 and should be numbered independently of tables. The figure number and title should appear at the bottom of the figure. When submitting a paper for publication each

Table A.4   A TYPICAL TABLE IN A RESEARCH ARTICLE

Table 1
Posttreatment Measures for the Three Treatment Approaches

Measures	Type of Therapy		
	Behavioral	Cognitive	Analytic
Number of activities[a]	4.6	3.8	2.1
Beck scores[b]	16.7	15.3	17.5
Insight ratings[c]	2.0	3.1	3.7

[a]The mean number of recreational activities in a one-week period.
[b]Mean Beck Depression Inventory scores--higher scores indicate greater depression.
[c]Rating based on an independent interview--ratings range from 1 (no insight) to 5 (maximum insight).

figure should be professionally drawn and submitted as a glossy print. The figures are numbered on the back of the print and the figure numbers and titles appear on a separate sheet. Figure A.1 presents an example.

In preparing a manuscript for publication tables and figures are assembled and placed at the end of the manuscript. In the manuscript the approximate placement of figures and tables is indicated with a centered instruction that is set off as follows:

Insert Figure X about here

There is no one correct way of presenting the results of a study. It is often useful for the researcher to try to organize results in various ways—testing both tables and figures to determine which method is most effective.

Discussion   The purpose of the discussion section is to interpret and evaluate the results. It is helpful to begin the discussion section by briefly summarizing the results in nontechnical language. Then the reader should be told what it is believed the results mean and how they should be interpreted. The interpretation of the results should follow logically from the actual data obtained in the study. It is useful in the discussion section to focus on the future directions that research might take. If there are weaknesses in the current study, we should describe ways that they may be overcome in future studies. If the study suggests new hypotheses, we should suggest ways in which the hypotheses might be adequately tested. The goal of any research project is to find answers to questions. But the outcome of most good research projects is to suggest new and important questions that still need to be answered. Suggesting directions for future research is a natural part of any well-designed, well-executed research project.

References   The reference section lists each study discussed in the paper in alphabetical order by the last name of the author(s). Works by the same author are arranged chronologically according to publication date. In addition to the author(s) and the title of the research study, a complete reference to the research report is included. The most

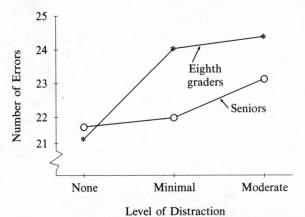

Figure A.1   LINE GRAPH OF DATA FROM A TWO-FACTOR STUDY

common reference is to an article in a research journal. The format for such a reference is to start by listing the author(s), last name first. The year the paper was published is listed in parentheses immediately after the authors' names, followed by the title of the article, the journal title, the volume of the journal, and the pages of the article. The journal title and the volume number are always underlined, but nothing else in the reference should be underlined. The typesetter will set any underlined material in italics. Here are two examples of references to *journal articles:*

> Beck, A. T. (1970). Role of fantasies in psychotherapy and psychopathology. Journal of Nervous and Mental Disease, 150, 3–17.
> Benbow, C. P., & Stanley, J. C. (1980). Sex differences in mathematical ability: Fact or artifact? Science, 210, 1262–1264.

A similar format is used for a reference to a book. Again, we list the author(s) followed by the year the book was published in parentheses. The title of the book follows and is underlined. After the title, we list the city in which the book was published and the publisher (i.e., city: publisher). Here are examples of references to *books:*

> Johnson, R. N. (1972). Aggression in man and animals. Philadelphia: Saunders.
> Welkowitz, J., Ewen, R. B., & Cohen, J. (1982). Introductory statistics for the behavioral sciences (3rd ed.). San Diego: Harcourt Brace Jovanovich.

The reference section of this text provides many other examples of the final typeset form for references. Remember, what appears as italicized in the published form is material that is underlined in the manuscript. A sample of a manuscript is presented in Figure A.2.

WRITING STYLE

Good writing is important whether you are writing a journal article or a letter home. It is one of the most difficult things to teach, and it can be learned only through practice. However, there are different kinds of writing. Writing a journal article requires technical writing. Precision, conciseness, and organization are important in technical writing. Flowery adjectives and a poetic style are best left to the creative writer.

The primary purpose of writing a research report is communication, and anything that obscures communication should be avoided. Pronouns should be used sparingly and should never be ambiguous. Abbreviations should also be used sparingly and should always be explained to the reader. Using the active voice and relatively simple sentence structure can help a writer avoid numerous communication pitfalls (such as dangling or misplaced modifiers). Traditionally, the research report is written in the past tense and primarily in the third-person point of view (e.g., "The experimenter assigned each subject. . . ."), although there is a current trend to use more first person in research reports. A good way to improve a research report is to have someone who was not involved in the research read the report. Anything that is unclear to them will

Individual Differences
1

Individual Differences in
Bimodal Processing and Text Recall
Bruce R. Dunn
University of West Flordia

Running head: INDIVIDUAL DIFFERENCES IN BIMODAL PROC

Individual Differences
2

Abstract

The differences in semantic recall among students with either an analytic or a
holistic cognitive style were investigated. The cognitive style was
determined by the amount of bilateral alpha activity (8-13 Hz) mesured from
the cerebral cortex of the brain during two eyes-open baseline recordings.
The results indicated that analytics (who produced less bilateral alpha
activity than holistics) recalled more of the logically or semantically
important information from structured expository text than did holistics.
Holistics recalled more of the semantically important information from high-
imagery poetry than did analytics. The findings are congruent with the
bimodal theory of conscious processing and support the position that
individual differences are important in memory research.

Individual Differences
3

Individual Differences in
Bimodal Processing and Text Recall

    A growing body of research has indicated that variations in the
electrical activity from the brain, as recorded by an electroencephalograph
(EEG), particularly the amount of alpha activity, can be used to identify a
person's manner of processing information, that is, a person's cognitive style
(e.g., Davidson & Schwartz, 1977; Doktor & Bloom, 1977; Ornstein & Galin,
1976). Much of this . . .

**Figure A.2   SAMPLE OF A MANUSCRIPT (*Source: APA Publication Manual, 1983,*
pp. 148–154; adapted by permission of the publisher.)**

that cognitive-style differences occur because individuals weight these two
modes differently when processing stimuli. Research (e.g., Dunn et al., 1981)
has indicated that processing style can be determined by the amount of alpha
activity (8-13 Hz) measured from . . .

qualitatively distinct styles implied by the terms _analytic_ and _holistic_.
In this study I attempted to identify the qualitative . . .

Subjects   Methods

Sixty upper division university students served as voluntary
participants. All participants were strongly right-handed, as determined by
Laterality Assessment Inventory (Sherman & Kulhavy, 1976). Volunteers
paid for their participation and . . .

were treated in accordance with the "Ethical Principles of Psychologists"
(American Psychological Association, 1981).

Materials

Two passages with approximately the same number of words were used. The
first passages, "Chemical Pesticides," was a 155-word expository passage
developed by Howell (1980), based on the work of . . .

Design and Procedure

Testing occurred in two sessions 1 week apart. In each session 3-min,
eyes-open EEG recordings were made for each participant. I used these
recordings as baseline recordings to determine cognitive style (see the
Results section).

leads through the outputs of the computer's A to D converter. A specially
written Fourier analysis program, independently tested by others (e.g., G.S.
Wolverton, personal communication, February . . .

Figure A.2 _(cont.)_

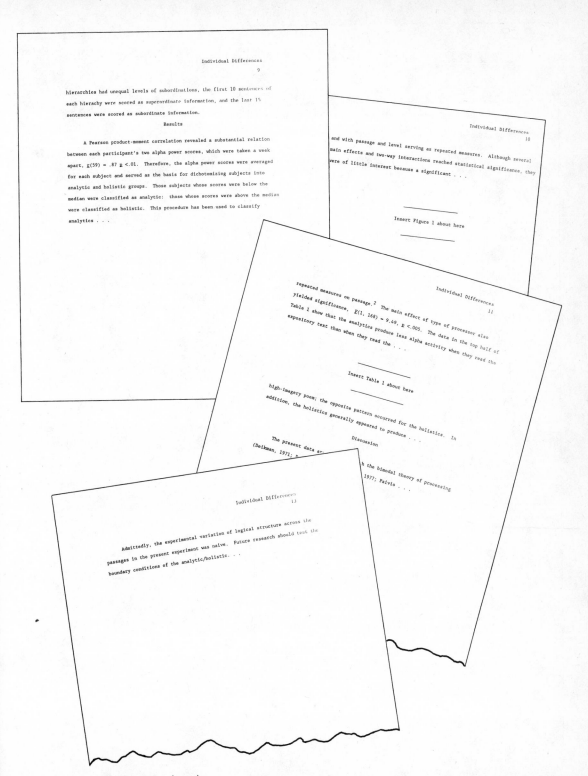

Individual Differences
9

hierarchies had unequal levels of subordinations, the first 10 sentences of
each hierachy were scored as superordinate information, and the last 15
sentences were scored as subordinate information.

Results

A Pearson product-moment correlation revealed a substantial relation
between each participant's two alpha power scores, which were taken a week
apart, $r(59) = .87$ $p <.01$. Therefore, the alpha power scores were averaged
for each subject and served as the basis for dichotomizing subjects into
analytic and holistic groups. Those subjects whose scores were below the
median were classified as analytic; those whose scores were above the median
were classified as holistic. This procedure has been used to classify
analytics . . .

Individual Differences
10

and with passage and level serving as repeated measures. Although several
main effects and two-way interactions reached statistical significance, they
were of little interest because a significant . . .

———————————

Insert Figure 1 about here

———————————

Individual Differences
11

repeated measures on passage 2. The main effect of type of processor also
yielded significance, $F(1, 168) = 9.49$, $p <.005$. The data in the top half of
Table 1 show that the analytics produce less alpha activity when they read the
expository text than when they read the . . .

———————————

Insert Table 1 about here

———————————

high-imagery poem; the opposite pattern occurred for the holistics. In
addition, the holistics generally appeared to produce . . .

Discussion

The present data ar[e] . . . h the bimodal theory of processing
(Deikman, 1971; p . . . 1977; Paivio . . .

Individual Differences
13

Admittedly, the experimental variation of logical structure across the
passages in the present experiment was naive. Future research should test the
boundary conditions of the analytic/holistic. . .

Figure A.2 *(cont.)*

339

Individual Differences

14

References

American Psychological Association (1981). Ethical principles of psychologist

(revised). *American Psychologist*, *36*, 633-638.

Brown, H., & Milstead, J. (1968). *Patterns in poetry: An introductory*

anthology. Glenview, IL: Scott, Foresman.

Cohen, G. (1975). Hemisphere differences in the effects of cuing in visual

recognition tasks. *Journal of Experimental Psychology*: *Human*

Perception and Performance, *1*, 366-373.

Davidson, R. J., & Schwartz, G. E. (1977). The influence of musical training

on patterns of EEG asymmetry during musical and non-musical self-

generation tasks. *Psychophysiology*, *14*, 58-63.

. . . . .

Individual Differences

19

Footnotes

[1]If poetry specialists had been consulted, I would have expressed
appreciation here to my colleagues Ronald V. Evans, University of West
Flordia; Harold Pepinsky, Ohio State University, . . .

Individual Differences

18

Author Notes

I fabricated these experiments for the *Publication Manual*. However, I
made the assumption, based on past research, that the hypotheses I examined
had face validity.

Figure A.2 *(cont.)*

probably also be unclear to other readers. A writing manual such as Strunk and White's *Elements of Style* (1979) is a valuable resource for any writer.

Although some researchers find the writing phase to be challenging and rewarding, for many researchers writing a good research report is a demanding task. It is made somewhat easier if the research itself is carefully conceived and well organized. For all researchers, however, telling people about something that they discovered can be truly exciting.

SUMMARY

The final stage of any research project is the communication of the results. Appendix A lists some of the basic features of the APA writing style for research reports. A journal article is a carefully organized presentation of the research and its findings. The body of the article is divided into introduction, method, results, and discussion sections, which help to organize the entire paper. In addition, the article should have an abstract that summarizes the study and a complete list of references.

STATISTICAL TABLES

Table B.1 AREA UNDER THE STANDARD NORMAL CURVE

(a) z	(b) Area between mean and z	(c) Area beyond z	(a) z	(b) Area between mean and z	(c) Area beyond z	(a) z	(b) Area between mean and z	(c) Area beyond z
0.00	.0000	.5000	0.55	.2088	.2912	1.10	.3643	.1357
0.01	.0040	.4960	0.56	.2123	.2877	1.11	.3665	.1335
0.02	.0080	.4920	0.57	.2157	.2843	1.12	.3686	.1314
0.03	.0120	.4880	0.58	.2190	.2810	1.13	.3708	.1292
0.04	.0160	.4840	0.59	.2224	.2776	1.14	.3729	.1271
0.05	.0199	.4801	0.60	.2257	.2743	1.15	.3749	.1251
0.06	.0239	.4761	0.61	.2291	.2709	1.16	.3770	.1230
0.07	.0279	.4721	0.62	.2324	.2676	1.17	.3790	.1210
0.08	.0319	.4681	0.63	.2357	.2643	1.18	.3810	.1190
0.09	.0359	.4641	0.64	.2389	.2611	1.19	.3830	.1170
0.10	.0398	.4602	0.65	.2422	.2578	1.20	.3849	.1151
0.11	.0438	.4562	0.66	.2454	.2546	1.21	.3869	.1131
0.12	.0478	.4522	0.67	.2486	.2514	1.22	.3888	.1112
0.13	.0517	.4483	0.68	.2517	.2483	1.23	.3907	.1093
0.14	.0557	.4443	0.69	.2549	.2451	1.24	.3925	.1075
0.15	.0596	.4404	0.70	.2580	.2420	1.25	.3944	.1056
0.16	.0636	.4364	0.71	.2611	.2389	1.26	.3962	.1038
0.17	.0675	.4325	0.72	.2642	.2358	1.27	.3980	.1020
0.18	.0714	.4286	0.73	.2673	.2327	1.28	.3997	.1003
0.19	.0753	.4247	0.74	.2704	.2296	1.29	.4015	.0985
0.20	.0793	.4207	0.75	.2734	.2266	1.30	.4032	.0968
0.21	.0832	.4168	0.76	.2764	.2236	1.31	.4049	.0951
0.22	.0871	.4129	0.77	.2794	.2206	1.32	.4066	.0934
0.23	.0910	.4090	0.78	.2823	.2177	1.33	.4082	.0918
0.24	.0948	.4052	0.79	.2852	.2148	1.34	.4099	.0901
0.25	.0987	.4013	0.80	.2881	.2119	1.35	.4115	.0885
0.26	.1026	.3974	0.81	.2910	.2090	1.36	.4131	.0869
0.27	.1064	.3936	0.82	.2939	.2061	1.37	.4147	.0853
0.28	.1103	.3897	0.83	.2967	.2033	1.38	.4162	.0838
0.29	.1141	.3859	0.84	.2995	.2005	1.39	.4177	.0823
0.30	.1179	.3821	0.85	.3023	.1977	1.40	.4192	.0808
0.31	.1217	.3783	0.86	.3051	.1949	1.41	.4207	.0793
0.32	.1255	.3745	0.87	.3078	.1922	1.42	.4222	.0778
0.33	.1293	.3707	0.88	.3106	.1894	1.43	.4236	.0764
0.34	.1331	.3669	0.89	.3133	.1867	1.44	.4251	.0749
0.35	.1368	.3632	0.90	.3159	.1841	1.45	.4265	.0735
0.36	.1406	.3594	0.91	.3186	.1814	1.46	.4279	.0721
0.37	.1443	.3557	0.92	.3212	.1788	1.47	.4292	.0708
0.38	.1480	.3520	0.93	.3238	.1762	1.48	.4306	.0694
0.39	.1517	.3483	0.94	.3264	.1736	1.49	.4319	.0681
0.40	.1554	.3446	0.95	.3289	.1711	1.50	.4332	.0668
0.41	.1591	.3409	0.96	.3315	.1685	1.51	.4345	.0655
0.42	.1628	.3372	0.97	.3340	.1660	1.52	.4357	.0643
0.43	.1664	.3336	0.98	.3365	.1635	1.53	.4370	.0630
0.44	.1700	.3300	0.99	.3389	.1611	1.54	.4382	.0618
0.45	.1736	.3264	1.00	.3413	.1587	1.55	.4394	.0606
0.46	.1772	.3228	1.01	.3438	.1562	1.56	.4406	.0594
0.47	.1808	.3192	1.02	.3461	.1539	1.57	.4418	.0582
0.48	.1844	.3156	1.03	.3485	.1515	1.58	.4429	.0571
0.49	.1879	.3121	1.04	.3508	.1492	1.59	.4441	.0559
0.50	.1915	.3085	1.05	.3531	.1469	1.60	.4452	.0548
0.51	.1950	.3050	1.06	.3554	.1446	1.61	.4463	.0537
0.52	.1985	.3015	1.07	.3577	.1423	1.62	.4474	.0526
0.53	.2019	.2981	1.08	.3599	.1401	1.63	.4484	.0516
0.54	.2054	.2946	1.09	.3621	.1379	1.64	.4495	.0505

Table B.1 (*cont.*)

(a) z	(b) Area between mean and z	(c) Area beyond z	(a) z	(b) Area between mean and z	(c) Area beyond z	(a) z	(b) Area between mean and z	(c) Area beyond z
1.65	.4505	.0495	2.22	.4868	.0132	2.79	.4974	.0026
1.66	.4515	.0485	2.23	.4871	.0129	2.80	.4974	.0026
1.67	.4525	.0475	2.24	.4875	.0125	2.81	.4975	.0025
1.68	.4535	.0465	2.25	.4878	.0122	2.82	.4976	.0024
1.69	.4545	.0455	2.26	.4881	.0119	2.83	.4977	.0023
1.70	.4554	.0446	2.27	.4884	.0116	2.84	.4977	.0023
1.71	.4564	.0436	2.28	.4887	.0113	2.85	.4978	.0022
1.72	.4573	.0427	2.29	.4890	.0110	2.86	.4979	.0021
1.73	.4582	.0418	2.30	.4893	.0107	2.87	.4979	.0021
1.74	.4591	.0409	2.31	.4896	.0104	2.88	.4980	.0020
1.75	.4599	.0401	2.32	.4898	.0102	2.89	.4981	.0019
1.76	.4608	.0392	2.33	.4901	.0099	2.90	.4981	.0019
1.77	.4616	.0384	2.34	.4904	.0096	2.91	.4982	.0018
1.78	.4625	.0375	2.35	.4906	.0094	2.92	.4982	.0018
1.79	.4633	.0367	2.36	.4909	.0091	2.93	.4983	.0017
1.80	.4641	.0359	2.37	.4911	.0089	2.94	.4984	.0016
1.81	.4649	.0351	2.38	.4913	.0087	2.95	.4984	.0016
1.82	.4656	.0344	2.39	.4916	.0084	2.96	.4985	.0015
1.83	.4664	.0336	2.40	.4918	.0082	2.97	.4985	.0015
1.84	.4671	.0329	2.41	.4920	.0080	2.98	.4986	.0014
1.85	.4678	.0322	2.42	.4922	.0078	2.99	.4986	.0014
1.86	.4686	.0314	2.43	.4925	.0075	3.00	.4987	.0013
1.87	.4693	.0307	2.44	.4927	.0073	3.01	.4987	.0013
1.88	.4699	.0301	2.45	.4929	.0071	3.02	.4987	.0013
1.89	.4706	.0294	2.46	.4931	.0069	3.03	.4988	.0012
1.90	.4713	.0287	2.47	.4932	.0068	3.04	.4988	.0012
1.91	.4719	.0281	2.48	.4934	.0066	3.05	.4989	.0011
1.92	.4726	.0274	2.49	.4936	.0064	3.06	.4989	.0011
1.93	.4732	.0268	2.50	.4938	.0062	3.07	.4989	.0011
1.94	.4738	.0262	2.51	.4940	.0060	3.08	.4990	.0010
1.95	.4744	.0256	2.52	.4941	.0059	3.09	.4990	.0010
1.96	.4750	.0250	2.53	.4943	.0057	3.10	.4990	.0010
1.97	.4756	.0244	2.54	.4945	.0055	3.11	.4991	.0009
1.98	.4761	.0239	2.55	.4946	.0054	3.12	.4991	.0009
1.99	.4767	.0233	2.56	.4948	.0052	3.13	.4991	.0009
2.00	.4772	.0228	2.57	.4949	.0051	3.14	.4992	.0008
2.01	.4778	.0222	2.58	.4951	.0049	3.15	.4992	.0008
2.02	.4783	.0217	2.59	.4952	.0048	3.16	.4992	.0008
2.03	.4788	.0212	2.60	.4953	.0047	3.17	.4992	.0008
2.04	.4793	.0207	2.61	.4955	.0045	3.18	.4993	.0007
2.05	.4798	.0202	2.62	.4956	.0044	3.19	.4993	.0007
2.06	.4803	.0197	2.63	.4957	.0043	3.20	.4993	.0007
2.07	.4808	.0192	2.64	.4959	.0041	3.21	.4993	.0007
2.08	.4812	.0188	2.65	.4960	.0040	3.22	.4994	.0006
2.09	.4817	.0183	2.66	.4961	.0039	3.23	.4994	.0006
2.10	.4821	.0179	2.67	.4962	.0038	3.24	.4994	.0006
2.11	.4826	.0174	2.68	.4963	.0037	3.25	.4994	.0006
2.12	.4830	.0170	2.69	.4964	.0036	3.30	.4995	.0005
2.13	.4834	.0166	2.70	.4965	.0035	3.35	.4996	.0004
2.14	.4838	.0162	2.71	.4966	.0034	3.40	.4997	.0003
2.15	.4842	.0158	2.72	.4967	.0033	3.45	.4997	.0003
2.16	.4846	.0154	2.73	.4968	.0032	3.50	.4998	.0002
2.17	.4850	.0150	2.74	.4969	.0031	3.60	.4998	.0002
2.18	.4854	.0146	2.75	.4970	.0030	3.70	.4999	.0001
2.19	.4857	.0143	2.76	.4971	.0029	3.80	.4999	.0001
2.20	.4861	.0139	2.77	.4972	.0028	3.90	.49995	.00005
2.21	.4864	.0136	2.78	.4973	.0027	4.00	.49997	.00003

Table B.2 CRITICAL VALUES OF STUDENT'S t

df	Level of Significance for Two-Tailed Test					
	0.20	0.10	0.05	0.02	0.01	0.001
1	3.078	6.314	12.706	31.821	63.657	636.619
2	1.886	2.920	4.303	6.965	9.925	31.598
3	1.638	2.353	3.182	4.541	5.841	12.941
4	1.533	2.132	2.776	3.747	4.604	8.610
5	1.476	2.015	2.571	3.365	4.032	6.859
6	1.440	1.943	2.447	3.143	3.707	5.959
7	1.415	1.895	2.365	2.998	3.499	5.405
8	1.397	1.860	2.306	2.896	3.355	5.041
9	1.383	1.833	2.262	2.821	3.250	4.781
10	1.372	1.812	2.228	2.764	3.169	4.587
11	1.363	1.796	2.201	2.718	3.106	4.437
12	1.356	1.782	2.179	2.681	3.055	4.318
13	1.350	1.771	2.160	2.650	3.012	4.221
14	1.345	1.761	2.145	2.624	2.977	4.140
15	1.341	1.753	2.131	2.602	2.947	4.073
16	1.337	1.746	2.120	2.583	2.921	4.015
17	1.333	1.740	2.110	2.567	2.898	3.965
18	1.330	1.734	2.101	2.552	2.878	3.922
19	1.328	1.729	2.093	2.539	2.861	3.883
20	1.325	1.725	2.086	2.528	2.845	3.850
21	1.323	1.721	2.080	2.518	2.831	3.819
22	1.321	1.717	2.074	2.508	2.819	3.792
23	1.319	1.714	2.069	2.500	2.807	3.767
24	1.318	1.711	2.064	2.492	2.797	3.745
25	1.316	1.708	2.060	2.485	2.787	3.725
26	1.315	1.706	2.056	2.479	2.779	3.707
27	1.314	1.703	2.052	2.473	2.771	3.690
28	1.313	1.701	2.048	2.467	2.763	3.674
29	1.311	1.699	2.045	2.462	2.756	3.659
30	1.310	1.697	2.042	2.457	2.750	3.646
40	1.303	1.684	2.021	2.423	2.704	3.551
60	1.296	1.671	2.000	2.390	2.660	3.460
120	1.289	1.658	1.980	2.358	2.617	3.373
∞	1.282	1.645	1.960	2.326	2.576	3.291

Source: R. A. Fisher and F. Yates (1974). *Statistical tables for biological, agricultural, and medical research* (2nd ed.), Table III. Edinburgh: Oliver and Boyd, Ltd.

Table B.3 CRITICAL VALUES OF THE F DISTRIBUTION

The obtained F is significant at a given level if it is equal to or *greater than* the value shown in the table. 0.05 (light row) and **0.01** (dark row) points for the distribution of F.

The values shown are the right tail of the distribution obtained by dividing the larger variance estimate by the smaller variance estimate. To find the complementary left or lower tail for a given df and α level, reverse the degrees of freedom and find the reciprocal of that value in the F table. For example, the value cutting off the top 5 percent of the area for df 7 and 12 is 2.85. To find the cutoff point of the bottom 5 percent of the area, find the value cutting off the top 5 percent of the area for df 12 and 7. This is found to be 3.57. The reciprocal is 1/3.57 = 0.28. Thus, 5 percent of the area falls *at or below an* $F = 0.28$.

Each cell shows the 0.05 (light) value over the **0.01** (dark) value as "light / dark".

Degrees of Freedom for Numerator

df (Denom.)	1	2	3	4	5	6	7	8	9	10	11	12	14	16	20	24	30	40	50	75	100	200	500	∞
1	161 / 4052	200 / 4999	216 / 5403	225 / 5625	230 / 5764	234 / 5859	237 / 5928	239 / 5981	241 / 6022	242 / 6056	243 / 6082	244 / 6106	245 / 6142	246 / 6169	248 / 6208	249 / 6234	250 / 6258	251 / 6286	252 / 6302	253 / 6323	253 / 6334	254 / 6352	254 / 6361	254 / 6366
2	18.51 / 98.49	19.00 / 99.01	19.16 / 99.17	19.25 / 99.25	19.30 / 99.30	19.33 / 99.33	19.36 / 99.34	19.37 / 99.36	19.38 / 99.38	19.39 / 99.40	19.40 / 99.41	19.41 / 99.42	19.42 / 99.43	19.43 / 99.44	19.44 / 99.45	19.45 / 99.46	19.46 / 99.47	19.47 / 99.48	19.47 / 99.48	19.48 / 99.49	19.49 / 99.49	19.49 / 99.49	19.50 / 99.50	19.50 / 99.50
3	10.13 / 34.12	9.55 / 30.81	9.28 / 29.46	9.12 / 28.71	9.01 / 28.24	8.94 / 27.91	8.88 / 27.67	8.84 / 27.49	8.81 / 27.34	8.78 / 27.23	8.76 / 27.13	8.74 / 27.05	8.71 / 26.92	8.69 / 26.83	8.66 / 26.69	8.64 / 26.60	8.62 / 26.50	8.60 / 26.41	8.58 / 26.30	8.57 / 26.27	8.56 / 26.23	8.54 / 26.18	8.54 / 26.14	8.53 / 26.12
4	7.71 / 21.20	6.94 / 18.00	6.59 / 16.69	6.39 / 15.98	6.26 / 15.52	6.16 / 15.21	6.09 / 14.98	6.04 / 14.80	6.00 / 14.66	5.96 / 14.54	5.93 / 14.45	5.91 / 14.37	5.87 / 14.24	5.84 / 14.15	5.80 / 14.02	5.77 / 13.93	5.74 / 13.83	5.71 / 13.74	5.70 / 13.69	5.68 / 13.61	5.66 / 13.57	5.65 / 13.52	5.64 / 13.48	5.63 / 13.46
5	6.61 / 16.26	5.79 / 13.27	5.41 / 12.06	5.19 / 11.39	5.05 / 10.97	4.95 / 10.67	4.88 / 10.45	4.82 / 10.27	4.78 / 10.15	4.74 / 10.05	4.70 / 9.96	4.68 / 9.89	4.64 / 9.77	4.60 / 9.68	4.56 / 9.55	4.53 / 9.47	4.50 / 9.38	4.46 / 9.29	4.44 / 9.24	4.42 / 9.17	4.40 / 9.13	4.38 / 9.07	4.37 / 9.04	4.36 / 9.02
6	5.99 / 13.74	5.14 / 10.92	4.76 / 9.78	4.53 / 9.15	4.39 / 8.75	4.28 / 8.47	4.21 / 8.26	4.15 / 8.10	4.10 / 7.98	4.06 / 7.87	4.03 / 7.79	4.00 / 7.72	3.96 / 7.60	3.92 / 7.52	3.87 / 7.39	3.84 / 7.31	3.81 / 7.23	3.77 / 7.14	3.75 / 7.09	3.72 / 7.02	3.71 / 6.99	3.69 / 6.94	3.68 / 6.90	3.67 / 6.88
7	5.59 / 12.25	4.74 / 9.55	4.35 / 8.45	4.12 / 7.85	3.97 / 7.46	3.87 / 7.19	3.79 / 7.00	3.73 / 6.84	3.68 / 6.71	3.63 / 6.62	3.60 / 6.54	3.57 / 6.47	3.52 / 6.35	3.49 / 6.27	3.44 / 6.15	3.41 / 6.07	3.38 / 5.98	3.34 / 5.90	3.32 / 5.85	3.29 / 5.78	3.28 / 5.75	3.25 / 5.70	3.24 / 5.67	3.23 / 5.65
8	5.32 / 11.26	4.46 / 8.65	4.07 / 7.59	3.84 / 7.01	3.69 / 6.63	3.58 / 6.37	3.50 / 6.19	3.44 / 6.03	3.39 / 5.91	3.34 / 5.82	3.31 / 5.74	3.28 / 5.67	3.23 / 5.56	3.20 / 5.48	3.15 / 5.36	3.12 / 5.28	3.08 / 5.20	3.05 / 5.11	3.03 / 5.06	3.00 / 5.00	2.98 / 4.96	2.96 / 4.91	2.94 / 4.88	2.93 / 4.86
9	5.12 / 10.56	4.26 / 8.02	3.86 / 6.99	3.63 / 6.42	3.48 / 6.06	3.37 / 5.80	3.29 / 5.62	3.23 / 5.47	3.18 / 5.35	3.13 / 5.26	3.10 / 5.18	3.07 / 5.11	3.02 / 5.00	2.98 / 4.92	2.93 / 4.80	2.90 / 4.73	2.86 / 4.64	2.82 / 4.56	2.80 / 4.51	2.77 / 4.45	2.76 / 4.41	2.73 / 4.36	2.72 / 4.33	2.71 / 4.31
10	4.96 / 10.04	4.10 / 7.56	3.71 / 6.55	3.48 / 5.99	3.33 / 5.64	3.22 / 5.39	3.14 / 5.21	3.07 / 5.06	3.02 / 4.95	2.97 / 4.85	2.94 / 4.78	2.91 / 4.71	2.86 / 4.60	2.82 / 4.52	2.77 / 4.41	2.74 / 4.33	2.70 / 4.25	2.67 / 4.17	2.64 / 4.12	2.61 / 4.05	2.59 / 4.01	2.56 / 3.96	2.55 / 3.93	2.54 / 3.91
11	4.84 / 9.65	3.98 / 7.20	3.59 / 6.22	3.36 / 5.67	3.20 / 5.32	3.09 / 5.07	3.01 / 4.88	2.95 / 4.74	2.90 / 4.63	2.86 / 4.54	2.82 / 4.46	2.79 / 4.40	2.74 / 4.29	2.70 / 4.21	2.65 / 4.10	2.61 / 4.02	2.57 / 3.94	2.53 / 3.86	2.50 / 3.80	2.47 / 3.74	2.45 / 3.70	2.42 / 3.66	2.41 / 3.62	2.40 / 3.60
12	4.75 / 9.33	3.88 / 6.93	3.49 / 5.95	3.26 / 5.41	3.11 / 5.06	3.00 / 4.82	2.92 / 4.65	2.85 / 4.50	2.80 / 4.39	2.76 / 4.30	2.72 / 4.22	2.69 / 4.16	2.64 / 4.05	2.60 / 3.98	2.54 / 3.86	2.50 / 3.78	2.46 / 3.70	2.42 / 3.61	2.40 / 3.56	2.36 / 3.49	2.35 / 3.46	2.32 / 3.41	2.31 / 3.38	2.30 / 3.36
13	4.67 / 9.07	3.80 / 6.70	3.41 / 5.74	3.18 / 5.20	3.02 / 4.86	2.92 / 4.62	2.84 / 4.44	2.77 / 4.30	2.72 / 4.19	2.67 / 4.10	2.63 / 4.02	2.60 / 3.96	2.55 / 3.85	2.51 / 3.78	2.46 / 3.67	2.42 / 3.59	2.38 / 3.51	2.34 / 3.42	2.32 / 3.37	2.28 / 3.30	2.26 / 3.27	2.24 / 3.21	2.22 / 3.18	2.21 / 3.16

Degrees of Freedom for Denominator

Table B.3 (cont.)

Degrees of Freedom for Numerator

Denom. df	1	2	3	4	5	6	7	8	9	10	11	12	14	16	20	24	30	40	50	75	100	200	500	∞
14	4.60 **8.86**	3.74 **6.51**	3.34 **5.56**	3.11 **5.03**	2.96 **4.69**	2.85 **4.46**	2.77 **4.28**	2.70 **4.14**	2.65 **4.03**	2.60 **3.94**	2.56 **3.86**	2.53 **3.80**	2.48 **3.70**	2.44 **3.62**	2.39 **3.51**	2.35 **3.43**	2.31 **3.34**	2.27 **3.26**	2.24 **3.21**	2.21 **3.14**	2.19 **3.11**	2.16 **3.06**	2.14 **3.02**	2.13 **3.00**
15	4.54 **8.68**	3.68 **6.36**	3.29 **5.42**	3.06 **4.89**	2.90 **4.56**	2.79 **4.32**	2.70 **4.14**	2.64 **4.00**	2.59 **3.89**	2.55 **3.80**	2.51 **3.73**	2.48 **3.67**	2.43 **3.56**	2.39 **3.48**	2.33 **3.36**	2.29 **3.29**	2.25 **3.20**	2.21 **3.12**	2.18 **3.07**	2.15 **3.00**	2.12 **2.97**	2.10 **2.92**	2.08 **2.89**	2.07 **2.87**
16	4.49 **8.53**	3.63 **6.23**	3.24 **5.29**	3.01 **4.77**	2.85 **4.44**	2.74 **4.20**	2.66 **4.03**	2.59 **3.89**	2.54 **3.78**	2.49 **3.69**	2.45 **3.61**	2.42 **3.55**	2.37 **3.45**	2.33 **3.37**	2.28 **3.25**	2.24 **3.18**	2.20 **3.10**	2.16 **3.01**	2.13 **2.96**	2.09 **2.89**	2.07 **2.86**	2.04 **2.80**	2.02 **2.77**	2.01 **2.75**
17	4.45 **8.40**	3.59 **6.11**	3.20 **5.18**	2.96 **4.67**	2.81 **4.34**	2.70 **4.10**	2.62 **3.93**	2.55 **3.79**	2.50 **3.68**	2.45 **3.59**	2.41 **3.52**	2.38 **3.45**	2.33 **3.35**	2.29 **3.27**	2.23 **3.16**	2.19 **3.08**	2.15 **3.00**	2.11 **2.92**	2.08 **2.86**	2.04 **2.79**	2.02 **2.76**	1.99 **2.70**	1.97 **2.67**	1.96 **2.65**
18	4.41 **8.28**	3.55 **6.01**	3.16 **5.09**	2.93 **4.58**	2.77 **4.25**	2.66 **4.01**	2.58 **3.85**	2.51 **3.71**	2.46 **3.60**	2.41 **3.51**	2.37 **3.44**	2.34 **3.37**	2.29 **3.27**	2.25 **3.19**	2.19 **3.07**	2.15 **3.00**	2.11 **2.91**	2.07 **2.83**	2.04 **2.78**	2.00 **2.71**	1.98 **2.68**	1.95 **2.62**	1.93 **2.59**	1.92 **2.57**
19	4.38 **8.18**	3.52 **5.93**	3.13 **5.01**	2.90 **4.50**	2.74 **4.17**	2.63 **3.94**	2.55 **3.77**	2.48 **3.63**	2.43 **3.52**	2.38 **3.43**	2.34 **3.36**	2.31 **3.30**	2.26 **3.19**	2.21 **3.12**	2.15 **3.00**	2.11 **2.92**	2.07 **2.84**	2.02 **2.76**	2.00 **2.70**	1.96 **2.63**	1.94 **2.60**	1.91 **2.54**	1.90 **2.51**	1.88 **2.49**
20	4.35 **8.10**	3.49 **5.85**	3.10 **4.94**	2.87 **4.43**	2.71 **4.10**	2.60 **3.87**	2.52 **3.71**	2.45 **3.56**	2.40 **3.45**	2.35 **3.37**	2.31 **3.30**	2.28 **3.23**	2.23 **3.13**	2.18 **3.05**	2.12 **2.94**	2.08 **2.86**	2.04 **2.77**	1.99 **2.69**	1.96 **2.63**	1.92 **2.56**	1.90 **2.53**	1.87 **2.47**	1.85 **2.44**	1.84 **2.42**
21	4.32 **8.02**	3.47 **5.78**	3.07 **4.87**	2.84 **4.37**	2.68 **4.04**	2.57 **3.81**	2.49 **3.65**	2.42 **3.51**	2.37 **3.40**	2.32 **3.31**	2.28 **3.24**	2.25 **3.17**	2.20 **3.07**	2.15 **2.99**	2.09 **2.88**	2.05 **2.80**	2.00 **2.72**	1.96 **2.63**	1.93 **2.58**	1.89 **2.51**	1.87 **2.47**	1.84 **2.42**	1.82 **2.38**	1.81 **2.36**
22	4.30 **7.94**	3.44 **5.72**	3.05 **4.82**	2.82 **4.31**	2.66 **3.99**	2.55 **3.76**	2.47 **3.59**	2.40 **3.45**	2.35 **3.35**	2.30 **3.26**	2.26 **3.18**	2.23 **3.12**	2.18 **3.02**	2.13 **2.94**	2.07 **2.83**	2.03 **2.75**	1.98 **2.67**	1.93 **2.58**	1.91 **2.53**	1.87 **2.46**	1.84 **2.42**	1.81 **2.37**	1.80 **2.33**	1.78 **2.31**
23	4.28 **7.88**	3.42 **5.66**	3.03 **4.76**	2.80 **4.26**	2.64 **3.94**	2.53 **3.71**	2.45 **3.54**	2.38 **3.41**	2.32 **3.30**	2.28 **3.21**	2.24 **3.14**	2.20 **3.07**	2.14 **2.97**	2.10 **2.89**	2.04 **2.78**	2.00 **2.70**	1.96 **2.62**	1.91 **2.53**	1.88 **2.48**	1.84 **2.41**	1.82 **2.37**	1.79 **2.32**	1.77 **2.28**	1.76 **2.26**
24	4.26 **7.82**	3.40 **5.61**	3.01 **4.72**	2.78 **4.22**	2.62 **3.90**	2.51 **3.67**	2.43 **3.50**	2.36 **3.36**	2.30 **3.25**	2.26 **3.17**	2.22 **3.09**	2.18 **3.03**	2.13 **2.93**	2.09 **2.85**	2.02 **2.74**	1.98 **2.66**	1.94 **2.58**	1.89 **2.49**	1.86 **2.44**	1.82 **2.36**	1.80 **2.33**	1.76 **2.27**	1.74 **2.23**	1.73 **2.21**
25	4.24 **7.77**	3.38 **5.57**	2.99 **4.68**	2.76 **4.18**	2.60 **3.86**	2.49 **3.63**	2.41 **3.46**	2.34 **3.32**	2.28 **3.21**	2.24 **3.13**	2.20 **3.05**	2.16 **2.99**	2.11 **2.89**	2.06 **2.81**	2.00 **2.70**	1.96 **2.62**	1.92 **2.54**	1.87 **2.45**	1.84 **2.40**	1.80 **2.32**	1.77 **2.29**	1.74 **2.23**	1.72 **2.19**	1.71 **2.17**
26	4.22 **7.72**	3.37 **5.53**	2.98 **4.64**	2.74 **4.14**	2.59 **3.82**	2.47 **3.59**	2.39 **3.42**	2.32 **3.29**	2.27 **3.17**	2.22 **3.09**	2.18 **3.02**	2.15 **2.96**	2.10 **2.86**	2.05 **2.77**	1.99 **2.66**	1.95 **2.58**	1.90 **2.50**	1.85 **2.41**	1.82 **2.36**	1.78 **2.28**	1.76 **2.25**	1.72 **2.19**	1.70 **2.15**	1.69 **2.13**
27	4.21 **7.68**	3.35 **5.49**	2.96 **4.60**	2.73 **4.11**	2.57 **3.79**	2.46 **3.56**	2.37 **3.39**	2.30 **3.26**	2.25 **3.14**	2.20 **3.06**	2.16 **2.98**	2.13 **2.93**	2.08 **2.83**	2.03 **2.74**	1.97 **2.63**	1.93 **2.55**	1.88 **2.47**	1.84 **2.38**	1.80 **2.33**	1.76 **2.25**	1.74 **2.21**	1.71 **2.16**	1.68 **2.12**	1.67 **2.10**
28	4.20 **7.64**	3.34 **5.45**	2.95 **4.57**	2.71 **4.07**	2.56 **3.76**	2.44 **3.53**	2.36 **3.36**	2.29 **3.23**	2.24 **3.11**	2.19 **3.03**	2.15 **2.95**	2.12 **2.90**	2.06 **2.80**	2.02 **2.71**	1.96 **2.60**	1.91 **2.52**	1.87 **2.44**	1.81 **2.35**	1.78 **2.30**	1.75 **2.22**	1.72 **2.18**	1.69 **2.13**	1.67 **2.09**	1.65 **2.06**
29	4.18 **7.60**	3.33 **5.42**	2.93 **4.54**	2.70 **4.04**	2.54 **3.73**	2.43 **3.50**	2.35 **3.33**	2.28 **3.20**	2.22 **3.08**	2.18 **3.00**	2.14 **2.92**	2.10 **2.87**	2.05 **2.77**	2.00 **2.68**	1.94 **2.57**	1.90 **2.49**	1.85 **2.41**	1.80 **2.32**	1.77 **2.27**	1.73 **2.19**	1.71 **2.15**	1.68 **2.10**	1.65 **2.06**	1.64 **2.03**

Degrees of Freedom for Denominator

Table B.3 (cont.)

Each cell shows the 5% point (top) / 1% point (bottom).

Degrees of Freedom for Numerator

Denom. df	1	2	3	4	5	6	7	8	9	10	11	12	14	16	20	24	30	40	50	75	100	200	500	∞
30	4.17 / 7.56	3.32 / 5.39	2.92 / 4.51	2.69 / 4.02	2.53 / 3.70	2.42 / 3.47	2.34 / 3.30	2.27 / 3.17	2.21 / 3.06	2.16 / 2.98	2.12 / 2.90	2.09 / 2.84	2.04 / 2.74	1.99 / 2.66	1.93 / 2.55	1.89 / 2.47	1.84 / 2.38	1.79 / 2.29	1.76 / 2.24	1.72 / 2.16	1.69 / 2.13	1.66 / 2.07	1.64 / 2.03	1.62 / 2.01
32	4.15 / 7.50	3.30 / 5.34	2.90 / 4.46	2.67 / 3.97	2.51 / 3.66	2.40 / 3.42	2.32 / 3.25	2.25 / 3.12	2.19 / 3.01	2.14 / 2.94	2.10 / 2.86	2.07 / 2.80	2.02 / 2.70	1.97 / 2.62	1.91 / 2.51	1.86 / 2.42	1.82 / 2.34	1.76 / 2.25	1.74 / 2.20	1.69 / 2.12	1.67 / 2.08	1.64 / 2.02	1.61 / 1.98	1.59 / 1.96
34	4.13 / 7.44	3.28 / 5.29	2.88 / 4.42	2.65 / 3.93	2.49 / 3.61	2.38 / 3.38	2.30 / 3.21	2.23 / 3.08	2.17 / 2.97	2.12 / 2.89	2.08 / 2.82	2.05 / 2.76	2.00 / 2.66	1.95 / 2.58	1.89 / 2.47	1.84 / 2.38	1.80 / 2.30	1.74 / 2.21	1.71 / 2.15	1.67 / 2.08	1.64 / 2.04	1.61 / 1.98	1.59 / 1.94	1.57 / 1.91
36	4.11 / 7.39	3.26 / 5.25	2.86 / 4.38	2.63 / 3.89	2.48 / 3.58	2.36 / 3.35	2.28 / 3.18	2.21 / 3.04	2.15 / 2.94	2.10 / 2.86	2.06 / 2.78	2.03 / 2.72	1.99 / 2.62	1.93 / 2.54	1.87 / 2.43	1.82 / 2.35	1.78 / 2.26	1.72 / 2.17	1.69 / 2.12	1.65 / 2.04	1.62 / 2.00	1.59 / 1.94	1.56 / 1.90	1.55 / 1.87
38	4.10 / 7.35	3.25 / 5.21	2.85 / 4.34	2.62 / 3.86	2.46 / 3.54	2.35 / 3.32	2.26 / 3.15	2.19 / 3.02	2.14 / 2.91	2.09 / 2.82	2.05 / 2.75	2.02 / 2.69	1.96 / 2.59	1.92 / 2.51	1.85 / 2.40	1.80 / 2.32	1.76 / 2.22	1.71 / 2.14	1.67 / 2.08	1.63 / 2.00	1.60 / 1.97	1.57 / 1.90	1.54 / 1.86	1.53 / 1.84
40	4.08 / 7.31	3.23 / 5.18	2.84 / 4.31	2.61 / 3.83	2.45 / 3.51	2.34 / 3.29	2.25 / 3.12	2.18 / 2.99	2.12 / 2.88	2.07 / 2.80	2.04 / 2.73	2.00 / 2.66	1.95 / 2.56	1.90 / 2.49	1.84 / 2.37	1.79 / 2.29	1.74 / 2.20	1.69 / 2.11	1.66 / 2.05	1.61 / 1.97	1.59 / 1.94	1.55 / 1.88	1.53 / 1.84	1.51 / 1.81
42	4.07 / 7.27	3.22 / 5.15	2.83 / 4.29	2.59 / 3.80	2.44 / 3.49	2.32 / 3.26	2.24 / 3.10	2.17 / 2.96	2.11 / 2.86	2.06 / 2.77	2.02 / 2.70	1.99 / 2.64	1.94 / 2.54	1.89 / 2.46	1.82 / 2.35	1.78 / 2.26	1.73 / 2.17	1.68 / 2.08	1.64 / 2.02	1.60 / 1.94	1.57 / 1.91	1.54 / 1.85	1.51 / 1.80	1.49 / 1.78
44	4.06 / 7.24	3.21 / 5.12	2.82 / 4.26	2.58 / 3.78	2.43 / 3.46	2.31 / 3.24	2.23 / 3.07	2.16 / 2.94	2.10 / 2.84	2.05 / 2.75	2.01 / 2.68	1.98 / 2.62	1.92 / 2.52	1.88 / 2.44	1.81 / 2.32	1.76 / 2.24	1.72 / 2.15	1.66 / 2.06	1.63 / 1.99	1.58 / 1.92	1.56 / 1.88	1.52 / 1.82	1.50 / 1.78	1.48 / 1.75
46	4.05 / 7.21	3.20 / 5.10	2.81 / 4.24	2.57 / 3.76	2.42 / 3.44	2.30 / 3.22	2.22 / 3.05	2.14 / 2.92	2.09 / 2.82	2.04 / 2.73	2.00 / 2.66	1.97 / 2.60	1.91 / 2.50	1.87 / 2.42	1.80 / 2.30	1.75 / 2.22	1.71 / 2.13	1.65 / 2.04	1.62 / 1.98	1.57 / 1.90	1.54 / 1.86	1.51 / 1.80	1.48 / 1.76	1.46 / 1.72
48	4.04 / 7.19	3.19 / 5.08	2.80 / 4.22	2.56 / 3.74	2.41 / 3.42	2.30 / 3.20	2.21 / 3.04	2.14 / 2.90	2.08 / 2.80	2.03 / 2.71	1.99 / 2.64	1.96 / 2.58	1.90 / 2.48	1.86 / 2.40	1.79 / 2.28	1.74 / 2.20	1.70 / 2.11	1.64 / 2.02	1.61 / 1.96	1.56 / 1.88	1.53 / 1.84	1.50 / 1.78	1.47 / 1.73	1.45 / 1.70
50	4.03 / 7.17	3.18 / 5.06	2.79 / 4.20	2.56 / 3.72	2.40 / 3.41	2.29 / 3.18	2.20 / 3.02	2.13 / 2.88	2.07 / 2.78	2.02 / 2.70	1.98 / 2.62	1.95 / 2.56	1.90 / 2.46	1.85 / 2.39	1.78 / 2.26	1.74 / 2.18	1.69 / 2.10	1.63 / 2.00	1.60 / 1.94	1.55 / 1.86	1.52 / 1.82	1.48 / 1.76	1.46 / 1.71	1.44 / 1.68
55	4.02 / 7.12	3.17 / 5.01	2.78 / 4.16	2.54 / 3.68	2.38 / 3.37	2.27 / 3.15	2.18 / 2.98	2.11 / 2.85	2.05 / 2.75	2.00 / 2.66	1.97 / 2.59	1.93 / 2.53	1.88 / 2.43	1.83 / 2.35	1.76 / 2.23	1.72 / 2.15	1.67 / 2.06	1.61 / 1.96	1.58 / 1.90	1.52 / 1.82	1.50 / 1.78	1.46 / 1.71	1.43 / 1.66	1.41 / 1.64
60	4.00 / 7.08	3.15 / 4.98	2.76 / 4.13	2.52 / 3.65	2.37 / 3.34	2.25 / 3.12	2.17 / 2.95	2.10 / 2.82	2.04 / 2.72	1.99 / 2.63	1.95 / 2.56	1.92 / 2.50	1.86 / 2.40	1.81 / 2.32	1.75 / 2.20	1.70 / 2.12	1.65 / 2.03	1.59 / 1.93	1.56 / 1.87	1.50 / 1.79	1.48 / 1.74	1.44 / 1.68	1.41 / 1.63	1.39 / 1.60
65	3.99 / 7.04	3.14 / 4.95	2.75 / 4.10	2.51 / 3.62	2.36 / 3.31	2.24 / 3.09	2.15 / 2.93	2.08 / 2.79	2.02 / 2.70	1.98 / 2.61	1.94 / 2.54	1.90 / 2.47	1.85 / 2.37	1.80 / 2.30	1.73 / 2.18	1.68 / 2.09	1.63 / 2.00	1.57 / 1.90	1.54 / 1.84	1.49 / 1.76	1.46 / 1.71	1.42 / 1.64	1.39 / 1.60	1.37 / 1.56
70	3.98 / 7.01	3.13 / 4.92	2.74 / 4.08	2.50 / 3.60	2.35 / 3.29	2.23 / 3.07	2.14 / 2.91	2.07 / 2.77	2.01 / 2.67	1.97 / 2.59	1.93 / 2.51	1.89 / 2.45	1.84 / 2.35	1.79 / 2.28	1.72 / 2.15	1.67 / 2.07	1.62 / 1.98	1.56 / 1.88	1.53 / 1.82	1.47 / 1.74	1.45 / 1.69	1.40 / 1.62	1.37 / 1.56	1.35 / 1.53
80	3.96 / 6.96	3.11 / 4.88	2.72 / 4.04	2.48 / 3.56	2.33 / 3.25	2.21 / 3.04	2.12 / 2.87	2.05 / 2.74	1.99 / 2.64	1.95 / 2.55	1.91 / 2.48	1.88 / 2.41	1.82 / 2.32	1.77 / 2.24	1.70 / 2.11	1.65 / 2.03	1.60 / 1.94	1.54 / 1.84	1.51 / 1.78	1.45 / 1.70	1.42 / 1.65	1.38 / 1.57	1.35 / 1.52	1.32 / 1.49

Degrees of Freedom for Denominator

Table B.3 *(cont.)*

Degrees of Freedom for Numerator

Denominator df	1	2	3	4	5	6	7	8	9	10	11	12	14	16	20	24	30	40	50	75	100	200	500	∞
100	3.94 / 6.90	3.09 / 4.82	2.70 / 3.98	2.46 / 3.51	2.30 / 3.20	2.19 / 2.99	2.10 / 2.82	2.03 / 2.69	1.97 / 2.59	1.92 / 2.51	1.88 / 2.43	1.85 / 2.36	1.79 / 2.26	1.75 / 2.19	1.68 / 2.06	1.63 / 1.98	1.57 / 1.89	1.51 / 1.79	1.48 / 1.73	1.42 / 1.64	1.39 / 1.59	1.34 / 1.51	1.30 / 1.46	1.28 / 1.43
125	3.92 / 6.84	3.07 / 4.78	2.68 / 3.94	2.44 / 3.47	2.29 / 3.17	2.17 / 2.95	2.08 / 2.79	2.01 / 2.65	1.95 / 2.56	1.90 / 2.47	1.86 / 2.40	1.83 / 2.33	1.77 / 2.23	1.72 / 2.15	1.65 / 2.03	1.60 / 1.94	1.55 / 1.85	1.49 / 1.75	1.45 / 1.68	1.39 / 1.59	1.36 / 1.54	1.31 / 1.46	1.27 / 1.40	1.25 / 1.37
150	3.91 / 6.81	3.06 / 4.75	2.67 / 3.91	2.43 / 3.44	2.27 / 3.13	2.16 / 2.92	2.07 / 2.76	2.00 / 2.62	1.94 / 2.53	1.89 / 2.44	1.85 / 2.37	1.82 / 2.30	1.76 / 2.20	1.71 / 2.12	1.64 / 2.00	1.59 / 1.91	1.54 / 1.83	1.47 / 1.72	1.44 / 1.66	1.37 / 1.56	1.34 / 1.51	1.29 / 1.43	1.25 / 1.37	1.22 / 1.33
200	3.89 / 6.76	3.04 / 4.71	2.65 / 3.38	2.41 / 3.41	2.26 / 3.11	2.14 / 2.90	2.05 / 2.73	1.98 / 2.60	1.92 / 2.50	1.87 / 2.41	1.83 / 2.34	1.80 / 2.28	1.74 / 1.17	1.69 / 2.09	1.62 / 1.97	1.57 / 1.88	1.52 / 1.79	1.45 / 1.69	1.42 / 1.62	1.35 / 1.53	1.32 / 1.48	1.26 / 1.39	1.22 / 1.33	1.19 / 1.28
400	3.86 / 6.70	3.02 / 4.66	2.62 / 3.83	2.39 / 3.36	2.23 / 3.06	2.12 / 2.85	2.03 / 2.69	1.96 / 2.55	1.90 / 2.46	1.85 / 2.37	1.81 / 2.29	1.78 / 2.23	1.72 / 2.12	1.67 / 2.04	1.60 / 1.92	1.54 / 1.84	1.49 / 1.74	1.42 / 1.64	1.38 / 1.57	1.32 / 1.47	1.28 / 1.42	1.22 / 1.32	1.16 / 1.24	1.13 / 1.19
1000	3.85 / 6.66	3.00 / 4.62	2.61 / 3.80	2.38 / 3.34	2.22 / 3.04	2.10 / 2.82	2.02 / 2.66	1.95 / 2.53	1.89 / 2.43	1.84 / 2.34	1.80 / 2.26	1.76 / 2.20	1.70 / 2.09	1.65 / 2.01	1.58 / 1.89	1.53 / 1.81	1.47 / 1.71	1.41 / 1.61	1.36 / 1.54	1.30 / 1.44	1.26 / 1.38	1.19 / 1.28	1.13 / 1.19	1.08 / 1.11
∞	3.84 / 6.64	2.99 / 4.60	2.60 / 3.78	2.37 / 3.32	2.21 / 3.02	2.09 / 2.80	2.01 / 2.64	1.94 / 2.51	1.88 / 2.41	1.83 / 2.32	1.79 / 2.24	1.75 / 2.18	1.69 / 2.07	1.64 / 1.99	1.57 / 1.87	1.52 / 1.79	1.46 / 1.69	1.40 / 1.59	1.35 / 1.52	1.28 / 1.41	1.24 / 1.36	1.17 / 1.25	1.11 / 1.15	1.00 / 1.00

Degrees of Freedom for Denominator

Source: G. W. Snedecor and William G. Cochran (1967). *Statistical Methods* (6th ed.). Ames, IA: Iowa State University Press.

Table B.4 CRITICAL VALUES OF THE PEARSON PRODUCT-MOMENT CORRELATION

If the observed value of r is greater than or equal to the tabled value for the desired level of significance and degrees of freedom (number of pairs of scores minus 2), we conclude that a statistically significant relationship between the variables does exist in the population sampled.

$df = N - 2$	Level of Significance for a Nondirectional (Two-Tailed) Test				
	0.10	0.05	0.02	0.01	0.001
1	0.9877	0.9969	0.9995	0.9999	1.0000
2	0.9000	0.9500	0.9800	0.9900	0.9990
3	0.8054	0.8783	0.9343	0.9587	0.9912
4	0.7293	0.8114	0.8822	0.9172	0.9741
5	0.6694	0.7545	0.8329	0.8745	0.9507
6	0.6215	0.7067	0.7887	0.8343	0.9249
7	0.5822	0.6664	0.7498	0.7977	0.8982
8	0.5494	0.6319	0.7155	0.7646	0.8721
9	0.5214	0.6021	0.6851	0.7348	0.8471
10	0.4973	0.5760	0.6581	0.7079	0.8233
11	0.4762	0.5529	0.6339	0.6835	0.8010
12	0.4575	0.5324	0.6120	0.6614	0.7800
13	0.4409	0.5139	0.5923	0.6411	0.7603
14	0.4259	0.4973	0.5742	0.6226	0.7420
15	0.4124	0.4821	0.5577	0.6055	0.7246
16	0.4000	0.4683	0.5425	0.5897	0.7084
17	0.3887	0.4555	0.5285	0.5751	0.6932
18	0.3783	0.4438	0.5155	0.5614	0.6787
19	0.3687	0.4329	0.5034	0.5487	0.6652
20	0.3598	0.4227	0.4921	0.5368	0.6524
25	0.3233	0.3809	0.4451	0.4869	0.5974
30	0.2960	0.3494	0.4093	0.4487	0.5541
35	0.2746	0.3246	0.3810	0.4182	0.5189
40	0.2573	0.3044	0.3578	0.3932	0.4896
45	0.2428	0.2875	0.3384	0.3721	0.4648
50	0.2306	0.2732	0.3218	0.3541	0.4433
60	0.2108	0.2500	0.2948	0.3248	0.4078
70	0.1954	0.2319	0.2737	0.3017	0.3799
80	0.1829	0.2172	0.2565	0.2830	0.3568
90	0.1726	0.2050	0.2422	0.2673	0.3375
100	0.1638	0.1946	0.2301	0.2540	0.3211

Source: R. A. Fisher and F. Yates (1974). *Statistical tables for biological, agricultural, and medical research* (2nd ed.), Table VII Edinburgh: Oliver and Boyd, Ltd.

Table B.5 CRITICAL VALUES OF THE SPEARMAN RANK-ORDER CORRELATION

If the observed value of r is greater than or equal to the tabled value for the desired level of significance and number of pairs, we conclude that a statistically significant relationship between these variables does exist in the population sampled.

N^a	Level of Significance for Two-Tailed Test			
	0.10	0.05	0.02	0.01
5	0.900	1.000	1.000	—
6	0.829	0.886	0.943	1.000
7	0.714	0.786	0.893	0.929
8	0.643	0.738	0.833	0.881
9	0.600	0.683	0.783	0.833
10	0.564	0.648	0.746	0.794
12	0.506	0.591	0.712	0.777
14	0.456	0.544	0.645	0.715
16	0.425	0.506	0.601	0.665
18	0.399	0.475	0.564	0.625
20	0.377	0.450	0.534	0.591
22	0.359	0.428	0.508	0.562
24	0.343	0.409	0.485	0.537
26	0.329	0.392	0.465	0.515
28	0.317	0.377	0.448	0.496
30	0.306	0.364	0.432	0.478

^aN = number of pairs.

Source: E. G. Olds (1949). The 5 percent significance levels for sums of squares or ranked differences and a correction. *Annals of Mathematical Statistics, 20,* 117–118; and E. G. Olds (1938). Distribution of sums of squares of ranked differences for small numbers of individuals. *Annals of Mathematical Statistics, 9,* 133–148.

Table B.6 PROBABILITY VALUES OF THE CHI-SQUARE DISTRIBUTION

If the observed chi-square is greater than or equal to the tabled value for the desired probability level and degrees of freedom, we should reject the null hypothesis.

Degrees of freedom (df)	0.10	0.05	0.02	0.01
1	2.706	3.841	5.412	6.635
2	4.605	5.991	7.824	9.210
3	6.251	7.815	9.837	11.341
4	7.779	9.488	11.668	13.277
5	9.236	11.070	13.388	15.086
6	10.645	12.592	15.033	16.812
7	12.017	14.067	16.622	18.475
8	13.362	15.507	18.168	20.090
9	14.684	16.919	19.679	21.666
10	15.987	18.307	21.161	23.209
11	17.275	19.675	22.618	24.725
12	18.549	21.026	24.054	26.217
13	19.812	22.362	25.472	27.688
14	21.064	23.685	26.873	29.141
15	22.307	24.996	28.259	30.578
16	23.542	26.296	29.633	32.000
17	24.769	27.587	30.995	33.409
18	25.989	28.869	32.346	34.805
19	27.204	30.144	33.687	36.191
20	28.412	31.410	35.020	37.566
21	29.615	32.671	36.343	38.932
22	30.813	33.924	37.659	40.289
23	32.007	35.172	38.968	41.638
24	33.196	36.415	40.270	42.980
25	34.382	37.652	41.566	44.314
26	35.563	38.885	42.856	45.642
27	36.741	40.113	44.140	46.963
28	37.916	41.337	45.419	48.278
29	39.087	42.557	46.693	49.588
30	40.256	43.773	47.962	50.892

Source: R. A. Fisher (1970). *Statistical methods for research workers.* (14th ed.). Reprinted by permission of Macmillan Publishing Company. Copyright © 1970 University of Adelaide.

Table B.7 RANDOM NUMBERS

To use the table of random numbers, select any starting point and any direction (up, down, left, right). For example, if we want to assign subjects randomly to each of five groups, we might start at the beginning of row 85 and move left to right. We number the groups 1 through 5. We assign the first subject to the group designated by the first digit we encounter that is between 1 and 5; the second subject is assigned to the group designated by the next suitable digit encountered, and so on. By this method, the first ten subjects are randomly assigned to the following groups: 1, 3, 1, 1, 2, 2, 4, 2, 1, 3.

It is also possible to randomize within blocks so that the same number of subjects is in each condition. For example, if we want to assign the first five subjects—one to each of the five groups—and we use the same starting point (beginning of row 85), we get the following assignment: 1, 3, 2, 4, 5. Our second block of five subjects are assigned to the following groups: 3, 2, 5, 4, 1. Variations of these procedures can be used for random selection of subjects from an accessible population, assignment of groups to conditions, or in some form of stratified random sampling.

Row number										
00000	10097	32533	76520	13586	34673	54876	80959	09117	39292	74945
00001	37542	04805	64894	74296	24805	24037	20636	10402	00822	91665
00002	08422	68953	19645	09303	23209	02560	15953	34764	35080	33606
00003	99019	02529	09376	70715	38311	31165	88676	74397	04436	27659
00004	12807	99970	80157	36147	64032	36653	98951	16877	12171	76833
00005	66065	74717	34072	76850	36697	36170	65813	39885	11199	29170
00006	31060	10805	45571	82406	35303	42614	86799	07439	23403	09732
00007	85269	77602	02051	65692	68665	74818	73053	85247	18623	88579
00008	63573	32135	05325	47048	90553	57548	28468	28709	83491	25624
00009	73796	45753	03529	64778	35808	34282	60935	20344	35273	88435
00010	98520	17767	14905	68607	22109	40558	60970	93433	50500	73998
00011	11805	05431	39808	27732	50725	68248	29405	24201	52775	67851
00012	83452	99634	06288	98033	13746	70078	18475	40610	68711	77817
00013	88685	40200	86507	58401	36766	67951	90364	76493	29609	11062
00014	99594	67348	87517	64969	91826	08928	93785	61368	23478	34113
00015	65481	17674	17468	50950	58047	76974	73039	57186	40218	16544
00016	80124	35635	17727	08015	45318	22374	21115	78253	14385	53763
00017	74350	99817	77402	77214	43236	00210	45521	64237	96286	02655
00018	69916	26803	66252	29148	36936	87203	76621	13990	94400	56418
00019	09893	20505	14225	68514	46427	56788	96297	78822	54382	14598
00020	91499	14523	68479	27686	46162	83554	94750	89923	37089	20048
00021	80336	94598	26940	36858	70297	34135	53140	33340	42050	82341
00022	44104	81949	85157	47954	32979	26575	57600	40881	22222	06413
00023	12550	73742	11100	02040	12860	74697	96644	89439	28707	25815
00024	63606	49329	16505	34484	40219	52563	43651	77082	07207	31790
00025	61196	90446	26457	47774	51924	33729	65394	59593	42582	60527
00026	15474	45266	95270	79953	59367	83848	82396	10118	33211	59466
00027	94557	28573	67897	54387	54622	44431	91190	42592	92927	45973
00028	42481	16213	97344	08721	16868	48767	03071	12059	25701	46670
00029	23523	78317	73208	89837	68935	91416	26252	29663	05522	82562
00030	04493	52494	75246	33824	45862	51025	61962	79335	65337	12472
00031	00549	97654	64051	88159	96119	63896	54692	82391	23287	29529
00032	35963	15307	26898	09354	33351	35462	77974	50024	90103	39333
00033	59808	08391	45427	26842	83609	49700	13021	24892	78565	20106
00034	46058	85236	01390	92286	77281	44077	93910	83647	70617	42941
00035	32179	00597	87379	25241	05567	07007	86743	17157	85394	11838
00036	69234	61406	20117	45204	15956	60000	18743	92423	97118	96338
00037	19565	41430	01758	75379	40419	21585	66674	36806	84962	85207
00038	45155	14938	19476	07246	43667	94543	59047	90033	20826	69541
00039	94864	31994	36168	10851	34888	81553	01540	35456	05014	51176

Table B.7 (*cont.*)

Row number										
00040	98086	24826	45240	28404	44999	08896	39094	73407	35441	31880
00041	33185	16232	41941	50949	89435	48581	88695	41994	37548	73043
00042	80951	00406	96382	70774	20151	23387	25016	25298	94624	61171
00043	79752	49140	71961	28296	69861	02591	74852	20539	00387	59579
00044	18633	32537	98145	06571	31010	24674	05455	61427	77938	91936
00045	74029	43902	77557	32270	97790	17119	52527	58021	80814	51748
00046	54178	45611	80993	37143	05335	12969	56127	19255	36040	90324
00047	11664	49883	52079	84827	59381	71539	09973	33440	88461	23356
00048	48324	77928	31249	64710	02295	36870	32307	57546	15020	09994
00049	69074	94138	87637	91976	35584	04401	10518	21615	01848	76938
00050	09188	20097	32825	39527	04220	86304	83389	87374	64278	58044
00051	90045	85497	51981	50654	94938	81997	91870	76150	68476	64659
00052	73189	50207	47677	26269	62290	64464	27124	67018	41361	82760
00053	75768	76490	20971	87749	90429	12272	95375	05871	93823	43178
00054	54016	44056	66281	31003	00682	27398	20714	53295	07706	17813
00055	08358	69910	78542	42785	13661	58873	04618	97553	31223	08420
00056	28306	03264	81333	10591	40510	07893	32604	60475	94119	01840
00057	53840	86233	81594	13628	51215	90290	28466	68795	77762	20791
00058	91757	53741	61613	62669	50263	90212	55781	76514	83483	47055
00059	89415	92694	00397	58391	12607	17646	48949	72306	94541	37408
00060	77513	03820	86864	29901	68414	82774	51908	13980	72893	55507
00061	19502	37174	69979	20288	55210	29773	74287	75251	65344	67415
00062	21818	59313	93278	81757	05686	73156	07082	85046	31853	38452
00063	51474	66499	68107	23621	94049	91345	42836	09191	08007	45449
00064	99559	68331	62535	24170	69777	12830	74819	78142	43860	72834
00065	33713	48007	93584	72869	51926	64721	58303	29822	93174	93972
00066	85274	86893	11303	22970	28834	34137	73515	90400	71148	43643
00067	84133	89640	44035	52166	73852	70091	61222	60561	62327	18423
00068	56732	16234	17395	96131	10123	91622	85496	57560	81604	18880
00069	65138	56806	87648	85261	34313	65861	45875	21069	85644	47277
00070	38001	02176	81719	11711	71602	92937	74219	64049	65584	49698
00071	37402	96397	01304	77586	56271	10086	47324	62605	40030	37438
00072	97125	40348	87083	31417	21815	39250	75237	62047	15501	29578
00073	21826	41134	47143	34072	64638	85902	49139	06441	03856	54552
00074	73135	42742	95719	09035	85794	74296	08789	88156	64691	19202
00075	07638	77929	03061	18072	96207	44156	23821	99538	04713	66994
00076	60528	83441	07954	19814	59175	20695	05533	52139	61212	06455
00077	83596	35655	06958	92983	05128	09719	77433	53783	92301	50498
00078	10850	62746	99599	10507	13499	06319	53075	71839	06410	19362
00079	39820	98952	43622	63147	64421	80814	43800	09351	31024	73167
00080	59580	06478	75569	78800	88835	54486	23768	06156	04111	08408
00081	38508	07341	23793	48763	90822	97022	17719	04207	95954	49953
00082	30692	70668	94688	16127	56196	80091	82067	63400	05462	69200
00083	65443	95659	18238	27437	49632	24041	08337	65676	96299	90836
00084	27267	50264	13192	72294	07477	44606	17985	48911	97341	30358
00085	91307	06991	19072	24210	36699	53728	28825	35793	28976	66252
00086	68434	94688	84473	13622	62126	98408	12843	82590	09815	93146
00087	48908	15877	54745	24591	35700	04754	83824	52692	54130	55160
00088	06913	45197	42672	78601	11883	09528	63011	98901	14974	40344
00089	10455	16019	14210	33712	91342	37821	88325	80851	43667	70883

Row number										
00090	12883	97343	65027	61184	04285	01392	17974	15077	90712	26769
00091	21778	30976	38807	36961	31649	42096	63281	02023	08816	47449
00092	19523	59515	65122	59659	86283	68258	69572	13798	16435	91529
00093	67245	52670	35583	16563	79246	86686	76463	34222	26655	90802
00094	60584	47377	07500	37992	45134	26529	26760	83637	41326	44344
00095	53853	41377	36066	94850	58838	73859	49364	73331	96240	43642
00096	24637	38736	74384	89342	52623	07992	12369	18601	03742	83873
00097	83080	12451	38992	22815	07759	51777	97377	27585	51972	37867
00098	16444	24334	36151	99073	27493	70939	85130	32552	54846	54759
00099	60790	18157	57178	65762	11161	78576	45819	52979	65130	04860
00100	03991	10461	93716	16894	66083	24653	84609	58232	88618	19161
00101	38555	95554	32886	59780	08355	60860	29735	47762	71299	23853
00102	17546	73704	92052	46215	55121	29281	59076	07936	27954	58909
00103	32643	52861	95819	06831	00911	98936	76355	93779	80863	00514
00104	69572	68777	39510	35905	14060	40619	29549	69616	33564	60780
00105	24122	66591	27699	06494	14845	46672	61958	77100	90899	75754
00106	61196	30231	92962	61773	41839	55382	17267	70943	78038	70267
00107	30532	21704	10274	12202	39685	23309	10061	68829	55986	66485
00108	03788	97599	75867	20717	74416	53166	35208	33374	87539	08823
00109	48228	63379	85783	47619	53152	67433	35663	52972	16818	60311
00110	60365	94653	35075	33949	42614	29297	01918	28316	98953	73231
00111	83799	42402	56623	34442	34994	41374	70071	14736	09958	18065
00112	32960	07405	36409	83232	99385	41600	11133	07586	15917	06253
00113	19322	53845	57620	52606	66497	68646	78138	66559	19640	99413
00114	11220	94747	07399	37408	48509	23929	27482	45476	85244	35159
00115	31751	57260	68980	05339	15470	48355	88651	22596	03152	19121
00116	88492	99382	14454	04504	20094	98977	74843	93413	22109	78508
00117	30934	47744	07481	83828	73788	06533	28597	20405	94205	20380
00118	22888	48893	27499	98748	60530	45128	74022	84617	82037	10268
00119	78212	16993	35902	91386	44372	15486	65741	14014	87481	37220
00120	41849	84547	46850	52326	34677	58300	74910	64345	19325	81549
00121	46352	33049	69248	93460	45305	07521	61318	31855	14413	70951
00122	11087	96294	14013	31792	59747	67277	76503	34513	39663	77544
00123	52701	08337	56303	87315	16520	69676	11654	99893	02181	68161
00124	57275	36898	81304	48585	68652	27376	92852	55866	88448	03584
00125	20857	73156	70284	24326	79375	95220	01159	63267	10622	48391
00126	15633	84924	90415	93614	33521	26665	55823	47641	86225	31704
00127	92694	48297	39904	02115	59589	49067	66821	41575	49767	04037
00128	77613	19019	88152	00080	20554	91409	96277	48257	50816	97616
00129	38688	32486	45134	63545	59404	72059	43947	51680	43852	59693
00130	25163	01889	70014	15021	41290	67312	71857	15957	68971	11403
00131	65251	07629	37239	33295	05870	01119	92784	26340	18477	65622
00132	36815	43625	18637	37509	82444	99005	04921	73701	14707	93997
00133	64397	11692	05327	82162	20247	81759	45197	25332	83745	22567
00134	04515	25624	95096	67946	48460	85558	15191	18782	16930	33361
00135	83761	60873	43253	84145	60833	25983	01291	41349	20368	07126
00136	14387	06345	80854	09279	43529	06318	38384	74761	41196	37480
00137	51321	92246	80088	77074	88722	56736	66164	49431	66919	31678
00138	72472	00008	80890	18002	94813	31900	54155	83436	35352	54131
00139	05466	55306	93128	18464	74457	90561	72848	11834	79982	68416

Table B.7 (*cont.*)

Row number										
00140	39528	72484	82474	25593	48545	35247	18619	13674	18611	19241
00141	81616	18711	53342	44276	75122	11724	74627	73707	58319	15997
00142	07586	16120	82641	22820	92904	13141	32392	19763	61199	67940
00143	90767	04235	13574	17200	69902	63742	78464	22501	18627	90872
00144	40ı88	28193	29593	88627	94972	11598	62095	36787	00441	58997
00145	34414	82157	86887	55087	19152	00023	12302	80783	32624	68691
00146	63439	75363	44989	16822	36024	00867	76378	41605	65961	73488
00147	67049	09070	93399	45547	94458	74284	05041	49807	20288	34060
00148	79495	04146	52162	90286	54158	34243	46978	35482	59362	95938
00149	91704	30552	04737	21031	75051	93029	47665	64382	99782	93478
00150	94015	46874	32444	48277	59820	96163	64654	25843	41145	42820
00151	74108	88222	88570	74015	25704	91035	01755	14750	48968	38603
00152	62880	87873	95160	59221	22304	90314	72877	17334	39283	04149
00153	11748	12102	80580	41867	17710	59621	06554	07850	73950	79552
00154	17944	05600	60478	03343	25852	58905	57216	39618	49856	99326
00155	66067	42792	95043	52680	46780	56487	09971	59481	37006	22186
00156	54244	91030	45547	70818	59849	96169	61459	21647	87417	17198
00157	30945	57589	31732	57260	47670	07654	46376	25366	94746	49580
00158	69170	37403	86995	90307	94304	71803	26825	05511	12459	91314
00159	08345	88975	35841	85771	08105	59987	87112	21476	14713	71181
00160	27767	43584	85301	88977	29490	69714	73035	41207	74699	09310
00161	13025	14338	54066	15243	47724	66733	47431	43905	31048	56699
00162	80217	36292	98525	24335	24432	24896	43277	58874	11466	16082
00163	10875	62004	90391	61105	57411	06368	53856	30743	08670	84741
00164	54127	57326	26629	19087	24472	88779	30540	27886	61732	75454
00165	60311	42824	37301	42678	45990	43242	17374	52003	70707	70214
00166	49739	71484	92003	98086	76668	73209	59202	11973	02902	33250
00167	78626	51594	16453	94614	39014	97066	83012	09832	25571	77628
00168	66692	13986	99837	00582	81232	44987	09504	96412	90193	79568
00169	44071	28091	07362	97703	76447	42537	98524	97831	65704	09514
00170	41468	85149	49554	17994	14924	39650	95294	00556	70481	06905
00171	94559	37559	49678	53119	70312	05682	66986	34099	74474	20740
00172	41615	70360	64114	58660	90850	64618	80620	51790	11436	38072
00173	50273	93113	41794	86861	24781	89683	55411	85667	77535	99892
00174	41396	80504	90670	08289	40902	05069	95083	06783	28102	57816
00175	25807	24260	71529	78920	72682	07385	90726	57166	98884	08583
00176	06170	97965	88302	98041	21443	41808	68984	83620	89747	98882
00177	60808	54444	74412	81105	01176	28838	36421	16489	18059	51061
00178	80940	44893	10408	36222	80582	71944	92638	40333	67054	16067
00179	19516	90120	46759	71643	13177	55292	21036	82808	77501	97427
00180	49386	54480	23604	23554	21785	41101	91178	10174	29420	90438
00181	06312	88940	15995	69321	47458	64809	98189	81851	29651	84215
00182	60942	00307	11897	92674	40405	68032	96717	54244	10701	41393
00183	92329	98932	78284	46347	71209	92061	39448	93136	25722	08564
00184	77936	63574	31384	51924	85561	29671	58137	17820	22751	36518
00185	38101	77756	11657	13897	95889	57067	47648	13885	70669	93406
00186	39641	69457	91339	22502	92613	89719	11947	56203	19324	20504
00187	84054	40455	99396	63680	67667	60631	69181	96845	38525	11600
00188	47468	03577	57649	63266	24700	71594	14004	23153	69249	05747
00189	43321	31370	28977	23896	76479	68562	62342	07589	08899	05985

Table B.7 (*cont.*)

Row number										
00190	64281	61826	18555	64937	13173	33365	78851	16499	87064	13075
00191	66847	70495	32350	02985	86716	38746	26313	77463	55387	72681
00192	72461	33230	21529	53424	92581	02262	78438	66276	18396	73538
00193	21032	91050	13058	16218	12470	56500	15292	76139	59526	52113
00194	95362	67011	06651	16136	01016	00857	55018	56374	35824	71708
00195	49712	97380	10404	55452	34030	60726	75211	10271	36633	68424
00196	58275	61764	97586	54716	50259	46345	87195	46092	26787	60939
00197	89514	11788	68224	23417	73959	76145	30342	40277	11049	72049
00198	15472	50669	48139	36732	46874	37088	63465	09819	58869	35220
00199	12120	86124	51247	44302	60883	52109	21437	36786	49226	77837

Source: RAND Corporation (1955). *A million random digits.* Glencoe, IL: Free Press of Glencoe.

STATISTICAL COMPUTATION PROCEDURES

Basic computational procedures are outlined here. Appendix C is not intended as a replacement for an introductory course in statistics. Further, issues in interpretation of statistical findings are covered in relevant chapters and are not duplicated here (see Chapters 5 and 10–12).

DESCRIPTIVE STATISTICS

Measures of Central Tendency

Mean   The mean is the arithmetic average of all scores. The mean is computed by adding the scores and dividing by the number of scores, as shown in Equation C.1. (A computational example is given in Chapter 5.)

$$\text{Mean} = \bar{X} = \frac{\Sigma X}{N} \tag{C.1}$$

Median   The median is the middle score or the score at the 50th percentile. To compute the median, first the scores are ordered from lowest to highest. If there is an odd number of scores, the median is the $(N + 1)/2$ score (where N is the number of scores). If there is an even number of scores, there are two middle scores. The median is the average of these two middle scores. When there are a large number of scores the median is computed from a frequency distribution using Equation C.2. A computational example using Equation C.2 is shown in Table C.1.

$$\text{Median} = \bar{X}_{ll} + i\frac{(N/2) - \text{cum } f_{ll}}{f_i} \tag{C.2}$$

Mode   The mode is the most frequently occurring score. With large data sets it is advisable to prepare a frequency distribution to simplify the task of finding the most frequent score. It is possible to have more than one mode in which case each mode is reported.

Measures of Variability

Variance   The computational formula for the variance (s^2) is given below. (A computational example is presented in Chapter 5.)

$$s^2 = \frac{\text{SS}}{N - 1} \tag{C.3}$$

where

$$\text{SS} = \Sigma X^2 - \frac{(\Sigma X)^2}{N} \tag{C.4}$$

Table C.1   COMPUTATIONAL EXAMPLE OF THE MEDIAN

Score	Frequency	Cum Freq
12	8	134
11	12	126
10	19	114
9	31	95 ←
8	29	64
7	16	35
6	11	19
5	5	8
4	3	3

Steps in Computing the Median

1. Find the interval containing the median by (a) dividing the total number of subjects by 2, and (b) moving up the Cum Freq column until you reach the first number as large or larger than $N/2$. $134/2 = 67$; therefore, median is in the interval with a score of 9.

2. Compute the lower real limit of the interval containing the median (X_{ll}). The real limits of the interval with a score of 9 are 8.50 and 9.50. The interval width (i) is 1.00. (Note that with grouped frequency distributions the interval may be wider.)

3. The values of cum f_{ll} and f_i can be read from the frequency or grouped frequency distribution. The frequency of scores that fall in the interval containing the median is f_i (in this case, 31). The frequency of scores that fall below the interval that contains the median is cum f_{ll} (in this case, 64).

4. Put these values into the median formula.

$$\text{Median} = X_{ll} + i \frac{(N/2) - \text{cum } f_{ll}}{f_i} = 8.50 + 1.00 \frac{(134/2) - 64}{31} = 8.60$$

Note: This procedure will not always give the same result as the algorithms discussed in the text. Differences in the two computational methods are apparent whenever the interval containing the median has more than one score. Both approaches to computing the median are widely used and there is no general consensus on which approach is best.

Standard deviation   The standard deviation (s) is equal to the square root of the variance.

$$s = \sqrt{s^2} \tag{C.5}$$

Measures of Relationship

Pearson Product-Moment Correlation   The Pearson product-moment correlation is used to index the relationship between two measures that produce score data. Equation C.6 gives the computational formula. X and Y in Equation C.6 are used to represent the two variables. The symbol for the correlation coefficient is r. Sometimes the subscript $_{xy}$ is included to clarify exactly what variables are being correlated. Table C.2 presents a computational example.

$$r_{xy} = \frac{\Sigma XY - \dfrac{(\Sigma X)(\Sigma Y)}{N}}{\sqrt{\left[\Sigma X^2 - \dfrac{(\Sigma X)^2}{N}\right]\left[\Sigma Y^2 - \dfrac{(\Sigma Y)^2}{N}\right]}} \tag{C.6}$$

Table C.2   COMPUTATION OF A PEARSON PRODUCT-MOMENT CORRELATION

Data include two scores from each of N people.

Person	X	Y	X^2	Y^2	XY
A	4	6	16	36	24
B	2	3	4	9	6
C	3	6	9	36	18
D	5	7	25	49	35
E	5	8	25	64	40
Sums	19	30	79	194	123

Compute the Correlation:

$$r_{xy} = \frac{\Sigma XY - \frac{(\Sigma X)(\Sigma Y)}{N}}{\sqrt{\left[\Sigma X^2 - \frac{(\Sigma X)^2}{N}\right]\left[\Sigma Y^2 - \frac{(\Sigma Y)^2}{N}\right]}} = \frac{123 - \frac{(19)(30)}{5}}{\sqrt{\left[79 - \frac{19^2}{5}\right]\left[194 - \frac{30^2}{5}\right]}}$$

$$r_{xy} = \frac{9}{\sqrt{[6.8][14]}} = \frac{9}{\sqrt{95.2}} = \frac{9}{9.76} = 0.92$$

The critical value of r can be found in Table B.4 of Appendix B. The degrees of freedom are equal to $(N - 2)$. If we assume an alpha of 0.05, the critical value of r is .8783. Because 0.92 exceeds the critical value of r, we conclude that there is a relationship between the two variables in the population from which the sample is drawn.

Spearman Rank-Order Correlation   If one or both variables produce ordered data and neither produce nominal data, the appropriate coefficient is the Spearman rank-order correlation. The formula for the rank-order correlation is given in Equation C.7. Table C.3 presents a computational example.

$$r_s = 1 - \frac{6 \Sigma d^2}{N(N^2 - 1)} \tag{C.7}$$

INFERENTIAL STATISTICS

Inferential statistics are used to draw conclusions about population characteristics on the basis of information from samples drawn from the population. In this section we assume that the student is familiar with the concepts of hypothesis testing. We present only the computational formulas with examples for some of the most widely used inferential statistics. (If more information is required, the student can consult Howell, 1987; Runyon & Haber, 1980; Shavelson, 1981; Welkowitz, Ewen, Cohen, 1982.)

Parametric Statistics

Parametric statistics test hypotheses about population parameters such as population means. Certain assumptions about the data must be met to use parametric statistics. In this section we describe parametric tests of differences in population means. The focus is on computation.

Table C.3 COMPUTATION OF A SPEARMAN RANK-ORDER CORRELATION

Student	(X) Class rank	Achievement test scores	(Y) Ranks for achievment test scores	(X − Y) d	d²
A	12	440	14	−2.0	4.00
B	8	580	8	0	0
C	15	400	16	−1.0	1.00
D	1	740	1	0	0
E	3	700	2.5	0.5	0.25
F	20	280	20	0	0
G	10	520	9.5	0.5	0.25
H	2	700	2.5	−0.5	0.25
I	9	500	11	−2.0	4.00
J	6	660	5	1.0	1.00
K	16	440	14	2.0	4.00
L	4	640	6	−2.0	4.00
M	11	520	9.5	1.5	2.25
N	5	680	4	1.0	1.00
O	14	460	12	2.0	4.00
P	17	320	18	−1.0	1.00
Q	7	600	7	0	0
R	19	300	19	0	0
S	13	440	14	−1.0	1.00
T	18	340	17	1.0	1.00
			Totals	0	29.00

Computation of Spearman-Rank Correlation

$$r_s = 1 - \frac{6 \, \Sigma \, d^2}{N(N^2 - 1)} = 1 - \frac{6(29)}{20(20^2 - 1)} = 1 - \frac{174}{7980} = 0.98$$

The critical value of r_s is found in Table B.5 in Appendix B. For an alpha of 0.01, the critical r_s is 0.591 (because $N = 20$). We conclude that there is a relationship between class ranking and achievement test scores in the population from which the sample is drawn.

Independent Samples *t*-Test The independent samples *t*-test is used to compare the means from two independent samples of subjects. The samples are independent if different subjects appear in each sample and the subjects in the two samples are not matched in any way. We test the null hypothesis that there is no difference between the population means. The computational formula is presented below. The subscripts $_1$ and $_2$ in Equation C.8 are used to designate the two groups. Table C.4 presents a computational example.

$$t = \frac{(\bar{X}_1 - \bar{X}_2)}{S_{\bar{X}_1 - \bar{X}_2}} \tag{C.8}$$

where

$$S_{\bar{X}_1 - \bar{X}_2} = \sqrt{\left[\frac{SS_1 + SS_2}{N_1 + N_2 - 2} \right] \left[\frac{1}{N_1} + \frac{1}{N_2} \right]} \tag{C.9}$$

The computed value of t is compared with the critical value of t, which is obtained from Table B.2 of Appendix B (df $= N_1 + N_2 - 2$). If the absolute value of the

Table C.4 COMPUTATION OF AN INDEPENDENT SAMPLES *t*-TEST

Data	Group 1	Group 2
	5	3
	8	5
	7	2
	8	3
	7	
ΣX	35	13
ΣX^2	251	47
N	5	4
Means	7.0	3.25
SS	6.0	4.75

Computational steps:

1. Compute the means and SSs for each group.
2. Compute the $S_{\bar{X}_1 - \bar{X}_2}$.
3. Compute t and compare it with the critical value of t. The dfs are equal to $N_1 + N_2 - 2$.

$$S_{\bar{X}_1 - \bar{X}_2} = \sqrt{\left[\frac{SS_1 + SS_2}{N_1 + N_2 - 2}\right]\left[\frac{1}{N_1} + \frac{1}{N_2}\right]}$$

$$S_{\bar{X}_1 - \bar{X}_2} = \sqrt{\left[\frac{6.00 + 4.75}{5 + 4 - 2}\right]\left[\frac{1}{5} + \frac{1}{4}\right]} = \sqrt{\left[\frac{10.75}{7}\right]\left[0.20 + 0.25\right]} = \sqrt{0.691} = .83$$

$$t = \frac{(\bar{X}_1 - \bar{X}_2)}{S_{\bar{X}_1 - \bar{X}_2}} = \frac{7.00 - 3.25}{0.83} = 4.52$$

Critical value of t is 2.365 (from Table B.2); assumes an alpha of 0.05; df = 7. Because the computed value of t (4.52) exceeds the critical value (2.365), we reject the null hypothesis and conclude that the two populations from which the samples are drawn do have different means.

computed value of t exceeds the critical value, we reject the null hypothesis and conclude that the means of the two populations are not equal.

Correlated *t*-Test A correlated *t*-test is used to analyze the results of either a within-subjects study with two groups or a matched-pairs study with two groups. The computational formula is given as Equation C.10. The formula uses the means and variances from each sample as well as the product-moment correlation of the scores for the two conditions.

$$t = \frac{\bar{X}_1 - \bar{X}_2}{\sqrt{S_{\bar{X}_1}^2 + S_{\bar{X}_2}^2 - 2rS_{\bar{X}_1}S_{\bar{X}_2}}} \tag{C.10}$$

where

$$S_{\bar{X}_1} = \frac{s_1}{\sqrt{N_1}} \quad \text{and} \quad S_{\bar{X}_2} = \frac{s_2}{\sqrt{N_2}} \tag{C.11}$$

The computed value of t is compared to a critical value of t from Table B.2 (df = Number of pairs of scores − 1). Table C.5 presents a computational example for the correlated t-test.

Analysis of Variance (ANOVA)

ANOVA procedures are used to test for differences in means between two or more groups. In this section we focus on the computational procedures for some of the more frequently used ANOVA models.

The results of an analysis of variance are summarized in a table, the structure of which is the same regardless of the complexity of the model. The first column lists the source of variance; the second, the degrees of freedom; the third, the sums of squares; the fourth, the mean squares; and the fifth, the F ratios. Often a sixth column is included that lists the p value for each F. In all cases the mean square for a particular source is computed by dividing the sum of squares for the source by the degrees of freedom for the source. The F is always a ratio of two mean squares. In the sections that follow, we summarize the computational formulas for everything but the sums of squares in a summary table format. The computational procedures for each of the sums of squares are listed as part of the discussion of the ANOVA model.

A *simple one-way ANOVA* is used to compare the group means of two or more independent groups. There are three sources of variance—variability between groups, variability within groups, and the total variability (the sum of the first two). The computational formulas for everything except the sums of squares are given in Table C.6.

Table C.5 COMPUTATION OF A CORRELATED *t*-TEST

Anxiety ratings are made before and after a brief treatment session. The ratings range from 1 (no anxiety) to 5 (extreme anxiety). Pre- and postratings of anxiety are made on 91 subjects. Listed here are the summary statistics computed from the raw data.

	Before	After
Mean ($\bar{X}$)	3.17	2.96
Standard Deviation (s)	0.893	0.975
Sample size (N) is 91	$r = 0.84$	

1. The next step is to compute the standard error of the mean for each group.

$$S_{\bar{X}_1} = \frac{s_1}{\sqrt{N_1}} = \frac{0.893}{\sqrt{91}} = 0.0936 \qquad S_{\bar{X}_2} = \frac{s_2}{\sqrt{N_2}} = \frac{0.975}{\sqrt{91}} = 0.1022$$

2. Now compute the value of t.

$$t = \frac{\bar{X}_1 - \bar{X}_2}{\sqrt{S^2_{\bar{X}_1} + S^2_{\bar{X}_2} - 2rS_{\bar{X}_1}S_{\bar{X}_2}}}$$

$$t = \frac{3.17 - 2.96}{\sqrt{(0.0936)^2 + (0.1022)^2 - 2(0.84)(0.0936)(0.1022)}} = \frac{0.21}{0.056} = 3.75$$

3. Look up the critical value of t (df = number of pairs − 1 = 91 − 1 = 90). With an alpha of 0.05, the critical value of t is between 1.98 and 2.00. Because the observed t (3.75) exceeds the critical value, we reject the null hypothesis and conclude that the treatment produced a significant reduction in anxiety.

Table C.6 COMPUTATIONAL FORMULAS FOR A ONE-WAY ANOVA SUMMARY TABLE

Source	df	SS	MS	F
Between	$k - 1$	SS_b	SS_b/df_b	MS_b/MS_w
Within	$N - k$	SS_w	SS_w/df_w	
Total	$N - 1$	SS_T		

Note: (1) k is the number of groups; N is the total number of subjects. (2) The sums of squares are computed using Equations C.12–C.14.

The computational formulas for the sum of squares within (abbreviated SS_w), the sum of squares between (SS_b) and the total sum of squares (SS_T) are given in Equations C.12–C.14. An important check on the computations involves verifying that $SS_w + SS_b = SS_T$. To clarify the notation, $(\Sigma X)_i$ refers to the sum of all the scores in the ith group and n_i refers to the sample size in the ith group. The term $(\Sigma X)_T$ refers to the total sum of X. SS_i is the sum of squares for the ith group. k refers to the number of groups. Table C.7 presents a computational example.

$$SS_b = \sum_{i = 1}^{k} \frac{((\Sigma X)_i)^2}{n_i} - \frac{((\Sigma X)_T)^2}{N} \tag{C.12}$$

$$SS_w = \sum_{i = 1}^{k} SS_i \tag{C.13}$$

$$SS_T = (\Sigma X^2)_T - \frac{((\Sigma X)_T)^2}{N} \tag{C.14}$$

A significant F ratio indicates that at least one mean is different from at least one other mean. Additional procedures are needed to evaluate which means are different from which other means. If we have a specific prediction about certain means, a *planned comparison* can be used to test that prediction. The planned comparison computes a *contrast,* which is a weighted sum of the means, and then compares that contrast with an error term, which is a function of the MS_w. Equation C.15 shows how to compute the contrast and Equation C.17 shows how to compute the test statistic. Table C.8 presents a computational example.

$$\hat{c} = \sum_{i = 1}^{k} w_i \bar{X}_i \tag{C.15}$$

where

$$\sum_{i = 1}^{k} w_i = 0 \tag{C.16}$$

$$t = \frac{\hat{c}}{\sqrt{MS_w \left[\sum_{i = 1}^{k} \frac{w_i^2}{n_i} \right]}} \tag{C.17}$$

Table C.7 COMPUTATION OF A SIMPLE ONE-WAY ANOVA

Raw Data

	Group 1	Group 2	Group 3
	3	4	9
	1	3	7
	3	5	8
	2	5	11
	4	4	9
	3		

Summary Statistics

				Totals
ΣX	16	21	44	81
ΣX^2	48	91	396	535
n	6	5	5	16
$\overline{X}$	2.67	4.20	8.80	
SS	5.33	2.80	8.80	

Computational steps

1. Compute the sums of squares.

$$SS_T = \Sigma X_T^2 - \frac{((\Sigma X)_T)^2}{N} = 535 - \frac{(81)^2}{16} = 124.94$$

$$SS_w = \sum_{i=1}^{k} SS_i = 5.33 + 2.80 + 8.80 = 16.93$$

$$SS_b = \sum_{i=1}^{k} \frac{((\Sigma X)_i)^2}{n_i} - \frac{((\Sigma X)_T)^2}{N} = \frac{162}{6} + \frac{212}{5} + \frac{442}{5} - \frac{812}{16} = 108.00$$

Double check the computation of the SSs by seeing if they add up. $SS_T = SS_b + SS_w = 108.00 + 16.93 = 124.93$ (there is a slight difference due to rounding).

2. Fill in the summary table using the Equations in Table C.6.

Source	df	SS	MS	F
Between	2	108.00	54.00	41.46
Within	13	16.93	1.30	
Total	15	124.94		

3. Critical value of F is 3.80. Because $41.46 > 3.80$, the differences are significant.

A *repeated measures ANOVA* is used to analyze within-subjects designs with two or more groups. The error term in this analysis takes into account the correlation between conditions. Three sums of squares are computed: sum of squares for the subjects (SS_s), sum of squares between conditions (SS_b), and the error term sum of squares (SS_E). Equations C.18–C.20 shows the computational formulas for each of these. Table C.9 shows the remaining computational formulas for the ANOVA summary table. Table C.10 presents a computational example.

Table C.8 COMPUTATION OF A PLANNED COMPARISON

This example uses the data from Table C.7. We test the hypothesis that group 3 is different from the average of groups 1 and 2. The weights for the contrast are $+1$, $+1$ and -2, which sum to zero.

Compute the contrast

$$\hat{c} = \sum_{i=1}^{k} w_i \bar{X}_i = (+1)(2.67) + (+1)(4.20) + (-2)(8.80) = -10.73$$

Compute the value of t

$$t = \frac{\hat{c}}{\sqrt{MS_w \left[\sum_{i=1}^{k} \frac{w_i^2}{n_i} \right]}} = \frac{-10.73}{\sqrt{1.30 \left[\frac{(+1)^2}{6} + \frac{(+1)^2}{5} + \frac{(-2)^2}{5} \right]}} = \frac{-10.73}{1.52} = -7.07$$

Compare the computed value of t with the critical value of t, which can be obtained from Table B.2. The degrees of freedom are $N - k$ where N is the total number of subjects and k is the number of groups. In this case the df $= 16 - 3 = 13$. The critical value of t (assuming an alpha of 0.05) is 2.160. Because the absolute value of the computed t exceeds the critical value, we conclude that group 3 is significantly different from the average of groups 1 and 2.

Table C.9 ONE-WAY REPEATED-MEASURES ANOVA SUMMARY TABLE

Source	df	SS	MS	F
Subjects	$n - 1$	SS_s	SS_s/df_s	
Between	$k - 1$	SS_b	SS_b/df_b	MS_b/MS_E
Error	$(n-1)(k-1)$	SS_E	SS_E/df_E	

Note: k is the number of conditions; n is the number of subjects, each of whom is tested under all k conditions.

$$SS_s = \frac{\sum_{i=1}^{n} \left(\sum_{j=1}^{k} X_{ij} \right)^2}{k} - \frac{\left(\sum_{i=1}^{n} \sum_{j=1}^{k} X_{ij} \right)^2}{(n)(k)} \tag{C.18}$$

$$SS_b = \frac{\sum_{j=1}^{k} \left(\sum_{i=1}^{n} X_{ij} \right)^2}{n} - \frac{\left(\sum_{i=1}^{n} \sum_{j=1}^{k} X_{ij} \right)^2}{(n)(k)} \tag{C.19}$$

$$SS_E = \sum_{i=1}^{n} \sum_{j=1}^{k} X_{ij}^2 - \frac{\left(\sum_{i=1}^{n} \sum_{j=1}^{k} X_{ij} \right)^2}{(n)(k)} - SS_s - SS_b \tag{C.20}$$

In a *simple two-way ANOVA* the SS_b is partitioned into three terms. Two of the terms represent the two factors, which are labeled A and B, and the third term represents the interaction of these factors (labeled AB). Because there are several terms, slightly more complex notation is needed. We use a as the number of levels of factor A and b as the number of levels of factor B. We use the subscripts $_i$ and $_j$ for the A

Table C.10 COMPUTATION OF A ONE-WAY REPEATED-MEASURES ANOVA

Data

Subject	Condition 1	Condition 2	Condition 3	Sum of scores
A	10	8	8	26
B	12	9	8	29
C	11	10	9	30
D	11	10	8	29
E	10	8	9	27
F	11	9	7	27

Summary statistics

ΣX	65	54	49	168
ΣX^2	707	490	403	4716
Mean	10.83	9.00	8.17	

$$SS_s = \frac{26^2 + 29^2 + 30^2 + 29^2 + 27^2 + 27^2}{3} - \frac{168^2}{(6)(3)} = 4.00$$

$$SS_b = \frac{65^2 + 54^2 + 49^2}{6} - \frac{168^2}{(6)(3)} = 22.33$$

$$SS_E = (707 + 490 + 403) - \frac{168^2}{(6)(3)} - 4.00 - 22.33 = 5.667$$

Source	df	SS	MS	F
Subjects	5	4.00	0.80	
Between	2	22.33	11.17	19.71
Error	10	5.67	0.567	

The critical value of F is 4.10 (from Table B.3). Because the observed F exceeds the critical value of F, we conclude that performance is different under the different conditions.

and B factors, respectively. We use the subscripts $_A$, $_B$, $_{AB}$, $_w$ and $_T$ to identify the source of variance.

The SS_T is computed by treating the data as if it came from one group. The SS_w is computed by summing the individual SSs from each of the $a \times b$ groups (i.e., treating it as if it were a one-way ANOVA with $a \times b$ groups). Equation C.21 looks more complicated than Equation C.13 because we have to sum across two instead of one factor. The term SS_{ij} refers to the sum of squares for the cell represented by the ith level of factor A and the jth level of factor B.

$$SS_w = \sum_{i=1}^{a} \sum_{j=1}^{b} SS_{ij} \qquad \text{(C.21)}$$

Computing the sums of squares for factors A and B involves ignoring (or collapsing across) the one factor while doing the computation for the other factor. The formulas for SS_A and SS_B are given in Equations C.22 and C.23. The notation is an extension of the notation used earlier. The term $(\Sigma X)_{ij}$ refers to the sum of scores from the cell formed by the ith level of A and the jth level of B. Therefore, the numerator in the first term of Equation C.22 represents the sum of scores collapsed across B for each level of A. The denominator represents the sample size for each level of A.

$$SS_A = \sum_{i=1}^{a} \frac{\left(\sum_{j=1}^{b} (\Sigma X)_{ij}\right)^2}{\sum_{j=1}^{b} n_{ij}} - \frac{((\Sigma X)_T)^2}{N} \qquad (C.22)$$

$$SS_B = \sum_{j=1}^{b} \frac{\left(\sum_{i=1}^{a} (\Sigma X)_{ij}\right)^2}{\sum_{i=1}^{a} n_{ij}} - \frac{((\Sigma X)_T)^2}{N} \qquad (C.23)$$

Computing the sum of squares for the interaction (SS_{AB}) requires the computation of four terms (Equation C.24), but three of them are familiar. The first term requires that we compute the sum of scores for each of the $a \times b$ cells, square the sum, divide by the sample size in the cell, and sum the terms for all $a \times b$ cells. The second and third terms are the first terms of Equations C.22 and C.23, respectively. The last term in Equation C.24 is the same as the last term in Equations C.22 and C.23.

$$SS_{AB} = \sum_{i=1}^{a} \sum_{j=1}^{b} \frac{((\Sigma X)_{ij})^2}{n_{ij}} - \sum_{i=1}^{a} \frac{\left(\sum_{j=1}^{b} (\Sigma X)_{ij}\right)^2}{\sum_{j=1}^{b} n_{ij}}$$

$$- \sum_{j=1}^{b} \frac{\left(\sum_{i=1}^{a} (\Sigma X)_{ij}\right)^2}{\sum_{i=1}^{a} n_{ij}} + \frac{((\Sigma X)_T)^2}{N} \qquad (C.24)$$

Again, it is important to check the accuracy of the computations of the sums of squares by seeing if $SS_T = SS_A + SS_B + SS_{AB} + SS_w$. Table C.11 presents the computational formulas for the remainder of the summary table. Table C.12 presents a computational example.

Table C.11 COMPUTATIONAL FORMULAS FOR A TWO-WAY ANOVA SUMMARY TABLE[a]

Source	df	SS	MS	F
A	$(a-1)$	SS_A	SS_A / df_A	MS_A / MS_w
B	$(b-1)$	SS_B	SS_B / df_B	MS_B / MS_w
AB interaction	$(a-1)(b-1)$	SS_{AB}	SS_{AB} / df_{AB}	MS_{AB} / MS_w
Within-groups	$N - ab$	SS_w	SS_w / df_w	
Total	$N-1$	SS_T		

[a]'a' is the number of levels of Factor A; b is the number of levels of Factor B; N is the total number of subjects.

Table C.12   COMPUTATION OF A TWO-WAY ANOVA

Raw Data:
Two factors (labeled A and B)

	B_1			B_2			B_3	
A_1	A_2	A_3	A_1	A_2	A_3	A_1	A_2	A_3
10	7	11	1	6	4	3	2	5
8	4	9	2	7	3	2	1	6
7	3	10	1	6	6	3	2	4
9	2	9	4	5	4	3	3	5
6		1	2		3	4		5

Summary Statistics

A levels	Terms	B levels B_1	B_2	B_3	Totals
	ΣX	40	16	50	106
	ΣX^2	330	78	504	912
A_1	n	5	4	5	14
	SS	10	14	4	
	$(\Sigma X)^2/n$	320	64	500	802.57
	Mean	8	4	10	7.57
	ΣX	10	24	20	54
	ΣX^2	26	146	86	258
A_2	n	5	4	5	14
	SS	6	2	6	
	$(\Sigma X)^2/n$	20	144	80	208.29
	Mean	2	6	4	3.86
	ΣX	15	8	25	48
	ΣX^2	47	18	127	192
A_3	n	5	4	5	14
	SS	2	2	2	
	$(\Sigma X)^2/n$	45	16	125	164.57
	Mean	3	2	5	3.43
	ΣX	65	48	95	208
	ΣX^2	403	242	717	1362
Totals	n	15	12	15	42
	SS				
	$(\Sigma X)^2/n$	281.67	192.00	601.67	1030.10
	Mean	4.33	4.00	6.33	4.95

Computational Steps
1. Compute the various sums of squares.

$$SS_A = \sum_{i=1}^{a} \frac{\left(\sum_{j=1}^{b} (\Sigma X)_{ij} \right)^2}{\sum_{j=1}^{b} n_{ij}} - \frac{((\Sigma X)_T)^2}{N}$$

369

Table C.12 (*cont.*)

$$SS_A = [281.67 + 192.00 + 601.67] - 1030.10 = 45.24$$

$$SS_B = \sum_{j=1}^{b} \frac{\left(\sum\limits_{i=1}^{a} (\Sigma\,X)_{ij}\right)^2}{\sum\limits_{i=1}^{a} n_{ij}} - \frac{((\Sigma\,X)_T)^2}{N}$$

$$SS_B = [802.57 + 208.29 + 164.57] - 1030.10 = 145.33$$

$$SS_{AB} = \sum_{i=1}^{a}\sum_{j=1}^{b} \frac{((\Sigma\,X)_{ij})^2}{n_{ij}} - \sum_{i=1}^{a} \frac{\left(\sum\limits_{j=1}^{b}(\Sigma\,X)_{ij}\right)^2}{\sum\limits_{j=1}^{b} n_{ij}} - \sum_{j=1}^{b} \frac{\left(\sum\limits_{i=1}^{a}(\Sigma\,X)_{ij}\right)^2}{\sum\limits_{i=1}^{a} n_{ij}} + \frac{((\Sigma\,X)_T)^2}{N}$$

$$SS_{AB} = [320 + 64 + 500 + 20 + 144 + 80 + 45 + 16 + 125] - [281.67 + 192.00 + 601.67]$$
$$- [802.57 + 208.29 + 164.57] + [1030.10] = 93.33$$

$$SS_T = (\Sigma\,X^2)_T - \frac{((\Sigma\,X)_T)^2}{N} = 1362 - \frac{208^2}{42} = 331.90$$

$$SS_w = \sum_{i=1}^{a}\sum_{j=1}^{b} SS_{ij} = 10 + 14 + 4 + 6 + 2 + 6 + 2 + 2 + 2 = 48.0$$

Check to make sure the sums of squares add up correctly.

$$SS_T = SS_A + SS_B + SS_{AB} + SS_w \;\rightarrow\; 331.90 = 45.24 + 145.33 + 93.33 + 48.0$$

2. Compute all the other terms in the summary table.

Source	df	SS	MS	F
A	2	45.24	22.62	15.55
B	2	145.33	72.67	49.96
AB interaction	4	93.33	23.33	16.04
Within-groups	33	48.00	1.45	
Total	41	331.90		

3. Identify the critical value of F for each test in this analysis. Assume an alpha of 0.05.

df	F_{crit}	
2, 33	3.29	For *A* and *B*
4, 33	2.66	For interaction term

Because each of the computed values of F exceeds the appropriate critical value, we draw the following conclusions:

There is a significant main effect for *A*.

There is a significant main effect for *B*.

There is a significant interaction between *A* and *B*.

Computation of more complex ANOVA models is generally done with the aid of a computer package such as SPSS or BMDP. The student is referred to advanced level statistics texts for details of more sophisticated designs (Myers, 1972; Winer, 1971).

Nonparametric Statistics

Nonparametric statistics are typically used to analyze either nominal or ordinal data.

Chi-Square Goodness-of-Fit Test   With nominal data each subject is categorized. The appropriate summary statistic is the frequencies in each of the categories. The chi-square (written χ^2) goodness-of-fit test evaluates the pattern of these frequencies against a specified hypothesis. The hypothesis is converted into expected frequencies (E in the formula) and then compared with the observed frequencies (O). The computed value of chi-square is compared with a critical value from Table B.6 in Appendix B. For a chi-square goodness-of-fit test the degrees of freedom are equal to the number of categories minus 1 ($k - 1$). Table C.13 presents a computational example.

$$\chi^2 = \sum_{i=1}^{k} \frac{(O_i - E_i)^2}{E_i} \tag{C.25}$$

Chi-Square Test for Independence   The chi-square test for independence is used for comparing two or more groups to determine if different patterns of frequencies exist in the groups. The chi-square formula is unchanged in the test for independence. The only change is in the way the expected cell frequencies are computed. In the test for

Table C.13 COMPUTATION OF A CHI-SQUARE GOODNESS-OF-FIT TEST

Problem: Suppose that in an ESP experiment the subject is to guess whether the experimenter is looking at a picture of a car or a picture of a tree. The subject guesses correctly 31 times and incorrectly 19 times. Do the data suggest that the person may have ESP?

1. Because the subject had a 50/50 chance of guessing correctly, we expect 25 correct guesses and 25 incorrect guesses with variations from that even split the result of sampling bias. Therefore, we set up the data matrix like so:

	Correct	Incorrect
Observed	31	19
Expected	25	25

2. We compute the value of chi-square:

$$\chi^2 = \sum_{i=1}^{k} \frac{(O_i - E_i)^2}{E_i} = \frac{(31 - 25)^2}{25} + \frac{(19 - 25)^2}{25} = \frac{36}{25} + \frac{36}{25} = 2.88$$

3. The calculated value of chi-square is compared with a critical value from Table B.6 in Appendix B. With an alpha of 0.05, degrees of freedom equal to the number of categories (in this case 2) minus 1, the critical value is 3.841. Because the observed chi-square (2.88) is less than the critical value (3.841), we fail to reject the null hypothesis and conclude there is not sufficient evidence to suggest the person tested has ESP powers.

independence we compute the expected cell frequencies based on the overall pattern of frequencies in the groups. This is more easily explained with an example (see Table C.14). The degrees of freedom in a test for independence are equal to the number of groups minus 1 times the number of categories minus 1 [(no. of groups − 1)(no. of categories − 1)].

Cautions Regarding Chi-Square Chi-square is an often misused statistical procedure. Caution is necessary. The data for chi-square are always frequencies—percentages are never used in the computations. To understand why, recompute the ESP example using percentages instead of frequencies (62 percent correct, 38 percent incorrect with a 50/50-percent hypothesis). Individual events or measures must be independent of one another. It is not legitimate to have a person contribute more than one data

Table C.14   COMPUTATION OF A CHI-SQUARE TEST FOR INDEPENDENCE

Problem: We have surveyed 50 males and 100 females and asked them whether they personally wanted to have kids. The choices available to each person were "yes," "no," and "undecided." Listed here are the results of the survey.

	Want kids	Don't want kids	Undecided	Row totals
Males	20	10	20	50
Females	20	20	60	100
Column totals	40	30	80	150

1. The first step is to compute the expected cell frequencies for each of the six cells. For each cell the expected cell frequency is equal to the row total multiplied by the column total and divided by the grand total. Following are the observed data with the expected cell frequencies in parentheses. Note that the expected cell frequencies, when added down the columns or across the rows, must give the same row and column totals of the original data. If they do not, we must have made a mistake in the computations.

	Want kids	Don't want kids	Undecided	Row totals
Males	20	10	20	50
	(13.33)	(10.00)	(26.67)	
Females	20	20	60	100
	(26.67)	(20.00)	(53.33)	
Column totals	40	30	80	150

2. Compute the value of chi-square:

$$\chi^2 = \sum_{i=1}^{k} \frac{(O_i - E_i)^2}{E_i} = \frac{(20 - 13.33)^2}{13.33} + \frac{(10 - 10)^2}{10} + \frac{(20 - 26.67)^2}{26.67}$$

$$+ \frac{(20 - 26.67)^2}{26.67} + \frac{(20 - 20)^2}{20} + \frac{(60 - 53.33)^2}{53.33}$$

$$= 3.34 + 0 + 1.67 + 1.67 + 0 + 0.83 = 7.51$$

3. Compare the computed value of chi-square with the appropriate critical value. Because df = (no. of categories − 1)(no. of groups − 1) = (3 − 1)(2 − 1) = 2, the critical value of chi-square is 5.991 (alpha = 0.05). Because the value of chi-square exceeds the critical value, we conclude that men and women differ in their stated preferences for having children.

point. Every subject or event must appear once and only once in the summary table. The most common violation of this principle is excluding nonoccurrences from the table.

It should be noted that many statistics texts, especially older textbooks, argue that chi-square should not be used if any expected cell frequencies are too small (usually a cutoff of five is used). More recent work (Camilli & Hopkins, 1978) suggests that such a rule is overly restrictive and that chi-square gives accurate results even when expected cell frequencies are quite small. Many older textbooks suggest using the Yates correction for continuity whenever there is one degree of freedom. Again, recent research suggests that such a procedure is unnecessarily restrictive and actually leads to less accurate conclusions.

Mann-Whitney U-Test   The Mann-Whitney U-test compares two groups on an ordinal measure (see Equation C.26). Table C.15 gives a computational example. Most statistics textbooks include tables giving critical values of U. The Mann-Whitney U-test is used less frequently today because research indicates that parametric statistics such as the t-test are appropriate and accurate even when major assumptions are violated (see Box 14.1).

$$U = n_1 n_2 + \frac{n_1(n_1 + 1)}{2} - R_1 \tag{C.26}$$

Table C.15   COMPUTATION OF THE MANN-WHITNEY U-TEST

1. Rank order the scores from the lowest (rank of 1) to the highest for the two groups combined. (The last rank used should be equal to $n_1 + n_2$.)
2. Sum the ranks for each group.

Group 1	Rank	Group 2	Rank
20	8	22	10.5
18	4	44	14
16	3	3	1
21	9	12	2
22	10.5	23	12
19	6	19	6
19	6	36	13
	46.5		58.5

3. Compute U:

$$U = n_1 n_2 + \frac{n_1(n_1 + 1)}{2} - R_1$$

$$U = 7(7) + \frac{7(7 + 1)}{2} - 46.5 = 49 + 28 - 46.5 = 30.5$$

4. Find the critical values of U by referring to a statistics textbook (such as Shavelson, 1981). With an alpha of 0.05, the critical values of U are 8 and 41. We reject the null hypothesis whenever U is outside the range set up by the two critical values of U. Because 30.5 does not fall outside the range, we fail to reject the null hypothesis and conclude there is no evidence that the groups differ.

Other Nonparametric Statistics   Nonparametric statistics have been developed to test almost any statistical hypothesis. Although once quite popular, nonparametric statistics are used today only when the dependent measure generates nominal or ordered data. Siegel (1956) is still one of the best summaries of the many nonparametric statistical procedures available to researchers.

SUMMARY

Statistics are tools that help interpret the results of studies. The appropriate statistic(s) depend on the nature of data and of the question being asked. Appendix C is designed to describe briefly some of the more commonly used statistics including appropriate computational procedures and rules for interpretation. (For a more detailed description of these procedures and other procedures not described here, the student is referred to entry level textbooks on statistics, such as Howell (1987) or Shavelson (1981).

SELECTED ANSWERS TO SECTION III EXERCISES

The following answers to selected exercises are intended to serve as basic ideas around which more complete answers should be elaborated.

CHAPTER 1

1. Knowledge obtained through science is always tentative because any idea may change in light of new knowledge.
2. A central task in both science and art is to represent *parts of the universe,* and there is much similarity in their processes of observation, abstraction, and representation.
3. All sciences use a combination of rational logic and empirical observation. As long as a social science uses these basic components, it is as much a science as any other. Science is not defined by its equipment or technology or even by its level of development, but by its way of thinking.
4. Again, science is defined by its way of thinking. This scientist could thus be operating in an eminently scientific manner.

CHAPTER 2

2. Useful information can be obtained at all levels of research, and it is important to know when to use each level of research.
4. (a) Case-study. (b) Experimental. (c) Experimental. (d) Differential. (e) Naturalistic. (f) Correlational.
5. To repeat, science is defined by its way of thinking.

CHAPTER 3

   2. (a) Variables are ethnic prejudices and socioeconomic status. Both are subject variables. Potential extraneous variables are age and sex of children. (b) Variables are amount of alcohol consumed (a stimulus variable) and number of driving errors (a behavioral variable). Potential extraneous variables might be the age and weight of the person, alcohol history, driving skill, and so on. (c) Variables include the laundry products to be compared and the condition under which the comparison is made (stimulus variables) and the subject's response (a behavioral variable). Possible confounding variables are the behavior of the interviewer and past history with the particular product. (d) Variables are size and peer status (subject variables). Possible extraneous variables include the child's appearance, intellect, personality, socioeconomic class, and differential behavior of the teacher toward the children.
   3. (a) Children in research are considered subjects at risk because, as minors, they are unable to give informed consent. The safeguard is to obtain informed consent from some responsible adult. (b) The ethical issue is the mild deception in not telling the subject that some of the other subjects are actually assistants of the experimenter. The usual safeguards are to initially obtain consent (even though complete information is not given) and to do a full debriefing once the experiment is completed. (c) There are two issues here. The first is that information is obtained from files of patients and it is not clear who should give permission to obtain such information. Secondly, information is obtained from these files about other people (i.e., the family) and it is not clear who should give permission for that. The safeguard is to obtain permission from a responsible administrator in the hospital and, if possible, from the patient and family.
   4. The risk to subjects is always balanced against the information obtained from the research. If the design is flawed, the information obtained is of no value and, therefore, virtually no risk is permissible. Consequently, the quality of the design is *an ethical issue.*

CHAPTER 4

   1. (a) IQ score; interval; score. (b) Number of disruptive outbursts; ratio; score. (c) The time for response to occur; ratio; score. (d) Position at end of race; ordinal; ordered. (e) Speed of each runner; ratio; score. (f) Income of subjects; ratio; score. (g) Number of people in each category of car preference; nominal; nominal.
   2. (a) Television violence; manipulated; number of aggressive acts; ratio/score; rating of aggression; ordinal/ordered. (b) What subjects are told about being paid; manipulated; time to solve the problems; ratio/score.
   3. IQ is based on an interval scale of measurement with no true zero point.

CHAPTER 5

   2. (a) Hours of food deprivation; manipulated; number of trials to learn the maze; ratio/score. (b) Age of the child; nonmanipulated; rating of enjoyment; ordinal/

ordered. (c) Diagnosis; nonmanipulated; frequency of birth complications; nominal/nominal.

CHAPTER 6

1. Freud's work is low-constraint, case-study research with no manipulation of independent variables and little chance to use controls to *rule out extraneous sources of variation.* Consequently, one cannot be sure of the causal relationship between variables.
2. *Useful information can be obtained from all levels of research.* Every level of research has its own advantages and disadvantages. High-constraint research can establish causal relationships effectively but it lacks the flexibility of lower constraint research.
3. The *ex post facto* fallacy is acceptance of a causal inference when such an inference cannot be properly made, because no variable is manipulated. *Alternative hypotheses cannot be ruled out* and, consequently, no causal relationship can be inferred.

CHAPTER 7

1. (a) Significant (0.001); 17 percent; age and height show a modest but significant relationship in grade-school females. (b) Not significant; 10 percent; there appears to be no relationship between depression and level of activity in hospitalized psychiatric patients. (c) Significant (0.05); 4 percent; there is a small but statistically significant relationship between the two assertiveness measures.
2. (a) One possible group is a nondelinquent group of boys of the same age. Possible confounding variables are social class, IQ, effects of labeling, size of family, presence of siblings, and the like. This group would control for the subject's sex and age but probably not for most of the other variables mentioned. A second control group could be nondelinquent boys of the same age who are matched on variables such as social class and IQ with the experimental group. This group would control for age, sex, social class, and IQ but none of the other variables mentioned. A third group could be boys of the same age and social class who had emotional difficulties other than juvenile delinquency. This group would control for factors such as having a deviant label. (b) One possible group might be loading dock personnel from the same company. However, this group would not be a good control because there are a number of differences between the experimental and control groups, such as sex of subjects, schooling, the type of job tasks, life-style, and so on. A better control group might be other clerks whose work does not include CRT work. This control group would control for most variables, although the possibility exists that there are differences between CRT clerks and other clerks in terms of their level of responsibility, degree of tension, and age. The best possible control group would be a group of clerks from the same or similar companies that are matched on such variables as age, social class, sex, and education but who do not work on CRTs. (c) One possible control group would be people randomly selected from an uncontaminated neighborhood. However, unless the neighborhood is selected to be of the same socioeconomic class, there are likely to be differences in health care. The best control

group would be a randomly selected sample from an uncontaminated neighborhood of the same socioeconomic class as the contaminated neighborhood. Yet another possible control group might be a group of individuals from the same neighborhood who had lived in that neighborhood for only a short period of time relative to the subjects in the experimental group. (d) One possible control group would be randomly selected individuals of the same age who are not depressed. Possible confounding variables, unless these were controlled, would be sex of the subject, socioeconomic class of the subject, and the roles that the individuals are in (e.g., parents, students, and so forth).

3. In both correlational and differential research we are interested in quantifying the degree of relationship between two or more variables.

CHAPTER 8

3. The statement of a problem identifies the major variables; operational definitions describe how the variables will be measured or manipulated. For example, anxiety may be operationally defined as a rating of anxiety level by the subject. The operational definition would lead to specific procedures for the conduct of the study. In a second study we might operationally define the same variable (anxiety) in a different way (such as pulse rate). The new operational definition would lead to a different set of procedures for the study, but the research itself would be focused on the same conceptual variable (anxiety). The two studies are looking at the same construct or theory but from different vantage points, and, thus, they give us new information about the same general phenomena.

CHAPTER 9

1. The general population includes all children in elementary schools throughout the country. The accessible population is the 473 students enrolled in this particular elementary school. The accessible population could be thought of as a sample from the general population except that it is not randomly drawn. Consequently, generalizing to the general population could be risky. The researcher draws the sample from the accessible population. If the sample is random, generalizing to the accessible population should be no problem. However, the researcher must be careful when extending the generalization to the general population.

2. Representativeness refers to the degree to which the sample is similar to the population from which it is drawn. It is not an absolute, and it is possible for a sample to be representative of a population on some variables while not being representative of the same population on other variables.

3. (a) Two levels, bright and dark illumination. (b) Four levels, different levels of noise. (c) Three levels, no clues, one clue, five clues. (d) Five levels, five different pain-relief medications.

CHAPTER 10

1. (a) Randomly assigning subjects to conditions increases our confidence that there will be no bias in the assignment of subjects. Random assignment is a good control for many threats to internal validity. (b) Adding a control group controls for specific threats to validity, such as maturation, history, and instrumentation. Because the control and the experimental groups are treated in the same manner and in the same time frame, any specific effect (such as maturation) should affect each group equally and hence not contribute to the comparison between groups.
2. Variability among people is part of nature. If we did not have variability, we would not have any reason for making comparisons between subjects. The degree of variability can be quantified. One widely used measure of variability is the variance, which is essentially equal to the average squared deviation from the mean.
3. Error variance is defined as random variation, which sometimes produces scores that are too large or too small. It is as likely that the scores will be too large as they will be too small. In contrast, systematic variation tends to move the scores in only one direction. Because all scores are affected in that one direction, the result is that the mean score is shifted. Error variation does not affect the mean score but can mask systematic variance. Therefore, it is important to maximize the systematic variance and to minimize the error variance.
5. The F ratio is designed to evaluate the effects of one variable on another by looking at the ratio of two variances: the mean square between is the function of both the error variance and the systematic variance and is the numerator of the ratio; the mean square within is a function of the error variance and is the denominator of the ratio. If there is no systematic effect of the independent variable on the dependent variable, both the mean square between and the mean square within will be estimates of the error variance only. In this case the expected F will be 1. To the extent that there is a systematic affect of the independent variable on the dependent variable, the numerator will be larger than the denominator and the F ratio will be greater than 1.

CHAPTER 11

3. With 3 conditions, 6 orders are possible; 5 conditions, 120 orders; 6 conditions, 720 orders. Because there are so many possible orders with 5 and 6 conditions, counterbalancing is usually not a feasible control for order effects.
4. Matching on a large number of variables is difficult. Therefore, we select only those variables on which matching will help to make the design sensitive. The type of variable to choose would be a variable that (a) is strongly related to the dependent measure and (b) shows a great deal of natural variability in the population we are sampling.
5. A major advantage of matched-subjects designs over within-subject designs is that there are no sequencing effects in the matched-subjects designs (such as practice and carry-over effects).

CHAPTER 12

1. When you have a factorial design with more than one independent variable, there are many possible effects to be evaluated. Each of the independent variables can have an effect on the dependent variables by itself (main effects). In addition, combinations of two or more independent variables can produce a joint effect (an interaction). The interaction effect is more than simply the additive effect of the two or more independent variables. It represents an enhancement created by the combination of the two or more variables. In most factorial studies the most interesting effects are the interactions.

3. There is no main effect for Factor A, but there is a main effect for Factor B and an interaction of A and B. As always, we begin by interpreting the interaction first. The matrix of cell means illustrates the effect of the interaction. In condition B_1, scores decrease from condition A_1 through A_4. The opposite trend is observed under the B_2 condition (scores tend to increase from A_1 through A_4). The main effect for B is reflected in the generally higher scores for B_2 as compared with B_1 regardless of the level of A.

4. (a) An A main effect; no B main effect; no interaction. (b) An A main effect; a B main effect; no interaction. (c) No A main effect; a B main effect; an interaction. (It always helps to draw the graphs.)

CHAPTER 13

1. (a) Both groups change in the same way and to the same degree. Therefore, we say there is no effect. (b) This is the classic crossover where the control group does not change but the experimental group, which was initially lower, is considerably higher at posttest. In this case we assume that the experimental condition did have an effect. (c) In this case both groups changed but the control group changed more. Therefore, it seems unlikely that the manipulation had an effect.

2. (a) There appears to be no effect of the manipulation. (b) There does appear to be an effect of the manipulation; scores that tended to be low prior to the manipulation increased after the manipulation.

3. Single-subject designs use procedures that allow each subject to serve as his or her own control. Hence, internal validity is protected and causality can be inferred for the particular subject in the study. The weakness of the single-subject design is that there is only one subject in the study. Consequently, the external validity of the study may be weak.

4. Controls available in the laboratory control threats to internal validity and, consequently, we are able to draw causal inferences between variables. In contrast, in natural settings it is difficult to apply these controls and, therefore, it is difficult to draw causal inferences. The trade-off is that laboratory control is achieved by simplifying real-life variables. Such simplification may or may not accurately represent the real world. As a result, one must be careful in generalizing laboratory studies to the real world.

CHAPTER 14

1. (a) Experimental. (b) Type of training. (c) Muscle relaxation; cognitive relaxation; no training. (d) Independent groups. (e) Blood pressure. (f) Systolic and diastolic blood pressure. (g) Ratio for both. (h) Score data for both. (i) "Relaxation training reduces hypertension" and "The two relaxation procedures will be differentially effective in reducing blood pressure." (j) For each hypothesis a test of differences. (k) For each hypothesis mean, variance, and standard deviation. (l) For the first hypothesis a one-way ANOVA; for the second hypothesis either a one-way ANOVA or a *t*-test.

3. (a) Experimental. (b) Type of feedback. (c) Immediate feedback, delayed feedback, and no feedback. (d) Correlated-groups, within-subjects design. (e) Reading accuracy. (f) Number of reading errors. (g) Ratio. (h) Score. (i) "The type of feedback will affect reading accuracy." (j) A test of differences between correlated groups. (k) Mean, standard deviation, and variance. (l) Repeated measures ANOVA.

G L O S S A R Y

ABA design   See *reversal design.*

abscissa   The *x*-axis on a graph.

accessible population   That subset of a target population that is available to the researcher and from which the sample is drawn.

ad hoc **sample**   Sample of subjects drawn from an accessible population. Characteristics of the *ad hoc* sample must be described to define the limits of generalizability.

alpha level   Level of Type I error (the probability of rejecting the null hypothesis when the null hypotheses is true).

analysis of covariance (ANCOVA)   Statistical procedure similar to *analysis of variance* used to evaluate whether two or more groups have different population means. Analysis of covariance statistically removes the effects of extraneous variables on the dependent variable and hence increases the power of the statistical test.

analysis of variance (ANOVA)   Statistical procedure used to analyze for mean differences between two or more groups. ANOVAs compare the variability between groups with the variability within groups. Many variations of analysis of variance are possible including *repeated measures ANOVAs* and *factorial ANOVAs.*

ANOVA summary table   Table that organizes the results of an analysis of variance computation. For each source of variation the appropriate *degrees of freedom, sums of squares, mean squares,* and *F ratios* are listed. (Examples are given in Chapters 10–12.)

applied research   Research to provide solutions to practical problems. Applied research is contrasted with *basic research.*

archival records   Any source of data (such as census data) for events that have already occurred.

artifact   In research, any apparent effect of a major conceptual variable that is actually the result of a confounding variable not properly controlled. Artifacts threaten the *validity* of research conclusions.

association   Relationship or correlation.

assumptions of science   Basic tenets that form the bases for more complex scientific theory and research.

attrition   Potential confounding variable in research. Attrition is the loss of subjects before or during the research. The subjects who remain may not be representative of the population. Hence, any conclusions drawn may not generalize to the entire population.

authority   A way of acquiring knowledge. New ideas are accepted as valid because some respected authority has declared the idea to be true.

automation   Use of equipment to conduct most or all aspects of presenting stimuli and to record subjects' responses. Automation can minimize the work required of the researcher, increase precision in data gathering, and minimize experimenter bias in gathering and recording data.

basic research   Fundamental or pure research. Basic research is carried out to add to knowledge but without applied or practical goals. Basic research is often contrasted with *applied research.*

behavioral variable   Variable representing an organism's behavior.

between-groups variance   Index of the variability among group means.

between-subjects design   Research design using two or more groups in which each subject appears in only one of the groups.

Biomedical Programs (BMDP)   Computer package of statistical data-analysis procedures.

case-study level of constraint   Research in which a few constraints are placed on subjects' behavior. Case-study research usually focuses on the behavior of a single subject.

categorical data   Synonymous with nominal data.

categorical variable   Synonymous with discrete variable. A categorical variable can have only a finite number of values.

causal hypothesis   Usual form of the research hypothesis in experimental research. It states that the independent variable has a causal relationship to the dependent variable. To accept this hypothesis one must have rejected the null hypothesis and all confounding variable hypotheses.

causal inference   Conclusion that the change in the independent variable resulted in a change in the dependent variable. It may be drawn only if all potential confounding variables are properly controlled.

causally related   Two variables are causally related if a change in one variable results in a predictable change in the other variable and the change occurs as a direct result of the action of the first variable.

ceiling effects   See *scale attenuation effects.*

central tendency   Average or typical score in a distribution. Three measures of central tendency are the *mean, median,* and *mode.*

classification variables   Organismic or subject variables used to classify subjects into discrete groups. Classification variables are used for assigning subjects to groups in differential research.

coding data   Process by which numerical or classification scores are assigned to a set of responses from a subject. The coded data are usually in a form that can be more easily analyzed statistically.

column means   In *factorial designs,* one factor is usually illustrated as separate columns of data where each column represents a different level of the factor. A second factor might be illustrated as rows of data, where the different rows represent levels of the second factor. Column means are computed by taking the mean of all subjects who appear in a given column regardless of their level on the second factor.

communication phase of research   Research phase in which the rationale, hypotheses, methods, results, and interpretations of the study are presented in oral or written form to other researchers.

computer-analysis packages   Sophisticated computer programs for many different statistical analyses of data sets. See also *Biomedical Programs (BMDP); Minitab; Statistical Analysis System (SAS)*

conceptual replication   See *systematic replication.*

confounding variable   Any uncontrolled variable that might affect the outcome of a study. A potential confounding variable exists only if (1) there is a mean *difference* between the groups on the variable and (2) there is a *correlation* between the variable and the dependent measure.

confounding variable hypothesis   Actually, a set of hypotheses. Each confounding variable hypothesis states that a particular confounding variable is responsible for the observed changes in the dependent measure. Each of the hypotheses must be rejected before one can safely conclude a causal relationship between the *independent* and *dependent variables.*

constructs Ideas constructed by the researcher to explain events observed in particular situations. Constructs are not necessarily direct representations of reality; they are not facts. They are explanatory fictions because, in most cases, we do not know the real reason for a particular event. Once formulated, constructs are used *as if* they are true (i.e., analogically) to predict relationships between variables in situations that had not previously been observed.

construct validity Validity of a theory. Most theories in science present broad conceptual explanation of relationship between variables and make many different predictions about the relationships between particular variables in certain situations. Construct validity is established by verifying the accuracy of each possible prediction that might be made from the theory. Because the number of predictions is usually infinite, construct validity can never be fully established. However, the more independent predictions from the theory verified as accurate, the stronger will be the construct validity of the theory.

contingency A particular relationship between two or more variables where, given that the first event occurs, the second event is highly probable. The relationship between the variables is a probabilistic one and does not necessarily imply a causal connection between them.

continuous variable Any variable that can theoretically take on an infinite numbers of values. Continuous variables are often contrasted with *discrete* or *categorical variables.*

control group A group of subjects used in either differential or experimental research that serves as a basis of comparisons for other (experimental) groups. The ideal control group is similar to the experimental group on all variables except the variable that defines the group *(independent variable).*

correlated-groups design Research design in which the subjects in each of the groups are related to the subjects in the other groups. Two variations of the correlated-groups design are (1) the *within-subjects design* and (2) the *matched-subjects design.* Correlated-groups designs provide more powerful tests of the hypotheses because they control for individual differences between subjects. They are contrasted with *independent-groups design.*

correlated *t*-test (or direct-difference *t*-test or matched-pairs *t*-test) Statistical procedure used to test for mean differences between two groups in a within-subjects or matched-subjects design.

correlation Degree of relationship between two or more variables.

correlational level of constraint Research designed to quantify the relationship between two or more variables. At this level there is no manipulation of variables and no attempt to draw causal inferences.

correlation coefficient Statistic that quantifies the degree of relationship between two or more variables. There are many kinds of correlation coefficients depending on the type of data and relationship predicted.

counterbalancing Control procedure used in within-subjects designs to control for sequencing effects. It is most practical when there is a small number of conditions in the study.

cross-tabulation Procedure for organizing frequency data that displays the relationship between two or more nominal variables. A cross-tabulation table contains individual cells, with the number in each cell representing the frequency of subjects who show that particular combination of characteristics.

data Plural noun that refers to information gathered in research. Research conclusions are drawn on the basis of an evaluation of the data gathered as part of a study.

data-analysis phase of research Research phase in which data gathered from observing subjects are analyzed, usually with statistical procedures.

data snooping Type of secondary analysis of data to help generate hypotheses for further study.

deception Procedures used in research to hide from the subject the true nature of the study. Many studies require deception to prevent subject expectancy effects, but the use of deception raises ethical issues that must be addressed by the researcher. Whenever deception is used, complete debriefing of the subjects at the end of the study is ethically required.

decision tree Flowchart model in which answers to specific questions lead to branching to a new set of questions or procedures. (Chapter 14 presents a decision-tree model designed to help students select appropriate statistical tests in a given research situation.)

deductive reasoning Reasoning from the general to the particular. In deductive reasoning specific predictions are made about future events.

degrees of freedom (df) Statistical concept; one degree of freedom is lost each time a population parameter is estimated on the basis of a sample of data from the population. The distribution of most statistics (t, F, and so on) are tabled by degrees of freedom (df).

demand characteristics Any aspect of the situation created by the researcher that suggests to the subject what behavior is expected.

dependent variable Variable that is hypothesized to have a relationship with the *independent variable.*

descriptive statistics Those statistics or statistical procedures that summarize and/or describe the characteristics of a sample of scores.

design notation (e.g., 2×2; 3×2; $2 \times 4 \times 3$) In factorial designs a way of indicating the number of factors and how many levels of each factor. For example, a $2 \times 4 \times 3$ design has three factors where the first factor has two levels, the second has four levels, and the third has three levels, for a total of 24 combinations.

difference score Arithmetic difference between scores at two points in time for a particular subject on the dependent measure.

differential level of constraint Research in which two or more groups defined on the basis of some preexisting organismic variables are compared on a dependent measure.

diffusion of treatment Potential confounding variable that occurs when subjects in one condition communicate information to subjects in another condition. This can be a particular problem in research settings where subjects are in close communication with one another (such as in a school or hospital or in the undergraduate psychology subject pool of a university).

direct differences *t*-test See *correlated t-test.*

discrete variable A discrete variable can take on only a finite number of values. Often contrasted with *continuous variable.*

dispersion Variability; how spread out the scores are in a sample.

double-blind procedure Research procedure in which neither the researcher nor the subject know in which condition the subject is tested. The purpose is to minimize the possibility of experimenter bias and of subject expectancies.

effective range Characteristic of any dependent measure; the range expressed in score units over which the dependent measure accurately reflects the level of the dependent variable.

empirical Based on *observed data.* A relationship between variables is empirically established if it has been observed to occur.

empiricism System of knowing about the world that is based solely on observation of the events around us.

enumerative data Synonymous with *nominal data.*

error term Generic term used in many different statistics, it provides a basis for comparing observed differences between groups. The error term is usually based on a measure of the variability of scores within each group.

error variance Type of error term that is a function of the variability of scores within groups.

***ex post facto* design** Nonexperimental research design in which the current situation of the subject is observed and related to previous events. Because there are no manipulations of variables and confounding variables cannot be controlled, alternative hypotheses cannot be ruled out. Therefore, it is a weak design and causal inferences cannot be drawn from it.

ex post facto **fallacy**   Error in reasoning where one assumes that the observed relationship between current events and some historical events represents a causal relationship.

exact replication   Repeating a study using exactly the same procedure used in the original study. See also *replication.*

experiment   High-constraint research procedure in which subjects in two or more conditions are compared on a dependent measure with subjects assigned without bias to each of the conditions. These may be either *within-subjects* or *between-subjects designs.* Experimental designs provide adequate control over virtually all possible confounding variables.

experimental design   Set of procedures that defines a research study at the experimental level of constraint. In experimental design subjects are assigned to groups or conditions without bias, such as with random assignment, and all appropriate control procedures are used.

experimental group   Group of subjects assigned to one or more conditions in an experiment where a specified level of the independent variable exists. The experimental group(s) is(are) usually contrasted with a *control group.*

experimental level of constraint   Research in which two or more groups or conditions (where subjects are assigned to groups or conditions without bias) are compared on at least one dependent measure. At the experimental level of constraint, the research design provides adequate controls for most confounding variables and, therefore, allows the researcher to draw causal inferences.

experimental variance   Degree of variability among the group means in a research study.

experimentation   Process by which a researcher studies the relationship between independent and dependent variables by systematically manipulating the independent variable, assigning subjects without bias to each level of the independent variable, and observing the effects of the independent variable on the dependent variable.

experimenter bias   Any effect that the expectations of the researcher might have on the measurement and recording of the dependent variable. Uncontrolled experimenter bias threatens the validity of research.

experimenter expectancies   Expectations of the researcher about the relationship between the variables being studied. Experimenter expectancies may affect the accuracy of the observations, especially in situations that require judgment on the part of the researcher.

experimenter reactivity   Any action by the researcher other than the manipulation of the independent variable that tends to influence the response of the subjects. A type of experimenter bias.

external validity   Extent to which the results of a study accurately indicate the true nature of a relationship between variables in the real world. If a study has external validity, the results are said to be generalizable to the real world.

extraneous variable   Any variable other than the independent variable that might affect the dependent measure in a study. Extraneous variables are potentially confounding and must be controlled.

extraneous variance   Variability in scores on the dependent measure that can be accounted for by the effects of extraneous variables.

F **ratio**   A test statistic computed by taking the ratio of two variances. *F* ratios are used most often in *analysis of variance* where the two variance estimates are an estimate based on (1) the difference between group means and (2) the difference among subjects within groups.

factorial ANOVA   Analysis of variance procedure for evaluating *factorial designs.*

factorial design Research designs employing more than one independent variable simultaneously. The major advantage of a factorial design is that it can measure the joint (interactive) effects of two or more independent variables.

factors In a factorial design, each of the independent variables is a factor.

facts Empirically observed events.

field research Research conducted outside the laboratory in natural settings. Field research might include low-constraint research (such as naturalistic or case-study research) or may include higher constraint procedures applied to natural settings. An advantage of field research is that results more easily generalize to the real world because observations are made in a real-world setting.

filler items Any questions or items that are asked along with items that make up the dependent measure in a study. Filler items are typically not scored as part of the dependent measure. Their purpose is to distract subjects from the true purpose of the study by making it unclear exactly what the dependent measure is.

floor effects See *scale attenuation effects*.

flowcharts Organizational device that allows one to reach a decision by following a path defined by answers to particular questions. (Chapter 14 illustrates the use of flowcharts to select the appropriate statistical test for any given research procedure.)

free random assignment Assignment of subjects to groups on a completely random basis so that the assignment of any given subject has no effect on the assignment of any other subject.

frequency data Synonymous with *nominal data*.

frequency distribution Organizational device used to simplify large data sets.

frequency polygon Graph that illustrates a frequency distribution. It is constructed by putting a dot above each possible score (which are listed on the x-axis) at a height that indicates the appropriate frequency of that score (which is indicated on the y-axis). The dots are then connected to form a graph of the frequency distribution.

generalizability Extent to which the findings from a research study are applicable to the outside world.

generalize Assuming that the findings of a particular research study will be found for other subjects or in other settings.

graphs of factorial data Graphs that provide a visual illustration of interaction effects and main effects in factorial studies.

group frequency distribution Frequency distribution that provides the frequency of scores in intervals of equal size. Group frequency distributions are used with continuous data or in situations where there is a large range of possible scores.

history Potential confounding variable. History represents any change in the dependent variable over the course of a research study that is a function of events other than the manipulation of the independent variable.

incidental learning Learning that occurs without specific reinforcement, usually while learning a different task.

idea-generating phase of research First step in any research project during which the researcher selects a topic to study.

independent variable Any variable in research that defines separate groups of subjects on which the dependent measure is taken. Subjects may be assigned to these groups on the basis of either (1) some preexisting characteristics (differential research) or (2) some form of random assignment (experimental research).

individual differences Natural differences between people on any variable. Individual differences between people on a dependent measure tend to obscure effects of an independent variable on the dependent measure(s).

inductive reasoning   Reasoning from the particular to the general. Used to generate theories or models based on particular observations or ideas.

inference   Any conclusion drawn on the basis of some set of information. In research we draw inferences on the basis of empirical data we collect and ideas we construct.

inferential statistics   Statistical procedures that compute the probability of obtaining the particular pattern of data in a study if all subjects were actually drawn from the same population. If the probability of obtaining such a pattern of scores is low, we reject the hypothesis that all subjects were drawn from the same population (null hypothesis) and conclude that there were meaningful differences between groups or conditions.

informed consent   Critical principle in the ethical treatment of subjects. Subjects have the right to know exactly what they are getting into and the right to refuse to participate.

institutional review board (IRB)   Formal body that operates in most institutions where research is conducted. The IRB reviews all research proposals to determine if they meet ethical guidelines.

instrumentation   Potential confounding variable involving any change in the measuring instrument over time that causes the instrument to give different readings when no change has occurred in the subject.

interaction   Combined effect of two or more independent variables on the dependent variable. Interactions can be measured only in factorial designs.

internal consistency reliability   Index of how homogeneous are the individual items of a measure. If the individual items are homogeneous, they will tend to correlate strongly with one another suggesting that all items are measuring the same characteristic.

internal validity   Accuracy of the research study in determining the relationship between the independent and the dependent variables. Internal validity can be assured only if all potential confounding variables have been properly controlled.

interpretation phase of research   Research phase in which the results of statistical analyses of data are interpreted in light of (1) the adequacy of control procedures in the research design, (2) previous research, and (3) existing theories about the behavior under study.

interrater reliability   Index of the consistency between two or more ratings made by separate raters. It is indexed by the correlation between the ratings of two raters.

interrupted time-series design   Type of research design suitable for either single subjects or groups in which multiple measures of the dependent variable are taken before and after some experimental manipulation. Time-series designs provide some control for history and maturation, even without the inclusion of a control group.

interval scale   Scale of measurement in which the distance between any two adjacent scores is the same as the distance between any other two adjacent scores, but zero is not a true zero. An example of an interval scale is temperature measured in either centigrade or fahrenheit.

invasion of privacy   Ethical issue in research. Researchers should avoid invading the privacy of subjects. When impossible, every effort should be made to protect subjects' privacy by maintaining confidentiality of records.

knowledge   Any information we have about the world around us. Knowledge may be achieved in different ways including the use of scientific research.

levels of constraint   Degree of systematic control applied in research. Research methods can range from low to high constraint. The labels assigned to these levels of constraint are *naturalistic, case study, correlational, differential,* and *experimental.*

linear relationship   Relationship between two or more variables which, when plotted in a standard coordinate system, tend to cluster around a straight line. Most correlation coefficients are sensitive only to linear relationships between variables.

logic   Set of operations that can be applied to statements and conclusions drawn from those statements to determine the internal accuracy of the conclusions.

main effects   In a factorial design, main effects refer to the individual effects of the independent variables. In contrast, interaction effects are the combined effects of two or more independent variables on the dependent variable.

manipulated independent variable   Type of independent variable found in an experimental research study. When manipulated independent variables are used, subjects are assigned to groups or conditions without bias.

manipulation check   Procedure designed to verify that the independent variable did occur at different levels in the different groups or conditions. A manipulation check is independent of any evaluation of the effect of the independent variable on the dependent variable.

matched-pairs *t*-test   See *correlated t-test.*

matched random assignment   Experimental procedure used to help insure that groups are equivalent at the beginning of the study. In matched random assignment subjects are matched in small groups (size is determined by the number of conditions in the study) on relevant variables and each member of the group is randomly assigned to one of the conditions of the study until all members have been assigned to one condition. Matched random assignment can be difficult if we attempt to match on more than one variable or if there are several conditions in the research study. Matched random assignment is an alternative to a *within-subjects design* and should be used whenever significant sequencing effects can be expected in a within-subjects design.

matched-subjects design   Research design in which subjects are matched on a variable that is highly correlated with the dependent measure. Once matched, each subject is randomly assigned to each of the groups defined by the independent variable. The design helps control for individual differences without introducing the sequencing problems inherent in a within-subjects design.

matrix of cells   Structure of cells in a factorial design.

maturation   Potential confounding factor involving changes in subjects on the dependent measure during the course of the study that results from normal growth processes.

mean   Arithmetic average of scores. The mean is the most commonly used measure of central tendency but should be computed only for *score data.*

mean square   In *analysis of variance (ANOVA),* the mean square is a variance estimate. Several different mean squares are computed in any ANOVA. It is the ratio of mean squares that is the F ratio and constitutes the inferential statistical test.

measurement error   Any inaccuracy found in the measurement of a variable. Although it is impossible to determine the precise degree and direction of measurement error for a given subject, it is possible to specify the average error associated with a particular measure.

measurement reactivity   Any effect on the subject's behavior that results from the subject being aware that he or she is being observed and measured. When measurement reactivity is excessive, a researcher may want to consider using unobtrusive measures to minimize the effect.

median   Middle score in a distribution.

Minitab   Computer package for statistical analysis of data.

mixed designs (between- and within-subjects variables)   Factorial design in which at least one of the factors is a between-subjects factor and at least one of the factors is a within-subjects factor. The pattern of between- and within-subjects factors affects the selection of the statistical analysis.

mixed designs (manipulated and nonmanipulated variables)   Factorial design in which at least one of the factors represents a nonmanipulated independent variable and at least one of the factors represents a manipulated independent variable. The distinction between manipulated and nonmanipulated variables does not effect the data analysis. However, the interpretation of the results must take into account the fact that at least some of the factors are nonmanipulated factors and, therefore, represent differential research.

mode Most frequent score in a distribution.

models In science, models are representations of the complex reality of the real world.

moderator variable Any variable that has an effect on the observed relationship between two or more other variables. When a moderator variable is operating, it is best to measure the relationship between variables separately in subgroups that are defined by the moderator variable. For example, relationships between variables are often evaluated separately in males and females (a commonly used moderator variable).

multiple baseline design Research design often used with single subjects when one wants to infer a causal relationship between the independent and dependent variables. Baselines on several different behaviors are taken and treatment strategies are applied at different points in time to each behavior being monitored.

multiple observers Control used to evaluate the accuracy of observations made by two or more independent observers.

multivariate analysis of variance (MANOVA) Extension of *analysis of variance* where more than one dependent measure is simultaneously evaluated.

multivariate techniques Advanced statistical procedures used to evaluate complex relationships between variables.

naturalistic level of constraint Research carried out in natural settings where the researcher makes no attempt to manipulate the environment as part of the research.

negative correlation Relationship between two variables in which an increase in one variable predicts a decrease in the other variable.

nominal data Data produced when a nominal scale of measurement is used. Nominal data are frequencies of subjects in each of the specific categories.

nominal scale Scale of measurement in which only categories are produced as scores. Examples are diagnostic classification, sex of the subject, and political affiliation.

nonequivalent control-group design Quasi-experimental design used in field settings. In this design two or more groups, which may not be equivalent at the beginning of the study, are compared on the dependent measure.

nonexperimental designs Any research design that fails to provide adequate controls for typical confounding.

nonlinear relationship Any relationship between two or more variables that is characterized by a scatter plot where the points tend to cluster around a curved instead of a straight line. Most correlations coefficients are insensitive to nonlinear relationships.

nonparametric statistics Inferential statistical procedures that do not rely on estimating population parameters such as the mean and variance.

nonreactive measure Any dependent measure that provides consistent scores regardless of whether the subject is aware or unaware of being measured.

normal distribution Distribution of scores that is characterized by a bell-shaped curve in which the probability of a score drops off rapidly from the midpoint to the tails of the distribution. A true normal curve is defined by a mathematical equation and is a function of two variables (the mean and variance of the distribution). Normal distributions are useful in psychology because psychological variables tend to show distributions that are close to normal.

null hypothesis States that the subjects from each group are drawn from populations with identical population parameters. The null hypothesis is tested by inferential statistics.

objective measure Any measure that requires little or no judgment on the part of the person making the measurement. Objective measures are more resistant to experimenter biases than *subjective measures*.

observation Empirical process in which data about the phenomenon of interest is gathered and reported. Careful observation is a central task in all research.

observation phase of research Research phase in which the actual data are gathered.

observational variable   Any variable that is observed and not manipulated in research. The term is usually used in low-constraint research where the independent and dependent variable distinction does not apply.

observed organismic variable   Any characteristic of the subject that can be measured and used for classification.

one-way ANOVA   Statistical procedure that evaluates differences in mean scores of two or more groups where the groups are defined by a single independent variable.

operational definition   Detailed set of procedures used to measure or manipulate the level of a variable.

ordered data   Data produced by ordinal scales of measurement.

orderliness belief   Belief dating from ancient artisans that events in nature are predictable.

ordinal scale   Scale of measurement where the scores can be rank ordered but the distance between any two adjacent scores will not necessarily be the same as the distance between any other two adjacent scores.

ordinate   The y-axis on a graph.

organismic variable   Any characteristic of the subject that can be used for classification. An organismic variable may be either directly observed *(observed organismic variable)* or may be inferred on the basis of the responses of the subject *(response-inferred organismic variable)*.

parametric statistics   Inferential statistical procedures that rely on sample statistics to draw inferences about population parameters such as the mean and variance.

participant observer   Any researcher gathering data in a setting in which the researcher is an active part. Participant observation tends to be less obtrusive than other observational procedures. However, the possibility for experimenter reactivity in participant observation is quite high.

Pearson product-moment correlation   Index of the degree of linear relationship between two variables where each variable represents score data.

percentile   Normative score that converts the raw score earned by a subject into a number from 0–100, which reflects the percentage of subjects who score lower than the subject in question.

perfect correlation   Correlation of $+1.00$ or -1.00. When two variables are perfectly correlated, knowing the score on one variable permits perfect prediction of the score on the other variable. In a scatter plot a perfect correlation is shown by all points falling on a straight line (but not a horizontal or vertical line).

phase of research   Every research project develops through phases in which certain types of questions are asked and answered. These phases are: *idea-generating phase, problem-definition phase, procedures-design phase, observation phase, data-analysis phase, interpretation phase,* and *communication phase.*

placebo effect   In a treatment study any observed improvement in response to a sham treatment. Placebo effects are probably the result of subjects' expectations for treatment effectiveness.

population   Any clearly defined set of objects or events (people, occurrences, animals, and so on). Populations usually represent all events in a particular class (e.g., all college students, all boys between the ages of 10 and 12, all headache sufferers).

population parameters   Any summary statistic computed on the entire population.

positive correlation   Relationship between two variables where one variable increases as the other variable increases.

post hoc **analyses**   Secondary analyses that evaluate relationships between variables not specifically hypothesized by the researcher prior to the study.

power of a statistical test   Ability of an inferential statistical procedure to detect differences between groups when such differences actually exist.

practice effects   Any change in performance on a dependent measure that results from previous exposure of the subject to the measurement procedure.

pretest-posttest design   Set of research designs in which subjects are tested at two points in time: before the administration of the independent variable and again after the administration of the independent variable.

pretest-posttest, natural control-group design   Nonexperimental research design in which preexisting groups are each measured before and after the manipulation of an independent variable. These naturally occurring groups are assigned to different levels of the independent variable.

problem-definition phase of research   Research phase where vague and general research ideas are converted into precise questions to be studied.

procedures-design phase of research   Research phase where the specific procedures to be used in the gathering of data are developed.

program evaluation   Specific area of field research for evaluating the effectiveness of a program in meeting its stated goals.

psychology   Scientific study of the behavior of organisms.

quasi-experimental design   Research designs which, although not true experimental designs with all experimental controls built in, provide experimental-like controls to minimize threats to internal validity. (Several quasi-experimental designs are discussed in Chapter 13.)

randomization   Any procedure that assigns a value or order in an unpredictable or random way such as by use of tables of random numbers. Randomization procedures may be used for selecting subjects, assigning subjects to groups or conditions, or assigning the order in which a subject will experience a number of successive conditions.

randomized, posttest-only, control-group design   Experimental design in which subjects are randomly assigned to two groups on the independent variable. Each group is tested on the dependent variable after the independent variable manipulation.

randomized, pretest-posttest, control-group design   Experimental design in which subjects are randomly assigned to two groups and each subject is tested on the dependent variable both before and after the manipulation of the independent variable.

random sampling   Procedure for the selection of subjects to be included in a research study where each subject in the population has an equal chance of being selected and where the selection of any one subject will not affect the probability of selecting any other subject. In most research random sampling from the population is not carried out because the procedure is not feasible. Instead, researchers rely on sampling from an accessible population.

range   Distance between the lowest score and the highest score inclusive of the scores.

rationalism   One of many ways of knowing about the universe. Relies on systematic logic and a set of premises from which logical inferences are made.

ratio scale   Scale of measurement in which the intervals between scores are equal (as in the *interval scale*) and the zero point on the scale represents none of the quality being measured (a *true zero*). Examples of ratio scales are height, weight, and frequency of an event.

reactive measure   Any measurement procedure that produces different scores depending on whether subjects are aware they are being measured.

regression to the mean   Potential confounding variable that occurs whenever subjects are selected because of extreme scores (either very high or very low) on some variable. When retested on the same or similar variable, the original extreme sample tends to be less extreme on average (scores will be generally closer to the mean).

reification of a construct   Incorrectly accepting a construct as a fact.

relationship   Any connection between two or more variables. In research there are many types of relationships from simple contingencies to established causal relationships.

reliability Index of the consistency of a measuring instrument in repeatedly providing the same score for a given subject. There are many different types of reliability, each referring to a different aspect of consistency. Types of reliability include *interrater reliability, test-retest reliability,* and *internal consistency reliability.*

repeated measures ANOVA Statistical procedure to evaluate the mean differences between two or more conditions where the same subjects contribute scores under each condition. Repeated measures ANOVA takes into account the fact that the same subjects appear in all conditions.

repeated measures factorials Factorial design in which all factors are within-subjects factors. Each subject is tested under every possible combination of conditions in the design.

replication To repeat a study with either no changes at all in the procedure *(exact replication)* or carefully planned changes in the procedure *(systematic* or *conceptual replication).*

representative sample Sample of subjects that adequately reflects the characteristics of the population from which the sample is drawn.

representativeness Degree to which a sample is representative of the population from which the sample is drawn.

research ethics Set of guidelines designed to protect human and nonhuman subjects from the risks of participating in research.

research hypothesis Precise and formal statement of a research question. The research hypothesis is constructed by adding operational definitions for each of the variables to the statement of the problem.

research setting Any characteristics of the situation and/or surroundings in which a research project is carried out. Settings may vary from natural, real-world settings to highly constrained and carefully controlled laboratory situations.

response-inferred organismic variable Construct referring to some hypothesized internal attribute of the organism that cannot be directly observed but, instead, is inferred on the basis of some observed behavior. Examples are intelligence, anxiety, anger, and love.

reversal design (ABA) Research design often used with single subjects where the effects of an independent variable on a dependent variable are inferred from observations made first without the independent variable present, then with the independent variable present, and again without the independent variable present. If an effect is noticed both when the independent variable is added and when it is later removed, it is likely that the independent variable is causally related to the dependent measure.

rival hypothesis Any feasible alternative hypothesis to the causal hypothesis.

row means In factorial designs, one factor is usually illustrated as separate rows of data where each row represents a different level of the factor. A second factor is illustrated as columns of data where the different columns represent various levels of the second factor. Row means are computed by taking the mean of all subjects who appear in a given row regardless of their level on the second factor.

sample Any subset drawn from a population. Researchers work with samples of subjects and draw inferences about the larger population.

sample statistic Descriptive index of some characteristic of the sample of subjects. Population parameters are estimated on the basis of statistics.

sampling Process of drawing a sample from a population. Many sampling techniques are available including *random sampling, stratified random sampling,* and various nonrandom sampling techniques.

sampling error Chance variation among different samples drawn from the same population.

scale attenuation effects Any limitation on the measuring instrument that limits the ability of the instrument to make discriminations at the top of the scale *(ceiling effects)* or the bottom of the scale *(floor effects).*

scales of measurement   Characteristics of the scores produced by a particular measurement instrument. Scales of measurement vary on how closely scores match the real number system. There are four generally recognized scales of measurement: *nominal scale, ordinal scale, interval scale,* and *ratio scale.*

scatter plot   Graphic technique that illustrates the relationship between two or more variables. In a two-variable situation the scatter plot is constructed by labeling the *x*-axis with one of the variables and the *y*-axis with the other variable and plotting each subject's pair of scores in the xy coordinate system. The scatter plot will illustrate the type of relation present (no relationship, *linear relationship,* or *nonlinear relationship*), the direction of the relationship, and the strength of the relationship.

science   Way of knowing about the universe around us, which combines rationalism and empiricism to form a system that places great demands on procedures, data, and theories.

Scientific Revolution   Period of time (the fifteenth through the seventeenth centuries) in which scientific methods and applications became independent from theology and developed rapidly into a generally recognized way of understanding nature.

score data   Data produced by *interval* or *ratio scales* of measurement.

secondary analyses   In the analysis of research data secondary analyses look at questions not directly stated in the original research hypothesis but that may be relevant to understanding some of the primary analyses.

selection   Potential confounding variable in any research project. Selection represents any process that may create groups not equivalent at the beginning of the study.

sequencing effects   Potential confounding variable in research involving repeated or multiple measures. Sequencing effects are the effects on the performance of subjects in later conditions as a consequence of their having previously participated in other conditions.

single-blind procedure   Research procedure in which the researcher is unaware of the condition to which each subject is assigned. The purpose of the single-blind procedure is to minimize measurement biases.

single-group, posttest-only design   Nonexperimental research design in which the researcher manipulates the independent variable and then takes a postmanipulation measure on the dependent variable. The difference between this design and an *ex post facto design* is the actual manipulation of the independent variable by the researcher.

single-group, pretest-posttest design   Nonexperimental design in which a group of subjects is measured on a dependent variable, the independent variable is manipulated, and a second measure on the dependent variable is taken. The design does allow comparison between pretest and posttest scores but, because no control group exists, confounding variables are not adequately controlled.

single-subject, randomized, time-series designs   Designs frequently used in naturalistic settings where multiple measures on the dependent variable are taken both before and after some manipulation of an independent variable. This type of design provides partial control of many potential confounding variables by allowing the researcher to see patterns in the movement of the dependent measure over time and specific changes in the dependent measure that appear to be a function of the manipulation of the independent measure.

single-subject design   Research design that seeks information sufficient to draw causal inferences about the relationship between an independent and dependent variable with a reasonable degree of confidence. The various types of single-subject design all have some form of built-in control to compensate for the fact that no control group exists. Typical examples of single-subject designs include *ABA design, single-subject, randomized time-series design,* and *multiple baseline design.*

skepticism   Unwillingness to accept information as valid knowledge without some documentation to confirm the information. Skepticism is one of the strongest tools available to a scientist.

skewed distribution   Any distribution of scores where the majority of scores in the distribution bunch up at the end of the distribution. Skewed distribution is often contrasted with *symmetric distribution.*

skewed negatively   Distribution in which scores are concentrated near the top of the scale with few scores near the lower end of the scale.

skewed positively   Distribution in which scores are concentrated near the bottom of the scale with few scores near the top of the scale.

social desirability   Response set that can have a powerful influence on information gathered from human subjects. Subjects showing a social desirability response set will tend to say what they believe is expected of them (i.e., they tend to present themselves in a socially desirable light).

Solomon four-group design   Sophisticated experimental design that combines the *randomized, posttest-only, control-group design* and the *randomized, pretest-posttest, control-group design.*

Spearman rank-order correlation   Correlation coefficient that indexes the degree of relationship between two variables, each of which is measured on an *ordinal scale* of measurement.

spread   Synonymous with *variability.*

standard deviation   Square root of variance. The standard deviation is an index of variability in the distribution of scores.

standard error of the differences between means   In statistics, the denominator in a *t*-test.

statement of the problem   First major refinement of initial research ideas in which a clear statement of the expected relationship between conceptual variables is made. The statement of the problem is refined into one or more research hypotheses by specifying the operational definitions of each conceptual variable in the statement.

Statistical Analysis System (SAS)   Computer package for statistical data analysis.

statistical hypothesis   Synonymous with *null hypothesis.*

Statistical Package for the Social Sciences (SPSS)   Computer package for statistical data analysis.

statistical validity   Accuracy of conclusions drawn from a statistical test. To enhance statistical validity one must meet critical assumptions and requirements of a statistical procedure.

statistics   Mathematical procedures used to evaluate the results of a research study. Some statistical procedures describe data *(descriptive statistics),* whereas others help draw conclusions about data *(inferential statistics).*

stimulus variable   Any variable part of the environment to which an organism reacts. A stimulus variable may be a natural part of the environment and observed by the researcher or may be actively manipulated by the researcher.

stratified random sampling   Variation of the random sampling procedure where a population is divided in narrow strata along some critical dimension. Subjects are then selected randomly from each of the strata in the same proportion that the strata are represented in the population. Stratified random sampling can increase the representativeness of the sample and is used extensively in sophisticated survey research.

subject assignment   Procedure of assigning subjects to a group or condition. Subject assignment may be made on the basis of some random procedure *(experimental research)* or on the basis of some preexisting condition in the subjects *(inferential research).*

subjects at risk   Any subject involved in a research project that poses some potential risk to the subject. When subjects are at risk, it is the responsibility of the researcher to inform them of the risks and to minimize the risks.

subjects' rights   Guarantees of proper treatment that subjects can justly expect in research.

subject variable Synonymous with *organismic variable.*

summary statistics Descriptive statistics that provide, in a single number, some general characteristic of the sample. Typical summary statistics are the *mean, median, variance,* and *standard deviation.*

sum of squares Sum of the squared differences from the mean. The sum of squares is the numerator in the variance formula.

symmetric distribution Graphical representation of any distribution in which the right half of the distribution is a mirror image of the left half. Symmetric distribution is often contrasted with *skewed distribution.*

systematic replication (or conceptual replication) Situation where a study is repeated with small, theory-based changes in the procedures. Systematic replication is more common than exact replication because it verifies original findings while also expanding knowledge of the phenomena.

t-**test** Statistical procedure designed to test for mean differences between two groups of subjects.

t-**test for independent groups** Statistical procedure designed to test for mean differences between two groups of subjects where all subjects in the study appear in one and only one group.

table Organizational device where information (often statistical information) is summarized briefly.

target population Population to which we hope to generalize the findings of a research study. In most research the entire target population is not accessible to the researcher.

technology Physical instruments or tools used by researchers. Note that technology does not define science; it merely provides tools for scientists to make and record observations, analyze data, and simplify their work.

tenacity Way of knowing about the universe. Tenacity is accepting an idea as true because it has been accepted as true for a long period of time.

testing Potential confounding variable in research. Testing represents any change in a subject's score on a dependent measure that is a function of the subject having been tested previously in the research project.

test-retest reliability Index of the consistency in scores over time. Test-retest reliability is computed by calculating the *Pearson product-moment correlation* between scores from two testings separated by some specified time interval.

theoretical concept Abstraction (thought or idea) that defines the relationship between two or more variables.

time-series design See *interrupted time-series design.*

true zero Characteristic of a measurement scale where zero represents none of the concept being measured.

two-way ANOVA Statistical procedure for the analysis of a factorial design with two independent variables.

Type I error Probability of rejecting the null hypothesis when the null hypothesis is true.

Type II error Probability of not rejecting the null hypothesis when the null hypothesis is false.

univariate Having to do with one variable. For example, a univariate distribution would provide the distribution for a single variable.

unobtrusive measure Any measure that can be taken on subjects without subjects being aware they are being measured.

unobtrusive observer Anyone who is able to observe the behavior of subjects without subjects being aware they are being observed.

validity Major concept in research that has several specific meanings *(internal validity, external validity, construct validity, statistical validity).* In a general sense validity refers to the methodological and/or conceptual soundness of research (i.e., in the case of an experiment, a question regarding validity is "Does this experiment really test what it is supposed to test?").

variability   Differences among subjects on any given variable.

variable   Any characteristic that can take on different values. Variables are sets of events measured in research. Research is aimed at defining the relationships between variables.

variance   Summary statistic that indicates the degree of variability among subjects for a given variable. The variance is essentially the average squared deviation from the mean and is the square of the standard deviation.

within-group variance   Variability among subjects within a particular group or condition. Provides a basis for comparing mean differences between groups in most statistical procedures.

within-subject design   Research design in which individual differences are controlled by having the same subjects tested under all conditions.

x-axis (abscissa)   In a graph the x-axis is the horizontal axis.

y-axis (ordinate)   In a graph the y-axis is the vertical axis.

REFERENCES

American Psychological Association. (1981). Ethical principles of psychologists. *American Psychologist, 36,* 633–638. Washington, DC: Author.

American Psychological Association. (1983). *Publication manual of the American Psychological Association* (3rd ed.). Washington, DC: Author.

American Psychological Association. (1986). *Guidelines for ethical conduct in the care and use of animals.* Washington, DC: Author.

Anastasi, A. (1982). *Psychological testing* (5th ed.). New York: Macmillan.

Bachrach, A. J. (1981). *Psychological research: An introduction.* New York: Random House.

Bandura, A. I. (1969). *Principles of behavior modification.* New York: Holt, Rinehart and Winston.

Barber, T. X., & Silver, M. J. (1968). Fact, fiction and the experimenter bias effect. *Psychological Bulletin Monograph Supplement, 70,* 1–29.

Barthel, C. N., & Holmes, D. S. (1968). High school yearbooks: A non-reactive measure of social isolation in graduates who later became schizophrenic. *Journal of Abnormal Psychology, 73,* 313–316.

Benbow, C. P., & Stanley, J. C. (1980). Sex differences in mathematical ability: Fact or artifact? *Science, 210,* 1262–1264.

Bergin, A. E. (1966). Some implications of psychotherapy research for therapeutic practice. *Journal of Abnormal Psychology, 71,* 235–246.

Bergin, A. E., & Strupp, H. H. (1970). New directions in psychotherapy research. *Journal of Abnormal Psychology, 76,* 13–26.

Bleuler, E. (1950). The fundamental symptoms. In E. Bleuler (Ed.), *Dementia praecox; or the group of schizophrenias* (J. Ziskin, Trans.) (pp. 14–54). New York: International University Press. (Original work published 1911.)

Boring, E. G. (1950). *A history of experimental psychology.* New York: Appleton-Century-Crofts.

Bornstein, P. H., & Quevillon, R. P. (1976). The effects of a self-instructional package on overactive preschool boys. *Journal of Applied Behavior Analysis, 9,* 179–188.

Bronowski, J. *The common sense of science.* New York: Random House. (Modern Library paperback edition, not dated.)

Brotemarkle, R. A. (1966). Fifty years of clinical psychology: Clinical psychology, 1896–1946. In I. N. Mensh (Ed.), *Clinical psychology: Science and profession* (pp. 63–68). New York: Macmillan.

Camilli, G., & Hopkins, K. D. (1978). Applicability of chi square to 2×2 contingency tables with small expected cell frequencies. *Psychological Bulletin, 85,* 163–167.

Campbell, A., Converse, P. E., & Rodgers, W. L. (1976). *The quality of American life: Perceptions, evaluations and satisfactions.* New York: Russell Sage Foundation.

Campbell, D. T. (1969). Reforms as experiments. *American Psychologist, 24,* 409–429.

Campbell, D. T., & Stanley, J. C. (1966). *Experimental and quasi-experimental designs for research on teaching.* Chicago: Rand McNally.

Caporaso, J. A. (1974). *The structure and function of European integration.* Pacific Palisades, CA: Goodyear.

Clagett, M. (1948). The medieval heritage: Religious, philosophic, scientific. In J. L. Blau, J. Buchler, & G. T. Matthews (Eds.), *Chapters in western civilization* (Vol. I, pp. 74–122). New York: Columbia University Press.

Cook, T. D., & Campbell, D. T. (1979). *Quasi experimentation: Design and analysis issues for field studies.* Chicago: Rand McNally.

Correa, V. I., Poulson, C. L., & Salzberg, C. L. (1984). Training and generalization of reach-grasp behavior in blind, retarded young children. *Journal of Applied Behavior Analysis, 17,* 57–69.

Curtis, D. R., & Crawford, J. M. (1969). Central synaptic transmission-microelectrophoretic studies. *Annual Review of Pharmacology, 9,* 209–240.

Daedalus. (1969, Spring). [Entire issue]. Boston, MA: American Academy of Arts and Sciences.

Daniken, E. v. (1970). *Chariots of the gods.* New York: Putnam.

Daniken, E. v. (1972). *Gods from outer space.* New York: Bantam Books.

Darley, J. M., & Latane, B. (1968). Bystander intervention in emergencies: Diffusion of responsibility. *Journal of Personality and Social Psychology, 8,* 377–383.

Darwin, C. (1859). *On the origin of species by means of natural selection, or the preservation of favored races in the struggle for life.* London: John Murray. (New York: Modern Library, 1967).

Edge, H.L., Morris, R.L., Rush, J.H., & Palmer, J. (1986). *Foundations of parapsychology: Exploring the boundaries of human capability.* Boston: Rutledge & Kegan Paul.

Edgington, E. S. (1974). A new tabulation of statistical procedures used in APA journals. *American Psychologist, 29,* 25–26.

Evans, C. (1979). *The micro millennium.* New York: Viking.

Farrington, B. (1949a). *Greek science: 1. Thales to Aristotle.* Harmondsworth: Pelican Books.

Farrington, B. (1949b). *Greek science: 2. Theophrastus to Galen.* Harmondsworth: Pelican Books.

Festinger, L. (1957). *A theory of cognitive dissonance.* Stanford, CA: Stanford University Press.

Fisher, R. A. (1935). *The design of experiments* (1st ed.). London: Oliver & Boyd.

Fossey, D. (1983). *Gorilla in the mist.* Boston, MA: Houghton Mifflin.

Freeman, M. (1984). History, narrative, and life-span developmental knowledge. *Human Development, 27,* 1–9.

Fuller, B. A. G. (1950). *A history of philosophy.* New York: Henry Holt & Co.

Glass, G. V., Peckham, P. D., & Sanders, J. R. (1972). Consequences of failure to meet assumptions underlying the fixed effects analyses of variance and covariance. *Review of Educational Research, 42,* 237–288.

Glass, G. V., Willson, V. L., & Gottman, J. M. (1975). *Design and analysis of time series.* Boulder, CO: Laboratory of Educational Research Press.

Goodall, J. (1971). *In the shadow of man.* Boston: Houghton-Mifflin.

Goodall, J. (1978). Chimp killings: Is it the man in them? *Science News, 113,* 276.

Goodall, J. (1986). *The Chimpanzees of Gombe.* Cambridge, MA: Belknap Press/Harvard University Press.

Graziano, A.M. (1963). *Relaxation training staff manual.* Unpublished paper, University of Bridgeport, Bridgeport, Conn.

Graziano, A. M. (1974). *Child without tomorrow.* Elmsford, NY: Pergamon Press.

Graziano, A. M., Gallipeau, K. A., & Graziano, S. G. (1982). *Death, taxes and spanking.* Unpublished manuscript, State University of New York at Buffalo.

Graziano, A. M., & Kean, J. (1968). Programmed relaxation and reciprocal inhibition with psychotic children. *Behaviour Research and Therapy, 6,* 433–437.

Graziano, A. M., & Mooney, K. C. (1982). Behavioral treatment of "nightfears," a 2-1/2 to 3 year follow-up. *Journal of Consulting and Clinical Psychology, 50,* 598–599.

Guerin, D., & MacKinnon, D. P. (1985). An assessment of the California Child Passenger Restraint Requirement. *American Journal of Public Health, 75,* 142–144.

Helmstadter, G. C. (1970). *Research concepts in human behavior.* New York: Appleton-Century-Crofts.

Heron, W., Doane, B. K., & Scott, T. H. (1956). Visual disturbance after prolonged perceptual isolation. *Canadian Journal of Psychology, 10,* 13–18.

Hersen, M., & Barlow, D. H. (1976). *Single-case experimental design: Strategies for studying behavioral change.* New York: Pergamon Press.

Howell, D. C. (1987). *Statistical methods for psychology* (2nd ed.). Boston: Duxbury.

Hull, C.L. (1943). *Principles of behavior.* New York: Appleton-Century-Crofts.

Hyman, R. (1964). *The nature of psychological inquiry.* Englewood Cliffs, NJ: Prentice-Hall.

Keith, A. (1954). Darwin and the "Origin of Species." In H. Shapley, S. Rapport, & H. Wright (Eds.), *A treasury of science* (pp. 437–446). New York: Harper and Brothers.

Kerlinger, F. N. (1964). *Foundations of behavioral research.* New York: Holt, Rinehart and Winston.

Kerlinger, F. N. (1986). *Foundations of behavioral research* (3rd ed.). New York: Holt, Rinehart and Winston.

Kerlinger, J. (1969). Research in "education." In R. Ebel, V. Nall, & R. Bauer (Eds.), *Encyclopedia of educational research* (4th ed., pp. 1127–1144). New York: Macmillan.

Kety, S. S., Rosenthal, D., Wender, P. H., & Schulsinger, F. (1968). The types and prevalence of mental illness in the biological and adoptive families of adopted schizophrenics. In D. Rosenthal & S. S. Kety (Eds.), *The transmission of schizophrenia* (pp. 345–362). Oxford: Pergamon.

Kimmel, M. J., Pruitt, D. G., Magenau, J. M., Konar-Goldband, E., & Carnevale, P. J. D. (1980). Effects of trust, aspiration, and gender on negotiation tactics. *Journal of Personality and Social Psychology, 38,* 9–22.

Kitto, H. D. F. (1951). *The Greeks.* Harmondsworth: Pelican Books.

Kraemer, D. L., Hastrup, J. L., Sobota, M., & Bornstein, R. F. (1985, April). *Adolescent crying: Norms and self-control.* Paper presented at the meeting of the Eastern Psychological Association, Boston, MA.

Kratochwill, T. R. (Ed.). (1978). *Single-subject research: Strategies for evaluating change.* New York: Academic Press.

Lawler, E. E., III, & Hackman, J. R. (1969). Impact of employee participation in the development of pay incentive plans: A field experiment. *Journal of Applied Psychology, 53,* 467–471.

Levine, A. G. (1982). *The Love Canal: Science, politics and people.* Lexington, MA: D. C. Heath.

Levine, M. (1974). Scientific method in the adversary model. *American Psychologist, 29,* 661–677.

Levine, M. (1980). Investigative reporting as a research method: An analysis of Bernstein and Woodward's "All the President's Men." *American Psychologist, 35,* 626–638.

Levine, M., & Howe, B. (1985). The penetration of social science into legal culture. *Law and Policy, 7,* 173–198.

Levy, K. (1980). A Monte Carlo study of analysis of covariance under violations of the assumptions of normality and equal regression slopes. *Educational and Psychological Measurement, 40,* 835–840.

Lick, J. (1973). Statistical versus clinical significance in research on the outcome of psychotherapy. *International Journal of Mental Health, 2,* 26–37.

Lord, F. M. (1967). A paradox in the interpretation of group differences. *Psychological Bulletin, 68,* 304–305.

Lovaas, O. I. (1973). *Behavioral treatment of autistic children.* Morristown, NJ: General Learning Press.

Marlatt, G. A., Demming, B., & Reid, J. B. (1973). Loss of control drinking in alcoholics: An experimental analogue. *Journal of Abnormal Psychology, 81,* 233–241.

Marr, D. (1982). *Vision: A computational investigation into the human representation and processing of visual information.* San Francisco: W. H. Freeman.

Marx, M. H. (Ed.). (1963). *Theories in contemporary psychology.* New York: Macmillan.

Masters, W. H., & Johnson, V. E. (1966). *Human sexual response.* Boston: Little, Brown.

Mazur-Hart, S. F., & Berman, J. J. (1977). Changing from fault to no-fault divorce: An interrupted time-series analysis. *Journal of Applied Social Psychology, 7,* 300–312.

McCain, G., & Segal, E. M. (1973). *The game of science.* Monterey, CA: Brooks/Cole.

McSweeny, A. J. (1978). The effects of response cost on the behavior of a million persons: Charging for directory assistance in Cincinnatti. *Journal of Applied Behavior Analysis, 11,* 47–51.

Mednick, S. A., & Schulsinger, F. (1968). Some powerful characteristics related to breakdown in children with schizophrenic mothers. In D. Rosenthal and S. S. Kety (Eds.), *The transmission of schizophrenia* (pp. 267–291). Oxford: Pergamon.

Miller, N. E. (1971). *Neal E. Miller: Selected papers.* Chicago: Aldine Atherton.

Miller, N. E. (1985). The value of behavioral research with animals. *American Psychologist, 40,* 423–440.

Myers, J. L. (1972). *Fundamentals of experimental design* (2nd ed.). Boston: Allyn & Bacon.

Nagel, E. (1948). The development of modern science. In J. L. Blau, J. Buchler, & G. T. Matthews (Eds.), *Chapters in western civilization* (Vol. 1, pp. 241–284). New York: Columbia University Press.

National Institute of Health. (1978). *Guide for the care and use of laboratory animals.* Washington, DC: Author.

Nelson, G. (1970). [Interview.] In S. Rosner & I. E. Abt (Eds.), *The creative experience* (pp. 251–268). New York: Grossman.

Nunnally, J. C. (1967). *Psychometric theory.* New York: McGraw-Hill.

Oppenheimer, J. R. (1956). Analogy in science. *American Psychologist, 11,* 127–135.

Orne, M. T. (1962). On the social psychology of the psychological experiment: With particular reference to demand characteristics and their implications. *American Psychologist, 17,* 776–783.

Parsons, J. E. (Ed.). (1980). *The psychology of sex differences and sex roles.* New York: McGraw-Hill.

Pauling, L. (1981). Cited in A. J. Bachrach, *Psychological research: An introduction* (4th ed., p. 3). New York: Random House.

Phillips, D. P. (1983). The impact of mass media violence on U.S. homicides. *American Sociological Review, 48,* 560–568.

Pruitt, D. G., & Lewis, S. A. (1975). Development of integrative solutions in bilateral negotiation. *Journal of Personality and Social Psychology, 31,* 621–633.

Raulin, M. L. (1984). Development of a scale to measure intense ambivalence. *Journal of Consulting and Clinical Psychology, 52,* 63–72.

Reese, W. L. (1980). *Dictionary of philosophy and religion: Eastern and Western thought.* Atlantic Highlands, NJ: Humanities Press.

Rohsenow, D. J., & Marlatt, G. A. (1981). The balanced placebo design: Methodological considerations. *Addictive Behavior, 6,* 107–122.

Rosenhan, D. L. (1973). On being sane in insane places. *Science, 179,* 250–258.

Rosenthal, R. (1976). *Experimenter effects in behavioral research.* New York: Halsted Press.

Rosenthal, R., & Fode, K. L. (1963a). The effect of experimenter bias on the performance of the albino rat. *Behavioral Science, 8,* 183–189.

Rosenthal, R., & Fode, K. L. (1963b). Three experiments in experimenter bias. *Psychological Reports, 12,* 491–511.

Rossi, P. H., Wright, J. D., & Anderson, A. B. (1983). *Handbook of survey research.* New York: Academic Press.

Runyon, R. P., & Haber, A. (1980). *Fundamentals of behavioral statistics.* Reading, MA: Addison-Wesley.

Salmon, W. C. (1963). *Logic.* Englewood Cliffs, NJ: Prentice-Hall.

Schulz, J. W., & Pruitt, D. G. (1978). The effects of mutual concern on joint welfare. *Journal of Experimental Social Psychology, 14,* 480–492.

Schuman, H., & Kalton, G. (1985). Survey methods. In G. Lindzey and E. Aronson (Eds.), *The handbook of social psychology* (Vol. 1, 3rd ed., pp. 635–698). New York: Random House.

Seigel, S. (1956). *Nonparametric statistics for the behavioral sciences.* New York: McGraw-Hill.

Shavelson, R. J. (1981). *Statistical reasoning for the behavioral sciences.* Boston: Allyn & Bacon.

Sidman, M. (1960). *Tactics of scientific research: Evaluating scientific data in psychology.* New York: Basic Books.

Skinner, B. F. (1938). *The behavior of organisms.* New York: Appleton-Century-Crofts.

Skinner, B. F. (1953). *Science and human behavior.* New York: Macmillan.

Skinner, B. F. (1956). A case history in scientific method. *American Psychologist, 11,* 221–233.

Skinner, B. F. (1972). *Cumulative record* (3rd ed.). New York: Appleton-Century-Crofts.

Skyrms, B. (1966). *Choice and change: An introduction to inductive logic.* Belmont, CA: Dickenson Publishing.

Solomon, R. L. (1949). An extension of control group design. *Psychological Bulletin, 46,* 137–150.

Spearman, C. (1904). "General intelligence" objectively determined and measured. *American Journal of Psychology, 15,* 201–293.

Stevens, S. S. (1946). On the theory of scales of measurement. *Science, 103,* 677–680.

Strunk, W., Jr., & White, E. B. (1979). *The elements of style* (3rd ed.). New York: Macmillan.

Szent-Gyorgi, A. (1971). Looking back. *Perspectives in Biology and Medicine, 13,* 1.

Timm, N. H. (1975). *Multivariate analysis with applications in education and psychology.* Monterey, CA: Brooks/Cole.

Tinbergen, N. (1951). *The study of instinct.* London: Oxford University Press.

Tinbergen, N. (1963). *The Herring Gull's world.* London: Collins.

Tukey, J. W. (1977). *Exploratory data analysis.* Reading, MA: Addison-Wesley.

Vinacke, E. A. (1954). Deceiving experimental subjects. *American Psychologist, 9,* 155.

Webb, E. J., Campbell, D. T., Schwartz, R. D., & Sechrest, L. (1966). *Unobtrusive measures: Nonreactive research in the social sciences.* Chicago: Rand McNally.

Welkowitz, J., Ewen, R. B., & Cohen, J. (1982). *Introductory statistics for the behavioral sciences* (3rd ed.). San Diego: Harcourt Brace Jovanovich.

Wender, P. H., Kety, S. S., Rosenthal, D., Schulsinger, F., Ortmann, J., & Lunde, I. (1986). Psychiatric disorder in the biological and adoptive families of adopted individuals with affective disorders. *Archives of General Psychiatry, 43,* 923–929.

Whitehead, A. N. (1925). *Science and the modern world.* New York: Macmillan.

Winer, B. (1971). *Statistical principles in experimental design.* New York: McGraw-Hill.

Wolpe, J. (1958). *Psychotherapy by reciprocal inhibition.* Stanford, CA: Stanford University Press.

Anastasi, A., 79
Anaximander, 12
Anderson, A. B., 297
Aquinas, Thomas, 14
Archimedes, 15, 33
Aristotle, 12

Bachrach, A. J., 4
Bacon, Roger, 14, 16
Bandura, A. I., 46
Barber, T. X., 174
Barlow, D. H., 284
Benbow, C. P., 165
Bergin, A. E., 283–284
Berman, J. J., 282
Bleuler, E., 145
Bornstein, P. H., 282
Bornstein, R. F., 189

Campbell, A., 295, 296
Campbell, D. T., 122, 164, 168, 268, 269,
   271, 272, 273–274, 275–276, 281, 282
Caporaso, J. A., 282
Carnevale, P. J. D., 126
Clagett, M., 14
Converse, P. E., 295
Cook, T. D., 164, 168, 268, 272, 273–274,
   275–276, 281
Copernicus, 8, 9, 29
Correa, V. I., 286
Crawford, J. M., 323
Curtis, D. R., 323

Daniken, Erich von, 164–165
Darley, J. M., 156–157
Darwin, Charles, 2, 3, 8, 111, 114
Demming, B., 186
DeNemore, Jordanus, 14
Dietrich of Frieberg, 14

Edge, H. L., 181
Edgington, E. S., 241
Empedocles, 12
Euclid, 15
Evans, Christopher, 324–325

Farrington, Benjamin, 10
Festinger, L., 46
Fisher, Sir Ronald, 217, 284
Fode, K. L., 174
Fossey, Diane, 111
Freeman, Mark, 324
Freud, Anna, 127

Freud, Sigmund, 8, 46, 114, 115, 126, 127,
   128

Gagarin, Yuri, 17
Galen, 8, 15
Galileo, 2, 8, 9, 29
Gallipeau, K. A., 189
Genovese, Kitty, 156–158
Glass, G. V., 281, 316
Goodall, Jane, 39, 111, 117
Gottman, J. M., 281
Graziano, A. M., 24, 25, 36, 68, 70, 76, 77,
   117, 118, 119, 136, 157, 162, 180, 189,
   192, 195
Graziano, S. G., 189
Guerin, D., 279, 281

Haber, A., 316
Hackman, J. R., 282
Hastrup, J. L., 189
Hersen, M., 284
Hippocrates, 8, 12, 15
Howe, B., 324
Hull, Clark, 31
Hyman, R., 32n

Johnson, V. E., 291

Kean, J., 117, 118, 119
Keith, Arthur, 3
Kerlinger, F. N., 76, 202
Kerlinger, J., 157
Kety, S. S., 122
Kimmel, M. J., 126
Konar-Goldband, E., 126
Kraemer, D. L., 189, 190
Kratochwill, T. R., 284

Latane, B., 156–157
Lawler, E. E., 111, 282
Levine, Adeline, 112–113, 121
Levine, M., 324
Levy, K., 316
Lick, J., 175
Lilienthal, Otto, 17n
Lovaas, O. I., 46
Lunde, I., 122

MacKinnon, D. P., 279, 281
McSweeny, A. J., 282
Magenau, J. M., 126
Marlatt, G. A., 181, 186
Marr, D., 326

Marx, M. H., 31
Masters, W. H., 291
Mazur-Hart, S. F., 282
Mead, Margaret, 111
Mednick, S. A., 323
Miller, N. E., 46, 62
Mooney, K. C., 180
Morris, R. L., 181

Nelson, George, 4–5
Nunnally, J. C., 78

Oppenheimer, J. Robert, 4
Ortmann, J., 122

Palmer, J., 181
Parsons, J. E., 165
Pasteur, Louis, 5
Pauling, Linus, 4, 34
Peckham, P. D., 316
Peter the Stranger of Maricourt, 14
Phillips, D. P., 282
Piaget, Jean, 115, 121
Plato, 12, 13
Poulson, C. L., 286
Pruitt, D. G., 126
Ptolemy, 15
Pythagoreans, 13

Quevillon, R. P., 282

Raulin, M. L., 145
Reese, W. L., 30n
Reid, J. B., 186
Rodgers, W. L., 295
Rohsenow, D. J., 186
Rosenhan, David, 113–114
Rosenthal, D. L., 122
Rosenthal, R., 174
Rossi, P. H., 297
Runyon, R. P., 316
Rush, J. H., 181

Salmon, W. C., 30n
Salzberg, C. L., 286
Sanders, J. R., 316
Schulsinger, F., 122, 323
Schulz, J. W., 126
Schwartz, R. D., 122
Sechrest, L., 122
Shavelson, R. J., 219
Sidman, M., 283, 284
Silver, J. J., 174

SUBJECT INDEX

ABA design (reversal design), 285–287
Abscissa (x-axis), 91
Abstract number system of measurement, 69
Accessible population, 187
Ad hoc samples, 189–190
Alpha levels, 104
American Psychological Association (APA), 18, 19, 269
  divisions within, 19
  ethical guidelines for research with human subjects, 57, 58–59
  writing style for research reports, 330–336
Analysis of covariance (ANCOVA), 263
Analysis of data, 148
Analysis of variance (ANOVA), 74, 104, 105–106, 215–218, 363–371
  computer-analysis programs for, 254–255, 325
  differential research and, 148
  in factorial design, 254–256
  multivariate, 263
  one-way, 106
  repeated measures, 106, 228–229, 258, 365–366, 367
  simple one-way, 363, 364, 365
  simple two-way, 366–368, 369–370
  specific means comparisons in, 219–221
  two-way, 106
Animals, research with, ethical principles in, 61–63
Annual Review of Psychology, 47
ANOVA summary table, 217, 255–256
Applied psychology, 47
Applied research, 47–48
  sensory deprivation and, 49
Archival records, 122
Art and science, 5
Artifact, 137
Artificial intelligence, 324
Asking questions, 2–5, 46
Assumptions of science, 23
Attrition (as confounding variable), 170–171
Authority, 6–7
Automation, 184–185

Babylonian civilization, 10
Basic research, 48
  sensory deprivation and, 49
Behavioral medicine, 324
Behavioral variables, 51

Behavior of organisms, 24
Bell-shaped (symmetric) curve, 92, 93
Between-groups variance, 202–203
Between-subjects designs, 211–212, 213
Between-subjects factors, 258–260
Bimodal distribution, 93
Biochemistry, 323
Biomedical Programs (BMDP), 254

Canadian Psychological Association (CPA), 18
Carry-over effects, 231–232
Case-study research, 41, 42, 110–111
  evaluating and interpreting data, 125–126
  examples of, 114–115
  limitations of, 126–130
  methods of, 121–125
  problem statements and hypotheses in, 120–121
Causal hypothesis, 161–163
Causal inferences, 127–129
Ceiling effect (scale attenuation effect), 80
Central tendency (of distribution), 93
  measures of, 93–95, 358
Chariots of the Gods (von Daniken), 164
Children's dark-fear study, 250–254, 257
Chi-square distribution, probability values of, 351
Chi-square goodness-of-fit test, 371
Chi-square test for independence, 371–372
Coefficient of determination, 143
Column means, 246–247
Communication phase, 33, 36–37
Computers, 324–327
  computer-analysis programs for ANOVA calculations, 254–255
Concept, 158
Conceptual models, 26–29
Confidentiality, 60
Confounding variable hypothesis, 160–161
Confounding variables, 136–138, 150, 166–168
  attrition, 170–171
  causal hypothesis and, 161
  diffusion of treatment, 171
  history, 168–169
  instrumentation, 169–170
  maturation, 168
  regression to the mean, 170
  selection, 170
  sequencing effects, 171–172
  testing, 169
  as threat to validity, 179

Constraint, levels of, 37–42
  case-study research, 41, 42, 110–111
  correlational research, 41, 42
  differential research, 41, 42
  experimental research, 41–42
  naturalistic observation, 40, 42
Constraint, validity and, 175
Constructs, 26, 158
Construct validity, 164–165, 179
Contingency, 119
Continuous variable, 90
Control, 179
  double-blind control procedures, 183–184
  single-blind control procedures, 183–184
  validity and, 175
Control-group design
  extension of, 214
  nonequivalent, 272–276
  pretest-posttest, 195
  randomized, 293
  randomized, posttest-only, 211–212
  randomized, pretest-posttest, 212–213
Control groups, 143–146, 205–207
  experimental designs and, 211
Controlled research, 54–55
Controls in research, 55
Correlated-groups design, 220, 225–237
  matched-subjects design, 233–237
  within-subjects design, 226–233
Correlated *t*-test, 104, 105, 362–363
Correlational research, 41, 42
  conducting, 140–143
  limitations of, 148–150
  methods of, 134–135
  when to use, 139–140
Correlation coefficient, 99–100
Correlations, 99–102
Counterbalancing, 227–228
Covariance, analysis of (ANCOVA), 263
Crossover effect, 275
Cross-sectional design, 297–298
Cross-sectional research, 298
Cross-tabulation, 89

Daedalus, 56
Data
  differential research and, 148
  graphical representation of, 90–93
  nominal, 74, 89
  ordered, 74
  ordinal, 89
  score, 74–75, 89–90
  types of, 73–75